Invitaciones

An Interactive Worktext for Beginning Spanish

SECOND EDITION

Deana Alonso
Southwestern College

Esther Alonso
Southwestern College

Brandon Zaslow
Occidental College

VISTA®
HIGHER LEARNING

Boston, Massachusetts

Publisher: José A. Blanco

President: Janet L. Dracksdorf

Managing Editors: Sarah Kenney, Paola Ríos Schaaf

Editorial Team: Christian Biagetti, Gabriela Ferland, Lauren Krolick

Design and Production Team: Susan Prentiss, Nick Ventullo

Student Text ISBN: 978-1-60007-950-4

Instructor's Annotated Edition ISBN: 978-1-60007-952-8

Library of Congress Control Number: 2008940881

4 5 6 7 8 9 RM 14 13

Maestro® and Maestro Language Learning System® and design are registered trademarks of Vista Higher Learning, Inc.

Dedication

At the time of his tragic death on August 15, 1996, my husband, **Costas Lyrintzis,** was a professor of Aerospace Engineering at San Diego State University. He was loved and respected by his students and colleagues because of his friendliness, his intelligence, and his ability to smile and make others feel better, even in the worst of times.

Even though his death made the process of writing this book so much more difficult, he has been with us all along the way. His memory gave us strength, his faith in us and our ability to contribute to the teaching of Spanish kept us going at times when we wanted to quit. Our desire to write a book worthy of him and his memory raised our spirits.

We all love you, Costas. Our lives will never be the same without you.

Deana Alonso

Introduction

Bienvenido a INVITACIONES, your invitation to the rich language and the diverse cultures of the Spanish-speaking world! This program takes a communicative approach to developing your ability to use and understand Spanish in practical, everyday contexts. It also aims at building your cultural knowledge and competency.

New to this Edition

- **More communicative practice** helps students develop interpersonal communication

- **New Revista cultural** section develops cultural knowledge through interesting and relevant readings

- **New video** content—the **Flash cultura** program and authentic TV clips—offers additional exposure to the cultures of the Spanish-speaking world

- **Updated culture** in the **Invitación a...** sections invites students to develop their interpretive communication skills and cultural competence

- **Online listening comprehension and pronunciation practice** provides students with opportunities to develop their interpretive skills and master pronunciation

- **Enhanced technology** delivers all audio and video content online, plus additional practice

Hallmark Features

▶ Unique interactive worktexts

INVITACIONES consists of two volumes, **Primera parte** and **Segunda parte**. Both are interactive worktexts, the first of their kind published for introductory college Spanish.

▶ All resources in one package

Each **INVITACIONES** worktext contains fifteen lessons, called **episodios**, and each episode is organized in exactly the same way: full-color lesson pages, immediately followed by black-and-white pages with workbook activities. As a result, the worktext offers you all the learning tools you need for learning Spanish in each self-contained volume. In addition, each new worktext comes packaged with a code for the **INVITACIONES** Supersite, a powerful new resource that contains all the audio and video material for the program, as well as lab practice with auto-grading.

▶ Video-driven program

Specially shot for **INVITACIONES**, the **Escenas de la vida** video revolves around the everyday lives and relationships of a group of Spanish-speaking friends as they attend college in the United States. Photos, events, and characters from the episodes are integrated into virtually every section of each lesson.

▶ Personalized learning experience

INVITACIONES invites you to interact with the worktext by filling in information that interests you, prompting personalized reactions, and by providing ideas for use with a partner, small groups, or the entire class. As you study, you will find that the worktext consistently gives you the support you need to carry out real-life tasks in Spanish.

To familiarize yourself with the worktext's organization and features, turn to page xiv and take the **INVITACIONES: Primera parte**-at-a-glance tour. For more information on **INVITACIONES: Segunda parte**, see page xxx.

Escenas de la vida	Para comunicarnos mejor

Escenas de la vida

opens every lesson with an input-driven *and* video-based introduction to the lesson's theme, vocabulary, and grammar.

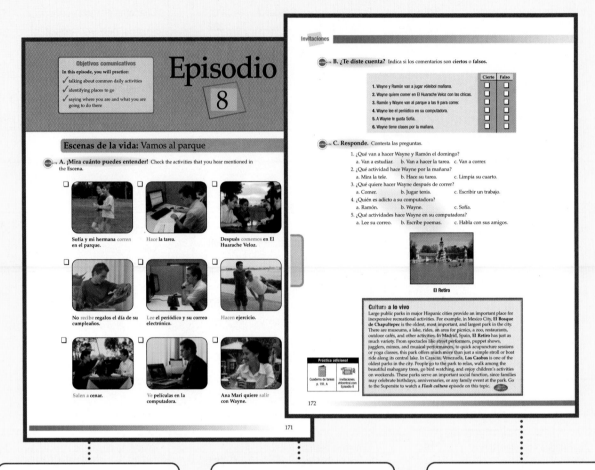

Objetivos comunicativos This brief list highlights the real-life tasks you will be able to carry out in Spanish by the end of the lesson.

Dramatic Video The **Escenas de la vida** sections in your worktext complement the corresponding **Escenas de la vida** episode from the **INVITACIONES** Video Program. The episodes tell the story of a group of Spanish-speaking friends attending college in the United States. To learn more about the video program, turn to pages xxvi–xxvii.

NEW! Authentic Video When applicable, **Flash cultura** video icons or a reference to an authentic TV clip indicate additional video material related to the **Cultura a lo vivo** sections. For more information, see pages xxvi–xxvii.

Activities The **Escenas de la vida** activities guide you through the lesson's video episode and check your understanding of the key events and ideas. **Práctica adicional** references let you know when activities from the **Cuaderno de tareas** and Supersite are available to reinforce **Escenas de la vida.**

Cultura a lo vivo Brief readings deepen your understanding of culture by providing an analysis of the video characters' behavior or by expanding on cultural concepts mentioned in the video.

NEW! Supersite The **INVITACIONES** Supersite (**invitaciones.vhlcentral.com**) provides you access to the entire **INVITACIONES** Video and Audio Programs, as well as additional practice and resources. See page xxviii for more information.

Para comunicarnos mejor

presents grammatical structures necessary for real-life tasks.

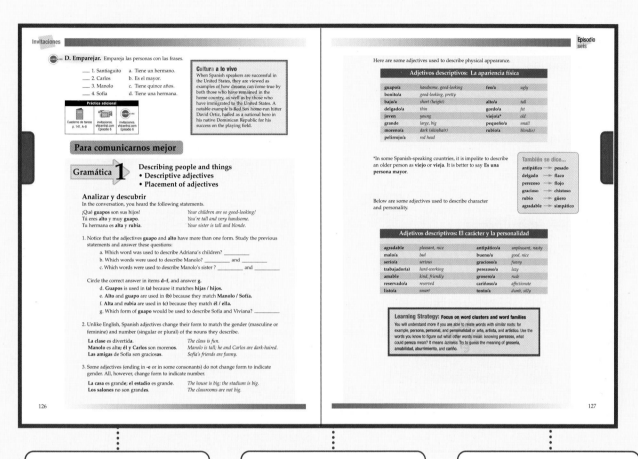

Gramática Formal presentations expand on grammatical concepts previewed in **Escenas de la vida** activities and featured in the corresponding **Escenas de la vida** video episode.

Analizar y descubrir This section appears, when appropriate, to guide you in analyzing and discovering grammatical structures and patterns featured in **Escenas de la vida**, before you use them in upcoming practice activities.

Examples Examples, frequently taken from the lesson's video episode, highlight the language and structures you are studying and put them in real-life contexts.

Charts Colorful, easy-to-use charts call out key grammatical structures and forms, as well as vocabulary fundamental to communicating with the structures at hand.

NEW! Gramática comunicativa When an explanation can be taken further, a **¡Fíjate!** note will refer you to a grammar appendix in the back of this book for more advanced explanations with practice.

Learning Strategy Learning strategy boxes present general techniques you can use to maximize your learning opportunities.

Para comunicarnos mejor
develops practical vocabulary for real-life applications.

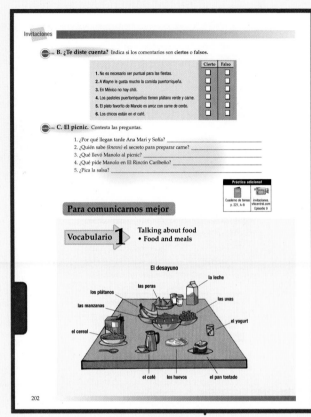

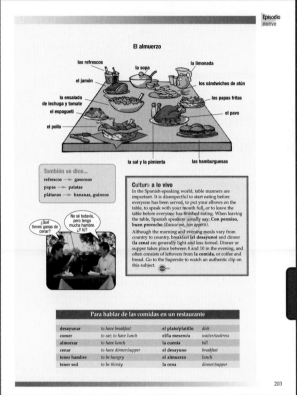

Vocabulario These sections present words and expressions taken from the lesson's video episode, as well as additional vocabulary related to the lesson's topic, using the same type of charts, examples, and other elements as in the **Gramática** sections.

Visual support New vocabulary is supported by illustrations, photographs, or images from the lesson's **Escenas de la vida** video episode.

También se dice In recognition of the richness and diversity of the Spanish language, this feature presents alternate words and expressions used throughout the Spanish-speaking world.

Cultura a lo vivo Brief cultural notes appear, where applicable, to provide background information related to the vocabulary topic.

Para comunicarnos mejor
provides varied types of guided, yet meaningful practice.

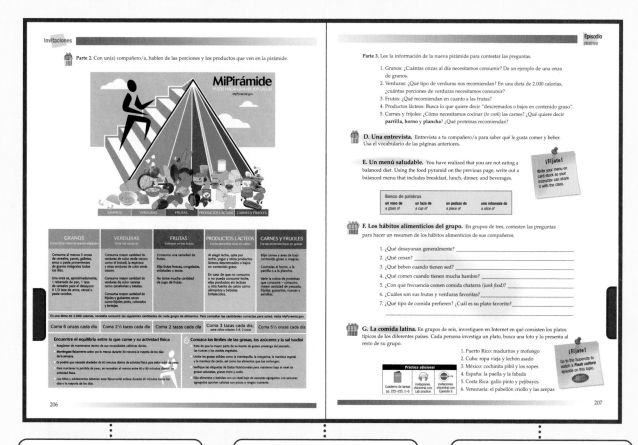

Práctica A wide variety of guided, yet meaningful activities develop your ability to express yourself in Spanish. Cultural information is also often embedded in these activities, as an integral part of their content.

NEW! Supersite The **INVITACIONES** Supersite (**invitaciones.vhlcentral.com**) has even more activities, including lab practice, to help you master the vocabulary and grammar. See page xxviii for more details.

Progression of activities To build your confidence and accurate use of Spanish, the activities begin with those that require only comprehension and progress to those in which you produce the language.

Activity types Activity types include oral exercises, written activities, listening practice, exercises that recycle previously learned vocabulary, pair work, and small group work. Activities are often set up to let you interact hands-on with the materials by writing directly in your worktext.

Banco de palabras These boxes provide you with on-the-spot vocabulary support directly related to the activities they accompany, so you may readily complete the language tasks at hand.

Icons Icons allow you to quickly identify the types of activities you are dealing with: reading, writing, pair work, and group work.

Para comunicarnos mejor
features personalized and video-related activities.

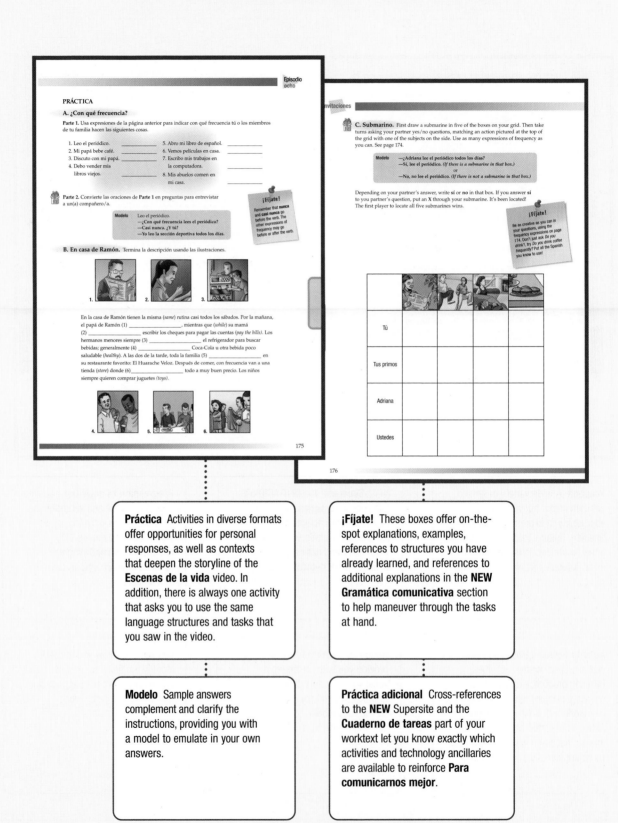

Práctica Activities in diverse formats offer opportunities for personal responses, as well as contexts that deepen the storyline of the **Escenas de la vida** video. In addition, there is always one activity that asks you to use the same language structures and tasks that you saw in the video.

¡Fíjate! These boxes offer on-the-spot explanations, examples, references to structures you have already learned, and references to additional explanations in the **NEW Gramática comunicativa** section to help maneuver through the tasks at hand.

Modelo Sample answers complement and clarify the instructions, providing you with a model to emulate in your own answers.

Práctica adicional Cross-references to the **NEW** Supersite and the **Cuaderno de tareas** part of your worktext let you know exactly which activities and technology ancillaries are available to reinforce **Para comunicarnos mejor**.

Actividades comunicativas

use information gap activities to strengthen your communication skills.

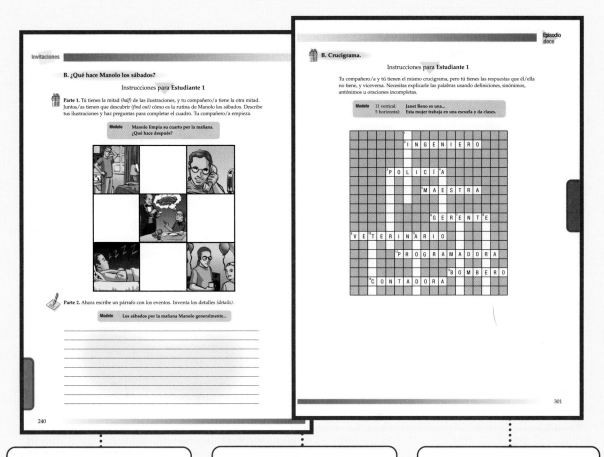

Information gap activities
Information gap activities support you as you practice the vocabulary and grammar of the lesson in problem-solving or other situations. These activities are frequently culturally-oriented. You and a partner each have only half of the information you need, so you must work together to accomplish the task at hand.

Unique Design These communicative activities, intended for classroom use, have a unique design that reflects this goal. From upside-down pages to protect information gap details to ample room for writing, the activities are carefully designed with communication in mind.

Varied activity types In **Crucigrama**, you and a partner give each other hints in order to complete a crossword puzzle, while in **En imágenes**, you work together to interpret a series of pictures. **Sopa de palabras** is based on scrambled sentences, and **Diferencias** deals with different versions of an illustration. Other information gap activities involve completing stories and enacting role-plays.

Actividades comunicativas
include other creative and interactive activities that build your communication skills.

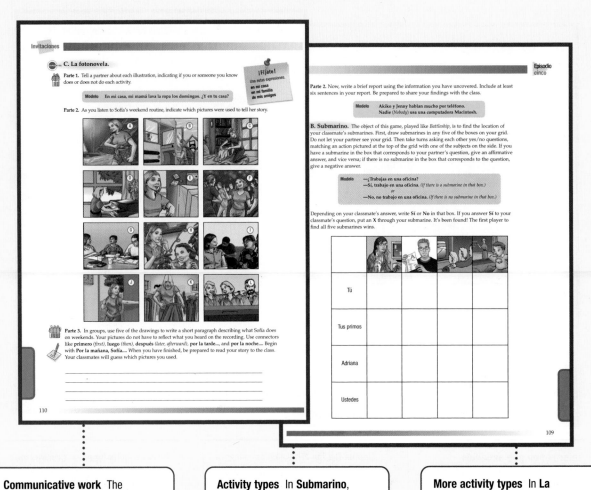

Communicative work The activities in this section require you to use all of the Spanish you have learned to accomplish the tasks at hand. As with the information gap activities, you are given the support you need: illustrations, models, graphs, and charts.

Activity types In **Submarino**, you and a partner ask each other questions in order to locate and sink each other's submarines, while in **Fotonovela**, you use illustrations to create or reconstruct a story.

More activity types In **La encuesta dice**, you and your teammates determine the most common answers to questions that elicit language you have studied. In **La historia va así**, you listen to a story and put a series of pictures in the correct order.

Other activity types Other activities involve surveying your classmates to find out certain information. Story completions and role-plays are also included.

La correspondencia

develops your reading and writing skills in the context of the lesson theme.

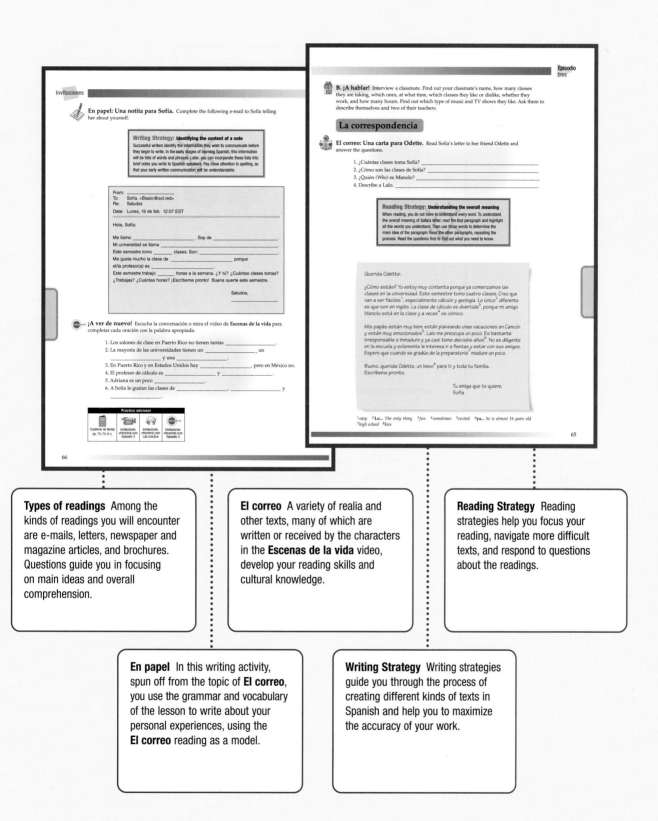

Types of readings Among the kinds of readings you will encounter are e-mails, letters, newspaper and magazine articles, and brochures. Questions guide you in focusing on main ideas and overall comprehension.

El correo A variety of realia and other texts, many of which are written or received by the characters in the **Escenas de la vida** video, develop your reading skills and cultural knowledge.

Reading Strategy Reading strategies help you focus your reading, navigate more difficult texts, and respond to questions about the readings.

En papel In this writing activity, spun off from the topic of **El correo**, you use the grammar and vocabulary of the lesson to write about your personal experiences, using the **El correo** reading as a model.

Writing Strategy Writing strategies guide you through the process of creating different kinds of texts in Spanish and help you to maximize the accuracy of your work.

La correspondencia
synthesizes the language of the lesson and spotlights culture.

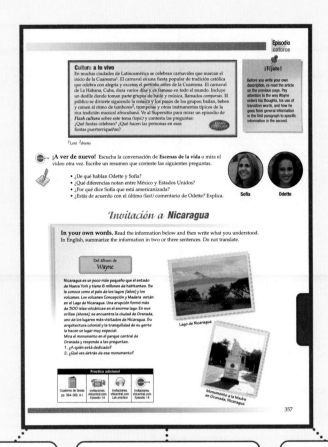

¡A ver de nuevo! In this final activity, you synthesize the vocabulary and grammar of the entire lesson by reviewing and summarizing the content of the lesson's **Escenas de la vida** video episode.

Invitación a... Captioned photos from the albums of the **INVITACIONES** characters introduce you to key places, customs, and artifacts from all twenty-one countries of the Spanish-speaking world, including the United States.

NEW! Video When applicable, a reference leads you to a *Flash cultura* episode or authentic TV clip on the Supersite. See page xxvii for more information.

Vocabulario and Español al instante
serve as important vocabulary references.

Objetivos comunicativos This list restates the communicative tasks that you practiced throughout the lesson and should now be able to perform in Spanish.

Vocabulario personal This unique feature allows you to personalize your language learning by providing you with space to write down vocabulary related to the lesson's theme that is important to your own experiences and interests.

Vocabulario A list of all new words and expressions summarizes the active vocabulary of the lesson, providing an easy reference for review and study.

Español al instante The appendix of your worktext conveniently lists practical vocabulary key to the successful navigation of both your worktext and your classroom. See page 400 for this handy reference.

Cuaderno de tareas
provides workbook activities that reinforce and expand on the materials in the lesson.

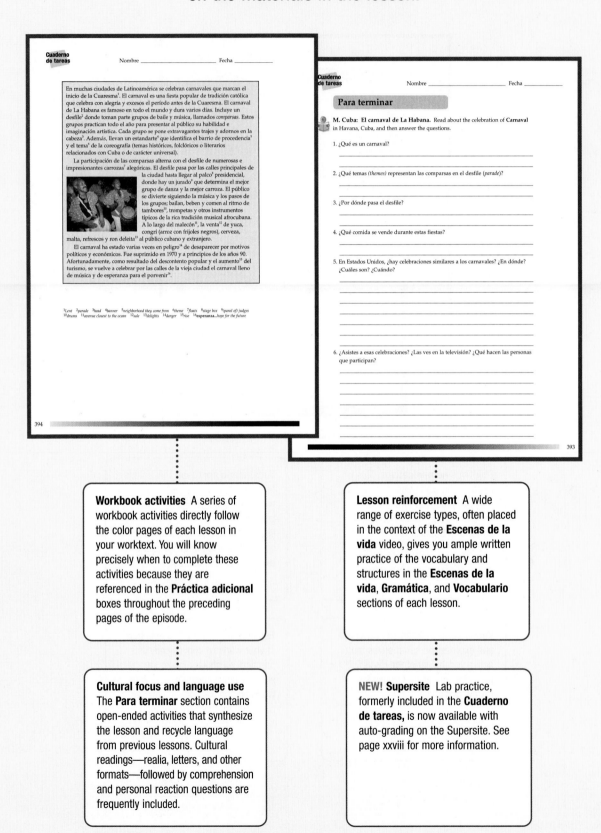

Cuaderno de tareas

Nombre _____ Fecha _____

En muchas ciudades de Latinoamérica se celebran carnavales que marcan el inicio de la Cuaresma[1]. El carnaval es una fiesta popular de tradición católica que celebra con alegría y excesos el período antes de la Cuaresma. El carnaval de La Habana es famoso en todo el mundo y dura varios días. Incluye un desfile[2] donde toman parte grupos de baile y música, llamados *comparsas*. Estos grupos practican todo el año para presentar al público su habilidad e imaginación artística. Cada grupo se pone extravagantes trajes y adornos en la cabeza[3]. Además, llevan un estandarte[4] que identifica el barrio de procedencia[5] y el tema[6] de la coreografía (temas históricos, folclóricos o literarios relacionados con Cuba o de carácter universal).

La participación de las comparsas alterna con el desfile de numerosas e impresionantes carrozas[7] alegóricas. El desfile pasa por las calles principales de la ciudad hasta llegar al palco[8] presidencial, donde hay un jurado[9] que determina el mejor grupo de danza y la mejor carroza. El público se divierte siguiendo la música y los pasos de los grupos; bailan, beben y comen al ritmo de tambores[10], trompetas y otros instrumentos típicos de la rica tradición musical afrocubana. A lo largo del malecón[11], la venta[12] de yuca, congrí (arroz con frijoles negros), cerveza, malta, refrescos y ron deleita[13] al público cubano y extranjero.

El carnaval ha estado varias veces en peligro[14] de desaparecer por motivos políticos y económicos. Fue suprimido en 1970 y a principios de los años 90. Afortunadamente, como resultado del descontento popular y el aumento[15] del turismo, se vuelve a celebrar por las calles de la vieja ciudad el carnaval lleno de música y de esperanza para el porvenir[16].

[1]*Lent* [2]*parade* [3]*head* [4]*banner* [5]*neighborhood they come from* [6]*theme* [7]*floats* [8]*stage box* [9]*(panel of) judges* [10]*drums* [11]*avenue closest to the ocean* [12]*sale* [13]*delights* [14]*danger* [15]*rise* [16]**esperanza**...*hope for the future*

394

Cuaderno de tareas

Nombre _____ Fecha _____

Para terminar

M. Cuba: El carnaval de La Habana. Read about the celebration of **Carnaval** in Havana, Cuba, and then answer the questions.

1. ¿Qué es un carnaval?
_____
_____

2. ¿Qué temas (*themes*) representan las comparsas en el desfile (*parade*)?
_____
_____

3. ¿Por dónde pasa el desfile?
_____
_____

4. ¿Qué comida se vende durante estas fiestas?
_____
_____

5. En Estados Unidos, ¿hay celebraciones similares a los carnavales? ¿En dónde? ¿Cuáles son? ¿Cuándo?
_____
_____
_____
_____
_____

6. ¿Asistes a esas celebraciones? ¿Las ves en la televisión? ¿Qué hacen las personas que participan?
_____
_____
_____
_____
_____
_____

393

Workbook activities A series of workbook activities directly follow the color pages of each lesson in your worktext. You will know precisely when to complete these activities because they are referenced in the **Práctica adicional** boxes throughout the preceding pages of the episode.

Lesson reinforcement A wide range of exercise types, often placed in the context of the **Escenas de la vida** video, gives you ample written practice of the vocabulary and structures in the **Escenas de la vida**, **Gramática**, and **Vocabulario** sections of each lesson.

Cultural focus and language use The **Para terminar** section contains open-ended activities that synthesize the lesson and recycle language from previous lessons. Cultural readings—realia, letters, and other formats—followed by comprehension and personal reaction questions are frequently included.

NEW! Supersite Lab practice, formerly included in the **Cuaderno de tareas,** is now available with auto-grading on the Supersite. See page xxviii for more information.

NEW SECTION!

Revistas culturales

provide a spotlight on the products, practices, and perspectives of the Spanish-speaking world.

Revista cultural Occurring every five lessons, these dynamic, four-page inserts take a thematic approach to culture. The magazine-like design, full of images, readings, and even multi-media components, is an engaging way to deepen your understanding of the cultures of the Spanish-speaking world.

Antes de leer Pre-reading support prepares you for the challenge of reading in a foreign language and practices important strategies on how to derive meaning from context and visual cues.

Lecturas A series of readings exposes you to the richness and diversity of each theme in the Spanish-speaking world. Each feature is carefully written to be comprehensible yet challenging. Dynamic photographs and realia support each feature.

Activities Each feature is complemented by activities that briefly check comprehension before moving on to personalized reactions. After each reading, you will be encouraged to compare and contrast the practices you have learned about to your own culture, and to explore further the topics that most interest you.

Flash cultura Fully-integrated with each **Revista cultural**, this video allows you to experience the sites and sounds of the Spanish-speaking world for yourself. On-page vocabulary support and comprehension activities ensure a successful viewing experience. See page xxvii for more information.

Video Program
Escenas de la vida

Fully integrated with your worktext, the **INVITACIONES: Primera parte** video contains fifteen episodes, one for each lesson in your worktext. The episodes follow a group of Spanish-speaking students attending college in the United States as they confront the challenges and experience the joys of daily life. The video, shot in southern California, follows the characters through an academic year and focuses on the Latino experience and influence in the United States.

Before you see each video episode, your instructor will use the **Escenas de la vida** section to preview the vocabulary and grammatical structures the characters will use and that you will study in the corresponding lesson. As the video progresses, the video conversations carefully combine new vocabulary and grammar with language taught in earlier lessons in your worktext. In this way, the video provides comprehensible input as it puts the language you are learning in action in real-life contexts.

A powerful and important learning tool, the video is integrated into every section of your worktext. The opening section of each lesson, **Escenas de la vida**, prepares you for the video episode and checks your comprehension. Language structures used in the video appear throughout **Para comunicarnos mejor.** The **Actividades comunicativas** and **La correspondencia** sections of each lesson reference the events and characters of the corresponding video episode, and both the **Cuaderno de tarea** workbook activities and online lab activities are often set in the context of the video episode.

The Cast

Here are the main characters you will meet when you watch the **Escenas de la vida: Primera parte** video.

From Mexico,
Sofía Blasio Salas

From Cuba,
Manolo Báez Rodríguez

From the United States, of Mexican and Honduran heritage,
Ana Mari Robledo Suárez

From Puerto Rico,
Adriana Ferreira de Barrón

Ana Mari's brother,
Ramón Robledo Suárez

From the United States,
Wayne Reilly

NEW! Flash cultura

The dynamic, new *Flash cultura* video is fully integrated with the **Revista cultural** section of your worktext, as well as with the **Cultura a lo vivo** and **Invitación a...** sections where possible. Shot all over the Spanish-speaking world, these contemporary and engaging episodes expand on the cultural themes presented in your worktext. Each episode is hosted by a correspondent from the featured country; the host provides valuable information on traditions, events, resources, and practices, and then talks with locals to get their opinions on the subject at hand. The episodes gradually move entirely into Spanish, but feature authentic Spanish interviews from the very beginning, exposing you to diverse and authentic accents from the Spanish-speaking world.

NEW! Video clips

New to this edition, **INVITACIONES** now features authentic video clips from the Spanish-speaking world for select lessons. Clip formats include commercials and news stories, and have been carefully chosen to be comprehensible for students learning Spanish. They offer another valuable window into the products, practices, and perspectives of the Spanish-speaking world, but more importantly, they are a fun and motivating way to improve your Spanish!

Episodio 1, p. 5: *Flash cultura*, Argentina

Episodio 5, p. 102: *Flash cultura*, Ecuador

Revista cultural 1, p. 124: *Flash cultura*, Mexico

Episodio 7, p. 149: Video clip, Argentina;
            p. 153: Video clip, Colombia

Episodio 8, p. 172: *Flash cultura*, Spain;
            p. 187: *Flash cultura*, Mexico

Episodio 9, p. 201: *Flash cultura*, US; p. 203: Video clip, US;
            p. 207: *Flash cultura*, Spain

Revista cultural 2, p. 256: *Flash cultura*, Costa Rica

Episodio 11, p. 271: *Flash cultura*, Ecuador

Episodio 12, p. 292: *Flash cultura*, Peru

Episodio 13, p. 316, *Flash cultura*, Costa Rica

Episodio 14, p. 357: *Flash cultura*, Puerto Rico

Episodio 15, p. 368: Video clip, Chile

Revista cultural 3, p. 398: *Flash cultura*, Argentina

The **INVITACIONES** video program is available in its entirety on the **INVITACIONES** Supersite (invitaciones.vhlcentral.com). To learn more about this exciting new resource, turn the page!

Ancillaries

Supersite

The **INVITACIONES** Supersite provides a wealth of resources for both students and instructors.

Access to the Supersite is free with the purchase of a new student worktext.

Learning tools available to students:

- Practice activities in addition to those in the worktext with auto-grading and real-time feedback

- Open-ended activities where students explore and search the Internet

- The complete **INVITACIONES** Video Program

  - **Escenas de la vida:** this dramatic storyline video follows a cast of characters through an academic year while providing comprehensible input for language acquisition

  - **Flash cultura:** shot on location all over the Spanish-speaking world, this video expands on the cultural themes presented in the worktext

  - **Video clips:** Real commercials and news stories offer you an authentic window into Spanish-language media

- **¡A escuchar!** Lab audio practice (formerly included in the **Cuaderno de tareas**)

  - Pronunciation and/or spelling activities for each lesson

  - Comprehension activities, frequently based on the **Escenas de la vida** video, that practice the lesson's grammar and vocabulary

- MP3 files for the entire **INVITACIONES** audio program

  - Lab audio files

  - Textbook audio files, including audio tracks of the **Escenas de la vida** video

- And more…

Access to all these great features comes built-in with every new worktext, so the Supersite is the only ancillary you need to be successful in your language class. MP3 CDs and the **Escenas de la vida** DVD are also available for purchase.

Resources for instructors:

- Student tracking and grading

- Instructor resources (see next page for more information)

Instructor Ancillaries

Instructor's Annotated Edition (IAE)

The **Instructor's Annotated Edition** provides a wealth of information designed to support classroom teaching and management. The same size as the student worktext, the **IAE** provides answers overprinted on the student pages, as well as resources and suggestions for implementing and extending the worktext activities.

Instructor's Resources (available on Supersite)

The **Instructor's Resources** include materials that reinforce and expand upon the lessons in the student worktext. **Comprehensible Input** provides guidance on what language to pre-teach before showing the video for the **Escenas de la vida** section. **Additional Activities** offer suggestions and materials for more activities to accompany the worktext episodes. The **Video Scripts** and **Audio Scripts** provide transcriptions of all three videos from the **Escenas de la vida** video program and the recorded activities, respectively.

Testing Program

The **Testing Program** contains a quiz for every lesson in **INVITACIONES**, as well as midterms and final exams.

Overhead Transparencies (available on Supersite)

This set of overhead transparencies contains maps of the Spanish-speaking world, as well as selected images from the student worktexts, for use in presenting and reinforcing the language introduced throughout the lessons.

Cuaderno de tareas Answer Key (available on Supersite)

The **Answer Key** provides answers to the workbook activities in the **Cuaderno de tareas** section of the worktext, should instructors wish to distribute them to students for self-correction.

DVD Set

These sets (one for **Primera parte**, one for **Segunda**) each contain a DVD for **Escenas de la vida** as well as one for the corresponding *Flash cultura* episodes for each volume.

Alternate delivery is available for many components. Textbook and Lab Audio material is also available on CD.

INVITACIONES: Segunda parte

This companion volume completes the course, continuing the video storyline and building on the grammatical structures and vocabulary presented in **INVITACIONES: Primera parte.**

INVITACIONES: Segunda parte offers the same features, input-driven instructional approach, and ancillary package as **Primera parte**, as it both reviews the first volume and rounds out the entire **INVITACIONES** program with **Episodios 16–30**.

Reviewers

The authors and the publishing professionals at Vista Higher Learning express their sincere appreciation to the college instructors nationwide who reviewed portions of the **INVITACIONES** program. Their comments and suggestions were invaluable to the final product. We would like to give a special thank-you to Bonnie Brunt from Spokane Falls Community College for her thorough, careful in-depth review of the program.

Susana Ackerman

Valerie Alvarado

Stacy Amling

Corinne Arrieta

Paul Bases

Bonnie Brunt

Nicole Carrier

Heidi Carrillo

Constance Cody

Carmelo Esterrich

Lillian Franklin

Judy Garson

Judy Getty

Norma Avery Hanson

Nora Kirchner

Kilby Kirkconnell

David Leavell

Lana Ledwig

Suzanne McLaughlin

Carrie Mulvihill

Sheryl Novacek

Graciela Pérez

Michele Picotte

Carol Pomares

Graziana Ramsden

José Rojas

Bert Roney

Claudia Schalesky

Lynda Southwick

Hernán J. Torres

Rosa Torres

Linda Tracy

Alexandria Waldron

Janice Wiberg

Judy Williams

Student Reactions

The authors would like to thank the students at California State University San Marcos, where the program was class tested in the summer of 1999, and at Southwestern College, where the **INVITACIONES** program was class-tested from the fall of 1999 until the time of the first edition. Their patience and candid remarks about the activities, the characters, and the philosophy of the text were invigorating and truly useful to the completion of the project. Below are some of their reactions.

"What I liked the most is that it was not a bunch of conjugating. It actually teaches you useful conversations."

"It is a brilliant idea to have everything in one book; I feel I am getting my money's worth."

"All the side notes helped me learn things!"

"I really liked the layout of the book. The activities help to break down your inhibitions about using the language."

"I loved having the vocabulary at the end of every episode."

"I enjoy learning about the characters and their lives; it helps to personalize the material for me."

"I really appreciate not carrying three books around!"

"I enjoyed being able to write all my notes directly on the book. I know that in the future, I can look back and review my Spanish."

"Everything in the episodes was relevant and related to what we were learning!"

"This book made it fun to learn, and the language is sticking to me."

Acknowledgments

The long process of writing this textbook was challenging and full of unexpected changes. It took a lot of tenacity, endurance, and our unappeasable dream that many more students would be successful in learning Spanish, if only the materials they used were more inviting, realistic, interactive, and fun.

Our most heartfelt gratitude goes to José Blanco, who shares our dream and was willing to take the inherent risk of bringing to the market a new, "out of the box" set of books. We are delighted to have been given the opportunity to work with him and his outstanding team of professionals, who made this program a reality.

We are grateful to Beverly Burdette, of Pellissippi State Community College, for creating lab activities to accompany our text; her conscientious contributions have always been in keeping with our own intentions and round-out our Spanish program.

We would like to thank our editors, Sarah Kenney and Gabriela Ferland, for their astute observations, unfaltering hard work and dedication, and, most of all, for their patience and cheery responses to our inquiries.

We are also indebted to our colleagues and friends, whose advice and contributions during the different stages of the manuscript helped us shape the book: Bonnie Brunt, of Spokane Falls Community College for unselfishly sharing her suggestions and observations while using the text in her classes; Dinorah Guadiana-Costa, for her sharp eye and generous time editing quizzes and exams, Concetta Calandra, Margarita Andrade, and Angelina Stewart of Southwestern College, for their support, constructive suggestions and enthusiasm while using our materials in their classes; Cuban poet Pedro Báez, Dr. Ana Hami, Founder of Orange County Children's Therapeutic ARTS Center, and Francisco Zabaleta, of Mesa College, for helping us create culturally and linguistically authentic Cuban, Puerto Rican, and Spanish characters, respectively; Diana Rossner and Nancy Barley, of Lake Tahoe Community College, for always offering sincere and encouraging remarks; Gary Anderson for sharing his ideas unselfishly; Virginia Young, of Grossmont College, for adding activities to our Instructor's Resources; Hal Wingard, the Executive Director of the California Language Teachers Association, for embracing our materials and speaking on our behalf at the Foreign Language Conference of the California Community Colleges. We thank Jonathan Brennan of Mission College for his ideas on exercises promoting Emotional Intelligence. We also give a special thanks to our colleagues and friends at the different institutions in San Diego, who have openly and warmly supported us, both personally and professionally.

A project of this magnitude could not be undertaken without the support of our families and close friends, who have unselfishly shared a piece of their lives by taking care of our children and pets, allowing us to use their pictures, their names, and their stories. Thank you for enduring the joys and sorrows of the past few years with us. We would also like to thank Southwestern College, for not only class testing our program, but also for being so cooperative and accommodating when we shot our video on the campus. Last but not least, we offer our sincere thanks to our wonderful team of adjunct instructors, who have served as anonymous reviewers.

Deana Alonso, Esther Alonso, and Brandon Zaslow

¡Bienvenidos al mundo hispano!

A. How much do you know about the Spanish language? Indicate whether you believe the following statements are true or false.

	Cierto	Falso
1. After English, Spanish is the most frequently spoken language in the United States.	☐	☐
2. One out of every ten United States residents speaks Spanish.	☐	☐
3. The United States has the fifth largest population of Spanish speakers in the world.	☐	☐
4. The first Europeans to settle in the modern-day United States were Spanish speakers.	☐	☐
5. There are over twenty Spanish-speaking countries.	☐	☐
6. More than 350 million people speak Spanish.	☐	☐
7. Spanish is a modern derivative of Latin.	☐	☐

B. Let's meet each other! Listen to your instructor model the pronunciation of the following exchange. Then practice the conversation with three or four classmates.

Estudiante 1:	¡Hola! ¿Cómo estás?
Estudiante 2:	Bien, ¿y tú?
Estudiante 1:	Bien, gracias.
Estudiante 2:	Me llamo _____ *(your name)*. Y tú, ¿cómo te llamas?
Estudiante 1:	Me llamo _____ ¡Mucho gusto!
Estudiante 2:	Igualmente.

C. The Spanish-speaking world. Spanish speakers are a diverse group of ethnicities, religions, and cultures. Learn about exciting places and facts, using your knowledge of English and of the world, as you read the captions under the photographs.

> **Learning Strategy: Using cognates**
>
> A cognate is a word that is similar in two or more languages because of a common origin. The English word *publication* and the Spanish word **publicación** are cognates. Cognates in Spanish and English are always pronounced differently, are often spelled differently, and sometimes differ in meaning. Most of the time, however, you can guess what a Spanish cognate means by associating it with an English word you know. Can you guess the meaning of these cognates?
>
> | colonial | falsos | indicar | contraste | fotografía | millones |
> |---|---|---|---|---|---|
> | comentarios | glaciares | moderna | construcciones | habitantes | montañas |
>
> You can use cognates to help you understand the overall meaning of Spanish sentences. To practice this strategy, read the captions under the following photographs.

En la Ciudad de México hay *(there are)* más de 20 millones de habitantes. Es la ciudad más poblada del mundo.

Chile y Argentina comparten *(share)* la Patagonia, donde hay glaciares e inmensas montañas.

En Puerto Rico, el contraste entre la arquitectura moderna y la arquitectura colonial es visible.

La Avenida 9 de Julio en Buenos Aires, Argentina, es enorme. Buenos Aires se considera el París de América.

Los mayas habitaron parte de México y de Centroamérica.

Las impresionantes murallas de Ávila fueron *(were)* construidas para proteger la ciudad después de expulsar a los árabes del territorio español.

El pueblo inca construyó Machu Picchu en las montañas de los Andes en el área que hoy es Perú.

D. Latinoamérica. Examina las fotografías para *(in order to)* indicar si los comentarios son **ciertos** o **falsos**.

	Cierto	Falso
1. En la Ciudad de México hay más de 20 millones de personas.	☐	☐
2. Puerto Rico tiene *(has)* muchas construcciones antiguas y modernas.	☐	☐
3. Los aztecas construyeron Machu Picchu.	☐	☐
4. El clima de Chile es tropical.	☐	☐
5. La Avenida 9 de Julio es enorme.	☐	☐
6. Los incas eran *(were)* habitantes de México y Guatemala.	☐	☐
7. Los árabes fueron expulsados de España.	☐	☐

Learning Strategy: How to be a successful language-learner

Learning to speak another language can be fun and exciting. Many successful language-learners share certain basic characteristics. Read the following statements to determine why these particular traits are useful in language learning.

1. Students who are excited about learning Spanish do better than students who are indifferent.
   Why do you think a positive attitude is important?

2. Students who are not afraid of speaking Spanish learn more than students who are reluctant to speak.
   Why do you think being willing to speak is important?

3. Students who take risks progress more rapidly than students who are inhibited.
   Why do you think taking risks is important?

4. Students who accept that uncertainty and inconsistency are a part of learning a language learn at a faster rate.
   Why do you think that tolerance of ambiguity is important?

Whether or not you possess these traits, you can learn to communicate well in Spanish. Throughout this book, you will encounter **Learning Strategy** sections designed to improve your study skills. Here are a few for starters.

Listen

Listen carefully in class. At first, you will not be able to understand everything you hear, but you will absorb a lot of Spanish without realizing it.

Speak

Speak as much Spanish as you can. Talk to your instructor and to your classmates in Spanish. Don't be afraid to make mistakes, as they will help you to identify things you need to learn.

Take Notes

Take notes in class. Your memory is going to get a workout, so write things down. Be sure to ask questions in class. Remember, there are no silly questions.

Practice

You will need to practice every day. Learning Spanish is like learning to swim or to play the guitar—the more you practice, the better you become. Cramming the night before an exam is a recipe for disaster!

Take Charge

The key element in shaping your success is you. Look for opportunities to practice Spanish outside of class: watch television in Spanish and listen to Spanish radio stations, talk to your neighbors, or use the Internet. Take charge of your own learning!

Have Fun

You are going to learn Spanish, but it will take time. After all, you didn't learn to speak English overnight! Your worktext is designed to make your learning enjoyable. Have fun and relax. If you do, you will learn faster and more easily.

Objetivos comunicativos

In this episode, you will practice:

✔ greeting and saying good-bye to others

✔ saying which classes you take

✔ saying how many credits/units you take and how many hours you work

Escenas de la vida: El primer día de clases

 A. ¡Mira cuánto puedes entender! *(See how much you can understand!)* As you watch the video, number the statements as you hear them in the conversations.

a. _____ Mucho gusto, señora.

b. _____ Buenos días.

c. _____ Igualmente.

d. _____ Soy de Puerto Rico. ¿Cómo te llamas?

Cultura a lo vivo

Did you notice that when the characters greet each other there is always some kind of physical contact? Hispanics use this contact (a kiss or two on the cheek, a pat on the back, or simply a handshake) to demonstrate openness and warmth. Go to the Supersite to watch a *Flash cultura* episode on this topic.

e. _____ ¡Que te vaya bien!

f. _____ ¿Cómo está usted?

g. _____ Gracias igualmente.

h. _____ Sí, ya sé. Hasta mañana.

i. _____ Encantada. Bueno, tengo clase de inglés ahora.

j. _____ ¿Cómo estás?

k. _____ Mira Manolo, te presento a Ana Mari. Es mi mejor amiga... y no tiene novio.

l. _____ Adiós.

B. ¿Te diste cuenta? *(Did you realize?)* Escucha las conversaciones otra vez para indicar si los comentarios son **ciertos** o **falsos.**

	Cierto	Falso
1. Adriana es de México.	☐	☐
2. Manolo necesita estudiar más.	☐	☐
3. Ana Mari es amiga de Manolo.	☐	☐
4. Manolo toma *(takes)* una clase de inglés.	☐	☐
5. Ana Mari no tiene novio *(doesn't have a boyfriend).*	☐	☐

C. ¿Quién lo dijo? *(Who said it?)* Indica quién hace estos comentarios: Adriana (**A**), Sofía (**S**), Ana Mari (**AM**), Manolo (**M**) o el profesor López (**pL**).

_____ 1. Soy de Puerto Rico.

_____ 2. Buenos días, profesor López.

_____ 3. Este semestre necesitas estudiar más.

_____ 4. Te presento a Ana Mari.

_____ 5. Encantada.

_____ 6. Tengo clase de inglés ahora.

_____ 7. Mucho gusto de conocerte.

_____ 8. ¡Que te vaya bien!

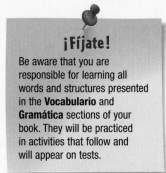

Práctica adicional		
Cuaderno de tareas p. 21, A	invitaciones. vhlcentral.com Episodio 1	invitaciones. vhlcentral.com Episodio 1

Para comunicarnos mejor

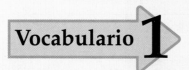

Vocabulario 1 ▷ **Greeting and saying good-bye to others • Greetings and good-byes**

Use these informal expressions when speaking to someone with whom you have a close relationship, such as a family member, friend, or someone your age or younger.

Para hablar con amigos	
¿Cómo estás?	*How are you?*
¿Y tú?	*And you?*
¿Cómo te llamas?	*What's your name?*
¡Que te vaya bien!	*Have a nice day!*
Te presento a...	*I'd like you to meet...*

¡Fíjate!
Be aware that you are responsible for learning all words and structures presented in the **Vocabulario** and **Gramática** sections of your book. They will be practiced in activities that follow and will appear on tests.

6

When speaking to someone with whom you do not have a close relationship, someone you would address with a title and a last name, or an older or higher–ranking person, use these formal expressions to show respect:

formal

Para hablar con respeto

¿Cómo está?	*How are you?*	**señor (Sr.)**	*Mr., sir*
¿Y usted?	*And you?*	**señora (Sra.)**	*Mrs., ma'am*
¿Cómo se llama?	*What's your name?*	**señorita (Srta.)**	*Miss*
¡Que le vaya bien!	*Have a nice day!*	**doctor(a) (Dr(a).)**	*Doctor*
Le presento a...	*I'd like you to meet...*	**profesor(a) (Prof(a).)**	*Professor*

¡Fíjate!

When in doubt about whether you should use **tú** or **usted**, use the formal **usted** forms to show respect.

Buenos días, profesor López.

Hola, Manolo. ¿Cómo estás?

Mira Manolo, te presento a Ana Mari.

Mucho gusto.

Más saludos, despedidas y expresiones de cortesía

Hola.	*Hi.*
Buenos días.	*Good morning.* (from dawn until noon)
Buenas tardes.	*Good afternoon.* (from noon until dusk)
Buenas noches.	*Good evening./Good night.* (from dusk until dawn)
Hasta luego.	*See you later.*
Hasta mañana.	*See you tomorrow.*
Nos vemos mañana.	*See you tomorrow.* (you have arranged to meet tomorrow)
Adiós.	*Good-bye.*
Me llamo...	*My name is...*
Mucho gusto.	*Nice to meet you.*
Encantado.	*Pleased to meet you.* (said by a man)
Encantada.	*Pleased to meet you.* (said by a woman)
Igualmente.	*Nice to meet you, too.*
Gracias.	*Thank you.*
De nada.	*You're welcome.*
Bien.	*Fine.*
Muy bien.	*Very well.*
Más o menos.	*So-so.*

Learning Strategy: Avoid word-for-word translation

Because English and Spanish are independent languages that often express the same thought in different ways, you should avoid translating word-for-word. For example, **¡Que te vaya bien!** might be translated as *May it go well with you.* The idea Spanish speakers mean to convey, however, is *Have a nice day!* So, learn the meaning of language "chunks," and avoid word-for-word translations.

PRÁCTICA

 A. ¡A actuar! With a classmate, act out the following conversations.

Después de la clase

Manolo	**Buenos días**, profesor López. **¿Cómo está usted?**
Profesor	¿Otra vez aquí? *((You) here again?)*
Manolo	Sí, necesito pasar esta clase.
Profesor	Este semestre necesitas estudiar más.
Manolo	Sí, ya sé. **Hasta mañana**.
Profesor	**¡Que te vaya bien!**
Manolo	**Gracias. Igualmente.**

Te presento a Ana Mari

Sofía	**Hola**, Ana Mari. **¿Cómo estás?**
Ana Mari	**Muy bien. ¿Y tú?**
Sofía	**Bien, gracias.**
Sofía	Mira, Manolo, **te presento** a Ana Mari. Es mi mejor amiga. Y no tiene novio.
Ana Mari	¡Sofía!
Manolo	**Mucho gusto.**
Ana Mari	**Encantada**. Bueno, tengo clase de inglés ahora. **Hasta luego.** Y **mucho gusto** de conocerte.
Manolo	**Gracias. Igualmente.**
Sofía	**Adiós**, Ana Mari. **¡Que te vaya bien!**

B. ¿Qué respondes? Imagina que conversas con Sofía. Responde apropiadamente.

1. Hola, ¿cómo te llamas? *Me llamo Anne Marie*
2. Te presento a Manolo. *Mucho gusto Manolo*
3. Hasta luego. *Adiós*
4. ¡Buenos días! *hola!*
5. Gracias. *De nada*
6. Adiós. *Que te vaya Bien*

C. Buenos días, profesor. Imagina que conversas con el profesor López. Responde apropiadamente.

1. Buenas tardes. *Buenas tardes*
2. ¿Cómo estás? *muy bien, gracias*
3. Mucho gusto. *encantada*
4. Hasta mañana. _____
5. ¡Que te vaya bien! _____
6. Buenas noches. *Buenas noches*

D. ¿Cómo respondes? *(How do you answer?)* Escucha las frases para seleccionar la respuesta apropiada.

1. a. Más o menos. b. Mucho gusto. c. Gracias.
2. a. Igualmente. b. ¡Que le vaya bien! c. Buenos días.
3. a. Igualmente. b. ¿Y usted? c. ¡Que te vaya bien!
4. a. ¿Y tú? b. ¿Cómo se llama? c. Muy bien, gracias.
5. a. Sí, gracias. b. Me llamo... c. Hasta luego.

E. Los nombres de mis compañeros. Imagina que estás en una fiesta. Saluda *(Greet)* a seis compañeros nuevos y escribe sus nombres.

Modelo	—Hola, ¿cómo estás?
	—Bien, ¿y tú?
	—Bien, gracias.
	—¿Cómo te llamas?
	—Me llamo Christy, ¿y tú?
	—Me llamo Paul.
	—Mucho gusto.
	—Igualmente.

_____ _____ _____

_____ _____ _____

F. ¡A conversar! Con un(a) compañero/a, usa las expresiones necesarias para inventar una conversación para cada *(each)* situación. *(Make sure each conversation has at least four exchanges.)*

1. You see your instructor at ten in the morning. Extend a greeting, ask how he/she is, and then say good-bye.

2. A new student has just joined the class. Greet the student and find out his/her name.

3. Your friend wants to meet the new student. Introduce him/her.

4. Class is over. Say good-bye to your friend and wish him/her a good day. Tell your friend you will see him/her tomorrow.

5. Your roommate returns home at four in the afternoon. Greet each other and ask each other how you are.

¡Fíjate!

In each conversation, use as many different expressions as you can.

Práctica adicional		

Cuaderno de tareas pp. 21–23, B–H	invitaciones. vhlcentral.com Lab practice	invitaciones. vhlcentral.com Episodio 1

Vocabulario 2

Saying which classes you take
- **The alphabet**
- **Class subjects**

You have probably noticed that in Spanish, there is a very close relationship between the way words are written and the way they are pronounced. This feature helps you learn how to spell and pronounce Spanish words. Spanish sounds, however, do not have exact equivalents in English, so do not rely on English sounds when you pronounce Spanish words.

A 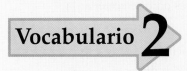 alfabeto	Be (grande) bandera	Ce cuaderno	CHe mochila	De diccionario
E escritorio	eFe fotocopias	Ge geografía	Hache hombre	I adiós good-bye au revoir ciao inglés
Jota mujer	Ka kiosko	eLe libro	eLLe silla	eMe mapa
eNe 1 2 3 4 5 6 números	eÑe baño	O oficina	Pe pluma	Q(cu) química
eRe librería	eRRe carro	eSe salón de clases	Te tenis	U USC UNIVERSITY OF SOUTHERN CALIFORNIA universidad
Ve (chica) video	W doble u Washington	X equis examen	Y (i griega) playa	Zeta lápiz

¡Fíjate!

Because the letters **b** and **v** have the same pronunciation in Spanish, Spanish speakers distinguish between the two by calling **b** "**Be grande**" and **v** "**Ve chica.**"

¡Fíjate!

To *say uppercase* and *lowercase*, use the terms **mayúscula** and **minúscula**, respectively. To indicate that a letter takes an accent, say **con acento** after the letter.

1. In 1994, the **Real Academia** subsumed **ch** and **ll** under **c** and **l** in alphabetized lists. For example, in dictionaries, entries starting with **ch** come between **ce** and **ci**, not under a separate letter between **c** and **d.** You should use **ch** and **ll** when spelling your name to Spanish speakers. You should also use **rr** to describe two **r**'s together, although **rr** is not technically a letter.

2. Ñ does not exist in English. The sound exists in words like *onion* and *canyon*.

3. The Spanish vowels **a, e, i, o,** and **u** are short and tense. Do not move your tongue, lips, or jaws when pronouncing them, to avoid the glide sound of English vowels.

PRÁCTICA

G. Pronunciación. Repeat the letters and the words in the alphabet box on page 10 after your instructor. Which words are cognates (words that are the same or almost the same in both languages)?

_____

H. ¿Tienes buena memoria? Write the words in Spanish.

1. pen _____   4. pencil _____   7. book _____
2. bookstore _____   5. dictionary _____   8. classroom _____
3. notebook _____   6. English _____   9. office _____

I. Dictado. You will hear eight famous last names. Write the names in the spaces provided.

1. _____   4. _____   7. _____
2. _____   5. _____   8. _____
3. _____   6. _____

J. ¿Quiénes son? *(Who are they?)* Match the last names from **Práctica I** with the first names below to describe eight Spanish-speaking celebrities.

John	Jennifer	Eva	Cristina
Sammy	Rafael	Javier	Salma

1. _____ es un actor colombiano.
2. _____ es una actriz de origen puertorriqueño.
3. _____ es una actriz de origen mexicoamericano.
4. _____ es una actriz mexicana.
5. _____ es un beisbolista dominicano.
6. _____ es una periodista y conductora cubana.
7. _____ es un actor español.
8. _____ es un tenista español.

• Class subjects

Listen carefully as your instructor pronounces the names of the class subjects **(las materias)** listed below. Repeat each word after him/her, reproducing the Spanish sounds as closely as you can.

Las materias			
antropología	economía	geografía	matemáticas
astronomía	(educación) física	historia	música
biología	español	inglés	química
drama	filosofía	literatura	psicología

PRÁCTICA

K. Personas famosas. Empareja las personas famosas con las materias.

_____	1. matemáticas	a. Jane Goodall
_____	2. astronomía	b. Sócrates
_____	3. economía	c. Adam Smith
_____	4. filosofía	d. Albert Einstein
_____	5. drama	e. Galileo
_____	6. antropología	f. Shakespeare

L. Asociaciones. ¿Qué materia(s) asocias con estas *(these)* personas?

1. Charles Darwin _____

2. Pitágoras *(Pythagoras)* _____

3. Toni Morrison/Isabel Allende _____

4. Álex Rodríguez/Oliver Pérez _____

5. Wolfgang Amadeus Mozart _____

6. Sigmund Freud _____

M. ¿Tomas una clase de...? *(Are you taking a... class?)* Use the list of classes from page 11 to find out if your partner is taking any of those courses.

Modelo	—¿Tomas *(Are you taking)* una clase de historia?

—Sí, ¿y tú?   —No, ¿y tú?
—Yo también *(Me too).*   or   Yo no.   —Yo tampoco *(Me neither).*   or   Yo sí.

Now write the classes your partner is taking.
Las clases de mi compañero/a son: ___economía, drama___

N. Mis clases. Escribe las clases que tomas *(you take)* este *(this)* semestre/trimestre y las clases que necesitas tomar *(you need to take)* el próximo *(next)* semestre/trimestre.

Este semestre/trimestre	El próximo semestre/trimestre
_____	_____
_____	_____
_____	_____
_____	_____
_____	_____

¡Fíjate!
Use the list of courses in **Vocabulario adicional**, p. 402, to find out the names of your classes in Spanish.

Ñ. Tus clases. Talk to a classmate to find out which classes he or she is currently taking and which classes they need to take next semester/trimester.

> **Modelo** —¿Qué clases tomas este semestre/trimestre (*Which classes are you taking this semester/trimester*)?
> —Historia, matemáticas y español.
> —¿Qué clases necesitas tomar el próximo semestre/trimestre (*Which classes do you need to take next semester/trimester*)?
> —Física, antropología y español. ¿Y tú, qué clases tomas este semestre?

Práctica adicional

Cuaderno de tareas
p. 23, I–J

SUPERSITE

invitaciones.
vhlcentral.com
Episodio 1

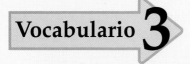 **Vocabulario 3**

Saying how many credits/units you take and how many hours you work
• **Numbers 0–40**

Los números del 0 al 40			
0 cero			
1 uno	11 once	21 veintiuno	31 treinta y uno
2 dos	12 doce	22 veintidós	32 treinta y dos
3 tres	13 trece	23 veintitrés	33 treinta y tres
4 cuatro	14 catorce	24 veinticuatro	34 treinta y cuatro
5 cinco	15 quince	25 veinticinco	35 treinta y cinco
6 seis	16 dieciséis	26 veintiséis	36 treinta y seis
7 siete	17 diecisiete	27 veintisiete	37 treinta y siete
8 ocho	18 dieciocho	28 veintiocho	38 treinta y ocho
9 nueve	19 diecinueve	29 veintinueve	39 treinta y nueve
10 diez	20 veinte	30 treinta	40 cuarenta

1. In some countries, the numbers from 16 through 19 and 21 through 29 are written as three separate words: **diez y seis, veinte y tres.**
2. The number *one* has three forms: **uno** (used when counting: **treinta y uno, treinta y dos...**), **un** (used before masculine nouns: **un libro, veintiún cuadernos**), and **una** (used before feminine nouns: **una pluma, treinta y una señoras**).
3. To ask and say how many classes you take and how many hours you work, use the following expressions:

¿Cuántas clases tomas? Tomo...   *How many classes are you taking? I take...*
¿Cuántas horas trabajas? Trabajo...   *How many hours do you work? I work...*

PRÁCTICA

O. Asociaciones. What number do you associate with...?

1. a week
2. the month of May
3. a triangle
4. all of your fingers
5. a square
6. the lives of a cat
7. an octopus
8. your eyes
9. your head

P. Sumas y restas. *(Addition and subtraction.)* Imagine you are a teacher **(maestro/a)** tutoring a first-grade student in math. Ask the student to give you the answers to the following problems.

Modelo	2 + 5 = ?		25 -12 = ?
	Maestro: **Dos más (*plus*) cinco son...**	Maestro:	**Veinticinco menos (*minus*) doce son...**
	Estudiante: **Siete.**	Estudiante:	**Trece.**

1. 8 + 6 = ?   5. 30 - 18 = ?   9. 47 - 14 = ?

2. 11 + 9 =?   6. 28 - 7 = ?   10. 15 + 17 = ?

3. 23 - 12 = ?   7. 18 + 4 = ?   11. 45 - 7 = ?

4. 12 + 13 = ?   8. 20 - 1 = ?   12. 26 - 16 = ?

Q. Trabajas demasiado. *(You work too much.)*

Parte 1. Find out from four of your classmates how many academic units/credits they are taking and how many hours per week they work. Fill out the chart below.

Modelo	—¿Cuántos créditos tomas este semestre?	—¿Cuántas horas trabajas?
	—12. ¿Y tú?	—25. ¿Y tú?
	—18.	—No trabajo.

	Nombre	Créditos este semestre	Horas de trabajo a la semana
1.	_____	_____	_____
2.	_____	_____	_____
3.	_____	_____	_____
4.	_____	_____	_____

> **¡Fíjate!**
>
> Native speakers use a variety of expressions to react to people's comments. Here are some you can use:
>
> **¡Pobrecito/a!** *Poor thing!*
> **¿En serio?** *For real?*
> **¿Qué te pasa?** *What's wrong (with you)?*

Parte 2. Now check the chart to see if your classmates follow the recommended work/study ratio per week. Comment on the results. You may use expressions from the **Banco de palabras**.

Si trabajas...	Debes tomar sólo...	Necesitas estudiar...
40 hrs.	6 créditos	12 horas por semana
30 hrs.	9 créditos	18 horas por semana
20 hrs.	12 créditos	24 horas por semana
10 hrs.	15 créditos	30 horas por semana
0 hrs.	18 créditos	36 horas por semana

> **Banco de palabras**
>
> **Trabajas demasiado.**
> *You work too much.*
>
> **Necesitas tomar menos clases.**
> *You need to take fewer classes.*
>
> **Vas a salir bien.**
> *You're going to do well.*

R. Juego de lotería. You are going to play the lottery. First write six numbers between 10 and 40 on the lines in your worktext. Then listen to the three sets of winning numbers, write them down, and circle the ones that match your selections.

Juego # 1 _____ _____ _____ _____ _____ _____

Juego # 2 _____ _____ _____ _____ _____ _____

Juego # 3 _____ _____ _____ _____ _____ _____

Invitación a **Estados Unidos**

S. In your own words. Comprehending main ideas in messages is an important skill to acquire when you are learning a second language. Read the information below in order to write, in your own words, what you understood. Use English, do not translate, summarize the information in one or two sentences.

Del álbum de
Sofía

La comunidad hispana más grande en Estados Unidos es la mexicoamericana. Su influencia en la cultura estadounidense es obvia en la comida, la música y el arte. La fiesta del 5 de mayo se celebra en muchas ciudades y prácticamente en todos los estados del suroeste del país. Los mariachis y grupos folclóricos son espectáculos comunes en muchos eventos norteamericanos.

T. Palabras. El inglés usa muchas palabras del español. Por ejemplo, *aficionado, alfalfa, bronco, cilantro, coyote, galleon* (galeón), *incommunicado, lasso* (lazo), *papaya, patio, plaza, stampede* (estampida), *tomato, vanilla*, etc.

Find at least ten more words of Spanish origin.

_____ _____ _____ _____ _____

_____ _____ _____ _____ _____

Práctica adicional		
Cuaderno de tareas p. 24, K–M	invitaciones. vhlcentral.com Lab practice	invitaciones. vhlcentral.com Episodio 1

15

Actividades comunicativas

In this activity, you will interact with another student. Decide who will take the role of **Estudiante 1,** and who will take the role of **Estudiante 2. Estudiante 1** follows one set of instructions, while **Estudiante 2** follows another set found on the following page. Neither you nor your partner should look at the other's instructions or information.

¡Fíjate!

The **Actividades comunicativas** require you to use all the Spanish you have learned to accomplish the task at hand. Do not be afraid of making mistakes. The purpose of these activities is to provide practice communicating in Spanish.

 A. Las agendas.

Instrucciones para **Estudiante 1**

You took home your co-worker's list of clients and left your own list at the office. By telephone, ask your co-worker to give you the names and phone numbers of your clients. Ask your partner to spell out the names. When asked, be ready to tell your co-worker the names and numbers of his/her clients. Alternate asking and answering questions. Use questions like the ones below.

Banco de palabras	
¿Cómo se llama el cliente número uno? *What is the first client's name?*	**¿Cuál es su teléfono?** *What is his/her phone number?*
¿Cómo se escribe su nombre? *How do you spell his/her name?*	

¡Fíjate!

Review **El alfabeto** on page 10 to prepare for this activity. Notice that telephone numbers are given in sets of two, except for the first number (4-21-05-25).

Mis clientes:

	Nombre	Teléfono
1.	_____	_____
2.	_____	_____
3.	_____	_____
4.	_____	_____

Los clientes de tu compañero/a:

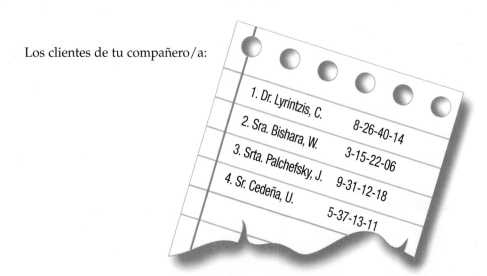

1. Dr. Lyrintzis, C.   8-26-40-14
2. Sra. Bishara, W.   3-15-22-06
3. Srta. Palchefsky, J.   9-31-12-18
4. Sr. Cedeña, U.   5-37-13-11

A. Las agendas.

Instrucciones para **Estudiante 2**

You took home your co-worker's list of clients and left your own list at the office. By telephone, ask your co-worker to give you the names and phone numbers of your clients. Ask your partner to spell out the names. When asked, be ready to tell your co-worker the names and numbers of their clients. Alternate asking and answering questions. Use questions like the ones below.

Banco de palabras

¿Cómo se llama el cliente número uno?
What is the first client's name?

¿Cómo se escribe su nombre?
How do you spell their name?

¿Cuál es su teléfono?
What is their phone number?

¡Fíjate!

Review **El alfabeto** on page 10 to prepare for this activity. Notice that telephone numbers are given in sets of two, except for the first number (4-21-05-25).

Mis clientes:

	Nombre	Teléfono
1.	_____	_____
2.	_____	_____
3.	_____	_____
4.	_____	_____

Los clientes de tu compañero/a:

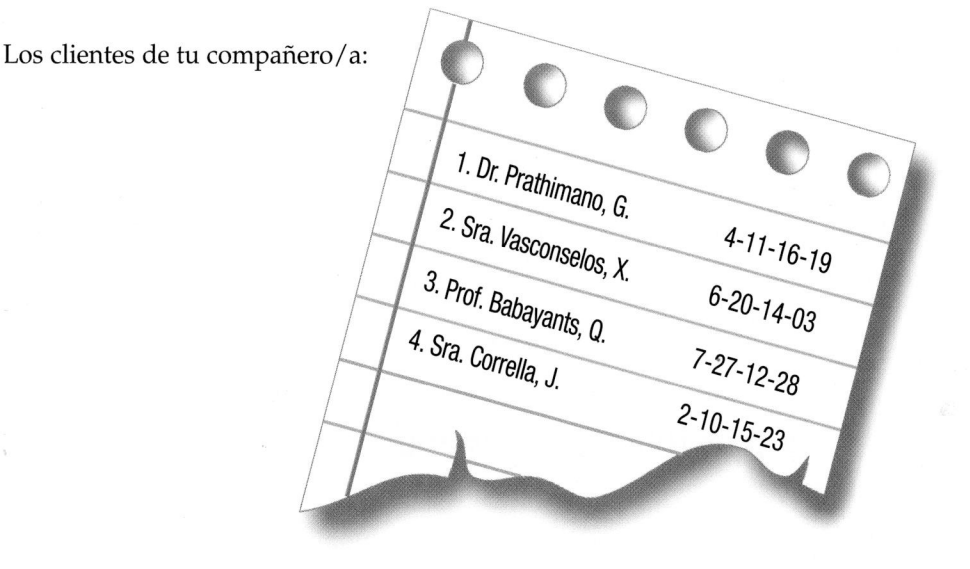

1. Dr. Prathimano, G.   4-11-16-19
2. Sra. Vasconselos, X.   6-20-14-03
3. Prof. Babayants, Q.   7-27-12-28
4. Sra. Corrella, J.   2-10-15-23

La correspondencia

El correo: La Universidad Autónoma de Guadalajara.

Parte 1. You received a brochure in the mail from the Universidad Autónoma de Guadalajara, but it was damaged and you cannot read all of the information. Call the university and listen to its automated message to fill out the missing information.

UNIVERSIDAD AUTÓNOMA DE GUADALAJARA

ÚNICO. Universidad en la comunidad ofrece las siguientes carreras:

- Fisioterapia
- Comercialización y ventas
- _____
- _____
- Prótesis dental
- Mercado de valores
- _____
- Fotografía
- Diseño y _____ de parques y _____
- Electromecánica industrial
- _____

VEN A FORMAR PARTE DE UNA UNIVERSIDAD

¡Con un estilo ÚNICO!

ÚNICO

UNIVERSIDAD EN LA COMUNIDAD

Parte 2. Read the complete brochure and answer the following questions in English.

1. Which areas of study look the most interesting to you? Why?

_____

2. Which areas appeal to you the least? Why?

_____

En papel: Presentación. Introduce yourself to your instructor! Fill out the card your instructor will give you with your personal information.

¡A ver de nuevo! Watch or listen to the **Escena** again to match the elements from the two columns.

I.
_____ 1. Adriana   a. es amiga de Ana Mari.
_____ 2. Sofía   b. necesita pasar la clase de cálculo.
_____ 3. Manolo   c. es de Puerto Rico.

II.
_____ 1. El Prof. López   a. tiene una clase de inglés.
_____ 2. Manolo   b. es profesor.
_____ 3. Ana Mari   c. necesita estudiar más (*needs to study more*).

III.
_____ 1. Sofía   a. no tiene novio (*doesn't have a boyfriend*).
_____ 2. Ana Mari   b. es de México.
_____ 3. El Prof. López   c. dice (*says*) "Manolo, ¿otra vez aquí?"

Práctica adicional			
Cuaderno de tareas pp. 25–28, N–P	invitaciones. vhlcentral.com Episodio 1	invitaciones. vhlcentral.com Lab practice	invitaciones. vhlcentral.com Episodio 1

Vocabulario del Episodio 1

Para hablar con amigos *To speak to friends*

¿Cómo estás?	How are you?
¿Y tú?	And you?
¿Cómo te llamas?	What's your name?
¡Que te vaya bien!	Have a nice day!
Te presento a...	I'd like you to meet...
¿Cuántas clases tomas? Tomo...	How many classes are you taking? I take...
¿Cuántas horas trabajas? Trabajo...	How many hours do you work? I work...

Para hablar con respeto *To speak with respect*

¿Cómo está?	How are you?	señor (Sr.)	Mr., sir
¿Y usted?	And you?	señora (Sra.)	Mrs., ma'am
¿Cómo se llama?	What's your name?	señorita (Srta.)	Miss
¡Que le vaya bien!	Have a nice day!	doctor(a) (Dr(a).)	Doctor
Le presento a...	I'd like you to meet...	profesor(a) (Prof(a).)	Professor

Más saludos, despedidas y expresiones de cortesía *More greetings, good-byes, and courtesy expressions*

Hola.	Hi.
Buenos días.	Good morning. (from dawn until noon)
Buenas tardes.	Good afternoon. (from noon until dusk)
Buenas noches.	Good evening. Good night. (from dusk until dawn)
Hasta luego.	See you later.
Hasta mañana.	See you tomorrow.
Nos vemos mañana.	See you tomorrow. (you have arranged to meet tomorrow)
Adiós.	Good-bye.
Me llamo...	My name is...
Mucho gusto.	Nice to meet you.
Encantado.	Pleased to meet you. (said by a man)
Encantada.	Pleased to meet you. (said by a woman)
Igualmente.	Nice to meet you, too.
Gracias.	Thank you.
De nada.	You're welcome.
Bien.	Fine.
Muy bien.	Very well.
Más o menos.	So-so.

Las materias *Class subjects*

antropología	economía	geografía	matemáticas
astronomía	(educación) física	historia	música
biología	español	inglés	química
drama	filosofía	literatura	sicología

19

Los números del 0 al 40

0 **cero**			
1 **uno**	11 **once**	21 **veintiuno**	31 **treinta y uno**
2 **dos**	12 **doce**	22 **veintidós**	32 **treinta y dos**
3 **tres**	13 **trece**	23 **veintitrés**	33 **treinta y tres**
4 **cuatro**	14 **catorce**	24 **veinticuatro**	34 **treinta y cuatro**
5 **cinco**	15 **quince**	25 **veinticinco**	35 **treinta y cinco**
6 **seis**	16 **dieciséis**	26 **veintiséis**	36 **treinta y seis**
7 **siete**	17 **diecisiete**	27 **veintisiete**	37 **treinta y siete**
8 **ocho**	18 **dieciocho**	28 **veintiocho**	38 **treinta y ocho**
9 **nueve**	19 **diecinueve**	29 **veintinueve**	39 **treinta y nueve**
10 **diez**	20 **veinte**	30 **treinta**	40 **cuarenta**

¡Fíjate!

This section is the place where you can write down and easily reference the vocabulary that applies to your own life and interests.

Vocabulario personal

Write the words that you need to know to talk about yourself in Spanish.

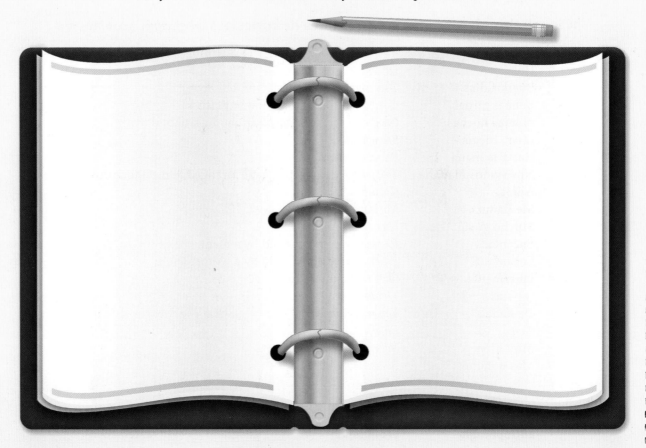

Episodio

Cuaderno de tareas

1

Escenas de la vida: El primer día de clases

 A. ¡Mira cuánto entendiste! See how much of the **Escena** you understood by matching the Spanish sentences with their English equivalents.

1. En la clase de cálculo

_____ 1. Mucho gusto.   a. And you?

_____ 2. ¿Hablas español?   b. Nice to meet you, too.

_____ 3. Igualmente.   c. Do you speak Spanish?

_____ 4. ¿Cómo te llamas?   d. I'm from...

_____ 5. Soy de...   e. What's your name?

_____ 6. ¿Y usted?   f. Nice to meet you.

2. Después de la clase

_____ 7. Hasta mañana.   g. I'd like you to meet...

_____ 8. ¡Que te vaya bien!   h. See you later.

_____ 9. Necesito pasar esta clase. i. I need to pass this class.

_____10. Es mi mejor amiga.   j. Have a nice day!

_____11. Hasta luego.   k. She's my best friend.

_____12. Te presento a...   l. See you tomorrow.

Vocabulario 1   **Greeting and saying good-bye to others**
• **Greetings and good-byes**

B. Para saludar. Select the appropriate greeting, according to the time of the day: **Buenos días, Buenas tardes,** or **Buenas noches.**

1. 1:45 pm _____.   3. 6:30 am _____.   5. 11:00 am _____.

2. 8:00 pm _____.   4. 10:30 pm _____.   6. 3:30 pm _____.

C. ¿Formal o informal? Write the expressions that you would use when talking to Manolo and those you would use when talking to Professor López in the appropiate column.

| ¿Cómo estás? | ¿Cómo se llama? | ¿Y tú? | ¿Y usted? |
| Te presento a... | ¿Cómo está? | ¿Cómo te llamas? | ¡Que le vaya bien! |

Manolo

_____
_____
_____
_____

Profesor López

_____
_____
_____
_____

D. Saludos. Match each statement with the appropriate response.

_____ 1. Hola. ¿Cómo te llamas?   a. Bien, ¿y usted?

_____ 2. Te presento a Roberto.   b. Martha.

_____ 3. Hasta luego.   c. Adiós.

_____ 4. ¿Cómo está usted?   d. Mucho gusto.

E. Te presento a Ana Mari. Order the statements so the dialogue makes sense.

_____ a. Igualmente.   _____ e. Muy bien. ¿Y tú?

__1__ b. Hola, Ana Mari. ¿Cómo estás?   _____ f. Bien, gracias.

_____ c. Mucho gusto.   _____ g. Adiós, Ana Mari. ¡Que te vaya bien!

_____ d. Pilar, te presento a Ana Mari.   _____ h. Bueno, hasta luego. Tengo clase ahora.

F. ¡Hola! Use the words from the list to complete the conversations between Adriana and Pilar, a counselor.

| Adriana | español | mucho | usted |
| cómo | igualmente | soy de | vaya |

Adriana   ¿Habla (1) _____?   Adriana   Me llamo (5) _____.

Pilar   Sí, (2) _____ España.   Pilar   (6) _____ gusto.

Adriana   ¿(3) _____ se llama?   Adriana   (7) _____.

Pilar   Pilar. ¿Y (4) _____?

G. Hablas con Sofía. Complete the conversation.

Sofía   ¡Hola! ¿Cómo estás?   Tú   (2) _____.

Tú   (1) _____   Manolo   Igualmente. Bueno, adiós.

Sofía   Bien, gracias. Mira, te presento a Manolo.   Tú   (3) _____.

H. Una conversación con tu profesor(a). Complete the conversation.

Profesor(a)   Buenas tardes. (1) ¿ _Cómo se llama_ ?

Tú   (2) Me llamo _Anne Marie_ .

Profesor(a)   Mucho gusto. ¿Cómo está hoy?

Tú   (3) _Bien,_

Profesor(a)   Bien, también. Hasta mañana.

Tú   (4) _¡Que te vaya bien_

Profesor(a)   Gracias. Igualmente.

Vocabulario 2 — Saying which classes you take
- The alphabet
- Class subjects

I. Ésa me gusta. *(I like that one.)* Indicate which subjects you like **(me gusta)** and which ones you do not like **(no me gusta).**

antropología	_me gusta_	economía	_no me gusta_
drama	_me gusta_	filosofía	_no me gusta_
literatura	_no me gusta_	? educación física	_me gusta lo_
astronomía	_me gusta_	geografía	_me gusta_
sicología	_me gusta_	química	_no me gusta_
biología	_me gusta_	historia	_me gusta_
música	_me gusta_	español	_me gusta_
botánica	_me gusta_	inglés	_no me gusta_

J. El alfabeto. Write the names of the underlined letters in the following words. Then write their English equivalents.

> **Modelo**   **Mi_ll_ones** se escribe con **elle** y significa *millions.*

1. **G_eo_grafía** se escribe con _____ y significa _____.

2. **E_x_amen** se escribe con _____ y significa _____.

3. **Ba_ñ_o** se escribe con _____ y significa _____.

4. **Mu_j_er** se escribe con _____ y significa _____.

5. **Di_cc_ionario** se escribe con _____ y significa _____.

6. **Ca_rr_o** se escribe con _____ y significa _____.

7. **Lápi_z_** se escribe con _____ y significa _____.

8. **_M_ochila** se escribe con _____ y significa _____.

9. **Fo_t_ocopia** se escribe con _____ y significa _____.

10. **Uni_v_ersidad** se escribe con _____ y significa _____.

Nombre _____ Fecha _____

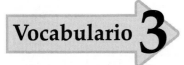

Vocabulario 3

Saying how many credits/units you take and how many hours you work
• Numbers 0–40

K. Los números. Match each number with its Spanish equivalent. Draw a line to link them.

14	doce
0	veinticinco
24	veintidós
12	dieciséis
7	cero
25	trece
13	catorce
37	once
40	veinticuatro
11	siete
22	treinta y siete
16	cuarenta

L. ¿Qué sigue? *(What's next?)* Write the numbers that precede and follow the given numbers.

1. _____cuatro_____   cinco   _____seis_____

2. _____   quince   _____

3. _____   dieciocho   _____

4 _____   veintiocho   _____

5. _____   treinta y tres   _____

6. _____   treinta y seis   _____

7. _____   treinta y nueve   _____

M. Preguntas personales. Answer the following questions.

1. ¿Qué *(Which)* clases tomas este semestre? _____

2. ¿Cuántas unidades *(units/credits)* son? _____

3. ¿Cuántas horas trabajas? _____

4. ¿Cuántas horas estudias? _____

5. ¿Qué clases necesitas tomar *(do you need to take)* el próximo *(next)* semestre?

_____

Para terminar

N. Una invitación de boda. *(A wedding invitation)* Examine the Mexican wedding invitation below in order to answer the following questions. You will also need to read the explanation that follows.

1. What is the name of the bride's father?

   _____

2. What is the name of the groom's mother?

   _____

3. What will be the traditional married name of the bride?

   _____

4. What is the groom's full name? (first name and last names)

   _____

Martha y Arturo

Ante Dios y con la bendición de sus padres

Eduardo Moreno Olivarria	*Arturo Hauter Salazar*
Martha Ibarra de Moreno	*Ana González de Hauter*

*Se unirán en matrimonio y los invitan
a la ceremonia religiosa el sábado
veintidós de octubre a las diecinueve horas
en la Iglesia del Espíritu Santo,
Fraccionamiento Chapultepec.*

*La fiesta, ofrecida por don Eduardo Moreno,
padre de la novia, se llevará a cabo
en el Lienzo Charro La Biznaga
después de la misa.*

*Impartiendo la Bendición
el Reverendo Alfonso González Quevedo S. E.*

Tijuana, Baja California

Cultura a lo vivo

You may have noticed that Spanish speakers often have long names. Most Spanish speakers have two first names, both of which they may or may not use. Some double names are common, however, such as Ana Mari and José Luis. In addition, Spanish speakers use two last names—their father's family name (which goes first), and their mother's family name (which goes second). For example, a brother and a sister, both single, might be called Ramón Robledo Suárez and Ana María Robledo Suárez (informally, they would be Ramón Robledo and Ana Mari Robledo). If Ana Mari marries, she will not change her last name. Traditionally, she will add her husband's last name, using **de**, which will replace her mother's last name. So, if Ana María Robledo Suárez marries Manolo Báez Rodríguez, her name will be Ana María Robledo de Báez. Today, many Hispanic women keep their maiden name; in this case, Mrs. Báez will be Ana María Robledo.

Ñ. Los personajes de Escenas de la vida. In **Escenas de la vida**, you will follow the lives of several Spanish speakers who live and study in the United States. As you learn about them, you will learn to communicate in Spanish, and you will get a glimpse into the rich and diverse culture of the Spanish-speaking world. Read the information for each character and answer the questions in **Práctica O**.

Sofía Blasio Salas

mexicana

20 años

arquitectura

extrovertida

Nombre

Nacionalidad

Edad

Carrera

Personalidad

Manolo Báez Rodríguez

cubano

25 años

no ha decidido[1]

bohemio

Wayne Andrew Reilly

norteamericano

23 años

computación

aventurero

Nombre

Nacionalidad

Edad

Carrera

Personalidad

Adriana Ferreira de Barrón

puertorriqueña

45 años

contabilidad[2]

reservada

Ana María Robledo Suárez

mexicoamericana

20 años

leyes[3]

sociable

Nombre

Nacionalidad

Edad

Carrera

Personalidad

Emilio Andrés Pradillo Salas

español

30 años

publicidad

serio

[1]*undecided* [2]*accounting* [3]*law*

O. ¡Mucho gusto! Based on the information about the characters, answer the following questions.

1. What is Sofía's mother's last name?

_____

2. Which of the female characters is married?

_____

3. Who has a double name?

_____

4. What is Manolo's father's last name?

_____

5. If Sofía married Wayne Reilly, what would be her traditional married name?

_____

6. Where is Sofía from?

_____

7. What is Manolo studying?

_____

8. What is Wayne studying?

_____

9. How old is Adriana?

_____

10. Where is Emilio from?

_____

11. How do you say *serious* in Spanish?

_____

12. What is the English equivalent of
    a. **aventurero?** _____
    b. **arquitectura?** _____

P. ¿Y tú? Now write your information.

Your picture goes here!

Apellido (*last name*): _____

Nacionalidad: _____

Edad: _____

Carrera: _____

Personalidad: _____

Episodio

2

Escenas de la vida: En la librería

 A. ¡Mira cuánto puedes entender!

Parte 1. Watch or listen to the **Escena** to indicate who needs to buy the following items: Manolo (**M**) or Sofía (**S**). Place an **X** next to the items no one mentions.

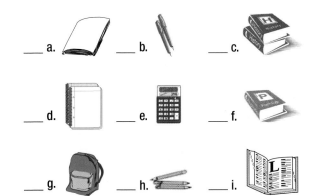

___ a. ___ b. ___ c.

___ d. ___ e. ___ f.

___ g. ___ h. ___ i.

Parte 2. First, place a check next to the classes Manolo has tomorrow. Then, write the time when the classes begin.

miércoles	
7:45	Cálculo
9:20	Geología
	Física

lunes/miércoles/viernes	
☐ Cálculo	7:45
☐ Sicología	
martes/jueves	
☐ Computación	8:45
☐ Historia	10:00
☐ Sociología	5:15

Cultura a lo vivo

In the Spanish-speaking world, a student must complete all general education requirements in high school in order to enter the university. The specifics vary from country to country, but before entering a university, a student must declare a major and frequently take an admissions exam to determine whether he or she qualifies for admission. Upon entering the university, a student begins a specific field of study; there are no undeclared majors.

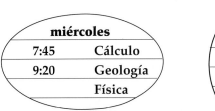

B. ¿Te diste cuenta? Review the **Escena** again to match these fragments.

_____ 1. Manolo gasta más de...   a. dos cuadernos.

_____ 2. Sofía necesita comprar...   b. al café mañana.

_____ 3. Los libros cuestan...   c. es sicología.

_____ 4. La clase favorita de Manolo... d. 200 dólares en libros.

_____ 5. Manolo y Sofía van...   e. mucho dinero.

C. ¿Quién lo dijo? Review the **Escena** and indicate whether the following phrases describe Sofía (**S**), Manolo (**M**), or both (**SM**).

_____ 1. Necesita novio.

_____ 2. Necesita libros.

_____ 3. Gasta mucho en libros.

_____ 4. Toma cinco clases.

_____ 5. Necesita ir a la biblioteca.

_____ 6. Va al café mañana.

Práctica adicional		
Cuaderno de tareas pp. 49–50, A–C	invitaciones. vhlcentral.com Episodio 2	invitaciones. vhlcentral.com Episodio 2

Para comunicarnos mejor

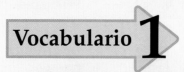
Vocabulario 1

Identifying university-related objects, places, and people
• **University-related vocabulary**

Las cosas, los lugares y las personas en la universidad			
Cosas	_Things_	**Lugares**	_Places_
la bandera	_flag_	**el auditorio**	_auditorium_
la calculadora	_calculator_	**el baño**	_bathroom_
el cuaderno	_notebook_	**la biblioteca**	_library_
el diccionario	_dictionary_	**la cafetería**	_cafeteria_
el escritorio	_desk_ (teacher's)	**la cancha de tenis**	_tennis court_
el lápiz	_pencil_	**de vóleibol**	_volleyball court_
el libro	_book_	**el edificio**	_building_
el mapa	_map_	**la enfermería**	_health center; infirmary_
la mochila	_backpack_	**el estacionamiento**	_parking lot_
el papel	_paper_	**el estadio**	_stadium_
la papelera	_wastebasket_	**el gimnasio**	_gym_
el pizarrón	_chalkboard_	**la librería**	_bookstore_
la pluma	_pen_	**la oficina**	_office_
la prueba	_quiz_	**la piscina**	_swimming pool_
la puerta	_door_	**la residencia estudiantil**	_dormitory_
el pupitre	_desk_ (student's)	**el salón de clase**	_classroom_

el reloj	clock
el reproductor de DVD	DVD player
la silla	chair
la tele(visión)	TV
la ventana	window
la videocasetera	VCR

También se dice...

el/la estudiante ⟶ el/la alumno/a

la papelera ⟶ el basurero, el bote/cubo/latón de basura

el pizarrón ⟶ la pizarra

la pluma ⟶ el bolígrafo

el/la profesor(a) ⟶ el/la maestro/a

el salón ⟶ el aula, la sala

Personas	People		
el compañero	la compañera	los/las compañeros/as	classmate(s)
el consejero	la consejera	los/las consejeros/as	counselor(s)
el estudiante	la estudiante	los/las estudiantes	student(s)

¡Fíjate!

You will see **También se dice** boxes throughout the text. Since Spanish is spoken in many countries, many times there are five or six different words for the same item. You do not need to learn all the variations; learn the ones your professor gives you or the ones you hear in your community.

PRÁCTICA

A. ¿Qué es? Identifica las cosas, los lugares y las personas en las ilustraciones.

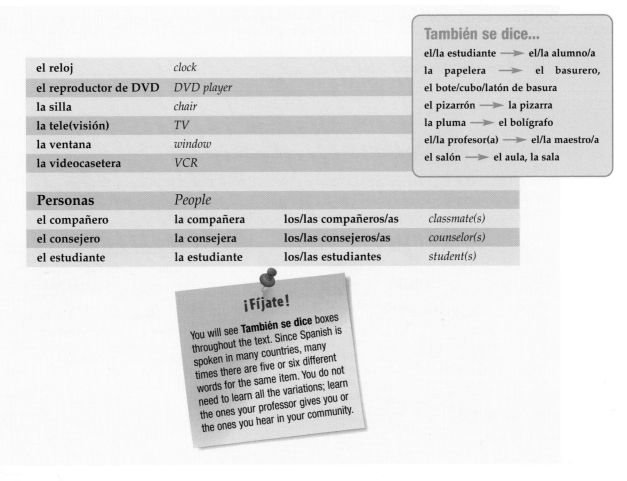

a 1. _____
2. _____
3. _____
4. _____
5. _____
6. _____
7. _____
8. _____
9. _____
10. _____

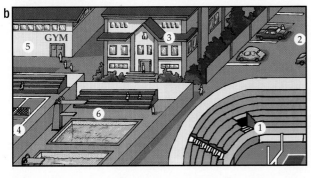

b 1. _____
2. _____
3. _____
4. _____
5. _____
6. _____

B. ¿Qué compraste? (*What did you buy?*) Write down the items you bought this semester for your classes.

Este semestre compré (*I bought*)..._____

_____

_____

C. ¿Adónde vas (*Where do you go*) con más frecuencia?

Parte 1. How often do you go to the following places? Write **0** next to places you never go to, **1** next to places you almost never go to, **2** next to places you sometimes go to, **3** next to places you often go to, and **4** next to places you go to every day.

¡Fíjate!

The words in **Banco de palabras** enable you to carry out specific classroom activities. You are not expected to memorize them or use them without support. However, begin to familiarize yourself with the words, since they may become part of your active vocabulary in later episodes.

Banco de palabras

(yo) voy	**(2) a veces**
I go	*sometimes*
(4) todos los días	**(1) casi nunca**
every day	*almost never*
(3) con frecuencia	**(0) nunca**
often	*never*

¿Con qué frecuencia vas...?

_____ 1. al auditorio
_____ 2. al gimnasio
_____ 3. a la piscina
_____ 4. a la librería
_____ 5. al estadio

_____ 6. a la cafetería
_____ 7. a la biblioteca
_____ 8. a las oficinas de los profesores
_____ 9. a la enfermería
_____ 10. a las canchas

Parte 2. Now interview a partner to find out how often they go to these places. Use the expressions from the **Banco de palabras.**

Modelo	—¿Con qué frecuencia vas al auditorio? —Casi nunca voy. ¿Y tú? —Yo voy todos los días.

¡Fíjate!

Use **nunca** and **casi nunca** before the verb **voy**; use the other expressions after it.

Práctica adicional

Cuaderno de tareas
pp. 50–51, D–G

invitaciones.
vhlcentral.com
Episodio 2

Gramática 1 — Talking about university-related objects, places, and people
- Gender of nouns
- Plural of nouns
- Hay

In the dialogue, Manolo mentioned **el libro de sicología** and **unos libros de historia.** They also mentioned **una mochila** and **la biblioteca. Libro, mochila,** and **biblioteca** are nouns. A noun is a word that names a person, a place, an animal, an object, or an idea. The articles **(los artículos)** *the* **(el, la)** or *a(n)* **(un, una)** usually accompany nouns.

• Gender of nouns

Nouns in Spanish have a gender (feminine or masculine) and number (singular or plural). When you learn a new noun, you must also learn whether that word is feminine or masculine, since the gender is arbitrary. See if you can make some helpful generalizations.

Analizar y descubrir

1. Look at the following feminine words:

la plum**a**	una televisi**ón**	la universid**ad**
la sill**a**	una conversac**ión**	la libert**ad**

Using these words, what observations can you make about the endings of feminine nouns? Most words that end in the letters _____ , _____, and _____ are feminine. Use **la** or **una** with feminine words.

2. Look at the following masculine words:

un libr**o**   un pupitr**e**   el pizarr**ón**   el inglé**s**   un profeso**r**   el pape**l**

Using these words, what observations can you make about the endings of masculine nouns? Most words that end in the vowels _____ and _____, or in a _____ are masculine. Use **el** or **un** with masculine nouns.

3. Although most words that end in **-e** are masculine, some are feminine. Therefore, it is best to learn the word along with its article:

(feminine)	**la clase**	**la noche**
(masculine)	**el pupitre**	**el coche** *(car)*

4. Most words that end in **-a** are feminine, but a few words (of Greek origin) that end in **-ma** are masculine. Notice that these words are cognates.

(masculine)	**el** proble**ma**	**el** progra**ma**	**el** siste**ma**

Los artículos				
	Singular		**Plural**	
Definidos	el, la	*the*	los, las	*the*
Indefinidos	un, una	*a(n)*	unos, unas	*some*

33

PRÁCTICA

D. ¿Masculino o femenino? Escribe **el** o **la**.

1. _______ estacionamiento
2. _______ pizarrón
3. _______ bandera
4. _______ drama
5. _______ oficina
6. _______ piscina
7. _______ teatro
8. _______ inglés
9. _______ cancha
10. _______ biblioteca
11. _______ computación
12. _______ pupitre

E. Artículos indefinidos. Escribe **un** o **una**.

1. _______ auditorio
2. _______ reloj
3. _______ silla
4. _______ libro
5. _______ profesor
6. _______ clase
7. _______ pluma
8. _______ ventana
9. _______ diccionario
10. _______ lápiz
11. _______ juego *(game)* de béisbol
12. _______ comunidad

• Plural of nouns

Analizar y descubrir

In a conversation with Adriana, Sofía said:

Las universidades aquí son muy diferentes...	*The universities here are quite different...*
Aquí **los salones** están muy bien equipados.	*Here, the classrooms are very well-equipped.*
¿En Puerto Rico hay **consejeros...?**	*Are there counselors in Puerto Rico...?*
Hablando de **profesores...**	*Speaking of professors...*

1. Examine the above examples to complete the following:
   a. What is added to the word **universidad** to make it plural? _______
   b. What is added to **salón** to make it plural? _______
   c. What is added to **consejero** to make it plural? _______
   d. What is added to **profesor** to make it plural? _______

2. Based on your answers, what observations can you make about how plural nouns are formed in Spanish?

Pluralizing rule:

a. When a word ends in a consonant, add _______ to make it plural.
b. When a word ends in a vowel, add _______ to make it plural.

Spelling rule: lápiz ➔ lápices

c. When a word ends in _______, change the **-z** to _______ in the plural form.

Accent marks: pizarr**ó**n ➔ pizarrones

d. When a word has an accent mark on the last syllable and it ends in a consonant, it loses _____________ in the plural form.

PRÁCTICA

F. En la universidad. Escribe la forma plural de estos sustantivos *(nouns)*.

1. el profesor _____

2. la silla _____

3. un estadio _____

4. la biblioteca _____

5. una cancha _____

6. un baño _____

G. Personas y cosas. Escribe la forma singular de estos sustantivos.

1. los consejeros _____   5. unos relojes _____

2. las compañeras _____   6. los cuadernos _____

3. unos mapas _____   7. unos lápices _____

4. las conversaciones _____   8. las bibliotecas _____

• Hay

Use **hay** + [*indefinite article*] to express the English equivalent of *there is/are* and to describe what you see. Use **unos/as** to say *some*.

Hay un diccionario en la mochila.   *There is a dictionary in the backpack.*

Hay unos estudiantes en la oficina.   *There are some students in the office.*

PRÁCTICA

H. ¿Qué hay en el escritorio? Escribe los nombres *(names)* de las cosas que hay en el escritorio.

Modelo

Hay una mochila.

1. _____
2. _____
3. _____
4. _____
5. _____
6. _____

I. ¿Qué hay en tu mochila? Escribe los nombres de cuatro cosas.

1. _____
2. _____
3. _____
4. _____

35

 **J. ¿Está bien equipado tu salón?** Describe what your classroom has and doesn't have, using the vocabulary on pages 30–31. Write your answers in your notebook.

Modelo   En el salón de... hay...
              En el salón de... no hay...

Práctica adicional
Cuaderno de tareas   invitaciones.
pp. 51–52, H–K   vhlcentral.com
Episodio 2

Gramática 2

Asking and telling when an event takes place
• Time of events

You heard the following statements and questions when Sofía and Manolo were discussing the times their classes meet.

¿A qué hora es tu clase de sicología?	*(At) What time is your psychology class?*
Es a la una y media.	*It's at one-thirty.*
¿Nos vemos mañana **a las doce?**	*See you tomorrow at twelve?*
...mi clase de física es **a las doce y cuarto.**	*...my physics class is at twelve-fifteen.*

Spanish, like English, depends on a few routine phrases to express time. One formula with **a** is used to say when events happen. Look at Ana Mari's weekly agenda to answer the following questions.

¿A qué hora?

¿A qué hora es...

la clase de horticultura?	**A la** una **de la tarde.**
la clase de inglés?	**A las** once y cuarto **de la mañana.**
la clase de biología?	**A las** siete y media **de la noche.**
el concierto?	**A las** cinco menos veinte **de la tarde.**
la fiesta?	**A las** diez menos cuarto **de la noche.**

Notice that **a la** is used with *one o'clock* and that **a las** is used for the rest of the hours.

AGOSTO/SEPTIEMBRE		
semana 36	1 martes	2 miércoles
31 lunes	8	8
8	9	9
9	10	10
10	11 :15 inglés	11
11	12	12
12	1	1
1 horticultura	2	2
2	3	3
3	4	4
4	5	5
5	6	6
6	7 :30 biología	7
7	8	8
8		

3 jueves	4 viernes	5 sábado
8	8	4:40 concierto
8	9	
9	10	
10	11	
12	1	6 domingo
1	2	
2	3	
3	4	
4	5	
5	6	
6	7	
7	8	
8	9:45 ¡fiesta!	

PRÁCTICA

K. ¿A qué hora...? When does Professor López teach this semester? Look at his schedule and write out when the calculus class meets. Note that the 24-hour clock (military time) is used.

> **Modelo**   16:40
> **El profesor tiene una clase a las cinco menos veinte de la tarde.**

Cálculo   a. 7:30   _____

b. 10:00   _____

c. 14:15   _____

d. 15:00   _____

e. 17:20   _____

f. 19:45   _____

> **¡Fíjate!**
>
> The 24-hour clock is generally used in newspapers, and in TV, train, flight, and class schedules throughout the Spanish-speaking world. To convert between a 24-hour and a 12-hour clock, subtract 12 from times after 12:00 p.m. (15:00-12 = 3:00 p.m.).

L. Vamos al cine. *(Let's go to the movies.)* Tienes planes para ir al cine con un(a) amigo/a. Pregúntale a qué hora son las funciones *(screenings)*. Túrnense.

> **Modelo**   *Mar adentro:* 11:30 / 18:20 / 21:55
> —¿A qué hora es *Mar adentro?*
> —Es a las once y media de la mañana, a las seis y veinte de la tarde y a las diez menos cinco de la noche.

> **¡Fíjate!**
>
> These films are highly acclaimed and are available in most video stores. Check them out!

★	1. El laberinto del fauno	14:45-16:30-18:05
★	2. María, llena eres de gracia	11:15-17:40-22:25
★	3. Diarios de motocicleta	14:30-16:15-19:10
★	4. Volver	10:50-12:15-21:20
★	5. La misma luna	17:25-19:35-20:17

M. ¡A conversar! Conversa con tres compañeros para saber quién sale de casa más temprano *(leaves home earliest)* y quién llega más tarde *(gets home latest)*.

> **Modelo**   —¿A qué hora sales de casa por la mañana?
> —A las siete y media. ¿Y tú?
> —A las seis y cuarto. ¿A qué hora llegas a casa?
> —A la una y media de la tarde. ¿Y tú?
> —A las ocho de la noche.

nombre *(name)*	**sale de casa**	**llega a casa**
1. _____	_____	_____
2. _____	_____	_____
3. _____	_____	_____

N. Organiza tu horario.
Successful students plan their schedules (**horarios**) carefully to allow for time to study and prepare for school.

Parte 1. Plan for your success. Consult the recommendations on page 14 (**Práctica Q**) to determine the number of hours you will need to schedule to prepare and study for school daily. Then fill in your weekly schedule with all of your activities: classes, work, rest, and study time.

Hora	lunes	martes	miércoles	jueves	viernes	sábado	domingo
8							
9							
10							
11							
12							
1							
2							
3							
4							
5							
6							
7							
8							
9							

Parte 2. Share your schedule with a partner and compare your study time allotment.

Modelo	Los lunes tengo clase a las ocho, a las nueve y a las diez de la mañana. Estudio para mis clases a la una y trabajo a las cuatro y media de la tarde. ¿Y tú?

Banco de palabras

Tengo *I have*
Trabajo *I work*
Estudio *I study*

De las... a las...
from... to...

Ñ. Tus actividades.

Parte 1. First, examine the images of daily activities. Then complete the sentences with the time you usually do each activity.

¿A qué hora...

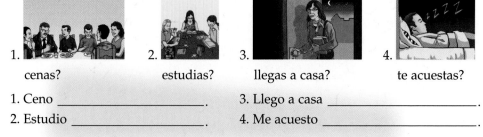

1. cenas?   2. estudias?   3. llegas a casa?   4. te acuestas?

1. Ceno _____.   3. Llego a casa _____.

2. Estudio _____.   4. Me acuesto _____.

Parte 2. Interview two or three classmates to find out the times they do the activities.

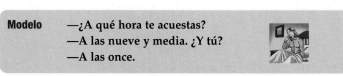

Modelo	—¿A qué hora te acuestas? —A las nueve y media. ¿Y tú? —A las once.

Práctica adicional

Cuaderno de tareas
p. 53 L–N

invitaciones.
vhlcentral.com
Lab practice

SUPERSITE

invitaciones.
vhlcentral.com
Episodio 2

Actividades comunicativas

A. Diferencias.

Instrucciones para **Estudiante 1**

The picture of the classroom below differs in several ways from your partner's picture. You and your partner will take turns saying what you see until you find seven differences. Check off the seven differences. Follow the model.

Modelo	—**Hay una profesora en el salón.**
	—**Aquí** (*Here*) **también.**
	or
	—**Aquí no hay una profesora. Hay un profesor.**

A. Diferencias.

Instrucciones para **Estudiante 2**

The picture of the classroom below differs in several ways from your partner's picture. You and your partner will take turns saying what you see until you find seven differences. Check off the seven differences. Follow the model.

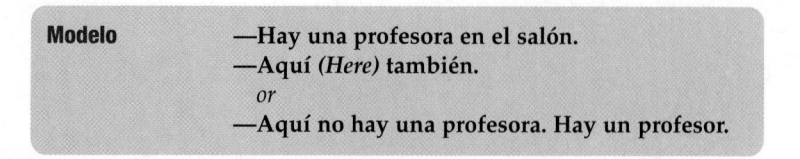

Modelo	—Hay una profesora en el salón.
	—Aquí (*Here*) también.
	or
	—Aquí no hay una profesora. Hay un profesor.

B. Los precios.

Instrucciones para **Estudiante 1**

You and a friend are tired of spending so much on school supplies. This semester you are shopping for the best prices. The prices you found in **Papelería Las Rosas** are shown in the drawing. Your partner found different prices in **Papelería El Trópico.** Share your information to determine the best price. Circle the items you decide to buy at your store. Follow the model.

Modelo	—¿**Cuánto cuesta** (*How much is*) **una calculadora ahí** (*there*)?
	—**Aquí** (*Here*) **cuesta veinte dólares y diecinueve centavos. ¿Y ahí?**
	—**Aquí cuesta veinte dólares y veintinueve centavos.**
	—**Ah, pues aquí es más barato** (*cheaper*).

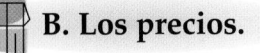

B. Los precios.

Instrucciones para **Estudiante 2**

You and a friend are tired of spending so much on school supplies. This semester you are shopping for the best prices. The prices you found in **Papelería El Trópico** are shown in the drawing. Your partner found different prices in **Papelería Las Rosas**. Share your information to determine the best price. Circle the items you decide to buy at your store. Follow the model.

Modelo	—¿**Cuánto cuesta** *(How much is)* **una calculadora ahí** *(there)*? —**Aquí** *(Here)* **cuesta veinte dólares y diecinueve centavos. ¿Y ahí?** —**Aquí cuesta veinte dólares y veintinueve centavos.** —**Ah, pues aquí es más barato** *(cheaper)*.

Papelería El Trópico

$ 23.15

DICCIONARIO
Español-
Inglés

$ 3.25

$ 2.11

Cien años
de
soledad

García Márquez

$13.29

$20.19

$ 14.10

$ .21

$ 1.25

C. El horario de clases.

Instrucciones para **Estudiante 1**

It is time to plan your class schedule for next semester. The chart shows the hours you will be at work **(trabajo)**. Before you graduate, you need to complete six courses:

antropología	**biología**	**historia**
álgebra	**español**	**sicología**

You will not be able to take all these classes this semester. Call your peer advisor for information and choose the four courses that best meet your needs. Use expressions like the ones below.

¿A qué hora es la clase de...?	*When is... class?*
¿Qué día es...?	*What day is...?*
Los lunes trabajo de... a...	*On Mondays I work from... to...*
¿Hay una clase de... a las...?	*Is there a... class at...?*
A esa hora no puedo.	*I can't do that time.*
¿Hay otra clase de...?	*Is there another... class?*

Banco de palabras
Los días de la semana

los lunes
on Mondays

los martes
on Tuesdays

los miércoles
on Wednesdays

los jueves
on Thursdays

los viernes
on Fridays

los sábados
on Saturdays

los domingos
on Sundays

	Lunes	Martes	Miércoles	Jueves	Viernes
8:00–9:00					
9:00–10:00					
10:00–11:00					
11:00–12:00		Trabajo		Trabajo	
12:00–1:00		Trabajo		Trabajo	
1:00–4:00					
4:00–6:00	Trabajo		Trabajo		
6:00–8:00	Trabajo		Trabajo		

C. El horario de clases.

Instrucciones para **Estudiante 2**

You are a peer advisor. By phone, help a student prepare a class schedule for next semester. Use expressions like the ones below.

¿Por qué no tomas...?	*Why don't you take...?*
Hay una clase de... a...	*There's a class from... to...*
¿Puedes tomar...?	*Can you take...?*
No hay clase de... a esa hora.	*There is no... class at that time.*
La clase de... es de... a...	*The class is from... to...*
Hay dos secciones de...	*There are two sections of...*

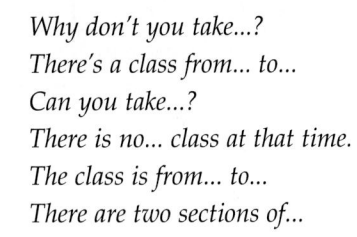

Clase/hora	Clase/hora
álgebra	**antropología**
lun. mar. miér. juev. vier. 9:00–10:00	lun. mar. miér. juev. 8:00–9:00
lun. mar. miér. juev. vier. 10:00–11:00	mar. juev. 16:00–17:30
biología	**español**
lun. mar. miér. juev. 8:00–9:00	lun. mar. miér. juev. vier. 8:00–9:00
mar. juev. 10:00–12:00	lun. mar. miér. juev. vier. 10:00–11:00
miér. 16:00–20:00	mar. juev. 12:00–14:30
historia	**sicología**
mar. juev. 11:00–12:15	lun. miér. vier. 10:00–11:00
lun. miér. vier. 17:00–19:30	lun. miér. vier. 16:00–18:15
	mar. juev. 10:00–11:15

La correspondencia

 El correo: El catálogo. Look over the brochure in order to answer the questions below.

Plan de estudios

1. What is the English equivalent of **Fisioterapia?** _____

2. How many quarters are necessary to complete a degree? _____

3. Indicate in which quarter students take the following courses:

   a. Human Anatomy _____   c. Introduction to Pathology _____

   b. Nutrition _____   d. Pharmacology _____

Mercado de trabajo

4. Where may a person with this degree work?

   a. _____   b. _____   c. _____   d. _____

COLEGIO DE CIENCIAS ASOCIADAS A LA SALUD

Fisioterapia

Perfil del egresado

El profesional en Fisioterapia estará capacitado para distinguir, en una evaluación física, los estados de normalidad e implementar, en su caso, el tratamiento de rehabilitación indicado, así como la aplicación del mismo, manejando el material y equipo necesarios en un área de medicina física y rehabilitación. Podrá participar conjuntamente con el médico fisiatra en la rehabilitación de casos especiales y en medicina del deporte.

PLAN DE ESTUDIOS

PRIMER TRIMESTRE
- Introducción a la Fisioterapia.
- Anatomía Humana.
- Fisiología General.

SEGUNDO TRIMESTRE
- Principios para el Cuidado del Paciente.
- Primeros Auxilios.
- Fisiología Especial.

TERCER TRIMESTRE
- Sicología Aplicada a la Fisioterapia.
- Física Aplicada a la Fisioterapia.
- Introducción a la Patología.

CUARTO TRIMESTRE
- Instrumentación a la Fisioterapia.
- Técnicas de Evaluación del Estado Físico Normal.
- Ejercicio Físico.

QUINTO TRIMESTRE
- Técnicas de Evaluación de Escuelas Patológicas.
- Medios en la Fisioterapia.
- Deontología.

SEXTO TRIMESTRE
- Rehabilitación Músculo-Esquelética.
- Técnicas de Rehabilitación Pediátrica.
- Técnicas de Rehabilitación Geriátrica.

SÉPTIMO TRIMESTRE
- El Deporte y la Fisioterapia.
- Nutriología.
- Terapia y Kinesiología.

OCTAVO TRIMESTRE
- Rehabilitación del Paciente Cardíaco.
- Rehabilitación del Paciente Neurológico.
- Farmacología.

Mercado de trabajo

El campo de trabajo del fisioterapeuta es amplio considerando su participación en programas dirigidos a personas sanas o enfermas y en el deporte, Escuelas de educación física, clubes deportivos, gimnasios, Hospitales y clínicas del sector público y privado, departamentos de medicina del deporte y atención a pacientes particulares.

En papel: ¿Qué hay en tu universidad? Write sentences describing what your school has and doesn't have, using the vocabulary on pages 30–31. Also indicate what classes you are taking and when they meet.

> **Modelo** En mi universidad hay una piscina, pero *(but)* no hay auditorios.
> Mi clase de matemáticas es a las ocho de la mañana.

¡A ver de nuevo! Contesta las preguntas.

1. ¿Qué necesita comprar Sofía? _____

_____

2. ¿Cuántas clases toma Manolo? _____

3. ¿Qué clases tiene Manolo mañana? _____

4. ¿Adónde va Sofía antes *(before)* de su clase de física? _____

5. ¿A qué hora es su clase de física? _____

6. ¿Adónde van mañana después de la clase de cálculo? _____

Invitación a **Honduras**

> Del álbum de
> *Ana Marí*

Honduras es un país pequeño; es un poco más grande que el estado de Tennessee. Copán es una bella ciudad maya en Honduras. Durante más de un milenio, Copán fue *(was)* el centro cultural y educativo más importante para los mayas.

Actualmente, Copán es Patrimonio de de la humanidad *(World Heritage)*. Un patrimonio es un lugar específico de importancia universal excepcional por su valor *(value)* cultural o natural. La UNESCO otorga *(gives)* esta prestigiosa designación; Copán la recibió *(received it)* en 1980.

1. How large is Honduras?
2. Why is Copán so important?
3. In your own words, summarize what is considered a World Heritage site.

Práctica adicional			
Cuaderno de tareas p. 54, Ñ	invitaciones. vhlcentral.com Episodio 2	invitaciones. vhlcentral.com Lab practice	invitaciones. vhlcentral.com Episodio 2

Vocabulario del Episodio 2

¿A qué hora es...?	*(At) What time is...?*
Es a las once y cuarto de la mañana.	*It's at eleven-fifteen in the morning.*
Es a la una y media de la tarde.	*It's at one-thirty in the afternoon.*
Es a las diez menos veinte de la noche.	*It's at twenty to ten in the evening.*
Hay...	*There is/are...*

En la universidad *At the university*

Cosas	*Things*	Lugares	*Places*
la bandera	*flag*	el auditorio	*auditorium*
la calculadora	*calculator*	el baño	*bathroom*
el cuaderno	*notebook*	la biblioteca	*library*
el diccionario	*dictionary*	la cafetería	*cafeteria*
el escritorio	*desk* (teacher's)	la cancha de tenis	*tennis court*
el lápiz	*pencil*	de vóleibol	*volleyball court*
el libro	*book*	el edificio	*building*
el mapa	*map*	la enfermería	*health center; infirmary*
la mochila	*backpack*	el estacionamiento	*parking lot*
el papel	*paper*	el estadio	*stadium*
la papelera	*wastebasket*	el gimnasio	*gym*
el pizarrón	*chalkboard*	la librería	*bookstore*
la pluma	*pen*	la oficina	*office*
la prueba	*quiz*	la piscina	*swimming pool*
la puerta	*door*	la residencia estudiantil	*dormitory*
el pupitre	*desk* (student's)	el salón de clase	*classroom*
el reloj	*clock*		
el reproductor de DVD	*DVD player*		
la silla	*chair*		
la tele(visión)	*TV*		
la ventana	*window*		
la videocasetera	*VCR*		

Personas *People*

el compañero	la compañera	los/las compañeros/as	*classmate(s)*
el consejero	la consejera	los/las consejeros/as	*counselor(s)*
el estudiante	la estudiante	los/las estudiantes	*student(s)*

Artículos definidos *Definite articles*

el	*the (for masculine singular nouns)*
la	*the (for feminine singular nouns)*
los	*the (for masculine plural nouns)*
las	*the (for feminine plural nouns)*

Artículos indefinidos *Indefinite articles*

un	*a/an (for masculine singular nouns)*
una	*a/an (for feminine singular nouns)*
unos	*some (for masculine plural nouns)*
unas	*some (for feminine plural nouns)*

Vocabulario personal

Write the words that you need to know to talk about your class schedule and academic life in Spanish.

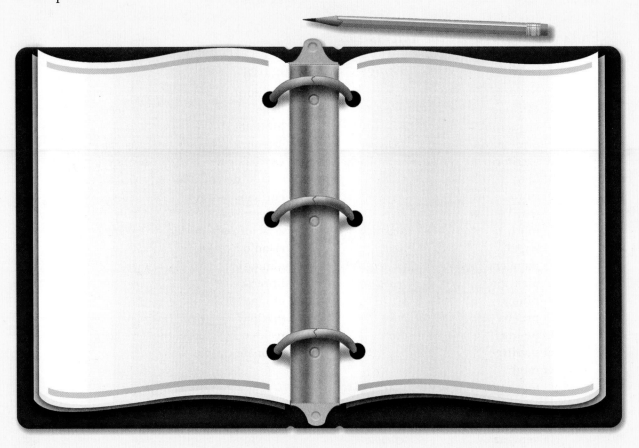

Cuaderno
de tareas

Cuaderno de tareas

Episodio

2

Escenas de la vida: En la librería

A. ¡Mira cuánto entendiste! See how much of the **Escena** you understood by matching the Spanish sentences with their English equivalents.

Los libros cuestan mucho dinero.

_____ 1. Necesito cuadernos y plumas.

_____ 2. Ya tengo los libros.

_____ 3. ¿Qué clases tienes mañana?

_____ 4. ¿Cuántas clases tomas?

_____ 5. ¿Qué necesitas comprar?

a. I already have my books.

b. I need notebooks and pens.

c. What do you need to buy?

d. How many classes are you taking?

e. What classes do you have tomorrow?

Vamos al café.

_____ 6. Necesito ir a la biblioteca.

_____ 7. Vamos después de clase.

_____ 8. Nos vemos mañana.

_____ 9. ¿Invito a Ana Mari?

_____10. ¿Por qué no vamos al café?

f. Why don't we go to the café?

g. Let's go after class.

h. Should I invite Ana Mari?

i. I need to go to the library.

j. See you tomorrow.

B. En la librería. Use the words below to complete the conversation.

comprar	cuadernos	historia	mochila
crimen	dinero	libros	plumas

Sofía   ¿Qué necesitas (1) _____?

Manolo   Unos libros de (2) _____. ¿Y tú?

Sofía   Necesito lápices, (3) _____, (4) _____ y una

(5) _____.

Manolo   Cada semestre gasto mucho (6)_____ en libros.

Sofía   No entiendo por qué los (7) _____ cuestan tanto.

Manolo   Es un (8) _____.

C. Después de clase. Order the statements so the dialogue makes sense.

_____ a. ¡Qué horror! Cinco clases, pobrecito. Oye, ¿qué clases tienes mañana?

_____ b. ¿A qué hora es tu clase de sicología?

_____ c. Cinco, y tres son horribles.

_____ d. ¿Cuántas clases tomas este semestre?

_____ e. Es a la una y media.

_____ f. Cálculo y sicología.

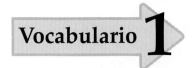 **Vocabulario 1**

Identifying university-related objects, places, and people
• University-related vocabulary

D. ¿Qué son? Examine the following words to determine whether they are **una cosa, un lugar,** or **una persona.** Write them in the appropriate column.

el auditorio	el consejero	la consejera
la bandera	el edificio	el reloj
el compañero	el mapa	la residencia estudiantil
la prueba	la piscina	las sillas

una cosa	un lugar	una persona
_____	_____	_____
_____	_____	_____
_____	_____	_____
_____	_____	_____
_____		

E. En el salón de clase. Identify the items in the illustration. Use the definite articles **el, la, los,** and **las.**

1. _____
2. _____
3. _____
4. _____
5. _____
6. _____
7. _____
8. _____
9. _____
10. _____
11. _____
12. _____

F. En la papelería. Identify the items in the illustration. Use the definite articles **el, la, los,** and **las**.

1. _____
2. _____
3. _____
4. _____
5. _____
6. _____
7. _____
8. _____

Papelería El Trópico

G. ¿Adónde vas? Say where you would go in each case.

| Modelo | to swim | la piscina |

1. to buy a book   _____

2. to exercise   _____

3. to eat something while at the university   _____

4. to park your car   _____

5. to watch a football game   _____

6. to play tennis   _____

7. to study while on campus   _____

8. to wash your hands   _____

Gramática 1

Talking about university-related objects, places, and people
- **Gender of nouns**
- **Plural of nouns**
- **Hay**

H. ¿Qué necesitas comprar? To express what you need to buy in Spanish, use indefinite articles, just as in English (*I need to buy* a *pen*). Fill in the missing articles.

Necesito comprar...

1. _____ libro
2. _____ reloj
3. _____ mochila
4. _____ mapas de Latinoamérica

5. _____ lápices
6. _____ cuaderno
7. _____ pluma
8. _____ videocaseteras

I. ¿Masculino o femenino?

Examine the following words to determine whether they are masculine or feminine. Write them in the appropriate column. Use the definite articles **el, la, los,** and **las.**

auditorio	comunidad	inglés	química	televisión
compañera	consejero	pizarrón	salón	ventana

Masculino		Femenino
1. _____		6. _____
2. _____		7. _____
3. _____		8. _____
4. _____		9. _____
5. _____		10. _____

J. El plural.

Make each statement plural.

> **Modelo**
> Hay <u>un lápiz</u> en la mochila.
> **Hay unos lápices en la mochila.**

1. Hay <u>un estudiante</u> en el salón.

_____

2. Hay <u>una piscina</u> en el gimnasio.

_____

3. Hay <u>una calculadora</u> en el pupitre.

_____

4. Hay <u>un edificio</u> en la universidad.

_____

5. Hay <u>un compañero</u> en la cafetería.

_____

K. Las opiniones.

In Spanish, when a general statement is made about something (a noun), the definite article is needed (i.e, **Los libros cuestan demasiado dinero.**). In English, the article is not needed (i.e., *Books cost too much.*). Provide the necessary article and state whether you agree (**estoy de acuerdo**) or disagree (**no estoy de acuerdo**).

1. _____ relojes son indispensables.   _____

2. _____ clases son difíciles *(difficult)*.   _____

3. _____ universidades son instituciones importantes.   _____

4. _____ profesores no ganan *(earn)* mucho dinero.   _____

5. _____ papeles necesitan reciclarse *(recycle)* siempre *(always)*.   _____

6. _____ papeleras están llenas *(full)*.   _____

7. _____ cafeterías en las universidades son caras *(expensive)*.   _____

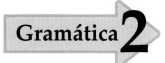

Nombre _____ Fecha _____

Gramática 2 **Asking and telling when an event takes place**
• **Time of events**

L. ¡Pon la hora! Set the clocks to the correct time.

las doce y cuarto

las tres y media

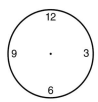

la una y veinte

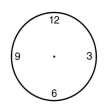

las cuatro menos diez

M. Los eventos universitarios. A Spanish-speaking friend has asked you to find out when the following events will take place. Write down what you would say in Spanish. Remember: *a las* **tres de la tarde**, but *a la* **una de la tarde**.

¿A qué hora es...

1. el concierto de música clásica? (9:00 p.m.) _____

2. el programa *(about)* sobre literatura moderna? (8:15 p.m.) _____

3. el partido *(game)* de fútbol? (5:45 p.m.) _____

4. la reunión del club latino? (10:30 a.m.) _____

5. la conferencia sobre el arte prehispánico? (1:30 p.m.) _____

6. la excursión al Museo de Ciencia y Tecnología? (8:10 a.m.)_____

N. Preguntas personales. Answer the following questions with the times requested; you do not need to use full sentences.

1. ¿A qué hora sales *(do you leave)* de casa por la mañana? _____

2. ¿A qué hora regresas *(do you return)*? _____

3. ¿A qué hora llegas *(do you arrive)* a la universidad? _____

4. ¿A qué hora es tu primera *(first)* clase los lunes? _____

5. ¿A qué hora miras *(do you watch)* la tele? _____

Para terminar

 Ñ. La Universidad en la Comunidad-Único. Read the following brochure for the **Universidad en la Comunidad** and answer the following questions.

Plan de estudios

1. What is the English word for **Nutrición**? _____
2. How many quarters are necessary to complete a degree? _____
3. Indicate in which quarter students take the following courses:

       a. Epidemiology _____

       b. Thesis Seminar _____

       c. Human Physiology _____

       d. Pediatric Nutrition _____

Mercado de trabajo

4. Where may a person with this degree work?

       a. _____

       b. _____

       c. _____

       d. _____

COLEGIO DE CIENCIAS ASOCIADAS A LA SALUD

Perfil del egresado

El profesional en Nutrición tendrá los conocimientos necesarios para colaborar en la solución de los problemas de nutrición y alimentación de México, ofreciendo apoyo nutricional, orientación y asesoría a todo individuo sano o enfermo.

Nutrición

Mercado de trabajo

El campo de trabajo del nutriólogo es amplio, ya que podrá prestar asesoría y desempeñar funciones de apoyo nutricional en hospitales y clínicas del sector público y privado, así como en otras disciplinas de interés: Salud pública, epidemiología, saneamiento ambiental e industria del alimento.

PLAN DE ESTUDIOS

PRIMER TRIMESTRE
- Bioquímica de la Nutrición.
- Morfología Humana.
- Fisiología Humana.

SEGUNDO TRIMESTRE
- Introducción a la Fisiopatología.
- Nutrición Básica.
- Salud Pública y Nutrición.

TERCER TRIMESTRE
- Química de los alimentos.
- Epidemiología.
- Métodos de la Investigación.

CUARTO TRIMESTRE
- Bioestadística.
- Principios de Dietocálculo.
- Principios Básicos de Administración.

QUINTO TRIMESTRE
- Nutrición Clínica en Adultos.
- Saneamiento Ambiental.
- Dietoterapia en Salud y Enfermedad.

SEXTO TRIMESTRE
- Apoyo Nutricional Especial.
- Nutrición Pediátrica.
- Salud Materno Infantil.

SÉPTIMO TRIMESTRE
- Sicología y Nutrición.
- Nutrición Comunitaria.
- Seminario de Tesis.

OCTAVO TRIMESTRE
- Tecnología Educativa en Nutrición.
- Administración de los Servicios de Alimentación y Nutrición.
- Nutrición Clínica Intrahospitalaria.

Episodio

3

Escenas de la vida: Los profesores y las clases

A. ¡Mira cuánto puedes entender!

Parte 1. Mira o escucha la **Escena** para indicar las cosas que hay en los salones de México.

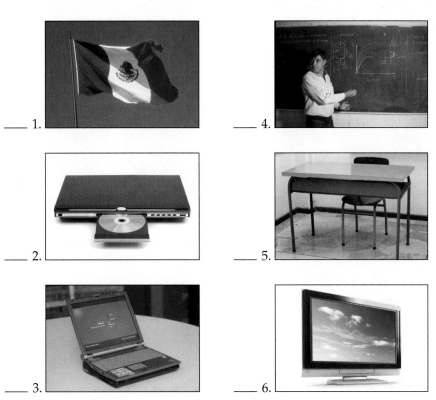

____ 1.

____ 2.

____ 3.

____ 4.

____ 5.

____ 6.

Parte 2. Mira o escucha la **Escena** para indicar las cosas que hay en las universidades de Puerto Rico.

La mayoría de las universidades de Puerto Rico tienen...

____ 1. una piscina

____ 2. una cafetería

____ 3. un gimnasio

____ 4. una biblioteca

____ 5. un auditorio

____ 6. canchas de tenis

B. Las características. As you listen to or watch the **Escena**, indicate the correct characteristic.

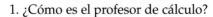

1. ¿Cómo es el profesor de cálculo?

☐ arrogante ☐ competente
☐ atractivo ☐ reservado
☐ estricto ☐ flexible

2. A Adriana le gusta la clase de composición porque el profesor es...

☐ extrovertido ☐ interesante
☐ paciente ☐ serio
☐ excelente ☐ flexible

Sofía   **Adriana**

3. A Adriana no le gusta la clase de contabilidad porque la profesora es...

☐ impaciente ☐ seria
☐ reservada ☐ arrogante
☐ pesimista ☐ tímida

4. Indica qué características aplican a Sofía (**S**) y cuáles a Adriana (**A**).

__ sociable   __ activa
__ tímida   __ responsable
__ madura   __ inteligente

Cultura a lo vivo

In the Spanish-speaking world, the concept of the nuclear family versus the extended family does not exist. The boundaries of the family extend beyond the immediate family to include grandparents, aunts and uncles, cousins, and others. Spanish speakers are widely assumed to have large families. However, Latin American families come in just as many sizes and varieties as families in the U.S. Many countries in Latin America have launched TV, radio, and billboard campaigns to promote smaller families; "**La familia pequeña vive mejor**" (*Smaller families live better*) is a popular slogan in Mexico.

C. ¿Te diste cuenta? Indica si los comentarios son **ciertos** o **falsos**.

	Cierto	Falso
1. En las universidades de México hay televisiones y videocaseteras en todos los salones.	☐	☐
2. En Puerto Rico, las universidades tienen un gimnasio, un auditorio y una biblioteca.	☐	☐
3. En México no hay consejeros.	☐	☐
4. A Adriana le gusta mucho la clase de composición.	☐	☐
5. El profesor de la clase de diseño es increíble.	☐	☐
6. La clase de geología es aburrida *(boring)*.	☐	☐
7. El esposo de Adriana es impaciente.	☐	☐

D. ¿Quién lo dijo? ¿Quién dijo las siguientes oraciones, Sofía (**S**) o Adriana (**A**)?

_____ 1. ¿Le gusta la clase de cálculo?

_____ 2. El cálculo es difícil.

_____ 3. A mí me gusta mucho la clase.

_____ 4. No me gusta la clase, pero la necesito porque es mi carrera.

_____ 5. ¿Cuál te gusta más?

Práctica adicional		
Cuaderno de tareas p. 69, A–B	invitaciones. vhlcentral.com Episodio 3	invitaciones. vhlcentral.com Episodio 3

Para comunicarnos mejor

Gramática 1

Expressing likes and dislikes
• Me gusta, te gusta, le gusta

In their conversation, Sofía and Adriana made the following statements:

> Me gusta mucho esta clase.

> No me gusta la clase.

La clase de composición **me gusta** mucho.	*I like composition class a lot.*
¿**Le gusta** la clase de cálculo?	*Do you like calculus class?*
A mí **me gusta** mucho la clase.	*I like the class a lot.*
¿Cuál **te gusta** más?	*Which one do you like better?*

1. Notice that you need to use the definite article after **gusta** when it is followed by a noun.

   ¿Le gusta **la** clase de cálculo?

2. When Sofía asks Adriana about her preferences, she does not use **¿te gusta?**; she uses **¿le gusta?** instead. Adriana is older, and Sofía just met her, so she wants to be polite. When you ask or tell a friend whether he/she likes something, use **te gusta.** Use **le gusta** with your instructor, and **me gusta** when referring to your own preferences.

   Me gusta estudiar español.

PRÁCTICA

A. ¿Qué clases te gustan? Use the list of class subjects on page 11 to interview a partner and find out your classmate's preferences. Remember, you need to use **el** or **la** before a noun.

> **Modelo**
> —¿Te gusta el drama?
> —Sí, me gusta. ¿Y a ti?
> —A mí también. *or* —A mí no.
>
> —¿Te gusta la biología?
> —No, no me gusta. ¿Y a ti?
> —A mí tampoco. *or* —A mí sí.

¡Fíjate!

Look at the ending of the class subjects to determine whether they are masculine or feminine.

B. Tus preferencias. Find out whether your classmate likes the activities listed below. Each activity begins with a verb. You can guess what the verbs mean from the context. For example, in **¿Te gusta jugar fútbol?** you can safely guess that **jugar** means *to play*.

> **Modelo**
> —¿Te gusta jugar fútbol?
> —No, no me gusta. ¿Y a ti?
> —A mí tampoco. *or* —A mí sí.
> ~ me neither
> —¿Te gusta comer ensaladas?
> —Sí, me gusta. ¿Y a ti?
> —A mí también. *or* —A mí no.

~ me too

1. jugar (vóleibol, béisbol, fútbol americano, fútbol *(soccer)*, tenis)
2. comer (pizza, tacos, enchiladas, hamburguesas, frutas, ensaladas)
3. estudiar (en casa, en la biblioteca, con compañeros de clase)
4. escuchar música (clásica, alternativa, rap, latina, moderna)
5. leer (novelas, poemas, el periódico *(newspaper)*, el horóscopo)
6. mirar programas (cómicos, policíacos, de suspenso)

> **También se dice...**
> These sports are also spelled without accent marks because many Spanish speakers stress the last syllable when pronouncing them:
>
> vóleibol ⟶ volibol
> béisbol ⟶ beisbol
> fútbol ⟶ futbol
> fútbol americano ⟶ futbol americano

C. Las preferencias de tu profesor(a). As a class, find out whether your instructor likes some of the same activities.

> **Modelo** —Profesor(a), ¿le gusta escuchar música rap?

D. Una entrevista. First fill in each column with your preferences. Then interview a classmate to find out if your preferences are similar.

| Modelo | —Me gusta la música de Rihanna. ¿Y a ti?
—A mí no me gusta. Pink me gusta más. ¿Te gusta el programa de *American Idol*?
—Sí, me gusta mucho. |

Práctica adicional

Cuaderno de tareas
p. 70, C–D

invitaciones.
vhlcentral.com
Episodio 3

Mis cantantes (*singers*) favoritos	Mis actores favoritos	Mis programas favoritos
_____	_____	_____
_____	_____	_____
_____	_____	_____

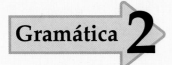 **Gramática 2**

Describing yourself and others
- **Ser** + [*adjectives*] (cognates)
- **Subject pronouns**

In the dialogue, Adriana says **soy un poco tímida** when describing herself and **el profesor es muy estricto** when describing her calculus instructor. **Soy** and **es** are forms of the verb **ser** (*to be*). Use the following forms to describe yourself and others.

Ser		
yo	**Soy** un poco tímida.	*I'm a little shy.*
tú	**Eres** muy pesimista.	*You are very pessimistic. (informal)*
usted (Ud.)	**Es** creativo.	*You are creative. (formal)*
él	**Es** ambicioso.	*He is ambitious.*
ella	**Es** seria.	*She is serious.*
nosotros nosotras	**Somos** inteligentes.	*We are intelligent.*
ustedes (Uds.)	**Son** impacientes.	
vosotros* vosotras	**Sois** impacientes.	*You are impatient. (plural)*
ellos ellas	**Son** muy sociables.	*They are easy-going.*

*Spain is the only country that uses **vosotros/as** for *you* (plural, informal) and **ustedes** for *you* (plural, formal). All other Spanish-speaking countries use **ustedes** for both formal and informal second-person plural.

1. Notice that **nosotros, vosotros,** and **ellos** may refer to a group of men or to a mixed group, whereas **nosotras, vosotras,** and **ellas** refer only to women.

2. Notice that there is no pronoun for *it*. Use **es** to convey the idea *it is*.

   Es mi libro.   *It is my book.*   **Son mis libros.**   *They are my books.*

¡Fíjate!
The **vosotros** forms are provided for your reference only; you are not responsible for learning them.

• Subject pronouns

In their conversation, Sofía and Adriana said:

Soy de Puerto Rico.   *I'm from Puerto Rico.*   Es mi mejor amiga.   *She is my best friend.*

Notice that the characters do not say *yo* **soy** or *ella* **es**. In Spanish, the verb form itself and/or the context indicates the person we are talking about *(I, you, he, she, we, they)*. Therefore, it is not necessary to use subject pronouns. The subject pronouns (**yo, tú, usted, él, ella, nosotros/as, vosotros/as, ustedes, ellos/as**) are used only when:

  a. you want to establish contrast or emphasis. **Tú no eres responsable, yo sí.**
  b. there is no verb. **Yo también, nosotros tampoco, tú no.**
  c. you are answering a "who" question. **¿Quién es romántico? Yo soy.**

Read the following descriptive adjectives. They are all cognates. Can you understand what they mean? The spelling of these adjectives stays the same whether they describe a man or a woman.

Para describir la personalidad I		
arrogante	increíble	pesimista
competente	interesante	(ir)responsable
excelente	materialista	sentimental
flexible	optimista	sociable
idealista	(im)paciente	terrible

The following adjectives end in **-o** when they refer to a man and in **-a** when they refer to a woman.

Para describir la personalidad II			
activo/a	discreto/a	(des)honesto/a	romántico/a
ambicioso/a	estudioso/a	(in)maduro/a	serio/a
atractivo/a	extrovertido/a	nervioso/a	tímido/a
creativo/a	generoso/a	reservado/a	tranquilo/a

To ask what someone is like, use the expression **¿Cómo es/son...?**
¿Cómo es la profesora de composición?   *What is your composition professor like?*

PRÁCTICA

E. Los amigos de Sofía. Complete Sofía's description and answer her questions using **ser**.

1. Mi mamá _____ extrovertida y sociable. ¿Y tú mamá?

   Mi mamá _____

2. Ana Mari y Ramón _____ responsables y maduros. ¿Cómo son tus amigos?

   Mis amigos _____

3. Manolo y yo _____ amigos; _____ muy diferentes.

4. ¿Cómo es tu mejor amigo/a? ¿Cómo eres tú? _____

5. Mi mejor amigo/a y yo _____

F. ¿Cómo eres? Chat with a partner about each other's characteristics. Use the adjectives from the previous page. Ask questions like:

Modelo	—¿Eres responsable?	—¿Eres reservado?
	—Sí, soy responsable. ¿Y tú?	—No, no soy reservado. ¿Y tú?
	—Yo también. *or* —Yo no.	—Yo tampoco. *or* —Yo sí.

G. ¿Cómo es tu profesor(a)? With your partner, try to determine the three characteristics that best describe your instructor. Then ask your instructor to tell whether your guesses are correct.

Invitación a **Bolivia**

Del álbum de
Sofía

Bolivia tiene aproximadamente tres veces *(times)* el tamaño *(size)* de Montana, y su población es de 9,1 millones de habitantes. Es el país más alto *(highest)* y aislado *(isolated)* de América. Bolivia tiene tres lenguas oficiales: el español, el quechua y el aymará. Hay estaciones de radio en quechua (lengua inca) y aymará (lengua pre-inca), y en la televisión se puede escuchar las noticias en quechua. Este país tiene suficiente gas natural para los próximos 400 años. Allí también encontramos el salar *(salt flat)* más grande del mundo, el salar de Uyuni. Se estima que contiene 10 billones de toneladas *(tons)* de sal.

Mujer quechua con llamas.

El salar de Uyuni.

1. How is the indigenous influence palpable in Bolivia?

2. What did you learn about Bolivia and the Salar de Uyuni?

3. What is one of Bolivia's natural resources?

Práctica adicional

Cuaderno de tareas
pp. 71–72, E–H

invitaciones.
vhlcentral.com
Lab practice

invitaciones.
vhlcentral.com
Episodio 3

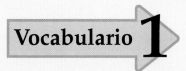

Vocabulario 1 Identifying Spanish-speaking countries

Study the map below to learn the locations, names, and capitals of the Spanish-speaking countries.

Los países de habla hispana y sus capitales

Estados Unidos, Washington D.C.
Océano Atlántico
España, Madrid
Cuba, La Habana
República Dominicana, Santo Domingo
Puerto Rico, San Juan
México, Ciudad de México
Honduras, Tegucigalpa
Guatemala, Ciudad de Guatemala
Colombia, Bogotá
Venezuela, Caracas
El Salvador, San Salvador
Nicaragua, Managua
Costa Rica, San José
Panamá, Ciudad de Panamá
Guinea Ecuatorial, Malabo
Ecuador, Quito
Perú, Lima
Paraguay, Asunción
Océano Pacífico
Bolivia, La Paz y Sucre
Uruguay, Montevideo
Chile, Santiago
Argentina, Buenos Aires

PRÁCTICA

H. El mundo hispano. Examina el mapa para completar las oraciones.

1. Los países hispanos de Centroamérica son: _____, _____, _____, _____, _____ y _____.
2. ¿En cuántos países (countries) se habla español? En _____.
3. En el Caribe, se habla español en _____, _____ y _____.
4. ¿Qué países de Sudamérica no tienen (do not have) acceso al océano? _____ y _____.
5. En Europa, un país de habla hispana es _____.
6. La capital de Guinea Ecuatorial es _____.
7. La capital de Chile es _____, la de Colombia es _____ y la de Nicaragua es _____.
8. San José es la capital de _____.

¡Fíjate!
Bolivia has two capitals: La Paz, the administrative capital and the center of government, and Sucre, the constitutional capital and judicial center.

Práctica adicional

Cuaderno de tareas p. 72, I–J

invitaciones. vhlcentral.com Lab practice

invitaciones. vhlcentral.com Episodio 3

Actividades comunicativas

A. Los habitantes en Latinoamérica.

Instrucciones para **Estudiante 1**

You have half of the information on populations in Latin America, and your partner
has the other half. First, write the names of the countries you are missing, then ask
your partner to give you the number of inhabitants for each one. Take turns and
use the following model.

Modelo —¿Cuántos habitantes hay en México?
—En México hay ciento trece punto tres
millones de habitantes.

¡Fíjate!
The numbers next to each
country represent the number of
people in millions. They are read
as follows:
**El Salvador, siete punto seis
millones de habitantes.**

En Estados Unidos hay
más de 40 millones de
hispanohablantes.

Cuba, 11.4

México, 113.3

El Salvador, 7.6

Costa Rica, 4.7

Panamá, 3.6

Ecuador, 14.2

Colombia, 49

Bolivia, 10.2

Uruguay, 3.7

Chile, 17.2

*Sources: U.S. Census Bureau and the Population Division, UN Secretariat.

A. Los habitantes en Latinoamérica.

Instrucciones para Estudiante 2

You have half of the information on populations in Latin America, and your partner has the other half. First, write the names of the countries you are missing, then ask your partner to give you the number of inhabitants for each one. Take turns and use the following model.

> **Modelo** —¿Cuántos habitantes hay en México?
> —En México hay ciento trece punto tres millones de habitantes.

¡Fíjate!
The numbers next to each country represent the number of people in millions. They are read as follows:
Honduras, ocho punto dos millones de habitantes.

En Estados Unidos hay más de 40 millones de hispanohablantes.

República Dominicana, 9.7

Puerto Rico, 4.1

Guatemala, 14.3

Honduras, 8.2

Nicaragua, 6.2

Venezuela, 30

Perú, 30.1

Paraguay, 7.1

Argentina, 40.8

*Sources: U.S. Census Bureau and the Population Division, UN Secretariat.

B. ¡A hablar! Interview a classmate. Find out your classmate's name, how many classes they are taking, which ones, at what time, which classes they like or dislike, whether they work, and how many hours. Find out which type of music and TV shows they like. Ask them to describe themselves and two of their teachers.

La correspondencia

El correo: Una carta para Odette. Read Sofia's letter to her friend Odette and answer the questions.

1. ¿Cuántas clases toma Sofía? _____

2. ¿Cómo son las clases de Sofía? _____

3. ¿Quién (Who) es Manolo? _____

4. Describe a Lalo. _____

Reading Strategy: Understanding the overall meaning

When reading, you do not have to understand every word. To understand the overall meaning of Sofía's letter, read the first paragraph and highlight all the words you understand. Then use those words to determine the main idea of the paragraph. Read the other paragraphs, repeating the process. Read the questions first to find out what you need to know.

Querida Odette:

¿Cómo estás? Yo estoy muy contenta porque ya comenzamos las clases en la universidad. Este semestre tomo cuatro clases. Creo que van a ser fáciles[1], especialmente cálculo y geología. Lo único[2] diferente es que son en inglés. La clase de cálculo es divertida[3], porque mi amigo Manolo está en la clase y a veces[4] es cómico.

Mis papás están muy bien; están planeando unas vacaciones en Cancún y están muy emocionados[5]. Lalo me preocupa un poco. Es bastante irresponsable e inmaduro y ya casi tiene dieciséis años[6]. No es diligente en la escuela y solamente le interesa ir a fiestas y estar con sus amigos. Espero que cuando se gradúe de la preparatoria[7] madure un poco.

Bueno, querida Odette, un beso[8] para ti y toda tu familia. Escríbeme pronto.

Tu amiga que te quiere,
Sofía

---

[1]*easy* [2]**Lo...** *The only thing* [3]*fun* [4]*sometimes* [5]*excited* [6]**ya...** *he is almost 16 years old*
[7]*high school* [8]*kiss*

En papel: Una notita para Sofía. Complete the following e-mail to Sofía telling her about yourself.

> **Writing Strategy: Identifying the content of a note**
> Successful writers identify the information they wish to communicate before they begin to write. In the early stages of learning Spanish, this information will be lists of words and phrases. Later, you can incorporate these lists into brief notes you write to Spanish speakers. Pay close attention to spelling, so that your early written communication will be understandable.

From: _____
To: Sofía. <Blasio@sol.red>
Re: Saludos

Date: Lunes, 19 de feb. 12:07 EST

Hola, Sofía:

Me llamo _____ . Soy de _____ .
Mi universidad se llama _____ .
Este semestre tomo _____ clases. Son: _____ .
Me gusta mucho la clase de _____ porque
el/la profesor(a) es _____ .
Este semestre trabajo _____ horas a la semana. ¿Y tú? ¿Cuántas clases tomas?
¿Trabajas? ¿Cuántas horas? ¡Escríbeme pronto! Buena suerte este semestre.

                                        Saludos,

                                        _____

¡A ver de nuevo! Escucha la conversación o mira el video de **Escenas de la vida** para completar cada oración con la palabra apropiada.

1. Los salones de clase en Puerto Rico no tienen tantas _____ .
2. La mayoría de las universidades tienen un _____ , un _____ y una _____ .
3. En Puerto Rico y en Estados Unidos hay _____ , pero en México no.
4. El profesor de cálculo es _____ y _____ .
5. Adriana es un poco _____ .
6. A Sofía le gustan las clases de _____ , _____ y _____ .

Práctica adicional			
Cuaderno de tareas pp. 73–74, K–L	invitaciones. vhlcentral.com Episodio 3	invitaciones. vhlcentral.com Lab practice	invitaciones. vhlcentral.com Episodio 3

Vocabulario del Episodio 3

Los gustos *Likes and dislikes*

¿Te gusta...?	*Do you like...?* (informal)	**No, no me gusta.**	*No, I don't like it.*
Sí, me gusta.	*Yes, I like it.*	**¿Le gusta...?**	*Do you like...?* (formal)

Para pedir descripciones *To ask for descriptions*

¿Cómo es tu profesor(a)?	*What is your teacher like?*
¿Cómo son tus amigos?	*What are your friends like?*

Los pronombres personales y el verbo <u>ser</u>

yo **soy**	*I am*
tú **eres**	*you are* (informal)
usted (Ud.) **es**	*you are* (formal)
él **es**	*he is*
ella **es**	*she is*
nosotros/as **somos**	*we are*
ustedes (Uds.) **son**	*you are* (plural)
vosotros/as **sois**	
ellos/as **son**	*they are*

Adjetivos

activo/a	excelente	(in)maduro/a	romántico/a
ambicioso/a	extrovertido/a	materialista	sentimental
arrogante	flexible	nervioso/a	serio/a
atractivo/a	generoso/a	optimista	sociable
competente	(des)honesto/a	(im)paciente	terrible
creativo/a	idealista	pesimista	tímido/a
discreto/a	increíble	reservado/a	tranquilo/a
estudioso/a	interesante	(ir)responsable	

Los países de habla hispana y sus capitales

Argentina, Buenos Aires	Guinea Ecuatorial, Malabo
Bolivia, La Paz y Sucre	Honduras, Tegucigalpa
Chile, Santiago	México, Ciudad de México
Colombia, Bogotá	Nicaragua, Managua
Costa Rica, San José	Panamá, Ciudad de Panamá
Cuba, La Habana	Paraguay, Asunción
Ecuador, Quito	Perú, Lima
El Salvador, San Salvador	Puerto Rico, San Juan
España, Madrid	República Dominicana, Santo Domingo
Estados Unidos, Washington D.C.	Uruguay, Montevideo
Guatemala, Ciudad de Guatemala	Venezuela, Caracas

Vocabulario personal

Write the words that you need to know to describe yourself and express your likes and dislikes in Spanish.

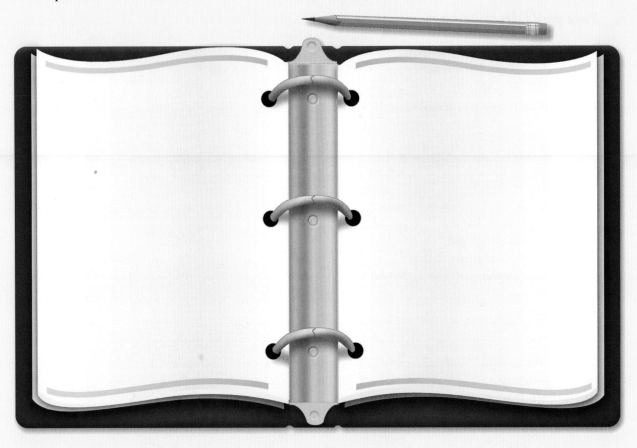

Cuaderno de tareas

Episodio

3

Escenas de la vida: Los profesores y las clases

A. ¡Mira cuánto puedes entender! See how much of the **Escena** you understood by matching the Spanish sentences with their English equivalents.

En la universidad

_____ 1. ¿Hay consejeros?

_____ 2. En México no hay.

_____ 3. Es mi carrera.

_____ 4. Los salones están bien equipados.

_____ 5. En Puerto Rico tampoco tienen tantas cosas.

a. It's my major.

b. Classrooms are well-equipped.

c. In Puerto Rico, they don't have as many things either.

d. Are there counselors?

e. In Mexico there aren't any.

Las clases

_____ 6. ¡Qué mala suerte!

_____ 7. El profesor explica bien.

_____ 8. Juego tenis con mi esposo.

_____ 9. Me gusta hacer ejercicio.

_____ 10. Por suerte, mi clase de composición me gusta mucho.

f. I like to exercise.

g. Luckily, I like my English Composition class a lot.

h. Too bad!

i. The professor gives good explanations.

j. I play tennis with my husband.

B. ¿Qué clase te gusta? Order the statements so the dialogue makes sense.

_____ a. A mí me gusta mucho la clase. La de vóleibol también. Me gusta mucho hacer ejercicio. ¿Y a usted?

_____ b. En Puerto Rico, sí. Y los profesores son excelentes.

_____ c. Pues, más o menos. El cálculo es difícil. ¿Y a ti?

__1__ d. ¿En Puerto Rico hay consejeros como en Estados Unidos? En México no hay.

_____ e. A veces juego tenis con mi esposo, pero no me gusta.

_____ f. Hablando de profesores, ¿le gusta la clase de cálculo?

Gramática 1   Expressing likes and dislikes
• <u>Me gusta, te gusta, le gusta</u>

C. ¿Qué materias te gustan? Indicate which subjects you like and which ones you do not like. You may use the subjects on the list below, or any subjects you wrote in your **Vocabulario personal** section. Remember to use the definite article after **gusta**.

cálculo	geología	inglés	contabilidad
economía	español	música	drama

1. Me gusta el arte.   No me gusta la astronomía.
2. _____   _____
3. _____   _____
4. _____   _____
5. _____   _____

D. ¿Qué te gusta hacer? Indicate six activities you like to do and six activities you do not like to do.

a. jugar (vóleibol, béisbol, fútbol americano, fútbol *(soccer)*, tenis)

b. comer (pizza, tacos, enchiladas, hamburguesas, frutas, ensaladas)

c. estudiar (en casa, en la biblioteca, con compañeros de clase)

d. escuchar música (clásica, alternativa, rap, latina, moderna)

e. leer (novelas, poemas, el periódico *(newspaper)*, el horóscopo)

f. mirar programas (cómicos, policíacos, de suspenso)

1. Me gusta estudiar en la biblioteca. _____
2. _____
3. _____
4. _____
5. _____
6. _____
7. _____
8. No me gusta escuchar música clásica. _____
9. _____
10. _____
11. _____
12. _____
13. _____
14. _____

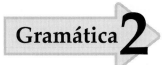

Gramática 2

Describing yourself and others
- **Ser** + [*adjective*] (cognates)
- **Subject pronouns**

E. Descríbelos. Describe what are the characteristics of a good professor and what are the characteristics of the best classmates or study buddies.

arrogante	idealista	optimista	sentimental
competente	increíble	(im)paciente	sociable
excelente	interesante	pesimista	terrible
flexible	materialista	(ir)responsable	tranquilo/a
activo/a	discreto/a	(des)honesto/a	romántico/a
ambicioso/a	estudioso/a	estricto/a	serio/a
atractivo/a	extrovertido/a	nervioso/a	tímido/a
creativo/a	generoso/a	reservado/a	inmaduro/a

1. Un buen profesor es _____

_____

2. Los mejores compañeros de clase son _____

_____

F. Mis amigos y yo: una descripción. Fill in the appropriate forms of **ser**.

(Yo) (1)_____ estudioso y ambicioso, pero no (2)_____ muy creativo.
Y tú, ¿cómo (3)_____ ? Tú (4) _____ un poco nerviosa, ¿no?
Sofía (5)_____ muy sociable y Manolo (6)_____ tímido. Ellos
(7)_____ buenos amigos. Ramón y yo (8)_____ inteligentes, pero también
(9)_____ materialistas. Y tus amigos, ¿cómo (10)_____?

G. ¿Cómo es… ? Describe the famous people below. To ask someone to describe a person/people, you ask **¿Cómo es/son… ?**

> **Modelo**   Barack Obama
> **¿Cómo es Barack Obama? Es inteligente y ambicioso.**

1. Brad Pitt y Angelina Jolie _____

2. Oprah Winfrey _____

3. Bill Gates _____

4. Michael Phelps _____

5. Mary-Kate y Ashley Olsen _____

H. Un poco sobre mí. (*A little about me.*) Write a paragraph with the following information: your name, the classes you take (**tomo...**), a description of your instructors (**Mi profesor de... es...**), the number of hours a week you work (**trabajo...**) and study (**estudio...**), and something you like to do.

_____

_____

_____

_____

_____

Vocabulario 1 ▷ Identifying Spanish-speaking countries

I. Capitales. Write the capitals of the following countries.

País	Capital
México	_____
Guatemala	_____
Costa Rica	_____
Panamá	_____
Chile	_____
España	_____
República Dominicana	_____
Puerto Rico	_____
Uruguay	_____

J. Los países. Look at the map in order to identify the countries.

1. _____   10. _____

2. _____   11. _____

3. _____   12. _____

4. _____   13. _____

5. _____   14. _____

6. _____   15. _____

7. _____   16. _____

8. _____   17. _____

9. _____   18. _____

Nombre _____ Fecha _____

Para terminar

K. La Universidad Estatal de San Marcos en California.

Parte 1. Read the description of the university and answer the questions.

La universidad está en la ciudad[1] de San Marcos, localizada a unas cuarenta millas[2] al norte de San Diego. Es la última[3] universidad (la número vientiuno) construída[4] en California por el sistema californiano de universidades estatales. California State University San Marcos es una universidad nueva y todavía es pequeña. La universidad no está totalmente terminada aún. Los salones son nuevos y modernos; todos están equipados con televisiones, computadoras, videocaseteras, pupitres y pizarrones nuevos, pero no hay piscinas. La cafetería y la biblioteca son muy bonitas[5] y modernas. Además hay un centro para el estudio de libros en español, Centro Barahona, que tiene una de las colecciones más grandes de libros infantiles y juveniles en español. Asisten aproximadamente 9,000 estudiantes. Ahora la universidad tiene tres edificios[6] para residencias estudiantiles, un gimnasio y una cancha de fútbol. También tiene muchos estacionamientos porque la mayoría de los estudiantes todavía[7] llegan a la universidad en coche[8]; menos de 600 estudiantes viven[9] en las residencias.

[1]city [2]miles [3]last [4]built [5]pretty [6]buildings [7]still [8]car [9]live

1. Describe the university, its size, and its facilities. _____

_____

2. Describe the classrooms. _____

_____

3. Why is this a good place to study? _____

_____

4. How many students are there? How many live on campus? How is parking?

_____

_____

Parte 2. Use the reading above as a model to write about your own university or college.

_____

_____

_____

_____

_____

L. Una miniprueba. Complete the following communicative tasks to test your knowledge of the content of this chapter.

1. Ask Sofía:
    a. how many classes she is taking.
    b. if she likes the calculus class.

2. Ask Adriana:
    c. when her composition class is.
    d. to describe her instructor.

3. Tell Manolo:
    e. the classes you take.
    f. which ones you like and why.

4. Describe:
    g. yourself.
    h. your favorite instructor.

a. _____

b. _____

c. _____

d. _____

e. _____

f. _____

_____

_____

_____

_____

_____

g. _____

_____

_____

_____

_____

_____

h. _____

_____

_____

_____

_____

Objetivos comunicativos

In this episode, you will practice:

✓ talking about your family

✓ telling and asking for someone's age

✓ saying and asking where someone is from

✓ asking for and giving phone numbers

Episodio 4

Escenas de la vida: ¡Qué internacionales!

 A. ¡Mira cuánto puedes entender!

1. Localiza los siguientes lugares *(places)* en el mapa.

a. México _____

b. Honduras _____

c. La Florida _____

d. Puerto Rico _____

e. Cuba _____

2. Mira la **Escena** para completar las oraciones.

f. La mamá de Ramón es de _____.

g. El papá de Ramón es de _____.

h. Los padres de Manolo son de _____.

i. Adriana es de _____.

3. Indicate who prefers to speak English and who prefers to speak Spanish.

Los papás y los hermanos de Ramón.

Cultura a lo vivo

Educational politics, when schools actively discourage the use of any language other than English, have intensified the problem of language loss within Hispanic families. Because of these procedures, many Hispanic children have stopped speaking Spanish and will be unable to pass the language on to their children. This trend has led many Spanish-speaking Americans to speak Spanish in their home as a way of preserving the links to their native countries. These families maintain their native language in order to enjoy the cultural and economic benefits of being bilingual and bicultural.

B. ¿Te diste cuenta? Escucha la conversación otra vez para indicar si los comentarios son **ciertos** o **falsos**.

	Cierto	Falso
1. A la hija de Adriana no le gusta hablar español.	☐	☐
2. Manolo está en la clase de cálculo.	☐	☐
3. Adriana y Sofía toman geología juntas *(together)*.	☐	☐
4. Ana Mari habla español muy bien.	☐	☐
5. Ramón y Sofía tienen una clase a las nueve.	☐	☐

C. Completa las oraciones. Complete the following sentences, according to what you heard in the **Escena**.

1. _____ es la hermana de Ramón.
2. Los padres de Manolo viven en _____.
3. Adriana _____ tres hijos.
4. Los _____ menores de Ramón no hablan español, pero lo entienden *(they understand it)*.
5. Manolo escribe _____ en español.

Práctica adicional		
Cuaderno de tareas p. 95, A–B	invitaciones. vhlcentral.com Episodio 4	invitaciones. vhlcentral.com Episodio 4

Para comunicarnos mejor

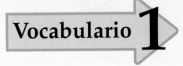

Vocabulario **1**

Identifying family members and friends
- **The family**
- **Expressing possession**

When Ramón and Adriana talked about their families, they made the following statements.

Mi **mamá** es de México.	*My mom is from Mexico.*
Mi **papá** es de Honduras.	*My dad is from Honduras.*
Mis **hijos** mayores hablan español.	*My older children speak Spanish.*
Mis **hermanos** menores lo entienden todo.	*My younger brothers understand everything.*

> **Learning Strategy: Make associations**
> Think of English words that sound similar to the Spanish words you are trying to learn. Then associate them with each other in some creative way. For example, the name *Sabrina* sounds a lot like the Spanish **sobrina** *(niece)*. Create a mental link: **Mi amiga Sabrina tiene una sobrina.** Recognize the relationships that exist in the two languages. For example, look at the words *apprentice (student)* and **aprender** *(to learn)*; to remember the Spanish, visualize an apprentice that must **aprender mucho.**

The following table contains the terms you use to identify the members of your family and your friends.

La familia, los familiares y más			
los abuelos	grandparents	el abuelo	la abuela
los amigos	friends	el amigo	la amiga
los chicos	adolescents, teenagers	el chico	la chica
los cuñados	brother(s)-in-law and sister(s)-in-law	el cuñado	la cuñada
los esposos	husband and wife	el esposo	la esposa
los familiares	relatives	el familiar	
los hermanos	brother(s) and sister(s)	el hermano	la hermana
los hijos	children (one's own): son(s) and daughter(s)	el hijo	la hija
el/la hijo/a único/a	only child		
los nietos	grandchildren	el nieto	la nieta
los niños	children: boy(s) and girl(s)	el niño	la niña
los novios	boyfriend and girlfriend; bride and groom; fiancés	el novio	la novia
los padres	parents	el padre	la madre
los primos	cousins	el primo	la prima
los sobrinos	nephew(s) and niece(s)	el sobrino	la sobrina
los suegros	in-laws: father-in-law and mother-in-law	el suegro	la suegra
los tíos	uncle(s) and aunt(s)	el tío	la tía

Las mascotas	Pets		
el/la gato/a	cat	el/la perro/a	dog
el pájaro	bird	el pez	fish

También se dice...

los padres ⟶ los papás (el papá, la mamá)

los familiares ⟶ los parientes

los chicos ⟶ los muchachos

¡Fíjate!

Ask your instructor for other family relationships you may need to describe your family. Write them in the **Vocabulario personal** at the end of **Episodio 4**.

• Expressing possession

1. Notice how Spanish uses the construction **el esposo de Adriana** to say *Adriana's husband*. Where English uses *'s* to express possession, Spanish uses [*article*] + [*noun*] **+ de +** [*noun*].

la hermana de Ramón   *Ramón's sister*
los hijos de Adriana   *Adriana's children*
el gato de Manolo   *Manolo's cat*

Ana Mari es la hermana de Ramón.

2. Another way of indicating possession or relationship is to use possessive adjectives. Read the following examples:

Mis padres son de México.	*My parents are from Mexico.*
¿De dónde son **tus** padres?	*Where are your parents from?*
Sus abuelos son de Irlanda.	*His/Her grandparents are from Ireland.*
Éstos son **nuestros** hijos.	*These are our children.*
No me gusta **su** gata. ⎱	*I don't like your cat.*
No me gusta **vuestra** gata. ⎰	
Su perro es un chihuahueño.	*Their dog is a chihuahua.*

3. Notice that the possessive adjectives agree in number with the noun possessed, not with the possessor. **Nuestro/a** and **vuestro/a** also agree in gender.

Los adjetivos posesivos

mi, mis	*my*	nuestro, nuestros	⎱ *our*
tu, tus	*your* (informal)	nuestra, nuestras	⎰
su, sus	*his, her, your* (formal)	vuestro, vuestros	⎱ *your* (informal)
	their, your (plural)	vuestra, vuestras	⎰

PRÁCTICA

A. La familia de Adriana. Indicate if the following statements are **cierto** (*true*) or **falso** (*false*), according to Adriana's family tree on the next page. Correct the false statements by replacing the incorrect word.

> **Modelo**　José Luis es el esposo de Adriana.
> **Falso. Es el hermano de Adriana.**

	Cierto	Falso
1. Doña Cristina es la esposa de don José Luis. _____	☐	☐
2. Beto y Esther son primos. _____	☐	☐
3. Roberto es el papá de Santiaguito. _____	☐	☐
4. Las sobrinas de José Luis son Tina, Esther y Viviana. _____	☐	☐
5. El abuelo de Beto se llama Roberto. _____	☐	☐
6. Don José Luis y doña Cristina tienen tres nietas. _____	☐	☐
7. Roberto es el tío de Santiaguito y Viviana. _____	☐	☐
8. Beto, Tina y Esther son hermanos. _____	☐	☐

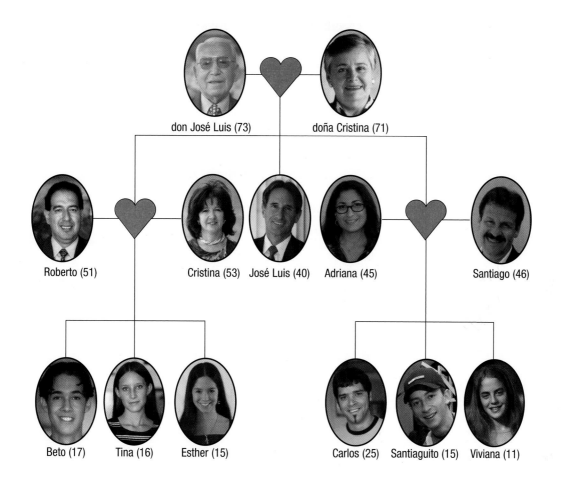

don José Luis (73)   doña Cristina (71)

Roberto (51)   Cristina (53) José Luis (40) Adriana (45)   Santiago (46)

Beto (17)   Tina (16)   Esther (15)   Carlos (25) Santiaguito (15) Viviana (11)

B. Relaciones familiares. ¿Cuál es la relación entre estas personas en la familia de Adriana?

> **Modelo**   Adriana y Santiago son **esposos.**

1. Santiaguito y Viviana son _____.

2. Esther y Viviana son _____.

3. Roberto y Cristina son los _____ de Esther.

4. Carlos, Santiaguito y Viviana son los _____ de Adriana.

5. Santiaguito y Beto son _____ de doña Cristina.

6. José Luis es el _____ de Santiaguito.

7. Don José Luis y doña Cristina son los _____ de Tina, Esther, Viviana, Beto, Carlos y Santiaguito.

8. Doña Cristina es la _____ de Roberto y Santiago.

C. ¿Quiénes son? *(Who are they?)* Completa las oraciones lógicamente.

¡Fíjate!

Be sure to use the appropriate forms of the possessive adjectives: **mi** and **tu** are singular, while **mis** and **tus** are plural.

> **Modelo**　La hija de mi mamá es **mi hermana.**
> Los papás de tus primas son **tus tíos.**

1. La madre de mi madre es _____.
2. Los hijos de mi hermana son _____.
3. La esposa de tu hermano es _____.

4. Las hijas de tus hijas son _____.
5. El hijo de mis tíos es _____.
6. El padre de tu esposa es _____.

D. ¿Y tus parientes? Who **(Quién)** do the following questions describe? Answer them yourself, and then interview a partner.

1. ¿Con qué familiares vives *(do you live)*? _____
2. ¿Qué *(Which)* familiares viven lejos *(far)*? _____
3. ¿Qué familiares ves *(do you see)* con frecuencia? _____
4. ¿Con quién celebras las fiestas del fin del año *(the holidays)*? _____

Práctica adicional	
Cuaderno de tareas pp. 96–98, C–G	invitaciones. vhlcentral.com Episodio 4

 **Gramática 1**

Expressing age
- **The verb tener**
- **Numbers 41–100**

In the conversation, you heard the following statements.

Yo **tengo** tres hijos.	*I have three children.*
¿Y **tienes** familia en Cuba?	*And do you have family in Cuba?*
En mi casa también **tenemos** ese problema.	*We also have that problem at home.*

Tengo, tienes, and **tenemos** are forms of the verb **tener** *(to have)*. You will use these forms, and the other forms of **tener,** to talk about the members of your family and to tell how old they are. Observe the conjugation of **tener** below.

Tener	
No **tengo** hijos.	*I don't have children.*
¿**Tienes** hermanos?	*Do you have brothers and sisters?*
Sofía **tiene** un hermano.	*Sofía has a brother.*
Tenemos mucha tarea.	*We have a lot of homework.*
¿Uds. **tienen** familia en España? ¿**Tenéis** familia en España?	*Do you have family in Spain?*
Ellos no **tienen** gatos, ¿verdad?	*They don't have cats, right?*
Tener is also used to indicate age.	
¿**Cuántos años tienes?**	*How old are you?*
Tengo treinta y seis **años.**	*I'm thirty-six years old.*
¿**Cuántos años tienen** tus papás?	*How old are your parents?*
Mi papá **tiene** sesenta y tres **años** y mi mamá **tiene** cincuenta y nueve.	*My dad is sixty-three years old, and my mom is fifty-nine.*

PRÁCTICA

E. ¿Cierto o falso? Completa cada oración con la forma apropiada del verbo **tener**. Después decide si la oración es **cierta** o **falsa**.

Basado en la conversación:	Cierto	Falso
1. Adriana y su esposo _____ dos hijas.	☐	☐
2. Ramón _____ una hermana.	☐	☐
3. Adriana dice *(says)*: "Yo _____ tres hijos."	☐	☐
4. Sofía no _____ novio.	☐	☐
5. Ramón y Sofía _____ una clase de cálculo.	☐	☐
Basado en tu experiencia personal:		
6. Mis compañeros y yo _____ mucha tarea *(homework)*.	☐	☐
7. Yo _____ cuatro clases este semestre.	☐	☐
8. Mis papás y yo _____ un perro.	☐	☐
9. Yo _____ veinte años.	☐	☐
10. Y tú, ¿_____ mascotas?	☐	☐

• Numbers 41–100

Más números			
41	cuarenta y uno	42, 43 . . .	cuarenta y dos, cuarenta y tres…
50	cincuenta	53, 54 . . .	cincuenta y tres, cincuenta y cuatro…
60	sesenta	64, 65 . . .	sesenta y cuatro, sesenta y cinco…
70	setenta	75, 76 . . .	setenta y cinco, setenta y seis…
80	ochenta	86, 87 . . .	ochenta y seis, ochenta y siete…
90	noventa	97, 98 . . .	noventa y siete, noventa y ocho…
100	cien		

PRÁCTICA

F. El inventario. You work in the bookstore at your university. Here is this week's inventory. Tell your co-worker how many of the following articles are in stock. When you are done, your co-worker will repeat them back to you.

> **Modelo**   48 calculadoras ⟶ **Hay cuarenta y ocho calculadoras.**

1. 86 libros de historia
2. 79 cuadernos
3. 100 mochilas
4. 65 calculadoras
5. 92 plumas
6. 43 diccionarios
7. 58 lápices
8. 74 libros de cálculo

G. ¿Cuántos años tiene...? Usa el árbol genealógico de la página 79 para contestar las preguntas.

1. ¿Quién (*Who*) es la persona que tiene setenta y un años? _____

2. ¿Quién tiene cuarenta y cinco años? _____

3. ¿Cuántos años tiene la hermana de Adriana? _____

4. ¿Cuántos años tiene el suegro de Santiago? _____

5. ¿Cuántos años tiene el menor (*the youngest*) de los primos? _____

H. ¿Cuál es tu teléfono? Write down the phone numbers of three of your classmates, and ask them when they are home.

> **¡Fíjate!**
> Pay attention to the way Spanish speakers give phone numbers. Look at the model.

Modelo	—¿Cuál (*What*) es tu teléfono?
	—Es el cuatro-veintitrés-sesenta y ocho-cuarenta y tres (423-6843).
	—¿A qué hora estás en casa (*are you at home*)?
	—A las seis.

	Nombre	Buena hora para llamar (*to call*)
1.	_____	_____
2.	_____	_____
3.	_____	_____

I. Preguntas personales. Answer the following questions about your family, your classes, and your social life. Afterwards, interview a partner. Bring photos of your family to share.

> **¡Fíjate!**
> Use expressions like:
> ¡Qué interesante!
> ¿En serio?
> ¡Qué bien/mal!

1. **Acerca de (*Concerning*) tu familia:** ¿Tienes una familia grande (*large*)? ¿Cuántos hermanos tienes? ¿Cuántos años tienen? ¿Cuántos años tienen tus papás? ¿Tienes mascotas?

_____

_____

_____

2. **Acerca de tus clases:** ¿Cuántas clases tienes este semestre? ¿Cuáles (*Which ones*) son? ¿Cómo son tus clases: interesantes o aburridas (*boring*)? ¿Qué clase te gusta más?

_____

_____

_____

3. **Acerca de ti:** ¿Tienes novio/a o esposo/a? ¿Cómo se llama? ¿Cuántos años tiene? ¿Cómo es: romántico/a o reservado/a?

_____

_____

_____

_____

Práctica adicional
Cuaderno de tareas pp. 98–100, H–J
SUPERSITE invitaciones. vhlcentral.com Episodio 4

Gramática 2

Saying where someone is from
• **Ser de**

In the conversation, you heard the following statements.

¿Y tú, **de dónde eres**?	*Where are you from?*
Soy de aquí.	*I'm from here.*
Mi papá **es de** Honduras.	*My dad is from Honduras.*

When asking and telling where someone is from, use the verb **ser**, plus the preposition **de**.

—¿**De** dónde **son** tus abuelos?   *Where are your grandparents from?*

—Mis abuelos **son de** España.   *My grandparents are from Spain.*

When asking where someone is from, **de** *(from)* is always at the beginning of the question.

—¿**De** dónde eres tu?   *Where are you from?*

PRÁCTICA

J. ¿De dónde son? Complete each description with the appropriate form of **ser**.

1. Adriana _____ de Puerto Rico.
2. Sofía y Lalo _____ de México.
3. Manolo _____ de Cuba.
4. ¿De dónde _____ tú?
5. Yo _____ de aquí.
6. ¿De dónde _____ ustedes?
7. Nosotros _____ de Estados Unidos.
8. Emilio y su esposa _____ de España, ¿verdad?

¡Fíjate!

You may want to review the conjugation of **ser** on page 59 before completing this activity.

K. Personas famosas. In pairs, ask questions to match these people to their countries.

Modelo	—¿De dónde es el jugador de los Lakers, Pau Gasol? —Es de España.	—¿De dónde son los directores de cine Del Toro y Cuarón? —Son de México.

_____ 1. el líder y activista Nelson Mandela   a. Colombia

_____ 2. los diseñadores Giorgio Armani y Donatella Versace   b. República Dominicana

_____ 3. la escritora Isabel Allende   c. Sudáfrica

_____ 4. los príncipes William y Harry   d. Italia

_____ 5. el escritor Gabriel García Márquez   e. España

_____ 6. la actriz Penélope Cruz   f. Inglaterra

_____ 7. el beisbolista David Ortiz   g. Japón

_____ 8. el emperador Akihito y su esposa   h. Chile

L. ¿De dónde es tu familia?

Parte 1. Interview three classmates to find out where their parents and grandparents are from (**de dónde son**). Write down their answers.

¡Fíjate!

See **Vocabulario adicional**, p. 402 to look up the Spanish names of other countries that you may need. Don't forget to write them in the **Vocabulario personal** section at the end of **Episodio 4**.

Modelo   —¿De dónde eres?
—Soy de...
—¿Y tus abuelos?
—Mi abuela materna es de... Mis abuelos paternos son de...
—¿De dónde son tus padres?
—Mi papá es de..., y mi mamá es de...

Banco de palabras

Soy adoptado/a.
I'm adopted.

No sé de dónde es/son.
I don't know where he/they is/are from.

Mi abuela murió.
My grandmother died.

Mis padres murieron.
My parents died.

Lo siento.
I'm sorry.

Parte 2. ¿Qué tan internacional es nuestra clase? Share with your instructor what you learned about your classmate's family.

Modelo   —La mamá de Erik es de Las Filipinas.
—Los abuelos de Kathy son de Alemania.

¡Fíjate!

Remember to highlight all of the words that you understand. Use the cognates, vocabulary, and structures you have learned in order to make sense of the rest of the information you read.

M. La familia real española.
Lee la información y contesta (*answer*) las preguntas.

En España, como en Inglaterra y otros países europeos, todavía[1] existe una monarquía constitucional. Desde 1975, el rey[2] de España representa a la nación y modera el funcionamiento de las instituciones legislativas. El rey Juan Carlos y la reina Sofía son el símbolo de la unidad española y realizan[3] muchas funciones ceremoniales.

La familia real español es una familia grande, ¿no? ¿Cuántas personas hay en la foto?

El rey Juan Carlos I es de España, aunque nació[4] en Roma por razones políticas. Su esposa, Sofía, es de Grecia. Los reyes tienen tres hijos: Elena, Cristina y Felipe. Elena es la mayor[5] y tiene dos hijos. Cristina tiene cuatro hijos, y Felipe, el menor[6], tiene dos.

[1]*still* [2]*king* [3]*carry out* [4]**aunque...** *although he was born* [5]*the oldest* [6]*the youngest*

1. ¿Cuántos nietos tienen los reyes?
2. ¿Cuántas hermanas tiene el príncipe Felipe?
3. ¿Cuántos primos tienen los hijos de Elena?
4. ¿Hay familias muy famosas en los Estados Unidos? ¿Quiénes son?
5. In your own words, explain the role of the royal family in Spain.

Práctica adicional

Cuaderno de tareas
p. 100, K

invitaciones.
vhlcentral.com
Lab practice

invitaciones.
vhlcentral.com
Episodio 4

Actividades comunicativas

 A. Los números de emergencia.

Instrucciones para **Estudiante 1**

Imagine you are going to Guadalajara, Mexico, with Sofía and her friends. As a precaution, you want the telephone numbers of various emergency services, and other important numbers. You were able to locate only a few. Ask your partner for the numbers you need and fill them in.

Modelo —¿Tienes el número de teléfono de los bomberos *(firefighters)*?

NOMBRE	TELÉFONO
La Cruz Roja	6-13-15-50 y 6-14-27-07
Los Ángeles Verdes (problemas mecánicos)	
La casa de Odette	
La policía federal	6-21-91-74 y 6-22-88-37
La casa de los abuelos de Ramón	5-54-13-90
Los bomberos *(firefighters)*	
La policía municipal	6-17-60-60 y 6-18-02-06
La defensa del consumidor	

A. Los números de emergencia.

Instrucciones para **Estudiante 2**

Imagine you are going to Guadalajara, Mexico, with Sofía and her friends. As a precaution, you want the telephone numbers of various emergency services, and other important numbers. You were able to locate only a few. Ask your partner for the numbers you need and fill them in.

> **Modelo** —¿Tienes el número de teléfono de la policía federal?

NOMBRE	TELÉFONO
La Cruz Roja	
Los Ángeles Verdes (problemas mecánicos)	5-13-26-64
La casa de Odette	5-82-99-24
La policía federal	
La casa de los abuelos de Ramón	
Los bomberos (*firefighters*)	6-19-52-41 y 6-23-08-33
La policía municipal	
La defensa del consumidor	6-14-94-16 y 6-14-94-01

B. Árbol genealógico: la familia de Ramón y Ana Mari Robledo.

Instrucciones para Estudiante 1

 Parte 1. With a partner, complete Ramón and Ana Mari's family tree. You have half of the information; your partner has the other half. Use the following expressions.

—¿Cuántos años tiene Luis?　　　　—¿Cuál es la profesión de Pilar?

—Tiene... años.　　　　　　　　　　—Es...

—¿De dónde es?　　　　　　　　　　—¿Cómo se llama el papá de Ana Mari?

—Es de...　　　　　　　　　　　　　—Se llama...

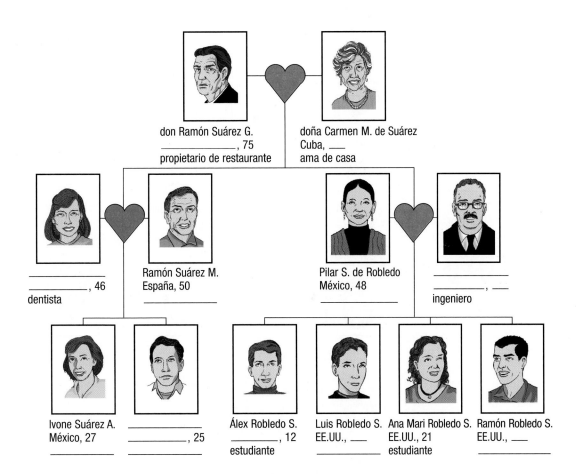

don Ramón Suárez G.
_____, 75
propietario de restaurante

doña Carmen M. de Suárez
Cuba, ___
ama de casa

_____, 46
dentista

Ramón Suárez M.
España, 50
_____

Pilar S. de Robledo
México, 48
_____

_____, ___
ingeniero

Ivone Suárez A.
México, 27
_____

_____, 25
_____

Álex Robledo S.
_____, 12
estudiante

Luis Robledo S.
EE.UU., ___
_____

Ana Mari Robledo S.
EE.UU., 21
estudiante

Ramón Robledo S.
EE.UU., ___
_____

 Parte 2. Now write a paragraph, describing Ramón and Ana Mari's family.

Modelo	Ramón tiene... hermanos. Sus hermanos son... Su papá se llama... Tiene... años...

B. Árbol genealógico: la familia de Ramón y Ana Mari Robledo.

Instrucciones para Estudiante 2

Parte 1. With a partner, complete Ramón and Ana Mari's family tree. You have half of the information; your partner has the other half. Use the following expressions.

—¿**Cómo se llama la mamá de Ana Mari?** —¿**Cuál es la profesión de Alejandro?**

—**Se llama...** —**Es...**

—¿**De dónde es?** —¿**Cuántos años tiene Álex?**

—**Es de...** —**Tiene... años.**

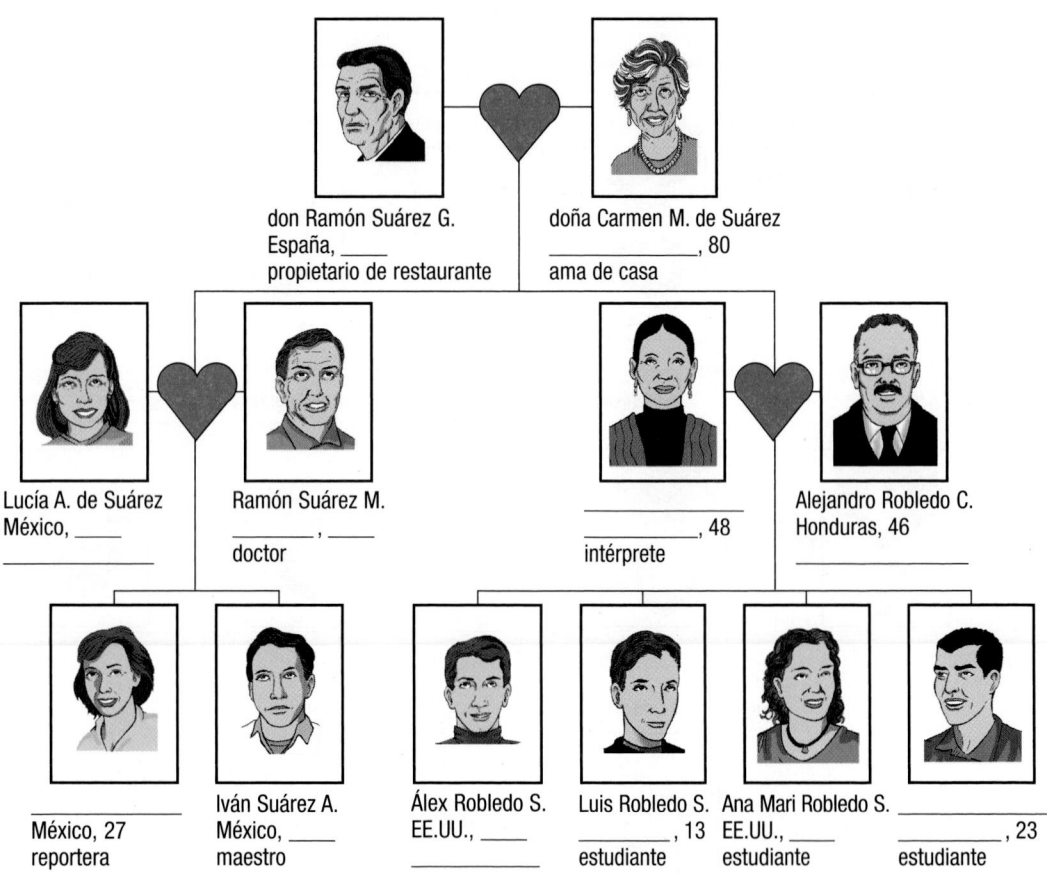

don Ramón Suárez G.
España, ____
propietario de restaurante

doña Carmen M. de Suárez
_____, 80
ama de casa

Lucía A. de Suárez
México, ____
_____

Ramón Suárez M.
_____, ____
doctor

_____, 48
intérprete

Alejandro Robledo C.
Honduras, 46
_____

_____
México, 27
reportera

Iván Suárez A.
México, ____
maestro

Álex Robledo S.
EE.UU., ____
_____

Luis Robledo S.
_____, 13
estudiante

Ana Mari Robledo S.
EE.UU., ____
estudiante

_____
_____, 23
estudiante

Parte 2. Now write a paragraph, describing Ramón and Ana Mari's family.

Modelo	Ramón tiene... hermanos. Sus hermanos son... Su papá se llama... Tiene... años, etc.

C. En imágenes.

Instrucciones para **Estudiante 1**

Use the following words and drawings to create logical sentences. When you know what your sentences are, read them to your partner, who will check the answer key to see if your sentences are correct. Take turns.

1. Necesito comprar un , dos y una para la clase de matemáticas.

2. En esa 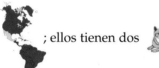 venden y .

3. Mis  paternos viven en ; ellos tienen dos , un y

muchos .

4. En las mañanas, es difícil encontrar en la **USC** UNIVERSITY OF SOUTHERN CALIFORNIA .

5. En la de mi novio hay muchos y .

Las respuestas de tu compañero/a:
1. En nuestro **salón de clases** hay treinta y ocho **pupitres**, tres **pizarrones**, una **bandera** y un **reloj**.
2. En la escuela de mi prima no hay **canchas de tenis**, **piscina** ni **gimnasio**.
3. Necesito ir al **baño** antes de mi clase de **química** porque hoy tenemos un **examen** difícil.
4. Mi **profesor** de **matemáticas** tiene cuarenta **chicos/estudiantes** en su clase.
5. Tengo una **familia** pequeña: mis **padres**, una **hermana** y un **perro**.

C. En imágenes.

Instrucciones para **Estudiante 2**

Use the following words and drawings to create logical sentences. When you know what your sentences are, read them to your partner, who will check the answer key to see if your sentences are correct. Take turns.

1. En nuestro  hay treinta y ocho , tres , una y un .

2. En la escuela de mi prima no hay 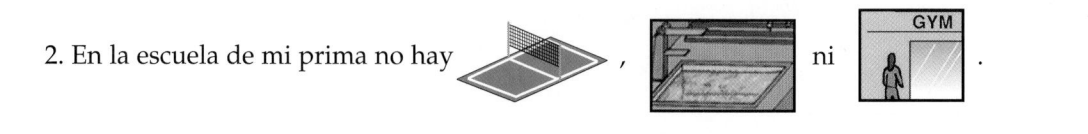 , ni .

3. Necesito ir al  antes de mi clase de porque hoy tenemos un difícil.

4. Mi 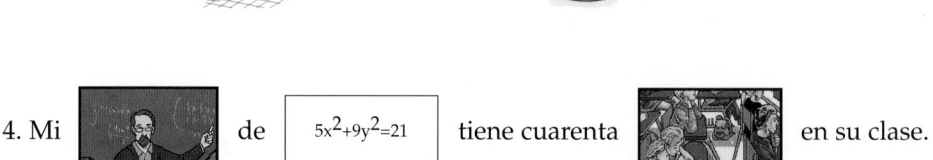 de $5x^2+9y^2=21$ tiene cuarenta en su clase.

5. Tengo una 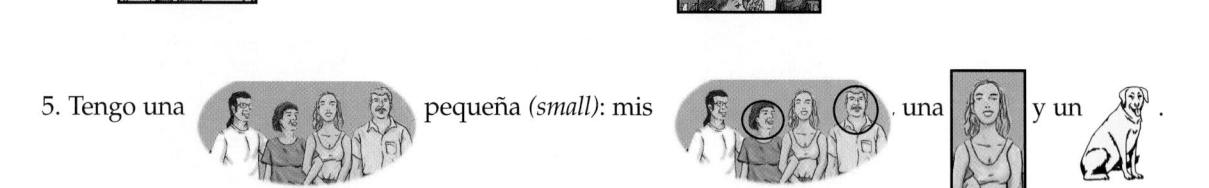 pequeña (*small*): mis , una y un .

Las respuestas de tu compañero/a:
1. Necesito comprar un **lápiz**, dos **plumas** y una **calculadora** para la clase de matemáticas.
2. En esa **librería** venden **escritorios** y **computadoras**.
3. Mis **abuelos** paternos viven en **México**; ellos tienen dos **gatos**, un **pájaro** y muchos **peces**.
4. En las mañanas, es difícil encontrar **estacionamiento** en la **universidad**.
5. En la **mochila** de mi novio hay muchos **libros** y **papeles**.

La correspondencia

El correo: Sofía te escribe. *(Sofía writes to you.)* Read the questions and Sofía's letter to you. Then answer the questions.

1. ¿Cuántas personas hay en la familia de Sofía? _____

2. ¿Por qué la abuela de Sofía es más generosa con Lalo? _____

3. ¿Qué profesiones tienen los padres de Sofía? _____

4. ¿Cómo es Lalo? ¿Conoces *(Do you know)* a una persona similar? ¿Quién *(Who)*?
_____

5. ¿La relación de Sofía y Lalo es buena *(good)* o mala *(bad)*? _____

Querido/a estudiante:

Tengo una familia pequeña[1]: mis abuelos, mis padres, un hermano y un perro. Mi abuela es mexicana y mi abuelo es español. Viven seis meses[2] en Guadalajara y seis meses en Estados Unidos con nosotros. Mi abuela es muy generosa, especialmente con Lalo, porque es su nieto favorito.

Mis padres son jóvenes[3]. Mi papá se llama Rubén. Tiene cuarenta y cuatro años. Es banquero; trabaja mucho y es muy estricto con nosotros. Mi mamá se llama Diana. Es una señora muy elegante e inteligente. Trabaja en un banco también, donde es supervisora de créditos comerciales.

Lalo, mi hermano, tiene quince años. Es estudiante. Es un poco irresponsable e inmaduro, pero es muy buen hermano. Le gustan los deportes y la música alternativa.

Con cariño,
tu amiga Sofía

[1]*small* [2]*months* [3]*young*

En papel: Una carta para Sofía. Sofía wants to know what your family is like. Use her letter as a model to write a simple description of your own family.

Modelo	Tengo una familia...: mi..., mi... y...
	Mi... se llama..., tiene... años. Es de...
	Le gusta... (actividades de la página 58, B)...

¡Fíjate!

Try to express yourself simply with the language you know. Although you may be tempted, avoid writing your letter in English and translating it into Spanish. At this point, your ability to write in English far exceeds your ability to communicate in Spanish; however, as time goes on, this will change!

¡A ver de nuevo! Review this episode's **Escena** to complete the summary that follows.

Adriana y Manolo están en la clase de (1)_____ con Sofía. Manolo es (2)_____ de Sofía. En este episodio, conocemos (we meet) a Ramón, el (3)_____ de Ana Mari. Él es de (4)_____, pero su papá es de (5)_____ y su (6)_____ es de México. Adriana no es de México; es de (7)_____. Tiene (8)_____ hijos. Sus hijos mayores (older) hablan español, pero a su (9)_____ no le gusta hablarlo. La familia de Ramón (10)_____ el mismo (same) problema. (11)_____ hermanos (12)_____ entienden español, pero no lo hablan.

Invitación a **Cuba**

Del álbum de
Manolo

Cuba es una isla grande; es un poco más grande que el estado de Pennsylvania. Hay aproximadamente 11,4 millones de habitantes. La mitad (half) de los cubanos es de ascendencia afro-española; el 11% es de ascendencia africana; el 37% es blanco y un pequeño porcentaje es de origen chino.

Un restaurante famoso, La Bodeguita del Medio, está en una calle (street) típica de la parte vieja (old) ciudad de La Habana, la ciudad capital. El escritor norteamericano Ernest Hemingway visitaba ese restaurante con frecuencia. En sus paredes (walls) puedes ver (see) muchas fotos de personalidades norteamericanas famosas de los años 50 que comían (used to eat) ahí; Frank Sinatra, entre otros. Hoy en día, todas las paredes además están decoradas con las fechas de vista y los nombres de todos las personas que comen (eat) en este restaurante.

In your own words. Answer the questions about Cuba in your own words.

1. How large is Cuba in size? _____

2. Is Cuba an ethnically diverse country? Explain.
_____
_____

3. Why is **La Bodeguita del Medio** famous?
_____
_____

4. Nowadays, what do visitors do in the restaurant, besides eating?
_____

Práctica adicional

Cuaderno de tareas
p. 100, L

invitaciones.
vhlcentral.com
Episodio 4

invitaciones.
vhlcentral.com
Lab practice

invitaciones.
vhlcentral.com
Episodio 4

Vocabulario del Episodio 4

La familia, los familiares y más

los abuelos	grandparents	el abuelo	la abuela
los amigos	friends	el amigo	la amiga
los chicos	adolescents, teenagers	el chico	la chica
los cuñados	brother(s)-in-law and sister(s)-in-law	el cuñado	la cuñada
los esposos	husband and wife	el esposo	la esposa
los familiares	relatives	el familiar	
los hermanos	brother(s) and sister(s)	el hermano	la hermana
los hijos	children (one's own): son(s) and daughter(s)	el hijo	la hija
el/la hijo/a único/a	only child		
los nietos	grandchildren	el nieto	la nieta
los niños	children: boy(s) and girl(s)	el niño	la niña
los novios	boyfriend and girlfriend; bride and groom; fiancés	el novio	la novia
los padres	parents	el padre	la madre
los primos	cousins	el primo	la prima
los sobrinos	nephew(s) and niece(s)	el sobrino	la sobrina
los suegros	in-laws: father-in-law and mother-in-law	el suegro	la suegra
los tíos	uncle(s) and aunt(s)	el tío	la tía

Las mascotas *Pets*

el/la gato/a	cat
el pájaro	bird
el/la perro/a	dog
el pez	fish

Posesivos

mi, mis	my
tu, tus	your
su, sus	his; her; their
nuestro/a(s)	our
la hija de Adriana	Adriana's daughter

Verbs

tener	to have
ser de	to be from
tener... años	to be... years old
¿Cuántos años tienes? Tengo... años.	How old are you? I'm... years old.
¿De dónde eres? Soy de...	Where are you from? I'm from...

Más números

41	**cuarenta y uno**	42, 43...	**cuarenta y dos, cuarenta y tres...**
50	**cincuenta**	53, 54...	**cincuenta y tres, cincuenta y cuatro...**
60	**sesenta**	64, 65...	**sesenta y cuatro, sesenta y cinco...**
70	**setenta**	75, 76...	**setenta y cinco, setenta y seis...**
80	**ochenta**	86, 87...	**ochenta y seis, ochenta y siete...**
90	**noventa**	97, 98...	**noventa y siete, noventa y ocho...**
100	**cien**		

Vocabulario personal

Write the words that you need to know to talk about yourself and your family in Spanish.

Cuaderno de tareas

Episodio 4

Escenas de la vida: ¡Qué internacionales!

 A. ¡A ver cuánto entendiste! See how much of the **Escena** you understood by matching the Spanish sentences with their English equivalents.

En casa

_____ 1. ¡Qué bueno que hablas español!

_____ 2. Los dos mayores hablan español muy bien.

_____ 3. A mi hija no le gusta hablar español.

_____ 4. También tenemos ese problema.

_____ 5. Mis hermanos menores lo entienden todo, pero no lo hablan.

a. The two older ones speak Spanish very well.

b. We also have that problem.

c. That's great that you speak Spanish!

d. My daughter doesn't like to speak Spanish.

e. My younger brothers understand everything, but they do not speak it.

Los amigos

_____ 6. ¿Sabías que Manolo es escritor?

_____ 7. Sí, algunos parientes.

_____ 8. Vamos a llegar tarde a clase.

_____ 9. Vámonos.

_____10. Tomamos geología juntos.

f. We are taking Geology together.

g. Let's go.

h. Did you know Manolo is a writer?

i. Yes, a few relatives.

j. We are going to be late to class.

B. ¡Qué internacionales! Complete the conversation based on what you saw in the video.

Manolo   Ramón, ¿tú, de dónde (1)_____?

Ramón   Soy de (2) _____. Mi mamá (3) _____ México y
(4) _____ es de Honduras. ¿Y tú?

Manolo   (5) _____ Cuba. Tengo algunos parientes en Cuba, pero
(6) _____ viven en la Florida.

Ramón   Señora, ¿usted también es de Cuba?

Adriana   No. Soy de (7) _____.

Ramón   ¡Qué (8) _____!

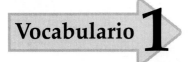

Vocabulario 1

Identifying family members and friends
- **The family**
- **Expressing possession**

C. ¿De quién son las cosas? Tell Adriana to whom the following objects belong.

> **Modelo** calculadoras/Manolo
> **Son las calculadoras de Manolo.**

1. mochila/Sofía _____

2. lápices/Santiaguito _____

3. reloj/Santiago _____

4. cuadernos/Viviana _____

5. diccionario/Manolo _____

6. plumas/Ana Mari _____

D. El primo Emilio. Lalo and Sofía talk about their cousin Emilio. Complete their description with the appropriate forms of the possessive adjectives.

Él es (1) _____ (nuestro/tu) primo. Se llama Emilio
y tiene treinta años. (2) _____ (Su/Mi) esposa está
en España. (3) _____ (Su/Sus) padres viven en
Madrid. (4) _____ (Nuestro/Nuestros) tíos, los padres
de Emilio, se llaman Laura y Emilio. Son muy buenos.
Emilio es (5) _____ (mis/mi) primo favorito.
¿Quién es (6) _____ (tu/tus) primo favorito?

Emilio

E. Tu familia. You are showing a family picture to a friend. Answer his/her questions using the appropriate forms of the possessive adjectives.

> **Modelo** ¿Ella es la hermana de tu mamá?
> Sí, es **su** hermana.

1. ¿Éste *(This)* es tu hermano? No, es _____ primo.

2. ¿Él es tu papá? Sí, es _____ papá.

3. Ah, y ellos son los papás de tus primos. Sí, son _____ *(their)* papás.

4. ¿Ellos son tus abuelos? Sí, son _____ abuelos paternos.

5. ¿De quién son estos perritos? Son _____ *(our)* mascotas.

6. ¿Los chicos son tus hermanos? No, él es _____ amigo, y ella es _____
   (his) novia._____ hermanos no están en la foto.

F. Crucigrama. You've been asked to create the clues for the crossword puzzle (**crucigrama**) in this week's school newspaper. Write a description or definition of the words in the puzzle.

horizontales

1. _____
4. _____
6. _____la hija de tus papás es tu..._____
7. _____
8. _____
9. _____
10. _____
14. _____
15. _____

verticales

1. _____
2. _____
3. _____
5. _____
11. _____un animal como Pluto_____
12. _____
13. _____

				C	U	Ñ	A	D	A	A					P
				H					B					Á
			H	I	J	O			U					J
		N		C				H	E	R	M	A	N	A
P	R	I	M	O	S			L					R
		E		S			N	O	V	I	A			O
G	A	T	O				S					
		O								
	E	S	P	O	S	O				P
		E		O					
		R		B			M	A	D	R	E
		R		R			D
		O		I			R
				N			E
			A	M	I	G	O	S

G. La familia de Manolo.

Parte 1. Read Manolo's description of his family. Then answer the questions.

> Hola, soy Manolo Báez Rodríguez. Soy estudiante y me gusta mucho tocar[1] la guitarra. Tengo una familia relativamente pequeña. Solamente somos mi hermana y yo. Mi hermana es dos años menor que[2] yo. Se llama Nancy. Mis papás son cubanos y ahora viven en Miami. Mi papá es doctor y mi mamá es profesora. Mi papá se llama Manuel Báez y mi mamá es Isabel Rodríguez de Báez. Los padres de mi papá son Arturo y Carlota. Ellos todavía viven en La Habana. Tengo un tío y una tía. Son los hermanos de mi papá. Mi tío Francisco es soltero y tiene 50 años; mi tía Perla es viuda[3] y tiene tres hijos: dos hombres y una mujer. Mi prima tiene 25 años, como yo; por eso, somos muy buenos amigos. Mis dos primos son menores que nosotros.

[1]to play [2]younger than [3]widowed

1. ¿Cuántos hermanos tiene Manolo? _____
2. ¿Dónde viven sus padres? ¿Como se llaman? _____

   _____
3. ¿Qué profesión tiene su papá? ¿Y su mamá? _____
4. ¿Cómo se llaman los abuelos de Manolo? ¿Dónde viven?

   _____
5. ¿De quién (Whose) son hermanos los tíos de Manolo? _____
6. ¿Cuántos años tiene Manolo? _____
7. ¿Cuántos primos tiene? _____

Parte 2. Use Manolo's letter as a model to write about your own family.

_____

_____

_____

_____

Gramática **1**	Expressing age • The verb <u>tener</u> • Numbers 41–100

H. ¿Cuántos años tienen tus familiares? Complete the sentences with the ages of different people in your own family, or an imaginary family.

1. Mi papá _____ años.
2. Mi mamá _____ años.
3. Mi hermano/a menor _____ años.
4. Mi _____ tiene _____ años.
5. Yo _____ años.

I. ¿Qué tiene? Create true statements or questions using an element from each column.

Manolo		mucha tarea
Sofía		cinco clases este semestre
las universidades		novio/a
mis amigos y yo	(no) tener	veintitrés años
mis compañeros		una clase de español
tú		coche *(car)*
Ana Mari		un hermano
yo		biblioteca y gimnasio

1. _____ .
2. _____ .
3. _____ .
4. _____ .
5. _____ .
6. _____ .
7. _____ .
8. _____ .

J. ¡Cuánto dinero! *(So much money!)* As the bookkeeper at your university bookstore, you have to pay the distributor of foreign books and movies. Complete the checks according to the invoices. Remember to make note of the items you are paying for (under *Memo*).

Libro/Video	Cantidad	Total
La colmena	23 libros	$98.35
Pedro Páramo	15 libros	$64.73
La misma luna	1 video	$51.69
¡Ay, Carmela!	1 video	$42.80

Tienda Universitaria   5322

Fecha _____

Páguese a la orden de   _Distribuidora Internacional_ $ _____

La cantidad de _____ dólares

Memo _____   _____

| 00231334: 232443 | | 2343243434

Tienda Universitaria	5323

Fecha _____

Páguese a la orden de ___Distribuidora Internacional___ $ _____

La cantidad de _____ dólares

Memo _____   _____

|00231334: 232443 | |2343243434

Tienda Universitaria	5324

Fecha _____

Páguese a la orden de ___Distribuidora Internacional___ $ _____

La cantidad de _____ dólares

Memo _____   _____

|00231334: 232443 | |2343243434

Tienda Universitaria	5325

Fecha _____

Páguese a la orden de ___Distribuidora Internacional___ $ _____

La cantidad de _____ dólares

Memo _____   _____

|00231334: 232443 | |2343243434

Gramática 2 — Saying where someone is from
- Ser de

K. ¿De dónde son? Complete the sentences based on what you know about the characters.

1. Sofía _____ mexicana. _____ la Ciudad de México.
2. Ramón y Ana Mari _____ mexicoamericanos. _____ Estados Unidos.
3. El papá de Ramón _____ Honduras. Su mamá es mexicana; es de _____.
4. Adriana y su familia _____ Puerto Rico.
5. Manolo es cubano. Él _____ Cuba.

Para terminar

L. Mi árbol genealógico. To preserve your heritage, you have decided to record the name, place of origin, and age of as many relatives as you can. Create your family tree. If you prefer not to do your own, you can interview a friend.

Episodio

5

Escenas de la vida: ¿Estudiamos el sábado?

 A. ¡Mira cuánto puedes entender! Listen to the conversation or watch the **Escena** to complete the tasks below.

1. ¿Qué días están libres *(are free)* Manolo y Adriana para estudiar?

	lunes	martes	miércoles	jueves	viernes	sábado	domingo
Manolo							
Adriana							

2. Adriana dice que nunca descansa; ¿por qué? ¿Qué hace Adriana los martes y jueves?

Compra la comida.

Trabaja en una oficina.

Llega tarde a casa.

3. ¿Qué hace la hija de Adriana los lunes?

Baila en un grupo.

Lava su ropa.

Limpia su cuarto.

101

4. ¿Qué hacen su hijo y sus amigos?

Miran **la tele.**

Visitan **a los abuelos.**

Tocan **la guitarra.**

B. ¿Te diste cuenta? Escucha la conversación o mira la **Escena** otra vez para indicar a quién se refieren los siguientes comentarios: Manolo **(M)**, Adriana **(A)**, Sofía **(S)** o todos **(T)** *(everybody)*.

_____ 1. No es pesimista.

_____ 2. Está libre los sábados por la tarde.

_____ 3. Necesitan estudiar para el examen.

_____ 4. Nunca tiene tiempo para descansar.

_____ 5. Está muy preocupada.

Cultura a lo vivo

In Spanish-speaking countries, most young adults do not move out to become "independent." It is common for them to stay home until they get married, or relocate to another city to work or pursue their studies. Go to the Supersite to watch a *Flash cultura* episode on this topic.

C. Responde. Contesta las siguientes preguntas.

1. ¿Qué día toca la guitarra el hijo de Adriana?

_____

2. ¿A qué hora trabaja Adriana?

_____

3. ¿Dónde tocan la guitarra el hijo de Adriana y sus amigos?

_____

4. ¿Por qué Adriana nunca descansa?

_____

5. ¿Dónde y cuándo van a estudiar?

_____

Práctica adicional		
Cuaderno de tareas p. 115, A	invitaciones. vhlcentral.com Episodio 5	invitaciones. vhlcentral.com Episodio 5

Para comunicarnos mejor

Gramática **1**

Talking about activities at school and at home
- **-ar** verbs
- **Days of the week**

In their conversation, you heard the following statements:

Trabajo en una oficina.	*I work in an office.*
Mi hija **baila** en un grupo folclórico.	*My daughter dances in a folk group.*
Mi hijo **toca** la guitarra.	*My son plays the guitar.*
Estudiamos el sábado a las dos, ¿de acuerdo?	*We'll study on Saturday at two, okay?*

To talk about the activities of her friends and family, Adriana uses different verb endings, which change depending on whom she is describing. In Spanish, verb forms consist of two parts: the stem **(la raíz)** and the ending **(la terminación)**. For example, the verb form **trabajo** *(I work)* is made up of the stem **trabaj-** and the ending **-o**. Different endings are attached to the stem to indicate who does the action *(I, you, he, she, it, we, they)*, when the action occurs *(today, yesterday, tomorrow)*, and how the action is carried out *(right now, only once, all the time)*. Attaching different endings to verb stems is called *conjugating the verb* **(conjugar el verbo)**. Study the following conjugation and use it to conjugate regular **-ar** verbs.

El presente de los verbos del grupo -ar		
yo	**Trabajo** en una oficina.	*I work in an office.*
tú	**Trabajas** mucho.	*You work a lot. (informal)*
usted	**Trabaja** por la mañana.	*You work in the morning. (formal)*
él/ella	**Trabaja** en un hospital.	*He/She works in a hospital.*
nosotros/as	**Trabajamos** juntos/as.	*We work together.*
ustedes	**Trabajan** de noche, ¿no?	*You work at night, right? (plural)*
vosotros/as	**Trabajáis** de noche, ¿no?	
ellos/as	**Trabajan** en un banco.	*They work in a bank.*

1. When the ending of the verb is **-ar** (as in **trabajar**), **-er**, or **-ir**, the verb has not been conjugated; that is, we do not know who is doing the action. This verb form is called the *infinitive* **(el infinitivo)**. In English, the infinitive is indicated by the word *to*, as in *to work*.

2. As a form of the present tense, **trabajo** may mean *I work* or *I am working*.

Trabajo en una oficina en Nueva York.	*I work in an office in New York.*
Trabajo en una oficina este semestre.	*I'm working in an office this semester.*

3. Every Spanish verb belongs to one of three groups, according to its infinitive ending.

• Verbs that end in **-ar**	**trabajar**	*to work*
• Verbs that end in **-er**	**comer**	*to eat*
• Verbs that end in **-ir**	**vivir**	*to live*

4. Remember that the **vosotros/as** form is used only in Spain.

5. The following verbs use the same endings as **trabajar**.

Actividades frecuentes

En la escuela

buscar información en Internet	*to look for information on the Internet*
estudiar mucho/poco	*to study a lot/a little*
llegar a tiempo	*to arrive (to get somewhere) on time*
necesitar libros	*to need books*
sacar buenas notas	*to get good grades*
tomar café	*to drink coffee*
tomar clases	*to take classes*
usar la computadora	*to use the computer*

Los fines de semana

bailar (bien/mal)	*to dance (well/badly)*
comprar cosas	*to buy things*
comida/ropa	*food/clothes*
descansar	*to rest*
hablar con los amigos	*to talk to friends*
llegar tarde/temprano/a tiempo a casa	*to get home late/early/on time*
tomar el autobús	*to take the bus*
trabajar en una tienda	*to work at a store*
visitar a los abuelos	*to visit one's grandparents*

En la casa

escuchar música	*to listen to music*
hablar por teléfono	*to talk on the phone*
lavar el coche	*to wash the car*
lavar la ropa	*to do the laundry*
limpiar la casa/el cuarto	*to clean the house/the (one's) room*
mirar la tele	*to watch TV*
tocar la guitarra	*to play the guitar*

También se dice...

el coche ⟶ el carro, el auto
la compu ⟶ el ordenador
mirar la tele ⟶ ver la tele
las notas ⟶ las calificaciones

Learning Strategy: Create flash cards

On one side, write a word in Spanish; on the other, write the English equivalent. If possible, draw a picture of the item and write a sentence where you use the word in a meaningful way. Study the words in both directions: from English to Spanish, and vice versa.

PRÁCTICA

A. ¿Qué hacen? Empareja las ilustraciones de la página siguiente con las oraciones apropiadas.

___ 1. Trabajo en una oficina.

___ 2. Los chicos siempre buscan información en Internet.

___ 3. Sofía escucha música alternativa.

___ 4. A veces tomamos el autobús a la escuela.

___ 5. Me gusta mucho comprar ropa.

___ 6. Los chicos sacan buenas notas.

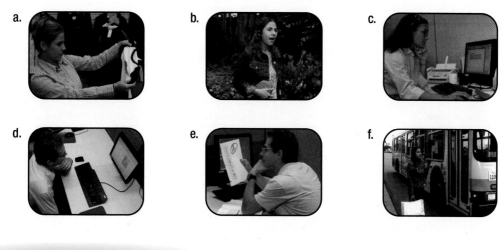

a.   b.   c.

d.   e.   f.

B. ¿Cuáles son tus actividades? Indica si las oraciones son **ciertas** o **falsas** para ti.

	Cierto	Falso
1. Mis amigos y yo necesitamos dinero.	☐	☐
2. Nunca lavo mi coche.	☐	☐
3. Mi mamá usa la computadora en casa.	☐	☐
4. Mi papá descansa por la noche.	☐	☐
5. Siempre llego a tiempo a la clase de español.	☐	☐
6. No trabajo este semestre.	☐	☐
7. Mis compañeros de clase estudian mucho.	☐	☐
8. Mi familia y yo visitamos a los abuelos los domingos.	☐	☐

C. Las actividades de mi familia. Look at the activities on page 104 in order to tell who among your family and friends does those activities. Write about as many different people as you can.

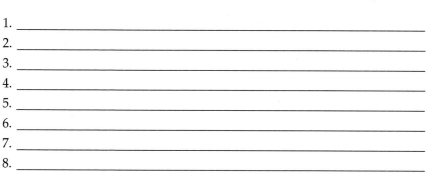

Modelo	Yo busco información en Internet.
	Mi novio Juan estudia mucho.
	Mis amigas Lucy y Bertha llegan a tiempo a clase.

¡Fíjate!

Remember to drop the **-ar** and add the appropriate ending to indicate who you are talking about.

1. _____

2. _____

3. _____

4. _____

5. _____

6. _____

7. _____

8. _____

• Days of the week

Los días de la semana y más			
los lunes	*on Mondays*	entre semana	*on weekdays*
los martes	*on Tuesdays*	los fines de semana	*on weekends*
los miércoles	*on Wednesdays*	por la mañana	*in the morning*
los jueves	*on Thursdays*	por la tarde	*in the afternoon*
los viernes	*on Fridays*	por la noche	*in the evening*
los sábados	*on Saturdays*	todos los días	*every day*
los domingos	*on Sundays*		

Note: In Spanish, the days of the week are not capitalized. **Los lunes** means *on Mondays*, but **el lunes** means *on Monday*.

PRÁCTICA

D. Mis actividades. Usa la tabla de arriba para escribir en tu cuaderno las actividades que haces. Escribe un total de 10 oraciones. Usa actividades diferentes.

> **Modelo** Los lunes lavo la ropa. Los martes trabajo cinco horas. Los miércoles...

Práctica adicional

Cuaderno de tareas
pp. 115–116, B–D

SUPERSITE

invitaciones.
vhlcentral.com
Episodio 5

Gramática 2

Asking yes/no questions
• Tag questions
• Infinitive constructions

Adding **¿no?** at the end of a statement is one of two ways of asking a yes/no question. When asking a question that need a yes/no answer, use the following two patterns.

1. Intonation. Raise your voice in a questioning tone at the end of the question.

Me gusta bailar salsa.	*I like dancing salsa.*
¿Te gusta bailar salsa?	*Do you like dancing salsa?*
Este semestre no trabajo.	*I don't work this semester.*
¿Este semestre no trabajas?	*You don't work this semester?*

2. Tag questions. Add **¿no?** or **¿verdad?** (*right?*) at the end.

Sus hijos podrían hacernos un *show*, **¿no?**	*Your kids could put on a show for us, right?*
Tus padres trabajan en un banco, **¿verdad?**	*Your parents work at a bank, right?*

PRÁCTICA

E. Una entrevista. Con un(a) compañero/a, convierte las oraciones de la **Práctica B** (página 105) a preguntas. Después, entrevista a otro/a compañero/a.

> **Modelo** Mis amigos y yo necesitamos dinero.
> —**¿Tus amigos y tú necesitan dinero?** *or*
> —**Tus amigos y tú necesitan dinero, ¿no?/¿verdad?**

F. Lotería. Find out who does the following things. Ask appropriate questions, according to the model. Write the name of a different classmate who responds **Sí** to your question in each box. The first student to form three straight lines wins the game.

> **Modelo** _____ visita a sus abuelos los domingos.
> —¿**Visitas a tus abuelos los domingos?**
> —**Sí, visito a mis abuelos los domingos.**

lava la ropa los viernes.	saca buenas notas en la clase de español.	no trabaja.	necesita comprar una computadora.
escucha música alternativa.	habla otro idioma *(another language)* con sus padres.	toma cuatro clases este semestre.	siempre llega tarde a clase.
toca bien el piano.	no es de aquí.	no estudia en la biblioteca.	visita a sus abuelos los domingos.
le gusta bailar los fines de semana.	descansa los lunes por la tarde.	busca información en Internet para las clases.	no tiene hermanos.

• Infinitive constructions

In the conversation, Adriana said:

Necesito repasar todo.   *I need to review everything.*
Necesito estar presente, porque si no...   *I need to be there, otherwise...*

In both English and Spanish, some verbs may be used in combination with other verbs in the infinitive. Notice that Adriana uses a combination of two verbs: the main verb, which is conjugated, and a second verb, which is in the infinitive form (the **-r** form). These combined verbs are called *infinitive constructions*, as in the following examples.

No **me gusta llegar** tarde a clase.   *I don't like to be late for class.*
Necesitamos buscar información en Internet.   *We need to look for information on the Internet.*
No **quiero sacar** F.   *I don't want to get an F.*

PRÁCTICA

G. Las actividades de Sofía. Sofía nos habla de sus actividades y las de *(those of)* su familia. Completa las oraciones.

1. Los sábados me gusta _____; por eso *(because of that)*, no trabajo por las tardes.
2. Los domingos necesito _____ la ropa y _____ mi cuarto.
3. Mi hermano nunca _____; por eso, no _____ buenas notas.
4. Mis papás _____ trabajar mucho para vivir *(to live)* bien.
5. Hoy no quiero lavar ropa porque necesito_____ la computadora.

H. Los fines de semana. Escribe seis cosas que **necesitas, te gusta** o **no te gusta** hacer *(to do)* durante los fines de semana. Comparte tus comentarios con un(a) compañero/a.

¡Fíjate!

Remember to use **los viernes** for *on Fridays* and **el viernes** for *on Friday*.

> **Modelo**   Los viernes por la noche no me gusta estudiar.

1. _____
2. _____
3. _____
4. _____
5. _____
6. _____

I. ¡A hablar! In groups of four, try to set a date and time to study Spanish together **(juntos/as)**. Indicate which days and times you can't meet, and why **(no puedo porque...)**. Use expressions like Estoy libre los..., Ese día no puedo..., ¿Estudiamos el...?, ¿Quién puede a las...?, etc.

Práctica adicional

Cuaderno de tareas
pp. 117–118, E–G

invitaciones.
vhlcentral.com
Lab practice

SUPERSITE

invitaciones.
vhlcentral.com
Episodio 5

Actividades comunicativas

A. Las actividades de mis compañeros.

Parte 1. First, answer the questions by writing **yo** in column **B** after any question to which you can respond *yes*. Then ask your classmates these questions and fill in the empty spaces in both columns with the names of those who answer *yes*.

	A	B
1. ¿Limpias tu cuarto los sábados?	_____	_____
2. ¿Usas una computadora Macintosh?	_____	_____
3. ¿Escuchas música *hip hop*?	_____	_____
4. ¿Miras mucho la tele?	_____	_____
5. ¿Necesitas estudiar más para esta clase?	_____	_____
6. ¿Hablas mucho por teléfono?	_____	_____

Parte 2. Now, write a brief report using the information you have uncovered. Include at least six sentences in your report. Be prepared to share your findings with the class.

> | Modelo | Akiko y Jenny hablan mucho por teléfono. |
> |---|---|
> | | Nadie (*Nobody*) usa una computadora Macintosh. |

 B. Submarino. The object of this game, played like *Battleship*, is to find the location of your classmate's submarines. First, draw submarines in any five of the boxes on your grid. Do not let your partner see your grid. Then take turns asking each other yes/no questions, matching an action pictured at the top of the grid with one of the subjects on the side. If you have a submarine in the box that corresponds to your partner's question, give an affirmative answer, and vice versa; if there is no submarine in the box that corresponds to the question, give a negative answer.

> | Modelo | —¿Trabajas en una oficina? |
> |---|---|
> | | —Sí, trabajo en una oficina. (*If there is a submarine in that box.*) |
> | | or |
> | | —No, no trabajo en una oficina. (*If there is no submarine in that box.*) |

Depending on your classmate's answer, write **Sí** or **No** in that box. If you answer **Sí** to your classmate's question, put an **X** through your submarine. It's been found! The first player to find all five submarines wins.

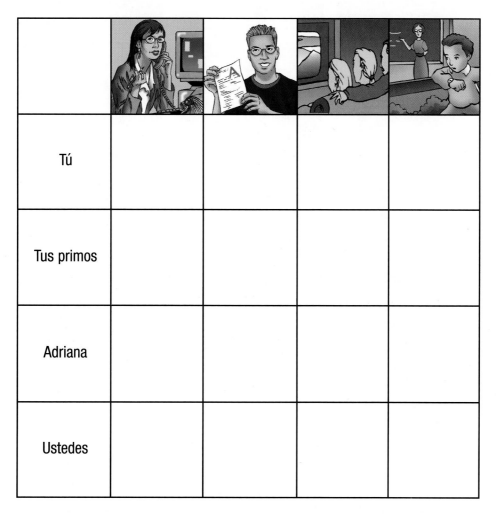

C. La fotonovela.

Parte 1. Tell a partner about each illustration, indicating if you or someone you know does or does not do each activity.

> **Modelo** En mi casa, mi mamá lava la ropa los domingos. ¿Y en tu casa?

Parte 2. As you listen to Sofía's weekend routine, indicate which pictures were used to tell her story.

Parte 3. In groups, use five of the drawings to write a short paragraph describing what Sofía does on weekends. Your pictures do not have to reflect what you heard on the recording. Use connectors like **primero** *(first)*, **luego** *(then)*, **después** *(later, afterward)*, **por la tarde...**, and **por la noche....** Begin with **Por la mañana, Sofía....** When you have finished, be prepared to read your story to the class. Your classmates will guess which pictures you used.

_____

_____

_____

_____

La correspondencia

El correo: Los problemas de Manolo. Lee las siguientes preguntas. Después, lee el correo electrónico *(email)* que Manolo le escribe a un amigo. Contesta las preguntas.

1. ¿Cuál es el peor *(What is the worst)* defecto del compañero de cuarto de Manolo?
   _____

2. ¿Qué cualidades tiene su compañero?
   _____

3. ¿Qué cosas tienen en común?
   _____

4. ¿Cuál es la rutina de Manolo?
   _____

> From: mbaez@casa.mía.red
> To: Amigo@dayton.fla.red
> Re: ¡Hola!
>
> En cuanto a[1] mi compañero de cuarto, tenemos algunos problemas. Es muy desordenado. Casi nunca[2] lava la ropa y no limpia su cuarto, que siempre está sucio[3]. Le gustan mucho las fiestas; con frecuencia invita a sus amigos y bailan y cantan toda la noche... ¡La música es horrible! Bueno, no todo es malo; él es muy generoso, compra todo para la casa y cocina muy rico[4]. También, tenemos varias cosas en común: los dos somos cubanos y tenemos conversaciones muy interesantes porque él es súper inteligente. A veces pasamos toda la noche conversando.
>
> Yo sigo con la misma[5] rutina; estudio por las mañanas y luego trabajo varias horas. Por la noche, lavo mi ropa y, los fines de semana, estudio y limpio la casa. Nada nuevo.

[1]*About* [2]*Almost never* [3]*dirty* [4]**cocina...** *he cooks delicious dishes* [5]*I follow the same*

Invitación a **Estados Unidos**

In your own words. Read the information below in order to write in English what you learned about Cuban-Americans. Summarize the information in one or two sentences without translating.

Del álbum de
Manolo

De los 45 millones de hispanos en Estados Unidos, aproximadamente 2 millones son cubanos. La mayor *(highest)* concentración de cubanos está en Miami y el condado *(county)* de Dade, en la Florida, pero hay comunidades cubanas en todos los estados.
La Pequeña Habana, en Miami, es el centro cultural de los cubanoamericanos. Muchas personalidades de la música y el cine son de origen cubano, como Gloria y Emilio Estefan, Andy García, Celia Cruz, Daisy Fuentes, Jon Secada y Cameron Díaz, entre otros *(among others)*.

En papel: Mi vida diaria. *(My daily life.)* In his e-mail, Manolo described his living situation. Use his letter as a model to write about your own situation. Write about your weekly activities and the activities of the people you live with.

 ¡A ver de nuevo!

Parte 1. Escucha la conversación de **Escenas de la vida** o mira el video para escribir un resumen *(summary)* del episodio.

> **¡Fíjate!**
> Express yourself simply with the Spanish you know. Do not write your summary in English.

Adriana está preocupada porque tiene un examen de cálculo y quiere sacar A...

 Parte 2. Now, compare your summary with a classmate's and add any information you might have left out.

Práctica adicional			
Cuaderno de tareas pp. 119–120, H–I	invitaciones. vhlcentral.com Episodio 5	invitaciones. vhlcentral.com Lab practice	invitaciones. vhlcentral.com Episodio 5

Vocabulario del Episodio 5

Verbos

bailar (bien/mal)	*to dance (well/badly)*
buscar información en Internet	*to look for information on the Internet*
comprar cosas	*to buy things*
comida/ropa	*food/clothes*
descansar	*to rest*
escuchar música	*to listen to music*
estudiar mucho/poco	*to study a lot/a little*
hablar con los amigos	*to talk to friends*
hablar por teléfono	*to talk on the phone*
lavar el coche	*to wash the car*
lavar la ropa	*to do the laundry*
limpiar la casa	*to clean the house*
el cuarto	*the (one's) room*
llegar a tiempo a casa	*to get home on time*
tarde	*late*
temprano	*early*
mirar la tele	*to watch TV*
necesitar libros	*to need books*
sacar buenas notas	*to get good grades*
tocar la guitarra	*to play the guitar*
tomar café	*to drink coffee*
tomar clases	*to take classes*
tomar el autobús	*to take the bus*
trabajar en casa	*to work at home*
usar la computadora	*to use the computer*
visitar a los abuelos	*to visit one's grandparents*

Los días de la semana y más

los lunes	*on Mondays*	entre semana	*on weekdays*
los martes	*on Tuesdays*	los fines de semana	*on weekends*
los miércoles	*on Wednesdays*	por la mañana	*in the morning*
los jueves	*on Thursdays*	por la tarde	*in the afternoon*
los viernes	*on Fridays*	por la noche	*in the evening*
los sábados	*on Saturdays*	todos los días	*every day*
los domingos	*on Sundays*		

113

Vocabulario personal

In this section, write all the words that you want to know in Spanish so that you can talk in greater detail about your activities and the activities of the people you know.

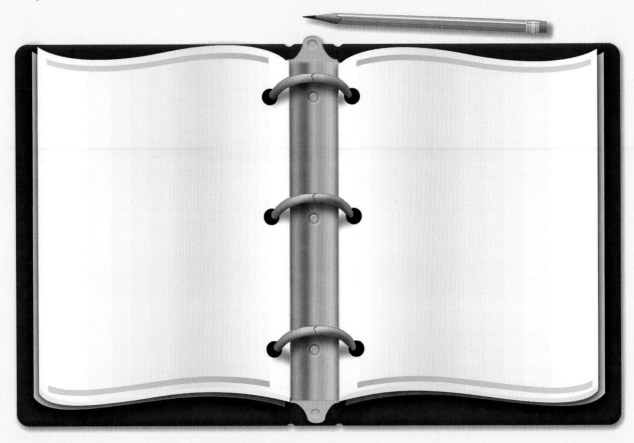

Cuaderno de tareas

Episodio 5

Escenas de la vida: ¿Estudiamos el sábado?

 A. ¡A ver cuánto entendiste! See how much of the **Escena** you understood by matching the Spanish sentences with their English equivalents.

Preguntas

_____ 1. ¿Está libre algún otro día?
_____ 2. ¿A qué hora descansa?
_____ 3. ¿En casa de quién?
_____ 4. ¿Cuándo estudiamos?
_____ 5. ¿Qué hace los sábados y domingos?

a. What do you do on Saturdays and Sundays?
b. Are you free any other day?
c. When are we going to study?
d. When do you rest?
e. At whose house?

Respuestas

_____ 6. Estudiamos el sábado.
_____ 7. ¡Qué ocupada está!
_____ 8. Necesito repasar todo.
_____ 9. Estoy muy preocupada.
_____10. Sus hijos podrían cantar
        y bailar para nosotros.

f. I'm very worried.
g. You are so busy!
h. Let's study on Saturday.
i. Your kids could sing and dance for us.
j. I need to review everything.

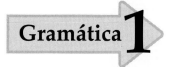 **Gramática 1**

Talking about activities at school and home
• **-ar verbs**
• **Days of the week**

B. La vida de Adriana. Use what you know about Adriana to answer Sofia's question.

¿Qué hace Adriana los otros días? (de lunes a viernes)

_____

_____

_____

_____

C. Los días de la semana. Complete these statements with the appropriate word.

1. En español, el primer día de la semana es el _____.

2. Si hoy es miércoles, mañana es _____.

3. Hay siete días en una _____.

4. Mi día favorito es el _____.

5. El Día de la Madre es el segundo *(second)* _____ de mayo.

6. Un día de mala suerte *(bad luck)* en Estados Unidos es el _____ trece.

7. El día preferido para hacer *(throw)* fiestas es el _____.

D. Las actividades de los estudiantes. Describe what the characters are doing in the illustrations. Use the verbs from **Episodio 5,** page 113 of your textbook. Use **porque** to justify the first part of your sentence. Keep the statements simple (e.g., *They study a lot because they have an exam*).

Modelo

Sofía toma el autobús porque no tiene coche.

1.
2.
3.

4.
5.
6.

1. _____

2. _____

3. _____

4. _____

5. _____

6. _____

Gramática 2

Asking yes/no questions
- **Tag questions**
- **Infinitive constructions**

E. ¡Preguntas! Imagine you and a classmate are talking about the characters in the video. Use the elements below to form questions. Then answer each question.

> **Modelo**   la hija de Adriana / tocar la guitarra / ¿no? (bailar)
> Q. La hija de Adriana toca la guitarra, ¿no?
> A. No, ella baila en un grupo folclórico puertorriqueño.

1. tú / estudiar italiano / ¿no? (español)

   Q. _____   A. _____

2. Adriana / trabajar en un restaurante (oficina)

   Q. _____   A. _____

3. los hermanos de Ramón / hablar español / ¿verdad? (inglés)

   Q. _____   A. _____

4. Manolo / ser de Puerto Rico / ¿no? (Cuba)

   Q. _____   A. _____

5. Sofía y Ana Mari / tener hermanas / ¿verdad? (no)

   Q. _____   A. _____

6. Ana Mari / tomar la clase de cálculo con Sofía y Manolo (Adriana)

   Q. _____   A. _____

F. Sofía y Adriana. You want to know more about Sofía and Adriana. Ask them questions using the cues. In each case, write an answer according to the drawing.

> **Modelo**
>
> if they study geology
> —¿Ustedes estudian geología?
> —No, estudiamos cálculo.

1. if they speak English

   _____

   _____

2. if Sofía uses the computer Friday nights

   _____

   _____

Nombre _____ Fecha _____

3. if Adriana always gets home late

_____

_____

4. if Sofía's mother does the laundry

_____

_____

G. ¿Qué hacen? Say what these people do at the places mentioned. Fill in the blanks with the appropriate forms of the verbs.

1. En la universidad

tomar	**hablar**	**llegar**
sacar	**estudiar**	**tocar**

Los lunes yo (1) _____ a la universidad a las 8:00 de la mañana.
(2) _____ una clase de español. Normalmente (3) _____
buenas notas cuando (4) _____ el vocabulario. Después de clase, me
gusta (5) _____ con mis amigos. A veces *(Sometimes)*, tomamos café y nos
quedamos *(we stay)* hablando en la cafetería.

2. En un café

escuchar	**bailar**	**lavar**
tocar	**cantar** *(to sing)*	**trabajar**

Los viernes en nuestro café favorito, mi amigo Miguel y yo (6) _____
la guitarra y la flauta en un grupo de jazz. También (7) _____ karaoke
cuando sabemos *(we know)* la letra *(lyrics)* de las canciones *(songs)*. A veces
(8) _____ y otras veces solamente *(only)* nos gusta (9) _____ la música.

3. En mi casa

visitar	**usar**	**lavar**	**mirar**
necesitar	**limpiar**	**trabajar**	**escuchar**

Los domingos mis hermanitos (10) _____ mi coche cuando ellos
(11) _____ dinero. Mi papá (12) _____ el garaje, mientras
(while) mi mamá (13) _____ en su jardín *(garden)*. Yo normalmente
necesito (14) _____ la computadora por la mañana. Por la tarde, mis
papás y mis hermanos (15) _____ a mis abuelos y yo visito a mis amigos.
Por la noche, todos nosotros (16) _____ una película *(movie)*.

Para terminar

H. Preguntas personales. Answer the following questions.

1. ¿Qué clases tomas? ¿Estudias todos los días?

   _____

   _____

2. ¿Te gusta bailar? ¿Dónde?

   _____

   _____

3. ¿Qué te gusta hacer *(to do)* los domingos?

   _____

   _____

4. ¿Cuántos años tienes? ¿Cuántos años tienen tus padres? ¿Cuántos años tiene tu novio/a /esposo/a?

   _____

   _____

5. ¿Qué programas miras en la tele?

   _____

6. ¿Trabajas? ¿Dónde? ¿Qué días trabajas?

   _____

   _____

7. ¿Qué días de la semana descansas?

   _____

8. ¿A qué hora llegas a tu casa los sábados?

   _____

   _____

9. ¿A qué hora llegas a la universidad los lunes?

   _____

   _____

10. ¿Sacas buenas notas en todas tus clases? ¿En qué clases sacas A y B? ¿Por qué?

   _____

   _____

I. La vida de Lorena. First read the questions, then read the following description of Lorena's activities, and then answer the questions.

1. ¿De dónde es Lorena?

_____

2. ¿Qué estudia? ¿Qué quiere estudiar en el futuro?

_____

3. ¿Cuáles son sus actividades favoritas?

_____

4. ¿Qué días tiene clase por la noche? ¿Qué clase es?

_____

5. ¿Qué hace *(does she do)* los fines de semana? ¿Con quién?

_____

Hola, me llamo Lorena; tengo 16 años. Soy de Tijuana, Baja California. Tengo un hermano mayor; se llama Iván y tiene 24 años. También tengo una gata y un hámster; ¡adoro a los animales! Estudio en una preparatoria que tiene un programa internacional; con ese programa puedo estudiar en cualquier universidad del mundo[1]. Quiero estudiar biología en San Diego. Algunas de mis clases me gustan mucho, otras no me gustan, pero tengo que[2] tomarlas. Aquí no tenemos muchas clases opcionales.

Durante las vacaciones trabajé[3] en una tienda de helados[4]. Ahora no trabajo, pero siempre tengo actividades. Por ejemplo, por las tardes, estudio o preparo mi tarea. Los martes por la noche, tomo una clase de actuación[5]. Me gusta mucho la clase, pero llego a las 10 de la noche a mi casa y el miércoles por la mañana no me puedo levantar[6]. Los jueves tengo mi clase de baile. Me gusta el jazz y el tap. Me gusta mirar películas[7] y escuchar música, especialmente el rock mexicano y la música alternativa. La música pop no me gusta mucho. Los viernes o los sábados voy a bailar con mis amigas (y amigos). Nos gusta bailar en una discoteca donde no hay bebidas[8] alcohólicas. Tengo muchas amigas, algunas son amigas de la escuela y otras son amigas de mi colonia[9]. También estudio piano con mi mamá porque ella es maestra de música en una escuela primaria y en la Normal[10].

Todavía no tengo licencia de manejar[11]. Mi papá dice[12] que soy muy joven[13]; ¡yo no opino lo mismo[14]! Los domingos normalmente es día de descanso, pero a veces visito a mi abuela o a mis tías.

[1]*world* [2]**tengo que...** *I have to* [3]*I worked* [4]*ice cream* [5]*acting* [6]**no me...***I can't get up* [7]*movies* [8]*drinks* [9]*neighborhood*
[10]*school that prepares teachers* [11]*driving license* [12]*says* [13]*young* [14]*the same*

Revista cultural

Graduaciones y horarios universitarios

Revistas culturales are designed to help you gain knowledge and understanding of the behaviors, traditions, products, practices, and perspectives of the people in the Spanish-speaking world. In the articles that follow, there will be words that you may not understand. As you read, highlight the words you *do* understand and try to make sense of the information presented with those words. If the pictures and/or the context do not help you, look up the words you need to know in a dictionary.

As you read the **Revistas culturales** in this book, reflect on the following:

1. What is culture?
2. Are your own cultural values and views sufficient to make assumptions and draw conclusions about other cultures?
3. What happens to students who learn languages but not the culture of the people who speak the languages?

Antes de leer

Mira las fotos de la revista para escribir lo que significan estas palabras.

birrete: _____

toga: _____

beca: _____

fogata para quemar: _____

las batas: _____

Las graduaciones se celebran en todos los países de habla hispana. Sin embargo, hay algunas diferencias en las ceremonias, la simbología y las actividades relacionadas con el acto de terminar la universidad.

A. ¿Te imaginas una graduación universitaria sin toga ni birrete?

En México

el birrete

la toga

Estos graduados llevan una toga y un birrete similar a los que se usan en los Estados Unidos.

En España

Los estudiantes reciben la beca el día de su graduación.

la beca

En muchos países hispanos los estudiantes se ponen togas y birretes, muy similares a los que se usan en Estados Unidos, el día de su graduación. En otros países no es costumbre usar la toga y el birrete para las graduaciones. En algunas regiones de España, por ejemplo, los estudiantes reciben una beca el día de su graduación como símbolo de que ya han terminado la carrera universitaria. Después de la graduación, donde se confiere la imposición de becas°, todos los graduados, sus familias y algunos profesores celebran con una cena elegante en un restaurante de moda de la ciudad.

° *In Spain, colored bands are placed around the shoulders of the graduates by the faculty conferring the degree. Graduates do not necessarily get a diploma.*

En México

La fogata para quemar...

... las batas.

Los estudiantes de la facultad de química queman sus batas.

B. ¿Te gustaría "quemar tu bata"?

En México, los estudiantes de la facultad de química celebran el último día de cursos quemando las batas de laboratorio que utilizaron durante los cinco años de la carrera. Todos los que van a graduarse, se juntan en un lugar específico y celebran bailando, cantando y quemando sus batas. Y después, claro, se van a celebrar con una gran fiesta.

Answer these questions in English.

1. Why would students burn their lab coats?
2. Would you be allowed to have a bonfire as a celebration in your community?
3. How will you celebrate your graduation?

C. Los horarios universitarios.

An important skill when learning a foreign language is to interpret the meaning of words based on your knowledge of the world. Let's practice this skill in the following section. Use your knowledge of universities to answer the questions on the next page about the calendar.

Revista
cultural

Algunos países tienen horarios muy similares a de Estados Unidos, otros tienen horarios un poco diferentes. Mira el horario de la UNAM en la página anterior para contestar estas preguntas.

1. When do classes begin at the UNAM? When do they end?
2. How many weeks are in each semester?
3. What does **días inhábiles** mean? (Look at the dates.)

16 de septiembre	**17 de noviembre**	**16 de marzo**
2 de noviembre	**2 de febrero**	**primero (1°) de mayo**

4. Use the Internet to find out the importance of these dates in Mexico.

D. ¿Te imaginas sólo tener dos semanas de vacaciones durante el mes de julio y agosto?

Buenos Aires, Argentina		
Inicio de cursos	Receso	Fin de cursos
03/03	28/07 al 08/08	13/12

En Argentina, las clases empiezan en marzo y terminan en diciembre. En invierno hay un receso de aproximadamente dos semanas durante julio y/o agosto.

1. Look at the school calendar for Argentinean schools. What can you tell about the way Argentineans write dates?
2. How would English speakers write the following dates?
   a. 28/07 _____   b. 13/12 _____   c. 08/05 _____

Los estudios

1. El video. Watch this *Flash cultura* episode from Mexico.

Estudio derecho en la UNAM.

¿Conoces algún (*any*) profesor famoso que dé clases... en la UNAM?

2. Emparejar. Match items from the first column with items from the second column to form complete sentences.

_____ 1. Los estudiantes de la UNAM no viven	a. una universidad muy grande.
_____ 2. México, D.F. es	b. 74 carreras de estudio.
_____ 3. La UNAM es	c. en residencias estudiantiles.
_____ 4. La UNAM ofrece	d. la ciudad más grande (*biggest*) de Latinoamérica.

Episodio 6

Escenas de la vida: ¡Qué guapos!

A. ¡Mira cuánto puedes entender! Use the spaces provided to describe Adriana and Sofía: what classes they take, what their families are like, where they are from, etc. Then select the statements that apply to the characters.

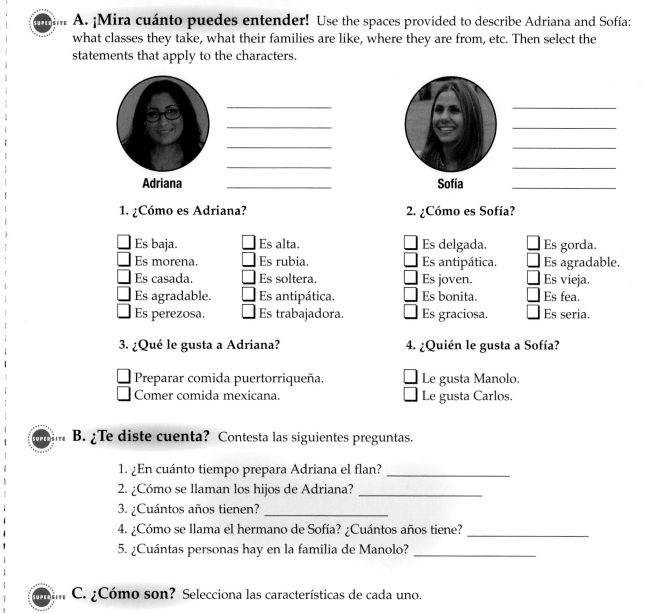

Adriana

Sofía

1. ¿Cómo es Adriana?

☐ Es baja.   ☐ Es alta.
☐ Es morena.   ☐ Es rubia.
☐ Es casada.   ☐ Es soltera.
☐ Es agradable.   ☐ Es antipática.
☐ Es perezosa.   ☐ Es trabajadora.

2. ¿Cómo es Sofía?

☐ Es delgada.   ☐ Es gorda.
☐ Es antipática.   ☐ Es agradable.
☐ Es joven.   ☐ Es vieja.
☐ Es bonita.   ☐ Es fea.
☐ Es graciosa.   ☐ Es seria.

3. ¿Qué le gusta a Adriana?

☐ Preparar comida puertorriqueña.
☐ Comer comida mexicana.

4. ¿Quién le gusta a Sofía?

☐ Le gusta Manolo.
☐ Le gusta Carlos.

B. ¿Te diste cuenta? Contesta las siguientes preguntas.

1. ¿En cuánto tiempo prepara Adriana el flan? _____
2. ¿Cómo se llaman los hijos de Adriana? _____
3. ¿Cuántos años tienen? _____
4. ¿Cómo se llama el hermano de Sofía? ¿Cuántos años tiene? _____
5. ¿Cuántas personas hay en la familia de Manolo? _____

C. ¿Cómo son? Selecciona las características de cada uno.

1. **Carlos**	alto	guapo	moreno	casado	joven	soltero
2. **La hermana de Manolo**	rubia	vieja	casada	alta	bonita	gorda
3. **Manolo**	bajo	feo	moreno	bueno	amable	guapo

D. Emparejar. Empareja las personas con las frases.

___ 1. Santiaguito   a. Tiene un hermano.

___ 2. Carlos   b. Es el mayor.

___ 3. Manolo   c. Tiene quince años.

___ 4. Sofía   d. Tiene una hermana.

Práctica adicional

Cuaderno de tareas
p. 141, A–B

invitaciones.
vhlcentral.com
Episodio 6

invitaciones.
vhlcentral.com
Episodio 6

Cultura a lo vivo

When Spanish speakers are successful in the United States, they are viewed as examples of how dreams can come true by both those who have remained in the home country, as well as by those who have immigrated to the United States. A notable example is Red Sox home-run hitter David Ortiz, hailed as a national hero in his native Dominican Republic for his success on the playing field.

Para comunicarnos mejor

Gramática 1

Describing people and things
- **Descriptive adjectives**
- **Placement of adjectives**

Analizar y descubrir

In the conversation, you heard the following statements.

¡Qué **guapos** son sus hijos!	*Your children are so good-looking!*
Tú eres **alto** y muy **guapo**.	*You're tall and very handsome.*
Tu hermana es **alta** y **rubia**.	*Your sister is tall and blonde.*

1. Notice that the adjectives **guapo** and **alto** have more than one form. Study the previous statements and answer these questions:

   a. Which word was used to describe Adriana's children? _____

   b. Which words were used to describe Manolo? _____ and _____

   c. Which words were used to describe Manolo's sister ? _____ and _____

   Circle the correct answer in items **d–f**, and answer **g**.

   d. **Guapos** is used in **(a)** because it matches **hijas / hijos.**

   e. **Alto** and **guapo** are used in **(b)** because they match **Manolo / Sofía.**

   f. **Alta** and **rubia** are used in **(c)** because they match **él / ella.**

   g. Which form of **guapo** would be used to describe Sofía and Viviana? _____

2. Unlike English, Spanish adjectives change their form to match the gender (masculine or feminine) and number (singular or plural) of the nouns they describe.

La clase es divertid**a**.	*The class is fun.*
Manolo es alt**o**; **él y Carlos** son moren**os**.	*Manolo is tall; he and Carlos are dark-haired.*
Las amigas de Sofía son gracios**as**.	*Sofía's friends are funny.*

3. Some adjectives (ending in **-e** or in some consonants) do not change form to indicate gender. All, however, change form to indicate number.

La casa es grand**e**; **el estadio** es grand**e**.	*The house is big; the stadium is big.*
Los salones no son grand**es**.	*The classrooms are not big.*

Here are some adjectives used to describe physical appearance.

Adjetivos descriptivos: La apariencia física			
guapo/a	handsome, good-looking	feo/a	ugly
bonito/a	good-looking, pretty		
bajo/a	short (height)	alto/a	tall
delgado/a	thin	gordo/a	fat
joven	young	viejo/a*	old
grande	large, big	pequeño/a	small
moreno/a	dark (skin/hair)	rubio/a	blond(e)
pelirrojo/a	red head		

*In some Spanish-speaking countries, it is impolite to describe an older person as **viejo** or **vieja**. It is better to say **Es una persona mayor**.

Below are some adjectives used to describe character and personality.

También se dice...

antipático	→	pesado
delgado	→	flaco
perezoso	→	flojo
gracioso	→	chistoso
rubio	→	güero
agradable	→	simpático

Adjetivos descriptivos: El carácter y la personalidad			
agradable	pleasant, nice	antipático/a	unpleasant, nasty
malo/a	bad	bueno/a	good, nice
serio/a	serious	gracioso/a	funny
trabajador(a)	hard-working	perezoso/a	lazy
amable	kind, friendly	grosero/a	rude
reservado/a	reserved	cariñoso/a	affectionate
listo/a	smart	tonto/a	dumb, silly

Learning Strategy: Focus on word clusters and word families

You will understand more if you are able to relate words with similar roots: for example, **persona**, **personal**, and **personalidad** or **arte**, **artista**, and **artístico**. Use the words you know to figure out what other words: knowing **perezoso**, what could **pereza** mean? It means *laziness*. Try to guess the meaning of **grosería**, **amabilidad**, **aburrimiento**, and **cariño**.

Here are some words and expressions used to describe people and things.

Descripciones: Las personas y las cosas			
nuevo/a	*new*	**viejo/a**	*old*
aburrido/a	*boring*	**divertido/a**	*fun*
desordenado/a	*messy, unorganized*	**ordenado/a**	*neat, organized*
fácil	*easy*	**difícil**	*hard, difficult*
rico/a	*wealthy; tasty*	**pobre**	*poor*
mayor	*older*	**menor**	*younger*
casado/a	*married*	**soltero/a**	*single*

PRÁCTICA

A. ¿Cómo son? Selecciona la característica que mejor describe a los personajes.

1. Manolo es (bajas / gordos / moreno / rubia).
2. Sofía es (vieja / joven / feo / bonitas).
3. Los hijos de Adriana son (soltera / nuevo / guapos / cariñosas).
4. Adriana es (rubios / moreno / mexicanas / trabajadora).
5. Manolo y su compañero de cuarto son (argentinas / cubano / jóvenes / casado).

B. Los opuestos. Completa cada frase con el adjetivo contrario.

> **Modelo**   Sofía no es seria; es **graciosa.**

1. La abuela de Sofía no es joven; es _____ .
2. Lalo no es antipático; es _____ .
3. Sofía no es tonta; es _____ .
4. Los hijos de Adriana no son gordos; son _____ .
5. Manolo no es serio; es _____ .
6. Sofía no es casada; es _____ .

C. Tu familia. Usa dos adjetivos diferentes para describir a tu familia o a una familia que conoces (*you know*).

> **Modelo**   Mis hermanas **son cariñosas y graciosas.**

1. Mis padres _____ .
2. Mi mamá _____ .
3. Mi papá _____ .
4. Mi hermano/a _____ .
5. Mis hermanos/as _____ .
6. Mis abuelos _____ .

• Placement of adjectives

An important difference between English and Spanish is the order of adjectives and nouns in a sentence. In English, the adjective comes *before* the noun (*I have a boring class*), whereas in Spanish, most adjectives go *after* the noun (**Tengo una clase** *aburrida*).

A few adjectives in Spanish do precede the noun.

1. Adjectives of quantity (**mucho, poco,** etc.) always come before the noun.

   Hay **pocos** estudiantes en la clase.   *There are few students in class.*
   Hoy tengo **mucha** tarea.   *I have a lot of homework today.*

2. Demonstrative adjectives also precede nouns.

   Necesito **este** libro.   *I need this book.*
   Sofía desea comprar **esa** mochila.   *Sofía wants to buy that backpack.*

Los adjetivos demostrativos			
este, esta	*this*	**ese, esa**	*that*
estos, estas	*these*	**esos, esas**	*those*

3. The adjectives **bueno** and **malo** may be used before the noun for emphasis. In this case, you must drop the **-o** from the masculine singular form.

   Tengo un **buen** coche.   *I have a good car.*
   ¿Tienes **buenos** profesores?   *Do you have good teachers?*
   No es un **mal** estudiante.   *He isn't a bad student.*

PRÁCTICA

D. ¿Qué adjetivo? Completa cada oración con el adjetivo demostrativo correcto.

> **Modelo**   **Este** *(This)* cuaderno es de Sofía.

1. Sofía compra _____ *(that)* mochila.
2. Adriana escucha _____ *(those)* canciones.
3. Carlos, Santiaguito y Viviana limpian _____ *(that)* cuarto.
4. Manolo toma _____ *(this)* clase.
5. Este semestre necesito _____ *(these)* libros.

E. La tarea de Johnny. Imagine you are helping Johnny, your eight-year-old neighbor, with his Spanish homework. He wants to write the following things about his family. Teach him how to do it in Spanish.

1. The blonde girl is my sister.

_____

2. She has a pretty friend, Lulú.

_____

3. Lulú is very funny.

_____

4. I have a married brother.

_____

5. He buys a lot of cars and all of them **(todos)** are ugly.

_____

6. I also have three pets: a big dog, a fat cat, and a dumb bird!

_____

F. Anuncios. Read the personal ads, which appeared in the Spanish-language newspaper *Diario del Club Latino*, in order to answer the questions that follow. First, read the questions so you can determine the purpose of the reading.

> **Reading Strategy: Using cognates and content to determine meaning**
> You can read Spanish with far greater ease if you guess at the meaning of cognates—words that look similar to English words. Before you read the personal ads below, consider these cognates: **americano, ingeniero, económicamente estable, español, inteligente, ejercicio, computadoras, atractiva, matrimonio, tel., bilingüe, sensual, educada, elegante, cine, responder**, and **electrónico**. The content of a text will provide clues to the meaning as well. Think about what you would expect to find in a personal ad and use this knowledge to help you understand the reading.

1. ¿Cómo es la persona del anuncio?

_____

2. ¿Qué le gusta a esta persona?

_____

3. ¿Qué tipo de persona busca?

_____

AMERICANO

Ingeniero económicamente estable; hablo español. Soy inteligente, cariñoso y trabajador. Me gusta hacer ejercicio, cocinar y trabajar con computadoras. Busco mujer atractiva, flaca. 20-30 años. ¿Amistad? ¿Matrimonio? Niño ok. Tel. 434-4444

4. ¿Cómo es la persona de este anuncio?

_____

5. ¿Cuántos años tiene?

_____

6. ¿Qué le gusta hacer?

_____

ATRACTIVA
Bilingüe, 30 años, sensual, educada, elegante y simpática. Me gusta viajar, bailar e ir al cine. Busco amigo para diversiones sanas[1]. Favor de responder vía correo electrónico. Atractiva@homemail.loc

[1]**diversiones...** *healthy fun*

G. ¡Un anuncio gratis! A local Spanish newspaper is offering free personal ads as a promotion for the weekend edition. Write an ad that will appeal to your ideal mate. Use the ads from **Práctica F** as models.

> **Writing Strategy: Using a text as a model for writing**
> To write successfully in Spanish, you will need to look at samples so you can identify the information you need to include when you write your own texts. Prepare to write your personal ad. First, reread the ads from the previous section and identify the information they provide, such as physical characteristics, personality traits, and hobbies. Then list the information you want to communicate in each of these categories in the space provided. Finally, write your ad.

Características físicas	Personalidad	Actividades
_____	_____	_____
_____	_____	_____
_____	_____	_____
_____	_____	_____
_____	_____	_____
_____	_____	_____

H. Mi personaje de televisión favorito. Describe your favorite TV character to the class. Include details such as: name, age, description of appearance and personality, description of the people the character interacts with in his/her show. Bring a picture of the actor or actress and tell your classmates when they can see the show and on what channel **(canal)**.

> **Modelo** Mi personaje favorito es Betty, del programa *Betty la fea*. Betty es una chica joven, un poco gorda y fea. La actriz, América Ferrera, no es fea, pero el personaje sí. Tiene 24 ó 25 años. Trabaja en una oficina. Betty es muy amable y buena con todas las personas; es cariñosa también. Vive *(She lives)* con su familia...

Práctica adicional	
Cuaderno de tareas pp. 142–144, C–G	invitaciones. vhlcentral.com Episodio 6

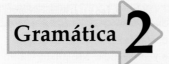

Gramática 2 — Asking for information • Interrogative words

Spanish, like English, uses inversion (placing the verb before the subject) to ask information questions. To change a statement into a *wh* question *(who, what, where, when, why)*, place the conjugated verb in front of the subject, and add the appropriate interrogative word.

Statement	Question
subject verb	verb subject
Adriana trabaja en una oficina. →	¿Dónde trabaja Adriana?
subject verb	verb subject
Manolo es alto y moreno. →	¿Cómo es Manolo?
subject verb	verb subject
Sofía toma cálculo y vóleibol. →	¿Qué clases toma Sofía?

¡Fíjate!

Cuál and **Qué** mean *what?* or *which?*. However, they are not interchangeable. Do not use **Cuál** + [*noun*]; use **Cuál** + [*verb to be*]. **¿Cuál es tu mochila?** Use **Qué** + [*nouns*].

¿Qué libro lees?
¿Qué coches te gustan?

Here is a summary of all the interrogative words you have been using.

Palabras interrogativas	
¿**Cómo** es Manolo?	*What is Manolo like?*
¿**Cuál** es tu clase favorita?	*What/Which is your favorite class?*
¿**Cuáles** son tus lápices?	*Which are your pencils?*
¿**Cuándo** descansa Adriana?	*When does Adriana rest?*
¿**Cuántos** hijos tiene?	*How many children does she have?*
¿**Cuántas** clases toma Manolo?	*How many clases does Manolo take?*
¿**Dónde** trabaja Adriana?	*Where does Adriana work?*
¿**Por qué** te gusta la clase?	*Why do you like the class?*
¿**Qué** clases toma Manolo?	*What/Which classes is Manolo taking?*
¿**Quién** es Carlos?	*Who is Carlos?*
¿**Quiénes** son tus amigos?	*Who are your friends?*

PRÁCTICA

I. Las respuestas. Empareja las preguntas de arriba *(above)* con las respuestas.

1. ¿_____? Son los hijos de Adriana.

2. ¿_____? La clase de español.

3. ¿_____? Tiene tres hijos.

4. ¿_____? Es alto y moreno.

5. ¿_____? Toma cuatro clases.

6. ¿_____? Porque es muy divertida.

7. ¿_____? En una oficina.

8. ¿_____? Nunca.

9. ¿_____? Cálculo, sicología e historia.

J. Preguntas. Completa las preguntas sobre Adriana.

1. ¿_____ estudia Adriana? En la biblioteca.

2. ¿_____ días a la semana trabaja? Dos días.

3. ¿_____ días? Martes y jueves.

4. ¿_____ descansa? Nunca.

5. ¿_____ es el profesor? Es agradable.

6. ¿_____ es Santiago? Es su esposo.

K. Preguntas personales. Responde apropiadamente a las preguntas. Después entrevista a un(a) compañero/a.

1. ¿Qué clases tomas este semestre?

2. ¿Cuál es tu clase favorita? ¿Por qué?

3. ¿Qué clase no te gusta? ¿Por qué?

4. ¿Cómo es tu profesor(a) de español? ¿Es divertida la clase?

5. ¿Dónde trabajas? ¿Cuántas horas a la semana trabajas? ¿Cuándo descansas?

6. ¿Cuándo estudias? ¿Dónde? ¿Con quién?

7. ¿A qué hora llegas a casa generalmente? ¿Qué haces (do you do) cuando llegas?

8. ¿Qué haces los fines de semana? ¿Lavas la ropa? ¿Limpias la casa? ¿Estudias? ¿Trabajas?

L. Veinte preguntas. Think of three famous people, but do not reveal their names to your partner. Your partner will ask you yes/no questions as they try to guess the names of each person. You get a point for every question your partner must ask you before he or she finds out who you are thinking of. Take turns. Write the names and physical and psychological characteristics below.

Modelo	¿Es hombre? ¿Es actor? ¿Es alto?

	Nombre	Características físicas	Características sicológicas
1.	_____	_____	_____
		_____	_____
		_____	_____
2.	_____	_____	_____
		_____	_____
		_____	_____
3.	_____	_____	_____
		_____	_____
		_____	_____

Práctica adicional

Cuaderno de tareas pp. 144–145, H–I	invitaciones. vhlcentral.com Lab practice	invitaciones. vhlcentral.com Episodio 6

Actividades comunicativas

 A. Crucigrama.

Instrucciones para **Estudiante 1**

You and your partner each have a copy of the same partially completed crossword puzzle. The words missing on your copy of the puzzle are filled in on your partner's copy. Give each other clues to complete the puzzle. Do not say the word your partner needs; instead, use definitions, examples, and incomplete sentences that provide a context for the missing word. Here are some examples:

Modelo
17 vertical: **La hija de mi hija es mi...**
15 horizontal: **Un niño no es viejo; es...**

¡Fíjate!

Find simple but creative ways of communicating the meaning of the words to your partner.

A. Crucigrama.

Instrucciones para **Estudiante 2**

You and your partner each have a copy of the same partially completed crossword puzzle. The words missing on your copy of the puzzle are filled in on your partner's copy. Give each other clues to complete the puzzle. Do not say the word your partner needs; instead, use definitions, examples, and incomplete sentences that provide a context for the missing word. Here are some examples:

Modelo	*17 vertical:* **La hija de mi hija es mi...**
	15 horizontal: **Un niño no es viejo; es...**

¡Fíjate!

Find simple but creative ways of communicating the meaning of the words to your partner.

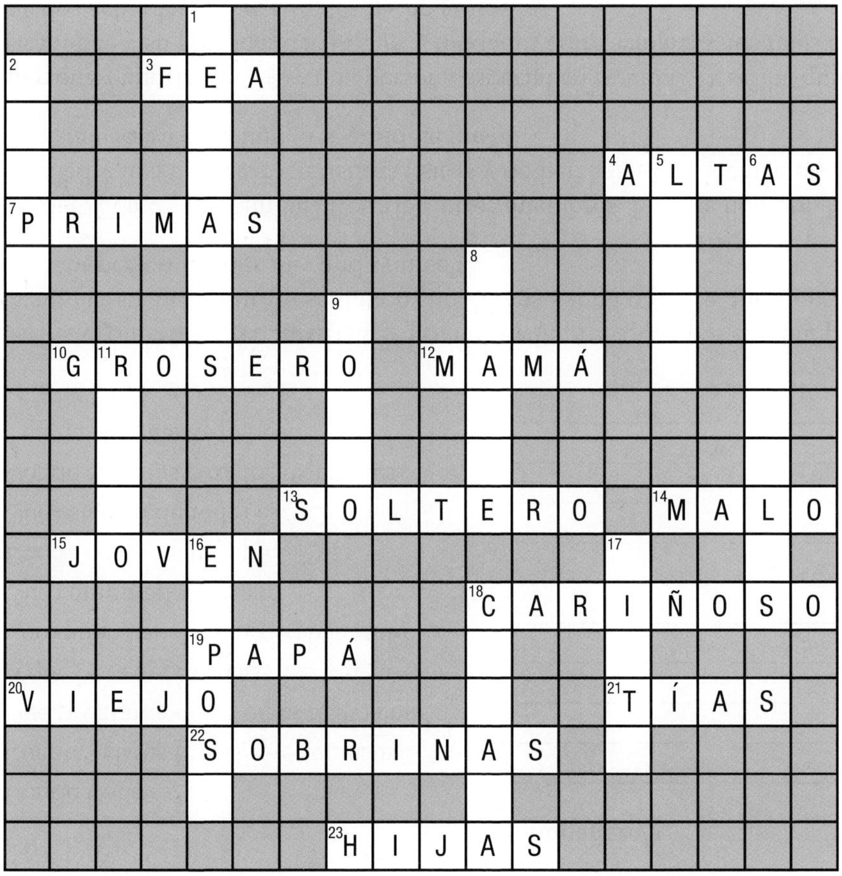

Crossword grid with the following filled entries:

- 3: FEA
- 4: ALTAS
- 7: PRIMAS
- 10: GROSERO
- 12: MAMÁ
- 13: SOLTERO
- 14: MALO
- 15: JOVEN
- 18: CARIÑOSO
- 19: PAPÁ
- 20: VIEJO
- 21: TÍAS
- 22: SOBRINAS
- 23: HIJAS

B. Actividades en común. First answer the questions in the column labeled **Yo**. Then look for classmates whose answers are the same as yours and write their names in the column labeled **Compañero/a**. Be prepared to share your findings with the class.

> **Modelo** —¿Dónde trabajas?
> —Trabajo en un banco. ¿Y tú?
> —Yo también. *or* Yo trabajo en una tienda.
> —Mary y yo trabajamos en un supermercado.

	Compañero/a	Yo
1. ¿Dónde trabajas?	_____	_____
2. ¿Cuántas clases tomas este semestre?	_____	_____
3. ¿Qué programa miras en la televisión?	_____	_____
4. ¿A qué hora llegas a casa los lunes?	_____	_____
5. ¿Con quién hablas más por teléfono?	_____	_____
6. ¿Qué computadora usas?	_____	_____
7. ¿Dónde compras tu ropa?	_____	_____
8. ¿Qué estación de radio escuchas?	_____	_____
9. ¿Dónde estudias para los exámenes?	_____	_____
10. ¿Cuántas hermanas tienes?	_____	_____

C. Una presentación oral: Mi familia y yo. You will prepare a four-minute presentation to share with your classmates. Your presentation should answer all of these questions about your family, an important person in your life, and yourself.

- **Tu familia:** ¿Cómo es tu familia? Describe a tres miembros. Incluye nombre, lugar de origen, edad y una o dos características físicas y de personalidad. Incluye una o dos cosas que le gusta hacer a cada uno/a usando **Le gusta…**

- **Una persona importante:** ¿Hay una persona especial en tu vida? Describe quién es, cómo es (físicamente y su personalidad) y sus actividades entre semana y los fines de semana. Incluye dos actividades que ustedes hacen juntos/as.

- **Tú:** ¿Cómo eres? Descríbete a ti mismo/a *(yourself)*. Incluye nombre, lugar de origen, edad y una o dos características físicas y de personalidad. Incluye una o dos cosas que te gusta hacer usando **Me gusta…**

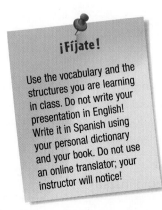

¡Fíjate!

Use the vocabulary and the structures you are learning in class. Do not write your presentation in English! Write it in Spanish using your personal dictionary and your book. Do not use an online translator; your instructor will notice!

¡Fíjate!

Prepare a poster board. Include pictures, photographs or drawings to illustrate what you are talking about. DO NOT READ! However, you may write a few words on the poster to guide your presentation, but DO NOT READ from notes as you go along.

Invitación a **Estados Unidos**

In your own words. Read the information below and then write what you understood. In English, summarize the information in two or three sentences. Do not translate.

_____

_____

_____

Del álbum de
Adriana

Después de los mexicanos, los puertorriqueños son la comunidad de hispanos más grande del país. Cada verano *(summer)* se celebra en Nueva York el desfile *(parade)* puertorriqueño al que asisten *(attend)* más de un millón de personas. Muchas personalidades famosas son de origen puertorriqueño, como Jennifer López, José Feliciano, Ricky Martin y Marc Anthony, entre otros.

Práctica adicional

SUPERSITE

invitaciones.
vhlcentral.com
Episodio 6

La correspondencia

El correo: Otra carta para Odette. Primero lee estas preguntas. Luego lee la carta (en la página 138) que Sofía le escribe a su amiga Odette en Guadalajara, México. Después contesta las preguntas.

1. ¿Cómo es el hijo de Adriana, según *(according to)* Sofía? _____

2. ¿Cómo es Lalo? _____

3. ¿Cómo es el ex novio de Odette? _____

4. ¿Cuándo van a Guadalajara? _____

Querida Odette:

Me da tanta alegría[1] recibir tus cartas. Estoy bien. Mis clases me gustan mucho. En mi clase de cálculo, tengo una compañera puertorriqueña. Se llama Adriana y es una señora muy agradable. Aunque[2] ya es mayor, somos buenas amigas. Además[3], ¡tiene un hijo guapísimo! Bueno, no lo conozco en persona, pero en las fotos es súper atractivo. Es piloto y ahora está en Chicago. ¿Te imaginas, poder visitar todo el mundo gratis[4]? Lalo, como siempre, llega tardísimo a casa, escucha una música horrorosa, nunca saca buenas notas en sus clases y siempre necesita dinero.

¡Qué bueno que terminaste[5] con tu ex novio! Era grosero y flojo. Tú mereces una persona buena y cariñosa como tú. No te preocupes, hay muchos muchachos. Yo no tengo novio, pero tengo muchos amigos.

Bueno, querida amiga, sí voy[6] a visitarte en diciembre. Ramón y Ana Mari van[7] a visitar a sus abuelos en Guadalajara. ¡Tal vez vamos juntos! Escríbeme pronto.

Tu amiga que te quiere,
Sofía

[1]**Me...** *It makes me so happy* [2]*Although* [3]*Besides* [4]*free* [5]*you finished (broke up)* [6]*I'm going*
[7]*are going*

En papel: Una notita para Odette. Write a letter to Odette telling her about friends, instructors, classmates, and other important people in your life. Include their name, their relationship to you, their physical description, their personality, and one or two interesting things about them.

¡Fíjate!

Create a simple outline, in Spanish, of the information you want to include in your letter before you begin to write.

¡A ver de nuevo!

Parte 1. Listen to or watch the **Escena** again and, on a separate piece of paper, write as much as you can about Manolo, Sofía, and Adriana, including: age, description, family, activities, etc.

Parte 2. Now compare your summary with a classmate's and add any information you may have left out.

Práctica adicional			
Cuaderno de tareas pp. 145–146, J–L	invitaciones. vhlcentral.com Episodio 6	invitaciones. vhlcentral.com Lab practice	invitaciones. vhlcentral.com Episodio 6

Vocabulario del Episodio 6

Para describir a las personas y las cosas

aburrido/a	*boring*	**joven**	*young*
agradable	*pleasant, nice*	**listo/a**	*smart*
alto/a	*tall*	**malo/a**	*bad*
amable	*kind, friendly*	**mayor**	*older*
antipático/a	*unpleasant, nasty*	**menor**	*younger*
bajo/a	*short (height)*	**moreno/a**	*dark (skin/hair)*
bonito/a	*good-looking, pretty*	**nuevo/a**	*new*
bueno/a	*good, nice*	**ordenado/a**	*neat, organized*
cariñoso/a	*affectionate*	**pelirrojo/a**	*red head*
casado/a	*married*	**pequeño/a**	*small*
delgado/a	*thin*	**perezoso/a**	*lazy*
desordenado/a	*messy, unorganized*	**pobre**	*poor*
difícil	*hard, difficult*	**reservado/a**	*reserved*
divertido/a	*fun*	**rico/a**	*wealthy; tasty*
fácil	*easy*	**rubio/a**	*blond(e)*
feo/a	*ugly*	**serio/a**	*serious*
gordo/a	*fat*	**soltero/a**	*single*
gracioso/a	*funny*	**tonto/a**	*dumb, silly*
grande	*large, big*	**trabajador(a)**	*hard-working*
grosero/a	*rude*	**viejo/a**	*old*
guapo/a	*handsome, good-looking*		

Los adjetivos demostrativos

este, esta	*this*	**ese, esa**	*that*
estos, estas	*these*	**esos, esas**	*those*

Palabras interrogativas

¿Cómo...?	*How...?*
¿Cuál/Cuales...?	*Which...?*
¿Cuándo...?	*When...?*
¿Cuántos/as...?	*How many...?*
¿Dónde...?	*Where...?*
¿Por qué...?	*Why...?*
¿Qué...?	*What...?*
¿Quién/Quiénes...?	*Who...?*

Vocabulario personal

In this section, write all the words that you want to know how to say in Spanish so that you can talk in greater detail about yourself, your family, your friends, and your activities.

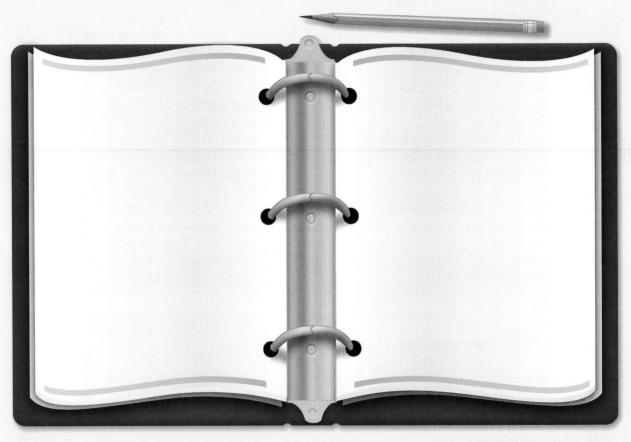

Cuaderno de tareas

Episodio

6

Escenas de la vida: ¡Qué guapos!

 A. ¡A ver cuánto entendiste! See how much of the **Escena** you understood by matching the Spanish sentences with their English equivalents.

El flan de queso

_____ 1. ¿Es difícil prepararlo?   a. It's easy to make.

_____ 2. ¡Qué rico!   b. Is it hard to make?

_____ 3. Lo preparo en media hora.   c. I like to cook a lot.

_____ 4. Es fácil prepararlo.   d. How delicious!

_____ 5. Me gusta mucho cocinar.   e. I make it in half an hour.

Los hermanos

_____ 6. Tu hermana es alta y rubia.   f. You're tall and very good-looking.

_____ 7. ¿Cuántos años tiene?   g. You're so different!

_____ 8. ¡Qué diferentes son!   h. I have her picture.

_____ 9. Tú eres alto y muy guapo.   i. How old is he?

_____ 10. Soy moreno y feo.   j. I have dark hair and I'm ugly.

_____ 11. Tengo su foto.   k. Your sister is tall and blonde.

B. Me gusta. Use the expressions to complete the following conversation.

fácil	seria	mexicano	rico	difícil
está	me encanta	media hora	joven	preparar comida

Manolo   ¡Qué (1) _____! (2) _____ el flan de queso.

Sofía   Es muy similar al flan (3) _____ . ¿Es (4) _____ prepararlo?

Adriana No, es muy (5) _____. Lo preparo en (6) _____.
         Me gusta (7) _____ puertorriqueña.

Sofía   ¡ (8) _____ delicioso!

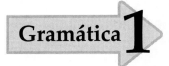

Nombre _____ Fecha _____

Gramática 1

Describing people and things
- **Descriptive adjectives**
- **Placement of adjectives**

C. ¡Qué caro! *(How expensive!)* Sofía and Ana Mari are at the bookstore gathering supplies. Complete the conversation with the appropriate forms of the demonstrative adjectives.

este	ese	estos	esos
esta	esa	estas	esas

Sofía   ¡Mira cuánto cuestan (1) _____ *(these)* lápices de grafito!

Ana Mari   ¡Qué horror! (2) _____ *(Those)* lápices son más caros que los libros. Bueno, (3) _____ *(this)* libro de diseño es carísimo también.

Sofía   A ver… ¡Ah! Por suerte ya *(already)* tengo (4) _____ *(that)* libro.

Ana Mari   ¿Y (5) _____ *(these)* plumas de colores?

Sofía   Ay, de (6) _____ *(those)* plumas necesito dos paquetes *(packages)*.

D. Voy a comprar… Sofía is shopping for school supplies. Fill in her list with the appropriate forms of the demonstrative adjectives for each column.

Voy a comprar…
1. __este__ libro de dibujo
2. _____ lápices
3. _____ plumas
4. _____ mochila
5. _____ diccionario

No necesito…
6. __esos__ papeles
7. _____ mapa
8. _____ banderitas
9. _____ calculadora
10. _____ cuadernos

E. Las descripciones. Write sentences using all the elements.

> **Modelo**   hay / poco / **coches** / bueno / bonito / barato *(inexpensive)*
> Hay pocos coches buenos, bonitos y baratos.

1. Ramón / tener / un / trabajo / fácil / bueno

_____

2. el compañero de cuarto de Manolo / ser / antipático / grosero

_____

3. la / **universidades** públicas en Latinoamérica / ser / muy / grande

_____

4. este semestre / yo / tener / bueno / **profesores**

_____

5. Sofía / tener / mucho / **amigas** / joven / soltero / guapo

_____

¡Fíjate!

Remember to use the appropriate articles to match the adjectives to the nouns, and to conjugate the verbs.

F. Mi familia. Adriana's adolescent daughter likes to talk about her own family. Use her family tree and the adjectives provided to describe her family. Then use your imagination and what you know about the family to create two original sentences.

> **Modelo**   Mi hermano menor es tímido.

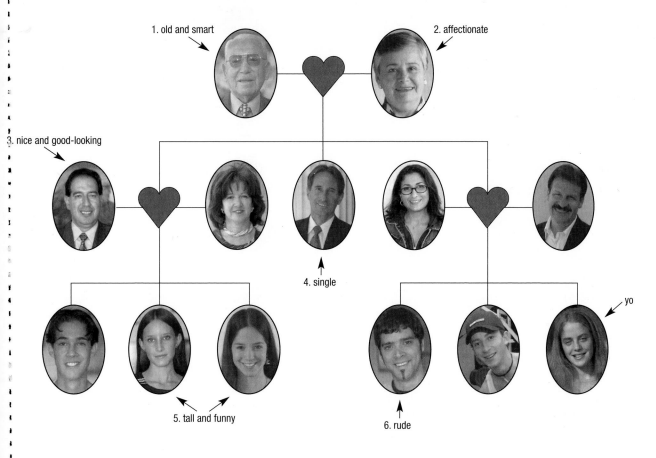

1. old and smart
2. affectionate
3. nice and good-looking
4. single
5. tall and funny
6. rude
yo

1. _____

2. _____

3. _____

4. _____

5. _____

6. _____

7. _____

8. _____

G. ¿Cómo son? Describe the characters of the book. Mention their physical appearance and their personality.

1. Sofía es _____

_____

_____

2. Manolo es _____

_____

_____

3. Ana Mari es _____

_____

_____

4. Adriana es _____

_____

_____

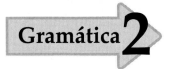 **Gramática 2** **Asking for information**
• **Interrogative words**

H. Preguntas y respuestas. Provide the appropriate interrogative expressions and answer the questions.

1. ¿ _____ te llamas?   Me llamo _____.
2. ¿ _____ eres?   Soy de _____.
3. ¿ _____ estudias?   En la universidad de _____.
4. ¿ _____ estudias?   Español y _____.
5. ¿ _____ hermanos tienes?   Tengo _____.
6. ¿ _____ es tu profesor(a)?   Es muy _____.
7. ¿ _____ son tus amigos?   Mis amigos se llaman _____.
8. ¿ _____ es tu teléfono?   Es el _____.
9. ¿ _____ estudias español?   Porque _____.
10. ¿ _____ es tu clase de español? Es a las _____ de la _____.

I. Una entrevista. You would like to know more about one of your classmates. Write four questions you might ask if you were to interview them.

1. _____
2. _____
3. _____
4. _____

Para terminar

J. Mi persona favorita. On a separate piece of paper, write a diary entry describing the person you like/admire the most. Explain why he/she is your favorite person: **Es mi persona favorita porque** (*because*)... Include the following information.

- name
- age
- where he/she is from
- physical appearance and personality
- activities
- occupation

Start like this: **Querido diario: Mi persona favorita se llama...**

K. El talento latino. Read the questions, then read the following articles and answer the questions.

Jennifer López: Una estrella (*star*) **puertorriqueña**

1. ¿De dónde son los padres de Jennifer? _____
2. ¿Cuántas hermanas tiene? ¿Qué profesiones tienen sus hermanas? _____
   _____
3. ¿Cómo es Jennifer? _____
4. ¿En qué idioma (*language*) canta? _____

Jennifer López nació[1] en el Bronx, Nueva York. Sus padres son puertorriqueños, originarios de la ciudad de Ponce. Jennifer tiene una hermana que es D. J. en una radiodifusora en Nueva York, y una hermana que es maestra de música, es casada y tiene un hijo. Jennifer toma clases de baile desde los seis años. Ella y sus hermanas hacían[2] presentaciones "artísticas" para la familia en su apartamento de Nueva York. La carrera artística de Jennifer se establece cuando hace la película[3] *Selena*. Su belleza física, típicamente latina, su talento y su ritmo musical la hacen famosa. Poco tiempo después graba[4] un disco que llega a tener ventas[5] de más de un millón. Además de cantar en inglés, ella ahora canta en español, aunque no lo habla muy bien. Por el momento, es la actriz y cantante latina más conocida y mejor pagada (*highest paid*) en Estados Unidos. Dos de sus películas son *Enough* y *Maid in Manhattan*. Hoy en día, ella y su también famoso esposo, Marc Anthony, están muy ocupados con sus hijos.

[1]*was born* [2]*used to do* [3]*movie* [4]*she records* [5]*sales*

Salma Hayek: Una estrella mexicana

1. ¿De dónde es Salma? _____

2. ¿Cómo es? _____

3. ¿De dónde son sus abuelos? _____

4. Según Salma, ¿qué es lo más importante para estar guapa? _____

5. ¿Cuál es su mejor película? _____

"Lo más importante en una relación es aceptar a la gente[1] como es."
–Salma Hayek

Esta bella actriz mexicana, es morena, tiene unos grandes ojos cafés y mide solamente 5' 2". Sus abuelos paternos son del Líbano, y su mamá es mexicana. Algunos de sus trabajos en Estados Unidos incluyen la serie de televisión *Ugly Betty* y las películas *Spy Kids 3-D, Once Upon a Time in Mexico* y *Across the Universe*. En una entrevista[2] reciente, Hayek dijo[3]: "Uno de los ingredientes imprescindibles para estar guapa es la felicidad". La mejor actuación de Salma es en la película *Frida*. La actriz trabajó[4] siete años para lograr[5] que filmaran la película. Hoy la actriz divide su tiempo entre su hija y su trabajo.

[1]*people* [2]*interview* [3]*said* [4]*worked* [5]*to achieve*

L. Una miniprueba para terminar. Complete the following communicative tasks to test your knowledge of the content of the chapter.

1. Ask Sofía:
   a. to describe her family.
   b. how old her brother is.
   c. where her grandparents are from.

2. Ask Adriana:
   d. when she works.
   e. if her children clean their rooms.
   f. when she usually gets home.

3. Ask Wayne and Ramón:
   g. if they get good grades.
   h. who does the laundry in their house.
   i. if they use the computer.

4. Tell the characters:
   j. what your typical day is like.
   k. something you do on the weekends.
   l. something about your family.

a. _____ g. _____

b. _____ h. _____

c. _____ i. _____

d. _____ j. _____

e. _____ k. _____

f. _____ l. _____

Episodio

7

Escenas de la vida: ¿Qué van a hacer el sábado?

 A. ¡Mira cuánto puedes entender! Listen to the conversation or watch the video to complete the tasks that correspond to each picture.

1. Indica qué nota creen que van a sacar en el primer examen de cálculo.

_____ _____ _____

2. Indica qué tiene ganas de hacer Ramón el sábado y por qué Sofía no puede hacer nada el sábado con Ramón. ¿Qué tiene que hacer Sofía?

☐ Tiene ganas de hacer un picnic.

☐ Tiene que trabajar.
☐ Tiene que limpiar su cuarto.
☐ Tiene que hacer una presentación.
☐ Tiene que estudiar.

☐ Tiene ganas de ir a la biblioteca.

3. Mira los planes de Manolo; completa la hora o la actividad necesaria.

sábado	domingo
_____ aeropuerto	¡nada!
después _____	
_____	
en la tarde _____	

4. ¿Qué va a hacer Adriana el domingo?

Cultura a lo vivo

Throughout the Spanish-speaking world, Sunday is considered a day to be spent with family. Some families attend religious services and then go to a restaurant; other families visit their parents and/or grandparents; still others go on outings such as a picnic, a visit to a nearby town, a day at the swimming pool, or a trip to the mountains, a river, or a park. These gatherings include family members of all ages, as well as close friends whose families may live elsewhere. Some parents feel so strongly about reserving Sunday for the family that teenage children are not allowed to go out with friends that day.

B. ¿Te diste cuenta? Escucha la conversación o mira el video otra vez para indicar quién hace estos comentarios: Sofía **(S),** Adriana **(A),** Ramón **(R)** o Manolo **(M).**

_____ 1. El examen fue muy fácil.

_____ 2. Para mí fue muy difícil.

_____ 3. Tenemos que hacer algo divertido.

_____ 4. No tengo nada que hacer el domingo.

_____ 5. Los domingos paso el día con la familia.

_____ 6. Todos están invitados.

C. ¡A responder! Contesta las preguntas.

1. ¿Quién tiene ganas de celebrar? ¿Por qué? _____

_____

2. ¿Qué quiere organizar Ramón? ¿Por qué? _____

_____

3. ¿Qué tiene que hacer Sofía el sábado por la tarde? _____

_____

4. ¿Qué hace Adriana los domingos? _____

_____

Práctica adicional		
Cuaderno de tareas p. 165, A–B	invitaciones. vhlcentral.com Episodio 7	invitaciones. vhlcentral.com Episodio 7

Para comunicarnos mejor

Gramática 1

Talking about weekend plans
- **Ir a** + [*infinitive*]
- **The personal a**

In the conversation, you heard Sofía, Ramón, and Adriana say the following:

Creo que **voy a sacar** A.   *I think I'm going to get an A.*

¿Qué **van a hacer** el sábado?   *What are you (all) going to do on Saturday?*

Vamos a visitar a los abuelos.   *We're going to visit our grandparents.*

Voy, van, and **vamos** are forms of the verb **ir** *(to go).* To talk about things and activities that are going to happen in the future, Spanish uses a form of **ir** followed by **a** and the infinitive (**-r** form) of a verb. In another conversation, the characters said the following about the things they are *going to do.*

¡Fíjate!
Go to the Supersite to watch an authentic TV commercial from Argentina that practices this structure.

Ir a + [*infinitive*]	
Hoy **voy a llevar** a Viviana a su clase de baile.	*Today I'm going to take Viviana to her dance class.*
¿**Vas a trabajar** el domingo?	*Are you going to work on Sunday?*
Sofía **va a comprar** un regalo.	*Sofía is going to buy a present.*
El próximo domingo **vamos a celebrar** el cumpleaños de Wayne.	*Next Sunday we're going to celebrate Wayne's birthday.*
¿Qué **van a hacer** mañana? ¿Qué **vais a hacer** mañana? }	*What are you going to do tomorrow? (pl.)*
Todos **van a ir** al parque.	*They are all going to go to the park.*

1. Notice that the verb **llevar** *(to take something or someone somewhere)* is followed by an **a** (**llevar a Viviana**). This is called the personal **a** (**la a personal**), and it has no English equivalent. You need to include **a** after verbs that have a person or a pet as the direct object.

> La familia de Adriana siempre visita **a** los abuelos los domingos.
> Los lunes Adriana **lleva a** su hija a la clase de baile folclórico.
> El sábado Manolo **lleva a** la gata al veterinario, ¿verdad?
> Escucho **a** mis padres.

2. To talk about your plans, use these expressions:

Expresiones de tiempo			
esta noche	*tonight*	**el próximo sábado**	*next Saturday*
hoy	*today*	**la próxima semana**	*next week*
mañana	*tomorrow*	**el año que viene**	*next year*
este jueves	*this Thursday*	**el lunes**	*on Monday*

Este jueves no voy a trabajar por la noche.   *This Thursday I am not going to work at night.*

PRÁCTICA

A. ¿Esto van a hacer ustedes?

Parte 1. Indica si vas a hacer *(to do)* las siguientes actividades.

	Sí	No
1. El sábado por la mañana voy a estudiar.	☐	☐
2. Voy a trabajar hoy.	☐	☐
3. Voy a salir *(to go out)* con mis amigos esta noche.	☐	☐
4. Voy a visitar a mi abuela el domingo.	☐	☐
5. Mi papá y yo vamos a jugar *(to play)* golf el próximo fin de semana.	☐	☐
6. Mi compañero/a y yo vamos a hacer ejercicio *(to exercise)*.	☐	☐
7. Mañana voy a mirar mi programa favorito en la televisión.	☐	☐
8. Voy a escribir *(to write)* una composición este fin de semana.	☐	☐

 Parte 2. Convierte las oraciones de la **Parte 1** en preguntas. Después entrevista a un(a) compañero/a.

B. ¿Qué van a hacer nuestros amigos?

Parte 1. Usa las fotos para escribir lo que *(what)* van a hacer los personajes la próxima semana y por qué. Usa **ir a** + **verbo** para expresar acciones futuras.

> **Modelo**   Ramón **va a buscar infomación en Internet esta noche porque necesita hacer una presentación oral.**

1. Sofía y Manolo...

2. Adriana...

3. Nosotros...

4. Manolo...

5. Sofía...

6. Ellos...

 Parte 2. Tell a partner if you are going to do the same activities sometime next week. Explain when and why.

Práctica adicional

Cuaderno de tareas pp.166–167, C–F

invitaciones. vhlcentral.com Episodio 7

 **Gramática** **2** **Expressing obligations and desires**
• Tener que, tener ganas de

You have used the verb **tener** to express ownership and possession.

Tenemos muy poco dinero.	*We have very little money.*
Tengo cuatro perros.	*I have four dogs.*
¿Tienes coche?	*Do you have a car?*

In every language, many common verb phrases have meanings which are independent of those same verbs. In English, these combinations are called *verb constructions*; in Spanish, they are called **construcciones verbales.** For example, when you use *have* as an independent verb, as in *I have a new car, have* means *to own* or *to possess*. When you use *have* in combination with an infinitive, as in *I have to buy a new car, have* does not mean *to possess*. The combination *have* + [*infinitive*] expresses an obligation, something you must do.

1. In Spanish, obligation is expressed by the verb construction **tener que** + [*infinitive*]. In this episode, you heard some of these statements containing **tener que**:

Tengo que trabajar por la mañana.	*I have to work in the morning.*
Tenemos que hacer algo divertido.	*We have to do something fun.*
Lalo **tiene que pagar** la cuenta de su celular.	*Lalo has to pay his cell phone bill.*

2. Another verb construction you heard is **tener ganas de** + [*infinitive*]. Use this construction to express what you feel or don't feel like doing.

Tengo ganas de celebrar.	*I feel like celebrating.*
No **tenemos ganas de estudiar.**	*We don't feel like studying.*
Lalo siempre **tiene ganas de salir** con sus amigos.	*Lalo always feels like going out with his friends.*

PRÁCTICA

C. Y ustedes, ¿qué tienen que hacer? Completa las oraciones lógicamente.

> **Modelo**   Los jueves mi hermana tiene que **lavar la ropa.**

1. Los lunes tengo que _____.

2. En la clase de español todos tenemos que _____.

3. Los sábados mis amigos y yo tenemos ganas de _____.

4. Los domingos no tengo ganas de _____.

5. Yo (no) _____ hacer la tarea.

6. Mi mejor amigo/a _____.

D. Seamos honestos. Mira la página 104 para hablar con un(a) compañero/a. Discutan cuándo tienen o no tienen ganas de hacer esas actividades.

Banco de palabras
Casi nunca
Almost never
Siempre
Always
Por suerte
Luckily
Tristemente
Sadly
Francamente
Honestly

> **Modelo** —Francamente, casi nunca tengo ganas de lavar la ropa. ¿Y tú?
> —A mí me gusta lavar la ropa, pero nunca tengo ganas de limpiar la casa.

E. ¿Por qué no quieres ir? Explícale a un(a) compañero/a por qué no quieres (*you don't want*) ir a esos lugares (*places*). Usa **no tengo ganas de** con los siguientes verbos.

nadar   hacer ejercicio   estudiar   comprar nada
correr   jugar tenis   leer libros   escribir correo electrónico (*e-mail*)

> **Modelo** a las canchas de tenis
> —¿Quieres ir a las canchas de tenis?
> —No, porque hoy no tengo ganas de jugar tenis.

1. al gimnasio
2. a la biblioteca
3. al laboratorio de computadoras

4. al centro comercial
5. al parque
6. a la piscina

Banco de palabras	
Quiero...	**nadar**
I want...	*to swim*
Quieres...	**correr**
You want...	*to run*

F. Las obligaciones académicas. Mira las fotos de las obligaciones típicas en la universidad. Dile (*Tell*) a un(a) compañero/a cuáles son tus obligaciones académicas. Explica tus respuestas.

> **Modelo** Este semestre no tengo que escribir trabajos de investigación porque sólo (*only*) tomo matemáticas y español.

sacar buenas notas

estudiar con mis compañeros/as

llegar a tiempo a clases

¡Fíjate!
Don't forget to write down the activities that apply to you in your personal dictionary on page 164.

hacer la tarea

leer mucho

escribir trabajos de investigación

G. Lo siento, pero no puedo. Imagina que un(a) amigo/a te invita a salir *(to go out)*, pero tú no tienes ganas. Por eso, inventas muchas obligaciones. ¡Inventa excusas!

> **Modelo**   ir al cine
> —¿Quieres ir al cine el próximo sábado?
> —Lo siento, pero no puedo porque tengo que trabajar.

1. ir al parque
2. ir al centro comercial
3. ir al concierto de Marc Anthony
4. ir a la cafetería
5. ir a un restaurante a comer *(to eat)*
6. mirar una película *(movie)* en mi casa

> **Banco de palabras**
>
> **No puedo**
> *I can't*
>
> **¿Puedes...?**
> *Can you...?*
>
> **Lo siento.**
> *I'm sorry.*
>
> **¿Quieres...?**
> *Do you want...?*

H. Preguntas personales. Contesta las preguntas. Luego entrevista a un(a) compañero/a.

1. ¿Qué tienes que hacer después de las clases?
2. ¿Qué tienes que hacer los fines de semana?
3. ¿Cuándo tienes ganas de estudiar? ¿Vas a estudiar esta noche? ¿Vas a mirar la tele?
4. ¿Qué tienes ganas de hacer este fin de semana?

Invitación a **Colombia**

In your own words. Read the information below and then write what you understood. In English, summarize the information in two or three sentences. Do not translate.

_____

_____

_____

> Del álbum de
> *Sofía*

Colombia tiene casi *(almost)* dos veces *(times)* el tamaño de Texas y aproximadamente 49 millones de habitantes. Es un bello *(beautiful)* país que ha dado *(has given)* al mundo *(world)* renombradas personalidades de fama mundial, como Gabriel García Márquez (Premio Nobel de Literatura) y Fernando Botero (pintor, escultor). Además de *(Besides)* artistas e intelectuales, Colombia es el lugar *(place)* de origen de los cantautores *(singer-songwriters)* Shakira, Juanes y Carlos Vives; y de los actores John Leguizamo y Sofía Vergara. ¿Te gusta el café? Pues Colombia produce, según los expertos, el mejor *(best)* café del mundo. El café es una de las exportaciones de mayor rendimiento *(greatest profitability)* económico del mundo. Para ver un anuncio auténtico de Colombia, ve al Supersitio.

I. Las actividades más comunes para relajarse. Habla con un(a) compañero/a de las actividades que generalmente tienes ganas de hacer durante los fines de semana.

> **Modelo** Los fines de semana, casi siempre tengo ganas de salir con mis amigos. A veces vamos a bailar o al centro comercial. ¿Y tú?

hacer ejercicio

dormir

jugar fútbol

ir a los partidos de fútbol americano

ir al cine

salir a cenar

> **¡Fíjate!**
>
> Don't forget to write down the activities that apply to you in your personal dictionary on page 164. You will learn the conjugations of these verbs in Episode 8. They are introduced here as vocabulary to talk about entertainment.

J. ¡A hablar! In groups of four, try to set a date and time to go out together to do something fun. Explain which days and times you have other commitments or obligations (**el martes no puedo porque...**). Discuss what you all feel like doing and agree on something you all want to do. Use the expressions from the list.

Banco de palabras

No tengo nada que hacer el [día].
I don't have anything to do on [day].

Ese día no puedo porque tengo que...
That day I can't because I have to...

Tengo muchas ganas de...
I would really like to...

¿Quién puede a las...?
Who is available at...?

Práctica adicional

| Cuaderno de tareas pp. 168–169, G–J | invitaciones. vhlcentral.com Lab practice | invitaciones. vhlcentral.com Episodio 7 |

Actividades comunicativas

 A. Los planes para el fin de semana.

Instrucciones para **Estudiante 1**

First, fill in the column marked **Yo** to indicate what you are going to do on the days and times indicated on the grid. Then talk to your partner in order to fill in the column marked **Mi compañero/a.** Finally, interview each other so you can fill in the empty boxes in the last two columns; you each have the information that the other needs.

Modelo   ¿Qué va a hacer Sofía el sábado por la tarde?

¡Fíjate!

Remember not to conjugate the verbs that follow **ir a**. Always use the infinitive **(-r)** form.

	Yo	Mi compañero/a	Sofía	Ramón y su familia
El viernes por la noche				
El sábado por la mañana				
El sábado por la tarde				
El domingo				

A. Los planes para el fin de semana.

Instrucciones para **Estudiante 2**

First, fill in the column marked **Yo** to indicate what you are going to do on the days and times indicated on the grid. Then talk to your partner in order to fill in the column marked **Mi compañero/a.** Finally, interview each other so you can fill in the empty boxes in the last two columns; you each have the information that the other needs.

| Modelo | ¿Qué va a hacer Sofía el sábado por la tarde? |

¡Fíjate!

Remember not to conjugate the verbs that follow **ir a.** Always use the infinitive **(-r)** form.

	Yo	Mi compañero/a	Sofía	Ramón y su familia
El viernes por la noche				
El sábado por la mañana				
El sábado por la tarde				
El domingo				

B. En imágenes.

Instrucciones para **Estudiante 1**

Use the first letter of the verb and the drawings to create logical sentences stating what you and the characters are going to do, have to do, or feel like doing during the weekend. Concentrate on the actions in the drawings. Then read your sentences to your partner, who will check the answer key to see if they are correct. Take turns.

¡Fíjate!

Try to interpret the whole sentence before attempting to give your partner the answer.

1. Mañana Sofía v _____ con sus amigas.

2. Adriana y Sofía t _____ para la clase de cálculo.

3. Wayne no t _____ de _____.

4. Manolo t _____ a la gata al veterinario.

5. ¿Este fin de semana tú v _____ en Internet?

Las respuestas de tu compañero/a:

1. Adriana **tiene que trabajar** todo el día.

2. Los hermanos de Ramón **tienen ganas de** ir a la **piscina** con sus amigos.

3. Sofía **va a tomar el autobús** porque su coche no funciona.

4. Ana Mari y yo **vamos a mirar** un programa de terror.

5. ¿Tú **tienes que comprar** muchos libros para tus clases como Manolo y Sofía?

B. En imágenes.

Instrucciones para **Estudiante 2**

Use the first letter of the verb and the drawings to create logical sentences stating what you and the characters are going to do, have to do, or feel like doing during the weekend. Concentrate on the actions in the drawings. Then read your sentences to your partner, who will check the answer key to see if they are correct. Take turns.

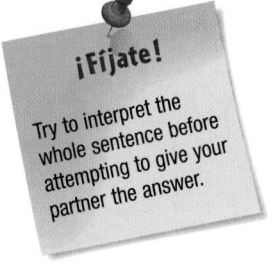

¡Fíjate!

Try to interpret the whole sentence before attempting to give your partner the answer.

1. Adriana t_____ todo el día.

2. Los hermanos de Ramón t_____ ir a la con sus amigos.

3. Sofía v_____ porque su coche no funciona.

4. Ana Mari y yo v_____ un programa de terror.

5. ¿Tú t_____ muchos libros para tus clases como Manolo y Sofía?

Las respuestas de tu compañero/a:

1. Mañana Sofía **va a bailar** con sus amigas.
2. Adriana y Sofía **tienen que estudiar** para la clase de cálculo.
3. Wayne no **tiene ganas de lavar el coche.**
4. Manolo **tiene que llevar** a la gata al veterinario.
5. ¿Este fin de semana tú **vas a buscar información** en Internet?

C. ¡Mucho gusto!

Instrucciones para **Estudiante 1**

Interview a classmate whom you have not had the opportunity to get to know. Find out:

- your partner's name
- if your partner has brothers and sisters; their names, ages, and physical descriptions
- if he/she works; where and what days
- if he/she uses a computer; what type **(tipo)**
- if he/she likes to watch TV; what programs
- what your partner usually feels like doing on weekends

You will need to report some of the information you learn about your partner to the rest of the class. Take notes.

C. ¡Mucho gusto!

Instrucciones para **Estudiante 2**

Interview a classmate whom you have not had the opportunity to get to know. Find out:

- your partner's name
- if your partner has a boyfriend/girlfriend; their name, age, and physical description
- how many classes they take, which ones, what days
- if your partner likes to listen to music; what kind
- what they have to do after school
- what they are going to do this weekend

You will need to report some of the information you learn about your partner to the rest of the class. Take notes.

La correspondencia

El correo: Una invitación para Wayne. Lee las preguntas. Luego lee el correo electrónico que recibe Wayne y contesta las preguntas.

1. ¿Quién invita a Wayne? _____

2. ¿Qué va a hacer Wayne el sábado por la mañana? _____

3. ¿Adónde va a llevar a su sobrino? _____

4. ¿Qué planes tiene Wayne para el próximo sábado? _____

From: Wayne Reilly <wreilly@micorreo.com>
To: "Guadalupe Amaré" <gamare@micorreo.com>
Re: Invitación para el sábado

Hola, Lupita:

Gracias por la invitación. Me gustaría[1] ir pero no puedo[2]. ¡Tengo muchísimas cosas
que hacer! Por la mañana tengo que reparar el coche de un amigo, porque no
puede ir a trabajar sin[3] coche. Por la tarde necesito estudiar, porque el lunes tengo
un examen de física que va a ser muy difícil y tengo que sacar A. A las siete de la
tarde, voy a llevar a mi sobrino a un juego de hockey. Así que muchas gracias de
todas maneras[4].

No tengo planes para el próximo fin de semana y tengo muchas ganas de verte[5].
¿Podemos organizar algo[6]?
¡Que te diviertas mucho![7]

Wayne

[1]*I would like* [2]*I can't* [3]*without* [4]**de...** *anyway* [5]*see you* [6]*something* [7]*Have fun!*

En papel: Lo siento, pero no puedo. A friend sends you an e-mail message inviting you to a
crafts fair (**una feria**) this weekend. You have a lot to do and cannot go. Write a reply explaining
your weekend plans. Use Wayne's letter as a model, paying special attention to the way that Wayne
politely declines the invitation.

161

¡A ver de nuevo!

Parte 1. Escribe de lo que se trató *(was about)* este episodio en tus propias *(own)* palabras.

¡Fíjate!

Your summary must include everybody's plans for the weekend. Be as specific as you can.

Ramón quiere organizar un picnic para Wayne porque…

Parte 2. Now compare your summary with a classmate's and add information you may have left out.

Práctica adicional			
Cuaderno de tareas pp. 169–170, K–L	invitaciones. vhlcentral.com Episodio 7	invitaciones. vhlcentral.com Lab practice	invitaciones. vhlcentral.com Episodio 7

Vocabulario del Episodio 7

ir a + [*infinitive*]   *to be going to +* [*infinitive*]
tener ganas de + [*infinitive*]   *to feel like...*
tener que + [*infinitive*]   *to have to...*

llevar a + [*person*]   *to take someone somewhere*
llevar + [*object*]   *to take something somewhere*
pagar la cuenta del celular   *to pay the cell phone bill*

Expresiones de tiempo

esta noche   *tonight*
hoy   *today*
mañana   *tomorrow*
este jueves   *this Thursday*
el próximo sábado   *next Saturday*
la próxima semana   *next week*
el año que viene   *next year*
el lunes   *on Monday*

Vocabulario personal

Write all the words that you need to know in Spanish so that you can talk in greater detail about your own obligations and weekend plans.

¡Fíjate!

Did you write down the activities that apply to you from pages 152 and 154?

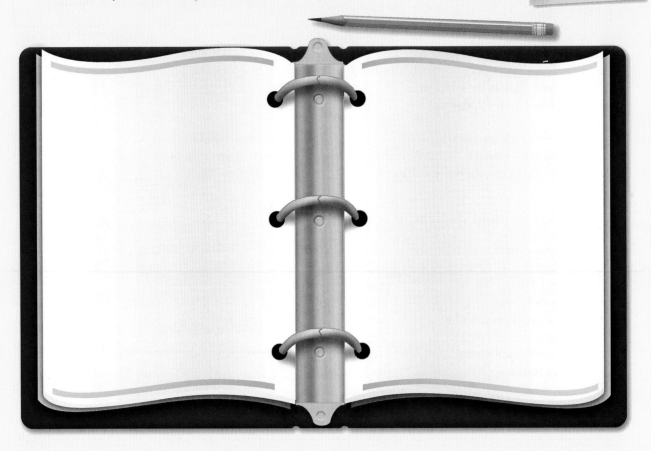

Cuaderno de tareas

Episodio

7

Escenas de la vida: ¿Qué van a hacer el sábado?

A. ¡A ver cuánto entendiste! See how much of the **Escena** you understood by matching the Spanish sentences with their English equivalents.

Después del examen

_____ 1. ¿Qué les parece a las dos?

_____ 2. Está solo y es su cumpleaños.

_____ 3. ¡Todos están invitados!

_____ 4. Paso el día con la familia.

_____ 5. Y usted, ¿puede ir?

_____ 6. Tenemos que hacer algo divertido
este fin de semana, ¿no?

_____ 7. Quiero organizar un picnic en el parque.

_____ 8. No tengo nada que hacer el domingo.

_____ 9. Hace años que no veo a Wayne.

_____10. Creo que no puedo ir.

a. I spend the day with my family.

b. I don't have to do anything
on Sunday.

c. How does two o'clock sound
to you?

d. We have to do something fun this
weekend, ok?

e. I want to organize a picnic in the park.

f. He's alone and it's his birthday.

g. Can you go?

h. I haven't seen Wayne in years.

i. I don't think I can go.

j. Everyone is invited!

B. ¿A quién se refieren? Indicate whether the statements refer to Manolo **(M)**,
Sofía **(S)**, Adriana **(A)**, or Ramón **(R)**.

_____ 1. Tiene que llevar a Jorge al aeropuerto.

_____ 2. Pasa el domingo con la familia.

_____ 3. Quiere organizar un picnic para Wayne.

_____ 4. Tiene que llevar a la gata al veterinario.

_____ 5. Tienen que trabajar el sábado.

_____ 6. Invita a todos al parque.

_____ 7. Tiene ganas de celebrar.

_____ 8. Tiene que estudiar más.

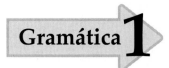

Gramática 1

Talking about weekend plans
- **ir a** + [*infinitive*]
- **The personal a**

C. Las actividades de la próxima semana. Describe what Sofía, her friends, and you are going to do next week.

Modelo   Mis hijos y yo

Mis hijos y yo vamos a visitar a los abuelos el domingo.

1.

2.

3.

4.

5.

6.

1. Viviana _____.

2. Ramón y su amiga _____.

3. Adriana y su familia _____.

4. Manolo y Ana Mari _____.

5. Nosotros _____.

6. Y tú, ¿ _____?

D. Los planes de Sofía y Manolo. Sofía and Manolo are making plans for the weekend. Look at the illustrations and describe what they are going to do. Sequence their activities in a cohesive paragraph. Use phrases like **por la mañana/tarde/noche, después, más tarde, también,** etc.

_____
_____
_____
_____
_____
_____
_____

E. ¿Y tus planes? Now describe your own weekend plans. Be specific and thorough.

_____
_____
_____
_____
_____
_____
_____

F. ¡En español! How would you say the following in Spanish?

1. Are you going to work next weekend?

_____

2. No, I am going to study for (**para**) a test.

_____

3. I am going to visit my grandmother in Utah next week, so (**entonces**) I am not going to be (**estar**) in class.

_____

4. But (**pero**) you are going to get an F.

_____

5. No, I am going to talk to the teacher tonight.

_____

Gramática 2 — Expressing obligations and desires
• Tener que, tener ganas de

G. Las actividades de nuestros amigos. Escribe la expresión necesaria para completar los comentarios. Después indica si son **ciertos** o **falsos.** Usa **tener que, tener ganas (de)** o **tener.**

	Cierto	Falso
1. Sofía dice: "Yo _____ hacer una presentación en el Club Latino."	☐	☐
2. Adriana _____ mucho trabajo en casa.	☐	☐
3. Manolo _____ llevar a Jorge al aeropuerto.	☐	☐
4. Los chicos _____ de ir al parque después de la clase.	☐	☐
5. Y tú, ¿_____ de ir a una fiesta este fin de semana?	☐	☐
6. Sí, pero (yo) _____ trabajar el domingo.	☐	☐

H. Las obligaciones. Describe the activities that you and the people you know usually have to do during the weekend.

> **Modelo**   Mi hijo **tiene que lavar su ropa.**

1. Yo _____.
2. Mi papá _____.
3. Mi mamá _____.
4. Mis hermanos/as _____.
5. Mi mejor amigo/a _____.

I. ¿Qué (no) tienen ganas de hacer? Indicate what the people feel like or don't feel like doing, according to the place or activity indicated.

> **Modelo**   Mi novia va a ir a la biblioteca.   **Tiene ganas de estudiar.**
> Yo voy a quedarme (*stay*) en casa.   **No tengo ganas de visitar a mis amigos.**

1. Voy a ir al centro comercial (*mall*)._____
2. Mis amigos y yo vamos a poner (*turn on*) el radio._____
3. Tú no vas a salir (*go out*) esta noche._____
4. Mis padres van a ir a la tienda de videos._____
5. Sofía y Ana Mari van a ir a una discoteca._____
6. Ramón va a usar la computadora._____

J. ¿Por qué no pueden salir? *(Why can't they go out?)* Explain why Ana Mari's brothers cannot go out to play on the days and at the times indicated.

> **Modelo**   lunes
> **El lunes a las doce tienen que ir a la biblioteca.**

semana 36		AGOSTO/SEPTIEMBRE
31 lunes	**1 martes**	**2 miércoles**
8	8	8
9	9	9
10	10	10
11	11	11
12 biblioteca	12	12
1	1	1
2	2	2
3	3	3
4	4	4
5	5	5
6 lavar el coche	6	6
7 de Ramón	7 estudiar	7
8	8	8

3 jueves	**4 viernes**	**5 sábado**
8	8	lavar la ropa
9	9	
10	10	
11	11	
12	12	**6 domingo**
1	1	
2	2 comprar	visitar a los
3	3 libros	abuelos
4	4	
5	5	
6	6	
7 limpiar el cuarto	7	
8	8	

1. _____
_____
2. _____
_____
3. _____
_____
4. _____
_____
5. _____
_____
6. _____
_____

Para terminar

K. Una invitación. Read the e-mail message Sofía's mother sent to her friend Liz. Then answer the questions in Spanish.

> From: Diana Blasio
> To: Liz Margolis
> Re: Invitación al teatro
>
> ───────────────────────────
>
> Hola Liz:
>
> Gracias por tu invitación al teatro esta noche, pero no voy a poder acompañarte. Tengo que trabajar hasta las cinco de la tarde y después voy a llevar a Lalo al doctor. No está bien. No tiene ganas de comer nada desde hace varios días y también tiene un poco de fiebre. Vamos a ver qué dice el doctor.
>
> Tengo muchas ganas de hablar contigo. ¿Tienes planes mañana por la noche? Llámame.
>
> Diana

1. Who is inviting Diana? _____

2. Where is she invited? _____

3. Why can't she go? _____

4. What is wrong with Lalo? _____

L. Para resumir la historia. Answer the questions about the **Escena**, using the images.

1. ¿Quién va a sacar A en el examen?

_____

2. ¿Quién tiene que estudiar mucho más?

_____

3. ¿Qué tiene ganas de hacer Ramón? ¿Por qué?

_____

4. ¿Por qué Adriana no puede (can't) ir al parque?

_____

5. ¿Qué tiene que hacer Manolo el sábado?

_____

6. ¿Quiénes van a ir al picnic?

_____

Episodio 8

Escenas de la vida: Vamos al parque

 A. ¡Mira cuánto puedes entender! Check the activities that you hear mentioned in the **Escena**.

☐

Sofía y mi hermana corren **en el parque.**

☐

Hace la tarea.

☐

Después comemos **en El Huarache Veloz.**

☐

No recibe **regalos el día de su cumpleaños.**

☐

Lee el periódico y su correo electrónico.

☐

Hacen ejercicio.

☐

Salen a **cenar.**

☐

Ve **películas en la computadora.**

☐

Ana Mari quiere salir **con Wayne.**

B. ¿Te diste cuenta? Indica si los comentarios son **ciertos** o **falsos**.

	Cierto	Falso
1. Wayne y Ramón van a jugar vóleibol mañana.	☐	☐
2. Wayne quiere comer en El Huarache Veloz con las chicas.	☐	☐
3. Ramón y Wayne van al parque a las 9 para correr.	☐	☐
4. Wayne lee el periódico en su computadora.	☐	☐
5. A Wayne le gusta Sofía.	☐	☐
6. Wayne tiene clases por la mañana.	☐	☐

C. Responde. Contesta las preguntas.

1. ¿Qué van a hacer Wayne y Ramón el domingo?

   a. Van a estudiar.　　b. Van a hacer la tarea.　　c. Van a correr.

2. ¿Qué actividad hace Wayne por la mañana?

   a. Mira la tele.　　b. Hace su tarea.　　c. Limpia su cuarto.

3. ¿Qué quiere hacer Wayne después de correr?

   a. Comer.　　b. Jugar tenis.　　c. Escribir un trabajo.

4. ¿Quién es adicto a su computadora?

   a. Ramón.　　b. Wayne.　　c. Sofía.

5. ¿Qué actividades hace Wayne en su computadora?

   a. Lee su correo.　　b. Escribe poemas.　　c. Habla con sus amigos.

El Retiro

Cultura a lo vivo

Large public parks in major Hispanic cities provide an important place for inexpensive recreational activities. For example, in Mexico City, **El Bosque de Chapultepec** is the oldest, most important, and largest park in the city. There are museums, a lake, rides, an area for picnics, a zoo, restaurants, outdoor cafés, and other activities. In Madrid, Spain, **El Retiro** has just as much variety. From spectacles like street performers, puppet shows, jugglers, mimes, and musical performances, to quick acupuncture sessions or yoga classes, this park offers much more than just a simple stroll or boat ride along its central lake. In Caracas, Venezuela, **Los Caobos** is one of the oldest parks in the city. People go to the park to relax, walk among the beautiful mahogany trees, go bird watching, and enjoy children's activities on weekends. These parks serve an important social function, since families may celebrate birthdays, anniversaries, or any family event at the park. Go to the Supersite to watch a *Flash cultura* episode on this topic.

Práctica adicional

Cuaderno de tareas
p. 191, A

invitaciones.
vhlcentral.com
Episodio 8

Para comunicarnos mejor

Gramática 1

Talking about common daily activities
- Regular **-er** and **-ir** verbs

You have used many regular **-ar** verbs, such as **trabajar** and **descansar**, to talk about some of your activities. When Ramón and Wayne talked, they used verbs ending in **-er** and **-ir** to talk about their activities. You will discover that the endings of these verbs are similar to the verbs you already know.

Analizar y descubrir

1. Complete these statements.

-ar verbs

a. invitar   Yo _____ a mis amigos al picnic.

b. descansar   ¿Tú _____ los fines de semana?

c. trabajar   Sofía _____ los sábados; por eso, no estudia.

d. celebrar   Nosotros _____ el cumpleaños de Wayne el domingo.

e. hablar   Los papás de Wayne _____ con él por teléfono.

2. Compare the verb endings you provided with the endings of the verb **comer** *(to eat)*.

Comer	
Yo **como** hamburguesas con frecuencia.	*I often eat hamburgers.*
¿Tú, qué **comes**?	*What do you eat?*
Sofía no **come** grasa.	*Sofía doesn't eat fat.*
Mi papá y yo no **comemos** carne.	*My dad and I don't eat meat.*
¿Ustedes también **comen** tortillas? ¿Vosotros también **coméis** tortillas? }	*Do you also eat tortillas?*
En Cuba no **comen** tacos.	*They don't eat tacos in Cuba.*

3. Now examine the endings of the verb **vivir** *(to live)*.

Vivir	
Yo **vivo** en San Diego.	*I live in San Diego.*
Tú, ¿dónde **vives**?	*Where do you live?*
Sofía **vive** cerca de la universidad.	*Sofía lives near the university.*
Mis hermanas y yo **vivimos** con mis papás.	*My sisters and I live with my parents.*
¿Dónde **viven** ustedes? ¿Dónde **vivís** vosotros? }	*Where do you live?*
Los abuelos de Ramón **viven** en México.	*Ramón's grandparents live in Mexico.*

4. In the following chart, fill in the endings of the **-ar (trabajar)**, **-er (comer)**, and **-ir (vivir)** verbs.

	-ar verbs	**-er verbs**	**-ir verbs**
yo	trabaj _____	com _____	viv _____
tú	trabaj _____	com _____	viv _____
usted/él/ella	trabaj _____	com _____	viv _____
nosotros/as	trabaj _____	com _____	viv _____
ustedes/ellos/ellas	trabaj _____	com _____	viv _____

5. Compare the endings of the **-ar** and **-er** verbs in the present tense. Where the **-ar** verbs have an **a**, the **-er** verbs have an _____ .

6. Compare the endings of the **-er** and **-ir** verbs. All endings of the **-er** and **-ir** verbs are the same except for the _____ and the _____ forms.

Here are some common **-er** and **-ir** verbs you may use to talk about your activities.

Más actividades: verbos **-er** e **-ir**

abrir	*to open*	**leer el periódico**	*to read the newspaper*
beber	*to drink*	**recibir correo electrónico**	*to receive (get) e-mail*
comer hamburguesas	*to eat hamburgers*	**regalos**	*gifts*
correr	*to run, to jog*	**salir* a cenar**	*to go out to dinner*
discutir (de/con)	*to discuss,*	**con los amigos**	*with friends*
	to argue (about/with)	**vender comida**	*to sell food*
escribir cartas	*to write letters*	**ver una película en casa**	*to watch a movie at home*
un trabajo	*a paper*	**vivir en/con**	*to live in/with*
hacer* la tarea	*to do homework*		
ejercicio	*to exercise*		

***hacer** and **salir** have a **g** in the **yo** form — **Yo hago** la tarea y **salgo** con mi novio.

7. Use these expressions to tell how often you do something.

¿Con qué frecuencia…?

todos los días	*every day*
con frecuencia	*often*
a veces	*sometimes*
una vez a la semana	*once a week*
dos veces al mes	*twice a month*
tres (cuatro…) veces al año	*three (four…) times a year*
siempre	*always*
(casi) nunca	*(almost) never*

Por la mañana siempre hago mi tarea y leo mi correo tranquilamente.

8. Use **deber** + [*infinitive*] to talk about what you *should/must do.*

Debo hacer la tarea todos los días.

PRÁCTICA

A. ¿Con qué frecuencia?

Parte 1. Usa expresiones de la página anterior para indicar con qué frecuencia tú o los miembros de tu familia hacen las siguientes cosas.

1. Leo el periódico. _____
2. Mi papá bebe café. _____
3. Discuto con mi papá. _____
4. Debo vender mis
   libros viejos. _____

5. Abro mi libro de español. _____
6. Vemos películas en casa. _____
7. Escribo mis trabajos en
   la computadora. _____
8. Mis abuelos comen en
   mi casa. _____

Parte 2. Convierte las oraciones de **Parte 1** en preguntas para entrevistar a un(a) compañero/a.

> **Modelo**   Leo el periódico.
> —¿Con qué frecuencia lees el periódico?
> —Casi nunca. ¿Y tú?
> —Yo leo la sección deportiva todos los días.

¡Fíjate!

Remember that **nunca** and **casi nunca** go before the verb. The other expressions of frequency may go before or after the verb.

B. En casa de Ramón. Termina la descripción usando las ilustraciones.

1.

2.

3.

En la casa de Ramón tienen la misma (*same*) rutina casi todos los sábados. Por la mañana, el papá de Ramón (1) _____, mientras que (*while*) su mamá (2) _____ escribir los cheques para pagar las cuentas (*pay the bills*). Los hermanos menores siempre (3) _____ el refrigerador para buscar bebidas; generalmente (4) _____ Coca-Cola u otra bebida poco saludable (*healthy*). A las dos de la tarde, toda la familia (5) _____ en su restaurante favorito: El Huarache Veloz. Después de comer, con frecuencia van a una tienda (*store*) donde (6) _____ todo a muy buen precio. Los niños siempre quieren comprar juguetes (*toys*).

4.

5.

6.

C. Submarino. First draw a submarine in five of the boxes on your grid. Then take turns asking your partner yes/no questions, matching an action pictured at the top of the grid with one of the subjects on the side. Use as many expressions of frequency as you can. See page 174.

> **Modelo**   —¿Adriana lee el periódico todos los días?
> —Sí, lee el periódico. *(If there is a submarine in that box.)*
> or
> —No, no lee el periódico. *(If there is not a submarine in that box.)*

Depending on your partner's answer, write **sí** or **no** in that box. If you answer **sí** to you partner's question, put an **X** through your submarine. It's been located! The first player to locate all five submarines wins.

¡Fíjate!

Be as creative as you can in your questions, using the frequency expressions on page 174. Don't just ask *Do you drink?*, try *Do you drink coffee frequently?* Put all the Spanish you know to use!

Tú				
Tus primos				
Adriana				
Ustedes				

D. Lotería.

Parte 1. Find out who does the following things. Write the name of a different classmate who respond *yes* to your question in each box. Ask appropriate questions according to the model. The first student to form three straight lines wins the game.

| Modelo | —¿Comes pizza con frecuencia? |
| | —Sí, como pizza dos veces a la semana. ¿Y tú? |

Come pizza con frecuencia.	No baila en las fiestas.	Corre tres veces a la semana.	Abre su libro de español todos los días.
Discute mucho con su hermano/a.	Hace la tarea en la biblioteca.	Recibe muchos correos de sus amigos.	Debe pagar (*pay*) la cuenta del celular.
Sale con su novio/a los sábados.	Vive con su familia.	No lee el periódico.	Vende sus libros viejos al final del semestre.
Nunca hace ejercicio.	Ve una película cada semana.	Debe visitar a los abuelos una vez al año.	Siempre escribe sus trabajos o tareas en la computadora.

Parte 2. Comparte las respuestas con la clase.

Modelo	Estudiante 1:	**John no baila en las fiestas.**
	Estudiante 2:	**¿Qué haces en las fiestas, John?**
	John:	**Hablo con mis amigos.**

Práctica adicional

Cuaderno de tareas
pp.192–196, B–G

invitaciones.
vhlcentral.com
Episodio 8

Gramática 2

Identifying places to go and places to be
• Ir a + [*place*] and estar en + [*place*]

You have used the verbs **ir** and **estar** already. We practiced **ir a** to express the future (**Mañana voy a bailar con mis amigos**). **Ir** is also used to indicate where someone is going: **Siempre voy al Museo de Historia los jueves.** We used **estar** to find out how someone is, as in ¿**Cómo estás**? **Estar** is also used to indicate where someone or something is located, as in ¿**Dónde estás**? **Estoy en la escuela.** Notice that you need the preposition **en**.

Read the following examples to examine the present-tense forms of **estar**.

Estar en	
Estoy en el Museo del Oro.	*I'm at the Museo del Oro.*
Estás en casa, ¿verdad?	*You're at home, right?*
El lago **está en** el centro del parque.	*The lake is in the center of the park.*
¿**En** qué museo **estamos**?	*What museum are we at?*
Uds. **están en** el Museo del Prado. Vosotros **estáis en** el Museo del Prado. }	*You are at the Prado Museum.*
Algunos cuadros de Picasso **están en** el Museo Nacional Reina Sofía.	*Some of Picasso's paintings are at the Reina Sofía National Museum.*

¡Fíjate!

Ser and **estar** both mean *to be*, but they are used differently. To learn about the differences between the two, go to **Apéndice A: Gramática comunicativa**, p. 408.

The verb **ir** usually requires the preposition **a.** Read the following examples.

Las personas van...	*People go...*
al parque	*to the park*
a los museos	*to the museums*
a la discoteca	*to the nightclub (disco)*
a las exhibiciones de arte	*to art exhibitions*

The word **el** forms contractions with the prepositions **a** and **de**: **al** (**a** + **el** = **al**) and **del** (**de** + **el** = **del**). These are used before masculine singular nouns.

¿Vamos a la oficina **del** profesor López?

Bueno, pero después vamos **al** laboratorio de computadoras.

¿Tienes el teléfono **del** doctor Aspin?

Sofía y Manolo están en la cafetería de la universidad.

Wayne está en su cama. Está enfermo.

You have already learned the names of many places at the university or college. Here are some places where people can go in the city.

Más lugares en la ciudad

(No) Voy...	I (don't) go...
al aeropuerto	to the airport
al boliche	to the bowling alley
al café	to the café
a la casa de mi novio/a	to my boyfriend's/girlfriend's house
a la casa de mis amigos/padres	to my friends'/parents' house
al centro comercial	to the mall
al cine	to the movie theater
a la discoteca	to the nightclub (disco)
al/a la doctor(a)	to the doctor
a la escuela	to school
a la exhibición de arte	to the art exhibition
a la iglesia/a misa	to church/Mass
al museo	to the museum
a ninguna parte	nowhere/anywhere
al partido de fútbol	to the soccer game
a la playa	to the beach
a un restaurante	to a restaurant
al supermercado	to the supermarket
a la tienda	to the store
al trabajo	to work

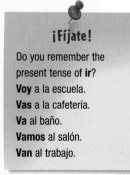

¡Fíjate!

Do you remember the present tense of **ir**?
Voy a la escuela.
Vas a la cafetería.
Va al baño.
Vamos al salón.
Van al trabajo.

También se dice...

discoteca ⟶ antro, club nocturno, bar

a la iglesia: depende de la religión, se usa **a la sinagoga** o **al templo.**

PRÁCTICA

E. Una llamada telefónica. Llama por teléfono a un(a) compañero/a para saber (to find out) dónde está y qué va a hacer allí. Empareja los lugares con las actividades.

Modelo	parque ⟶ hacer ejercicio un rato
	—¿Dónde estás ahora?
	—Estoy en el parque.
	—¿Qué vas a hacer allí?
	—Voy a hacer ejercicio un rato.

1. playa
2. casa de mi novio/a
3. supermercado
4. boliche
5. casa
6. cine
7. restaurante
8. discoteca

a. ver una película española
b. escribir un trabajo en la computadora
c. comer con una amiga
d. correr con unos amigos
e. bailar con mis amigos/as
f. jugar boliche con mis primas
g. mirar la tele y descansar un rato
h. comprar la comida para la fiesta

F. ¿Es fácil localizarte? Indica dónde estás en los días y a las horas mencionadas. Después compara tus respuestas con las de un(a) compañero/a.

¿Dónde estás...	_Estoy en mi casa._
1. los lunes a las siete de la mañana?	_____
2. los miércoles a las diez de la mañana?	_____
3. los jueves a las dos de la tarde?	_____
4. los viernes por la noche?	_____
5. los sábados por la mañana?	_____
6. los domingos al mediodía?	_____

G. ¿Cuántas veces? *(How often?)*

Parte 1. En grupos de tres personas, contesten las preguntas para decidir quién es la persona **más activa** o **más tranquila**.

Nombres _____   _____   _____

En el transcurso *(course)* de un mes, ¿con qué frecuencia...

1. vas al cine?	_____	_____	_____
2. comes en un restaurante?	_____	_____	_____
3. vas a las discotecas?	_____	_____	_____
4. vas al centro comercial?	_____	_____	_____
5. vas al parque?	_____	_____	_____
6. vas a casa de tus amigos?	_____	_____	_____
7. vas al boliche?	_____	_____	_____

Parte 2. Ahora compartan la información con el resto de la clase. Usen expresiones como:

Modelo	Nancy es la más activa porque va a las discotecas tres veces al mes. Larry es el más tranquilo porque nunca va al cine ni a las discotecas.

¡Fíjate!

When using **a ninguna parte** *(nowhere/anywhere)*, place **no** before the verb. **Los domigos no voy a ninguna parte.**

H. ¿Adónde vas? Indica adónde vas en cada situación. Usa **voy**.

¿Adónde vas...

1. cuando tienes ganas de beber algo? _____

2. cuando tienes que estudiar? _____

3. cuando tienes ganas de comer comida italiana? _____

4. cuando estás enfermo/a *(sick)*? _____

5. después de tus clases? _____

6. cuando no tienes ganas de hablar con nadie *(anybody)*? _____

7. cuando estás aburrido/a? _____

I. ¿Dónde estás ahora y adónde vas después? Usa las ilustraciones para indicar a un(a) compañero/a dónde están las personas ahora, adónde van después y por qué. Usa **tener ganas de, tener que** u otros verbos.

Mis hermanos pero después porque...

Modelo	Mis hermanos están en casa ahora, pero después van al aeropuerto porque tienen ganas de ver a sus abuelos de México.

1. Adriana pero después porque...

¡Fíjate!

Remember to use **en** after **estar** and **a** after **ir.** Be as creative as you can in your explanations. Use all the Spanish you have acquired!

2. Mi mamá pero después porque...

3. Yo pero después porque...

4. Mis amigas y yo pero después porque...

5. Mis compañeros de clase pero después porque...

J. La historia va así.

Parte 1. Look carefully at each of the eight images. Then, as you listen to Wayne's plans for Saturday, identify the sequence of events by placing the numbers 1 through 8 next to the appropriate image. Check your answers when you listen to Wayne's plans the second time.

Parte 2. En grupos de tres, escriban la historia en diferente orden.

Práctica adicional

Cuaderno de tareas
pp. 196–200, H–N

invitaciones.
vhlcentral.com
Lab practice

invitaciones.
vhlcentral.com
Episodio 8

Actividades comunicativas

 A. Actividades, obligaciones, deseos y planes semanales.

Instrucciones para **Estudiante 1**

First, ask your partner the necessary questions in order to fill in all the missing information. You each have the information your partner needs. Then, ask your partner about their activities and write them under **Mi compañero/a** column.

Modelo	¿Qué hace Sofía por las tardes?
	¿Qué tienen ganas de hacer Ramón y Wayne...?
	¿Dónde estás...?

	Sofía	Ramón y Wayne	Wayne	Mi compañero/a
Actividades de rutina	una vez a la semana			
Deseos (tener ganas de)		los sábados por la noche	los viernes después de clase	
Obligaciones (tener que...)	tres veces a la semana	Account Number 0123456 Phone Bill Summary Access Charges $69.99 Usage Charges Voice $0.00 Data $6.00 Total Charges $75.99	para sus clases	
Lugares (estar en...)		los domingos		

A. Actividades, obligaciones, deseos y planes semanales.

Instrucciones para Estudiante 2

First, ask your partner the necessary questions in order to fill in all the missing information. You each have the information your partner needs. Then, ask your partner about their activities and write them under the **Mi compañero/a** column.

Modelo	¿Qué hace Wayne los sábados por la tarde?
	¿Qué tienen ganas de hacer Ramón y Wayne...?
	¿Dónde está Sofía...?

	Sofía	Ramón y Wayne	Wayne	Mi compañero/a
Actividades de rutina		los sábados por la mañana	a las cinco	
Deseos (tener ganas de)	los sábados por la mañana			
Obligaciones (tener que...)		cada mes		
Lugares (estar en...)	de 4 a 6 de la tarde		los jueves a las seis y cuarto de la tarde	

B. Cosas en común.

Parte 1. First answer the questions in the column labeled **Yo**. Then look for classmates whose answers are the same as yours and write their names in the column labeled **Compañero/a**.

> **Modelo** —¿Qué bebes en las fiestas?
> —Coca–Cola. ¿Y tú?
> —Yo también.   or   —Yo bebo agua.

	Yo	Compañero/a
1. Generalmente, ¿qué bebes en las fiestas?	_____	_____
2. ¿Con quién discutes más?	_____	_____
3. ¿Dónde vives?	_____	_____
4. ¿A qué hora comes los sábados?	_____	_____
5. ¿Qué vas a hacer hoy después de clase?	_____	_____
6. ¿A qué hora llegas a la escuela los martes?	_____	_____
7. ¿Recibes regalos el día de San Valentín?	_____	_____
8. ¿Dónde estás los lunes a las 8:00 de la mañana?	_____	_____
9. ¿Con quién sales los fines de semana?	_____	_____
10. ¿Con qué frecuencia haces ejercicio?	_____	_____

Parte 2. Be prepared to share your findings with the class.

> **Modelo**   Lupe y yo bebemos Coca–Cola en las fiestas.

C. ¡A hablar! In groups of four, find out who has the healthiest lifestyle. You will determine this based on the number of times per week they exercise, eat fruits and vegetables (**frutas y verduras**), go out, rest, how many hours they watch TV, read, listen to music, talk to their family, study, and do homework. Be ready to share your findings with the class.

Nombre	Actividad	Frecuencia
_____	_____	_____
_____	_____	_____
_____	_____	_____
_____	_____	_____
_____	_____	_____
_____	_____	_____
_____	_____	_____
_____	_____	_____

La correspondencia

 El correo: El regreso a la escuela. Lee las preguntas; luego lee la carta que Adriana le escribe a su hermana en Puerto Rico. Después contesta las preguntas.

1. ¿Cómo está Adriana?

_____

2. ¿Cómo son los compañeros según *(according to)* Adriana?

_____

3. ¿Por qué Adriana no tiene tiempo para cocinar ni limpiar?

_____

4. ¿Ahora quién tiene que lavar y cocinar?

_____

5. ¿Quién apoya y ayuda a Adriana?

_____

Querida hermana: 15 de octubre

¿Cómo estás? Yo estoy muy bien. Estudiar en la universidad es una experiencia fabulosa.

Éste es el segundo mes de clases y todavía[1] estoy muy nerviosa. Tengo clases muy interesantes, pero tengo que dedicar mucho tiempo a leer y estudiar. Los fines de semana no salgo mucho porque tengo que escribir trabajos y buscar información en Internet constantemente.

Por suerte[2] tengo unos compañeros de clase muy buenos y siempre me invitan a estudiar con ellos. Aunque[3] son muy jóvenes (tienen la edad de Carlos, ¿te imaginas?), son responsables e inteligentes, y siempre me incluyen en sus actividades.

Desafortunadamente para Santiago, ahora él tiene que cocinar[4] y lavar, pues yo no tengo tiempo (ni ganas) para cocinar, limpiar y lavar. No le gusta mucho la situación. También creo que está un poco celoso[5] de mis actividades y mis nuevos amigos. Por suerte, a Viviana, a Santiaguito y a Carlos les gusta mucho que yo estudie, y por eso me apoyan y me ayudan[6] en la casa. Escríbeme pronto.

Tu hermana que te quiere,
Adriana

[1]*still* [2]*Luckily* [3]*Although* [4]*to cook* [5]*jealous* [6]***me...*** *support me and help me*

Invitación a **México**

In your own words. Read the information below in order to write what you understood. In English, summarize the information in two or three sentences. Do not translate.

_____

_____

Del álbum de
Sofía

Con más de 20 millones de habitantes, la Ciudad de México tiene actividades recreativas, culturales y de entretenimiento las 24 horas del día. Los fines de semana, la gente (*people*) va al Bosque de Chapultepec, a Coyoacán o a Xochimilco, donde encuentran diversas actividades para toda la familia. La ciudad está llena (*full*) de museos famosos, como el Museo de Antropología, el de Arte Moderno, el Museo Casa de Frida Kahlo, el Museo del Niño o el Museo Nacional de Historia en el Castillo de Chapultepec. Ve al Supersitio para mirar un episodio de *Flash cultura* sobre este tema.

Puerta del Museo Casa de Frida Kahlo.

1. What kind of place do you think the *Bosque de Chapultepec* is, given the activities people can do there?
2. What is the *Museo del Niño*?
3. When you visit a new city, what kind of places do you visit?

En papel: Los fines de semana. Write to Adriana about how you and your family and friends spend your weekends. Describe where you go, what you do at home, and how you prepare for school.

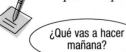

¡A ver de nuevo!

Parte 1. In your own words, write a description of what Ramón wants to do with Wayne at the park. Explain why he wants Wayne to go.

¿Qué vas a hacer mañana?

Tengo muchas cosas que hacer.

Ramón llama a Wayne por teléfono…

Parte 2. Now work with a partner to add any information you may have left out.

Práctica adicional			
Cuaderno de tareas p. 200, Ñ	invitaciones. vhlcentral.com Episodio 8	invitaciones. vhlcentral.com Lab practice	invitaciones. vhlcentral.com Episodio 8

Vocabulario del Episodio 8

Expresiones verbales

estar en	*to be (at/in)*
ir a + [*place*]	*to go to*
al	*to the*
a la (los, las)	*to the*

Más actividades: verbos **-er** e **-ir**

abrir	*to open*
beber	*to drink*
comer hamburguesas	*to eat hamburgers*
correr	*to run, to jog*
deber	*should/must*
discutir (de/con)	*to discuss, to argue (about/with)*
escribir cartas	*to write letters*
un trabajo	*a paper*
hacer ejercicio	*to exercise*
la tarea	*to do homework*
leer el periódico	*to read the newspaper*
recibir correo electrónico	*to receive (get) e-mail*
regalos	*gifts*
salir a cenar	*to go out to dinner*
con los amigos	*with friends*
vender comida	*to sell food*
ver una película en casa	*to watch a movie at home*
vivir en/con	*to live in/with*

¿Con qué frecuencia...? *How often…?*

todos los días	*every day*
con frecuencia	*often*
a veces	*sometimes*
una vez a la semana	*once a week*
dos veces al mes	*twice a month*
tres (cuatro...) veces al año	*three (four...) times a year*
siempre	*always*
(casi) nunca	*(almost) never*

Los lugares en la ciudad *Places in the city*

el aeropuerto	*airport*
el boliche	*bowling alley*
el café	*café*
la casa de mi novio/a	*my boyfriend's/girlfriend's house*
la casa de mis amigos/padres	*my friends'/parents' house*

189

el centro comercial	mall
el cine	movie theater
la discoteca	nightclub (disco)
el/la doctor(a)	doctor
la escuela	school
la exhibición de arte	art exhibition
la iglesia/misa	church/Mass
el museo	museum
ninguna parte, (a)	nowhere/anywhere
el parque	park
el partido de fútbol	soccer game
la playa	beach
el restaurante	restaurant
el supermercado	supermarket
la tienda	store
el trabajo	work

Vocabulario personal

Write the words you need to know to talk about the places you like to go to and the activities you like to do.

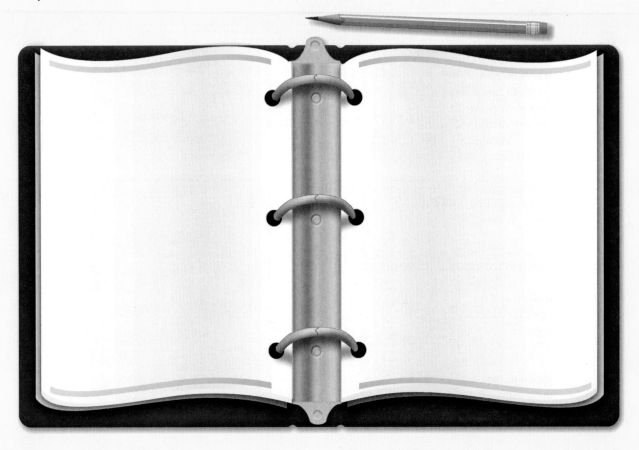

Cuaderno de tareas

Episodio 8

Escenas de la vida: Vamos al parque

 A. ¡A ver cuánto entendiste! See how much of the **Escena** you understood by matching the Spanish sentences with their English equivalents.

En el parque

_____ 1. Hace mucho que no hacemos ejercicio juntos.

_____ 2. Además, ¿no quieres ver a Sofía?

_____ 3. Todo listo. Ya convencí a Wayne de ir al parque mañana.

_____ 4. Bueno, ¿y cómo lo convenciste?

_____ 5. Le dije que Sofía muere por salir con él.

a. I told him that Sofía is dying to go out with him.

b. Besides, don't you want to see Sofía?

c. We haven't exercised together for a while.

d. All done! I convinced Wayne to go to the park tomorrow.

e. Good, and how did you convince him?

¿Dónde y cuándo?

_____ 6. Qué, ¿la usa mucho?

_____ 7. ¿Vamos a correr un par de millas?

_____ 8. Vamos a vernos a las dos.

_____ 9. Leo mi correo tranquilamente.

_____ 10. Hace todo en su computadora.

f. I read my mail in peace.

g. He does everything on his computer.

h. Should we run a couple of miles?

i. What, does he use it a lot?

j. We are going to meet at two.

Gramática 1

Taking about common daily activities
• **Regular -er and -ir verbs**

B. Actividades para todos. Use the expressions to complete the description of the park.

venden	museos
ejercicio	familias
restaurantes	correr
comer	celebrar
leer	discutir

El Bosque de Chapultepec

Muchas personas van al Bosque de Chapultepec en la Ciudad de México a hacer (1) _____ o van a (2) _____ alrededor del lago (*around the lake*). Otros simplemente van a descansar, estudiar, (3) _____, escribir o conversar bajo los árboles (*trees*). Los domingos muchas (4) _____ hacen picnics para (5) _____ cumpleaños y aniversarios. Alrededor del lago hay bares, cafés y (6) _____ donde la gente va a (7) _____, a beber y a escuchar música. Hay centros culturales donde (8) _____ artesanía (*handicrafts*) mexicana y recuerdos (*souvenirs*). Hay conciertos de música al aire libre (*outdoor*), exhibiciones en los (9) _____ y clases de pintura (*painting*) y teatro.

C. Manolo y su compañero de cuarto.

Parte 1. Escribe los verbos necesarios de la página 189 para completar el texto acerca de la vida de Manolo y su compañero de cuarto.

Manolo, el amigo cubano de Sofía, no (1) _____ con su familia. Sus padres (2) _____ en Miami, y él (3) _____ en California con un amigo. Manolo les (4) _____ correos electrónicos a sus padres con frecuencia, pues es más barato[1] que llamarlos por teléfono. Él también (5) _____ muchos correos electrónicos de sus padres y de sus familiares de Cuba.

Manolo y Jorge, su compañero de cuarto, a veces (6) _____ de política cubana. Pero en general, ellos tienen muchas cosas en común; por ejemplo, la comida y el gusto por los libros.

A Jorge le gusta estar siempre en buena condición física[2]; por eso, él (7) _____ dos millas todos los días. A Manolo no le gusta (8) _____, pero le gusta jugar fútbol. Manolo y Jorge desean estar saludables[3]; por eso, ellos siempre (9) _____ comida nutritiva y (10) _____ mucha agua[4].

[1]**más...** *cheaper* [2]**en...** *in good shape* [3]*healthy* [4]*water*

Parte 2. Ahora contesta las preguntas.

1. ¿Por qué Manolo escribe y recibe muchos correos electrónicos?

_____

_____

2. ¿Qué es importante para Manolo y Jorge?

_____

_____

3. ¿Qué hacen para estar en buena condición física?

_____

_____

D. Más actividades. Sofía habla de las actividades de los fines de semana. Escribe frases lógicas.

1. mis padres / leer / periódico / la mañana

_____

2. mi mamá / escribir / cartas

_____

3. yo / ver / películas / con Ana Mari / viernes

_____

4. Lalo / nunca / abrir / libros / fines de semana

_____

5. Lalo y mi papá / discutir / porque / Lalo / ser / irresponsable

_____

6. por la noche / nosotros / deber / hacer / ejercicio

_____

Sofía

¡Fíjate!
Remember to conjugate the verbs appropriately!

E. Actividades frecuentes. Write a complete sentence describing each illustration. Include how often the activity takes place.

Modelo

Adriana a veces habla por teléfono con los clientes.

1.

2.

3.

1. Y tú, ¿ _____ ?
2. Adriana y su esposo _____
3. Wayne _____
4. Ana Mari y Sofía _____
5. Yo siempre _____
6. Mi primo y yo _____

4.

5.

6.

F. ¿Qué hacen? Write five true statements about your family, friends, or instructors using elements from the columns. If you like, add additional information.

> **Modelo**   Mi amiga Angie come hamburguesas una vez a la semana.

	comer		
siempre	hacer la tarea	en la casa	una vez a la semana
a veces	salir con	hamburguesas	con frecuencia
casi nunca	leer novelas	amigos	todos los días
nunca	discutir con	novio/a	por la noche

¡Fíjate!
Notice that some frequency expressions are placed before the verb and some are placed at the end of the sentence. For **Práctica F**, use only one expression per sentence.

1. _____
2. _____
3. _____
4. _____
5. _____

G. Las obligaciones y los deseos. Explain what the characters and you feel like doing but can't and why.

> **Modelo**   Adriana tiene ganas de descansar, pero debe trabajar porque necesita dinero.

1. Wayne _____
_____
_____
_____

2. Ana Mari y Ramón _____

_____

_____

_____

3. Manolo y yo _____

_____

_____

_____

Gramática 2   **Identifying places to go and places to be**
- <u>ir a</u> + [*place*] and <u>estar en</u> + [*place*]

H. ¿Dónde están? Sofía reveals where she and her friends are on different days and at different times. Complete her statements with the appropriate forms of **estar**.

1. Los lunes por la mañana, mis amigos y yo _____ en la clase de cálculo.

2. Los martes a las seis, la Sra. Barrón _____ en el trabajo.

3. Los miércoles por la tarde, generalmente Ramón y Wayne _____ en casa.

4. Los jueves a las doce, (yo) _____ en la clase de geología.

5. Y tú, ¿dónde _____ a esa hora?

Nombre _____ Fecha _____

I. ¿Y a qué hora, Sofía? Sofía's mother always wants to know where her daughter is going and when she will come back. Complete the mother's questions and Sofía's answers, using contractions where necessary.

> **Modelo**   —¿Adónde vas, Sofía?
> —Voy **al** cine.
> —¿Y a qué hora llegas **del cine**?

Sofía   **Mamá**

1. —Voy _____ casa de Ana Mari.

   —¿Y a qué hora llegas _____?

2. —Voy _____ biblioteca.

   —¿Y a qué hora llegas _____?

3. —Voy _____ trabajo.

   —¿Y a qué hora llegas _____?

4. —Voy _____ museo.

   —¿Y a qué hora llegas _____?

5. —Voy _____ exhibición de arte.

   —¿Y a qué hora llegas _____?

¡Fíjate!

Del indicates *where you arrive or return from*, with the expression **llegar de**.
Vamos a llegar *del* **aeropuerto a las dos.**

J. ¿Adónde vas? Indicate where you go when you want to do the following things.

> **Modelo**   Voy **a la biblioteca** cuando tengo ganas de estudiar.

1. Voy _____ cuando tengo ganas de correr.

2. Voy _____ cuando tengo ganas de escuchar música.

3. Voy _____ cuando necesito hablar con un profesor.

4. Voy _____ cuando necesito comprar un regalo.

5. Voy _____ cuando tengo ganas de nadar y tomar el sol.

6. Voy _____ cuando necesito comprar la comida para toda la semana.

7. Voy _____ cuando tengo que trabajar.

8. Voy _____ cuando no tengo ganas de comer en mi casa.

K. ¿De quién son las cosas? Say to whom the following things belong. Use an element from each column.

Modelo	Estos pacientes son del Dr. Pérez.

gato			profesor
mochilas		del	estudiante de literatura
oficina	es	de la	jugadores/as (*players*)
novela	son	de los	Sr. López
video		de las	niño

¡Fíjate!

de + el = del

Del is used to express *to whom something belongs*, often with the expression **ser de.**

¿Este coche nuevo es *del* hijo de Adriana?

1. _____

2. _____

3. _____

4. _____

5. _____

L. ¡Adivina! (*Guess!*) Look at the images and write where the characters are now.

> **Modelo**
>
> Manolo va a hablar con el doctor.
> **Está en la clínica veterinaria.**

1. Sofía va a lavar su ropa.

_____

2. Adriana va a comprar la comida.

_____

3. Ramón y yo vamos a mirar una película.

_____

4. Ana Mari va comprar ropa nueva.

_____

5. Yo voy a hacer un poco de ejercicio.

_____

6. Adriana va a comprar libros para sus hijos.

_____

7. ¿Tú vas a ver a tus amigos?

_____

8. Wayne y Ramón van a tomar el sol y jugar vóleibol.

_____

M. ¿Cuándo vas? Write how often you go to the following places and explain why.

cine	**casa de mis abuelos**	**iglesia (a misa)**
trabajo	**centro comercial**	**tienda de videos**

> **Modelo**   a ninguna parte
> **Muchos domingos no voy a ninguna parte porque tengo que hacer tarea.**

1. _____

_____

2. _____

_____

3. _____

_____

4. _____

_____

5. _____

_____

6. _____

_____

N. ¿Qué tienes que hacer? Explain what you have to do at each place using **tengo ganas de** or **tengo que**.

> **Modelo**   ¿Estás en el aeropuerto?
> **Sí, porque tengo que llevar a Jorge; va a Miami.**

1. ¿Estás en la discoteca? _____

_____

2. ¿Estás en el parque? _____

_____

3. ¿Estás en la librería? _____

_____

4. ¿Estás en el supermercado? _____

_____

5. ¿Estás en la casa de tus padres? _____

_____

6. ¿Estás en un restaurante? _____

_____

Para terminar

Ñ. Una miniprueba para terminar. Complete the following communicative tasks to test your knowledge of the content of the episode.

1. Ask Sofía and Ana Mari:

    a. if they watch TV programs in Spanish.
    b. how many times a week they run.
    c. if they argue with their parents.
    d. where they live.

2. Ask Adriana:

    e. if she sells her books at the end of the (**al final del**) semester.
    f. what she feels like doing this weekend.
    g. what her kids have to do on Sundays.

1.

    a. _____
    b. _____
    c. _____
    d. _____

2.

    e. _____
    f. _____
    g. _____

Episodio

9

Escenas de la vida: ¡Qué rica comida!

 A. ¡Mira cuánto puedes entender! Mira el video o escucha la **Escena** para contestar las preguntas.

1. ¿Qué comida llevan los chicos al parque?

sándwiches	carne para asar
salsa	pasteles puertorriqueños
refrescos	pastel
helado	flan
frutas	tortillas
verduras	arroz
guacamole	papas

2. ¿Cómo se prepara la carne en casa de Ramón? Selecciona los ingredientes.

Cultura a lo vivo

In the Spanish-speaking world, meals are important social events. **La comida,** the principal meal, usually begins at one and lasts until three in the afternoon. People generally go home to eat with family members and rest before returning to work for a few more hours. In Spain, for example, most small stores are closed between one and three so people can return home.

Since Spanish speakers like to relax and to enjoy the food and conversation, a meal in a restaurant may last as long as three hours. For this reason, it would be extremely rude for the server to bring the check right after the meal has been served. Servers wait until the customer asks for the check. These days, Latin food has become so popular in the United States that you can find the dishes you desire in many local restaurants. Go to the Supersite to watch a *Flash cultura* episode on this topic.

3. ¿Qué comida pide Wayne cuando sale a comer?

 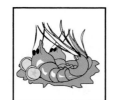 

4. ¿Qué comida sirven en El Rincón Caribeño?

a. mexicana   c. china

b. cubana   d. puertorriqueña

B. ¿Te diste cuenta? Indica si los comentarios son **ciertos** o **falsos.**

	Cierto	Falso
1. No es necesario ser puntual para las fiestas.	☐	☐
2. A Wayne le gusta mucho la comida puertorriqueña.	☐	☐
3. En México no hay chili.	☐	☐
4. Los pasteles puertorriqueños tienen plátano verde y carne.	☐	☐
5. El plato favorito de Manolo es arroz con carne de cerdo.	☐	☐
6. Los chicos están en el café.	☐	☐

C. El picnic. Contesta las preguntas.

1. ¿Por qué llegan tarde Ana Mari y Sofía? _____
2. ¿Quién sabe *(knows)* el secreto para preparar carne? _____
3. ¿Qué llevó Manolo al picnic? _____
4. ¿Qué pide Manolo en El Rincón Caribeño? _____
5. ¿Pica la salsa? _____

Práctica adicional
Cuaderno de tareas p. 221, A–B   invitaciones.vhlcentral.com Episodio 9

Para comunicarnos mejor

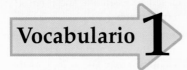

Vocabulario 1

Talking about food
• **Food and meals**

El desayuno

la leche

las peras

los plátanos

las manzanas

las uvas

el yogurt

el cereal

el café   los huevos   el pan tostado

El almuerzo

los refrescos
la sopa
la limonada
el jamón
los sándwiches de atún
la ensalada
de lechuga y tomate
las papas fritas
el espagueti
el pavo
el pollo
la sal y la pimienta
las hamburguesas

También se dice...

refrescos ➔ gaseosas

papas ➔ patatas

plátanos ➔ bananas, guineos

¿Qué tienes ganas de cenar?

No sé todavía, pero tengo mucha hambre. ¿Y tú?

Cultura a lo vivo

In the Spanish-speaking world, table manners are important. It is disrespectful to start eating before everyone has been served, to put your elbows on the table, to speak with your mouth full, or to leave the table before everyone has finished eating. When leaving the table, Spanish speakers usually say: **Con permiso, buen provecho** (*Excuse me, bon appétit*).

Although the morning and evening meals vary from country to country, breakfast **(el desayuno)** and dinner **(la cena)** are generally light and less formal. Dinner or supper takes place between 8 and 10 in the evening, and often consists of leftovers from **la comida,** or coffee and bread. Go to the Supersite to watch an authentic clip on this subject.

Para hablar de las comidas en un restaurante

desayunar	*to have breakfast*	el plato/platillo	*dish*
comer	*to eat; to have lunch*	el/la mesero/a	*waiter/waitress*
almorzar	*to have lunch*	la cuenta	*bill*
cenar	*to have dinner/supper*	el desayuno	*breakfast*
tener hambre	*to be hungry*	el almuerzo	*lunch*
tener sed	*to be thirsty*	la cena	*dinner/supper*

La cena

el vino tinto
la cerveza
el agua
los dulces
las galletas
los camarones
el arroz
los frijoles
el pescado
el pastel
el helado
la carne de cerdo
las zanahorias
el brócoli
las papas al horno
el bistec de res
la langosta

Otro vocabulario

la bebida	drink	la fruta	fruit
la carne	meat	el jugo de naranja	orange juice
la carne de res	beef	los mariscos	seafood
la dona	donut	el postre	dessert
la ensalada de	lettuce and tomato	el queso	cheese
lechuga y tomate	salad	el té	tea
el flan	flan	la verdura	vegetable

PRÁCTICA

A. Asociaciones. ¿Qué platos y bebidas asocias con las siguientes comidas?

1. la comida china
2. la comida italiana
3. la comida mexicana
4. la comida norteamericana
5. la comida japonesa
6. la comida vegetariana

B. ¿Tienes una dieta saludable (healthy)? Marca con un círculo la mejor (best) respuesta según tus hábitos de comida.

Un "test" de nutrición

1. Generalmente, desayuno...
a. leche y cereal.
b. café y pan tostado.
c. huevos con frijoles.
d. nada.

2. Generalmente, ceno...
a. pescado y verduras.
b. pollo con arroz.
c. espagueti, o arroz y frijoles.
d. carne con papas.

3. En una fiesta prefiero beber...
a. jugo.
b. refresco.
c. vino.
d. cerveza.

4. Me gusta comer sándwiches de...
a. atún.
b. pavo.
c. jamón y queso.
d. mantequilla de cacahuate[1] con mermelada.

5. Generalmente, para el almuerzo como...
a. sopa y ensalada.
b. un yogurt con fruta.
c. un sándwich de jamón y queso.
d. una hamburguesa con papas fritas.

6. Cuando tengo sed, bebo...
a. agua.
b. limonada.
c. jugo de fruta.
d. refrescos.

7. Mi postre favorito es...
a. frutas.
b. galletas.
c. dulces.
d. helado con pastel.

Convierte las letras en números
(1 por cada a, 2-b, 3-c, 4-d) y suma
tus preguntas.

Marcador[2] _____

Interpreta tus resultados

De 7 a 14. ¡Bravo! Seguramente eres una persona consciente de la salud[3]. Tienes buenos hábitos de comida. Probablemente eres muy organizado/a y haces ejercicio regularmente.

De 15 a 22. ¡Muy bien! Probablemente eres una persona consciente de la salud, pero a veces sucumbes a la tentación de comer cosas con muchas calorías o grasas. Seguramente haces ejercicio para compensar.

De 23 a 28. ¡Qué barbaridad! Seguramente no tienes tiempo de preparar comidas saludables. Tienes que incluir en tu dieta más frutas y verduras. Debes evitar las cosas dulces y grasosas.

[1]peanut butter [2]score [3]health

C. La nueva pirámide de la salud.

Parte 1. Primero indica cuántas porciones comes de las siguientes categorías. Luego lee *La nueva pirámide de la salud* para completar la información y determinar si llevas una dieta saludable.

Generalmente como...

1. ___ porciones de frutas.

2. ___ porciones de carnes.

3. ___ porciones de verduras.

4. ___ porciones de panes y cereales.

5. ___ porciones de productos lácteos.

6. ___ porciones de dulces y grasas.

Parte 2. Con un(a) compañero/a, hablen de las porciones y los productos que ven en la pirámide.

GRANOS	VERDURAS	FRUTAS	PRODUCTOS LÁCTEOS	CARNES Y FRIJOLES
Consuma la mitad en granos integrales	Varíe las verduras	Enfoque en las frutas	Coma alimentos ricos en calcio	Escoja proteínas bajas en grasas
Consuma al menos 3 onzas de cereales, panes, galletas, arroz o pasta provenientes de granos integrales todos los días. Una onza es, aproximadamente, 1 rebanada de pan, 1 taza de cereales para el desayuno ó 1/2 taza de arroz, cereal o pasta cocidos.	Consuma mayor cantidad de verduras de color verde oscuro como el brócoli, la espinaca y otras verduras de color verde oscuro. Consuma mayor cantidad de verduras de color naranja como zanahorias y batatas. Consuma mayor cantidad de frijoles y guisantes secos como frijoles pinto, colorados y lentejas.	Consuma una variedad de frutas. Elija frutas frescas, congeladas, enlatadas o secas. No tome mucha cantidad de jugo de frutas.	Al elegir leche, opte por leche, yogur y otros productos lácteos descremados o bajos en contenido graso. En caso de que no consuma o no pueda consumir leche, elija productos sin lactosa u otra fuente de calcio como alimentos y bebidas fortalecidos.	Elija carnes y aves de bajo contenido graso o magras. Cocínelas al horno, a la parrilla o a la plancha. Varíe la rutina de proteínas que consume – consuma mayor cantidad de pescado, frijoles, guisantes, nueces y semillas.

En una dieta de 2.000 calorías, necesita consumir las siguientes cantidades de cada grupo de alimentos. Para consultar las cantidades correctas para usted, visite MyPyramid.gov.

Coma 6 onzas cada día	Coma 2½ tazas cada día	Coma 2 tazas cada día	Coma 3 tazas cada día; para niños edades 2-8, 2 tazas	Coma 5½ onzas cada día

Encuentre el equilibrio entre lo que come y su actividad física

- Asegúrese de mantenerse dentro de sus necesidades calóricas diarias.
- Manténgase físicamente activo por lo menos durante 30 minutos la mayoría de los días de la semana.
- Es posible que necesite alrededor de 60 minutos diarios de actividad física para evitar subir de peso.
- Para mantener la pérdida de peso, se necesitan al menos entre 60 y 90 minutos diarios de actividad física.
- Los niños y adolescentes deberían estar físicamente activos durante 60 minutos todos los días o la mayoría de los días.

Conozca los límites de las grasas, los azúcares y la sal (sodio)

- Trate de que la mayor parte de su fuente de grasas provenga del pescado, las nueces y los aceites vegetales.
- Limite las grasas sólidas como la mantequilla, la margarina, la manteca vegetal y la manteca de cerdo, así como los alimentos que los contengan.
- Verifique las etiquetas de Datos Nutricionales para mantener bajo el nivel de grasas saturadas, grasas *trans* y sodio.
- Elija alimentos y bebidas con un nivel bajo de azúcares agregados. Los azúcares agregados aportan calorías con pocos o ningún nutriente.

Parte 3. Lee la información de la nueva pirámide para contestar las preguntas.

1. Granos: ¿Cuántas onzas al día necesitamos consumir? Da un ejemplo de una onza de granos.
2. Verduras: ¿Qué tipo de verduras nos recomiendan? En una dieta de 2.000 calorías, ¿cuántas porciones de verduras necesitamos consumir?
3. Frutas: ¿Qué recomiendan en cuanto a las frutas?
4. Productos lácteos: Busca lo que quiere decir "descremados o bajos en contenido graso".
5. Carnes y frijoles: ¿Cómo necesitamos cocinar (*to cook*) las carnes? ¿Qué quiere decir **parrilla, horno** y **plancha**? ¿Qué proteínas recomiendan?

 D. Una entrevista. Entrevista a tu compañero/a para saber qué le gusta comer y beber. Usa el vocabulario de las páginas anteriores.

E. Un menú saludable. You have realized that you are not eating a balanced diet. Using the food pyramid on the previous page, write out a balanced menu that includes breakfast, lunch, dinner, and beverages.

¡Fíjate!

Write your menu on card stock so your instructor can share it with the class.

Banco de palabras			
un vaso de	**un taza de**	**un pedazo de**	**una rebanada de**
a glass of	*a cup of*	*a piece of*	*a slice of*

 F. Los hábitos alimenticios del grupo. En grupos de tres, contesten las preguntas para hacer un resumen de los hábitos alimenticios de sus compañeros.

1. ¿Qué desayunan generalmente? _____
2. ¿Qué cenan? _____
3. ¿Qué beben cuando tienen sed? _____
4. ¿Qué comen cuando tienen mucha hambre? _____
5. ¿Con qué frecuencia comen comida chatarra (*junk food*)? _____
6. ¿Cuáles son sus frutas y verduras favoritas? _____
7. ¿Qué tipo de comida prefieren? ¿Cuál es su plato favorito? _____
_____

 G. La comida latina. En grupos de seis, investiguen en Internet en qué consisten los platos típicos de los diferentes países. Cada persona investiga un plato, busca una foto y lo presenta al resto de su grupo.

1. Puerto Rico: maduritos y mofongo
2. Cuba: ropa vieja y lechón asado
3. México: cochinita pibil y los sopes
4. España: la paella y la fabada
5. Costa Rica: gallo pinto y pejibayes
6. Venezuela: el pabellón criollo y las arepas

¡Fíjate!

Go to the Supersite to watch a *Flash cultura* episode on this topic.

Práctica adicional		
Cuaderno de tareas pp. 222–225, C–G	invitaciones. vhlcentral.com Lab practice	invitaciones. vhlcentral.com Episodio 9

Gramática 1

Ordering a meal
• <u>Pedir</u>, <u>servir</u>, and <u>almorzar</u>

Analizar y descubrir

In the conversation, you heard the following:

¿Por qué siempre **pides** chili?	*Why do you always order chili?*
Ahí siempre **pido** arroz con pollo.	*I always order chicken with rice there.*
También **sirven** comida cubana.	*They also serve Cuban food.*

Pides, pido, and **sirven** are forms of the stem-changing verbs **pedir** *(to ask for, order a meal)* and **servir** *(to serve).*

1. Read the following examples to complete the conjugation of the verbs **pedir, servir,** and **almorzar.**

Pedir

¿Desea **pedir** algo más?	*Do you want to order something else?*
Nunca **pido** el plato más caro del menú.	*I never order the most expensive dish on the menu.*
¿Qué **pides** cuando cenas aquí?	*What do you order when you eat dinner here?*
Ana Mari a veces **pide** postre.	*Ana Mari sometimes orders dessert.*
¿**Pedimos** vino para todos?	*Should we order wine for everyone?*
Ustedes siempre **piden** lo mismo. Vosotros siempre **pedís** lo mismo. }	*You always order the same thing.*
Ellos siempre **piden** la cuenta primero.	*They always ask for the check first.*

Servir

¿Qué van a **servir?**	*What are you going to serve?*
Casi nunca **sirvo** nada tan tarde.	*I almost never serve anything so late.*
Y tú, ¿qué **sirves?**	*And what do you serve?*
Mi mamá siempre nos **sirve** un desayuno saludable.	*My mom always serves us a healthy breakfast.*
En casa **servimos** tamales para las fiestas.	*At home we serve tamales for parties.*
Y ustedes, ¿qué **sirven?** Y vosotros, ¿qué **servís?** }	*And what do you serve?*
¿Con qué **sirven** el bistec aquí?	*What do they serve the steak with here?*

Almorzar

¿Dónde van a **almorzar** hoy?	*Where are you going to have lunch today?*
Generalmente **almuerzo** en mi casa.	*I usually have lunch at home.*
Si **almuerzas** en la cafetería gastas más dinero.	*If you have lunch at the cafeteria, you spend more money.*
Sofía **almuerza** con Ana Mari los martes y jueves.	*Sofía has lunch with Ana Mari on Tuesdays and Thursdays.*
Ramón y yo nunca **almorzamos** temprano.	*Ramón and I never eat lunch early.*
Y ustedes, ¿a qué hora **almuerzan?** Y vosotros, ¿a qué hora almorzáis? }	*And at what time do you have lunch?*
Mis hijos **almuerzan** juntos los domingos.	*My kids have lunch together on Sundays.*

2. Now complete the conjugations of **pedir**, **servir**, and **almorzar**.

	Pedir	Servir	Almorzar
yo	_____	_____	_____
tú	_____	_____	_____
usted/él/ella	_____	_____	_____
nosotros/as	_____	_____	_____
vosotros/as	pedís	servís	almorzáis
ustedes/ellos/ellas	_____	_____	_____

3. In which forms of **pedir** and **servir** does the -**e**- of the infinitive change to an -**i**-?

_____

4. In which forms does the -**e**- remain unchanged? _____

5. In which forms of **almorzar** does the -**o**- of the infinitive change to a -**ue**-?

_____

The verb **poder** means *to be able to* and has the same stem change as **almorzar**. You will learn more about this verb in Episode 10, p. 231.

PRÁCTICA

H. Recomendaciones. En grupos de tres personas, hagan (*make*) recomendaciones sobre los mejores lugares de la ciudad para comer. Incluye muchos detalles. Después comparte tu opinión con tus compañeros.

> **Modelo** comida italiana
> **Si tienes ganas de comer comida italiana, tienes que ir al Mamma Lucia. El restaurante está en la calle Juárez. Generalmente pido la pizza vegetariana. También sirven un espagueti delicioso.**

1. comida mexicana (cubana, china, japonesa, etc.)
2. hamburguesas
3. espagueti
4. pastel de chocolate

5. desayuno
6. café
7. helados
8. ensaladas

I. Adriana y Santiago van a cenar. Usa estas palabras para completar el diálogo entre el mesero, Adriana y Santiago.

ensalada	mariscos	pides	cerveza	pido
servir	vino	pedir	pescado	sirven

Mesero   Buenas tardes, señores. ¿Están listos para (1) _____?

Adriana   Pues más o menos. ¿Qué nos recomienda?

Mesero   Bueno, la especialidad de la casa es el pescado y los (2) _____.

Santiago   ¿Con qué (3) _____ el filete de pescado?

Mesero   Lo servimos con arroz y verduras. Tenemos un pescado excelente.

Adriana   Yo no tengo ganas de comer (4) _____ hoy. Voy a pedir carne.

Santiago   ¿Por qué no pedimos una (5) _____ César para los dos?

Tú (6) _____ un filete miñón y yo (7) _____ el filete de pescado.

Adriana   También queremos una botella de (8) _____ tinto. Gracias.

J. ¿Qué te gusta comer en ocasiones especiales? En grupos de tres, hablen de las cosas que comen en algunas ocasiones especiales (cumpleaños, aniversarios, graduaciones, etc.). Incluyan en su conversación:

- qué hacen, adónde van, con quién(es), qué sirven en casa
- cuando van a restaurantes, qué piden, cuál es su plato favorito
- si van al parque, qué llevan para almorzar, a qué parque van, qué hacen allí

K. En el restaurante. En grupos de tres, escriban las conversaciones entre las personas; inventen todos los detalles. Después actúen los diálogos para el resto de la clase.

1.

2.

Invitación a **Argentina**

In your own words. Read the information below and then write what you understood. In English, summarize the information in two or three sentences. Do not translate.

_____

_____

_____

Del álbum de
Sofía

Argentina tiene aproximadamente 40 millones de habitantes. Es el país de habla hispana más grande (en extensión) de Sudamérica, y es famosa por su carne, el mate y el tango. El asado es uno de los platos principales de la comida argentina. ¿En qué consiste este famoso 'asado'? La carne de res es su principal ingrediente. Los argentinos asan (barbecue) la carne y la sazonan con una deliciosa salsa llamada chimichurri. En este plato se incluyen también los chorizos y la morcilla. El mate (un té verde) es la bebida argentina por excelencia, aunque se bebe en Uruguay y otros países también. Para beber mate, se necesita una taza (cup) especial y un popote (straw) metálico. Para los argentinos, el mate es más que una simple bebida; es una tradición, una sensación y un modo de vida.

El famoso asado argentino.

La típica bombilla para el mate.

Práctica adicional		
Cuaderno de tareas p. 226, H–I	invitaciones. vhlcentral.com Lab practice	invitaciones. vhlcentral.com Episodio 9

Actividades comunicativas

A. ¿Cuánto ejercicio necesito hacer?

Instrucciones para Estudiante 1

Parte 1. You have decided to get in shape, so you are counting calories. You are making sure that you burn the calories you eat by exercising. As you look at these food items, you will notice that you have only half of the information. Your partner has the other half. Fill in all the missing information by interviewing your partner.

> **Modelo** —¿Cuántas calorías tiene la hamburguesa grande con queso?

COMIDA	Cal.	VERDURAS	Cal.
Burrito de frijoles y arroz	380	brócoli	_____
		zanahorias	22
Hamburguesa grande con queso	_____	coliflor	_____
Papas fritas tamaño grande	540	**POSTRES**	
		Frutas	
Pizza de 12"	1.080	pera (1 fruta mediana)	_____
Sándwich de atún con mayonesa	_____	manzana	75
		plátano	_____
Tacos de carne	280	**BEBIDAS**	
Tacos de pollo	_____	Jugo de naranja	105
Un *bagel* de cebolla con queso crema	250	Cerveza	150
Un bistec de 12 oz.	_____	Café laté descremado	_____

Parte 2. Decide what you are going to eat for dinner. Write down the calories in each item and add them all up.

Voy a comer _____. _____ cal.

Voy a beber _____. _____ cal.

Para postre _____. _____ cal.

Calorías para quemar: _____ cal.

Parte 3. Look at the chart to see how many calories you burn per hour for the activities listed. Now talk to your partner to decide which activities you will do in order to burn all the calories you ate. Your partner has a list of different activities that you may also choose from. Consult with each other in order to choose.

	Cal.		Cal.
Hacer aeróbicos	396	Cortar el pasto *(to mow the lawn)*	324
Andar en bicicleta	240		
Hacer una caminata *(to go for a hike)*	432	Jugar tenis	400
		Limpiar la casa	252
Correr	740	Nadar *(to go swimming)*	500

A. ¿Cuánto ejercicio necesito hacer?

Instrucciones para **Estudiante 2**

Parte 1. You have decided to get in shape, so you are counting calories. You are making sure that you burn the calories you eat by exercising. As you look at these food items, you will notice that you have only half of the information. Your partner has the other half. Fill in all the missing information by interviewing your partner.

Modelo —¿Cuántas calorías tiene el burrito de frijoles con arroz?

COMIDA	Cal.	VERDURAS	Cal.
Burrito de frijoles y arroz	_____	brócoli	15
		zanahorias	_____
Hamburguesa grande con queso	700	coliflor	30
Papas fritas tamaño grande	_____	**POSTRES**	
		Frutas	
Pizza de 12"	_____	pera (1 fruta mediana)	50
Sándwich de atún con mayonesa	640	manzana	_____
		plátano	80
Tacos de carne	_____	**BEBIDAS**	
Tacos de pollo	190	Jugo de naranja	_____
Un *bagel* de cebolla con queso crema	_____	Cerveza	_____
Un bistec de 12 oz.	900	Café laté descremado	220

Parte 2. Decide what you are going to eat for dinner. Write down the calories in each item and add them all up.

Voy a comer _____. _____ cal.

Voy a beber _____. _____ cal.

Para postre _____. _____ cal.

Calorías para quemar: _____ cal.

Parte 3. Look at the chart to see how many calories you burn per hour for the activities listed. Now talk to your partner to decide which activities you will do in order to burn all the calories you ate. Your partner has a list of different activities that you may also choose from. Consult with each other in order to choose.

	Cal.		Cal.
Esquiar	576	Sembrar plantas (to garden)	324
Jugar frisbi	216		
Levantar pesas (to lift weights)	216	Jugar vóleibol	288
		Jugar vóleibol de playa	576
Jugar ráquetbol	720	Jugar waterpolo	720

B. ¿Es comida saludable?

Instrucciones para **Estudiante 1**

First, ask your partner the necessary questions in order to fill in all the missing information. You each have the information your partner needs. Then ask your partner about his/her eating habits and write them under the **Mi compañero/a** column.

Modelo	¿Qué desayuna Sofía?
	¿Qué almuerzan Adriana y su familia?
	¿Cuál es tu postre favorito?

	Sofía	Adriana y su familia	Wayne	Mi compañero/a
El desayuno				
El almuerzo				
La cena				
Postres favoritos				

B. ¿Es comida saludable?

Instrucciones para **Estudiante 2**

First, ask your partner the necessary questions in order to fill in all the missing information. You each have the information your partner needs. Then ask your partner about his/her eating habits and write them under the **Mi compañero/a** column.

Modelo **¿Qué desayunan Adriana y su familia?**
¿Qué almuerza Sofía?
¿Cuál es tu postre favorito?

	Sofía	Adriana y su familia	Wayne	Mi compañero/a
El desayuno				
El almuerzo				
La cena				
Postres favoritos				

C. Diferencias.

Instrucciones para **Estudiante 1**

Hay varias diferencias entre tu restaurante y el restaurante de tu compañero/a. Para encontrar las diferencias, necesitas describir qué hay en el restaurante, qué comen o beben las personas, qué piden o qué sirven los meseros. Anota siete diferencias.

Modelo En este restaurante, un mesero sirve el jugo de naranja.

C. Diferencias.

Instrucciones para Estudiante 2

Hay varias diferencias entre tu restaurante y el restaurante de tu compañero/a. Para encontrar las diferencias, necesitas describir qué hay en el restaurante, qué comen o beben las personas, qué piden o qué sirven los meseros. Anota siete diferencias.

Modelo   En este restaurante, un mesero sirve el jugo de naranja.

La correspondencia

El correo: La Estancia Santa Gertrudis. A friend of yours wants to go to a place to relax, eat a healthy diet, and relieve stress. She found this brochure in Spanish. First, read the questions. Then read the brochure for her and answer the questions in English.

1. Where is the resort? _____

2. What is the spa like? _____

3. What is the food like? _____

4. What are the daily activities? Describe them. _____
_____

5. What do you think are some special features of this spa? Would it be a place for relaxation and meditation? Why? _____

Reading Strategy: Scanning for specific information

When reading a Spanish text for specific information, you can disregard information that does not correspond to your purpose for reading. Be content with understanding the overall meaning. *Scan* the text—that is, locate and read carefully only the information you are looking for. For example, in the following article, you need to know where **la Estancia Santa Gertrudis** is. *Scan* the first paragraph to locate the country or state. Be sure to read the questions first so you know what specific information you are looking for. Remember to look for cognates to help you understand the text.

Lo último en salud y descanso:

Un fin de semana en la Estancia Santa Gertrudis

La Estancia Santa Gertrudis es un spa ecológico de 1.660 hectáreas, con enormes arboledas[1], un lago de 200 hectáreas y actividades para todos los gustos. Está localizada en el partido[2] de Chascomús, a 165 kilómetros de la capital, en Argentina. La estancia recibe un máximo de diez personas cada fin de semana: seis en la casa principal y cuatro en la casa de huéspedes[3].

En un oasis de tranquilidad, comida saludable, ejercicio diario, safaris fotográficos y observación de varias clases de animales silvestres, la Estancia Santa Gertrudis es una "opción ideal para un fin de semana saludable y activo".

Las actividades del día incluyen caminatas alrededor del lago, fútbol, natación, caballos, bicicletas y, la especialidad de la casa, clases de yoga (método Iyengar).

La comida es natural y casera, elaborada con harinas integrales, verduras cultivadas en la estancia y, para quienes lo deseen, carne ecológica de producción propia. Por la tarde, usted puede descansar en la vieja arboleda que rodea la casa, leer, conversar con los otros huéspedes, remar[4] en el lago o simplemente relajarse.

Un fin de semana de dieta saludable, ejercicio diario, descanso total y cuidados especiales hacen que usted se sienta[5] extraordinariamente bien y feliz.

Para recibir más información, llame a Darío Sarachaga, teléfono (0242) 3-21-33, fax 8-06-14.

---

[1]forests [2]state or province [3]guests [4]row [5]you feel

En papel: Una visita por la ciudad. A good friend of yours from high school is coming to visit you for a week next month. Write a letter telling your friend what you have planned during his/her stay—places you will see, activities you have planned, new restaurants you will visit, and so on.

Writing Strategy: Recombining learned material

As your ability to communicate in Spanish increases, you will be able to link the words and phrases you know to express more complex messages. When responding to a writing task—in this case, a letter to a friend—you should devise an appropriate plan to organize your ideas effectively. First, determine the information that needs to be included in the letter. Then identify the places you want to go. Organize your letter by linking those places with activities you plan to do. Finally, write your letter.

¡A ver de nuevo!

Parte 1. Escribe un resumen del episodio. Incluye la comida que llevan al parque y las cosas que les gusta comer.

Parte 2. Después trabaja con un(a) compañero/a para añadir más información.

Vocabulario del Episodio 9

Para hablar de las comidas

almorzar (o → ue)	*to have lunch*	**el almuerzo**	*lunch*
cenar	*to have dinner/supper*	**la cena**	*dinner/supper*
comer	*to eat; to have lunch*	**la cuenta**	*bill, check*
desayunar	*to have breakfast*	**el desayuno**	*breakfast*
pedir (e → i)	*to ask (for), order* (a meal)	**el/la mesero/a**	*waiter/waitress*
servir (e → i)	*to serve*	**el plato/platillo**	*dish*
tener hambre	*to be hungry*		
tener sed	*to be thirsty*		

La comida

Un desayuno internacional *An international breakfast*

el cereal	*cereal*	**el pan tostado**	*toast*
la dona	*donut*	**la pera**	*pear*
el huevo	*egg*	**el plátano**	*banana*
la fruta	*fruit*	**la uva**	*grape*
la manzana	*apple*	**el yogurt**	*yogurt*

Un almuerzo norteamericano *An American lunch*

la ensalada de lechuga y tomate	*lettuce and tomato salad*
el espagueti	*spaghetti*
la hamburguesa	*hamburger*
el jamón	*ham*
las papas fritas	*French fries*
el pavo	*turkey*
la pimienta	*pepper*
el pollo	*chicken*
el queso	*cheese*
la sal	*salt*
el sándwich de atún	*tuna sandwich*
la sopa	*soup*

La cena *Dinner*

el arroz	*rice*	**la carne de res**	*beef*
el bistec de res	*roast beef*	**la langosta**	*lobster*
los camarones	*shrimp*	**los mariscos**	*seafood*
la carne de cerdo	*pork*	**el pescado**	*fish*

Las verduras *Vegetables*

el brócoli	*broccoli*
los frijoles	*beans*
la papa al horno	*baked potato*
la zanahoria	*carrot*

Los postres *Desserts*

los dulces	*candy, sweets*
el flan	*flan*
las galletas	*cookies*
el helado	*ice cream*
el pastel	*cake*

Las bebidas *Drinks*

el agua	*water*
el café	*coffee*
la cerveza	*beer*
el jugo de naranja	*orange juice*
la leche	*milk*
la limonada	*lemonade*
los refrescos	*sodas/soft drinks*
el té	*tea*
el vino tinto	*red wine*

Vocabulario personal

Write all the words you need to know in Spanish so that you can talk in greater detail about your eating habits and the foods you like/dislike.

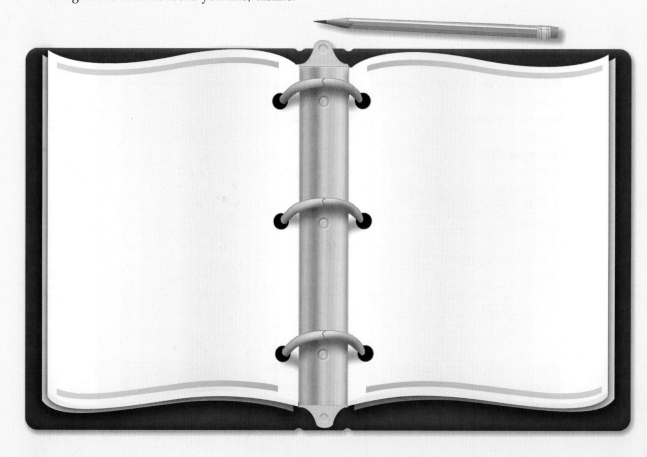

Cuaderno de tareas

Episodio

9

Escenas de la vida: ¡Qué rica comida!

 A. ¡A ver cuánto entendiste! See how much of the **Escena** you understood by matching the Spanish sentences with their English equivalents.

El picnic

_____ 1. Es hora latina.

_____ 2. Para fiestas no es necesario ser puntual.

_____ 3. Si no es el trabajo.

_____ 4. ¡Ya era hora!

_____ 5. Eso dice mi papá.

a. For parties, it's not necessary to be punctual.

b. But it's not work.

c. It's Latin time.

d. That's what my dad says.

e. It's about time!

La comida

_____ 6. La carne está muy buena.

_____ 7. El secreto es prepararla la noche anterior.

_____ 8. La salsa no pica nada.

_____ 9. Pensé que se les había olvidado.

_____ 10. ¿Por qué siempre pides chili?

f. Why do you always order chili?

g. I thought you had forgotten.

h. The meat is very good.

i. The secret is to prepare it the night before.

j. The sauce isn't spicy at all.

 B. Todos en el parque. Order the statements so the dialogue makes sense.

_____ a. El secreto para que la carne esté perfecta es prepararla la noche anterior con cerveza, sal y limón. Bueno, eso dice mi papá.

_____ b. Ana Mari, ¿pica la salsa?

__1__ c. La carne está muy buena.

_____ d. Tu papá tiene razón. Me gusta mucho la comida mexicana.

_____ e. No, no pica nada.

_____ f. ¿Entonces por qué siempre pides chili? En México no hay chili.

_____ g. *No way!*

Nombre ______________________________ Fecha ______________

Vocabulario 1

Talking about food
• Food and meals

C. Las categorías. Your 10-year-old niece has asked you to help her with her school project on food groups in Spanish. Fill in each of the categories with the names of foods in Spanish.

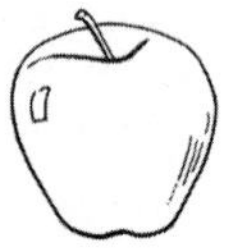

Frutas

____
____
____
____
____
____
____

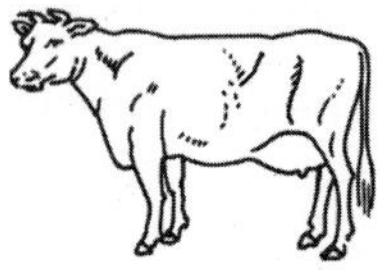

Productos lácteos

____
____
____
____
____
____
____

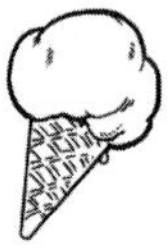

Postres

____
____
____
____
____
____
____

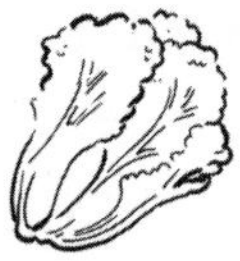

Verduras

____
____
____
____
____
____
____

D. Cuerpo sano, mente sana. *(Healthy body, healthy mind.)* Look at the foods in the illustrations. Then write the foods you consider healthy under **Saludable** and write the reason why each is considered good: vitamins **(vitaminas)**, proteins **(proteínas)**, calcium **(calcio)**, or low in fat **(poca grasa)**. Under **No muy saludable,** list the foods and beverages that are high in fat **(grasa),** sugar **(azúcar),** salt **(sal),** or cholesterol **(colesterol)**.

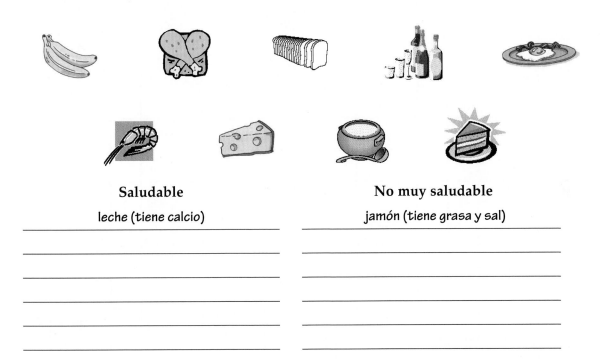

Saludable	No muy saludable
leche (tiene calcio)	jamón (tiene grasa y sal)

E. Tres menús. You are planning three different breakfasts for the restaurant where you work. Write down the appropriate foods and beverages.

Un desayuno norteamericano

**Un desayuno dominguero
(Sunday brunch)**

Un desayuno ligero

Nombre _____ Fecha _____

F. Un crucigrama. Fill out the crossword puzzle by writing the appropriate word for each item.

Definiciones

Verticales

1. Una bebida de fruta común para el desayuno.
2. Se sirven con la comida mexicana; son pequeños y negros o cafés.
3. Se comen fritos o en omelet; tienen mucho colesterol.
4. Es común hacer sándwiches de _____ y queso.
5. La comida del mediodía.
7. Todo lo que comemos; los alimentos.
9. Se come en el desayuno con leche; tiene fibra.
10. Lo que se come en KFC.
12. Una bebida similar al té.
13. La primera comida del día.
14. Los vegetarianos nunca comen _____.
15. La Coca-Cola y el 7-UP son _____.

Horizontales

6. Los camarones y la langosta son _____.
8. Una bebida blanca; tiene calcio.
10. Se necesita para hacer un sándwich.
11. Se usa mucho en la comida china; es blanco.
14. Un marisco pequeño y caro (en la forma plural).
16. Vive en el agua; se come en filetes.
17. Un producto lácteo; se come con o sin frutas.
18. La última comida del día.
19. Tienen vitaminas; no son dulces; se usan para hacer ensaladas.

G. Las definiciones. Write the food item that best fits the description.

> **Modelo**   La comida favorita de los chimpancés.   **Los plátanos.**

1. Una bebida anaranjada (*orange*), no tiene alcohol. _____
2. Son unas verduras anaranjadas. A Bugs Bunny le gustan. _____
3. Es un marisco rojo muy caro. _____
4. Un pescado que se usa para hacer sándwiches. _____
5. Tienes que beber ocho vasos de este líquido al día. _____
6. A los niños les gusta mucho; es frío, de chocolate o vainilla. _____
7. Escribe dos ejemplos de carne. _____
8. Es la comida más común para Acción de Gracias (*Thanksgiving*). _____
9. Un plato de verduras frescas. _____
10. De esta bebida, hay tinto, blanco y rosado. _____

Gramática 1

Ordering a meal
• Pedir, servir, and almorzar

H. ¡Qué desastre! Lalo and Santiaguito are working at a cafeteria during their vacation. Unfortunately, they bring the wrong things to Sofía and her friends. Complete the sentences with the appropriate forms of **pedir** and **servir**. (Note: **me** means *[to] me*, **te** means *[to] you*, **le** means *[to] him/her*, and **les** means *[to] them*.)

> **Modelo** Los niños **piden** una pizza de queso, pero Lalo les **sirve** una pizza vegetariana.

1. Sofía _____ un café, pero Santiaguito le _____ un té.
2. Adriana y Ana Mari _____ frutas, pero los chicos les _____ pastel.
3. Yo _____ pastel, pero ellos me _____ yogurt.
4. Nosotras _____ limonadas para todas, pero Lalo nos _____ refrescos.
5. ¿Tú _____ helado de fresa? ¡De seguro *(for sure)*, Lalo y Santiaguito te van a _____ helado de vainilla!

I. ¡Vamos a cenar! Imagine you are at an Argentinian restaurant. Answer the waiter's questions.

1. Buenas tardes, ¿qué plato principal va a pedir? _____
2. ¿Y quiere pedir algo *(something)* antes del plato principal? _____
_____
3. ¿Qué va a beber? _____
4. ¿Va a pedir postre? _____

Para terminar

J. ¡Vivir bien con poca grasa[1]! Lee las preguntas, después lee el anuncio del libro *Vivir bien con poca grasa* y responde a las preguntas.

1. ¿Qué beneficios puede tener el comer con poca grasa? _____
_____
2. ¿Qué ayuda a que la grasa se queme más rápidamente? _____
3. ¿Qué actividad hace que engordemos *(makes us get fat)*? _____

¡Disfrute[2] de la mejor salud de toda su vida!
Una vez que usted viva con poca grasa, su
calidad de vida va a mejorar inmediatamente. Va
a tener mejor humor y más energía. Va a dejar de[3]
preocuparse por su peso y va a comenzar a disfrutar de los
beneficios de un cuerpo más delgado y sano, sin los peligros
propios[4] de las dietas. ¡No espere más! Envíe el **Certificado
de Inspección GRATUITA** ¡hoy mismo!

INSPECCIÓN GRATUITA DE 21 DÍAS

Secreto para controlar la GRASA automáticamente

Nº 1

Tomar agua puede ayudar a reducir los depósitos de
grasa. Cuando usted está totalmente hidratada, su
cuerpo transporta más rápidamente la grasa a los
músculos para ser quemada[5] allí. En la PÁGINA 107
de VIVIR BIEN CON POCA GRASA, descubra cómo el
AGUA HELADA puede servir durante todo el día como
¡SÚPER estimulante de la combustión de grasa!

Secreto para controlar la GRASA automáticamente

Nº 2

La TV hace aumentar de peso: Increíble, pero es ¡la
pura verdad! Estar sentada[6] delante del televisor la
hace engordar más que el estar solamente sentada.
Además, si usted mira TV por cuatro horas o más, es
DOS VECES más probable que sufra[7] de sobrepeso.
Antes de prender[8] el "control de producción de grasa"
de su televisor, lea la PÁGINA 71 para saber cuántas
horas de televisión puede usted mirar.

[1]*fat*   [2]*enjoy*   [3]**dejar***... stop*   [4]**peligros***... inherent risks*   [5]*burned*   [6]*sitting*   [7]*suffer*   [8]*turn on*

K. Una miniprueba para terminar. Give Ramón the following information about yourself. Write it in the form of a paragraph. Then write how you would ask him for the information in **2.** Remember that you have to create the questions that would elicit the information you need.

1. Tell Ramón:
    a. about your eating habits.
    b. the places you usually go after school.
    c. who you live with.
    d. everything you are going to do tomorrow.

2. Ask Ramón:
    e. what they serve at his home for lunch.
    f. what his favorite dish is.
    g. what he usually eats between meals (**entre comidas**).
    h. where he goes when he feels like eating his favorite food.
    i. if he has to work on Sundays.

1. a.–d. _____

_____

_____

_____

_____

_____

_____

_____

_____

2. e. _____

    f. _____

    g. _____

    h. _____

    i. _____

Episodio 10

Escenas de la vida: Una invitación confusa

 A. ¡Mira cuánto puedes entender! As you listen, indicate the order in which you hear these statements.

La película empieza a las 8:30.

Podemos **tomar café antes de la película.**

Ana Mari, ¿puedes venir conmigo **al cine?**

Bueno, voy contigo, **pero necesitas modernizarte.**

Me invita y no viene por mí **a la casa.**

Es difícil encontrar **estacionamiento.**

Prefiero no manejar **de noche.**

Además, por la noche no me gusta salir sola.

Bueno, entonces nos vemos el sábado.

B. Los hechos. Selecciona la respuesta correcta.

Sofía   **Wayne**   **Ana Mari**

1. Wayne dice *(says)*...
   a. Voy por ti.
   b. ¿Dónde dan la película?
   c. ¿Quieres ir al cine el sábado?

2. Wayne dice...
   a. ¿Quieres visitar el Centro Cultural
      de la universidad?
   b. ¿Puedes llegar a las 7:30?
   c. Mi coche no funciona.

3. Ana Mari…
   a. no entiende a Sofía.
   b. piensa que Sofía es muy moderna.
   c. puede ir en su coche.

4. Sofía…
   a. sale sola por la noche con
      frecuencia.
   b. va al cine en el coche de Ramón.
   c. no cree que Wayne la invite a salir
      otra vez.

 C. ¿Te diste cuenta? Contesta las preguntas.

1. ¿Por qué quiere Wayne llegar temprano al cine?
   _____

2. ¿Dónde y a qué hora van a verse?
   _____

3. ¿Por qué Sofía invita a Ana Mari?
   _____

4. ¿Qué piensa Ana Mari de Sofía?
   _____

5. ¿Por qué invitan también a Ramón?
   _____

Cultura a lo vivo
In many traditional
families of Latin American
countries, when a young
man invites a girl out
on a date, he is expected
to pick her up at home.
This custom provides
an opportunity for the
parents of the girl to
meet the young man.

Learning Strategy: Making an educated guess

To understand the general meaning of a message, you do not have to understand every
word you hear or read. In most situations, you can use the context, your knowledge of
the world and of how people communicate, and visual cues such as facial expressions,
gestures, and body language to make an educated guess about meaning.

Use the context to derive meaning. More often than not, you can correctly guess the
meaning of a word by focusing on the words that precede and follow it. For example,
when Wayne said to Sofía, "**quiero llegar temprano porque es difícil encontrar
estacionamiento**," you had not seen **encontrar** before, but you know that **quiero llegar
temprano** means *I want to arrive early* and that **estacionamiento** means *parking*.
Therefore, by using context, you can easily guess that **encontrar** means *to find*.

Práctica adicional

Cuaderno de tareas	invitaciones.
p. 247, A	vhlcentral.com
	Episodio 10

Para comunicarnos mejor

Gramática **1**

Accepting and declining invitations
• Stem-changing verbs (<u>e</u> → <u>ie</u>) and (<u>o</u> → <u>ue</u>)

In the conversation, Wayne said **¿Quieres ir al cine el sábado?** to ask Sofía if she wanted to go to the movies. Sofía responded **Sí, puedo. Quieres** and **puedo** are forms of the verbs **querer** and **poder**.

Analizar y descubrir

1. Study the following exchanges:

Querer y poder	
—¿**Quieres** tomar un café?	*Do you want some coffee?*
—Sí, **quiero**, pero no **puedo** tomar cafeína.	*Yes, I want some, but I can't have any caffeine.*
—¿Ana Mari **quiere** llevar su coche?	*Does Ana Mari want to take her car?*
—No **puede**, porque no funciona.	*She can't, because it doesn't work.*
—¿Sofía y Ana Mari **quieren** ir al cine?	*Do Sofía and Ana Mari want to go to the movies?*
—Sí, **quieren**, pero no **pueden**.	*Yes, they want to, but they can't.*
—¿**Quieren** ustedes ir al cine? —¿**Queréis** ir al cine?	*Do you want to go to the movies?*
—**Queremos** ir pero no **podemos**, porque tenemos que trabajar.	*We want to go but we can't, because we have to work.*

2. Write the forms of **querer** and **poder**.

	querer	poder
yo	_____	puedo
tú	_____	_____
usted/él/ella	quiere	_____
nosotros/as	_____	_____
vosotros/as	queréis	podéis
ustedes/ellos/ellas	_____	_____

3. Look at the endings of **querer** and **poder.** Are they the same as other **-er** verbs you know, such as **comer** and **beber?** _____

4. Look at the stems of the two verbs (**quer-, pod-**) and answer the questions.

   a. What happens to the **-e-** of **querer?** It becomes _____.

   b. What happens to the **-o-** of **poder?** It becomes _____.

   c. Does the **-e-** of **querer** change in all the verb forms? _____.

   d. Does the **-o-** of **poder** change in all the verb forms? _____.

5. Complete these rules for stem-changing verbs.

    a. In stem-changing verbs like **querer**, **-e-** changes to _____ in all forms except the _____ and _____ forms.

    b. In stem-changing verbs like **poder**, **-o-** changes to _____ in all forms except the _____ and _____ forms.

6. The following expressions contain other common stem-changing verbs:

Para hacer planes con los amigos			
e ➤ ie		**o/u ➤ ue**	
empezar a...	*to start...*	**almorzar**	*to have lunch*
entender el problema	*to understand the problem*	**dormir bien/mal**	*to sleep well/poorly*
pensar en	*to think about* (someone or something)	**encontrar**	*to find*
pensar que...	*to think that...* (phrase)	**jugar*** (al) tenis**	*to play tennis*
preferir* no manejar	*to prefer not to drive*	**(no) poder ir**	*to (not) be able to go*
querer	*to want; to love*	**recordar**	*to remember*
venir** por mí	*to pick me up*		

*Note that the second **-e-** in **preferir** is the one that changes to **-ie-**. **¿Prefieres el té o el café?**

****venir** has a **g** in the **yo** form—**yo vengo. Venir** alone means *to come*. **Vengo a clase todos los días.**

***Note that **jugar** is the only verb that has the **u ➤ ue** stem change.

PRÁCTICA

A. Otra invitación. Organiza el diálogo de forma lógica. Después actúa la conversación con un(a) compañero/a.

_____ a. A las cuatro es muy temprano. Tengo que trabajar hasta las seis.

_____ b. Bueno, ¿qué película quieres ver?

_____ c. ¿Quieres ir al cine conmigo el viernes?

_____ d. No sé. ¿Qué tipo de películas prefieres, románticas o de terror?

_____ e. Puedo ir por ti a las siete. Si quieres, podemos cenar después de la peli.

_____ f. Perfecto, estoy en tu casa a las siete en punto. Hasta el viernes.

_____ g. Bueno, pues tú decides qué película vemos. ¿Voy por ti a las cuatro?

_____ h. Definitivamente o románticas o cómicas. No de terror.

_____ i. Si encuentro una película entre siete y ocho, podemos cenar después. Pero si la película empieza después de las ocho, prefiero cenar antes. ¿Te parece?

B. Problemas de familia. Completa la conversación entre Adriana y su esposo con los verbos de la lista. Después contesta las preguntas.

empiezas	almuerzas	quieres
puedes	duermes	prefiero
encontrar	jugar	vienes

Santiago Adriana, no entiendo por qué (1) _____ trabajar y estudiar. Si quieres estudiar para contadora, es mejor *(better)* que no trabajes hasta que termines.

Adriana Si no tengo experiencia, no voy a poder (2) _____ trabajo cuando termine.

Santiago Es cierto, pero tú (3) _____ adquirir *(acquire)* experiencia más adelante *(later)*. Recuerda que tienes esposo, casa e hijos. No tienes tiempo para nada. La casa es un desastre.

Adriana Ay, Santiago, limpiar la casa es muy aburrido. (4) _____ trabajar y estudiar. Con el dinero que gano le puedo pagar *(pay)* a una empleada *(maid)*.

Santiago No es sólo la casa; últimamente *(lately)* tú no (5) _____ lo suficiente, a veces sólo cinco o seis horas por noche. Además (6) _____ mal, porque no tienes tiempo ni para ir al supermercado. Casi nunca hay comida en el refrigerador.

Adriana Santiago, (7) _____ a hablar como esos hombres que no quieren que sus esposas progresen.

Santiago No es verdad. Quiero que tú progreses, pero...

1. ¿Por qué quiere trabajar Adriana?

   _____

   _____

2. ¿Qué piensa Santiago que Adriana debe hacer?

   _____

   _____

3. En tu opinión, ¿quién tiene razón *(is right)*?

   _____

   _____

C. Hombres y mujeres.

Parte 1. Indica si estás de acuerdo *(if you agree)* con estos estereotipos.

¡Fíjate!

Use these expressions to react to your partners' opinions:

Estoy de acuerdo.
I agree.

No estoy de acuerdo.
I disagree.

Tienes razón.
You are right.

¡Ya quisieras!
¡You wish!

¡Sí, cómo no!
¡Yeah, right!

Los hombres...	Sí	No	Depende
1. nunca encuentran las cosas.	☐	☐	☐
2. no pueden vivir solos.	☐	☐	☐
3. no entienden a las mujeres.	☐	☐	☐
4. prefieren no casarse *(to get married)*.	☐	☐	☐
5. no pueden aceptar sus errores.	☐	☐	☐
Las mujeres...			
6. siempre piensan que están gordas.	☐	☐	☐
7. no entienden a los hombres.	☐	☐	☐
8. quieren tener hijos.	☐	☐	☐
9. no pueden hacer mucho ejercicio.	☐	☐	☐
10. no encuentran interesantes los deportes *(sports)*.	☐	☐	☐

Parte 2. En grupos de tres compartan sus respuestas y hablen de sus ideas.

> **Modelo** No estoy de acuerdo con el comentario número dos. Mis amigos y yo vivimos solos y estamos muy bien. No necesitamos a las mujeres.

D. Lotería.

Parte 1. Walk around the class and find a classmate who fits each description. Write his/her name in the space provided; the first student with two lines of four in a row wins.

> **Modelo** —¿Haces ejercicio tres veces a la semana?
> —Sí, hago ejercicio tres veces a la semana. ¿Y tú?

casi nunca almuerza en la cafetería.	juega vóleibol una vez a la semana.	prefiere no manejar por la noche.	empieza a estudiar tres días antes del examen.
hace ejercicio tres veces a la semana.	a veces no entiende la tarea.	quiere ir al cine este fin de semana.	no tiene ganas de hacer la tarea hoy.
ve videos en casa de su novio/a.	no duerme ocho horas por noche.	recuerda a su primer(a) maestro/a.	vive en casa de sus abuelos.
encuentra estacionamiento cuando llega.	sirve tamales en Navidad.	no puede tomar clases por las noches.	piensa que esta clase es muy fácil.

Parte 2. Comparte la información con la clase.

Invitación a **España**

In your own words. Read the information below and then write what you understood. In English, summarize the information in two or three sentences. Do not translate.

Del álbum de
Sofía

España tiene aproximadamente 42 millones de habitantes y dos veces el tamaño *(size)* del estado de Oregón. Salamanca, en España, es una ciudad *(city)* con una larga tradición intelectual y cultural. La Universidad de Salamanca se fundó en 1218 y es la más antigua *(oldest)* del país. Hoy en día, la ciudad tiene innumerables academias, institutos, escuelas, colegios y universidades, por lo que estudian ahí miles *(thousands)* de estudiantes nacionales e internacionales. Salamanca es una ciudad con muchas actividades. Los jóvenes van a conciertos, discotecas y obras de teatro *(plays)*. Las discotecas abren sus puertas a las once o doce de la noche y las cierran a las tres o cuatro de la mañana.

E. Preguntas personales. Contesta las preguntas en tu cuaderno y después entrevista a un(a) compañero/a y escribe sus respuestas aquí.

En la universidad

1. ¿Qué quieres estudiar? ¿Por qué?

_____

2. ¿Vas bien en tus clases? ¿Cuáles son las más difíciles?

_____

3. ¿Empiezas a estudiar con tiempo para un examen? ¿Qué cosas haces para prepararte?

_____

4. ¿Dónde prefieres estudiar? ¿Por qué te gusta estudiar ahí?

_____

Los fines de semana

5. ¿En qué ocasiones prefieres estar con tus amigos? ¿Y con tu familia?

_____

6. ¿Puedes hacer todas las cosas que quieres? Si no, ¿por qué no?

_____

_____

7. ¿Cuántas horas duermes? ¿Piensas que es importante dormir lo suficiente? ¿Por qué sí o por qué no?

_____

_____

8. ¿Almuerzas en casa? ¿Qué almuerzas generalmente? ¿Con quién?

_____

9. ¿Qué deportes *(sports)* practicas? ¿Juegas béisbol?, ¿tenis?, ¿fútbol americano?

_____

10. ¿Sales mucho? ¿Con quién? ¿Qué hacen?

_____

_____

11. Cuando sales con alguien por primera vez, ¿piensas que el chico tiene que ir por la chica a su casa? ¿En qué casos sí y en qué casos no? Explica.

_____

_____

Banco de palabras
Para hablar del trabajo

el horario flexible/fijo *flexible/fixed schedule*	**el tiempo libre** *free time*
el sueldo alto/bajo *high/low salary*	**el turno de la mañana/** **tarde/noche** *morning/afternoon/evening* *(night) shift*
tiempo completo/parcial *full-time/part-time*	

¡Fíjate!

You will need these words to answer the questions. Familiarize yourself with them, since they will become active in the next episode.

En el trabajo

12. ¿Es fácil encontrar trabajo en tu ciudad *(city)*? ¿Qué tipo de trabajos hay? ¿Te gusta tu trabajo? ¿Por qué?

_____

_____

13. ¿Trabajas tiempo completo o tiempo parcial? ¿Recibes buen sueldo o quieres ganar más *(to earn more)*?

_____

_____

14. ¿Cuántas horas a la semana puedes trabajar? ¿Qué días no puedes trabajar?

_____

_____

15. ¿Prefieres trabajar el turno de la tarde o el de la mañana? ¿Tienes un horario flexible?

_____

_____

Práctica adicional

Cuaderno de tareas
pp. 247–249, B–F

SUPERSITE

invitaciones.
vhlcentral.com
Episodio 10

16. ¿Quieres encontrar otro trabajo este semestre? ¿Por qué?

_____

_____

Gramática **2** **Extending invitations**
• Prepositional pronouns

In other conversations, the characters said the following statements.

Pronombres preposicionales

¿Quieres ir **conmigo** a cenar?	*Do you want to go to dinner with me?*
Bueno, voy **contigo** si vienes **por mí**.	*Fine, I'll go with you if you pick me up.*
Wayne siempre habla **de ti**.	*Wayne always talks about you.*
¿Y Sofía? ¿Piensa **en él**?	*And Sofía? Does she think about him?*
Ramón va a jugar **con nosotros**.	*Ramón is going to play with us.*
¿Wayne vive **con ustedes**? ¿Wayne vive **con vosotros**? }	*Does Wayne live with you?*
No, él vive **con ellos**.	*No, he lives with them.*

Los pronombres preposicionales

mí	*me* (but: *conmigo*)	**nosotros/as**	*us*
ti	*you* (but: *contigo*)	**ustedes**	*you* (pl.)
usted	*you*	**vosotros/as**	*you* (pl.)
él/ella	*him/her*	**ellos/ellas**	*them*

1. Notice that the subject pronouns (**yo, tú, usted, él, ella, nosotros/as, ustedes, vosotros/as,** and **ellos/ellas**) and pronouns that follow prepositions (**a, con, de, en, para, por**) are the same, with two exceptions: **yo/mí** (**Vienes** *por mí.*) and **tú/ti** (**Lo siento, no puedo ir** *por ti.*).
2. Notice that **conmigo** means *with me* and **contigo** means *with you*.
3. Some prepositions in Spanish have different translations depending on the verb they follow. Learn the verb with its preposition. Some verbs you already know may be followed by prepositions: **hablar de, discutir con, vivir con, jugar con, pensar en, ir por,** and **venir por.**

Las preposiciones

a	*to, at (with time)*	*Voy **a** tu casa **a** las tres de la tarde.*
con	*with*	*Wayne juega fútbol **con** Ramón los domingos.*
de	*from; about (with **hablar**)*	*Manolo no habla **de** sus planes profesionales.*
en	*in, on; about (with **pensar**)*	*Wayne piensa **en** Sofía con frecuencia.*
para	*for (destination/purpose)*	*La computadora es **para** Wayne.*
por	*for (with **ir** and **venir**)*	*¿Quién va a venir **por** mí?*

PRÁCTICA

F. ¿De quién habla? Sofía hizo *(made)* estos comentarios. ¿A quién(es) se refiere(n) los pronombres preposicionales? Empareja las dos columnas.

_____ 1. Necesito hablar *con ella*.

_____ 2. Lalo va a jugar fútbol *con ellos*.

_____ 3. Mi abuela vive *con nosotros*.

_____ 4. Quiero hablar *contigo*.

_____ 5. No comparte *(he doesn't share)* sus cosas *con ellas*.

a. amigos

b. Ana Mari y Adriana

c. mis padres y yo

d. la profesora

e. tú

G. Un poco de lógica. Empareja cada pregunta o declaración con la respuesta lógica.

_____ 1. ¿Está Sofía en casa?

_____ 2. ¿Quieres ir conmigo al cine?

_____ 3. Su hijo es muy considerado, ¿no?

_____ 4. ¿Puedo ir contigo?

_____ 5. Estas flores son para ti.

a. Lo siento, pero no puedo.

b. Claro que puedes venir conmigo.

c. Sí. ¿Quieres hablar con ella?

d. Sí. Siempre piensa en nosotros primero.

e. Gracias. Siempre piensas en mí.

H. Traducción. Escribe estas oraciones en español.

1. I have tickets for the game tonight—do you want to go? Manolo and Jorge are also coming with us. We can go in Jorge's car.

_____

_____

2. Sure I want to go, but I'd rather take my own car. I don't understand why you always invite Jorge—he's silly!

_____

_____

¡Fíjate!

Remember not to translate word-for-word; translate ideas

I. Escribe sobre las personas queridas. Contesta todas las preguntas en forma de párrafo. Después comparte tus respuestas con un(a) compañero/a.

> **Modelo** Tu hermano/a: ¿Ves a tu hermano/a? ¿Qué haces con él/ella? ¿Vives con él/ella?
> **Veo a mi hermana casi todos los días. Tomo café con ella por las mañanas. A veces salgo con ella a cenar. Nunca discuto con ella. Y tampoco voy por ella con frecuencia. Prefiere manejar su coche. No vivo con ella, vivo con mi hija.**

Práctica adicional

Cuaderno de tareas
pp. 250–251, G–K

invitaciones.
vhlcentral.com
Episodio 10

1. Tus abuelos: ¿Ves a tus abuelos? ¿Sales con ellos? ¿Qué haces con ellos?

2. Tu novio/a /mejor amigo/a: ¿Hablas mucho con él/ella? ¿Discutes con él/ella?

3. Tus compañeros de clase: ¿Qué actividades haces con ellos? ¿Estudias con ellos? ¿Dónde y cuándo?

4. Tu mamá o tu papá: ¿Vives con él/ella? ¿Discuten con frecuencia? ¿Por qué? ¿Qué actividades hacen juntos/as *(together)*?

Actividades comunicativas

A. La historia va así.

Parte 1. Mira las ilustraciones y escucha los comentarios de Manolo con respecto a su trabajo. Indica el orden cronológico en que menciona las actividades. Después escucha los comentarios otra vez para verificar tus respuestas.

 Parte 2. En grupos de tres, escriban la historia en diferente orden.

B. ¿Qué hace Manolo los sábados?

Instrucciones para **Estudiante 1**

 Parte 1. Tú tienes la mitad *(half)* de las ilustraciones, y tu compañero/a tiene la otra mitad. Juntos/as tienen que descubrir *(find out)* cómo es la rutina de Manolo los sábados. Describe tus ilustraciones y haz preguntas para completar el cuadro. Tu compañero/a empieza.

| Modelo | Manolo limpia su cuarto por la mañana. ¿Qué hace después? |

 Parte 2. Ahora escribe un párrafo con los eventos. Inventa los detalles *(details)*.

| Modelo | Los sábados por la mañana Manolo generalmente... |

_____

_____

_____

_____

_____

_____

_____

_____

_____

B. ¿Qué hace Manolo los sábados?

Parte 1. Tú tienes la mitad *(half)* de las ilustraciones, y tu compañero/a tiene la otra mitad. Juntos/as tienen que descubrir *(find out)* cómo es la rutina de Manolo los sábados. Describe tus ilustraciones y haz preguntas para completar el cuadro. Tú empiezas.

> **Modelo**   ¿Qué hace Manolo primero?

Parte 2. Ahora escribe un párrafo con los eventos. Inventa los detalles *(details)*.

> **Modelo**   Los sábados por la mañana Manolo generalmente...

_____

_____

_____

_____

_____

_____

_____

_____

_____

C. Un programa de intercambio.

Instrucciones para **Estudiante 1**

You are considering becoming a host family for an international student. Interview the student applying to stay at your home for a summer immersion program. Based on his/her responses, decide if you wish to accept this student.

Find out this information about the student:

- activities he/she prefers to do after school and on weekends
- eating habits and dietary requirements
- family and hometown or country
- personality traits

¡Fíjate!

You may take time to prepare written questions for your partner before you begin this activity, i.e., **¿Te gusta bailar? ¿Qué te gusta comer? ¿Haces ejercicio?**

C. Un programa de intercambio.

Instrucciones para **Estudiante 2**

You are applying for an exchange program and are being interviewed by a prospective host. Based on this interview, you will decide if you will stay with this family or look for another one. Answer all the questions you are asked, and ask a few of your own.

Ask about:

- the members of the host family
- their activities
- their eating habits
- anything else you think may be important

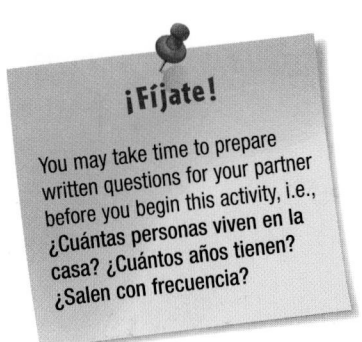

¡Fíjate!

You may take time to prepare written questions for your partner before you begin this activity, i.e., ¿Cuántas personas viven en la casa? ¿Cuántos años tienen? ¿Salen con frecuencia?

D. Te invito a salir. Vas a salir con tu compañero/a. Selecciona una cartera *(wallet)* para saber cuánto dinero pueden gastar *(spend)*. Inventen una conversación que incluya (1) adónde van a ir, (2) cuándo y a qué hora van y (3) cómo van a gastar todo el dinero. Estén listos para actuar su diálogo en clase.

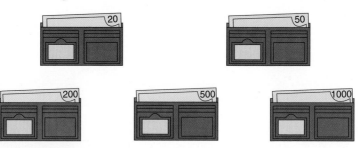

La correspondencia

El correo: ¡Los hombres! Primero, lee las siguientes preguntas. Después, lee la página del diario de Sofía y contesta las preguntas.

1. ¿Por qué invita Sofía a sus amigos al cine?

_____

2. ¿Por qué cree Sofía que Wayne va a pensar que está loca?

_____

3. ¿Crees que es interesante salir con una persona de otra cultura? ¿Por qué?

_____

_____

_____

Querido diario: 9 de octubre

Hoy me llamó Wayne para invitarme al cine, pero pienso que acabo de[1] tener un malentendido[2] cultural con él. Creo que Wayne quiere salir conmigo, y yo quiero salir con él, pero como no conoce[3] mis costumbres, no se ofreció a venir a la casa por mí. Creo que él no entiende que tiene que venir por mí a mi casa; así mis papás pueden conocerlo[4]. Wayne va a pensar que no quiero salir con él o que estoy loca. ¡Llegar con Ana Mari y Ramón a nuestra primera cita! ¡Qué problema! Bueno, los dos tenemos que recordar que tenemos culturas y costumbres diferentes. ¡Así es más interesante! ¡A ver qué pasa el sábado!

[1]*I have just* [2]*misunderstanding* [3]*he doesn't know* [4]*meet him*

En papel: ¡Un viaje a Salamanca! Vas a ir a Salamanca a estudiar el próximo verano *(summer)*. Escríbele una carta a la familia con quien vas a vivir para presentarte *(introduce yourself)*. Incluye esta información:

- tu nombre, tu edad y una descripción de tu familia
- tu rutina diaria y cosas que quieres hacer en Salamanca
- los platos que te gusta comer y los que no puedes comer
- las actividades que te gusta hacer después de las clases y los fines de semana

 ¡A ver de nuevo!

 Parte 1. Escucha **Escenas de la vida** otra vez para escribir un resumen del episodio.

El resumen debe contestar estas preguntas:

¿A qué hora quiere Wayne ir al cine?
¿Cómo van a llegar al cine?
¿Qué error comete *(makes)* Wayne?
¿Sofía acepta ir al cine?
¿Por qué llama Sofía a Ana Mari inmediatamente?
¿Qué piensa Ana Mari?
Por fin, ¿quiénes van al cine?

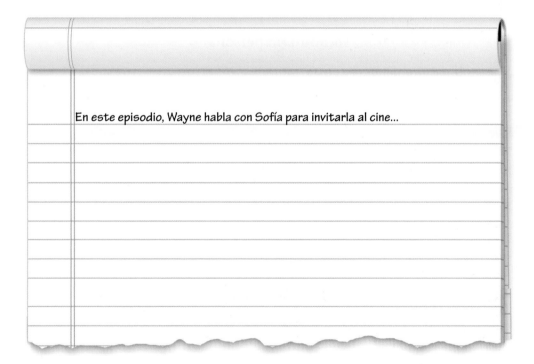

En este episodio, Wayne habla con Sofía para invitarla al cine...

 Parte 2. Ahora trabaja con un(a) compañero/a para comparar la información y añadir lo que te haya faltado.

Práctica adicional			
Cuaderno de tareas p. 252, L	invitaciones. vhlcentral.com Episodio 10	invitaciones. vhlcentral.com Lab practice	invitaciones. vhlcentral.com Episodio 10

Verbos

almorzar (o → ue)	*to have lunch*	**pensar (e → ie) en**	*to think about (someone or something)*
dormir (o → ue) bien/mal	*to sleep well/poorly*		
empezar a... (e → ie)	*to start...*	**pensar (e → ie) que...**	*to think that...*
encontrar (o → ue)	*to find*	**poder (o → ue)**	*to be able to, can*
entender (e → ie)	*to understand*	**(no) poder (o → ue) ir**	*to (not) be able to go*
el problema	*the problem*	**preferir (e → ie)**	*to prefer*
invitar a	*to invite*	**querer (e → ie)**	*to want; to love*
jugar (u → ue) (al) tenis	*to play tennis*	**recordar (o → ue)**	*to remember*
manejar	*to drive*	**venir (e → ie)**	*to come*
		venir (e → ie) por mí	*to pick me up*

Las preposiciones y los pronombres preposicionales

a mí	*to me*	**por él**	*for him*	**de ellos/ellas**	*from/about them*
para ti	*for you*	**de nosotros/as**	*from/about us*	**conmigo**	*with me*
con ella	*with her*	**de ustedes**	*from/about you* (pl.)	**contigo**	*with you*

Vocabulario personal

Write all the words you need to know in Spanish so that you can talk in greater detail about your dates and your weekend plans.

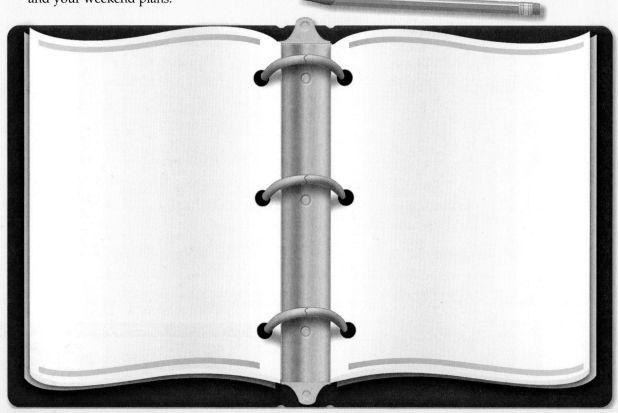

Cuaderno de tareas

Episodio

10

Escenas de la vida: Una invitación confusa

A. ¡A ver cuánto entendiste! See how much of the **Escena** you understood by matching the Spanish sentences with their English equivalents.

_____ 1. No viene por mí.

_____ 2. Es normal hacer eso en una cita.

_____ 3. Vamos a encontrarnos ahí.

_____ 4. La película empieza temprano.

_____ 5. Voy contigo.

_____ 6. ¿Puedes ir conmigo?

_____ 7. La próxima vez te apuesto que viene por mí.

_____ 8. ¡A ver si hay una próxima vez!

_____ 9. En una cita, el muchacho viene a la casa.

_____ 10. ¿Puedes creer que no viene por mí?

a. The movie starts early.

b. Next time I bet you he'll come to pick me up.

c. Can you believe he won't pick me up?

d. We'll see if there's a next time!

e. He's not going to pick me up.

f. It's normal to do that on a date.

g. We're going to meet there.

h. On a date, the guy comes to your house.

i. Can you go with me?

j. I'll go with you.

Gramática 1

Accepting and declining invitations
• **Stem-changing verbs (e → ie) and (o → ue)**

B. Una invitación a jugar. Use the verbs to complete the conversation.

quieres	puedo	empieza	encuentro
venir	prefiero	preferir	puedes

Ramón   Hola, Wayne, ¿(1) _____ ir a jugar fútbol esta tarde?

Wayne   Me gustaría (*I would like to*), pero no (2) _____ porque no
(3) _____ mis tenis (*sneakers*) de fútbol.

Ramón   Tengo dos pares de tenis. Si quieres, (4) _____ usar los míos.

Wayne   Gracias, pero (5) _____ buscar bien mis tenis o ir a comprar otros.

Ramón   ¡Como quieras (*As you wish*)! El juego (6) _____ a las seis.
Si decides ir conmigo, puedes (7) _____ a mi casa.

C. ¿Qué hacen? Write a complete sentence for each illustration.

1.　　　　　2.　　　　　3.　　　　　4.

1. Wayne y su amiga/almorzar

_____

2. Adriana/(no) entender

_____

3. Manolo/encontrar trabajo

_____

4. ¿Tú/venir por mí?

_____

D. Un anuncio de periódico.

Parte 1. Adriana siempre lee el periódico para estar bien informada. Hoy encuentra este anuncio *(ad)* de un restaurante nuevo cerca de su casa. Completa el anuncio con las formas apropiadas de los verbos.

Restaurante El Huarache Veloz
Calle Rancho del Rey 345   Tel. 2-A-COMER

Si usted (1) _____ (querer) almorzar bien y sin *(without)* trabajo, venga a nuestro restaurante, El Huarache Veloz. Nosotros (2) _____ (entender) las necesidades de la mujer moderna que trabaja y que no (3) _____ (tener) tiempo para cocinar *(cook)*. Ud. y sus compañeros de trabajo (4) _____ (poder) comunicarse con nosotros por teléfono al número 2-A-COMER. Es muy fácil (5) _____ (recordar) nuestro número. Si usted (6) _____ (preferir), comuníquese por correo electrónico al hv@acomer.com. Nuestro restaurante se (7) _____ (encontrar) en las calles *(streets)* de Rancho del Rey y Paseo Ladera. Nosotros (8) _____ (empezar) a tomar órdenes desde *(from)* las ocho de la mañana.

Parte 2. Encuentra un restaurante en Internet que acepte las órdenes por correo electrónico. Escribe una descripción del restaurante. Incluye estos datos y otros que creas importantes.

- **nombre del restaurante**　　　• **dónde está**
- **qué tipo de comida sirven**　　• **qué platos te gustaría** *(would you like)* **ordenar**

E. ¡Ay, Lalo!

Parte 1. Use the appropriate forms of the verbs to complete the description.

tener	entender	llegar	preferir
recordar	querer	empezar	jugar

¡Lalo es tremendo! Sus clases (1) _____ a las siete y media de la mañana; por eso, (2) _____ que salir de casa a las seis y cuarto a más tardar *(at the latest)*. Pues nunca lo hace. Siempre (3) _____ tarde a sus clases. No (4) _____ que es muy importante ser puntual y responsable. Pero cuando (5) _____ salir con una chica, entonces sí (6) _____ que ser puntual es importante. Le dice a mi mamá: "Mami, (7) _____ salir temprano de casa porque a las chicas no les gusta que llegue tarde." ¡Vaya inconsistencia!

Parte 2. What is the inconsistency in Lalo's behavior? Explain in your own words.

_____

_____

_____

_____

F. Las actividades. Make up six true statements using elements from each column.

Modelo

Mi amigo Roberto piensa que su trabajo es aburrido.

yo	dormir	los libros
mi novio/a	entender	los problemas de matemáticas
mis profesores/as	jugar	(a) los/las estudiantes
mi hermano/a	encontrar	la tarea
mi amigo/a y yo	pensar (en/que)	comer
		bien
		hasta tarde los domingos

1. _____

2. _____

3. _____

4. _____

5. _____

6. _____

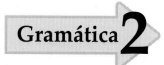

Nombre _____ Fecha _____

Gramática 2

Extending invitations
• Prepositional pronouns

G. ¡Ramón está celoso (*jealous*)! Use five of these words to complete the conversation.

ti	usted	conmigo	mí	contigo	ella	él	nosotros

Laura   Ramón, ¿quién va a ir (1) _____ a la fiesta?

Ramón   Nadie (*Nobody*). ¿Quieres ir (2) _____ ?

Laura   Lo siento, pero voy a ir con Jorge.

Ramón   ¿¡Con quién!? ¿Por qué vas con (3) _____ ? Es un antipático.

Laura   Pues sí, un poco, pero viene por (4) _____ a mi casa, me
paga (*he pays for*) todo y me lleva a lugares elegantes.

Ramón   A (5) _____ sólo te interesa lo material y eso no está bien.

H. Hablando de Wayne. Choose the appropriate words to complete the conversation.

contigo	ella	nosotros	ustedes
ti	ellos	él	mí

Ramón   Sofía, Wayne habla mucho de (1) _____ .

Sofía   ¿Ah sí? ¿Y qué cosas dice de (2) _____ ?

Ramón   Pues… que quiere salir (3) _____ .

Sofía   Él es muy agradable. ¿Por qué no lo invitas a salir con (4) _____
con más frecuencia? Así puedo conocerlo mejor.

Ramón   Creo que tú debes salir sola con (5) _____ .

I. Preguntas personales. Answer the questions using prepositional pronouns.

> **Modelo**   ¿Discutes mucho con tus hermanos?
> **Sí, a veces discuto con ellos.**

1. ¿Vives con tus padres?

_____

2. ¿Piensas mucho en tu novio/a?

_____

3. ¿Qué deporte (*sport*) juegas con tus amigos/as?

_____

4. ¿Hablas con tus profesores/as con frecuencia?

_____

5. ¿Vas por tu mejor (*best*) amigo/a a su casa cuando salen?

_____

J. Traducción. Write the following sentences in Spanish.

1. —Do you want to go out with me on Friday or Saturday?
   —I prefer Saturday, because Friday I can't.

   _____

   _____

2. —I am going to have lunch with him, and then we are going to watch a movie.
   —Is he going to pick you up?

   _____

   _____

3. —Are you going to start going out with him?
   —Yes, I think he is a good guy.

   _____

   _____

K. ¿Quieres salir? Manolo finally calls Ana Mari to go out. However, they have very different ideas about what kind of date it is. Write their conversation using the illustrations; take either Manolo's or Ana Mari's role. Make sure you use **poder, preferir,** and **querer** to express your preferences and desires. Finish up by agreeing to meet at a time and place.

Manolo	Hola, Ana Mari. ¿Cómo estás? Habla Manolo.
Ana Mari	¡Hola, qué milagro!
Manolo	_____
Ana Mari	_____
Manolo	_____
Ana Mari	_____
Manolo	_____
Ana Mari	_____
Manolo	_____
Ana Mari	_____

Nombre _____ Fecha _____

Para terminar

L. Chiquita.

Parte 1. Lee la historia de una joven liliputiense cubana llamada Espiridona "Chiquita" Cenda, basada en la novela *Chiquita* de Antonio Orlando Rodríguez°.

La familia Cenda vive en la ciudad de Matanzas, Cuba. El señor Ignacio Cenda es doctor, y su esposa Cirenia es una dama de sociedad. Ellos tienen cuatro hijos. Uno es una niña muy, muy pequeñita. Los hijos crecen[1] normalmente, pero Chiquita no. A los cuatro años, todavía parece[2] un bebé, aunque ya habla y camina[3]. Los papás están muy preocupados[4] y no entienden por qué su hija no crece igual que sus hermanos. Hacen lo imposible por lograr que la niña crezca; su papá la mide[5] todas las semanas y le da todo tipo de remedios, y su mamá está obsesionada con alimentarla[6] excesivamente con granos, proteínas y mucha leche. Chiquita no crece ni un centímetro; con tan sólo veinte pulgadas[7], parece una perfecta muñequita[8]. Mortificados, la llevan con muchos médicos, quienes determinan que la niña está perfectamente saludable, pero nunca va a crecer a un tamaño[9] normal.

Cuando Chiquita cumple[10] 15 años, sólo mide 26 pulgadas. Es una perfecta y bella señorita en miniatura, pero lo único pequeño en ella es su tamaño. Tiene la inteligencia, personalidad y voluntad[11] de un gigante. Habla, además de español, francés, inglés y alemán, canta ópera, baila y lee casi todo el día (a esa edad ya ha leído[12] a todos los clásicos de la literatura), porque no va a la escuela y no tiene amigos.

Antes de que Chiquita cumpla los dieciocho años, sus papás mueren[13] en un accidente y, poco después, ella queda en la ruina. Chiquita sabe que en Cuba una persona como ella no va a poder encontrar trabajo, entonces decide ir a vivir a Nueva York, pues quiere ser una gran artista de los teatros de variedades.

[1]**crecer** *to grow,* **crecen** *and* **crezca** *are conjugations of the verb* [2]**todavia...** *she still looks like/seems like* [3]*walks* [4]*worried* [5]*measures her* [6]*feeding her* [7]*inches* [8]*doll* [9]*size* [10]*turns* [11]*will* [12]**ha...** *she has read* [13]*die*

°Antonio Orlando Rodríguez es un escritor cubano que reside en Miami y que ganó el premio Alfaguara 2008.

Parte 2. Contesta las preguntas.

1. ¿Cómo es Chiquita? _____

2. ¿Por qué están preocupados sus padres? _____

3. ¿Qué hace Chiquita durante el día? _____

4. ¿Por qué Chiquita quiere ir a Nueva York? _____

5. ¿Qué opinas de la decisión de Chiquita de salir de Cuba a Estados Unidos?

_____

Parte 3. Investiga en Internet dónde trabajó Chiquita en Nueva York. Escribe un párrafo con la información que encontraste *(you found)*.

Revista
Cultural

La comida

pupusa

pabellón criollo

pastel de tres leches

Antes de leer

Mira las fotos de la revista para escribir lo que significan estas palabras.

maíz: _____

licuado: _____

cultivo: _____

alimentación humana: _____

---

1. Ahora mira la foto de la pupusa. ¿Qué crees que es? ¿Qué ingredientes crees que tiene? ¿La sirven en el desayuno, la comida o la cena?

2. Mira la foto del pabellón criollo. ¿Qué es y qué sirven con ese platillo? ¿Tú comes algo similar?

3. Mira la foto del pastel de tres leches. ¿Por qué crees que se llama 'tres leches'? ¿Qué leches son esas tres?

4. ¿Cuáles son tus postres favoritos?

A. La papa, el maíz y el cacao.

¿Sabías (*did you know*) que muchas de nuestras comidas básicas son de origen americano? ¿Cómo sería tu vida sin papas, maíz y chocolate?

La papa o patata ya se consumía (*was already eaten*) en América hace 13.000 años. Se han encontrado (*they have found*) evidencias de esto en un poblado prehistórico al sur de Chile, donde una comunidad comía (*used to eat*), entre otros vegetales, la papa silvestre (*wild*). Su cultivo empezó (*began*) en la región entre Bolivia y Perú de 7.000 a 10.000 años antes de nuestra era (*age*). Hay más de doscientos tipos de papa, de las cuales se  cultivan principalmente siete. La papa es muy nutritiva y de alto valor calórico. Forma, junto con el maíz, el trigo (*wheat*) y el arroz, el grupo básico alimentario de la especie humana.

Se cree que el maíz se cultiva desde hace 9.000 años en la región central de México. Como la papa, el maíz forma parte del grupo de productos esenciales para la alimentación humana por su valor nutritivo y versatilidad. Estados Unidos, China, Brasil, México y Argentina son algunos de los mayores productores.

El cultivo del cacao (planta con la que se hace el chocolate) se originó en América Central hace más de 3.000 años. Los mayas fueron (*were*) los primeros en documentar el uso del cacao como bebida de uso diario y ritual. La palabra **chocolate** es de origen azteca (*xocolatl*) y significa **agua amarga** (*bitter water*). Según datos históricos, el emperador azteca Moctezuma II (1480-1520) no bebía otra cosa que (*wouldn't drink anything but*) chocolate, preparado  con vainilla, chile y otras especias (*spices*). Como símbolo de amistad, Moctezuma II ofreció (*offered*) chocolate al conquistador español Hernán Cortés.

licuado de chocolate

Answer these questions in English to show your understanding of what you read.

1. How do we know that potatoes were eaten 13.000 years ago?
   _____

2. Why are potatoes an important part of the human diet?
   _____

3. When and where did humans begin to grow corn? _____

4. What countries are currently some of the major producers of corn?
   _____

5. Where did the cultivation of cocoa start? _____

6. Who were the first people to document its use? _____

7. What is the origin of the word **chocolate**? _____

8. What do we know about the use of chocolate by Moctezuma?
   _____

B. La comida hispana actual.

En el mundo hispano puedes encontrar comidas deliciosas y muy variadas. Entre muchísimos otros platos, en México tienen los tacos, las enchiladas y el mole (salsa donde se combinan las especias, los chiles y el chocolate). En América Central, las pupusas (tortillas rellenas [*filled*] de queso o de carne), el gallopinto (arroz y frijoles cocinados con cebolla [*onion*], cilantro y especias). En el Caribe, el mofongo (bananas verdes [(*green*) fritas [*fried*] mezcladas con especias y carne de puerco) y la ropa vieja (carne de res en salsa de tomate con cebolla y pimiento [*pepper*] verde). En América del Sur, el asado (*barbecue*) y el ceviche (pescado cocido [*cooked*] en jugo de limón con cebolla, maíz y camote [*sweet potato*]). Y en España, la paella (arroz con carne, mariscos y verduras) y las tapas (pequeños platos que van desde aceitunas [*olives*] o queso, hasta camarones o tortilla de patatas [*Spanish omelet*]).

1. Use the Internet to locate photographs of two dishes from each of these regions: Mexico, Central America, the Caribbean, South America and Spain. Label the dishes and list the ingredients.

C. El lado (*side*) dulce de la comida hispana.

¿Quién no disfruta los postres?

¿Quién no disfruta de un trozo (*piece*) de fruta fresca, un licuado (*shake*), un helado o un dulce de papaya, maracuyá (*passion fruit*), piña (*pineapple*), pitahaya (*dragon fruit*) o guayaba (*guava*)? Son numerosas y exquisitas las frutas americanas. Por su parte, el mango, el coco y la uva fueron (*were*) introducidas a nuestro continente por los colonizadores y comerciantes europeos.

Tomando como base muchas de estas frutas, en los países hispanos se han creado postres como los dulces de nopal (*cactus native from Mexico*), los pastelitos de guayaba o de coco, los tamales dulces y los panes dulces y galletas rellenos de mermelada de mango o de piña. Éstos y muchos más forman parte de la variedad de postres americanos y de España. ¡Qué rico!

Revista cultural

1. Use the Internet to locate photographs of several fruits and dishes containing fruits common in Spain, and Latin America. Label the fruits and the ingredients of the products/dishes you discovered.

2. Use the Internet to locate photographs of two desserts from each of the following regions: Mexico, Central America, the Caribbean, South America, and Spain. Label the desserts and list the ingredients.

D. Si quieres explorar más...

1. Prepare a list of drinks commonly found in the Spanish-speaking world.
2. Prepare a recipe from the Spanish-speaking world to share with the class. Reproduce the recipe so others can prepare the dish at home.
3. Make recommendations for healthy living by listing the ingredients in common foods and dishes of a Spanish-speaking country.
4. Participate in a competition in which you and your classmates prepare recipes for the same dish from different Spanish-speaking countries. As a class decide on the tastiest variation.
5. Make a list of national dishes and meal time traditions of ten countries in the Spanish-speaking world.
6. Explore mealtime practices in the Spanish-speaking world. Find out when meals are served, who is usually present and what is usually served.

Comprar en los mercados

1. El video. Watch this *Flash cultura* episode from Costa Rica.

... pero me hace un buen descuento.

¿Qué compran en el Mercado Central?

2. Comprensión. Select the option that best summarizes this episode.

    a. Randy Cruz va al mercado al aire libre para comprar papayas. Luego va al Mercado Central. Él les pregunta a clientes qué compran, prueba (*tastes*) platos típicos y busca la heladería.

    b. Randy Cruz va al mercado al aire libre para comprar papayas y pedir un descuento. Luego va al Mercado Central para preguntarles a los clientes qué compran en los mercados.

Episodio

11

Escenas de la vida: ¡A ganarse la vida![1]

A. ¡Mira cuánto puedes entender! Indica qué dicen (*what they say*) sobre sus trabajos.

Wayne:

☐ Me pagan bien. ☐ Me pagan mal.

☐ Salgo tarde. ☐ Salgo temprano.

☐ Mi jefe es agradable. ☐ Mi jefe es antipático.

☐ No me gusta mi trabajo. ☐ Me gusta mucho.

☐ Me dan propinas. ☐ No me dan propinas.

☐ No busco otro trabajo. ☐ Necesito encontrar otro trabajo.

Sofía:

☐ A ti te dan propinas. ☐ A mí no me dan propinas.

☐ A ti te dan problemas. ☐ A mí sólo me dan problemas.

☐ Los niños que cuido. ☐ Los clientes que atiendo.

☐ Ellos van a comer con nosotros. ☐ Ellos van al cine con nosotros.

Ana Mari:

☐ A mí me gusta mi trabajo. ☐ A mí tampoco me gusta mi trabajo.

☐ Me pagan bien. ☐ Me pagan poco.

☐ Mis compañeros me ayudan. ☐ Mis compañeros no me ayudan.

☐ Mis compañeros me invitan a almorzar. ☐ Mis compañeros me invitan a salir.

Ramón:

☐ Soy chofer de taxis. ☐ Soy chofer de limusinas.

☐ Tengo clientes europeos. ☐ Tengo clientes latinoamericanos.

☐ Siempre me dan buenas propinas. ☐ No me dan buenas propinas.

[1]*Making a living*

257

B. ¿Te diste cuenta? Indica quién hace los siguientes comentarios: Sofía **(S)**, Ramón **(R)**, Ana Mari **(AM)** o Wayne **(W)**.

_____ 1. ¿Qué tal el trabajo?

_____ 2. ¿Quién te da problemas?

_____ 3. Por suerte, mi trabajo es bueno.

_____ 4. La verdad es que no sé qué hacer.

_____ 5. Sabemos que son trabajos de tiempo parcial.

_____ 6. Ramón y Ana Mari, adiós, que les vaya bien.

_____ 7. Ellos van al cine con nosotros.

> **Cultura a lo vivo**
> Traditionally in the Spanish-speaking world, students don't always work while going to school. However, depending on the family's economic situation, many students help out in the family business and/or work during school vacations.

C. Los compañeros Completa las oraciones.

1. Los compañeros de Ana Mari son _____.

2. Sofía trabaja con _____.

3. Ramón es _____ de limusinas, sus clientes son _____ con él.

4. Ana Mari y Ramón van _____ con Sofía y Wayne.

5. Wayne le dice a Sofía: "Ya vámonos. Vamos a _____ al cine."

Práctica adicional		
Cuaderno de tareas pp. 275–276, A–C	invitaciones. vhlcentral.com Episodio 11	invitaciones. vhlcentral.com Episodio 11

Para comunicarnos mejor

Gramática 1

Talking about your job
• **Saber**, **salir**, **poner**, and job-related vocabulary

Empleos, ocupaciones y trabajos	
el/la ama de casa	_homemaker_
el/la chofer	_driver_
el/la empleado/a	_clerk, employee_
el/la jefe/a	_boss_
el/la mesero/a	_waiter/waitress_
el/la niñero/a	_baby-sitter_
el/la supervisor(a)	_supervisor_

Para hablar del trabajo	
el horario flexible/fijo	_flexible/fixed schedule_
las prestaciones	_benefits_
el puesto	_position_
el sueldo alto/bajo	_high/low salary_
el tiempo completo/parcial/libre	_full-time/part-time/free time_
el turno de la mañana/tarde/noche	_morning/afternoon/night shift_
las vacaciones	_vacation_
la ventaja/desventaja	_advantage/disadvantage_

Read the following examples:

¿**Saben** usar la computadora?	*Do they know how to use a computer?*
No **sé** si **saben** usarla.	*I don't know if they know how to use it.*
Yo **pongo** las cosas en su lugar.	*I put everything in its place.*
Salgo muy bien en mis clases de historia.	*I do very well in my history classes.*

Note that *only* the **yo** forms of the verbs have a spelling change. The rest of the forms are conjugated as regular **-er** or **-ir** verbs. So far you have learned the following verbs with irregular **yo** forms in the present tense: **estar (estoy), saber (sé), salir (salgo), poner (pongo), tener (tengo),** and **venir (vengo)**.

En el trabajo o la escuela

atender (e → ie) a los clientes	*to attend to customers/clients*
contestar los teléfonos/los correos	*to answer the phone/e-mails*
cuidar a los niños/ los ancianos	*to take care of (to watch) kids/the elderly*
poner* atención	*to pay attention*
poner* las cosas en su lugar	*to place (put) things in their place*
saber + [verbo]	*to know how to + [verb]*
salir bien/mal en las clases/los exámenes	*to do well/badly in class/exams*
salir temprano/tarde	*to get off (leave) early/late*

poner, like salir, has a g in the yo form. **Pongo atención en mis clases; por eso salgo bien.*

Learning Strategy: Advanced organizers

To maximize your learning before class, take a few minutes to look at the material that will be presented that day. Read the titles of the sections in the episode and look at the illustrations to get an idea of the story and to see what vocabulary and grammatical structures you will find. When you organize in advance, you will understand better and retain more information.

PRÁCTICA

A. Las personas y sus trabajos. Empareja la(s) persona(s) con el trabajo que sabe(n) hacer.

_____ 1. Una secretaria		a. organizar una casa.
_____ 2. Una doctora		b. entender los problemas de las personas.
_____ 3. Los sicólogos		c. manejar y reparar coches.
_____ 4. Un chofer		d. usar la computadora.
_____ 5. Una veterinaria	sé	e. ayudar y cuidar a los niños.
_____ 6. Las niñeras	sabe	f. combinar colores y formas.
_____ 7. Las amas de casa	saben	g. hacer operaciones médicas.
_____ 8. Un diseñador		h. abrir las botellas de vino.
_____ 9. Los meseros		i. trabajar con animales.
_____ 10. Yo		j. hablar inglés.
		k. cocinar *(to cook)*.

B. ¡Cuánto sabes de Latinoamérica! En grupos de tres personas, contesten las preguntas. Decidan quién sabe más de Latinoamérica.

1. ¿Sabes dónde están las pirámides mayas?

_____

2. ¿Sabes quién es el presidente de México?

_____

3. ¿Sabes cuál es la capital de Argentina?

_____

4. ¿Sabes cuándo es el Día de los Muertos *(The Day of the Dead)*?

_____

5. ¿Sabes a qué hora se comen las uvas el 31 de diciembre?

_____

6. ¿Sabes cómo se dice *"I love you"* en español?

_____

7. ¿Sabes cuántos países hay en Centroamérica?

_____

8. ¿Sabes en cuántos países se habla español?

_____

C. Ana Mari y Sofía hablan de sus trabajos. Completa las descripciones.

Ana Mari:

1. Me gusta mi trabajo porque me pagan bien. Tengo un _____ alto.

2. Trabajo tiempo _____, sólo 24 horas a la semana. Soy empleada de una tienda.

3. Tengo el _____ de la tarde: empiezo a las 2:30 y termino a las 7:30 de la tarde.

4. No me dan _____; tengo que trabajar todo el año.

5. Desafortunadamente, no tengo _____: no tengo seguro médico, pensión ni vacaciones.

Es divertido jugar con las niñas.

A veces son groseras conmigo, pero sé cómo controlarlas.

Sofía:

6. Soy _____; por las tardes y los fines de semana cuido niñas y niños. Me gusta mi trabajo porque tiene muchas _____: es flexible, trabajo las horas que yo quiero y es divertido estar con los niños pequeños. Con frecuencia los padres me dan regalos.

7. Las _____ son que no me pagan muy bien, tengo que _____ todas las cosas en su lugar y a veces los niños son groseros conmigo.

Práctica adiciona

Cuaderno de tareas
pp. 276–277, D–G

invitaciones.
vhlcentral.com
Episodio 11

Gramática **2**

Saying what people do for you
• The object pronouns <u>me</u> and <u>te</u>

Analizar y descubrir

In the video, you heard these statements. Study the examples and answer the questions.

Me pagan bien.	*They pay me well.*
Mis compañeros **me invitan** a salir y **me ayudan.**	*My co-workers invite me out and help me.*
Por lo menos a ti **te dan** propinas; a mí sólo **me dan** problemas.	*At least they give you tips; they only give me problems.*

1. Where are **me** and **te** placed in relation to the verb **(pagan, invitan, ayudan, dan)** in Spanish? _____

   Where are *me* and *you* placed in relation to the verb in English? _____

2. Notice the use of **a ti** and **a mí** in the third example. Use them for emphasis or contrast.

A mí me pagan mal, pero **a ti te pagan** una fortuna. ¡No es justo!	*They pay me poorly, but they pay you a fortune. It's not fair!*

Here are some common verbs used with **me** and **te.**

Las cosas que mi familia y mis amigos hacen		
ayudar	*to help*	Mi mamá **me ayuda** mucho.
contar (o → ue) los problemas	*to tell one's problems*	Mis hermanos no **me cuentan** sus problemas.
dar consejos/un regalo	*to give advice/a gift*	Mi abuela **me da** buenos consejos.
dejar usar su coche	*to let someone use one's car*	Mi novio **me deja** usar su coche.
invitar a salir	*to ask/invite someone out*	Tus compañeros, ¿**te invitan** a salir?
llamar	*to call*	Mi profesora no **me llama** a la casa.
mandar mensajes de texto	*to send text messages*	Mis amigos siempre **me mandan** mensajes de texto.
pagar	*to pay*	¿**Te pagan** bien en el trabajo?
pedir (e → i) cosas prestadas	*to borrow things*	Mi sobrina **me pide** ropa *(clothes)* prestada.
prestar dinero	*to lend money*	¿Quién **te presta** dinero cuando necesitas?

3. Now observe where **me** (or **te**) is placed in expressions with multiple verbs.

   Me tienes que ayudar.
   Tienes que ayudar**me.** } *You have to help me.*

   No va a invitar**me** a salir otra vez.
   No **me** va a invitar a salir otra vez. } *He's not going to ask me out again.*

4. In an expression with a conjugated verb and an unconjugated verb, you may place **me** and **te** _____ the first verb or attach it to the _____ .

5. Many other verbs you know may be used to express what people do for you: **Mi novia me escucha; ¿Te llevan a la universidad?; Mi mamá me lava la ropa;** etc.

¡Fíjate!

The verb **contar** is conjugated like **recordar**. ¿Recuerdas? ¿Me cuentas ese problema?

PRÁCTICA

D. Otra cita. Después de dos semanas, Wayne llama a Sofía para invitarla a salir otra vez. Lee la conversación y escribe la forma apropiada de los verbos en la lista. Después contesta las preguntas con un(a) compañero/a.

saber	salir	estar	querer
ver	invitar	poder	hablar

¿A qué hora voy por ti?

A las 12, ¿te parece?

¡Fíjate!
Remember that some verbs have irregular **yo** forms.

Sofía   ¿Bueno?

Wayne   ¿Sofía? Habla Wayne.

Sofía   ¡Hola, Wayne! ¿Cómo (1) _____?

Wayne   Bien, gracias. Oye, te (2) _____ al cine mañana por la noche.

Sofía   Gracias, pero por la noche no (3) _____. Voy a (4)_____ a mis abuelos. Pero si quieres, podemos (5) _____ a almorzar.

Wayne   Bueno, ¿a qué hora voy por ti?

Sofía   A las doce, ¿te parece? Esta vez (tú) no (6) _____ que invite a todos mis amigos, ¿verdad?

Wayne   ¡No, por favor! Ya (7) _____ cuál fue *(was)* mi error.

Sofía   No te preocupes. Fue un malentendido *(misunderstanding)*. Yo tampoco quiero ir con ellos esta vez.

1. ¿Adónde quiere ir Wayne mañana?

   _____

2. ¿Qué va a hacer Sofía por la noche?

   _____

3. ¿Adónde van a ir Sofía y Wayne?

   _____

4. ¿Sabes cuál fue el error de Wayne?

   _____

E. ¡Tengo suerte! *(I am lucky!)* Escribe el nombre de la(s) persona(s) que hace(n) estas cosas por ti. Después comparte *(share)* tus respuestas con un(a) compañero/a.

> **Modelo**   **Mis primos** me hablan por teléfono el día de mi cumpleaños *(birthday)*.

1. _____ me deja(n) usar su coche.

2. _____ me habla(n) por teléfono el día de mi cumpleaños.

3. _____ me manda(n) mensajes constantemente.

4. _____ me invita(n) a salir los fines de semana.

5. _____ me ayuda(n) con la tarea.

6. _____ me lleva al doctor cuando estoy enfermo/a *(sick)*.

7. _____ me cuenta los problemas de su familia.

¡Fíjate!
Use **nadie** for *nobody*. Remember to respond to your classmate's comments using these expressions.
¡Pobrecito/a! *Poor thing!*
¡Qué suerte! *What luck!*
¡Qué consentido/a! *How spoiled!*

F. ¡Qué consentido! (*How spoiled!*) Indica si los siguientes comentarios son **ciertos** o **falsos**.

	Cierto	Falso
1. Mi mamá me prepara el desayuno entre semana.	☐	☐
2. Mi compañero/a de cuarto me ayuda en todo.	☐	☐
3. Mi familia siempre me escucha cuando tengo problemas.	☐	☐
4. Mis profesores no me dan mucha tarea.	☐	☐
5. Todos me quieren mucho.	☐	☐
6. Mis amigas siempre me prestan dinero.	☐	☐
7. Mi jefe/a me deja salir temprano.	☐	☐
8. Mis abuelos me dan muchos regalos.	☐	☐
9. Mis amigos vienen por mí cuando vamos a las fiestas.	☐	☐

G. ¿Quién? Contesta las siguientes preguntas. Después entrevista a tu compañero/a para ver si tienen algo en común.

> **Modelo** ¿Quién te manda mensajes?
> **Mi amiga Irene me manda mensajes casi todos los días.**

1. ¿Quién te presta dinero? _____

2. ¿Quién te escribe cartas de amor? _____

3. ¿Quién te da buenos consejos? _____

4. ¿Quién te manda mensajes? _____

5. ¿Quién te pide cosas prestadas? _____

6. ¿Quién te deja usar su computadora? _____

7. ¿Quién te necesita más? _____

8. ¿Quién te escucha cuando tienes problemas? _____

¡Fíjate!
Remember to place **me** before the conjugated verb.

H. Una entrevista. Convierte a preguntas las oraciones de la **Práctica F** para entrevistar a un(a) compañero/a. Haz los cambios necesarios. Después decide si tu compañero/a es un(a) consentido/a (*spoiled*) o no.

> **Modelo** Mi mamá me prepara el desayuno entre semana.
> **¿Tu mamá te prepara el desayuno entre semana?**

I. Una persona especial. Habla con un(a) compañero/a de una persona importante en tu vida. Explica las cosas que esta persona hace por ti. Usa los verbos de la página 261.

> **Modelo** **Mi hermana es muy importante para mí. Siempre me
> ayuda cuando tengo problemas. Hablo mucho con ella
> porque siempre me da buenos consejos. Nunca me presta
> dinero; no tiene porque compra mucha ropa. Pero me
> deja usar su coche y su computadora cuando los necesito.**

J. El trabajo de Adriana.

Parte 1. Escucha la narración de Adriana para completar el párrafo.

(1) _____ que tengo algunos problemas con mi esposo porque trabajo y también (2) _____, pero para mí es importante adquirir experiencia y aprender cosas relacionadas con mi carrera. Mi jefe es muy bueno. (3) _____ mucho y me explica (4) _____ no sé hacer algo que él desea. (5) _____ muchas cosas interesantes en la oficina. Llamo por teléfono a (6) _____ clientes para saber si todo está bien con nuestros productos. Analizo muchos expedientes *(files)* y (7) _____ los documentos importantes en orden. Mi jefe también (8) _____ su computadora cuando necesito (9) _____ mis trabajos de la universidad. Además, (10) _____ salir temprano cuando termino todo el trabajo a tiempo.

Adriana

Parte 2. Ahora responde a las preguntas.

1. ¿Por qué quiere Adriana trabajar?

_____

2. ¿Cómo es su jefe?

_____

3. ¿Qué hace Adriana en la oficina donde trabaja?

_____

4. ¿Tu jefe te presta su computadora? ¿Te deja salir temprano? ¿Te ayuda cuando no entiendes algo?

_____

K. El trabajo.

Parte 1. Primero contesta las preguntas en tu cuaderno. Después entrevista a un(a) compañero/a para determinar quién tiene el mejor *(the best)* trabajo. Si no trabajas, entrevista a una persona de tu familia que trabaja. Escribe sus respuestas.

1. ¿Dónde trabajas? ¿Qué días trabajas? ¿Qué haces en tu trabajo?
2. ¿Tienes buen sueldo? ¿Trabajas tiempo completo o tiempo parcial?
3. ¿Qué prestaciones tienes? ¿Cuándo te dan vacaciones? ¿Cuántos días?
4. ¿Cómo es tu jefe/a?
5. ¿Por qué trabajas ahí? ¿Qué ventajas/desventajas tienes?
6. ¿Te dejan hablar por teléfono? ¿Qué cosas no te dejan hacer?

Parte 2. Ahora escribe una descripción para tu profesor(a).

L. Preguntas personales. Usa las siguientes preguntas para conversar con tu compañero/a.

> **Modelo**   ¿Haces ejercicio? ¿Dónde? ¿Con qué frecuencia?
> **Hago ejercicio tres veces a la semana.**
> **Mi amigo Ramón me llama para ir al gimnasio. ¿Y tú?**

1. ¿Haces ejercicio? ¿Dónde? ¿Con qué frecuencia? ¿Quién te invita a hacer ejercicio?

   _____

   _____

2. ¿Sabes cocinar? ¿Qué platos haces? ¿Con qué frecuencia cocinas? ¿Te gusta cocinar?

   _____

   _____

3. ¿A qué hora sales del trabajo? ¿Qué días sales tarde? Si tú no trabajas, ¿quién sale tarde del trabajo entre tus familiares y amigos? ¿Quién sale temprano? ¿A qué hora?

   _____

   _____

4. ¿Ves a tus familiares con frecuencia? ¿Cuándo ves a tus tíos y primos? ¿Qué actividades haces con ellos? ¿Te llaman con frecuencia?

   _____

   _____

5. ¿Pones tu ropa en el clóset o en el suelo (*floor*) cuando llegas tarde a casa? ¿Dónde pones tu mochila? ¿Y tus libros? En general, ¿pones las cosas en su lugar?

   _____

   _____

6. Normalmente, ¿sales bien en tus clases? ¿A veces sales mal en algunas clases? ¿En cuáles? ¿Por qué? ¿Qué necesitas hacer para salir bien en los exámenes?

   _____

   _____

Práctica adicional

Cuaderno de tareas
pp. 278–279, H–K

invitaciones.
vhlcentral.com
Episodio 11

invitaciones.
vhlcentral.com
Episodio 11

Actividades comunicativas

A. La fotonovela.

 Parte 1. Con un(a) compañero/a, habla de las actividades en cada ilustración.

> **Modelo**   Generalmente llego a mi casa a las seis. Tengo clase a las
> cuatro y el profesor me deja salir temprano. ¿Y tú?

  Parte 2. En grupos de cuatro, seleccionen cinco de las siguientes actividades para escribir una descripción de lo que hace Adriana entre semana. Después tu grupo va a leer la descripción a la clase y tus compañeros deben adivinar (*guess*) las letras de las actividades que usaron en la descripción. Usen expresiones como **generalmente, con frecuencia, casi siempre** y **muchas veces.**

> **Modelo**   Hay semanas que son terribles para mí. A veces…

B. Sopa de palabras.

Instrucciones para **Estudiante 1**

First, create logical sentences out of the scrambled words (the first and last words of each sentence are already in place). Then read your sentences to your partner, who will tell you whether they are correct. You have your partner's unscrambled sentences. Do not tell your partner the right word order immediately; let them try to correct any mistakes.

Modelo

Mis a compañeros invitan me **salir.**
Mis compañeros me invitan a salir.

En mi trabajo.

1. **Mi** hace horas a la supervisora me trabajar veinte más de **semana**.

_____

_____

2. **Mis** salen me cuando amigos escriben de no **vacaciones**.

_____

_____

3. **Mis** cuando soy clientes me dan buenas con propinas amable **ellos**.

_____

_____

4. ¿**Tu** cuando ayuda problemas jefe te tienes **económicos**?

_____

_____

5. **Mis** con agradables; compañeros con son muy ellos salgo **frecuencia**.

_____

_____

¡Fíjate!
Remember to place **me** and **te** before the conjugated verb.

Las respuestas de mi compañero/a

1. Mis papás no me dan suficiente dinero; por eso, trabajo.
2. Mis abuelos siempre me mandan chocolates el día de mi cumpleaños.
3. Mi hermano me llama por teléfono cuando necesita algo.
4. ¿Tus amigos te visitan cuando estás enfermo?
5. Mi prima estudia conmigo; por eso, voy por ella todos los días.

B. Sopa de palabras.

Instrucciones para Estudiante 2

First, create logical sentences out of the scrambled words (the first and last words of each sentence are already in place). Then read your sentences to your partner, who will tell you whether they are correct. You have your partner's unscrambled sentences. Do not tell your partner the right word order immediately; let them try to correct any mistakes.

Modelo

Mi ayuda primo me a la limpiar **casa.**
Mi primo me ayuda a limpiar la casa.

En mi casa.

1. **Mis** dinero; no me por suficiente eso, papás dan **trabajo**.

_____

_____

2. **Mis** chocolates el día me siempre abuelos mi mandan de **cumpleaños**.

_____

_____

¡Fíjate!

Remember to place **me** and **te** before the conjugated verb.

3. **Mi** teléfono necesita me por hermano llama cuando **algo**.

_____

_____

4. ¿**Tus** te cuando amigos visitan estás **enfermo**?

_____

_____

5. **Mi** conmigo; los por eso, estudia por ella todos prima voy **días**.

_____

_____

Las respuestas de mi compañero/a

1. Mi supervisora me hace trabajar más de veinte horas a la semana.
2. Mis amigos no me escriben cuando salen de vacaciones.
3. Mis clientes me dan buenas propinas cuando soy amable con ellos.
4. ¿Tu jefe te ayuda cuando tienes problemas económicos?
5. Mis compañeros son muy agradables; salgo con ellos con frecuencia.

C. Dos familias diferentes.

Instrucciones para **Estudiante 1**

You and a friend are spending the summer in Ecuador as exchange students. Call your friend to find out how things are going with his/her Ecuadorian family. You will start by finding out if:

- they take your friend to school
- they prepare good food for your friend
- they let him/her use the computer
- they help him/her with homework
- your friend's parents call him/her often

¡Fíjate!

Review the verbs in **Las cosas que mi familia y mis amigos hacen** on page 261.

| Modelo | ¿Te preparan buena comida? ¿Te llevan a...? |

Then read about your own situation at home so you can answer your partner's questions.

> This is your situation at home:
>
> Your host family is nice, but they are all very busy. They do not have time to cook for you, so you prepare your own meals. About three times a week, they take you out to dinner and do not let you pay for anything. They are generous, and buy you many small presents. They do not take you to school, nor do they pick you up from school; you have to take the bus. They are very busy people, and they have little time to help you with your Spanish homework. You do your own laundry and clean your own room.

Decide who is the luckiest! Be ready to explain your reasoning to the class; take notes in the space provided.

_____

_____

_____

_____

_____

_____

_____

_____

C. Dos familias diferentes.

Instrucciones para **Estudiante 2**

You and a friend are spending the summer in Ecuador as exchange students. Your friend calls you to find out how things are going with your Ecuadorian family. Read about your own situation at home so you can answer your partner's questions:

> This is your situation at home:
>
> Your host family is nice. They take you to school every morning and they pick you up. Your Ecuadorian mother prepares all your meals for you, does your laundry, and makes your bed. Your sister helps you with your homework and lets you use her computer. Your host family does not take you out much, nor do they give you gifts. Your parents back home do not call you, but they write e-mails to you every day.

Now find out how your friend is doing.

Find out if:
- they take him/her out to dinner
- they do your friend's laundry and clean his/her room
- they pick your friend up from school
- they help with homework
- they buy things for your friend

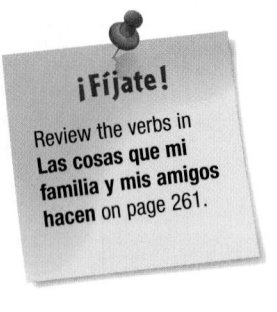

¡Fíjate!

Review the verbs in **Las cosas que mi familia y mis amigos hacen** on page 261.

Modelo ¿Te invitan a cenar? ¿Te llevan a... ?

Decide who is the luckiest! Be ready to explain your reasoning to the class; take notes in the space provided.

_____

_____

_____

_____

_____

_____

_____

_____

_____

Invitación a **Ecuador**

In your own words. Read the information below and then write what you understood.
In English, summarize the information in two or three sentences. Do not translate.

> Del álbum de
> *Sofía*

Ecuador tiene unos 14 millones de habitantes y es un poco más
pequeño que Nevada. En la pequeña ciudad de Otavalo, a unas
horas de Quito, vemos un excelente ejemplo de cómo los
indígenas ecuatorianos han logrado una prosperidad inigualable
(unequaled). Esta industriosa comunidad de indígenas (el 25% de
la población es indígena) otavalenses ha logrado establecer
contactos comerciales en Europa para la venta de sus productos
artesanales y textiles, sin la necesidad de intermediarios. En
Ecuador (que quiere decir *equator*) se encuentra también el
monumento de la Mitad del Mundo, donde la latitud es 0" 0" 0".
Miles de turistas visitan este monumento cada año. Ve al
Supersitio para ver un episodio de *Flash cultura* sobre este país.

La correspondencia

El correo: El club de corazones solitarios. *(Lonely Hearts Club.)* Acabas de recibir esta
carta. Lee las preguntas y la carta; luego contesta las preguntas.

1. ¿Qué hacen en **El club de corazones solitarios**? _____
2. ¿Qué ofrecen en el club para ayudarte? _____
3. ¿Cómo te preparan para la primera cita? _____

> ¿No tienes pareja[1]? No te preocupes: nosotros te encontramos la
> pareja perfecta. No es necesario ir a bares de solteros para encontrar
> la pareja ideal. Nosotros te encontramos pareja sin ningún peligro[2].
> Te hacemos un video donde puedes hablar de tus gustos, tus
> preferencias, tus actividades, tu personalidad y las características
> que deseas encontrar en tu pareja ideal. También te preparamos para
> la primera cita: te damos consejos prácticos en cuanto a la ropa, los
> temas[3] de conversación, los mejores restaurantes y las actividades
> culturales de la ciudad ese día. Solamente tienes que contestar las
> preguntas del cuestionario, y nosotros hacemos el resto.

[1]*partner* [2]**sin...** *safely* [3]*topics*

Invitaciones

 En papel: El club de corazones solitarios. Completa el cuestionario.

Club de corazones solitarios

1. Nombre: _____ 2. Edad: _____ 3. Sexo: ☐ hombre ☐ mujer

4. **Estatura (en pies):**   5. **Peso (en libras):**

☐ entre 4' y 5'   ☐ entre 6'7" y 7'   ☐ 100–125   ☐ 191–205
☐ entre 5'1" y 5'6"   ☐ más de 7'   ☐ 126–140   ☐ 206–225
☐ entre 5'7" y 6'   ☐ 141–165   ☐ 226+
☐ entre 6'1" y 6'6"   ☐ 166–190

6. **Color de pelo:**   7. **Profesión u ocupación:** _____

☐ negro   ☐ rubio
☐ castaño   ☐ pelirrojo

8. **Sueldo (en dólares):**

☐ 5.000–15.000   ☐ 26.000–35.000   ☐ 46.000–55.000
☐ 16.000–25.000   ☐ 36.000–45.000   ☐ 55.000+

9. **Marca sí o no según tus preferencias.**

Sí	No		Sí	No	
☐	☐	¿Fumas?	☐	☐	¿Viajas?
☐	☐	¿Haces ejercicio?	☐	☐	¿Te interesa el matrimonio?
☐	☐	¿Cocinas?	☐	☐	¿Prefieres sólo una amistad?
☐	☐	¿Lees?	☐	☐	¿Quieres tener hijos?

10. ¿Qué deportes haces/practicas? _____

11. ¿Tienes mascotas (*pets*)? ¿Cuáles? _____

12. ¿Cómo es tu personalidad? _____

13. ¿Cuáles son tus actividades favoritas? _____

14. ¿Qué características de la personalidad son importantes en tu pareja?
_____

15. ¿Qué características físicas prefieres en tu pareja? _____
_____

¡Fíjate!
To convert meters to feet (**pies**):
meters x 3.2808

To convert kilos to pounds (**libras**):
kilos x 2.2046

Parte 2. Ahora escribe un breve perfil para enviar al Club de corazones solitarios.

¡A ver de nuevo! Escribe un resumen del episodio. Incluye detalles que describen los trabajos de los amigos. Después, trabaja con un(a) compañero/a para añadir más información.

Práctica adicional			
Cuaderno de tareas pp. 279–282, L–M	invitaciones. vhlcentral.com Episodio 11	invitaciones. vhlcentral.com Lab practice	invitaciones. vhlcentral.com Episodio 11

Vocabulario del Episodio 11

Empleos, ocupaciones y trabajos

el/la ama de casa	*homemaker*
el/la chofer	*driver*
el/la empleado/a	*clerk, employee*
el/la jefe/a	*boss*
el/la mesero/a	*waiter/waitress*
el/la niñero/a	*baby-sitter*
el/la supervisor(a)	*supervisor*

Para hablar del trabajo

el horario flexible/fijo	*flexible/fixed schedule*
las prestaciones	*benefits*
el puesto	*position*
el sueldo alto/bajo	*high/low salary*
el tiempo completo/parcial/libre	*full-time/part-time/free time*
el turno de la mañana/tarde/noche	*morning/afternoon/night shift*
las vacaciones	*vacation*
la ventaja/desventaja	*advantage/disadvantage*

En el trabajo o la escuela

atender (e ⟶ ie) a los clientes	*to attend the customers/clients*
contestar los teléfonos/los correos	*to answer the phone/e-mails*
cuidar a los niños/los ancianos	*to take care of (to watch) kids/the elderly*
poner atención	*to pay attention*
poner las cosas en su lugar	*to place (put) things in their place*
saber + [verbo]	*to know how to + [verb]*
salir bien/mal en las clases/los exámenes	*to do well/badly in class/exams*
salir temprano/tarde	*to get off, to leave early/late*

Las cosas que mi familia y mis amigos hacen

ayudar	*to help*
contar (o ——► ue) los problemas	*to tell one's problems*
dar consejos/un regalo	*to give advice/a present*
dejar usar su coche	*to let someone use one's car*
invitar a salir	*to ask/invite someone out*
llamar	*to call*
mandar mensajes de texto	*to send text messages*
pagar	*to pay*
pedir (e ——► i) cosas prestadas	*to borrow things*
prestar dinero	*to lend money*

Vocabulario personal

In this section, write the words you want to know in Spanish so you can talk about your own job.

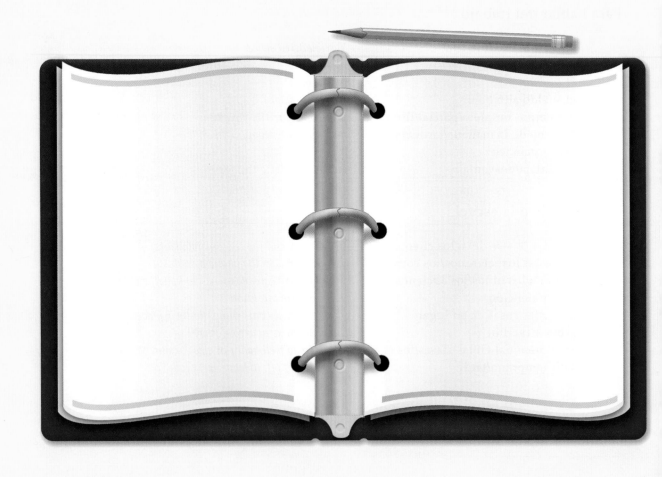

Cuaderno de tareas

Episodio

11

Escenas de la vida: ¡A ganarse la vida!

A. ¡A ver cuánto entendiste! See how much of the **Escena** you understood by matching the Spanish sentences with their English equivalents.

_____ 1. Cuido niños por la tarde.

_____ 2. A ti te dan propinas.

_____ 3. Me invitan a salir.

_____ 4. ¿Qué tal el trabajo?

_____ 5. La verdad es que no sé qué hacer.

_____ 6. ¿Te pagan bien?

_____ 7. Sabemos que son trabajos de tiempo parcial.

_____ 8. Yo creo que necesito encontrar otro trabajo.

_____ 9. Como hablo español, son generosos conmigo.

_____ 10. ¿Cómo que adiós?

a. They invite me out.

b. Since I speak Spanish, they are generous with me.

c. I baby-sit children in the afternoons.

d. Do they pay you well?

e. What do you mean "goodbye"?

f. The truth is, I don't know what to do.

g. We know that they're part-time jobs.

h. They give you tips.

i. How's your job?

j. I think I need to find another job.

B. ¡Tenemos que trabajar! Complete each phrase in column **A** with the appropriate element from column **B**. Then identify the speaker.

1. ¿Quién lo dijo? *(Who said it?)*

A	B
_____ 1. Soy mesero…	a. mal.
_____ 2. Tengo que trabajar de...	b. en un restaurante.
_____ 3. Me pagan…	c. tarde.
_____ 4. Salgo…	d. noche.

_____ **lo dijo.**

C. Los trabajos de Ramón y Sofía. Indicate whether the statements are **cierto** or **falso**.

	Cierto	Falso
1. Sofía trabaja durante las tardes y los fines de semana.	☐	☐
2. A Sofía le dan buenas propinas.	☐	☐
3. Ramón es chofer de autobuses.	☐	☐
4. A Ramón le dan buenas propinas.	☐	☐
5. Ramón practica el español en su trabajo.	☐	☐
6. A Sofía le gustan los niños, pero le dan problemas.	☐	☐

Gramática 1

Talking about your job
• Saber, salir, poner, and job-related vocabulary

D. Manolo va a una agencia de colocación *(employment agency)*. Use the expressions to complete Manolo's conversation with his counselor.

ventajas	tiempo parcial	sueldo	el puesto	el turno de la tarde
tiempo libre	vacaciones	desventajas	horario fijo	el empleado

Consejero   Bueno, Manolo, ¿qué tipo de trabajo deseas encontrar?

Manolo   Pues, no sé. Quiero un trabajo que me permita tener un poco de

(1) _____ para poder continuar con mi poesía y mi música.

Consejero   ¿Cuántas horas quieres trabajar y qué días?

Manolo   Pues, unas veinte o veinticinco horas a la semana. Puedo trabajar

cualquier día de la semana.

Consejero   Creo que tengo (2) _____ perfecto para ti: asistente de maestro.

Este trabajo tiene muchas (3) _____: sólo son veinte horas de

trabajo a la semana, por las mañanas; tienes (4) _____ con

frecuencia. Además *(Besides)*, te da la oportunidad de ver si te gustaría ser

maestro en el futuro. Y el (5) _____ es bastante bueno, quince

dólares la hora.

Manolo   ¡Qué lástima! *(What a pity!)*, pero por las mañanas no puedo. Sólo puedo

trabajar (6) _____. Definitivamente no puedo trabajar el turno

de la mañana.

Consejero   Bueno, hay muchos trabajos de (7) _____ en restaurantes. El

sueldo no es malo, pero una de las (8) _____ es que no te dan

muchas vacaciones.

Manolo   ¿Y el horario?

Consejero   Bueno, no es un (9) _____. Ellos te informan cuál es tu horario

para cada semana.

Manolo   Gracias por su ayuda, pero creo que por ahora voy a quedarme con *(keep)*

mi trabajo.

E. ¿Qué sabes hacer? Indicate whether you (or the people you know) know how to do the following things, using the verb **saber**.

jugar tenis	**esquiar**	**usar las computadoras**
patinar en línea *(rollerblade)*	**cocinar**	**hablar bien español**

> **Modelo**   Mis primos Mark y Jim saben patinar en línea.

1. _____
2. _____
3. _____
4. _____
5. _____
6. _____

F. ¿Qué quiere saber Wayne? Sofía and Wayne are talking on the phone. Judging from Sofía's answers, write down what Wayne asks her.

1. Wayne   _____

   Sofía   Hago la tarea en la biblioteca.

2. Wayne   _____

   Sofía   Los sábados salgo con Ana Mari y Ramón o con Manolo.

3. Wayne   _____

   Sofía   No, no veo mucho la tele. Prefiero leer o usar Internet.

4. Wayne   _____

   Sofía   Sí, me gusta mucho ver películas extranjeras.

5. Wayne   _____

   Sofía   Pues, pongo atención en clase y por eso salgo bien.

6. Wayne   _____

   Sofía   No, no sé cocinar, pero quiero aprender.

G. Justificaciones. Complete the sentences logically.

> **Modelo**   No sé tocar el piano porque **no tengo tiempo para aprender.**

1. No hago la tarea cuando _____.
2. A veces no pongo atención en clase porque _____.
3. Mis amigos y yo vemos películas en casa cuando _____.
4. Hago ejercicio porque _____.
5. Salgo con mis amigos cuando_____.
6. Voy a salir bien en esta clase porque_____.
7. No pongo mi ropa en el clóset cuando_____.
8. No sé jugar fútbol porque _____.

Gramática 2

Saying what people do for you
• **The object pronouns <u>me</u> and <u>te</u>**

H. Adriana está muy ocupada. Everybody wants Adriana's help today. Use the expressions to complete the questions her family asks her.

me lees	ayudarme	me llamas
me prestas	me cuentas	comprarme
pagarme	invitarme	me dejas

Viviana	Mami, ¿vas a (1) _____	con la tarea esta noche?
Santiago	Cariño, ¿vas a (2) _____	a salir esta noche?
Carlos	Mami, ¿(3) _____	usar tu coche esta noche?
Viviana	Mami, ¿(4) _____	la carta de tía Cristina?
Santiaguito	Mami, ¿(5) _____	veinte dólares?
Viviana	Mami, ¿vas a (6) _____	un uniforme nuevo?

I. Mi mejor amiga.

Parte 1. Ana Mari explains why Sofía is her best friend. Complete the description, using verbs and object pronouns from this episode.

> Sofía es mi mejor amiga. Ella (1) _____ con mis problemas. Hay mucha confianza (*trust*) entre nosotras. Ella (2) _____ sus problemas y secretos también. Además (*Besides*), (3) _____ consejos cuando los necesito. Si mi coche no funciona, ella (4) _____ usar el suyo (*hers*). Los fines de semana, (5) _____ a salir al cine o a cenar. A veces vamos a tomar café o a visitar a Adriana. Una amiga así (*like her*) no es fácil de encontrar.

Parte 2. Now write what *your* best friend does for you.

_____

_____

_____

_____

_____

_____

J. Mi profesor(a) favorito/a. Answer the questions in a paragraph to describe your favorite teacher.

¿Quién es tu profesor(a) favorito/a? ¿Qué clase enseña? ¿Te da mucha tarea? ¿Te deja entregar *(turn in)* la tarea tarde? ¿Te ayuda cuando no entiendes? ¿Te deja salir temprano? ¿Te escucha cuando haces una pregunta? ¿Necesitas estudiar mucho?

_____

_____

_____

_____

_____

K. Las personas que (no) me ayudan. Make up true statements about the people who do or do not do the following things for you.

mandarte mensajes	prestarte dinero	llamarte con frecuencia
dejarte usar su computadora	darte consejos	invitarte a salir

> **Modelo** Mi hermano Rubén nunca me presta dinero.

1. _____
2. _____
3. _____
4. _____
5. _____
6. _____

Para terminar

L. La curiosa de Ana Mari. Ana Mari wants to know more about Manolo, so she is asking Sofía many questions. How would Ana Mari ask the following in Spanish?

1. Do you know where he works? _____

2. Do you know who lives with him? _____

3. Do you know which days he works? _____

4. Do you know how many classes he takes? _____

5. Does he know how to play volleyball? _____

6. Does he know how to cook? _____

7. Do you know if he has a girfriend? _____

8. Do you know if he is going to ask me out? _____

M. Gustos y aptitudes. Read and complete the following survey to find out if your chosen career suits your talents and interests. Do not spend time thinking about your responses; instead, select the first answer that comes to mind.

Parte 1. Ocupaciones y profesiones. Para cada ocupación, selecciona la posibilidad de hacer ese trabajo: **(S) Sí:** me gustaría; **(I) Indiferente:** ni me gusta ni me disgusta; **(N) No:** no me gustaría.

	S	I	N			S	I	N	
1.	☐	☐	☐	Abogado/a *(Lawyer)*	13.	☐	☐	☐	Ingeniero/a
2.	☐	☐	☐	Director(a) de ventas	14.	☐	☐	☐	Contador(a)
3.	☐	☐	☐	Político/a	15.	☐	☐	☐	Gerente *(Manager)*
4.	☐	☐	☐	Ejecutivo/a internacional	16.	☐	☐	☐	Analista de sistemas
5.	☐	☐	☐	Educador(a)	17.	☐	☐	☐	Guardia de seguridad *(Security guard)*
6.	☐	☐	☐	Maestro/a	18.	☐	☐	☐	Mecánico/a
7.	☐	☐	☐	Líder religioso	19.	☐	☐	☐	Guardabosques *(Park ranger)*
8.	☐	☐	☐	Sicólogo/a	20.	☐	☐	☐	Ingeniero/a mecánico/a
9.	☐	☐	☐	Farmacéutico/a	21.	☐	☐	☐	Fotógrafo/a
10.	☐	☐	☐	Cirujano/a *(Surgeon)*	22.	☐	☐	☐	Músico/a
11.	☐	☐	☐	Asistente dental	23.	☐	☐	☐	Dibujante o Diseñador(a)
12.	☐	☐	☐	Investigador(a) científico/a	24.	☐	☐	☐	Escritor(a) de libros para niños

Parte 2. Materias de la escuela. Para cada materia, selecciona la mejor opción, aunque nunca hayas estudiado esa materia. *(It does not matter if you have never taken a class in that subject.)* **(S) Sí:** me interesa; **(I) Indiferente:** ni me gusta ni me disgusta; **(N) No:** no me interesa.

	S	I	N			S	I	N	
1.	☐	☐	☐	Leyes *(Law)*	13.	☐	☐	☐	Ley de impuestos *(taxes)*
2.	☐	☐	☐	Administración	14.	☐	☐	☐	Administración laboral
3.	☐	☐	☐	Ciencias políticas	15.	☐	☐	☐	Computación
4.	☐	☐	☐	Idiomas	16.	☐	☐	☐	Composición
5.	☐	☐	☐	Salud	17.	☐	☐	☐	Educación física
6.	☐	☐	☐	Sicología infantil	18.	☐	☐	☐	Geología
7.	☐	☐	☐	Pedagogía	19.	☐	☐	☐	Reparación automotriz *(auto mechanics)*
8.	☐	☐	☐	Sicología	20.	☐	☐	☐	Electricidad
9.	☐	☐	☐	Filosofía	21.	☐	☐	☐	Arte visual
10.	☐	☐	☐	Química	22.	☐	☐	☐	Historia de la música
11.	☐	☐	☐	Matemáticas	23.	☐	☐	☐	Diseño gráfico/dibujo
12.	☐	☐	☐	Estadística	24.	☐	☐	☐	Literatura

Parte 3. Actividades. Selecciona las actividades que te gustan o te interesan.

	S	I	N			S	I	N	
1.	☐	☐	☐	Hablar en público	13.	☐	☐	☐	Preparar tus propios impuestos
2.	☐	☐	☐	Entrevistar *(To interview)* personas	14.	☐	☐	☐	Trabajar en la computadora
3.	☐	☐	☐	Discutir de política	15.	☐	☐	☐	Escribir tus gastos del mes
4.	☐	☐	☐	Ver las noticias de otros países	16.	☐	☐	☐	Organizar tus documentos
5.	☐	☐	☐	Ayudar a personas con problemas	17.	☐	☐	☐	Ir a exposiciones de armas
6.	☐	☐	☐	Cuidar niños	18.	☐	☐	☐	Ir de campamento
7.	☐	☐	☐	Ser voluntario/a en tu comunidad	19.	☐	☐	☐	Limpiar el motor de tu coche
8.	☐	☐	☐	Organizar actividades en grupo	20.	☐	☐	☐	Participar en actividades deportivas
9.	☐	☐	☐	Hablar del significado de la vida	21.	☐	☐	☐	Ir a conciertos/galerías de arte
10.	☐	☐	☐	Hacer experimentos químicos	22.	☐	☐	☐	Hacer trabajos manuales/dibujar
11.	☐	☐	☐	Ver una operación de corazón *(heart)*	23.	☐	☐	☐	Ir a desfiles de modas *(fashion shows)*
12.	☐	☐	☐	Leer artículos de medicina	24.	☐	☐	☐	Escribir historias

Parte 4. Tipo de personas. Piensa si te interesa socializar con personas con las siguientes características.

	S	I	N			S	I	N	
1.	☐	☐	☐	Personas ricas	8.	☐	☐	☐	Personas estables y tranquilas
2.	☐	☐	☐	Personas de distintas culturas	9.	☐	☐	☐	Personas deportistas
3.	☐	☐	☐	Ancianos	10.	☐	☐	☐	Personas a las que les gusta el peligro *(danger)*
4.	☐	☐	☐	Personas con problemas de salud					
5.	☐	☐	☐	Científicos	11.	☐	☐	☐	Genios musicales
6.	☐	☐	☐	Personas famosas o importantes	12.	☐	☐	☐	Personas con talentos artísticos
7.	☐	☐	☐	Personas que tienen tus mismos intereses					

Parte 5. Tus características. Selecciona las respuestas que describan el tipo *(kind)* de persona que eres. **(S) Sí:** me describe; **(D) Depende:** depende de la situación: a veces sí, a veces no; **(N) No:** no me describe.

	S	D	N			S	D	N	
1.	☐	☐	☐	Puedes resolver problemas entre dos personas.	7.	☐	☐	☐	Prefieres trabajar horas regulares.
					8.	☐	☐	☐	Prefieres trabajar solo/a que en comités.
2.	☐	☐	☐	Te comunicas fácilmente con personas de otras culturas.					
					9.	☐	☐	☐	Tienes habilidades mecánicas.
3.	☐	☐	☐	Te gusta organizar actividades en tu grupo.	10.	☐	☐	☐	Prefieres estar al aire libre que en una oficina.
4.	☐	☐	☐	Tienes paciencia para enseñar.	11.	☐	☐	☐	Prefieres trabajar sin horario fijo.
5.	☐	☐	☐	Te gusta aprender cosas nuevas.					
6.	☐	☐	☐	Sabes escribir bien; de forma clara y concisa.	12.	☐	☐	☐	Te gusta crear cosas originales.

Parte 6. Interpretación de resultados. Basado en el examen *STRONG: Strong Interest Inventory* (publicado por *Consulting Psychologists Press, Inc.*), el inventario de preferencias, gustos e intereses puede dividirse en seis áreas principales:

Mecánica: construcción, reparación, trabajar al aire libre
Investigativa: investigación y análisis
Artística: crear y disfrutar el arte, drama, música, escribir
Social: ayudar, enseñar y cuidar a otros
Comercial: ventas, administración, persuasión
Tradicional: contabilidad, organizar, procesamiento de datos

Para saber en qué área están tus intereses, sigue los siguientes pasos:

1. Primero examina las **Partes 1, 2 y 3;** escribe el número total de veces en las que marcaste la columna (**Sí**) de las preguntas:

Preguntas	1–4	5–8	9–12	13–16	17–20	21–24
	____	____	____	____	____	____

2. Ahora determina el área de interés predominante. Por ejemplo, si en las preguntas 13–16 tienes el número más alto, entonces quiere decir que tus intereses están en el área tradicional. Busca arriba las carreras y profesiones del área tradicional.

Partes 1, 2 y 3

1–4: Comercial	13–16: Tradicional
5–8: Social	17–20: Mecánica
9–12: Investigativa	21–24: Artística

3. Ahora examina las **Partes 4 y 5** y haz lo mismo: escribe el número total de veces en las que marcaste la columna (**Sí**) de las preguntas.

Preguntas	1–2	3–4	5–6	7–8	9–10	11–12
	____	____	____	____	____	____

4. Ahora determina el área de interés predominante. Luego busca las carreras o profesiones de esa área.

Partes 4 y 5

1–2: Comercial	7–8: Tradicional
3–4: Social	9–10: Mecánica
5–6: Investigativa	11–12: Artística

Resultado final: Mi(s) área(s) de interés es/son _____, y las carreras que podría (*I could*) estudiar son: _____

Objetivos comunicativos

In this episode, you will practice:

✓ discussing professional plans

✓ talking about people and places you know

✓ talking about salaries

✓ avoiding repetition when answering questions

Episodio 12

Escenas de la vida: Los planes profesionales

 A. ¡Mira cuánto puedes entender! Escucha a los personajes expresar sus planes para saber...

a. ¿Qué quiere ser Sofía?

☐

contadora

☐

arquitecta

Sofía dice que...

☐ quiere trabajar con números.

☐ quiere diseñar edificios modernos.

☐ conoce a un arquitecto que gana más de $80.000.

☐ conoce a un contador que gana más de $8.000.

b. ¿Qué quiere ser Wayne?

☐

periodista

☐

analista de sistemas

Wayne dice que...

☐ entiende mejor a las personas.

☐ entiende mejor las computadoras.

☐ va a empezar con un sueldo bajo.

☐ va a ganar $45.000.

c. ¿Qué quiere ser Ana Mari?

☐

abogada

☐

maestra

1. ¿A quién quiere ayudar?

_____

_____

2. ¿A quién admira, y por qué?

_____

_____

d. ¿Qué quiere ser Ramón?

oficial de prisión

hombre de negocios

1. ¿Qué quiere estudiar?

_____

2. ¿Qué necesitan los profesionales del siglo XXI?

_____

3. ¿Cuántos idiomas sabe hablar?

_____

e. ¿Qué debe ser Manolo?

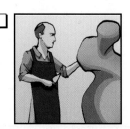

artista

veterinario

1. ¿Qué quiere ser Manolo?

_____

2. ¿Qué cosas le gusta hacer?

_____

_____

3. ¿Qué debería (should he) estudiar?

_____

_____

B. ¿Te diste cuenta? Escucha los comentarios otra vez para indicar si las oraciones son **ciertas** o **falsas**.

	Cierto	Falso
1. Sofía toma una clase de diseño de circuitos.	☐	☐
2. Ana Mari no va a defender criminales.	☐	☐
3. Ana Mari es idealista.	☐	☐
4. Muchos trabajos requieren comunicación en tres idiomas.	☐	☐
5. Manolo va a ser maestro de primaria.	☐	☐

C. ¿Quién? Escucha para indicar a quién se refieren estos comentarios: Ana Mari (**AM**), Manolo (**M**), Ramón (**R**) o Wayne (**W**).

_____ 1. Habla japonés, pero no lo sabe escribir.

_____ 2. Va a empezar con 40.000 ó 45.000 dólares de sueldo.

_____ 3. Dice que hay pocos abogados bilingües.

_____ 4. Tiene muchos talentos artísticos.

Práctica adicional

Cuaderno de tareas pp. 309–310, A–C	invitaciones. vhlcentral.com Episodio 12	invitaciones. vhlcentral.com Episodio 12

Cultura a lo vivo

In both Hispanic and Anglo cultures, most people are creative and productive; they take pride in their work and strive to support their families and improve their communities. Spanish speakers, however, do not typically define themselves by their work; they rather tend to place greater value on their relationships with family and friends. Spanish speakers typically do not find personal self-esteem in the amount of money they earn; far more important is the knowledge and level of education they have acquired. Although in Latin America, for example, teachers do not earn a lot of money, they are greatly respected and appreciated by the community.

Para comunicarnos mejor

 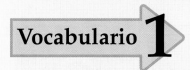

Discussing professional plans
- Careers and professions

¿Tiene futuro mi carrera?

Projections from the U.S. Department of Labor indicate that these professions will continue to experience growth.

Higienista dental
Título: licencia
Sueldo promedio: $24,63
por hora

Bombero
Título: licencia
Sueldo promedio: $865
a la semana

Enfermero/a
Título: universitario
Sueldo promedio: $4.934
al mes (*month*)

Carreras, ocupaciones y profesiones

el/la abogado/a	*lawyer*	**el/la ingeniero/a ambientalista**	*environmental engineer*
el/la administrador(a) de empresas	*business administrator*	**el/la ingeniero/a en computación**	*computer engineer*
el/la analista de sistemas	*systems analyst*	**el/la investigador(a) (forense)**	*(forensic) investigator*
el/la bombero	*firefighter*	**el/la maestro/a**	*teacher*
el/la contador(a)	*accountant*	**el/la médico/a**	*physician*
el/la diseñador(a) gráfico/a	*graphic designer*	**el/la oficial de prisión**	*prison guard/(parole) officer*
el/la educador(a)	*pre-school teacher*	**el/la periodista**	*journalist*
el/la enfermero/a	*nurse*	**el/la policía**	*police officer*
el/la fisioterapeuta	*physical therapist*	**el/la profesor(a) de idiomas**	*language professor*
el/la gerente	*manager*	**el/la programador(a)**	*computer programmer*
el/la higienista dental	*dental hygienist*	**el/la sicólogo/a**	*phychologist*
ganar bien	*to make a good living, to earn good money*	**el/la técnico/a en computación**	*computer technician*
		el/la veterinario/a	*veterinarian*

PRÁCTICA

A. Los profesionales. Empareja la descripción con la profesión.

_____ 1. Defiende a los criminales y a los inocentes.
_____ 2. Diseña productos buenos para el medio ambiente.
_____ 3. Escribe artículos para periódicos.
_____ 4. Cuida a los pacientes.
_____ 5. Enseña en las escuelas.
_____ 6. Repara las computadoras.
_____ 7. Administra compañías y empresas.
_____ 8. Protege a la comunidad.
_____ 9. Cuida y cura a los animales.
_____ 10. Programa computadoras.

a. ingeniera ambientalista
b. enfermero
c. maestro
d. programadora
e. periodista
f. veterinario
g. policía
h. abogada
i. administrador de empresas
j. técnica en computación

B. Estereotipos sobre las profesiones. Completa las oraciones lógicamente; algunas pueden tener varias respuestas.

1. Los _____ ganan mucho dinero.
2. Las _____ analizan a todas las personas con quienes hablan.
3. Las _____ son dulces y pacientes con los niños.
4. Los _____ saben hablar muchos idiomas.
5. Los _____ son estrictos y muy ordenados.

C. Adivina quién lo hace. Identifica la profesión que corresponde a cada descripción.

1. Este profesional le ayuda al dentista. También
les limpia los dientes a los pacientes. _____

2. Diseña sistemas de computación específicos
a las necesidades de las compañías. _____

3. Toma las decisiones importantes de una empresa.
Diseña e implementa planes económicos y de trabajo. _____

4. Representa a la organización; resuelve problemas
entre personas y grupos. _____

5. Ayuda a los pacientes con problemas
físicos y de rehabilitación. _____

D. Aspectos personales. Contesta las preguntas y comparte la información con un(a) compañero/a para ver si tienen cosas en común.

1. ¿Qué ocupaciones o profesiones tienen tus familiares y amigos?

_____

2. ¿Y tú, qué quieres ser?

_____

3. ¿Por qué quieres estudiar esa carrera *(major)*?

_____

4. ¿Cuáles son algunas ventajas de tu carrera?

_____

5. ¿Cuáles son algunas desventajas?

_____

6. ¿Cuántos años de preparación necesitas?

_____

7. ¿Dónde quieres trabajar?

_____

8. ¿Qué sueldo vas a ganar? ¿Qué prestaciones vas a tener?

_____

9. ¿Qué es más importante, ganar muy bien o tener una profesión que te gusta mucho?

_____

Práctica adicional
Cuaderno de tareas pp. 310–311, D–E	invitaciones. vhlcentral.com Episodio 12

 **Gramática 1**

Talking about people and places you know
• The verb <u>conocer</u>

¡Fíjate!

If you want to learn more about **conocer** and contrast it with **saber**, go to Appendix A, p. 408, at the end of this book.

Analizar y descubrir

Study the examples and answer the questions.

Conocer	
¿Quieres **conocer a** Wayne?	*Do you want to meet Wayne?*
Conozco a un arquitecto que gana mucho.	*I know an arquitect who earns a lot.*
¿**Conoces** Guadalajara?	*Do you know (Have you been to) Guadalajara?*
Ramón no **conoce a** mi abogado.	*Ramón doesn't know my lawyer.*
Mi hija y yo **conocemos a** una diseñadora excelente.	*My daughter and I know an excellent designer.*
¿Ustedes **conocen** Miami? ¿**Conocéis** Miami? }	*Do you know (Have you been to) Miami?*
Ellos no **conocen a** Emilio.	*They don't know Emilio.*

1. What do you need to place after **conocer** when referring to a *specific person*?

_____

2. Do you do the same when you are talking about a place? _____

PRÁCTICA

E. Personas y lugares.

Parte 1. Busca entre tus compañeros quiénes te pueden dar la información que necesitas. Usa el verbo **conocer**.

Banco de palabras
estilista *hair dresser/stylist*
consultorio *doctor's office*
taller *(repair) shop*
salón de belleza *beauty shop/parlor*

Modelo   un buen dentista
—Sarah, ¿conoces un buen dentista?
—Sí, conozco una. Se llama Elvia Cárdenas.
—¿Sabes dónde está su consultorio?
—Está en la ciudad de Chula Vista.

	¿Quién lo/la conoce?	¿Cómo se llama?	¿Dónde está?
1. un buen dentista	Sarah	Elvia Cárdenas	Chula Vista
2. una buena manicurista			
3. un buen restaurante chino			
4. un buen veterinario			
5. una buena discoteca			
6. un buen café			
7. un buen mecánico			
8. una buena estilista			

Parte 2. Comparte las respuestas con la clase.

Modelo   Frank conoce a una buena estilista. Se llama Gloria
y su salón de belleza está en Imperial Beach.

F. La familia de Sofía.
La familia de Sofía viaja mucho y conoce muchos lugares famosos. Completa las oraciones para saber a qué lugares ya fueron.

Modelo   Sofía **conoce** la pirámide de Giza porque fue a **Egipto**.

Banco de palabras
fui a *I went to*
fuiste a *you went to*
fue a *he/she went to*
fuimos a *we went to*
fueron a *they/you went to*

a. Perú
b. Chicago
c. París
d. Puerto Rico
e. Guatemala
f. Nueva York
g. ¿?

1. Mi familia y yo _____ la torre Eiffel porque fuimos a _____
2. Mis padres _____ las pirámides de Tikal porque fueron a _____
3. La profesora _____ Machu Picchu porque fue a _____
4. Mis primos _____ la Estatua de la Libertad porque fueron a _____
5. Mi tío _____ el Yunque porque fue a _____
6. ¿Tú _____ la torre de Sears? Sí, porque fuiste a _____
7. Yo _____ _____ porque fui a _____

Práctica adicional

Cuaderno de tareas pp. 311–312, F–G
SUPERSITE invitaciones. vhlcentral.com Episodio 12

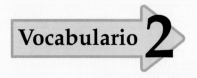

Vocabulario 2

Talking about salaries
• Numbers 101–100,000

When Wayne was thinking about his future career, he predicted that his entry-level salary would be between **cuarenta** and **cuarenta y cinco mil dólares.** Sofía said that she knows an architect who earns **más de ochenta mil dólares.** When talking about salaries, you will need to use numbers such as the following:

Más números			
101 **ciento uno**	200 **doscientos**	700 **setecientos**	10.000 **diez mil**
102 **ciento dos**	300 **trescientos**	800 **ochocientos**	20.000 **veinte mil**
103 **ciento tres**	400 **cuatrocientos**	900 **novecientos**	30.000 **treinta mil**
104 **ciento cuatro**	500 **quinientos**	1.000 **mil**	80.000 **ochenta mil**
110 **ciento diez**	600 **seiscientos**	2.000 **dos mil**	100.000 **cien mil**
120 **ciento veinte**			

1. The numbers from **doscientos** to **novecientos**, when followed by nouns, are adjectives and agree in gender with those nouns. Observe these masculine/feminine distinctions.

> Necesito quinient**os** pes**os**.
>
> Mi primo trabaja en Londres y gana seiscient**as** libr**as** *(pounds)* a la semana.

2. In some Latin American countries and in Spain, a period is used instead of a comma to indicate thousands, and a comma is used instead of a period to indicate decimals.

> En España: **2.367,00** euros   En México: **2,367.00** pesos

PRÁCTICA

G. Los cheques de la señora Blasio. Ayuda a la abuela de Sofía a pagar sus cuentas. Escribe en números la cantidad a pagar que falta en cada cheque.

1.

2.

Banco Santander Mexicano

Páguese por este cheque a:

Automotriz Salas

8 de noviembre de 2010

Fecha

$ _____

Moneda nacional

Noventa y siete mil ochocientos cuarenta y cinco.

La cantidad de

Sara Blasio

Cuenta personal
SARA BLASIO

Firma

2810-2182-4-12-2000

Cuenta   Cheque

7406-:11991715:(0011307993)-(0031) Santander S.A. Institución de Banca Múltiple

3.

Banco Santander Mexicano

Páguese por este cheque a:

Palacio de Gobierno

8 de noviembre de 2010

Fecha

$ _____

Moneda nacional

Dieciocho mil quinientos treinta y ocho.

La cantidad de

Sara Blasio

Cuenta personal
SARA BLASIO

Firma

2810-2182-4-12-2000

Cuenta   Cheque

7406-:11991715:(0011307993)-(0032) Santander S.A. Institución de Banca Múltiple

4.

Banco Santander Mexicano

Páguese por este cheque a:

Cablevisión

8 de noviembre de 2010

Fecha

$ _____

Moneda nacional

Quince mil doscientos sesenta y nueve.

La cantidad de

Sara Blasio

Cuenta personal
SARA BLASIO

Firma

2810-2182-4-12-2000

Cuenta   Cheque

7406-:11991715:(0011307993)-(0033) Santander S.A. Institución de Banca Múltiple

H. ¿Cuánto cuesta? You are helping an administrator with the budget for a new university classroom. Tell him/her the price of the items you have selected. Take turns with your partner.

> **Modelo** 10 calculadoras / $135.25
> **Diez calculadoras cuestan ciento treinta y cinco dólares con veinticinco centavos** *(cents).*

¡Fíjate!
The verb **costar**
(o ⟶ **ue**) means
to cost:
cuesta *it costs*
cuestan *they cost*

1. 1 televisión / $326.64
2. 1 reproductor de DVD / $213.00
3. 1 pizarrón / $111.99
4. 2 escritorios / $449.83
5. 2 sillas ergonómicas / $755.30
6. 6 programas de multimedia / $508.22
7. 15 diccionarios bilingües / $126.40
8. 1 computadora / $970.68
9. 1 cámara digital / $664.00
10. La Enciclopedia Hispánica / $843.10

I. Eventos históricos. Empareja las fechas con los eventos. Compara tus respuestas con las de tu compañero/a.

1. La conquista de México ocurre en _____ .
2. El hombre va a la luna *(moon)* por primera vez en _____ .
3. El muro *(wall)* de Berlín es destruido en _____ .
4. La Guerra Civil de Estados Unidos empieza en _____ .
5. Estamos en el año de _____ .
6. La Segunda Guerra Mundial empieza en _____ .
7. La independencia de Estados Unidos es en _____ .
8. Cristóbal Colón llega a América en _____ .
9. Las Olimpiadas en China son en _____ .

a. 1492
b. 1521
c. 1776
d. 1860
e. 1939
f. 1969
g. 1989
h. 2008
i. _____

J. ¿Cuánto ganan estos profesionales? Cada dos años la Oficina de Estadística Laboral proyecta los sueldos promedio de las profesiones con más futuro. Escucha el informe *(report)* para completar la información.

A la semana...

1. Un diseñador gana _____ a la semana.
2. Un doctor gana _____ a la semana.

Al mes *(month)***...**

3. Un policía gana _____ al mes.
4. Un piloto gana _____ al mes.

Al año...

5. Un administrador de empresas gana _____ al año.
6. Un técnico en computación gana _____ al año.
7. Un fisioterapeuta gana _____ al año.
8. Un bombero gana _____ al año.

K. Infórmate sobre tu carrera.

Parte 1. Busca información en Internet sobre una de las carreras o profesiones en la página 285 y prepara un reporte escrito. Busca el sitio del *Occupational Outlook Handbook*.

Parte 2. Prepara la información en español para compartir con tus compañeros. Incluye el mercado (*market*) de trabajo, la preparación académica, las prestaciones, las ventajas, las desventajas, el sueldo y el horario que tienen esos profesionales.

> **¡Fíjate!**
> Make a poster with the information so it can be displayed for the whole class to see.

Writing Strategy: Creating a simple plan

Planning to respond to a writing task in Spanish requires several steps:
1. First, you must be sure you understand what is being asked of you. To do this, you should read the instructions several times and make a brief outline of what is required. In this section, you are asked to use what you know about yourself—your interests, your abilities, the activities you enjoy—to explain why you have selected a certain career path. Perhaps you will focus on your personality as a key aspect of your choice.
2. Next, you need to determine the ideas you want to communicate. These must be simple enough to be communicated with the language you have learned: descriptive adjectives, verbs, and connecting words such as **por eso** and **porque.**
3. Finally, you need to organize your sentences in such a way that your meaning is clearly communicated. Use the outline you prepared to organize your writing.

Parte 3. En grupos de cuatro, compartan la información que encontraron *(you found)*.

Invitación a **Perú**

In your own words. Read the information below and then write what you understood. In English, summarize the information in two or three sentences. Do not translate.

_____

_____

_____

Del álbum de
Ana Mari

Perú es la tierra de los incas. Su cultura, ropa, idioma, comida y costumbres continúan influenciando al peruano moderno. Esta antigua y avanzada cultura construyó *(built)* increíbles fortalezas en remotos lugares de los Andes. Hoy en día *(Nowadays)* los descendientes de los incas usan la tecnología moderna. Para contestar estas preguntas, ve al Supersitio para mirar un episodio de *Flash cultura* sobre este tema *(topic)*.

1. ¿Para qué usan la tecnología en Cusco?
2. ¿Dónde hay acceso a Internet?
3. ¿Cómo ayuda (beneficia) la tecnología a la comunidad local de Cusco?

Práctica adicional		
Cuaderno de tareas p. 312, H	invitaciones. vhlcentral.com Lab practice	invitaciones. vhlcentral.com Episodio 12

Gramática 2 — Avoiding repetition when answering questions
- ## The direct object pronouns <u>lo</u>, <u>la</u>, <u>los</u>, and <u>las</u>

Analizar y descubrir

In their remarks, the characters used the words **lo**, **la**, **los**, and **las** to avoid repeating words already mentioned. Study the following examples and answer the questions.

Condoleezza Rice fue la primera mujer afroamericana en llegar al puesto de Secretaria de Estado. ¿La recuerdan?

¿Las computadoras? Las entiendo mejor que a las personas.

Voy a trabajar con computadoras.	*I'm going to work with computers.*
Las entiendo mucho mejor que a las personas.	*I understand them much better than people.*
Admiro mucho a Janet Reno.	*I admire Janet Reno a lot.*
¿**La** recuerdan?	*Do you remember her?*
También hablo japonés. Bueno, en realidad no **lo** hablo bien y no **lo** sé escribir.	*I also speak Japanese. Well, actually I don't speak it well, and I don't know how to write it.*
Todos mis amigos ya saben qué quieren ser.	*All my friends already know what they want to be. I envy them.*
Los envidio.	

1. In the first example, what word does **las** replace? _____

2. In the second example, what words does **la** replace? _____

3. In the third example, what word does **lo** replace? _____

4. In the fourth example, what words does **los** replace? _____

5. Where, with respect to the verb, are **lo, la, los,** and **las** placed? _____

6. Which other pronouns that you know are also placed before the conjugated verb?

_____

7. In a construction with multiple verbs **(En poco tiempo voy a hablar*lo* bien. / En poco tiempo *lo* voy a hablar bien.),** where may the object pronoun be placed?

_____

In summary, direct object pronouns match in gender (masculine or feminine) and number (singular or plural) with the nouns they replace, and are placed in the same position as the object pronouns **me** and **te**—that is, before conjugated verbs or attached to infinitives.

PRÁCTICA

¡Yo no los tengo!

L. ¿Dónde está? Como ya sabes, el compañero de cuarto de Manolo es muy desordenado; él nunca sabe dónde están sus cosas. ¿Qué cosas busca ahora? Completa los diálogos con la(s) palabra(s) apropiada(s) de la lista.

¡Fíjate!

Remember that object pronouns match the nouns they replace in gender and in number.

discos compactos	calculadora	diccionarios
el cheque de la renta	las fotografías	plumas

1. —¿Tienes _____?
   —No, ¡tú lo tienes!

2. —¿Dónde está mi _____?
   —No sé. No la necesito para nada.

3. —¿Tienes mis _____?
   —No, no las tengo. Yo uso lápices.

4. —¿Dónde están mis _____?
   —No sé. Yo no los tengo. No escucho tu música.

5. —¿Tienes _____ de la fiesta?
   —No, Sofía las tiene.

6. —¿Tienes mis _____?
   —No, yo nunca los uso.

M. La comida. Habla con un(a) compañero/a acerca de lo que les gusta comer y beber. No repitan la comida; usen **lo, la, los** o **las**.

> **Modelo** —¿Prefieres las hamburguesas con queso o sin queso?
> —**Las prefiero sin queso. ¿Y tú?**

1. ¿Cómo sirven el pollo en tu casa, frito (*fried*) o asado (*roasted*)? _____

2. ¿Cómo tomas el café, negro o con leche? _____

3. ¿Bebes la leche fría (*cold*) o caliente (*hot*)? _____

4. ¿Prefieres los huevos fritos o en *omelette*? _____

5. ¿Prefieres las enchiladas de pollo o de queso? _____

6. ¿Cómo sirven el espagueti en tu casa, con carne o con mantequilla (*butter*)?

_____

N. En la casa. Entrevista a un(a) compañero/a. No repitas el objeto directo (*it is underlined*). Usa **lo, la, los** o **las** en tus respuestas, según sea necesario.

> **Modelo** —¿Cuándo limpias <u>tu cuarto</u>?
> —**Lo limpio cuando tengo tiempo. ¿Y tú?**

1. ¿Cuándo visitas a <u>tus abuelos</u>? _____

2. ¿A qué hora haces <u>la tarea</u>? _____

3. ¿Qué día limpias <u>tu cuarto</u>? _____

4. ¿Con quién ves <u>películas</u> (*movies*)? _____

5. ¿Para qué usas <u>tu computadora</u>? _____

Ñ. ¡Cuánta repetición! The following comments are too repetitive. Use **lo, la, los,** and **las** to make the exchanges less repetitive. Then practice the dialogue with a classmate.

> **Modelo** —¿Adónde va **tu novio**?
> —Va a San Francisco. Mañana tengo que llevar a **mi novio** al aeropuerto y no voy a ver a **mi novio** hasta el domingo.
>
> **Sin repetición**
> —Va a San Francisco. Mañana **lo** tengo que llevar al aeropuerto y no **lo** voy a ver hasta el domingo.
>   or
> —Va a San Francisco. Mañana tengo que llevar**lo** al aeropuerto y no voy a ver**lo** hasta el domingo.

1. — ¡Qué bonita **pluma**!

   — Gracias. ¿Quieres **la pluma**? Tengo muchas.

   — ¿Puedo usar **la pluma**?

   — Sí, es tuya *(it's yours)*.

   Sin repetición

   — ¡Qué bonita pluma!

   — _____

   — _____

   — _____

> **¡Fíjate!**
> Remember that object pronouns are placed before a conjugated verb or attached to an infinitive.

2. — ¿Ves **a tus padres** con frecuencia?

   — No mucho, veo **a mis padres** dos o tres veces al año.

   — ¿Tú visitas **a tus padres** en Miami o ellos te visitan aquí?

   — Yo visito **a mis padres**. Ellos no pueden viajar.

   Sin repetición

   — ¿Ves a tus padres con frecuencia?

   — _____

   — _____

   — _____

3. — Mamá, **tu coche** siempre está limpio.

   — Por supuesto, lavo **mi coche** con mucha frecuencia. También pongo **mi coche** en el garaje. Además, cuido mucho **mi coche.**

   Sin repetición

   — Mamá, tu coche siempre está limpio.

   — _____

   _____

   _____

O. La encuesta dice... Esta actividad es similar al programa *Family Feud*. En grupos de tres, escriban las cinco respuestas que ustedes creen que son las más comunes. Tu profesor(a) tiene las respuestas correctas.

1. ¿Qué hacen los estudiantes con el libro de español?

> **Modelo**   Lo compran en la librería.

a. _____
b. _____
c. _____
d. _____
e. _____

2. ¿Cómo debe comportarse *(should behave)* un buen hijo con su mamá?

> **Modelo**   Un buen hijo debe invitarla a comer o al cine.

Un buen hijo debe...

a. _____
b. _____
c. _____
d. _____
e. _____

3. ¿Qué hacen las personas con sus coches?

> **Modelo**   Las personas los manejan con cuidado.

a. _____
b. _____
c. _____
d. _____
e. _____

4. ¿Qué necesita hacer Wayne para conquistar *(win over)* a Sofía?

> **Modelo**   Wayne necesita invitarla a salir otra vez.

a. _____
b. _____
c. _____
d. _____
e. _____

P. Josefina y Bo.

Parte 1. Mira las fotos y contesta las preguntas antes de leer el texto sobre Josefina y Bo.

1. ¿Qué profesión tiene Josefina? _____

2. ¿En qué otras profesiones usan perros para trabajar? _____
_____

3. ¿Crees que la carrera de policía es buena? Explica. _____
_____

Parte 2. Lee las preguntas, después lee el texto y por último contesta las preguntas.

1. ¿Qué hace Josefina y quién es Bo? _____

2. ¿Qué hacen antes de empezar su turno? _____

3. ¿Cómo cuida Josefina a Bo? _____

4. ¿Por qué le gusta su carrera? _____

5. ¿Cuáles son las desventajas de ser policía? _____

6. ¿Qué hace en su tiempo libre? _____

Me llamo Josefina López. Soy policía y ésta es mi compañera, Bo, una perra policía. Bo y yo hacemos mucho ejercicio, pues para hacer bien nuestro trabajo tenemos que estar en buena condición física. En la comisaría hay un gimnasio para los empleados; yo voy todos los días, y después Bo y yo salimos a correr antes de empezar nuestro turno. Me gusta mucho trabajar con Bo, es una perra muy inteligente y una excelente policía. Bo es mi responsabilidad y por eso la cuido mucho. La baño, la llevo al veterinario, le doy de comer y también la entreno para ser obediente.

Me gusta mucho mi carrera, pues sé que puedo ayudar a muchas personas en mi comunidad y también ayudo a combatir el crimen. Mi trabajo a veces es peligroso (*dangerous*), pero por suerte trabajo con personas muy competentes y buenas. Uno de los aspectos negativos de ser policía es que tenemos turnos muy largos. A veces trabajo doce horas. También es una desventaja que el horario no es fijo. Con frecuencia tengo que trabajar en el turno de la noche y tengo que estar siempre preparada por si hay una emergencia. El sueldo no es malo; ganas entre 40.000 y 60.000 dólares, dependiendo de los años de experiencia.

Ahora estudio criminología. Los cursos que tomo son cursos a distancia (*online*) y son muy interesantes. Aprendo mucho, aunque (*although*) los exámenes son difíciles porque hay mucha información. Lo bueno de hacer exámenes en línea es que los puedo presentar cuando estoy segura de que sé toda la información y cuando tengo el tiempo para hacerlo. En unos años quiero ser detective. Los detectives ganan mejor y es más interesante que ser policía.

Parte 3. Investiga cuánto ganan los policías y los detectives en tu comunidad. Entrevista a uno/a si puedes. Usa algunas de las preguntas de la página 159. Luego, presenta tu información ante la clase.

Q. Preguntas personales. Usa las preguntas como guía para hablar con tu compañero/a; escribe sus respuestas. Usa **lo, la, los** y **las** para evitar la repetición cuando sea posible.

> **Modelo** — ¿Tienes muchos amigos? ¿Cuándo los ves? ¿Los visitas con frecuencia?
> — Me gusta tener amigos; por eso, tengo muchos. Los veo en la escuela todos los días, pero también los veo los fines de semana. Estudio con ellos con frecuencia. Casi nunca los visito porque ellos prefieren venir a mi casa.

¡Fíjate!

Be as creative as you can with your answers. Put all the Spanish you have acquired to work!

1. ¿Tienes muchos amigos? ¿Cuándo los ves? ¿Los visitas con frecuencia?

_____

_____

_____

2. ¿Qué computadora usas? ¿La usas con mucha frecuencia? ¿Dónde la tienes?

_____

_____

_____

3. ¿Siempre haces tu tarea? ¿A qué hora prefieres hacerla? ¿Dónde?

_____

_____

_____

4. ¿Tienes novio/a? ¿Cómo se llama? ¿Lo/La ves todos los días? ¿Tus padres lo/la conocen? ¿Qué piensan de él/ella?

_____

_____

_____

5. ¿Vives con tus padres? ¿Los ayudas en la casa? Si no vives con ellos, ¿los invitas a tu casa? ¿Los llamas por teléfono con frecuencia?

_____

_____

_____

_____

Práctica adicional		
Cuaderno de tareas p. 313, I–J	invitaciones. vhlcentral.com Lab practice	invitaciones. vhlcentral.com Episodio 12

Actividades comunicativas

A. Larga distancia.

Instrucciones para **Estudiante 1**

Trabajas para la compañía de teléfonos más grande de Estados Unidos. Hay un problema con tu computadora y no puedes obtener el área telefónica de las siguientes regiones. Llama a tu compañero/a y pídele *(ask him/her for)* la información que necesitas. Él/Ella también te va a hacer preguntas; lee las respuestas como un solo número **(617 = seiscientos diecisiete)**.

> **Modelo** —¿Me puedes dar el área telefónica de Illinois?
> —Es setecientos setenta y tres.

	Área
1. Juneau, Alaska	_____
2. Portland, Oregon	_____
3. Cheyenne, Wyoming	_____
4. Tucson, Arizona	_____
5. Fargo, North Dakota	_____
6. Little Rock, Arkansas	_____
7. Miami, Florida	_____
8. Portland, Maine	_____

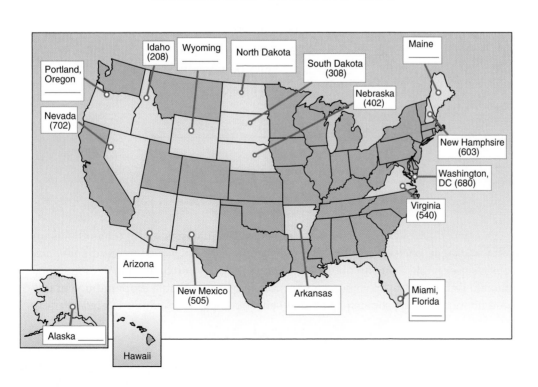

A. Larga distancia.

Instrucciones para **Estudiante 2**

Trabajas para la compañía de teléfonos más grande de Estados Unidos. Hay un problema con tu computadora y no puedes obtener el área telefónica de las siguientes regiones. Tu compañero/a te llama para pedirte las áreas de teléfono que necesita. Dáselas *(Give them to him/her)* y pídele *(ask him/her for)* la información que tú necesitas; lee las respuestas como un solo número **(617 = seiscientos diecisiete)**.

Modelo —¿Me puedes dar el área telefónica de Illinois?
—Es setecientos setenta y tres.

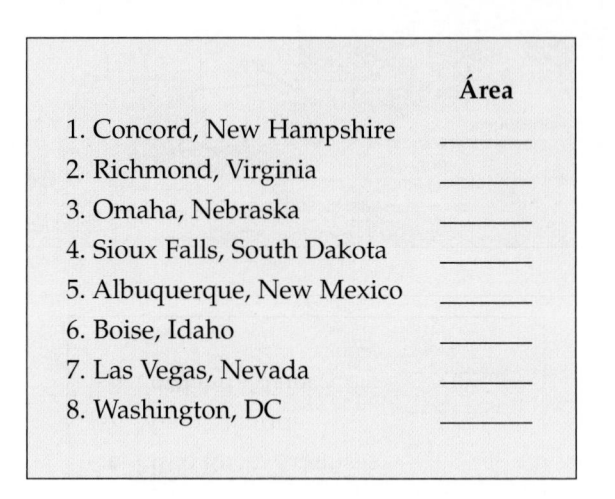

	Área
1. Concord, New Hampshire	_____
2. Richmond, Virginia	_____
3. Omaha, Nebraska	_____
4. Sioux Falls, South Dakota	_____
5. Albuquerque, New Mexico	_____
6. Boise, Idaho	_____
7. Las Vegas, Nevada	_____
8. Washington, DC	_____

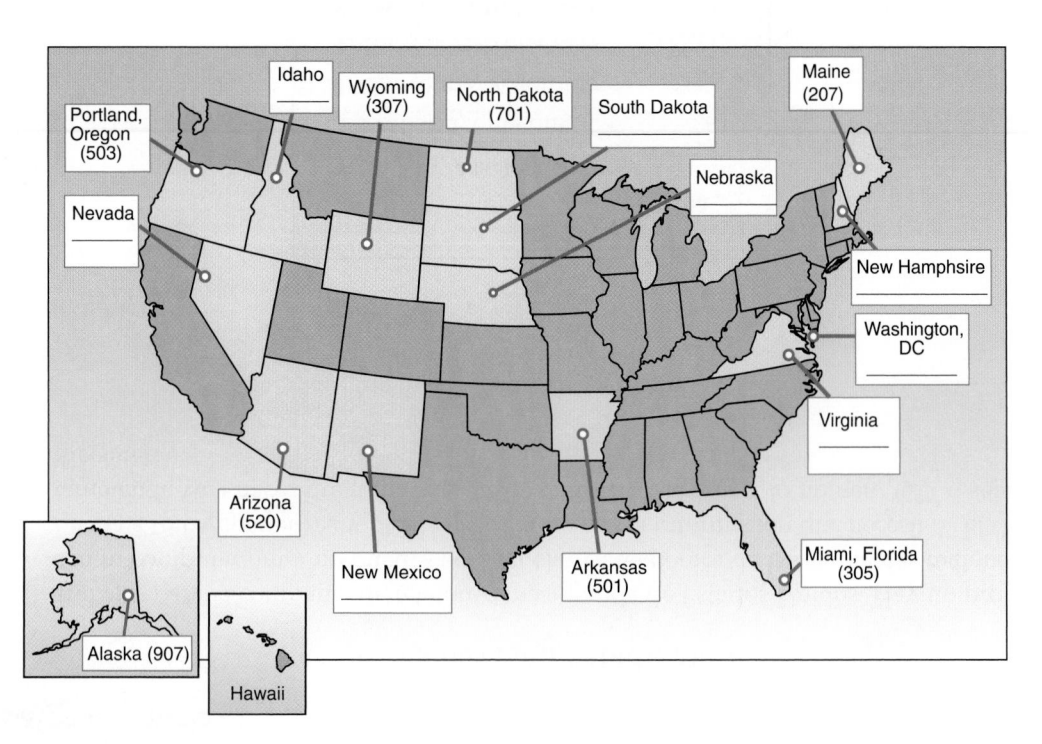

B. Crucigrama.

Instrucciones para **Estudiante 1**

Tu compañero/a y tú tienen el mismo crucigrama, pero tú tienes las respuestas que él/ella no tiene, y viceversa. Necesitas explicarle las palabras usando definiciones, sinónimos, antónimos u oraciones incompletas.

Modelo	11 vertical:	**Janet Reno es una...**
	5 horizontal:	**Esta mujer trabaja en una escuela y da clases.**

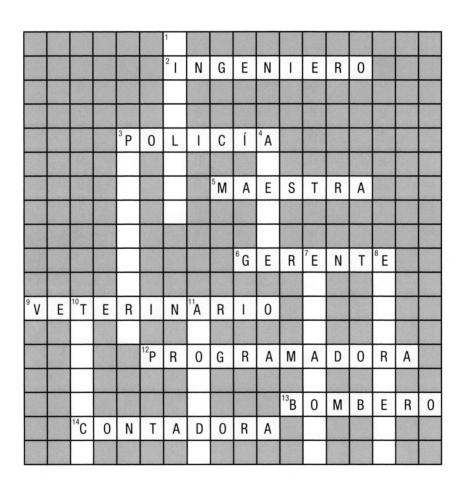

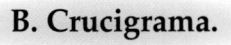

B. Crucigrama.

Instrucciones para **Estudiante 2**

Tu compañero/a y tú tienen el mismo crucigrama, pero tú tienes las respuestas que él/ella no tiene, y viceversa. Necesitas explicarle las palabras usando definiciones, sinónimos, antónimos u oraciones incompletas.

Modelo	11 vertical:	**Janet Reno es una...**
	5 horizontal:	**Esta mujer trabaja en una escuela y da clases.**

Crossword grid:

Vertical word at column 1: S-I-C-Ó-L-O-G-O (starting at ¹S, ²I, C, Ó, L, O, G, O)

³P-R-O-F-E-S-O-R-A (vertical)

⁴A-G-E-N-T-E (vertical) with 6, ⁷E... ⁸E...

Column words: ¹⁰T-É-C-N-I-C-O (vertical), R-A (at ¹⁰ area), ¹¹A-B-O-G-A-D-A (vertical)

⁷E-D-U-C-A-D-O-R-A (vertical)

⁸E-N-F-E-R-M-E-R-A (vertical)

¹⁴C-O (vertical)

C. ¿Quién hace las cosas?

Instrucciones para Estudiante 1

Parte 1. Cuando Sofía y sus amigos celebran algo (*something*), generalmente hacen una fiesta. Habla con tu compañero/a para saber quién hace las siguientes actividades para la fiesta. Tu compañero/a tiene la información que tú necesitas. Hazle las siguientes preguntas. Después, mira las imágenes y contesta las preguntas de tu compañero/a sobre un viaje (*trip*).

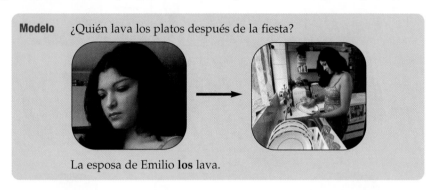

Modelo ¿Quién lava los platos después de la fiesta?

La esposa de Emilio **los** lava.

1. ¿Quién lleva el pastel? _____

2. ¿Quién prepara la ensalada? _____

3. ¿Quién compra las bebidas? _____

4. ¿Quién llama por teléfono a los invitados? _____

5. ¿Quién hace las hamburguesas? _____

6. ¿Quién limpia la casa? _____

La información para tu compañero/a:

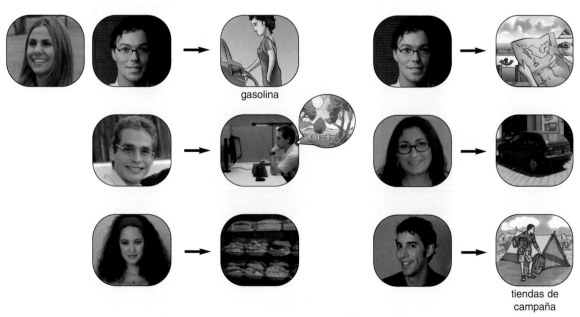

gasolina

tiendas de
campaña

Parte 2. Ahora hablen de quién hace las cosas cuando organizan una fiesta en sus casas. Después, hablen de quién hace las cosas cuando ustedes organizan un viaje.

Modelo —En mi casa, yo hago el pastel. ¿Y en tu casa?
          —En mi casa, mi mamá lo hace.

303

-C. ¿Quién hace las cosas?

Instrucciones para Estudiante 2

Parte 1. Mira las imágenes y contesta las preguntas de tu compañero/a sobre una fiesta. Después, habla con tu compañero/a sobre un viaje (*trip*) que Sofía y sus amigos están organizando. Hazle las siguientes preguntas para saber quién hace las siguientes cosas para el viaje. Tu compañero/a tiene la información que tú necesitas.

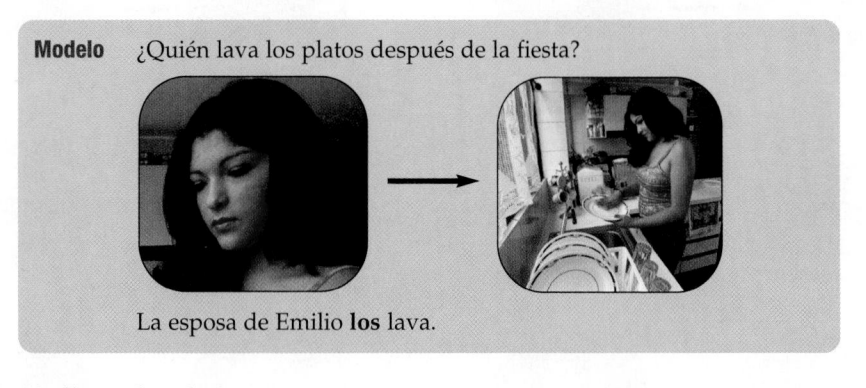

Modelo ¿Quién lava los platos después de la fiesta?

La esposa de Emilio **los** lava.

1. ¿Quién lleva el coche? _____

2. ¿Quién lleva el mapa? _____

3. ¿Quién busca la información del clima y el campamento? _____

4. ¿Quién paga la gasolina? _____

5. ¿Quién compra los sándwiches para el camino (*road*)? _____

6. ¿Quién pone las tiendas de campaña (*tents*)? _____

La información para tu compañero/a:

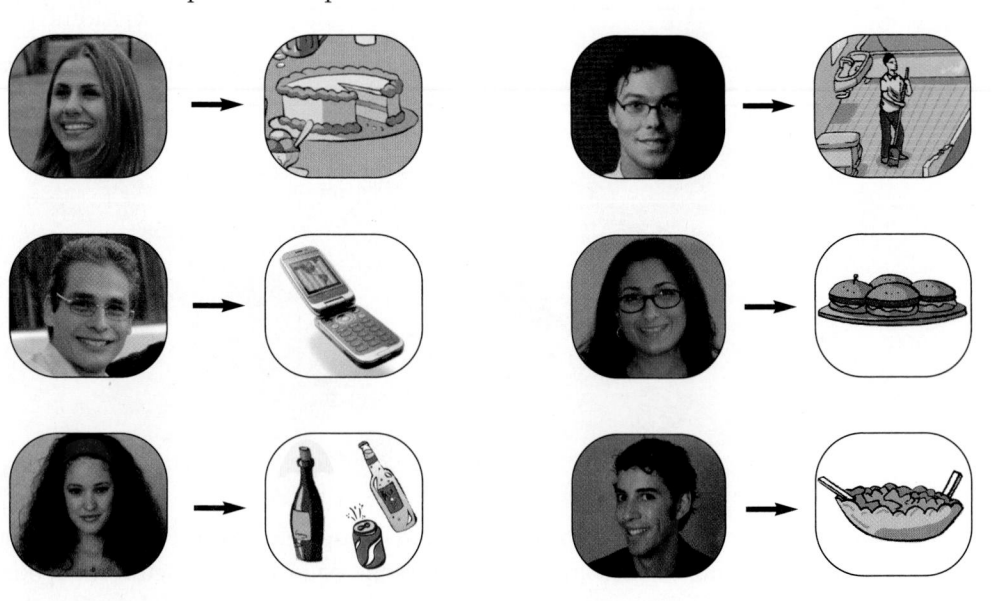

Parte 2. Ahora hablen de quién hace las cosas cuando organizan una fiesta en sus casas. Después, hablen de quién hace las cosas cuando ustedes organizan un viaje.

Modelo —En mi casa, yo busco la información del clima y las actividades. ¿Y en tu casa?
—En mi casa, mi papá la busca.

La correspondencia

El correo: Premio (*Award*) escolar "Espíritu de Superación". Acabas de recibir este artículo por correo. Lee las preguntas y después lee el artículo para contestarlas.

1. ¿Quién otorga los premios? _____

2. ¿Cuántos estudiantes solicitaron *(applied for)* este premio? _____

3. ¿Cuál es el estado con mayor número de ganadores *(winners)*? _____

4. ¿Cuánto dinero van a recibir los estudiantes ganadores? _____

5. ¿A quién admira la ganadora Silvia Posada? _____

Reading Strategy: Using context to determine meaning

Authentic Spanish texts will always contain words and structures you do not know. To understand them, you will have to use the context—the words that surround the unknown vocabulary and grammar—to accomplish the tasks you need to perform. Before reading the text below, pick out the words in the article that you do understand.

1. Underline the parts of the text you understand.
2. Write down the expressions you do not understand.
3. Use the parts of the text you do understand to guess the meaning of the unknown expressions.
4. Write down your guesses.
5. Compare your guesses with a partner and discuss your reasoning.

Then use this information to guess at the meaning of the text. Not only will you understand the article better, but you will also learn more Spanish.

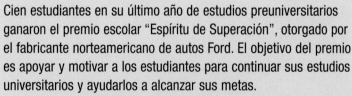

Cien estudiantes ganaron el premio
"Espíritu de Superación"

Cien estudiantes en su último año de estudios preuniversitarios ganaron el premio escolar "Espíritu de Superación", otorgado por el fabricante norteamericano de autos Ford. El objetivo del premio es apoyar y motivar a los estudiantes para continuar sus estudios universitarios y ayudarlos a alcanzar sus metas.

En colaboración con la cadena televisiva Univisión, un panel de jueces seleccionó a los cien mejores estudiantes de entre 35.000 participantes. Los requisitos eran: escribir una composición que hablara de la persona que más admiran y de cómo esta persona se ha superado, estar en el último año de estudios secundarios y de tener un promedio mínimo de 3,0. La selección de los ganadores se basó en la originalidad, creatividad, relevancia del tema y uso correcto del idioma.

Los ganadores van a recibir $1.200 cada uno y representan varios grupos étnicos de todas partes de la nación; el 88% de los ganadores son hispanos. Los estados con mayor número de ganadores son California con un 38%; Texas con 16%, Nueva York y Nueva Jersey con 13%, Illinois con 11% y Florida con 6%.

"Para nosotros es un honor premiar a estudiantes que han demostrado esfuerzo y dedicación en sus estudios. Su espíritu de superación nos inspira", declaró Ross Roberts, Vicepresidente y Gerente General de la División Ford.

La ganadora Silvia Posada de Los Ángeles, California, escribe: "Yo la admiro [a mi hermana] por todos sus logros en la escuela y por nunca dudar de sí misma. La seguridad y confianza que ella tiene en sus habilidades es la misma que tiene para mí, y ése es el mejor regalo que me pueden ofrecer."

En papel: Mi futuro. Escribe una carta a la Ford, basándote en la lectura de **El correo**, en la que describas:

- tus estudios, tus notas y tus planes profesionales
- por qué necesitas $1.200 dólares y qué vas a hacer con el dinero

 ¡A ver de nuevo!

 Parte 1. Escucha la conversación de **Escenas de la vida** o mira el video para hacer un resumen de los planes profesionales de cada personaje en tu cuaderno.

 Parte 2. Ahora trabaja con un(a) compañero/a para comparar la información y añadir la que no tienes.

Práctica adicional			
Cuaderno de tareas p. 314, K	invitaciones. vhlcentral.com Episodio 12	invitaciones. vhlcentral.com Lab practice	invitaciones. vhlcentral.com Episodio 12

Vocabulario del Episodio 12

Objetivos comunicativos

You should now be able to do the following in Spanish:

✓ discuss professional plans

✓ talk about people and places you know

✓ talk about salaries

✓ avoid repetition when answering questions

Las profesiones y las ocupaciones

el/la abogado/a	*lawyer*
el/la administrador(a) de empresas	*business administrator*
el/la analista de sistemas	*systems analyst*
el/la bombero	*firefighter*
el/la contador(a)	*accountant*
el/la diseñador(a) gráfico/a	*graphic designer*
el/la educador(a)	*pre-school teacher*
el/la enfermero/a	*nurse*
el/la fisioterapeuta	*physical therapist*
el/la gerente	*manager*
el/la higienista dental	*dental hygienist*
el/la ingeniero/a ambientalista	*environmental engineer*
el/la ingeniero/a en computación	*computer engineer*
el/la investigador(a) (forense)	*(forensic) investigator*
el/la maestro/a	*teacher*
el/la médico/a	*physician*
el/la oficial de prisión	*prison guard/(parole) officer*
el/la periodista	*journalist*
el/la policía	*police officer*
el/la profesor(a) de idiomas	*language professor*
el/la programador(a)	*computer programmer*
el/la sicólogo/a	*psychologist*
el/la técnico/a en computación	*computer technician*
el/la veterinario/a	*veterinarian*

Verbos

conocer	*to know; to meet someone*
ganar bien	*to make a good living, to make good money*

Pronombres de complemento directo

¿Me ayudas?	*Will you help me?*
Sí, te ayudo.	*Yes, I'll help you.*
Lo sé.	*I know it.*
La veo, Lo veo.	*I see her, I see him.*
Los conozco.	*I know them.* (m)
Las ayudo.	*I help them.* (f)

Más números

101	**ciento uno**	600	**seiscientos**
102	**ciento dos**	700	**setecientos**
103	**ciento tres**	800	**ochocientos**
104	**ciento cuatro**	900	**novecientos**
105	**ciento cinco**	1.000	**mil**
110	**ciento diez**	2.000	**dos mil**
120	**ciento veinte**	10.000	**diez mil**
200	**doscientos**	20.000	**veinte mil**
300	**trescientos**	30.000	**treinta mil**
400	**cuatrocientos**	80.000	**ochenta mil**
500	**quinientos**	100.000	**cien mil**

Vocabulario personal

In this section, write the words you want to know in Spanish so you can talk about your professional plans.

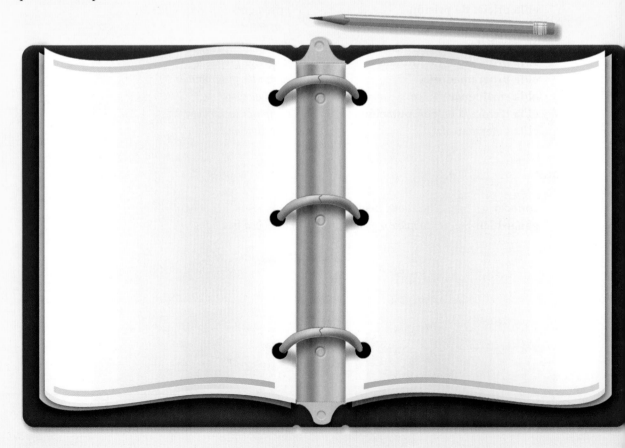

Cuaderno de tareas

Episodio

12

Escenas de la vida: Los planes profesionales

A. ¡A ver cuánto entendiste! See how much of the **Escena** you understood by matching the Spanish sentences with their English equivalents. Then identify the speakers.

_____ 1. Los envidio. _____

_____ 2. Tengo que ganarme la vida. _____

_____ 3. Me gusta cuidar a los animales. _____

_____ 4. Las entiendo mucho mejor que
     a las personas. _____

_____ 5. Me gustaría diseñar edificios
     modernos. _____

_____ 6. Voy a diseñar mi propia casa. _____

_____ 7. Voy a ser la mejor abogada
     del estado. _____

_____ 8. Estoy seguro que pronto voy a hablarlo
     perfectamente. _____

a. I like to take care of animals.

b. I understand them much
   better than people.

c. I am going to be the best
   lawyer in the state.

d. I have to earn a living.

e. I am sure that soon I am going
   to speak it perfectly.

f. I envy them.

g. I would like to design
   modern buildings.

h. I am going to design my
   own house.

B. Los planes profesionales de Sofía y Wayne. Use the words from the list to complete the monologues.

casa	arquitecta	diseñar	sueldo	computadoras
suerte	las	ochenta mil	abogada	edificios

Sofía   Quiero ser (1) _____ porque me gusta diseñar

       (2) _____ modernos. Algún día voy a

       (3) _____ mi propia (4) _____.

       Conozco a un arquitecto que gana más de (5) _____ dólares

       al año.

Wayne   Voy a trabajar con (6) _____. (7) _____

       entiendo mucho mejor que a las personas. Sé que voy a empezar con

       (8) _____ bueno, y con un poco de suerte...

C. Los planes profesionales de Ana Mari y Ramón. Answer the questions.

1. ¿Qué quiere ser Ana Mari? ¿A quién quiere ayudar? ¿A quién admira, por qué? ¿A quién nunca va a defender?

_____

_____

_____

2. ¿Por qué estudia Ramón negocios internacionales? ¿Qué dice *(says)* el artículo de periódico? ¿Qué idiomas habla? ¿Qué pasa con el japonés? ¿Cuándo lo va a hablar perfectamente?

_____

_____

_____

Vocabulario 1

Discussing professional plans
• **Careers and professions**

D. ¿Qué profesión tienen? Match the definitions with the illustrations; then write the correct profession.

a 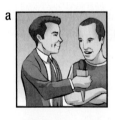 b 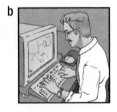 c  d

e  f  g  h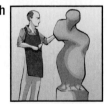

_____ 1. La persona que escribe para los periódicos. También hace entrevistas. _____

_____ 2. Una persona que trabaja en hospitales. Ayuda a los doctores. _____

_____ 3. Una persona que protege a la sociedad y busca a los criminales. _____

_____ 4. Esta persona diseña casas y edificios. _____

_____ 5. Las personas que nos ayudan y protegen de los incendios. _____

_____ 6. Una persona que diseña sistemas de computación para empresas. _____

_____ 7. Una persona que crea esculturas y pinturas. _____

_____ 8. Las personas que llevan la contabilidad de una empresa. _____

Nombre _____ Fecha _____

E. Ventajas y desventajas. Based on what you know about the following professions, list the advantages, disadvantages, and rate the salary.

Carrera	Ventajas	Desventajas	Sueldo
policía	• prestaciones buenas • poder ayudar a las personas	• muchas horas de trabajo • horario de noche • peligroso (*dangerous*)	• bajo al empezar • buen sueldo con los años
gerente			
niñero/a (**babysitter**)			
escritor(a) de novelas (como Stephen King)			
sicólogo			

Gramática 1

Talking about people and places you know
• **The verb** <u>conocer</u>

F. Las grandes ciudades norteamericanas. You are talking to Sofía, who is interested in traveling in the United States. Tell her about cities you know.

Modelo	¿Conoces la ciudad de Chicago? **No, no la conozco, pero sé que es muy grande, interesante y que hay muchos mexicanos.**

¿Conoces la ciudad de...

1. Los Ángeles? _____
_____

2. Miami? _____
_____

3. San Francisco? _____
_____

4. Atlanta? _____
_____

5. Seattle? _____
_____

6. Washington, DC? _____

_____

7. San Antonio? _____

_____

G. ¿A quién conocemos? Complete Manolo and Ana Mari's conversation using **conocer**.

Ana Mari

Manolo

Ana Mari   Manolo, ¿tú (1) _____ a alguien famoso?

Manolo   Pues no, pero mi hermana que vive en Miami (2) _____ al hermano de Luis Miguel.

Ana Mari   Huy, ¡qué interesante! Yo tampoco (3) _____ a nadie famoso, pero mis papás (4) _____ a varios actores mexicanos.

Manolo   Wayne y yo (5) _____ la casa de alguien famoso... El castillo de Hearst.

Ana Mari   ¿El castillo de Hearst? ¡Ay Manolo, pero si eso es un museo!

Manolo   Bueno, pero era su casa, ¿no?

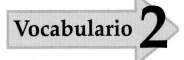
Vocabulario 2

Talking about salaries
• Numbers 101–100,000

H. ¿Cuánto?

Parte 1. Match each number with its written equivalent.

_____ 1. 54.641   a. cincuenta y cuatro mil setecientos cuarenta y uno

_____ 2. 183.835   b. dieciséis mil cuatrocientos noventa y seis

_____ 3. 16.496   c. veinte mil trescientos sesenta y tres

_____ 4. 54.741   d. cincuenta y cuatro mil seiscientos cuarenta y uno

_____ 5. 20.363   e. ciento ochenta y tres mil ochocientos treinta y cinco

Parte 2. Fill in the missing parts of the numbers.

1. 92.517   _____ y dos _____ _____ diecisiete

2. 75.409   _____ y cinco mil _____ nueve

3. 39.212   treinta y _____ mil_____ doce

4. 116.578   _____ dieciséis _____ _____

_____ y ocho

5. 48.024   cuarenta _____ ocho mil _____

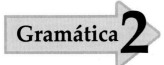

Nombre _____ Fecha _____

Gramática 2

Avoiding repetition when answering questions
- **The direct object pronouns <u>lo</u>, <u>la</u>, <u>los</u>, and <u>las</u>**

I. El primer día de clases. Ana Mari's little brothers are preparing for their first day of school. Answer their questions using direct object pronouns.

> **Modelo** ¿Tengo que llevar la calculadora?
> No, **no la tienes que llevar/no tienes que llevarla.**

1. ¿Necesito el papel?
   Sí, _____.

2. ¿Podemos llevar al perro a la escuela?
   No, _____.

3. ¿Voy a usar mis lápices de colores?
   No, _____.

4. ¿Tengo que llevar las plumas?
   Sí, _____.

5. ¿Necesitamos los libros de texto?
   Sí, _____.

J. ¡Qué ocupados! Answer the questions about the characters, using direct object pronouns. You may make up some answers.

> **Modelo**
>
> ¿Con quién hace Sofía la tarea?
> **La hace con Adriana y Manolo.**

¡Fíjate!
Remember to place the direct object pronoun before the verb (**la hace**) and to match the gender and number with the object it replaces (**la** because **tarea** is feminine and singular).

1.   2.   3.   4. **1:00 pm**   5. **Los sábados**

1. ¿Con quién mira Sofía la tele? _____

2. ¿Qué va a hacer con la ropa? _____

3. ¿Adónde va a llevar a Manolo? _____

4. ¿A qué hora va a hacer Adriana el flan? _____

5. ¿Visitan a los abuelos entre semana? _____

Para terminar

K. La CIA: Agencia Central de Inteligencia. Read the article on the CIA, taken from *Hispanic Business* magazine. Then answer the questions.

1. ¿Qué características personales necesita tener un agente de la CIA?

_____

2. ¿Qué preparación académica necesitas para hacer una carrera en la CIA?

_____

3. ¿Qué tipo de experiencia o habilidades especiales son deseables?

_____

4. ¿Te parece interesante trabajar para la CIA? ¿Por qué sí o por qué no?

_____

Lo máximo en carreras internacionales

Para el individuo que quiere más que un simple trabajo, ésta es una carrera única; un estilo de vida que prueba[1] los límites de la inteligencia, la autosuficiencia[2] y la responsabilidad. Requiere un espíritu aventurero, una personalidad bien definida, una habilidad intelectual superior, fuerza[3] mental y un alto grado de integridad. Se necesitan habilidades especiales y disciplina profesional para producir resultados. Usted debe resolver situaciones volátiles, ambiguas y poco estructuradas que prueben al máximo su ingenio[4].

El Programa de Entrenamiento de la CIA es la puerta de entrada a una carrera internacional. Para entrar, usted debe poseer calificaciones de primera: título universitario con excelente historial académico, sólidas habilidades interpersonales, la capacidad de escribir clara y precisamente y un inagotable interés en asuntos internacionales. Las personas con estudios de posgrado,

viajes[5] al extranjero, que hablen otros idiomas, que hayan vivido[6] en otros países o con experiencia militar tienen ya cierta ventaja.

El sueldo va de $31.459 a $48.222, dependiendo de la experiencia y preparación. Los solicitantes deben someterse a un riguroso examen psicológico y médico, una entrevista poligráfica y una investigación completa de antecedentes. La edad máxima para ingresar a la agencia es de 35 años, y se requiere la ciudadanía[7] estadounidense para usted y su pareja. La CIA busca hombres y mujeres de todas las razas y de todos los sectores culturales de la población. La CIA representa a Estados Unidos, y el personal debe ser representativo de la diversidad cultural del país.

Para solicitar empleo, mande su currículum[8] (incluya promedio[9] académico) y una carta que explique sus destrezas[10] y habilidades. En treinta días nos pondremos en contacto con los solicitantes mejor calificados.

---

[1]*tests* [2]*self-sufficiency* [3]*strength* [4]**prueban...** *test your resourcefulness to the limit* [5]*trips* [6]*have lived* [7]*citizenship*
[8]*résumé* [9]*average* [10]*skills*

Episodio 13

Escenas de la vida: Las vacaciones

 A. ¡Mira cuánto puedes entender! Escucha la conversación o mira el video para indicar quién hace los siguientes comentarios: Sofía, Manolo, Ramón o Ana Mari.

¿Necesitamos pasaporte y visa para ir a México?

Ya tenemos las reservaciones de avión.

El boleto de ida y vuelta cuesta $390,00.

Durante el día, hace calor.

Pero es invierno y llueve mucho, ¿no?

Por la noche baja la temperatura y hace bastante frío.

Te ayudo con tus maletas.

Enero

D	L	M	M	J	V	S
		(1)	2	3	4	5
6	7	8	9	10	11	12
13	14	15	16	17	18	19
20	21	22	23	24	25	26
27	28	29	30	31		

Regresamos el primero de enero.

Yo voy a llevar pantalones cortos y traje de baño.

315

B. ¿Te diste cuenta? Escucha la conversación otra vez para indicar si las oraciones son ciertas o falsas.

	Cierto	Falso
1. El pasaporte de Manolo está vencido *(has expired)*.	☐	☐
2. Ana Mari conoce Guadalajara.	☐	☐
3. Manolo paga su boleto con tarjeta de crédito.	☐	☐
4. En Guadalajara siempre hace calor.	☐	☐
5. Los chicos regresan el dos de enero.	☐	☐

C. Preguntas. Escucha la conversación de nuevo y contesta las preguntas.

1. ¿Qué día salen para Guadalajara? _____

2. ¿Cuándo tienen que pagar los boletos? _____

3. ¿Por qué Manolo no puede pagar su boleto ahora? _____
   _____

4. ¿Qué ropa necesitan llevar a Guadalajara? _____
   _____

5. ¿En qué estación del año llueve en Guadalajara? _____

6. ¿Quién va a ayudar a Sofía con sus maletas? _____
   _____

Invitación a **Costa Rica**

In your own words. Read the information below and then write what you understood. In English, summarize the information in two or three sentences. Do not translate.

Del álbum de
Sofía

Costa Rica es un paraíso para los amantes *(lovers)* de la naturaleza y del turismo de aventura. Este país ayuda a solucionar o, por lo menos, a disminuir los efectos del calentamiento *(warming)* global; sólo en el año 2007, plantó siete millones de árboles *(trees)*, siete veces más que los que se plantaron en Estados Unidos. Los numerosos parques ecológicos del país ofrecen actividades para todos los gustos: desde caminatas *(hikes)* en las selvas *(jungles)*, exploración de volcanes (activos e inactivos), 'canopy' y surf, hasta paseos en balsas *(rafts)* por rápidos. Ve al Supersitio para mirar un episodio de *Flash cultura* sobre este tema *(topic)*.

Práctica adicional		
Cuaderno de tareas p. 337, A–B	invitaciones. vhlcentral.com Episodio 13	invitaciones. vhlcentral.com Episodio 13

316

Learning Strategy: Looking for similarities and differences in language structure

Noticing similarities and differences between English and Spanish word order will help you understand and learn Spanish. For instance, look at the placement of adverbs in the following examples:

¡Tú **nunca** vas al gimnasio!   You **never** go to the gym!

Yo hago ejercicio **todos los días.**   I exercise **every day.**

Notice that the placement of *never* (**nunca**) and *every day* (**todos los días**) is the same in English and in Spanish. You do not have to learn a different word order when using these words.

However, there are other differences in word order that you should learn. These include:

- the placement of the direct object pronouns **me, te, lo, la, los,** and **las.**

Te doy un cheque la próxima semana.   I'll give **you** a check next week.

In Spanish, these pronouns are placed before a conjugated verb; in English, they are placed after the verb.

- the placement of descriptive adjectives

Lleva ropa **ligera** para el día...   Take **light** clothing for daytime...

In Spanish, most descriptive adjectives are placed after the noun; in English, they come before the noun.

When you study, concentrate on the differences and just make a mental note of the similarities.

Para comunicarnos mejor

 **Vocabulario 1**

Talking about dates and the weather
• Seasons, months, and the weather

In the conversation, you heard the following statements.

Salimos **el 18 de diciembre.**	*We're leaving on the 18th of December.*
Regresamos **el primero de enero.**	*We're returning on the first of January.*
Durante el día **hace calor.**	*During the day it's hot.*
Por la noche **hace** bastante **frío.**	*At night it's rather cold.*
Llueve durante el verano.	*It rains during the summer.*

1. Use **el** + [*number*] + **de** + [*month*] to talk about dates.
2. Use **el primero** to say *the first of* [*month*].
3. Notice that months are not capitalized in Spanish.

¿Qué tiempo hace en Guadalajara?

Generalmente hace buen tiempo.

• Seasons, months, and the weather

Cultura a lo vivo

In both Hispanic and Anglo cultures, the climate, the weather, and the formality of the occasion determine the appropriateness of a particular outfit. Although it varies from country to country, in general, Spanish speakers dress more formally than people in the U.S.

Spanish speakers tend to dress formally for parties and social events. Depending on the country, Spanish speakers may not wear shorts or sandals unless they are at the beach. Even in the most informal situations, they do not go barefoot or shirtless.

¡Fíjate!

In Latin America, like in most of the world, Celsius degrees are used instead of Fahrenheit degrees. You can practice converting from Celsius to Fahrenheit using the following formula: $F = (C \times 1.8) + 32$

To say the temperature, say **Está a... grados** (it is... degrees).

Las estaciones del año	¿Qué tiempo hace?	La temperatura	Los meses
el invierno Hace frío. Llueve o nieva. Hace mal tiempo.		-15° – 10°	diciembre enero febrero
la primavera Hace fresco. Llueve. Hace viento.		10° – 18°	marzo abril mayo
el verano Hace calor. Hace sol. Hace buen tiempo.		20° – 30°	junio julio agosto
el otoño Hace viento. Está nublado. Hace fresco.		10° – 22°	septiembre octubre noviembre

PRÁCTICA

A. ¿Cuándo se celebra? Escribe la fecha de estas celebraciones.

> **Modelo** El Día de los Muertos es **el dos de noviembre.**

1. El Día de San Valentín es _____.
2. El Día de la Independencia de Estados Unidos es _____.
3. La Navidad es _____.
4. El Día de los Inocentes *(April Fool's Day)* es _____.
5. El Día de Año Nuevo es _____.
6. El día de mi cumpleaños es _____.

B. Fechas importantes. Escribe cinco fechas importantes para ti. Incluye dos cumpleaños, un aniversario y dos días festivos *(holidays)*. Después comparte con un(a) compañero/a las actividades que haces en esos días.

> **Modelo** **El 9 de octubre es importante para mí porque es el cumpleaños de mi mamá. Mi familia y yo salimos a cenar con ella. Generalmente vamos a un restaurante elegante.**

1. _____
   _____
2. _____
   _____
3. _____
   _____
4. _____
   _____
5. _____
   _____

C. ¿Dónde? Indica en qué ciudades de Estados Unidos existen estas condiciones climatológicas.

Tampa   **Seattle**   **Chicago**   **Buffalo**

1. En esta ciudad llueve todo el año. Hace fresco. La
   temperatura promedio durante la primavera es de 60°F.   _____
2. En esta ciudad hace mucho frío durante el invierno. Nieva
   mucho. La temperatura promedio es de 5°F bajo cero.   _____
3. En esta ciudad el clima es húmedo y hace mucho
   calor en el verano.   _____
4. En esta ciudad hace viento. El clima es extremo: hace calor
   en el verano y hace frío en el invierno.   _____

D. El pronóstico del tiempo. When you listen to a weather forecast, you will hear words that you would not normally use in talking about the weather with a friend. Using your knowledge of the weather expressions will help you derive meaning from words with common roots. With a partner, try to guess the meaning of the following expressions commonly used by the news media. Be ready to explain your choices.

_____ 1. Un ambiente soleado

_____ 2. Un día caluroso

_____ 3. Cielos despejados

_____ 4. Cielos parcialmente nublados

_____ 5. Días lluviosos

_____ 6. Nieblas matinales

_____ 7. Puede caer algún chubasco

a. rainy days

b. clear skies

c. sunny days

d. morning fog

e. possible showers

f. partially cloudy skies

g. a very hot day

¡Fíjate!

To see some weather forecasts from different countries, go to YouTube and search **prónostico del tiempo.**

Práctica adiciona

Cuaderno de tareas
pp. 338–339, C–F

invitaciones.
vhlcentral.com
Episode 13

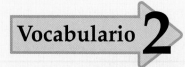

Vocabulario 2

Planning your wardrobe
• Clothing and colors

La ropa que Sofía quiere llevar a Guadalajara

el abrigo

la falda roja

el vestido negro

la blusa morada

las botas

los zapatos de tacón

la camiseta azul

las sandalias verdes

los pantalones anaranjados

La ropa que Manolo va a llevar a Guadalajara

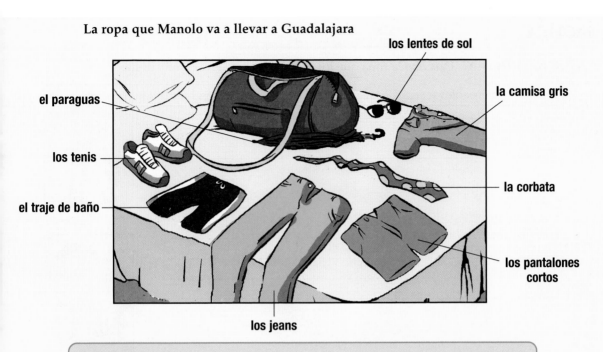

el paraguas

los tenis

el traje de baño

los jeans

los lentes de sol

la camisa gris

la corbata

los pantalones cortos

También se dice...

la chaqueta ⟶ la chamarra, el saco, la cazadora

color café ⟶ marrón, pardo

la falda ⟶ la pollera

la maleta ⟶ la valija, la petaca, el veliz

los jeans ⟶ los pantalones de mezclilla, los bluejeans, los mahones, los vaqueros

Más ropa

la bolsa	*bag*	los guantes	*gloves*	el sombrero	*hat*
la bufanda	*scarf*	llevar	*to wear*	usar	*to wear*
los calcetines	*socks*	la maleta	*suitcase*		

La maleta de Ana Mari

la blusa blanca

la chaqueta azul

el bikini

el suéter café

el impermeable gris

el/la pijama

el traje

la minifalda amarilla

321

PRÁCTICA

E. ¿Qué ropa llevan? Describe la ropa que los chicos piensan llevar a una fiesta.

1. Manolo piensa llevar _____

_____

_____

_____

2. Sofía quiere llevar _____

_____

_____

_____

¡Fíjate!
Remember to use **un, una, unos,** and **unas** when talking about the clothes people wear.

3. Ana Mari va a llevar _____

_____

_____

_____

4. Ramón quiere llevar _____

_____

_____

_____

F. ¿Qué llevan? Comenta con un(a) compañero/a la ropa que llevan los chicos para salir en Guadalajara.

Manolo   Sofía   Ramón   Ana Mari

G. Las estaciones. Describe la ropa que usas en las siguientes situaciones; menciona colores cuando sea posible. Después de contestar las preguntas, comparte tus respuestas con un(a) compañero/a.

1. En el invierno para ir a la universidad, uso _____
   _____.

2. En la primavera para ir al trabajo, llevo _____
   _____.

3. Cuando la temperatura es de 80°F, me pongo _____
   _____.

4. Cuando la temperatura es de -10°F, llevo _____
   _____.

5. Cuando voy a la playa, me pongo _____
   _____.

6. Cuando voy al supermercado, uso _____
   _____.

7. Cuando voy a una fiesta elegante, me pongo _____
   _____.

8. Para ir a una entrevista de trabajo, uso _____
   _____.

¡Fíjate!

Me pongo... is another way of expressing what you put on. You will learn this reflexive verb in **Episodio 14**.

H. ¿Qué tiempo hace? Tú eres un(a) agente de viajes y tu trabajo es informar a tus clientes qué clima hay en diferentes ciudades de Latinoamérica. Mira el mapa para saber la información necesaria. Túrnate con un(a) compañero/a.

F= (C × 1.8) + 32

1. ¿Qué tiempo hace en Bariloche en junio? ¿Qué estación del año es? ¿Qué ropa necesitan llevar?
   _____
   _____

2. ¿Qué tiempo hace en Viña del Mar en enero? ¿Qué estación del año es? ¿Qué ropa necesitan llevar?
   _____
   _____
   _____

3. ¿Qué tiempo hace en Cusco en marzo? ¿Qué estación del año es? ¿Qué ropa necesitan llevar?
   _____
   _____
   _____

4. ¿Qué tiempo hace en Quito en septiembre? ¿Qué estación del año es? ¿Qué ropa necesitan llevar?
   _____
   _____
   _____

I. Tres diseñadores famosos. Lee la información sobre estos tres importantes diseñadores hispanos y escribe un resumen *(summary)*. Después, comparte tu resumen con un(a) compañero/a.

Carolina Herrera

Óscar de la Renta

Carolina Herrera es una de las diseñadoras más famosas de Nueva York. Es de Caracas, Venezuela, y vive en Nueva York desde hace muchos años. Carolina tiene cuatro hijas: Mercedes, Ana Luisa, Carolina, Adriana y Patricia. Carolina es también una excelente mujer de negocios. Sus bellas colecciones de ropa se presentan en las pasarelas *(runways)* más prestigiosas del mundo. Además de ropa, en 1988 lanzó *(she launched)* su primera fragancia para mujer y en 1991, una segunda, *"Carolina Herrera for Men"*. Su último lanzamiento *(launch)* fue una línea de fragancias para hombres llamada *"212 Men"*. Su hija Carolina Adriana es su colaboradora. Carolina la considera una inspiración y reconoce que esta última línea de fragancias es creación de su hija.

Carolina también es una mujer con conciencia social; ella dona dinero y representa a una fundación que ayuda a llevar comida a niños en países pobres.

1. En inglés, escribe un resumen de lo que aprendiste *(you learned)* sobre Carolina Herrera.

2. Ahora, mira las fotografías para hablar con un(a) compañero/a.

   a. ¿Qué ropa llevan estos modelos?

   b. ¿De qué colección es esta ropa, otoño, primavera o verano? Explica.

   c. ¿Te gusta la ropa? ¿En qué ocasión podrías *(would you be able to)* usar ropa así?

Los diseñadores y creadores de la casa Custo Barcelona son los hermanos Custodio y David Dalmau. Los hermanos Dalmau son de Barcelona, España, y de ahí viene el nombre. Los hermanos empiezan a diseñar camisetas mezclando *(mixing)* materiales, colores y estampados *(patterns)*. Las camisetas se hicieron *(became)* muy famosas porque las usaron *(were worn)* en varios episidios de las series de televisión *Friends* y *Sex and the City*. Otros actores famosos que usan sus camisetas son Julia Roberts, Brad Pitt y Penélope Cruz.

Custo Barcelona

Ahora también hay tiendas Custo Barcelona en países como Italia, Corea y Puerto Rico, y en ciudades de los EE.UU. como Nueva York, Los Ángeles y Chicago.

3. En inglés, escribe un resumen de lo que aprendiste *(you learned)* sobre los hermanos Dalmau y su línea de ropa.

4. Ahora, mira las fotografías para hablar con un(a) compañero/a.

   a. ¿Qué ropa llevan estos modelos?

   b. ¿De qué colección es esta ropa, otoño, primavera o verano? Explica.

   c. ¿Te gusta esta ropa? ¿En qué ocasión podrías usar ropa así?

Óscar de la Renta es de Santo Domingo, República Dominicana. A los dieciocho años se va a vivir a Madrid, España. Originalmente estudia pintura, pero después empieza a trabajar como diseñador de ropa. También trabaja en París. Fue el primer latinoamericano en diseñar ropa para una famosa empresa francesa. Finalmente llega a Nueva York, donde establece su propia firma y se hace un diseñador famoso internacionalmente. Su ropa para mujer es muy elegante, y es común ver sus diseños en las entregas de los premios Óscar.

Este diseñador y su esposa Annette tienen un hijo, Moisés; un niño que adoptaron en la República Dominicana.

5. En inglés, escribe un resumen de lo que aprendiste *(you learned)* sobre Óscar de la Renta.

6. Ahora, mira las fotografías para hablar con un(a) compañero/a.

   a. ¿Qué ropa llevan estos modelos?

   b. ¿De qué colección es esta ropa, la colección de otoño, primavera o verano? Explica.

7. ¿Cuál es tu diseñador(a) favorito/a de los tres? Explica por qué.

J. Un desfile de modas. Work with a partner to put on a runway fashion show. Introduce your partner and describe what they are wearing. Be creative!

Modelo	Compañeros, les presento a Rosa. Hoy Rosa lleva una falda negra de H&M, una blusa amarilla de Zara y unas botas de tacón de Aldo, por supuesto.

K. De vacaciones. Talk to your partner about a place you like to go to when you are on vacation. Describe the season, month or date you like to go, the weather, the clothing you usually take with you, who you go with, and what you do there.

Banco de palabras

la bahía	los lagos	el parque de atracciones	remar
bay	*lakes*	*amusement park*	*to row*
esquiar	las montañas	el planetario	el zoológico
to ski	*mountains*	*planetarium*	*zoo*

Práctica adicional

Cuaderno de tareas
pp. 339–341, G–J

SUPERSITE
invitaciones.
vhlcentral.com
Episodio 13

Actividades comunicativas

A. Un viaje a México.

Instrucciones para **Estudiante 1**

You want to go to Mexico on vacation. Call your travel agent to plan your trip. Look at the map and ask about places that interest you. Your requirements: a destination that is hot and sunny, and a price of $600 or less. You want to leave on Monday, July 20, and return on Friday, July 25, at night.

Modelo	—¿Qué tiempo hace en... ?
	—¿Cuánto cuesta el viaje *(the trip)* a...?

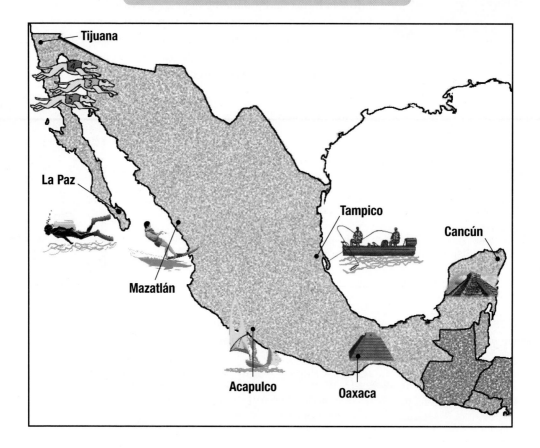

A. Un viaje a México.

Instrucciones para **Estudiante 2**

You are a travel agent. Your job is to help your client plan a vacation. Answer your client's questions about the weather conditions of the place he or she would like to visit, and give the prices. Once you know where your client wants to go, fill in the card.

VIAJES MAJESTIC

Acapulco $450   Tijuana $520   Cancún $870   Tampico $640

Mazatlán $465   La Paz $500   Oaxaca $395

Cliente _____ Teléfono _____

Viaja a _____

Quiere salir el _____

Quiere regresar el _____

Viajan _____ personas

Precio _____

¡Cinco días en México!

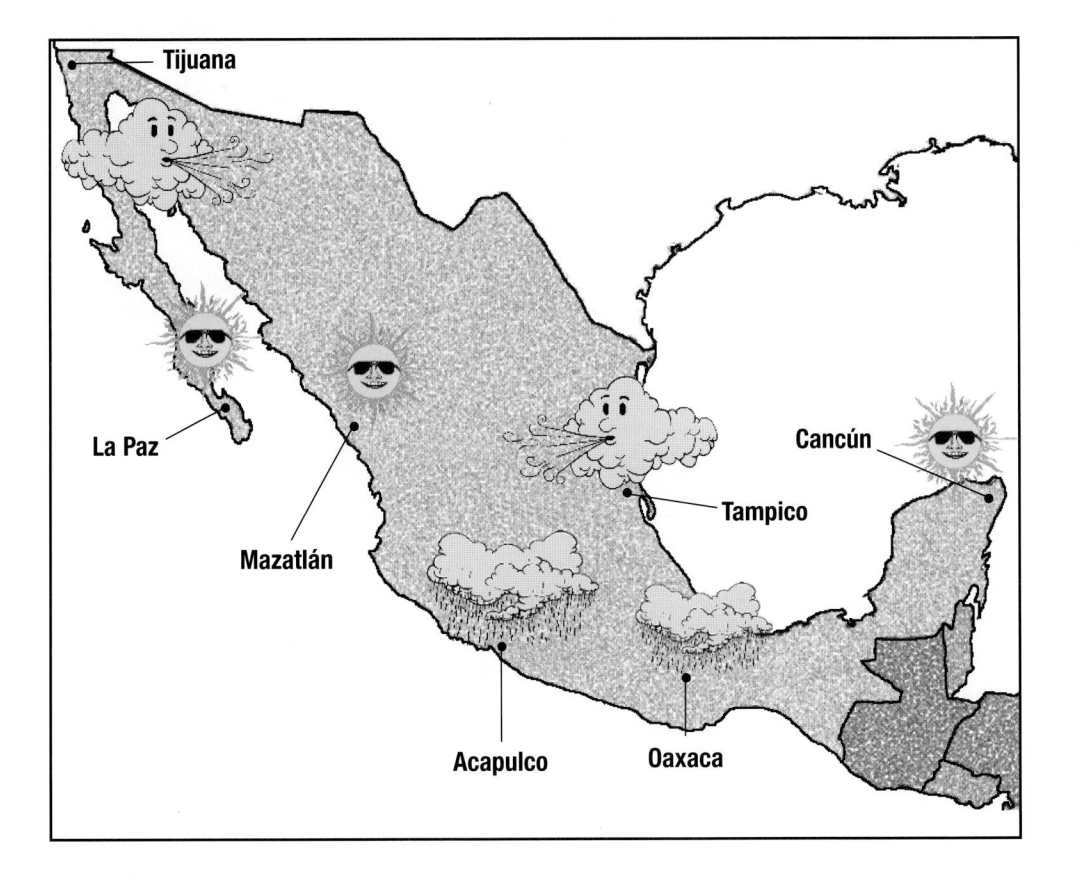

B. Diferencias.

Instrucciones para **Estudiante 1**

Aquí tienes un dibujo de Sofía y sus amigos en la playa de Puerto Vallarta. Hay varias diferencias entre tu dibujo y el de tu compañero/a. Para encontrarlas, describe el clima, las actividades y la ropa. Escribe siete diferencias que encontraste.

Modelo	**Manolo duerme en la hamaca. Lleva unos pantalones azules cortos, ¿no?**

B. Diferencias.

Instrucciones para **Estudiante 2**

Aquí tienes un dibujo de Sofía y sus amigos en la playa de Puerto Vallarta. Hay varias diferencias entre tu dibujo y el de tu compañero/a. Para encontrarlas, describe el clima, las actividades y la ropa. Escribe siete diferencias que encontraste.

Modelo   Manolo lleva unos pantalones cortos azules, ¿no? Lee el periódico.

C. El trabajo en la clínica.

Instrucciones para **Estudiante 1**

Trabajas en la clínica de salud Del Prado. Tu turno va a empezar, y sólo tienes la mitad de la información de los pacientes que va a atender el doctor hoy. Habla con un(a) compañero/a para escribir la información que necesitas.

Modelo	—¿Conoces a la chica que lleva unos pantalones verdes y un suéter negro?
	—Sí, la conozco. Se llama Lucía Morales.
	—¿Sabes cuántos años tiene y cuánto pesa?
	—Tiene veintiocho años y pesa 136 libras.
	—¿Sabes cuál es su profesión?
	—Sí, es sicóloga.

Banco de palabras

¿Cuánto pesa?   *How much does he/she weigh?*

Lucía Morales
28 años
136 libras
Sicóloga

Emiliano Llano
53 años
186 libras
Programador

Felipe Rosas
3 años
38 libras
Ninguna

Irma Pérez
80 años
153 libras
Ama de casa

C. El trabajo en la clínica.

Instrucciones para **Estudiante 2**

Trabajas en la clínica de salud Del Prado. Tu turno va a empezar, y sólo tienes la mitad de la información de los pacientes que va a atender el doctor hoy. Habla con un(a) compañero/a para escribir la información que necesitas.

Modelo	—¿Conoces a la chica que lleva unos pantalones verdes y un suéter negro? —Sí, la conozco. Se llama Lucía Morales. —¿Sabes cuántos años tiene y cuánto pesa? —Tiene veintiocho años y pesa 136 libras. —¿Sabes cuál es su profesión? —Sí, es sicóloga.

Banco de palabras

¿Cuánto pesa?   *How much does he/she weigh?*

Lucía Morales
28 años
136 libras
Sicóloga

Jordi Olimón
7 años
62 libras
Estudiante de primaria

CLÍNICA DEL PRADO

RECEPCIÓN

Pedro Estrada
41 años
192 libras
Oficial de prisión

Abril Jiménez
30 años
125 libras
Periodista

La correspondencia

 El correo: Aprenda español en Costa Rica. Lee la información acerca de los programas para aprender español en Costa Rica. Después contesta las preguntas.

Instituto Forester

El Forester Instituto Internacional, en San José, Costa Rica, ofrece varios programas de instrucción en español. El instituto está localizado en una zona exclusiva de la ciudad, a sólo veinte minutos del centro.

Nuestros estudiantes. El Instituto recibe estudiantes de diversos países, diferentes edades y necesidades de aprendizaje:
- personas que buscan unas vacaciones diferentes y productivas
- ejecutivos de corporaciones e instituciones
- estudiantes de preparatorias y universidades
- diplomáticos
- doctores y enfermeros
- personas jubiladas[1] que desean mantenerse activas
- empleados de líneas aéreas

Nuestros profesores. La lengua materna de todo el profesorado es el español. Además, tienen títulos universitarios y amplia experiencia en enseñar el español como segunda lengua.

Las familias anfitrionas[2]. El Instituto selecciona cuidadosamente a las familias anfitrionas. Son muy amables y abiertas[3], les gusta relacionarse con personas de otros países y tienen interés en ayudar a los estudiantes extranjeros. El estudiante tendrá[4] cuarto privado, desayuno y cena. Todas las familias viven a menos de veinte minutos del Instituto, y es fácil llegar en autobús o a pie[5].

Días festivos. El Instituto está cerrado[6] durante algunos días festivos nacionales[7] que se celebran en Costa Rica: el primero de enero, el Jueves Santo y el Viernes Santo[8], el primero de mayo (Día del Trabajo), el 15 de agosto (la Asunción y Día de las Madres), el 15 de septiembre (Día de la Independencia) y el 25 de diciembre.

Clima. La temperatura varía muy poco durante el año. Obviamente, hace más frío en las montañas que en la costa (San José está a 4.000 pies de altura). La temporada de lluvias[9] es de mayo a noviembre, y generalmente hace sol por las mañanas y llueve por las tardes. La temporada seca[10] es de diciembre a abril.

Sugerencias para la ropa. Los costarricenses usan ropa informal. Es una buena idea llevar ropa ligera y una chaqueta o un suéter. Es recomendable llevar un paraguas o un impermeable si va a visitar el país durante la temporada de lluvias. Durante la temporada seca, las noches pueden ser bastantes frías. Mujeres: jeans, camisetas, pantalones y blusas, un suéter y/o una chaqueta. Uno o dos vestidos para ocasiones especiales. Hombres: jeans, camisetas, pantalones y camisas. Se recomienda llevar un saco y una corbata para eventos especiales. Tanto las mujeres como los hombres deben llevar zapatos cómodos, tenis o sandalias. Y por supuesto, ¡los trajes de baño son indispensables!

---

[1]*retired* [2]*host* [3]*open* [4]*will have* [5]*on foot* [6]*closed* [7]**días...** *national holidays*
[8]*Holy Thursday and Good Friday* [9]*rainy season* [10]*dry season*

1. ¿A qué van personas de diferentes profesiones y edades a Costa Rica?

_____

2. ¿Qué características tienen las familias anfitrionas?

_____

_____

_____

_____

3. ¿Qué fiestas nacionales se celebran en Costa Rica?

_____

_____

4. ¿Qué clima tiene San José? ¿Qué ropa recomiendan para viajar en Costa Rica?

_____

_____

_____

5. ¿Por qué es importante aprender un segundo idioma? ¿Qué ventajas tiene?

_____

_____

_____

6. ¿Te gustaría participar en un programa así? ¿Por qué sí o por qué no?

_____

_____

_____

En papel: ¡Ven, visita mi ciudad! Muchos costarricenses tienen interés en visitar Estados Unidos. Escribe un artículo sobre tu ciudad para una revista de turismo en Costa Rica. Incluye la siguiente información:

- el clima en las diferentes estaciones
- la ropa que uno debe llevar
- atracciones y lugares de interés
- actividades interesantes

¡Fíjate!
Create a simple outline of the information you want to include before you begin to write.

Banco de palabras

el zoológico	**el planetario**	**las montañas**
zoo	*planetarium*	*mountains*
los lagos	**el parque de atracciones**	**la bahía**
lakes	*amusement park*	*bay*

¡A ver de nuevo!

Parte 1. Con tus propias palabras, haz un resumen del episodio.

Parte 2. Ahora trabaja con un(a) compañero/a para comparar la información y añadir la que no tienes.

Práctica adicional			
Cuaderno de tareas pp. 342–344, K–L	invitaciones. vhlcentral.com Episodio 13	invitaciones. vhlcentral.com Lab practice	invitaciones. vhlcentral.com Episodio 13

Vocabulario del Episodio 13

Los meses *The months*

enero	*January*
febrero	*February*
marzo	*March*
abril	*April*
mayo	*May*
junio	*June*
julio	*July*
agosto	*August*
septiembre	*September*
octubre	*October*
noviembre	*November*
diciembre	*December*

Las estaciones *The seasons*

la primavera	*spring*
el verano	*summer*
el otoño	*fall*
el invierno	*winter*

¿Qué tiempo hace? *What's the weather like?*

Está nublado.	*It's cloudy.*
Hace buen/mal tiempo.	*The weather is nice/bad.*
Hace (mucho) calor.	*It's (very) hot.*
Hace fresco.	*It's cool.*
Hace frío.	*It's cold.*
Hace sol.	*It's sunny.*
Hace viento.	*It's windy.*
llover (o ⟶ ue), llueve	*to rain, it rains*
nevar (e ⟶ ie), nieva	*to snow, it snows*

La ropa *Clothes*

el abrigo	*coat*	**los pantalones**	*pants*
el bikini	*bikini*	**los pantalones cortos**	*shorts*
la blusa	*blouse*	**el paraguas**	*umbrella*
la bolsa	*bag*	**el/la pijama**	*pajamas*
las botas	*boots*	**las sandalias**	*sandals*
la bufanda	*scarf*	**el sombrero**	*hat*
los calcetines	*socks*	**el suéter**	*sweater*
la camisa	*shirt*	**el traje**	*suit*
la camiseta	*T-shirt*	**el traje de baño**	*bathing suit*
la chaqueta	*jacket*	**usar**	*to wear*
la corbata	*tie*	**el vestido**	*dress*
los guantes	*gloves*	**los zapatos (de tacón)**	*(high-heeled) shoes*
el impermeable	*raincoat*	**los (zapatos) tenis**	*tennis shoes*
los jeans	*jeans*		
los lentes de sol	*sunglasses*		
llevar	*to wear*		
la maleta	*suitcase*		
la minifalda	*mini-skirt*		

Los colores *Colors*

amarillo/a	*yellow*
anaranjado/a	*orange*
azul	*blue*
blanco/a	*white*
café	*brown*
gris	*gray*
morado/a	*purple*
negro/a	*black*
rojo/a	*red*
verde	*green*

Vocabulario personal

Write all the words you need to know in Spanish so that you can talk in greater detail about the clothes you like to wear, the weather in your city, and important dates in your family.

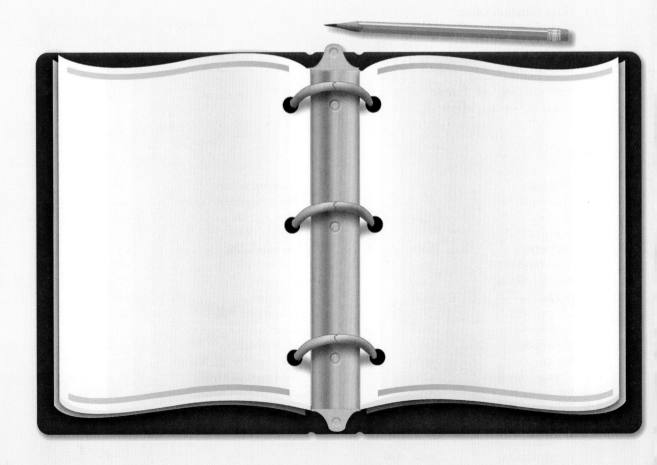

Episodio

Cuaderno de tareas

13

Escenas de la vida: Las vacaciones

 A. ¡A ver cuánto entendiste! Match the Spanish sentences with their English equivalents.

_____ 1. Te doy un cheque la próxima semana.

_____ 2. Tienes que pagarlo antes de diciembre.

_____ 3. Salimos el 18 de diciembre.

_____ 4. Cuesta trescientos noventa dólares.

_____ 5. Ya tenemos las reservaciones de avión.

_____ 6. No te voy a ayudar con las maletas.

_____ 7. ¿Cuánto cuesta el boleto?

_____ 8. Todavía no me pagan.

_____ 9. Mi pasaporte está vencido.

a. We're leaving on the 18th of December.

b. We already have the plane reservations.

c. My passport has expired.

d. I'll give you a check next week.

e. You have to pay it before December.

f. They haven't paid me yet.

g. I'm not going to help you with your suitcases.

h. It costs three hundred and ninety dollars.

 i. How much does a ticket cost?

 B. Las vacaciones. Choose the correct answer.

1. El boleto cuesta…
   a. cincuenta dólares.
   b. quinientos treinta dólares.
   c. trescientos noventa dólares.

2. Para ir a México, los chicos necesitan…
   a. permiso de turista.
   b. pasaporte y visa.
   c. visa.

3. Manolo le pide a Sofía pagar su boleto con...
   a. dinero.
   b. un cheque.
   c. su tarjeta de crédito.

4. En invierno en Guadalajara…
   a. hace frío y nieva.
   b. hace calor durante el día.
   c. hace calor por la noche.

5. Los chicos salen…
   a. el 10 de diciembre.
   b. el primero de enero.
   c. el 18 de diciembre.

6. Para usar durante el día, los chicos deben llevar…
   a. un impermeable.
   b. un abrigo.
   c. ropa ligera.

Vocabulario 1

Talking about dates and the weather
• Seasons, months, and the weather

C. Algunas fechas importantes en Hispanoamérica. Write the following dates in Spanish. Do you know what holidays they are?

1. January 6 _____
2. February 14 _____
3. May 1 _____

4. March 21 _____
5. July 4 _____
6. October 12 _____

D. El hemisferio sur. Indicate the seasons in which these holidays take place in the Southern Hemisphere. Remember that it is not the same as in the United States.

1. En Argentina las vacaciones de diciembre son en_____.
2. En Uruguay, en las vacaciones de julio es_____.
3. En Paraguay, el 21 de marzo es el primer día de_____.
4. En Perú, el 21 de septiembre es el primer día de_____.

E. ¿Qué tiempo hace? Indicate the weather conditions and the temperature in the following places for the month in question, based on the temperature and the illustration. Remember, to convert from Celsius to Fahrenheit: **F = (C × 1.8) + 32.**

> **Modelo**
>
> Ciudad de México, México / /17°C /septiembre
>
> **En la Ciudad de México generalmente llueve en el mes de septiembre. Hace fresco, la temperatura promedio es de sesenta y tres grados Fahrenheit.**

1. Managua, Nicaragua / / 30°C/ enero

_____

_____

2. San Juan Bautista, Paraguay / / 37°C / febrero

_____

_____

3. Bariloche, Argentina / / 10°C / julio

_____

_____

4. Barcelona, España / / abril / 27°C

_____

_____

5. La Habana, Cuba / / diciembre / 32°C

_____

_____

F. Odette quiere saber. Answer Odette's questions about weather in the United States.

1. ¿Qué tiempo hace en Nueva York en invierno?

_____

2. ¿Qué tiempo hace en Las Vegas en verano?

_____

3. ¿Qué tiempo hace en San Francisco en primavera?

_____

4. ¿Qué tiempo hace en Minneapolis en otoño?

_____

Vocabulario 2 → **Planning your wardrobe**
• Clothing and colors

G. Las cosas para Guadalajara. Write the names of the items the characters are bringing to Guadalajara.

a. La ropa de Sofía

1. _____
2. _____
3. _____
4. _____
5. _____
6. _____
7. _____

b. La ropa de Manolo

1. _____
2. _____
3. _____
4. _____
5. _____
6. _____
7. _____
8. _____

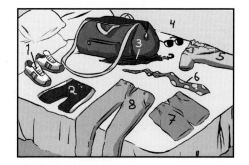

c. La ropa de Ana Mari

1. _____
2. _____
3. _____
4. _____
5. _____
6. _____
7. _____
8. _____

H. ¿Qué color? What colors do you associate with the following foods?

1. el arroz _____
2. las uvas _____
3. el plátano _____
4. la naranja _____

5. la lechuga _____
6. el tomate _____
7. los frijoles _____
8. el chocolate _____

I. Lo que no debe llevar. Indicate the item that does not belong. Then explain your choice.

> **Modelo** Hoy Lynn va a la playa; por eso, lleva: un traje de baño, unas sandalias blancas, un sombrero, un suéter amarillo y unos lentes de sol.
> **En la playa hace calor; no necesita llevar un suéter.**

1. Hoy hace frío; Nancy lleva: un abrigo largo, unos pantalones cortos, un suéter verde, unos zapatos verdes y un sombrero.

_____

2. Esta noche Joe va a una fiesta; por eso, lleva: una corbata roja, un traje negro, una camisa blanca y unos lentes de sol.

_____

3. Es verano. Para trabajar Carlos lleva: unos zapatos de tacón, unos pantalones cortos y una camisa ligera.

_____

4. Hoy llueve; por eso, Larry lleva: un impermeable gris, una blusa anaranjada, una chaqueta azul, pantalones grises y una camisa azul.

_____

5. Es otoño en Nueva York. Valerie lleva: una blusa morada, una falda negra, un traje de baño y unos tenis morados.

_____

6. Hoy hace sol y buen tiempo. Para ir con sus amigos al parque, Joe lleva una camiseta blanca, unos jeans, unos tenis y un paraguas café.

_____

J. ¿Qué me pongo? Imagine this is the city where you live. For each illustration, describe the weather, the season, and the clothes you wear during that season.

a.
_____
_____
_____
_____
_____
_____

b.
_____
_____
_____
_____
_____
_____

c.
_____
_____
_____
_____
_____
_____

Para terminar

K. Cruceros Festival. Read the brochure and answer the questions.

> **Reading Strategy: Looking for specific information**
>
> As you become a proficient reader in Spanish, you will learn to not be disturbed by "noise"—language you do not yet understand. Instead, you will be aware of your purpose for reading a text and will only need to use a dictionary if understanding the details is important to your purpose. Most often, you will use your background knowledge—what you know about the world—and the context of the words to guess the meaning.
>
> You are about to read a travel brochure. The information you will most likely find in a travel brochure includes activities to do, interesting places to see, special events, and facts about weather, costs, currency, passport, visas, and vaccinations. Your purpose in reading is to gather details about the Mexican cruise in order to answer the following questions.

1. ¿Qué día llega el barco a Cabo San Lucas? ¿Cuántas horas se queda *(does it stay)* ahí?

   _____

2. ¿A qué hora se va el barco de Puerto Vallarta?

   _____

3. ¿Dónde está Cabo San Lucas?

   _____

4. ¿Qué lugares interesantes puedes visitar en Cabo San Lucas?

   _____

5. ¿Cómo es Mazatlán?

   _____

6. ¿En qué mes hace más calor? ¿Cuál es la temperatura durante el invierno?

   _____

7. ¿Qué actividades puedes hacer en Mazatlán?

   _____

8. ¿Qué característica especial tiene Puerto Vallarta?

   _____

9. ¿Qué es Yelapa y cómo puedes llegar allí?

   _____

10. ¿Conoces alguna de estas ciudades? ¿Cuál(es)? ¿Cuál te gustaría *(would you like)* conocer? ¿Por qué?

    _____

    _____

    _____

¡Descubra los tesoros[1] de México!

Ud. descubrirá tesoros en sus playas y ciudades, en sus atardeceres[2] dorados, en la sonrisa de la gente, en la comida y en la famosa artesanía mexicana.

Itinerario

Día	Puerto	Llegada	Salida
domingo	San Diego		16:00
lunes	Travesía del Mar		
martes	Cabo San Lucas	07:00	22:00
miércoles	Mazatlán	07:00	24:00
jueves	Puerto Vallarta	07:00	23:00
viernes	San Diego	22:00	

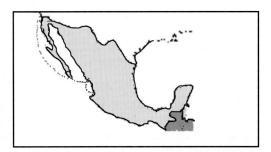

El primer tesoro: Cabo San Lucas

Cabo San Lucas está en el extremo sur de la península de Baja California, que se extiende 1.500 kilómetros al sur de la frontera con Estados Unidos. Esta pequeña ciudad, bañada[3] por el sol los 365 días del año, tiene docenas de playas vírgenes y de aguas templadas, de arena[4] blanca, y las doradas montañas del desierto a la distancia. Cabo San Lucas es famoso por sus enormes rocas en forma de arco, donde se bañan al sol las focas[5] y los leones marinos; y donde las ballenas[6] grises de Alaska pasan el invierno.

El segundo tesoro: Mazatlán

Mazatlán, en el estado de Sinaloa, es el puerto con la mayor flota camaronera[7] del país. Es muy popular entre los turistas mexicanos, estadounidenses y canadienses por la pesca y la navegación a vela[8]. Esta ciudad relativamente nueva y moderna tiene playas magníficas. También hay hoteles de la mejor calidad y la Zona Dorada, en el centro de la ciudad, tiene una gran variedad de tiendas. Pero principalmente, Mazatlán ofrece una excelente vida nocturna: restaurantes, terrazas, bares y discotecas. Es fácil y barato[9] transportarse del puerto al centro.

Temperaturas

mes	alta	baja
ene.	73	63
feb.	73	63
mar.	73	63
abr.	77	66
may.	81	72
jun.	84	77
jul.	91	79
ago.	88	79
sep.	86	77
oct.	80	76
nov.	81	70
dic.	73	64

El tercer tesoro: Puerto Vallarta

Puerto Vallarta es una pequeña ciudad de la Riviera mexicana que conserva su aire tradicional de pequeño pueblo mexicano. Tiene estrechas calles empedradas[10], una linda plaza a la orilla del mar[11], donde se hacen representaciones de pastorelas[12] durante la época de Navidad y donde tocan bandas musicales el resto del año. Tiene que visitar la catedral de Nuestra Señora de Guadalupe y caminar por la zona central de la ciudad. También hay pequeñas tiendas de artesanías, artículos de piel[13], cerámica y joyerías[14]. Tiene que visitar Yelapa. Debe tomar un pequeño barco local que visita la Isla de las Rocas y la playa de Mismaloya antes de llegar a la playa de Yelapa. Ahí Ud. debe nadar hasta la playa (está muy cerca) e ir a caballo[15] hasta el nacimiento[16] del río.

[1]*treasures* [2]*sunsets* [3]*bathed* [4]*sand* [5]*seals* [6]*whales* [7]*shrimp population* [8]**pesca...** *fishing and sailing* [9]*cheap* [10]**estrechas...** *narrow cobblestone streets* [11]*seashore* [12]*humorous popular plays representing the struggle between good and evil* [13]*leather* [14]*jewelry stores* [15]*horse* [16]*start*

L. Un lugar bonito que tú conoces. Write a description of a vacation place you have visited. Talk about the weather in the season when you usually go, the activities you usually do, etc.

> **Writing Strategy: Using simple language to express your ideas**
>
> You may feel frustrated when you cannot communicate your ideas in written Spanish as well as you can in English. For this reason, you may make the mistake of using a dictionary and creating sentences that Spanish speakers would not be able to understand. A much more effective strategy is to limit your messages to what you are able to communicate.
>
> You have just read a tourist brochure in Spanish. By using the illustrations, your background knowledge, and context, you were probably able to understand most of the text. But you are probably not yet able to use that level of language to communicate your own ideas. For example, in the brochure you read this about Cabo San Lucas: **Esta pequeña ciudad, bañada por el sol los 365 días del año, tiene docenas de playas vírgenes...** Although you cannot yet write a similar description, you can write something like: **Cabo San Lucas es una ciudad pequeña. Siempre hace sol y calor y hay muchas playas bonitas,** which any Spanish speaker would understand. Using simple language enables you to express yourself effectively while you build your writing communication skills.

_____

_____

_____

_____

_____

_____

_____

_____

_____

_____

_____

_____

_____

_____

_____

_____

_____

_____

Episodio 14

Escenas de la vida: ¡Estás muy americanizada!

 A. ¡Mira cuánto puedes entender! Sofía y Odette hablan de sus rutinas diarias. Escucha la conversación o mira el video para indicar si las oraciones son **ciertas (C)** o **falsas (F).**

1. Sofía se pone **pantalones de mezclilla para ir a la universidad.**

2. Odette se pone **ropa elegante sólo para salir.**

3. Odette no sale de casa sin pintarse.

4. Odette sale con **sus amigos entre semana.**

5. Sofía se queda **en casa entre semana.**

6. Sofía siempre se pinta **para ir a la universidad.**

7. Sofía se acuesta **tarde y** se levanta **temprano.**

8. Sofía y Odette se van a divertir **en el teatro esta noche.**

9. Sofía prefiere bañarse **por la noche.**

B. ¿Quién lo dijo? Escucha la conversación o mira el video otra vez para indicar quién hizo los siguientes comentarios: Odette (**O**) o Sofía (**S**).

_____ 1. ¿Adónde vas tan elegante?

_____ 2. Si me acuesto tarde, no puedo levantarme temprano.

_____ 3. En Estados Unidos hay más oportunidades profesionales para las mujeres.

_____ 4. Para mí, es muy importante tener vida social.

_____ 5. Casi todos salen del trabajo, van a casa, ven la tele y se acuestan.

_____ 6. Aquí nos acostamos tarde y nos levantamos temprano.

C. ¿Te diste cuenta? Escucha la conversación o mira el video para responder.

1. ¿Por qué dice Sofía que la vida en Estados Unidos es aburrida entre semana?

_____

2. ¿Por qué dice Sofía que está muy americanizada?

_____

3. ¿Por qué dice Sofía que le gusta vivir en Estados Unidos?

_____

4. ¿Qué van a hacer Sofía y Odette esta noche?

_____

Cultura a lo vivo

In Spanish-speaking countries, people are used to going out regularly on weekday evenings. For Hispanics, it is very important to keep in touch with their family and friends, so informal get-togethers are a constant. It's very common to hold impromptu parties or gatherings for the pleasure of seeing each other again, regardless of the day of the week or time of day.

Práctica adicional		
Cuaderno de tareas p. 359, A	invitaciones. vhlcentral.com Episodio 14	invitaciones. vhlcentral.com Episodio 14

Para comunicarnos mejor

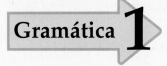

Gramática **1**

Describing your daily routine
• **Reflexive pronouns**

Analizar y descubrir

In the conversation, you heard the following:

Sólo **me pongo** camisetas…   *I only wear T-shirts...*
¿Y **te pintas**?   *And do you wear makeup?*
La gente **se acuesta** temprano.   *People go to bed early.*
Nos levantamos temprano.   *We get up early.*

1. The verb forms **me pongo**, **te pintas**, **se acuesta**, and **nos levantamos** each include a reflexive pronoun. You will know that a verb is conjugated with a reflexive pronoun when **se** appears in the infinitive form: **ponerse**, **pintarse**, **acostarse**, **levantarse**. Reflexive verbs have the same endings as other **-ar**, **-er**, and **-ir** verbs.

Study the following examples and answer the questions.

Verbos con pronombres reflexivos

Los sábados **me levanto** tarde.	*On Saturdays I get up late.*
¿A qué hora **te levantas**?	*What time do you get up?*
Usted nunca **se acuesta** temprano, ¿verdad?	*You never go to bed early, do you?*
Sofía **se quita** los lentes de contacto para dormir.	*Sofía takes off her contact lenses to sleep.*
Nosotros **nos bañamos** por la mañana.	*We take a shower/bathe in the morning.*
¿Ustedes **se divierten** en la clase ¿no? ¿Vosotros **os divertís** en la clase ¿no? }	*You have fun in class, right?*
Los niños no **se lavan** las manos antes de comer.	*The kids do not wash their hands before eating.*

2. Which reflexive pronoun is used...

    a. with the **yo** form of the verb? _____   e. with the **nosotros/as** form? _____

    b. with the **tú** form? _____   f. with the **ustedes** form? _____

    c. with the **usted** form? _____   g. with the **ellos/as** form? _____

    d. with the **él/ella** form? _____

3. Spanish uses the definite article (**el, la, los, las**) when reflexive verbs are used with parts of the body and clothing. English uses a possessive adjective (*my, your, her*). Identify the statements above that illustrate this rule.

    a. _____

    b. _____

4. Reflexive pronouns, like direct object pronouns, may be placed before a conjugated verb or attached to the infinitive.

        Tengo que **levantarme** temprano porque voy a trabajar.

    or   **Me** tengo que **levantar** temprano porque voy a trabajar.

5. Reflexive pronouns are not optional. Verbs used reflexively have different meanings than those used without reflexive pronouns; for example, while **ir** means *to go*, **irse** means *to leave*.

Para hablar de tu rutina diaria

acostarse (o ➤ ue) tarde	*to go to bed late*	levantarse temprano	*to get up early*
bañarse por la noche	*to take a bath / shower at night*	pintarse	*to put on makeup*
divertirse (e ➤ ie)	*to have fun*	ponerse la ropa	*to put on/wear clothing*
irse (a)	*to leave*	quedarse en casa	*to stay home*
irse de vacaciones	*to go on vacation*	quitarse los zapatos	*to take off one's shoes*
juntarse	*to get together*		
lavarse las manos	*to wash one's hands*		
los dientes	*to brush one's teeth*		

> **También se dice...**
>
> pintarse ➤ maquillarse
>
> lavarse los dientes ➤ cepillarse los dientes

PRÁCTICA

A. ¿Qué hacen?

Parte 1. Empareja las ilustraciones con las descripciones.

a

b

c

d

e

f

_____ 1. Sofía se levanta tarde los sábados.

_____ 2. ¿Te pintas todos los días?

_____ 3. Me baño por la noche cuando hace frío.

_____ 4. Todos se divierten cuando se juntan para salir.

_____ 5. Nosotros nos quedamos en casa esta noche.

_____ 6. Me pongo pantalones para ir a la universidad.

Parte 2. Con un(a) compañero/a, habla de estas actividades.

| **Modelo** | Yo me levanto a las seis. ¿Y tú? |

B. La rutina diaria. Ordena las oraciones del uno al diez en una secuencia lógica.

_____ a. Y me acuesto porque ya es tarde.

_____ b. Luego me voy a la universidad.

_____ c. Luego me pongo el pijama.

_____ d. Después me baño.

_____ e. Voy a mi cuarto a ponerme la ropa.

_____ f. Me lavo los dientes antes de acostarme.

_____ g. Me quedo en la universidad todo el día.

_____ h. Me levanto temprano porque es lunes.

_____ i. Me voy a casa porque ya estoy cansado.

_____ j. Me divierto un rato *(for a little while)* mirando mi programa cómico favorito.

C. Lotería.

Parte 1. Encuentra un(a) compañero/a que haga las siguientes cosas. Escribe su nombre en el cuadro *(box)* apropiado. La persona que llene todas las líneas sin repetir nombres gana el juego.

> **Modelo** _____ prefiere bañarse por la noche.
> —¿Te bañas por la noche?
> —No, me baño por la mañana. ¿Y tú?

_____ se acuesta antes de las once de la noche.	_____ sabe jugar golf.	_____ se levanta tarde los domingos.	_____ no se pone pijama para dormir.
_____ se divierte en su trabajo.	_____ no conoce a los padres de su novio/a.	_____ se queda en casa los sábados por la tarde.	_____ no se pinta todos los días.
_____ prefiere bañarse por la noche.	_____ se va de vacaciones todos los años.	_____ se junta con la familia el día de su cumpleaños.	_____ ayuda a su mamá en la casa.
_____ se quita los zapatos cuando llega a casa.	_____ se lava los dientes con *Aquafresh*.	_____ nunca pide postre en los restaurantes.	_____ usa lentes de contacto.

¡Fíjate!

Remember to use reflexive pronouns only with reflexive verbs!

Parte 2. Comparte *(share)* la información con la clase.

> **Modelo** Estudiante 1: **Rick se va de vacaciones todos los años.**
> Estudiante 2: **¿Adónde vas?**
> Rick: **Generalmente vamos a Utah a esquiar.**

D. En casa de Ramón y Ana Mari.

Parte 1. Ana Mari describe la rutina diaria de su familia. Conjuga los verbos para formar oraciones completas y haz los cambios necesarios.

En mi casa:

1. mis padres / levantarse / antes que todos
   _____

2. a mí / me / gustar / acostarse / temprano
   _____

3. por eso / (yo) / bañarse / por la noche
   _____

4. mis hermanos / preferir / bañarse / por la mañana
   _____

5. mi mamá / pintarse / mientras que mi papá / preparar / el desayuno
   _____

6. a las ocho / todos / (nosotros) / desayunar / juntos
   _____

7. luego / todos / irse / al trabajo o a la escuela
   _____

Parte 2. Ahora contesta las preguntas.

1. ¿Quién se levanta primero en casa de Ramón y Ana Mari? ¿Y en tu casa?
   _____

2. ¿Quién se baña por la noche? Y tú, ¿cuándo te bañas?
   _____

3. ¿Quién prepara el desayuno? ¿Y en tu casa?
   _____

E. ¿Cómo cambia tu rutina cuando estás de vacaciones?

Parte 1. Adriana describe cómo cambia *(changes)* su rutina cuando está de vacaciones. Lee la descripción en la siguiente página y contesta las preguntas.

1. ¿Cuáles son las diferencias principales en sus actividades?
   _____
   _____

2. ¿Por qué se levanta temprano durante las vacaciones?
   _____
   _____

3. ¿Adónde se va de vacaciones generalmente? ¿Por qué va allí? ¿Qué hacen?
   _____
   _____

Durante el verano
me divierto más
porque no tengo
tantas obligaciones.

Yo no me divierto
tanto porque estudio
y trabajo igual que el
resto del año.

¡Pobrecito!

Cuando estoy de vacaciones mi rutina de las mañanas no cambia[1] mucho.
Generalmente me levanto temprano porque mi esposo siempre se levanta
temprano, vacaciones o no.

La ropa que me pongo sí es diferente: para ir a trabajar me pongo vestidos, faldas o
pantalones más formales. En cambio[2], cuando estoy de vacaciones me pongo jeans,
camisetas y ropa muy informal. No me pinto todos los días, si no tengo que trabajar o ir a
la universidad.

La diferencia más importante es lo que hago después de trabajar: en las
vacaciones me divierto mucho más porque hago lo que yo quiero. No tengo tantas (as
many) obligaciones y me puedo quedar tranquila en casa o juntarme con amigos si
tengo ganas. Cuando estoy en clases siempre estudio y hago la tarea antes de
acostarme.

En invierno, generalmente me voy de vacaciones a Puerto Rico a ver a mi hermana.
Allá, nos acostamos muy tarde porque nos gusta mucho salir o juntarnos con la familia
para hablar, cantar y bailar hasta la madrugada[3].

¡Fíjate!

Notice that verbs
are not conjugated
after prepositions:
**para hablar, cantar...,
después de trabajar,
antes de acostarme.**

[1]*doesn't change* [2]*on the other hand* [3]*dawn*

Parte 2. Usa la descripción de Adriana como modelo para escribir cómo cambia tu rutina
cuando estás de vacaciones.

F. ¡Qué divertido! Listen to the story Ana Mari's younger brothers tell about when they
visited their grandmother. Indicate whether their behaviors are good or bad. Share your
answers with a partner.

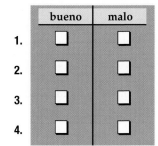

	bueno	malo
1.	☐	☐
2.	☐	☐
3.	☐	☐
4.	☐	☐

	bueno	malo
5.	☐	☐
6.	☐	☐
7.	☐	☐
8.	☐	☐

Práctica adicional

Cuaderno de tareas
pp. 360–364, B–G

invitaciones.
vhlcentral.com
Lab practice

invitaciones.
vhlcentral.com
Episodio 14

G. ¡A hablar! En grupos de cuatro, hablen de sus rutinas durante el año escolar y
describan cómo cambia esa rutina durante las vacaciones de verano. Piensen en la ropa que
se ponen, la hora a la que se levantan y acuestan, las obligaciones que tienen, etc.

Actividades comunicativas

 A. Un sondeo (*survey*). Vamos a descubrir cuáles son los hábitos de nuestros/as compañeros/as para poder hablar de las tendencias entre los/las chicos/as universitarios/as.

Parte 1. Contesta cada pregunta con precisión (*accuracy*) en la columna **YO**.

HÁBITOS	YO					PROMEDIO
1. ¿Cuántas horas duermes generalmente?						
2. ¿A qué hora te acuestas entre semana?						
3. ¿Cuántas veces a la semana te quedas en la biblioteca para hacer tarea o trabajos?						
4. ¿A qué hora te levantas los fines de semana?						
5. Entre semana, ¿cuántas noches sales con amigos?						
6. ¿Cuántas horas a la semana usas la computadora?						
7. ¿Cuántos mensajes mandas al día?						
8. ¿Cuántas horas de televisión ves a la semana?						
9. ¿Cuánto tiempo pasas (*spend*) con tu familia?						
10. ¿Cuántos días al año te vas de vacaciones?						

Parte 2. En grupos de cuatro o cinco personas, hablen sobre cada pregunta. Escriban los nombres y las respuestas de cada uno/a para sacar un promedio (*an average*) de grupo.

Parte 3. Compartan la información con la clase. Saquen un promedio de la clase entera (*whole*).

Modelo	—En nuestro grupo dormimos un promedio de 6.9 horas por noche. —La persona que duerme más es Laurie; ella duerme 8 horas, y la persona que duerme menos es Joe; él duerme 6 horas.

B. Sopa de palabras.

Instrucciones para Estudiante 1

Primero escribe oraciones lógicas usando todas las palabras. La primera y la última palabras ya están en su lugar. Después léele tus oraciones a tu compañero/a para verificar las respuestas. Si tiene errores, ayúdalo/la a encontrarlos, pero no le des *(don't give them)* la respuesta correcta inmediatamente. Deja que trate *(let them try)* de solucionar los problemas. Túrnense.

Modelo

Sofía pinta los se solamente **sábados.**
Sofía se pinta solamente los sábados./Sofía solamente se pinta los sábados.

Los fines de semana

1. **Los** tarde, mis esposo acuestan se pero sábados, acuesta se mi hijos **temprano**.

   _____

2. **Me** llego cuando quitarme los a zapatos gusta **casa.**

   _____

3. **Me** para ir solamente las pinto a **fiestas**.

   _____

4. **Es** con importante con la muy familia juntarse **frecuencia**.

   _____

5. **Los** vestido pongo me domingos mi **favorito**.

   _____

Las respuestas de tu compañero/a:

1. Los lunes me levanto temprano, pero los sábados prefiero levantarme tarde./Los sábados me levanto temprano, pero los lunes prefiero levantarme tarde./Los lunes prefiero levantarme temprano, pero los sábados me levanto tarde./Los sábados prefiero levantarme temprano, pero los lunes me levanto tarde.
2. Mis hijos se divierten mucho en la clase de karate.
3. No me gusta quedarme en casa los sábados; prefiero salir.
4. Mi esposo se acuesta muy tarde; yo necesito acostarme antes de las diez.
5. Siempre nos bañamos por la noche/mañana porque por la mañana/noche no tenemos tiempo.

B. Sopa de palabras.

Instrucciones para Estudiante 2

Primero escribe oraciones lógicas usando todas las palabras. La primera y la última palabras ya están en su lugar. Después léele tus oraciones a tu compañero/a para verificar las respuestas. Si tiene errores, ayúdalo/la a encontrarlos, pero no le des *(don't give them)* la respuesta correcta inmediatamente. Deja que trate *(let them try)* de solucionar los problemas. Túrnense.

> **Modelo**
> **Wayne** la camiseta ejercicio en se la pone hacer para **parque.**
> **Wayne se pone la camiseta para hacer ejercicio en el parque.**

Las actividades en casa

1. **Los** me temprano, lunes prefiero levanto sábados levantarme pero los **tarde.**

   _____

2. **Mis** divierten clase en la mucho se de hijos **karate.**

   _____

3. **No** me quedarme prefiero los sábados; casa gusta en **salir.**

   _____

4. **Mi** muy esposo tarde; se yo las acostarme antes acuesta necesito de **diez.**

   _____

5. **Siempre** bañamos mañana noche nos por la tenemos no porque por la **tiempo.**

   _____

Las respuestas de tu compañero/a:

1. Los sábados, mis hijos se acuestan tarde, pero mi esposo se acuesta temprano./Los sábados, mi esposo se acuesta tarde, pero mis hijos se acuestan temprano.
2. Me gusta quitarme los zapatos cuando llego a casa.
3. Me pinto solamente para ir a las fiestas.
4. Es muy importante juntarse con la familia con frecuencia.
5. Los domingos me pongo mi vestido favorito.

C. La fotonovela.

 Parte 1. Habla con un(a) compañero/a sobre cada imagen. Indica cuándo, dónde, a qué hora o con qué frecuencia haces tú estas actividades.

> **Modelo**   **Mi novia me llama todos los días. Hablamos durante horas por teléfono.**

¡Fíjate!

Have a real conversation with your partner. Make sure to react to his/her statements or ask a follow-up question. Try and use the following phrases:

¡Qué romántico!
How romantic!

¡Qué parrandero!
You are a party animal!

¡Qué madrugador!
You're an early bird!

¡Qué dormilón!
You're a sleepy head!

¡Ojalá!
I wish!

¡Qué envidia!
I'm jealous!

 Parte 2. En grupos de cuatro personas, seleccionen cinco actividades para escribir una descripción de lo que hacen Sofía y sus amigos los fines de semana. Después, tu grupo va a leer la descripción a la clase y tus compañeros van a adivinar (*guess*) las letras de las actividades que usaron en la descripción.

Empiecen su descripción así: **Los viernes por la tarde, Sofía generalmente…**

La correspondencia

El correo: La gritería nicaragüense. Lee el artículo del periódico *(paper)* escolar sobre la más famosa celebración nicaragüense. Después contesta las preguntas.

1. ¿Qué es la gritería? ¿Cuándo se celebra?

_____

2. ¿Qué hacen las personas durante la gritería?

_____

3. ¿Qué hacen ese día por la mañana? ¿A qué hora se levantan? ¿Por qué?

_____

_____

4. ¿Qué hacen ese día por la tarde?

_____

_____

La gritería, celebración nacional nicaragüense

Por Wayne Reilly

Hace dos años, visité[1] Managua, la capital de Nicaragua. Una de mis mejores experiencias fue[2] participar en "la gritería". La gritería es una fiesta dedicada a la Virgen María que se celebra el 7 de diciembre. Las personas van de casa en casa cantando y alabando[3] a la Virgen. Cuando un grupo llega a una casa, pregunta, "¿Qué causa tanta alegría?", y las personas de la casa contestan, "¡La concepción de María!".

En la casa de mi familia adoptiva, los preparativos empezaron[4] muy temprano. Nos levantamos a las siete de la mañana, limpiamos toda la casa (tiene que estar todo muy limpio para los visitantes) y preparamos las canastas[5] de dulces para regalar. A las cinco de la tarde, salimos a la calle y fuimos a la casa de varios vecinos[6]. Cantamos, disparamos cohetes[7], vimos los fuegos artificiales[8], comimos caña de azúcar, gofios (dulces hechos de masa de maíz) y dulces de leche. Después volvimos[9] a la casa para esperar a que llegaran otras personas del barrio. Fue una noche fabulosa; cantamos, bailamos y conversamos. Yo me acosté a las tres de la mañana y mi familia se acostó todavía más tarde.

Los nicaragüenses me dicen que la gritería es la celebración más esperada del año. Algunos años se celebra aun[10] en medio de situaciones violentas. La gente olvida la violencia y los conflictos políticos por un día y se dedica a celebrar con alegría.

[1] *I visited* [2] *was* [3] *praising* [4] *started*
[5] *baskets* [6] *neighbors* [7] *we shot firecrackers*
[8] *fireworks* [9] *we returned* [10] *even*

En papel: Una celebración importante en mi país. Usa el artículo de Wayne como modelo para escribir sobre una celebración importante en la que tú participas con frecuencia. Debes hacer un bosquejo *(outline)* primero con la información que quieres escribir.

Cultura a lo vivo

En muchas ciudades de Latinoamérica se celebran carnavales que marcan el inicio de la Cuaresma[1]. El carnaval es una fiesta popular de tradición católica que celebra con alegría y excesos el período antes de la Cuaresma. El carnaval de La Habana, Cuba, dura varios días y es famoso en todo el mundo. Incluye un desfile donde toman parte grupos de baile y música, llamados *comparsas*. El público se divierte siguiendo la música y los pasos de los grupos; bailan, beben y comen al ritmo de tambores[2], trompetas y otros instrumentos típicos de la rica tradición musical afrocubana. Ve al Supersitio para mirar un episodio de *Flash cultura* sobre este tema *(topic)* y contesta las preguntas: ¿Qué fiestas celebran? ¿Qué hacen las personas en esas fiestas puertorriqueñas?

Flash CULTURA

[1]Lent [2]drums

¡A ver de nuevo! Escucha la conversación de **Escenas de la vida** o mira el video otra vez. Escribe un resumen que conteste las siguientes preguntas.

- ¿De qué hablan Odette y Sofía?
- ¿Qué diferencias notan entre México y Estados Unidos?
- ¿Por qué dice Sofía que está americanizada?
- ¿Estás de acuerdo con el último *(last)* comentario de Odette? Explica.

Sofía   **Odette**

Invitación a **Nicaragua**

In your own words. Read the information below and then write what you understood. In English, summarize the information in two or three sentences. Do not translate.

Del álbum de
Wayne

Nicaragua es un poco más pequeño que el estado de Nueva York y tiene 6 millones de habitantes. Se le conoce como el país de los lagos *(lakes)* y los volcanes. Los volcanes Concepción y Madera están en el Lago de Nicaragua. Una erupción formó más de 300 islas volcánicas en el enorme lago. En sus orillas *(shores)*, se encuentra la ciudad de Granada, uno de los lugares más visitados de Nicaragua. Su arquitectura colonial y la tranquilidad de su gente la hacen un lugar muy especial.

Mira el monumento en el parque central de Granada y responde a las preguntas.
1. ¿A quién está dedicado?
2. ¿Qué ves detrás de ese monumento?

Lago de Nicaragua

Práctica adicional			
Cuaderno de tareas pp. 364–366, H–I	invitaciones. vhlcentral.com Episodio 14	invitaciones. vhlcentral.com Lab practice	invitaciones. vhlcentral.com Episodio 14

Monumento a la Madre en Granada, Nicaragua

357

Vocabulario del Episodio 14

Para hablar de tu rutina diaria

acostarse (o ➔ ue) tarde	*to go to bed late*
bañarse por la noche	*to take a bath/shower at night*
divertirse (e ➔ ie)	*to have fun*
irse (a)	*to leave*
irse de vacaciones	*to go on vacation*
juntarse	*to get together*
lavarse las manos	*to wash one's hands*
los dientes	*to brush one's teeth*
levantarse temprano	*to get up early*
pintarse	*to put on makeup*
ponerse la ropa	*to put on/wear clothing*
quedarse en casa	*to stay home*
quitarse los zapatos	*to take off one's shoes*

Vocabulario personal

▼

Write the words you need to know to talk about your daily routine and important celebrations in your family.

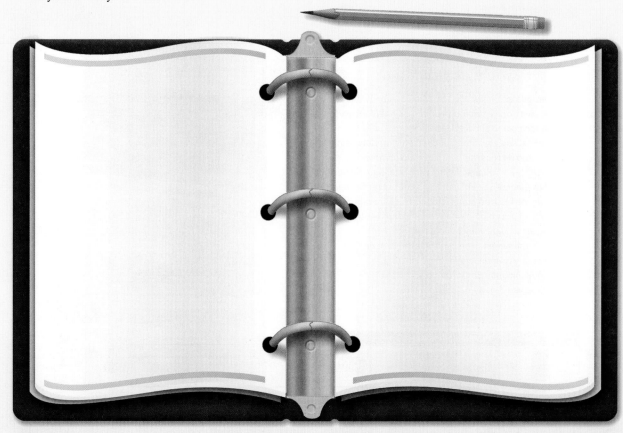

Episodio

Cuaderno de tareas

Escenas de la vida: ¡Estás muy americanizada!

 A. ¡A ver cuánto entendiste! See how much of the **Escena** you understood by matching the Spanish sentences with their English equivalents. At the end, identify the speaker.

1. ¿Quién lo dijo? *(Who said it?)*

_____ 1. Sólo salen los fines de semana.

_____ 2. Yo estoy tan americanizada.

_____ 3. Me pinto cuando voy a salir.

_____ 4. Sólo me pongo camisetas.

_____ 5. Entre semana la gente se
　　　　　acuesta temprano.

a. I'm so Americanized.

b. I only wear T-shirts.

c. I put on makeup when
　 I go out.

d. They only go out on
　 weekends.

e. During the week, people go
　 to bed early.

_____ **lo dijo.**

2. ¿Quién lo dijo?

_____ 1. Es mi ropa normal.

_____ 2. Pareces viejita.

_____ 3. Aquí la gente sale casi todos los días.

_____ 4. No necesitas levantarte todavía.

_____ 5. Aquí nos acostamos tarde.

a. Here people go out almost
　 every day.

b. You're like an old woman.

c. You don't need to get up yet.

d. Here we go to bed late.

e. These are my normal clothes.

_____ **lo dijo.**

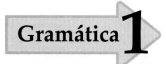
Gramática 1 Describing your daily routine
• Reflexive pronouns

B. ¿En qué secuencia? Put the following activities in the order in which the people indicated do them. Use **primero**, **después**, and **por último**.

> **Modelo** (yo)/ponerse el pijama, acostarse, mirar la tele
> **Primero miro la tele, después me pongo el pijama y por último me acuesto.**

1. (Sofía)/bañarse, ponerse la ropa, levantarse

_____

_____

2. (mi esposo y yo)/lavarse los dientes, acostarse, quitarse la ropa

_____

_____

3. (yo)/irse de vacaciones, comprar ropa, pagar mis cuentas *(bills)*

_____

_____

4. (los niños)/ponerse el pijama, cenar, dormirse

_____

_____

5. (las mujeres)/peinarse, levantarse, pintarse

_____

_____

¡Fíjate!

Notice the difference between transition words like **después** and prepositions like **después de**.
a. Odette se pinta **después de ponerse** la ropa.
b. Odette se pinta, **después se pone** la ropa.
In **a**, Odette puts her clothes on first; in **b**, Odette puts makeup on first.
Also notice that the verb is not conjugated after the preposition **de**.

Verbs are not conjugated after prepositions: e.g., **para, antes de**, and **después de**.
Verbs are conjugated after transition words: e.g., **cuando, por eso, después**, and **antes**.

C. ¿Qué hacen? Join the actions shown below using a preposition and a conjunction (**por eso**, **para**, **cuando, antes de,** and **después de**) to express the order in which you do these activities. Review the **¡Fíjate!** on conjugating verbs on the previous page.

> **Modelo**
>
> Primero me lavo los dientes, después me acuesto.
>
>

1. _____

_____

_____

2. _____

_____

_____

3. _____

_____

_____

4. _____

_____

_____

D. La rutina de Manolo.

Parte 1. Manolo is spending a week back home with his parents. As he talks about his routine, complete the description with the appropriate forms of the verbs. Then answer the questions that follow.

Ahora estoy de vacaciones en casa de mis papás. Mi rutina aquí es un poco diferente que en mi casa. Usualmente (1) _____ (bañarse) por las noches, pero en la Florida hace muchísimo calor. Por eso prefiero (2)_____ (bañarse) por las mañanas. Aquí todos (3) _____ (levantarse) temprano. Mis papás (4) _____ (levantarse) temprano porque trabajan, y yo también (5) _____ (levantarse) porque voy a surfear con mis primos. Durante mi semestre regular, generalmente (6) _____ (acostarse) temprano porque tengo una clase de cálculo a las siete de la mañana. En casa de mis papás, (7) _____ (acostarse) tardísimo porque hay muchísimas cosas que hacer.

Bueno, por las tardes vienen mis primos y tíos de visita (¡viven en la casa de al lado!). Jugamos cartas o Monopolio. Mis primos y yo (8) _____ (quitarse) los zapatos, (9) _____ (ponerse) cómodos y (10) _____ (quedarse) en casa toda la tarde y parte de la noche. A la una o una y media, mis primos y tíos (11) _____ (irse) a sus casas. La verdad es que yo (12) _____ (divertirse) con ellos.

Parte 2. Answer the following questions.

1. ¿Qué cosas diferentes hace Manolo en la casa de sus papás?

_____

2. ¿Por qué se acuesta tarde?

_____

3. ¿Por qué todos se levantan temprano?

_____

4. ¿Qué hacen Manolo y sus primos por las tardes?

_____

5. ¿A qué hora se van sus tíos y primos?

_____

E. Mi rutina de las vacaciones. Use Manolo's description as a model to write a description of your routine when you are on vacation.

_____

_____

_____

_____

_____

_____

F. ¡Pobre Carlos! In a letter to her sister in Puerto Rico, Adriana describes Carlos' life in the military. Write the appropriate forms of the verbs from the list to complete her letter. Then answer the questions.

1. ¿Por qué está preocupada Adriana? _____

2. ¿Cómo es la rutina de Carlos? ¿Te gusta esa rutina? ¿Por qué sí o por qué no?

_____

_____

3. ¿Por qué crees que se duerme inmediatamente? _____

4. ¿Por qué es buena la Fuerza Aérea para Carlos? _____

acostarse	bañarse	dormir	irse	ponerse
ser	divertirse	hacer	levantarse	verte

...por otra parte, también estoy un poco preocupada por Carlos. ¿Recuerdas que te dije *(I told you)* que está en un entrenamiento[1] especial con la Fuerza Aérea? Pues, hoy recibí una tarjeta *(card)* de él, y me cuenta que está contento, pero que él y todos sus compañeros están cansados, con hambre y con sueño.

Los pobres chicos (1) _____ a las cuatro de la mañana y (2) _____ con agua fría. Después (3) _____ la ropa y (4) _____ sus camas en menos de quince minutos, pues a las cuatro y cuarto deben reportarse con el sargento en el patio. Empiezan a hacer ejercicios físicos y prácticas militares; ¡todo esto antes de desayunar! Después, toda la mañana toman clases de aviación. Por la tarde hacen sus prácticas de vuelo *(flight)*. Tienen que (5) _____ a las ocho de la noche.

Me dice que en cuanto se acuesta, se (6) _____ inmediatamente. ¡Pobre de mi hijito, con lo dormilón que es! Me dice que también ha bajado de peso[2], pobrecito, con esa rutina. Lo bueno es que va a aprender a tener disciplina y a (7) _____ ordenado.

Bueno, Cristina, escríbeme pronto y cuéntame cómo va todo por allá. ¿Cuándo vas a venir? Tengo muchas ganas de (8) _____ .

Recibe un fuerte abrazo de tu hermana que te quiere,

Adriana

[1]*training* [2]*has lost weight*

G. Un poco de lógica.

The verbs you are learning in this section use a reflexive pronoun. However, many of these same verbs may also be used without a reflexive pronoun. Compare the following models and then complete the sentences. Decide whether the reflexive pronoun is necessary or not.

¡Fíjate!

Notice that in the first photo, **Laura lava los platos**, no reflexive pronoun is needed because Laura is washing something else. In grammatical terms, a reflexive pronoun is necessary only when the subject and the object are the same person. In the second photo, **Laura se lava las manos**, Laura is washing her own hands, requiring the use of the reflexive pronoun.

Modelo

Laura lava los platos.

Laura se lava las manos.

Sofía/bañar

1. _____

Carlos/bañar

2. _____

Sofía/poner/lavadora

3. _____

Odette/poner

4. _____

Para terminar

H. Venezuela: Los diablos danzantes de Yare. Read about **Los diablos danzantes de Yare**. Then answer the questions. You may answer in English or in Spanish.

1. Before you read, look at the picture of **Los diablos**. What do you think **diablos** mean? What kind of celebration might it be?

   _____

   _____

2. When and where does this celebration take place?

   _____

   _____

3. What do participants do on the first day?

   _____

   _____

4. What do they wear on the second day?

   _____

   _____

5. What do they do after mass on the second day?

_____

_____

6. What do they do after the ceremony?

_____

_____

Los diablos danzantes de Yare

Una tradición medieval española que llega en 1619 a varias ciudades de Venezuela es la de los diablos danzantes[1]. Estos diablos celebran el Corpus Christi con ceremonias simbólicas de cómo la cruz (la religión católica) derrota el mal y los pecados[2] de la humanidad. El pueblo de San Francisco de Yare es famoso por su celebración de los diablos danzantes.

La celebración empieza el día anterior al jueves de Corpus Christi. Los participantes bailan por las calles del pueblo y por la noche van al Calvario[3]. Al día siguiente, por la mañana, se ponen sus trajes rojos de diablo y van al cementerio a visitar a algunos diablos anteriores. Después van a misa *(mass)*. Al terminar la misa, cada diablo se acerca bailando al sacerdote[4] y le dice qué sacrificios va a hacer. El sacerdote le pregunta cuál es el motivo del ofrecimiento y la duración de la promesa.

Al finalizar esta ceremonia, todos los diablos salen a bailar otra vez por las calles del pueblo. Este ritual combina elementos indígenas y africanos con la tradición católica romana.

Los diablos danzantes bailan por las calles de San Francisco de Yare, en Venezuela.

Los músicos, vestidos de rojo, acompañan a los diablos danzantes.

[1]*dancing devils* [2]*defeats evil and the sins* [3]*Calvary (symbolizing the place where Jesus was crucified)* [4]*priest*

I. Una miniprueba. Complete the following tasks in Spanish; write your answers below.

1. Ask Sofía
    a. when she gets up on Sundays
    b. if she goes to bed later on weekends
    c. what she wears to go to the gym

Sofía

2. Ask Adriana
    d. how often she gets together with her sister
    e. if she is going to go on vacation this winter
       or if she is going to stay home
    f. what the weather is like where she lives

Adriana

a. _____

_____

b. _____

_____

c. _____

_____

d. _____

_____

e. _____

_____

f. _____

_____

Episodio 15

Escenas de la vida: La posada

 A. ¡Mira cuánto puedes entender! Indica en qué secuencia ocurrieron las actividades de la posada, según la **Escena**.

Ana Mari está feliz porque todos quieren bailar con ella.

La mitad de los invitados están en el jardín.

Manolo tocó la guitarra.

Empezó a llover y los mayores corrieron a la casa.

Sofía se queda en su cuarto. Ramón y Ana Mari se van.

Los niños se quedaron afuera. Están ocupados recogiendo dulces.

Todos cantaron los versos tradicionales.

Ramón está molesto con Ana Mari.

Sofía está enferma porque comió demasiado pozole.

B. ¿Te diste cuenta? Indica si los comentarios son **ciertos** o **falsos,** según la **Escena.**

	Cierto	Falso
1. Los niños no recogen *(gather)* los dulces de la piñata.	☐	☐
2. Todos los invitados llegaron a la casa de Odette.	☐	☐
3. Empezó a llover, pero los niños corrieron por sus dulces.	☐	☐
4. Las personas de afuera se quedan afuera toda la noche.	☐	☐
5. Al pedir posada, hay personas dentro y fuera de la casa.	☐	☐
6. Hay comida, bebidas y música toda la noche.	☐	☐

C. ¿Quién? Indica quién se siente *(feels)* así en la posada: Sofía (**S**), Ana Mari (**AM**), Manolo (**M**), Ramón (**R**), Odette (**O**) o los niños (**LN**).

Sofía **Ana Mari** **Manolo** **Ramón** **Odette**

_____ 1. Están emocionados de comer dulces y jugar en la lluvia.

_____ 2. Está muy contenta porque todo va muy bien.

_____ 3. Está feliz porque está de vacaciones.

_____ 4. Está enojado porque llegaron una hora tarde.

_____ 5. Está emocionado porque es la primera vez que va a México.

_____ 6. Está en cama y solamente escucha la música y la risa *(laughter)* de los invitados.

Cultura a lo vivo

Even though Spanish speakers and English speakers, like all cultural groups, get together to enjoy each other's company, their parties differ in substantial ways. For most Spanish speakers, a party is only a **fiesta** if there is music, dancing, food, and drinks. Gatherings without dancing are called **reuniones** in Mexico and **tertulias** in Spain.

A **posada** is a special **fiesta** common in Mexico that takes place between December 16 and 23. Family and friends of all ages reenact the biblical story of Mary and Joseph's search for shelter before the birth of Jesus. Go to the Supersite to watch an authentic video clip on this subject.

En esta fiesta, los niños están emocionados porque ya es hora de romper la piñata. Todos están listos con sus bolsitas para poner los dulces que van a recoger *(gather)*.

Práctica adicional		
Cuaderno de tareas p. 387, A	invitaciones. vhlcentral.com Episodio 15	invitaciones. vhlcentral.com Episodio 15

Para comunicarnos mejor

Gramática **1**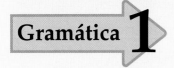

Saying how you feel and where you are
• **Estar** + [*adjective*], **estar** + [*location*]

In the **Escena**, you heard these statements:

Ahora **estoy enferma**.	*Now I'm sick.*
Odette **está** muy **contenta**.	*Odette is very happy.*
Estoy feliz; estoy de vacaciones.	*I'm happy; I'm on vacation.*
Ramón **está molesto** conmigo...	*Ramón is upset with me...*
Los niños **están emocionados** de comer dulces.	*The kids are excited about eating candies.*

1. You have used the verb **estar** to find out how someone is (**¿Cómo estás?**). **Estar** is also used to express how you are feeling at a particular time.
2. **Enferma, contenta, molesto,** and **emocionados** are adjectives and match the gender (masculine or feminine) and number (singular or plural) of the nouns they describe.
3. Adjectives ending in **-e** or **-z**, such as **feliz**, match with nouns only in number.

Para describir cómo estás o cómo te sientes (*To describe how you feel*)			
A veces estoy.../Hoy me siento...		*Sometimes I am.../Today I feel...*	
aburrido/a	*bored*	**enfermo/a**	*sick*
borracho/a	*drunk*	**enojado/a**	*angry*
cansado/a	*tired*	**estresado/a**	*stressed*
contento/a	*happy*	**molesto/a**	*upset*
deprimido/a	*depressed*	**nervioso/a**	*nervous*
desilusionado/a	*disappointed*	**preocupado/a**	*worried*
emocionado/a	*excited*	**tranquilo/a**	*calm*
ocupado/a	*busy*	**triste**	*sad*

4. You have also used **estar** to tell where someone is (**Estoy en mi casa**); here are some more expressions of location that are used with **estar**.
5. Use **dentro de** and **fuera de** followed by a place; use **adentro** and **afuera** when no location follows.

—¿Quién dejó la leche **fuera del** refrigerador?   —Ay, perdón, yo la dejé **afuera**.

Estar + [*location*]	
Están de vacaciones.	*They are on vacation.*
Odette está adentro.	*Odette is inside.*
Ramón está afuera, en el jardín.	*Ramón is outside, in the garden.*
Yo estoy en cama.	*I am in bed.*

6. **Sentirse (e ⟶ ie)** (*to feel*) may also be used with these expressions. It is conjugated like other reflexive verbs.

—¿Comó **te sientes** hoy?   —**Me siento** más tranquila.

PRÁCTICA

A. Los opuestos. Completa las descripciones de las personas en la posada.

1. Odette no está triste; está _____.

2. Ramón no está contento; está _____.

3. Sofía no se siente bien; está _____.

4. Los niños no están desilusionados; están _____.

5. Manolo no está preocupado; está _____.

B. Causas. Con un(a) compañero/a empareja cada columna para formar oraciones lógicas en voz alta *(out loud)*. Usa **porque** or **por eso** para unir las ideas.

> **Modelo**   Odette está emocionada porque su amiga Sofía va a estar en su casa dos semanas.

1. Odette está preocupada	a. van a ir a Guadalajara de vacaciones.
2. Ramón y Ana Mari están emocionados	b. llueve y no pueden salir a jugar.
3. Los niños están enojados por eso	c. Sofía está enferma.
4. Wayne está muy ocupado porque	d. Ana Mari no quiere bailar con ellos.
5. Manolo está un poco nervioso	e. no puede ir a Guadalajara con Ramón.
6. Los amigos de Odette están desilusionados	f. no le gusta tocar la guitarra en público.

C. ¿Cómo estás? Usa expresiones con **estar** o **sentirse** para describir cómo estás en las siguientes situaciones.

> **Modelo**   Hoy salimos de vacaciones, **estamos emocionados**.
> No encuentro a mi perrito; por eso, **me siento triste**.

1. Mañana tengo un examen muy difícil; por eso, _____.

2. Los martes tengo cuatro clases y trabajo seis horas; por eso, _____.

3. Mi pareja admira a otras/os chicas/os; _____.

4. Mis padres me dan dinero; _____.

5. Mis amigos/as no me llaman; _____.

6. Quiero ir al parque y empieza a llover; _____.

7. Hace muchísimo calor; _____.

8. La semana que viene compro un coche nuevo; _____.

D. La inteligencia emocional. Lee el artículo sobre la inteligencia emocional y contesta las preguntas.

> La inteligencia emocional es la habilidad de conocer, entender y controlar nuestras emociones y sentimientos (*feelings*). Muchos sicólogos opinan que la inteligencia emocional juega un papel (*plays a role*) más importante en la vida y la felicidad de las personas que la inteligencia cognitiva. ¡Tú puedes desarrollar la capacidad de controlar y usar tus emociones a tu favor! Las cinco dimensiones de la inteligencia emocional son: (1) conocimiento de uno mismo (*oneself*), (2) autocontrol, (3) automotivación, (4) empatía y (5) habilidades para relacionarse.
>
> Conocer tus propias emociones es lo más importante en el desarrollo (*development*) de tu inteligencia emocional. En cada decisión que tomas en la vida, tus emociones y sentimientos están presentes. Reconocer las expresiones faciales de otros te ayuda a saber identificar sus emociones y así actuar adecuadamente.

1. Summarize what you understood about emotional intelligence.

_____

_____

2. Name a situation in which you let your emotions "get in the way" of your desired outcome.

_____

_____

Parte 1. Reflexiona sobre tus sentimientos durante todo un día. Escribe las seis emociones que sientes con más frecuencia en tu vida (en casa, en el trabajo, con los amigos, en las fiestas, etc.). Para cada una, anota el porcentaje de tiempo en que te sientes así. Por ejemplo, el 50% del día estoy contento. Después, identifica la intensidad con la que sientes cada emoción. Usa **A** (alta intensidad), **M** (mediana intensidad) y **B** (baja intensidad). Recuerda que el total de las seis emociones debe sumar 100%.

¿Cómo te sientes?	%	Intensidad	¿Cómo te sientes?	%	Intensidad

Parte 2. En el siguiente cuadro, anota los sentimientos más frecuentes en tu vida de estudiante (durante tus clases, cuando haces la tarea, cuando estudias, etc.).

¿Cómo te sientes?	%	Intensidad	¿Cómo te sientes?	%	Intensidad

Parte 3. Dibuja (*draw*) una cara con cada una de las emociones que tienes en la **Parte 1**.

| Me siento triste. | Estoy enojado. | Me siento _____. | Estoy _____. |

| Me siento _____. | Estoy _____. | Me siento _____. | Estoy _____. |

Parte 4. Reconocer las expresiones faciales de otros te ayuda a saber identificar sus emociones. Con un(a) compañero/a, usa tus dibujos (*drawings*) para tratar de identificar sus expresiones faciales. ¿Eres bueno/a para 'leer' los sentimientos de otros?

> **Modelo** (*Make a facial expression with an emotion you are feeling to your partner.*)
> —¿Estás enojado?

Parte 5. Tú tienes el control de tus emociones. ¿Cómo te gustaría sentirte (*How would you like to feel*) cada día? Si tú pudieras escoger (*to choose*) tus sentimientos (y sí que puedes), ¿qué emociones te gustaría (*would you like*) sentir durante cada día?

En tu vida   **En tu vida de estudiante**

_____   _____
_____   _____
_____   _____
_____   _____
_____   _____
_____   _____
_____   _____
_____   _____
_____   _____

Práctica adicio

Cuaderno de tarea
pp. 388–389, B–

SUPERSITE

invitaciones.
vhlcentral.com
Episodio 15

Gramática 2

Talking about past activities
• Introduction to the preterit tense

Analizar y descubrir

In the **Escena**, you heard these statements:

Manolo **tocó** la guitarra y **cantó...**   *Manolo played the guitar and sang...*
Comí demasiado pozole.   *I ate too much **pozole**.*
... los mayores **corrieron** a la casa.   *...the grown-ups ran into the house.*

1. **Tocó, cantó, comí,** and **corrieron** are preterit (past tense) forms of the verbs **tocar, cantar, comer,** and **correr.**

Study the examples and answer the questions.

Bailar	
Yo **bailé** toda la noche.	*I danced all night.*
Y tú, ¿**bailaste** con Manolo?	*And you, did you dance with Manolo?*
Manolo no **bailó** con Ana Mari.	*Manolo didn't dance with Ana Mari.*
Nosotras **bailamos** con Ramón.	*We danced with Ramón.*
¿Ustedes **bailaron** hasta tarde? ¿Vosotros **bailasteis** hasta tarde? }	*Did you dance until late?*
Los niños también **bailaron**.	*The kids also danced.*

2. In the preterit, the endings of **-er** verbs and **-ir** verbs are identical.

Comer	
Yo **comí** mucho.	*I ate a lot.*
Y tú, ¿**comiste** tamales?	*And you, did you eat tamales?*
Sofía **comió** demasiado pozole.	*Sofía ate too much **pozole**.*
Nosotros no **comimos** dulces.	*We didn't eat candy.*
¿Ustedes **comieron** pastel? ¿Vosotros **comisteis** pastel? }	*Did you eat cake?*
¡Los niños **comieron** muchos dulces!	*The kids ate a lot of candy!*

3. Now complete the conjugations of **hablar, beber,** and **escribir.**

El pretérito de los verbos regulares		
-ar	**-er**	**-ir**
hablar	beber	escribir
yo _____	_____	_____
tú _____	_____	_____
usted/él/ella _____	_____	_____
nosotros/as _____	_____	_____
ustedes/ellos/as _____	_____	_____

a. What are the preterit endings for regular verbs in the **yo** form? _____

b. What are the endings for the **tú** form? _____

c. What are the endings for the **él, ella,** and **usted** form? _____

d. What are the endings for regular verbs in the **nosotros/as** form? _____

e. How are the **-ar nosotros/as** forms different from the present tense endings? _____

f. What are the preterit endings for the **ellos, ellas,** and **ustedes** form? _____

4. The following are three common irregular verbs.

El pretérito de **ir, hacer** y **tener**	
ir	fui, fuiste, fue, fuimos, fueron
hacer	hice, hiciste, hizo, hicimos, hicieron
tener	tuve, tuviste, tuvo, tuvimos, tuvieron

—¿Adónde **fue** Adriana durante las vacaciones?   *Where did Adriana go during her vacation?*

—No **fue** a ninguna parte porque **tuvo** que trabajar.   *She didn't go anywhere because she had to work.*

—Y tú, ¿qué **hiciste**?   *What did you do?*

—**Fui** a Guadalajara.   *I went to Guadalajara.*

5. Verbs ending in **-ar** and **-er** that have stem changes (**e ⟶ ie, o ⟶ ue, u ⟶ ue**) in the present tense will not have those changes in the preterit tense. Compare the two tenses:

present   preterit

Ramón **juega** fútbol, pero durante las vacaciones no **jugó**.

El partido nunca **empieza** a tiempo, y ayer tampoco **empezó** a tiempo.

Manolo **duerme** cinco horas por las noches, pero el sábado **durmió** diez.

La tienda Marisol **cierra** a las seis de la tarde, pero el 31 de diciembre **cerró** a las dos.

6. Verbs ending in **-gar (llegar, pagar), -car (sacar, tocar),** and **-zar (empezar, organizar)** have spelling changes in the **yo** form.

El semestre pasado lle**gué** a tiempo a todas mis clases. Pa**gué** todas mis deudas *(debts)*. También to**qué** la guitarra en la banda de la escuela. Y lo mejor es que sa**qué** buenas notas porque empe**cé** a trabajar menos y a estudiar más; hasta organi**cé** un grupo de estudio con mis compañeros.

7. The following are some of the expressions used with the preterit tense to indicate the past.

Algunas expresiones para hablar del pasado			
ayer	*yesterday*	hace dos semanas	*two weeks ago*
anoche	*last night*	hace tres meses	*three months ago*
la semana pasada	*last week*	hace cuatro años	*four years ago*
el mes pasado	*last month*	esta mañana	*this morning*
el año pasado	*last year*	durante cinco años	*for five years*

PRÁCTICA

E. ¿Por qué estás así? Une las columnas con una línea para crear oraciones lógicas usando la palabra **porque**.

> **Modelo** Estoy contenta porque saqué A en mi examen de inglés.

1. Estoy nerviosa
2. Mi hija está triste
3. Estoy enfermo
4. Los niños están felices
5. Manolo y yo estamos cansados
6. Ramón está enojado

porque

a. recibieron mucho dinero en su cumpleaños.
b. comí demasiados mariscos.
c. jugamos fútbol toda la mañana.
d. tuvo que comprar muchos libros este semestre.
e. no encontró su bolsa.
f. no estudié para el examen que voy a tomar hoy.

F. ¿Qué hiciste el domingo pasado?

Parte 1. Indica si hiciste estas actividades el domingo pasado.

	Sí	No
1. Me bañé muy temprano.	☐	☐
2. Lavé la ropa.	☐	☐
3. Limpié mi cuarto.	☐	☐
4. Comí en un restaurante elegante.	☐	☐
5. Visité a mis abuelos/papás.	☐	☐
6. Me quedé en casa toda la tarde.	☐	☐
7. Fui a un lugar divertido.	☐	☐
8. Tuve que trabajar.	☐	☐
9. Hice toda mi tarea.	☐	☐
10. Me acosté a las diez de la noche.	☐	☐

Parte 2. Cambia las oraciones a preguntas para entrevistar a un(a) compañero/a. Después escribe acerca de lo que hizo tu compañero/a.

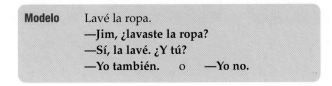

> **Modelo** Lavé la ropa.
> —Jim, ¿lavaste la ropa?
> —Sí, la lavé. ¿Y tú?
> —Yo también.   o   —Yo no.

¡Fíjate!

Use **lo, la, los,** and **las** when you have a direct object. Remember, not all verbs take a direct object.

G. Las actividades de mi compañero.

Parte 1. Usa las expresiones de la página 374 para escribir cuándo hiciste estas cosas.

¿Cuándo fue la última vez que...	Yo	Mi compañero/a
1. compraste ropa?	_____	_____
2. llegaste tarde a una clase?	_____	_____
3. hiciste ejercicio?	_____	_____
4. almorzaste en la cafetería?	_____	_____
5. fuiste a una fiesta?	_____	_____
6. comiste comida italiana?	_____	_____
7. jugaste ráquetbol?	_____	_____
8. saliste con tus amigos a cenar?	_____	_____
9. te levantaste antes de las 5 de la mañana?	_____	_____
10. te juntaste con toda la familia?	_____	_____

Parte 2. Entrevista a un(a) compañero/a para comparar la información. Escribe sus respuestas y hablen de cada actividad.

> **Modelo**
> —¿Cuándo fue la última vez que compraste ropa?
> —La semana pasada.
> —¿Qué compraste?
> —Unos pantalones y unos tenis. ¿Y tú?

H. ¿Qué hicieron? Usa las fotos para escribir qué hicieron Sofía y Wayne el domingo. Ordena los eventos lógicamente. Usa **por la mañana, después, a las... de la noche,** etc.

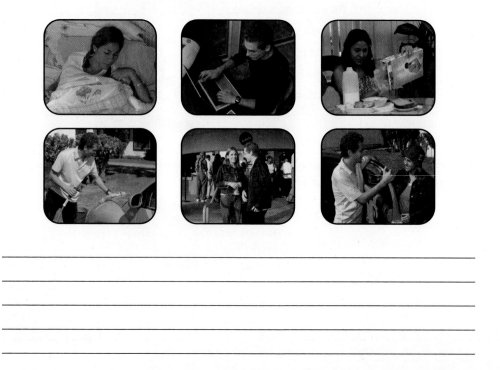

_____

_____

_____

_____

_____

I. ¡A hablar! En grupos de tres, hablen de un fin de semana divertido. Por lo menos, tienen que mencionar cinco actividades.

> **Modelo** Hace un mes fui a un juego de vóleibol. Después, mis compañeros y yo fuimos a comer. Por la noche, salí con unas amigas; vimos una película muy buena...

Invitación a **México**

In your own words. Read the information below and then write what you understood. In English, summarize the information in two or three sentences. Do not translate.

_____

_____

_____

Del álbum de
Sofía

Muchos de los elementos de la cultura mexicana conocidos en todo el mundo provienen del estado de Jalisco, cuya capital es Guadalajara. De ahí vienen los mariachis y las charreadas. Estas fiestas en rodeos combinan las habilidades artísticas con el colorido y belleza de la ropa, las técnicas en el manejo del caballo y la elegancia del jinete *(rider)*. Los palenques (ferias donde hay cantantes) y mucha de la "comida mexicana" también son originarios de Jalisco. Además, grandes escritores mexicanos como Juan Rulfo y Mariano Azuela, y muralistas importantes como José Clemente Orozco son jaliscienses. En Guadalajara se encuentra el Hospicio Cabañas que sirvió de hospital y asilo para cientos de niños huérfanos (niños sin padres) hasta el año 1980. Orozco pintó algunos de sus famosos murales allí. Ahora, este edificio es la sede *(seat)* del Instituto Cultural Cabañas, que promueve *(promotes)* el arte y la cultura.

Hospicio Cabañas

Práctica adicional		
Cuaderno de tareas pp. 389–392, F–L	invitaciones. vhlcentral.com Lab practice	invitaciones. vhlcentral.com Episodio 15

Actividades comunicativas

A. Un día en la guardería "El Porvenir".

Instrucciones para Estudiante 1

Tú eres el/la supervisor(a) en la guardería "El Porvenir". Hoy hablas con un(a) empleado/a. Dile cómo se llaman los niños que tú conoces y pregúntale sobre los niños que no conoces. Pregunta por qué están contentos, tristes, preocupados, enojados, etc. Escribe la información que necesitas. Tu compañero/a empieza con una pregunta.

Modelo
—¿Cómo se llama la niña que lleva una blusa rosa y un vestido verde?
—(tú) Se llama Eliana.
—¿Por qué esta contenta?
—(tú) Porque hoy es su cumpleaños y recibió muchos regalos.

Eliana
Today is her birthday and she got many presents.

Juan
He does not like the music.

Iván and Rubén
They do not know anybody because it's their first day.

disappointed

excited

angry

happy

sick

Mario
He went to bed at midnight.

Brandon
Noni and Laura do not want to talk to him.

A. Un día en la guardería "El Porvenir".

Instrucciones para **Estudiante 2**

Tú eres un(a) empleado/a de la guardería "El Porvenir". Hoy hablas con el/la supervisor(a). Dile cómo se llaman los niños que tú conoces y pregúntale sobre los niños que no conoces. Pregunta por qué están contentos, tristes, preocupados, enojados, etc. Escribe la información que necesitas. Tú empiezas.

Modelo	—*(tú)* ¿Cómo se llama la niña que lleva una blusa rosa y un vestido verde? —Se llama Eliana. —*(tú)* ¿Por qué esta contenta? —Porque hoy es su cumpleaños y recibió muchos regalos.

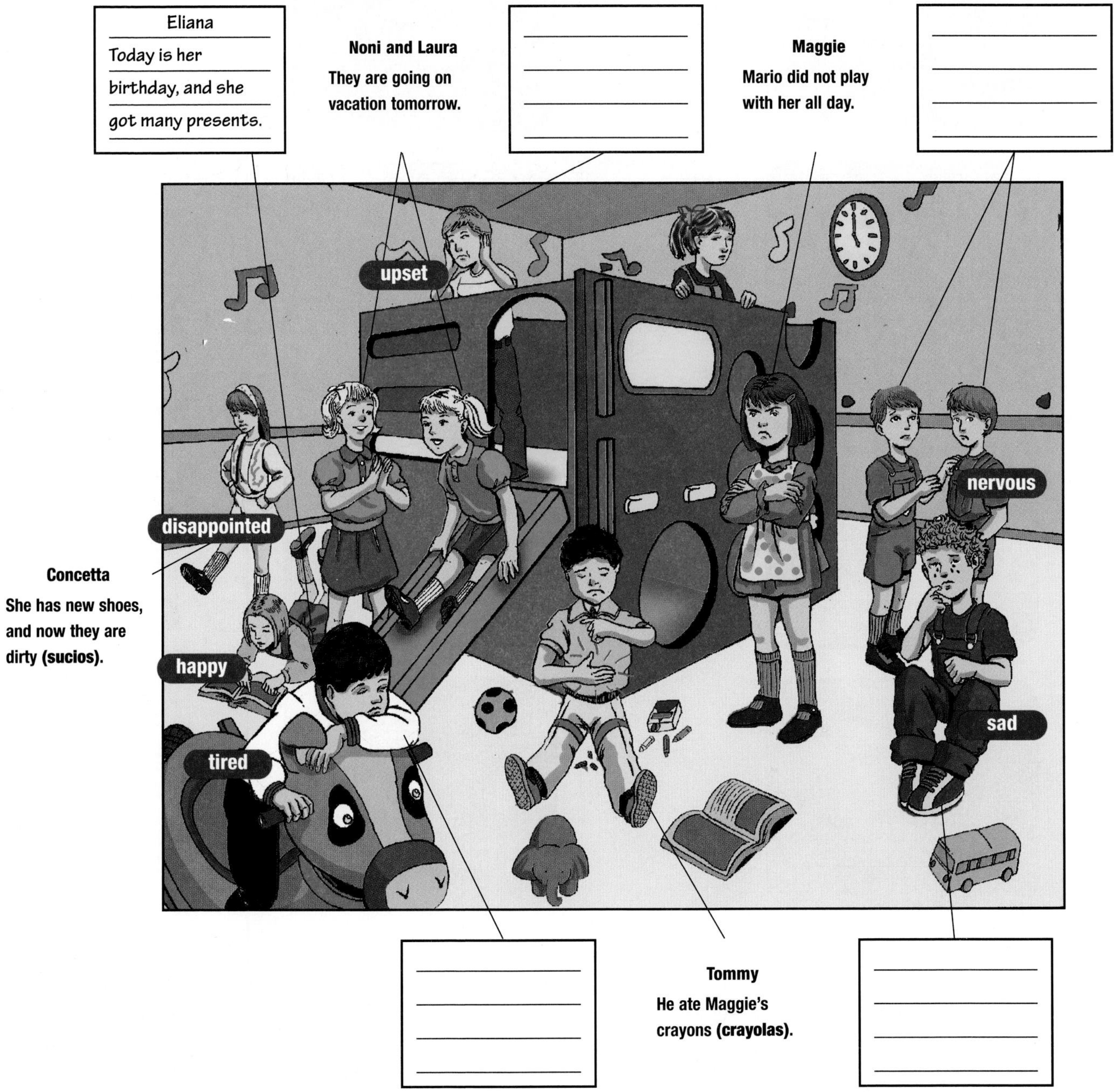

Eliana

Today is her birthday, and she got many presents.

Noni and Laura
They are going on vacation tomorrow.

Maggie
Mario did not play with her all day.

Concetta
She has new shoes, and now they are dirty (sucios).

upset
disappointed
happy
tired
nervous
sad

Tommy
He ate Maggie's crayons (crayolas).

B. La historia va así.

Parte 1. Escucha lo que hizo Sofía la semana pasada y mira las ilustraciones. Identifica el orden, del uno al ocho, en que ocurrieron los eventos. Escucha una vez más para verificar tus respuestas.

___ a

___ e

___ b

___ f

___ c

___ g

___ d

___ h

Parte 2. Ahora en grupos escriban una historia diferente.

_____

_____

_____

_____

_____

_____

C. El chisme (*gossip*). Imagina que un(a) compañero/a nuevo/a no sabe nada ni conoce a Sofía ni a sus amigos. Tu compañero/a y tú le van a decir todo lo que saben de ellos. Escriban la información y todos los detalles posibles sobre los personajes y sobre la situación en cada foto.

1. Todo lo que saben de Adriana, de su esposo y de su situación en casa.

_____
_____
_____
_____
_____
_____

2. Todo lo que saben de las clases y los estudios de Sofía, Adriana y Manolo.

_____
_____
_____
_____
_____
_____

3. Todo lo que saben de Wayne, sus actividades y su fiesta de cumpleaños.

_____
_____
_____
_____
_____
_____

4. Todo lo que saben de la cita de Wayne y Sofía.

_____
_____
_____
_____
_____
_____

La correspondencia

 El correo: Manolo escribe desde Guadalajara. Manolo les escribe a sus padres una carta desde Guadalajara comentándoles su visita a México. Léela y contesta las preguntas.

1. ¿Qué es una posada? ¿Qué hacen los invitados en una posada? _____
_____

2. ¿Dónde está Manolo? ¿Qué tiempo hace allí? _____
_____

3. ¿Adónde van Manolo y sus amigos por las noches? _____
_____

4. ¿Adónde fueron? ¿Qué lugares conocieron? _____
_____

Queridos papás: Guadalajara, 26 de diciembre

Espero que estén bien. Yo nunca he pasado[1] mejores vacaciones. Odette y su familia son muy amables. Anteayer[2] hicieron una posada fabulosa aquí en la casa de Odette. Comí muchos platos típicos mexicanos que no conocía. Me estoy divirtiendo como no tienen idea.

Guadalajara es una ciudad realmente bonita. Tiene zonas supermodernas y zonas coloniales; tiene árboles y flores por todas partes, pues el clima es ideal para las plantas (llueve bastante y hace calor, pero no tiene clima tropical). El lunes pasado fuimos al Museo Regional de Guadalajara, donde hay una colección de artículos de la revolución y de la independencia mexicana. También hay unas pinturas fabulosas de los mejores artistas regionales y nacionales.

Otro día visitamos el mercado de Tlaquepaque, donde venden artesanía, comida típica y todo lo que se puedan imaginar. Yo no sabía que la artesanía mexicana era tan bonita y fina. Hacen unas cosas de plata, cobre, latón, barro y vidrio[3] que son unas obras de arte[4]. Compré muchas cosas y no pagué mucho.

Por las noches hay mil cosas que hacer. Una noche cantamos y bailamos en la Plaza del Mariachi, donde se pueden escuchar varios grupos de mariachis y no se paga nada a menos que uno pida que canten algo. También fuimos a escuchar al grupo de rock Maná, unos músicos con mucho talento, que son de Guadalajara.

Otra noche fuimos al Teatro Degollado a ver el ballet folclórico de la Universidad de Guadalajara. Compré un video del ballet para ustedes. Les va a gustar mucho el vestuario, la música, los bailes, la alegría… ¡tienen que verlo!

En el Hospicio Cabañas están los famosos murales de Orozco. Hay unos frescos enormes, llenos de color y, lo más importante, con contenido social.

Bueno, ya tengo que irme a dormir porque mañana tenemos que madrugar[5]; salimos para Puerto Vallarta. Les mando un beso y los llamo cuando regrese a Estados Unidos.

Su hijo que los quiere,
Manolo

[1]*have spent* [2]*the day before yesterday* [3]**plata,...** *silver, copper, brass, clay, and glass* [4]*works of art* [5]*get up early (at dawn)*

En papel: Una celebración familiar. Escríbele una carta a Odette sobre un evento o una fiesta que celebraste con tu familia.

Incluye la siguiente información:

- dónde fue
- cuándo fue
- qué celebraron
- qué actividades hicieron
- quiénes fueron
- qué ropa llevaste
- qué comiste

Writing Strategy: Using simple language to express your ideas

You may feel frustrated when you cannot communicate your ideas in written Spanish as well as you can in English. For this reason, you may make the mistake of using a dictionary and creating sentences that Spanish speakers would not be able to understand. A much more effective strategy is to limit your messages to what you are able to communicate.

You have just read Manolo's letter. By using your background knowledge, and context, you were probably able to understand most of the text. But you are probably not yet able to use that level of language to communicate your own ideas.

For example, in the letter you read this about Guadalajara: **En el Hospicio Cabañas están los famosos murales de Orozco. Hay unos frescos enormes, llenos de color y... contenido social...** Although you cannot yet write a similar description, you can write something like: **En el Hospicio Cabañas hay unos murales muy bonitos e interesantes,** which any Spanish speaker would understand. Using simple language enables you to express yourself effectively while you build your written communication skills.

¡Fíjate!

Remember to create an outline in simple Spanish. Write a first draft with your ideas. Then use connectors to join your sentences. In the final draft, check vocabulary and grammar.

¡A ver de nuevo!

 Parte 1. Escucha la narración de **Escenas de la vida** o mira el video para hacer un resumen que conteste todas las preguntas.

1. ¿Qué hacen las personas a la hora de pedir posada?
2. ¿Por qué está contenta Odette?
3. ¿Por qué está feliz Ana Mari?
4. ¿Qué hizo Manolo en la posada?
5. ¿Qué pasó con Sofía? ¿Por qué no fue a la posada?

 Parte 2. Ahora trabaja con un(a) compañero/a para comparar la información y añadir la que no tienes.

Práctica adicional			
Cuaderno de tareas pp. 393–394, M	invitaciones. vhlcentral.com Episodio 15	invitaciones. vhlcentral.com Lab practice	invitaciones. vhlcentral.com Episodio 15

Vocabulario del Episodio 15

Objetivos comunicativos

You should now be able to do the following in Spanish:

✓ say how you feel and where you are

✓ talk about past activities

Para describir cómo estás

A veces estoy...	Sometimes I am...
Hoy me siento...	Today I feel...
aburrido/a	bored
borracho/a	drunk
cansado/a	tired
contento/a	happy
deprimido/a	depressed
desilusionado/a	disappointed
emocionado/a	excited
enfermo/a	sick
enojado/a	angry
estresado/a	stressed
molesto/a	upset
nervioso/a	nervous
ocupado/a	busy
preocupado/a	worried
tranquilo/a	quiet, calm
triste	sad

Sentirse (e ⟶ ie) + [emotions]

Estar + [location]

estar...	to be...
adentro/dentro de	inside
afuera/fuera de	outside
en cama	in bed
en clase	in class
de vacaciones	on vacation

Algunas expresiones para hablar del pasado

ayer	yesterday	hace dos semanas	two weeks ago
anoche	last night	hace tres meses	three months ago
la semana pasada	last week	hace cuatro años	four years ago
el mes pasado	last month	esta mañana	this morning
el año pasado	last year	durante cinco años	for five years

Vocabulario personal

In this section, write all the words you need to know in order to talk in greater detail about your own activities.

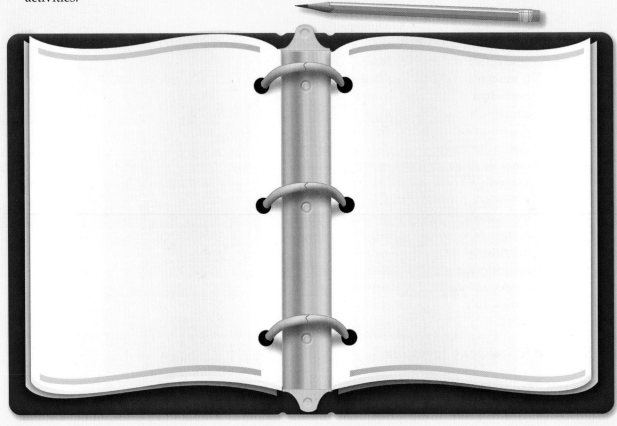

Cuaderno de tareas

Episodio

15

Escenas de la vida: La posada

 A. ¡A ver cuánto entendiste! Match the sentences with their translations.

La posada

_____ 1. La otra mitad se queda adentro de la casa.

_____ 2. Ya es hora de pedir posada.

_____ 3. Los niños decidieron recoger los dulces y juguetes.

_____ 4. Están emocionados de romper la piñata.

_____ 5. Empezó a llover.

_____ 6. Todos tienen una vela y los versos tradicionales.

a. They're excited about breaking the piñata.

b. It began to rain.

c. It's time to ask for shelter.

d. Everyone has a candle and the traditional verses.

e. The kids decided to gather the candies and toys.

f. The other half stays in the house.

¡Los hermanos!

_____ 7. ¿No me dijiste que no llueve en el invierno?

_____ 8. ¿Y cómo va la fiesta?

_____ 9. Ramón está molesto conmigo.

_____ 10. Llegamos a tiempo para pedir posada.

_____ 11. Llegamos una hora tarde.

_____ 12. A Manolo le gustó una chica.

g. We got here on time to ask for shelter.

h. Manolo liked a girl.

i. And how is the party going?

j. Ramón is upset with me.

k. We got here an hour late.

l. Didn't you tell me it doesn't rain in the winter?

<table>
<tr><td>**Gramática 1**</td><td>**Saying how you feel and where you are**
•<u>Estar</u> + [*adjective*], <u>estar</u> + [*location*]</td></tr>
</table>

B. Usa la lógica. Combine elements from the three columns to make logical sentences.

> **Modelo** Comiste muchos tacos de pescado, por eso estás enfermo.
>
> o
>
> Estás enfermo porque comiste muchos tacos de pescado.

1. estoy aburrido/a		no sé si voy a pasar el examen
2. estamos cansados/as		vamos a descansar y dormir un rato
3. estoy estresado/a		comiste muchos tacos de pescado
4. mi novio/a está molesto/a	porque	todos están en casa
5. mi papá está tranquilo	por eso	sacaron F en el examen
6. los chicos están preocupados		mis amigos están ocupados y no
7. estás enfermo/a		pueden salir conmigo
		no lo/la llamé por teléfono anoche

1. _____

2. _____

3. _____

4. _____

5. _____

6. _____

C. ¿Por qué estás así? Complete the following statements in a logical manner.

> **Modelo** Estoy triste porque mis amigos no me invitan a sus fiestas.

1. Estoy aburrido/a porque _____.

2. Estoy cansado/a porque _____.

3. Mi mamá está enojada conmigo porque _____.

4. Estoy molesto/a porque _____.

5. Estoy contento/a porque _____.

6. Mis padres están preocupados porque _____.

D. Un día muy interesante. Describe how people in the images feel, where they are, and the reason they feel that way using any expression with **estar.**

| Julia | Ana | Jorge | Eva | Paco |

_____

_____

_____

_____

_____

_____

E. ¿Dónde está Migdalia? Describe where Manolo's cat, Migdalia, is using **en, dentro del,** and **afuera.**

1.   **2.**    **3.**

1. Migdalia, la gata de Manolo, a veces está _____.

2. Otras veces está _____ la cama de Manolo.

3. Pero cuando Manolo no está, a la gata le gusta estar _____ cajón

   (drawer) de los suéteres.

 **Gramática 2**   **Talking about past activities**
• Introduction to the preterit tense

F. ¡Dime más! When Manolo mentions the things he did last week, Ramón follows every statement with a question. What does Ramón ask?

| **Modelo** | Manolo | **Hablé por teléfono con mis padres.** |
| | Ramón | **¿Y cómo están?** |

Manolo	**Ramón**
_____ 1. Salí con Ana Mari.	a. ¿Para quién?
_____ 2. Fui a un concierto.	b. ¿Adónde fueron?
_____ 3. Vi una buena película.	c. ¿A qué grupo escuchaste?

_____ 4. Aprendí una canción nueva en la guitarra.

_____ 5. Almorcé comida cubana.

_____ 6. Llegué tarde a clase.

_____ 7. Trabajé hasta las tres de la mañana.

_____ 8. Escribí un poema.

d. ¿Y tienes que trabajar hoy también?

e. ¿Tuviste que practicar mucho?

f. ¿Qué comiste?

g. ¿Ah sí, cuál?

h. ¿Hablaste con la profesora?

G. Explicaciones. Complete the statements logically using verbs in the preterit.

> **Modelo**   Estoy cansada porque **ayer trabajé mucho.**

1. Mi mamá está enferma porque _____.

2. Estoy desilusionado/a porque _____.

3. Tú estás molesto porque _____.

4. Estamos nerviosos porque _____.

5. Estoy deprimido/a porque _____.

6. Ella está emocionada porque _____.

H. ¿Qué hicieron en la playa? Use the illustration to complete Sofía's description with the following verbs in the preterit: **jugar, hacer, hablar, comer, ir, beber,** and **descansar.**

Ayer, (1) _____ a la playa con todos mis amigos. Por suerte (2) _____ muy buen tiempo: calor y sol. Ana Mari y yo (3) _____ vóleibol un par de horas. Manolo no (4) _____ con nosotras; leyó el periódico y (5) _____ en una hamaca. Odette (6) _____ mucho con Ramón. Ellos (7) _____ camarones y (8) _____ refrescos.

I. Los problemas de Adriana. Describe what happened in Adriana's house last weekend. Use the illustrations to describe what she did.

El sábado por la mañana Adriana (1) _____ a Viviana a su clase de baile. Luego regresó a casa. Primero (2) _____ los platos y luego (3) _____ un trabajo en la computadora para su clase de composición. También (4) _____ con Santiago un par de horas. Llegó a casa muy cansada, así que (5) _____ un rato en el sofá de la sala. Por la noche Adriana y su amiga (6) _____. Vieron una película de misterio. El domingo en la mañana todos (7) _____ a los abuelos. Cuando llegaron a casa, ella (8) _____ con Santiago otra vez; por eso, se fue a la biblioteca de la universidad a estudiar y no (9) _____ hasta las diez de la noche.

J. Ahora te toca a ti. Tell what you did last weekend. Write at least six sentences.

_____
_____
_____
_____
_____
_____

K. ¿Cuándo fue la última vez? Use the expressions to tell when you last did the following activities. Include direct object pronouns when possible.

ayer	**anoche**	**la semana pasada**
hace tres meses	**el mes pasado**	**hace un año**

> **Modelo** ¿Cuándo hiciste la tarea?
> **La hice ayer por la mañana.**

1. ¿Cuándo lavaste tu coche?

_____

2. ¿Cuándo fuiste al supermercado?

_____

3. ¿Cuándo viste a tus padres?

_____

4. ¿Cuándo limpiaste tu cuarto?

_____

5. ¿Cuándo almorzaste con toda tu familia?

_____

L. La semana pasada. Answer the questions with as much detail as you can.

1. ¿Adónde fuiste la semana pasada? ¿Con quién(es)? ¿Qué hiciste/hicieron ahí?

_____

_____

_____

_____

2. ¿Tuviste que trabajar? ¿Qué otras cosas tuviste que hacer?

_____

_____

_____

_____

3. ¿Te levantaste tarde o temprano? ¿Te bañaste por la mañana o por la noche?

_____

_____

_____

_____

4. ¿Comiste en un restaurante? ¿Qué comiste?

_____

_____

_____

_____

5. ¿Hiciste tarea o estudiaste? ¿Dónde? ¿Para qué clase?

_____

_____

_____

_____

Para terminar

 M. Cuba: El carnaval de La Habana. Read about the celebration of **Carnaval** in Havana, Cuba, and then answer the questions.

1. ¿Qué es un carnaval?

_____

_____

2. ¿Qué temas *(themes)* representan las comparsas en el desfile *(parade)*?

_____

_____

3. ¿Por dónde pasa el desfile?

_____

_____

4. ¿Qué comida se vende durante estas fiestas?

_____

_____

5. En Estados Unidos, ¿hay celebraciones similares a los carnavales? ¿En dónde? ¿Cuáles son? ¿Cuándo?

_____

_____

_____

_____

_____

_____

_____

6. ¿Asistes a esas celebraciones? ¿Las ves en la televisión? ¿Qué hacen las personas que participan?

_____

_____

_____

_____

_____

_____

_____

En muchas ciudades de Latinoamérica se celebran carnavales que marcan el inicio de la Cuaresma[1]. El carnaval es una fiesta popular de tradición católica que celebra con alegría y excesos el período antes de la Cuaresma. El carnaval de La Habana es famoso en todo el mundo y dura varios días. Incluye un desfile[2] donde toman parte grupos de baile y música, llamados *comparsas*. Estos grupos practican todo el año para presentar al público su habilidad e imaginación artística. Cada grupo se pone extravagantes trajes y adornos en la cabeza[3]. Además, llevan un estandarte[4] que identifica el barrio de procedencia[5] y el tema[6] de la coreografía (temas históricos, folclóricos o literarios relacionados con Cuba o de carácter universal).

La participación de las comparsas alterna con el desfile de numerosas e impresionantes carrozas[7] alegóricas. El desfile pasa por las calles principales de

la ciudad hasta llegar al palco[8] presidencial, donde hay un jurado[9] que determina el mejor grupo de danza y la mejor carroza. El público se divierte siguiendo la música y los pasos de los grupos; bailan, beben y comen al ritmo de tambores[10], trompetas y otros instrumentos típicos de la rica tradición musical afrocubana. A lo largo del malecón[11], la venta[12] de yuca, congrí (arroz con frijoles negros), cerveza, malta, refrescos y ron deleita[13] al público cubano y extranjero.

El carnaval ha estado varias veces en peligro[14] de desaparecer por motivos políticos y económicos. Fue suprimido en 1970 y a principios de los años 90. Afortunadamente, como resultado del descontento popular y el aumento[15] del turismo, se vuelve a celebrar por las calles de la vieja ciudad el carnaval lleno de música y de esperanza para el porvenir[16].

---

[1]*Lent* [2]*parade* [3]*head* [4]*banner* [5]*neighborhood they come from* [6]*theme* [7]*floats* [8]*stage box* [9]*(panel of) judges*
[10]*drums* [11]*avenue closest to the ocean* [12]*sale* [13]*delights* [14]*danger* [15]*rise* [16]**esperanza...***hope for the future*

Revista cultural

La música y los ritmos latinos

Antes de leer

Veamos qué sabes de la música y el baile hispanos. Mira estas fotos para contestar las preguntas.

1. ¿Qué países crees que representan estas fotos?
   _____

2. ¿Qué tipo de música crees que tocan?
   _____

3. ¿Qué ritmos bailan?
   _____

4. ¿Qué instrumentos musicales usan?
   _____

5. ¿Qué influencias se ven en la música y el baile?
   _____

6. Prepara una lista de todos los ritmos latinos que conoces.

   _____ _____ _____

   _____ _____ _____

A. La música latinoamericana.

Hoy en día, los ritmos latinoamericanos se escuchan por todo el mundo.

La música de los diferentes países latinoamericanos es el resultado de la fusión de la música española con elementos de las músicas de la América precolombina, África, Asia y, más recientemente, las influencias de Estados Unidos y países de Europa Occidental.

Hoy en día, los ritmos latinoamericanos se escuchan por todo el mundo. Entre los más populares están la salsa, predominante en los países caribeños, la rumba, el danzón, el chachachá y el mambo de origen cubano. El tango argentino, los corridos y canciones rancheras mexicanos, la cumbia colombiana, el joropo venezolano y los valses peruanos son mundialmente conocidos e identifican las ricas tradiciones musicales de estos países. En España, el canto flamenco, el fandango andaluz y las coplas están entre los ritmos peninsulares que más influyeron en la música del continente americano.

1. ¿Qué influencias hay en la música latinoamericana?

   _____

2. ¿Qué ritmos arriba mencionados conoces o escuchas?

   _____

3. En grupos, usen Internet para escuchar algunos de éstos: una rumba cubana, un tango argentino, una ranchera mexicana, una cumbia colombiana o un canto flamenco. Si es posible, traigan *(bring)* la música para compartir con sus compañeros de clase.

el tango (Argentina)

B. Los bailes tradicionales.

La diversidad musical y cultural española y de la América hispana dieron origen al surgimiento *(rise)* de bailes y danzas tradicionales. Entre estos bailes típicos o folclóricos de España y las naciones hispanoamericanas se encuentran: el jarabe (México), el pericón (Argentina y Uruguay), el danzón (Cuba), el flamenco (España), el xuc (El Salvador), el tamborito (Panamá), el palo de mayo (Nicaragua) y el merengue (República Dominicana).

Actualmente, el reggaetón es uno de los ritmos con más difusión entre los jóvenes de Estados Unidos, América Latina y Europa. Surgido en Panamá con influencias del *reggae* jamaiquino y la música *dancehall*, el reggaetón incorpora elementos de muy diversos ritmos musicales como el *rap* y el *reggae*.

la cueca (Bolivia y Chile)

1. ¿Conoces el reggaetón? ¿Tienes algún grupo favorito?

2. Descubre quiénes son algunos de los intérpretes más conocidos de vallenato, mariachi y reggaetón para presentarlos a la clase.

la bomba (Puerto Rico)

3. Busca la música que acompaña algunos de los bailes mencionados para compartir con la clase.

4. En parejas, escojan la salsa, el flamenco o el tango y hagan una demonstración de baile en clase, enseñando a sus compañeros los pasos del baile.

C. El rock en español.

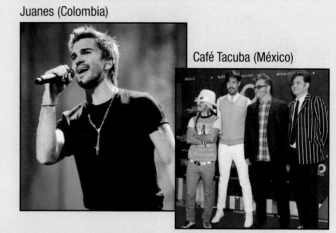

Juanes (Colombia)

Café Tacuba (México)

En México, a fines de los años 50 se organizan las primeras bandas que escriben y cantan rock en español. A fines de los años 60, Argentina ocupa un lugar preeminente en el mundo rockero en español y se convierte en el país que más rock exporta en el mundo. Hoy día existen movimientos de rock en español importantes en Bolivia, Chile, Colombia, Cuba, España, Estados Unidos, Venezuela y Uruguay.

Rockeros hispanos	
Argentina	Luis Alberto Spinetta, Miranda!, El otro yo, Catupecu Machu y Bersuit Vergarabat
Colombia	Juanes, Aterciopelados, Doctor Krápula, 1280 almas y Tr3s de corazón
Cuba	Moneda Dura, Los Kent, Viento Solar y Gens
España	Enrique Bunbury, Muchachito bombo infierno, Amparanoia y Marea
México	Julieta Venegas, Maná, Camila, Jaguares, Café Tacuba y Jumbo
Venezuela	Desorden Público, Los amigos invisibles y Papashanty SaundSystem

1. Investiga a uno de los rockeros que canta en español. Describe su apariencia física y su música. ¿Qué semejanzas y diferencias encuentras con los rockeros de Estados Unidos? ¿Te gusta su música? Explica tu respuesta.

2. Investiga los movimientos rockeros de Bolivia, Chile o Uruguay. ¿Quiénes son los cantantes más famosos? ¿Cómo son físicamente? ¿Te gusta su música? Explica por qué sí o no.

D. Los instrumentos musicales.

Los instrumentos musicales precolombinos incluyen la quena, las maracas y los caracoles marinos (*conch shells*). En las civilizaciones precolombinas no existían los instrumentos de cuerda (*string*). Éstos fueron traídos (*were brought*) por los españoles: la guitarra, el violín y el arpa. Los africanos contribuyeron con instrumentos de percusión y ritmo, entre ellos las congas, los tambores batá, el güiro y los tambores bongó.

la quena

Revista cultural

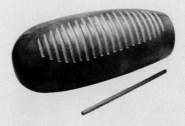

el güiro

1. ¿Tocas algún instrumento? Explica tu repuesta.

_____

2. ¿Qué tipo de instrumento es la quena?

_____

3. ¿Qué tipo de instrumento es el güiro?

_____

E. Si quieres explorar más...

1. Imita ante la clase a tu artista o grupo hispano favorito y explica por qué te gusta su música y/o su forma de interpretarla.
2. Explora los ritmos y bailes de otros países hispanos no mencionados en esta revista e ilustra una presentación con fotos, música y videos.
3. Imagina cómo va a evolucionar tu música hispana favorita en los próximos veinte años y crea tu propia música mediante la fusión de ritmos y tendencias musicales.
4. Descubre cuáles compositores e intérpretes de música y baile clásicos han sobresalido en el mundo hispano e ilustra tu investigación con fotos y música.
5. Investiga los carnavales latinoamericanos más famosos y divertidos. Trae fotos de la ropa, música y bailes típicos.

Lo mejor de Argentina

1. El video. Watch this *Flash cultura* episode from Argentina.

Para bailar el tango hay que ser más elegante que atlético.

Bienvenidos al campo argentino.

2. Emparejar. Find the items in the second column that correspond to the ones in the first.

_____ 1. Grupo de personas que comparte una actividad.	a. estancia
_____ 2. Pequeño acordeón que se usa en el tango.	b. bombilla
_____ 3. Cilindro metálico para beber mate.	c. tertulia
_____ 4. Carne preparada en una parrilla al aire libre.	d. asado
	e. bandoneón

Vocabulario adicional

Para hablar con el/la profesor(a)

¿Podría explicar eso otra vez/repetirlo?
Perdone que haya llegado tarde.
No sé.
No entiendo.
Lo siento, se me olvidó.
¿Hay tarea?
¿Cuándo es la prueba?
No voy a venir a clase mañana.
Gané./Nosotros ganamos.
No hemos terminado.
Más despacio, por favor.
Tengo una duda/pregunta.
¿Cómo se escribe?

To talk to your teacher

Could you explain that again/repeat that?
Excuse me for being late.
I don't know.
I don't understand.
I'm sorry, I forgot.
Is there any homework?
When is the test?
I won't be in class tomorrow.
I won./We won.
We have not finished yet.
Slower, please.
I have a question.
How do you spell that?

Para interactuar con tus compañeros

¿Trabajas conmigo?
¿En qué página estamos?
Yo empiezo./Empieza tú.
Te toca./Me toca.
Dímelo otra vez./¿Cómo?

To interact with your classmates

Do you want to work with me?
What page are we on?
I'll start./You start.
Your turn./My turn.
Say that again.

Tu profesor(a) dirá...

¿Listos para empezar?
Abran/Cierren sus libros.
Para mañana, hagan...
Escuchen./Repitan.
Escríbanlo en sus cuadernos.
¿Entienden?
¿Quién ganó?
No hablen inglés.
Felicidades.
¿Con quién vas a trabajar?
Quiero que hables con otro compañero.
Mañana van a entregar...
Pasen la tarea hacia el frente.
¿Han terminado?/¿Ya terminaron?
¿Hay preguntas/dudas?
¿Puedo continuar?
Escribe en la pizarra/el pizarrón...

Your professor will say...

Are you ready to start?
Open/Close your books.
For tomorrow, do…
Listen./Repeat.
Write it in your notebooks.
Do you understand?
Who won?
Don't speak English.
Congratulations.
Who are you going to work with?
I want you to talk to a different classmate.
Tomorrow you are going to turn in…
Pass the homework to the front.
Have you finished?
Are there any questions?
May I continue?
Write on the board…

Frases de cortesía

Muchas gracias.
De nada.
Con permiso.
Perdone.
No es nada.
No importa.
¡Salud!
¿Puedo pasar?
Perdona la molestia.
A sus órdenes.
Es un placer.

Courtesy phrases

Thanks alot.
You're welcome.
Excuse me.
Pardon me.
No problem.
No problem.
Cheers! Bless you!
May I get by?
Pardon the interruption.
At your service.
It's a pleasure.

En instrucciones

Fecha	*Date*
Con un(a) compañero/a…	*With a partner…*
En grupos…	*In groups…*
Escribe un resumen/una oración/frase.	*Write a summary/a sentence.*
…de lo que se trató.	*…what it was about.*
Primero escucha la conversación.	*First listen to the conversation.*
Después mira el video otra vez.	*Then watch the video again.*
Lee la siguiente carta.	*Read the following letter.*
Empareja/Corrige las frases.	*Match/Correct the phrases.*
…cambiando…	*…by changing…*
Según el árbol genealógico…	*According to the family tree…*
Contesta las preguntas.	*Answer the questions.*
Comparte tus respuestas.	*Share your answers.*
Túrnense para saber…	*Take turns to find out…*
Entrevista a tres personas.	*Interview three people.*
Haz una encuesta para encontrar…	*Do a survey to find…*
Pregúntale/Dile a tu profesor(a).	*Ask/Tell your professor.*
Convierte oraciones/frases a preguntas.	*Change the statements to questions.*
Ella quiere/desea saber…	*She wants to know…*
Usa su carta como modelo.	*Use her letter as a model.*
Haz los cambios necesarios.	*Make the necessary changes.*
…para añadir lo que te haya faltado.	*…to add whatever you are missing.*
Indica si estás de acuerdo.	*Indicate if you agree.*

Réplicas / Rejoinders

¡Caramba!	*Wow!*
¡Qué bien!	*Great!*
¡No me digas!	*You don't say!*
¡Qué esperanza!	*Fat chance!*
¡Qué pena!	*What a pain!*
¡Qué lío!	*What a mess!*
¡Ojalá!	*Hopefully!*
¿De veras?	*Really?*
¿En serio?	*Seriously?*
Por supuesto.	*Of course.*
¡Qué fastidio!	*What a drag!*
¡Qué gracioso!	*How funny!*
De acuerdo.	*Okay.*

LOS PAÍSES

Alemania	*Germany*
Angola	*Angola*
Arabia Saudí	*Saudi Arabia*
Australia	*Australia*
Austria	*Austria*
Bélgica	*Belguim*
Brasil	*Brazil*
Bulgaria	*Bulgaria*
Canadá	*Canada*
China	*China*
Corea del Norte	*North Korea*
Corea del Sur	*South Korea*
Croacia	*Croatia*
Dinamarca	*Denmark*
Egipto	*Egypt*
Escocia	*Scotland*
Eslovaquia	*Slovakia*
Etiopía	*Ethiopia*
Filipinas	*Philippines*
Finlandia	*Finland*
Francia	*France*
Gran Bretaña	*Great Britain*
Grecia	*Greece*
Haití	*Haiti*
Hungría	*Hungary*
India	*India*
Inglaterra	*England*
Irán	*Iran*
Iraq, Irak	*Iraq*
Irlanda	*Ireland*
Israel	*Israel*
Italia	*Italy*
Japón	*Japan*
Kuwait	*Kuwait*
Países Bajos	*Netherlands*
Pakistán	*Pakistan*
Polonia	*Poland*
Rusia	*Russia*
Siria	*Syria*
Somalia	*Somalia*
Sudáfrica	*South Africa*
Sudán	*Sudan*
Suecia	*Sweden*
Suiza	*Switzerland*
Tailandia	*Thailand*
Taiwán	*Taiwan*
Turquía	*Turkey*
Vietnam	*Vietnam*

LAS MATERIAS

la agronomía	*agriculture*
el alemán	*German*
el álgebra	*algebra*
la anatomía	*anatomy*
la antropología	*anthropology*
la arqueología	*archaeology*
la arquitectura	*architecture*
la astronomía	*astronomy*
la bioquímica	*biochemistry*
la botánica	*botany*
el cálculo	*calculus*
el chino	*Chinese*
las ciencias políticas	*political science*
las comunicaciones	*communications*
el derecho	*law*
el desarrollo infantil	*child development*
la educación	*education*
la educación física	*physical education*
la enfermería	*nursing*
la ética	*ethics*
la filosofía	*philosophy*
el francés	*French*
la geología	*geology*
el griego	*Greek*
el hebreo	*Hebrew*
la informática	*computer science*
la ingeniería	*engineering*
el italiano	*Italian*
el japonés	*Japanese*
el latín	*Latin*
las lenguas clásicas	*classical languages*
las lenguas romances	*romance languages*
la lingüística	*linguistics*
la lógica	*logic*
la medicina	*medicine*
el mercadeo	*marketing*
la música	*music*
los negocios	*business*
el portugués	*Portuguese*
el ruso	*Russian*
la salud física	*physical health*
los servicios sociales	*social services*
la trigonometría	*trigonometry*
la zoología	*zoology*

LA COMIDA

Frutas

el albaricoque	*apricot*
la cereza	*cherry*
la ciruela	*plum*
la frambuesa	*raspberry*
la fresa	*strawberry*
la mandarina	*tangerine*
el mango	*mango*
la papaya	*papaya*
la piña	*pineapple*
el pomelo, la toronja	*grapefruit*
la sandía	*watermelon*

El pescado y los mariscos

la almeja	*clam*
el calamar	*squid*
el cangrejo	*crab*
el langostino	*prawn*
el lenguado	*sole, flounder*
el mejillón	*mussel*
la ostra	*oyster*
el pulpo	*octopus*
la sardina	*sardine*
la vieira	*scallop*

Vegetales

la aceituna	*olive*
el aguacate	*avocado*
la alcachofa	*artichoke*
el apio	*celery*
la berenjena	*eggplant*
el brócoli	*broccoli*
la calabaza	*squash; pumpkin*
la col, el repollo	*cabbage*
las espinacas	*spinach*
las judías verdes	*string beans*
el pepino	*cucumber*
el rábano	*radish*
la remolacha	*beet*

La carne

la albóndiga	*meatball*
el chorizo	*pork sausage*
el cordero	*lamb*
los fiambres	*cold meats*
el filete	*fillet*
el hígado	*liver*
el perro caliente	*hot dog*
el puerco	*pork*
la ternera	*veal*
el tocino	*bacon*

Otras comidas

el batido	*milkshake-like drink*
los fideos	*noodles; pasta*
la harina	*flour*
la mermelada	*marmalade; jam*
la miel	*honey*
la tortilla	*omelet (Spain)*

Adjetivos relacionados con la comida

ácido/a	*sour*
amargo/a	*bitter*
caliente	*hot*
dulce	*sweet*
duro/a	*tough*
fuerte	*strong; heavy*
ligero/a	*light*
picante	*spicy*
salado/a	*salty*

LAS CELEBRACIONES

Celebraciones en familia

la amistad	*friendship*
el anfitrión/ la anfitriona	*host/hostess*
el bizcocho	*cake*
la fiesta sorpresa	*surprise party*
el globo	*balloon*
la invitación	*invitation*
la reunión	*social gathering*
la serpentina	*streamers*
la torta	*cake*
las velas	*candles*

Celebraciones religiosas

el bautismo, el bautizo	*baptism, christening*
el funeral	*funeral*
la madrina	*godmother*
el padrino	*godfather*
la Pascua	*Easter*
la primera comunión	*first communion*
el/la sacerdote	*priest*

Días feriados

el Año Nuevo	*New Year's*
el día de acción de gracias	*Thanksgiving Day*
el día de la independencia	*Independence Day*
el día de San Valentín	*Valentine's Day*

Más palabras de celebraciones

las bodas de oro	*golden wedding anniversary*
las bodas de plata	*silver wedding anniversary*
los fuegos artificiales	*fireworks*
el pastel de bodas	*wedding cake*
el ramo de flores	*bouquet, cut flowers*
el reconocimiento	*recognition*
agradecer	*to thank*
festejar	*to celebrate*
gozar	*to enjoy*

Expresiones para brindar

¡Por los años que pasamos juntos!	*To many years together!*
¡Por tu futuro!	*To your future!*
¡Por una carrera brillante!	*To a brilliant career!*
¡Te felicito!	*Congratulations!*
¡Felicidades!	*Happiness to you!*
¡Larga vida y prosperidad para _____!	*Long life and prosperity to _____!*

LA CASA

En la casa

el aire acondicionado	*air conditioning*
la buhardilla	*attic*
la calefacción central	*central heating*
el calentador	*hot water heater*
la decoración de interiores	*interior design*
la despensa	*pantry*
el gas	*gas*
la madera	*wood*
la sala de estar	*common room*
el techo	*roof*
el tendedero	*clothesline*
arriba	*upstairs*
abajo	*downstairs*

Los quehaceres

la limpieza	*cleaning*
el mantenimiento	*maintenance*
enjabonar	*to soap up*
enjuagar	*to rinse*
pulir	*to polish*
regar las plantas	*to water the plants*
tender la cama	*to make one's bed*
ventilar	*to ventilate*

Objetos de la casa

el baúl	*chest*
el bombillo/ la bombilla	*lightbulb*
la licuadora	*blender*
el perchero	*coat rack*
la persiana	*blinds*
la repisa	*shelf*
la vajilla	*dishes*

Otras palabras

el/la niñero/a	*babysitter*
el/la plomero/a	*plumber*
acogedor(a)	*cozy*
amplio/a	*spacious*
mixto/a	*co-ed*
prefabricado/a	*prefabricated*

LA SALUD

El gimnasio

la adrenalina	*adrenaline*
el baño de vapor	*steam room*
el baño turco	*Turkish bath*
la bicicleta de ejercicio	*exercise bike*
la correa	*strap, belt*
el/la entrenador(a)	*trainer*
el jacuzzi	*jacuzzi*
la meta	*goal*
la perseverancia	*perseverance*
la presión sanguínea	*blood pressure*
el pulso	*pulse*
la rapidez	*speed*
el ritmo	*rhythm*
cansar(se)	*to tire (to get tired)*
progresar	*to progress*
(re)bajar de peso	*to lose weight*
benéfico/a	*beneficial*
musculoso/a	*muscular*

El bienestar

el ánimo	*spirits*
el bienestar	*well-being*
la concentración	*concentration*
la meditación	*meditation*
la relajación	*relaxation*
la respiración	*breathing*
la tranquilidad	*tranquility, peace*
reposar	*to rest*

La nutrición

la diabetes	*diabetes*
la fibra	*fiber*
el fluido	*fluid*
la información nutricional	*nutritional information*
el líquido	*liquid*

EL TRABAJO

Las ocupaciones

el/la administrador(a)	*administrator*
el/la agente de bienes raíces	*real estate agent*
el/la agente de seguros	*insurance agent*
el/la agricultor(a)	*farmer*
el albañil	*construction worker*
el/la artesano/a	*artisan*
el/la auxiliar de vuelo	*flight attendant*
el/la basurero/a	*garbage collector*
el/la bibliotecario/a	*librarian*
el/la cajero/a	*bank teller; cashier*
el/la camionero/a	*truck driver*
el/la cantinero/a	*bartender*
el/la carnicero/a	*butcher*
el/la cirujano/a	*surgeon*
el/la cobrador(a)	*bill collector*
el/la comprador(a)	*buyer*
el/la diplomático/a	*diplomat*
el/la empresario/a de una funeraria	*funeral director*
el/la fisioterapeuta	*physical therapist*
el/la fotógrafo/a	*photographer*
el/la intérprete	*interpreter*
el/la juez	*judge*
el/la marinero/a	*sailor*
el/la nutricionista	*dietician*
el/la obrero/a	*manual laborer*
el/la optometrista	*optometrist*
el/la panadero/a	*baker*
el/la paramédico/a	*paramedic*
el/la piloto	*pilot*
el/la plomero/a	*plumber*
el/la quiropráctico/a	*chiropractor*
el/la redactor(a)	*editor*
el/la sastre	*tailor*
el/la supervisor(a)	*supervisor*
el/la vendedor(a)	*sales representative*
el/la veterinario/a	*veterinarian*

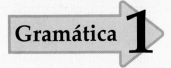

Gramática comunicativa

Gramática **1**   ¿Cómo es?
   • **Ser** and **estar**

¿Cómo es tu hermana?

Es muy guapa.

Ramón	¿Cómo **es** tu hermana?
Emilio	**Es** muy guapa. **Es** alta y delgada. Pero lo importante **es** que **es** buena e inteligente. **Es** contadora.
Ramón	**Es** casada, ¿verdad?
Emilio	Pues... era *(she was)*. Ahora **está** divorciada, pero **está** contenta. **Está viviendo** en casa de mi madre para ahorrar *(save)* y comprarse un piso *(apartment)*.

1. Remember that you have learned the forms and several uses of the verbs **ser** and **estar**. Here is a detailed summary of their uses.

Ser
a. to identify people, places, or objects
Ésa es mi casa. Ella es Ana Mari.
b. to identify characteristics that define people and objects, including profession, nationality and religion
La mamá de Sofía es banquera. Sus abuelos son mexicanos.
Toda la familia es católica. Todos son muy amables.
c. to give a definition
—¿Qué es eso? —Es un regalo para Sofía.
d. to tell time
—¿Qué hora es? —Son las tres.
e. to tell when and where an event takes place
—¿Dónde es la fiesta? —Es en el parque Bolívar.
—¿Cuándo es? —Es el sábado próximo.

Estar
f. to talk about how someone feels
Ramón está enfermo.
g. to express your opinion about something you perceive with your senses
¡Qué guapa estás hoy! Los tacos están muy buenos. La música está muy alta.
h. to tell where something or someone is located
—¿Dónde está Wayne? —Está en casa de Ramón.
i. with the present progressive
Estoy hablando con Manolo.

Note: with **divorciado/a** and **casado/a**, you may use either **ser** or **estar**.
Emilio es casado.
Adriana no está divorciada.

Ser and **estar** may be confusing to English speakers when they try to describe a person or an object. **Ser** and **estar** both mean *to be*, but have very distinct uses in Spanish.

2. **Ser** is used to talk about traits that characterize a person or thing. For example, you may think of yourself as generous, intelligent, funny, shy or easy-going; tall or short; Protestant or buddhist. You may be a student, a clerk, or a teacher. All these are qualities and properties that describe you as a person in a long-term or permanent sense. Use **ser** to talk about these qualities.

Soy alto/a, generoso/a, inteligente y tímido/a.
Soy budista y soy estudiante.

3. **Estar** is used to describe how you feel, your state of mind, or a resulting condition. For example, you may be tired, sick or very busy, you may feel angry or happy, or you may be nervous because you are waiting for your grades. **Estar** is used with adjectives that tell how you feel. They do not describe you as a person.

Estoy cansado/a y un poco enfermo/a.
¿Estoy enojado/a o contento/a?
Estoy nervioso/a.

4. Looking at the uses of **ser** and **estar,** you will see this tendency of permanent/long-term vs. temporary qualities prevails over some of the uses. However, some other uses of **ser** and **estar** are somewhat arbitrary, and you will need to learn them without looking for an explanation.

5. One adjective that does not follow the patterns outlined here is **muerto/a** *(dead)*. Although death is a permanent state, **muerto/a** takes **estar**.

Mi abuelo está muerto.   *My grandfather is dead.*

PRÁCTICA

A. El coche de Ana Mari. Completa cada oración con el verbo correcto.

Modelo	El coche de Ana Mari **está** en la calle.

El coche de Ana Mari es/está...

1. _____ nuevo.
2. _____ en el garaje.
3. _____ rojo.
4. _____ un Toyota.
5. _____ limpio.
6. _____ japonés.

B. Completar. Completa las conversaciones con la forma correcta de **ser** o **estar**. Lee la respuesta primero.

1. —¿Cómo _____ tu novio?

   —_____ muy agradable y guapo.

2. —Hola Adriana, ¿cómo _____?

   —_____ bien, pero un poco ocupada.

3. —¿Ustedes _____ aficionados al fútbol?

   —Sí, los tres _____ seguidores (*fans*) del Real Madrid.

4. —¿Qué _____ haciendo los abuelos?

   —_____ escribiendo las invitaciones porque la próxima semana

   _____ su aniversario.

C. Un poco de la vida de Adriana. Completa el párrafo con la forma correcta de **ser** o **estar** para saber un poco de la vida de Adriana.

Adriana (1) _____ en la universidad, porque (2) _____ muy responsable y necesita estudiar. (3) _____ un poco nerviosa porque mañana tiene el examen de cálculo. Por suerte, la universidad (4) _____ cerca de su casa y sus hijos (5) _____ muy comprensivos (*understanding*) y la ayudan en la casa. Santiago a veces no (6) _____ tan comprensivo como sus hijos; por eso, algunas veces Adriana (7) _____ enojada con él.

D. Situación. Your university is going to choose two student ambassadors to welcome a group of students visiting from Argentina. Work in groups of three and practice telling each other what you will say to prove that you are the ideal candidate. Describe yourself, talk about how you feel about your current activities, and identify the qualities that make you a good choice.

E. Adivinar. Write a description of a celebrity without mentioning his or her name. Share your description with a partner. Can your partner guess who you are describing? Use these questions as a guide when writing your description.

- ¿Cómo es?
- ¿Cómo está?
- ¿De dónde es?
- ¿Dónde está?
- ¿Qué está haciendo?
- ¿Cuál es su profesión?

_____

_____

_____

_____

_____

_____

_____

_____

 **Gramática 2** ¿Conoces a Wayne?
• **Saber** and **conocer**

Mamá   Sofía, ¿quién es Wayne?

Sofía   No **lo conoces**, mami. Es amigo de Ramón. Vamos al cine esta tarde.

Mamá   ¡Ah! ¿Y de dónde es este chico?

Sofía   Bueno, es americano, pero no **sé** de dónde. Lo que **sé** es que hace mucho tiempo que **conoce** a Ramón. Y habla español bastante bien.

Mamá   Supongo que **voy a conocerlo** cuando venga por ti.

Sofía   Ay, pues no, mami. Wayne **sabe** muchas cosas de la cultura hispana, **conoce** varios países, y a veces, **sabe** más historia de Latinoamérica que yo... ¡pero no **sabe** que tiene que venir por mí! Por eso invité *(I invited)* a Ramón y a Ana Mari; no estaba *(I wasn't)* segura de que él me estaba invitando a una cita.

You have learned two verbs that mean *to know*: **saber** and **conocer**. However, these verbs are used for "knowing" different things.

1. The verb **saber** means *to know information* and *to know how to do something.*

> **Wayne sabe mucho de historia latinoamericana.**
> *Wayne knows a lot about Latin American history.*

> **Sofía sabe manejar, pero no quiere llevar su coche.**
> *Sofía knows how to drive, but she doesn't want to take her car.*

> **Sé hablar inglés, español y francés.**
> *I know how to speak English, Spanish, and French.*

2. The verb **conocer** means *to know* in the sense of being acquainted or familiar with people (to have met this person), places (to have been to a place), or things.

> **Wayne conoce varios países latinoamericanos.**
> *Wayne knows (has been to) several Latin American countries.*

> **La mamá de Sofía no conoce a Wayne.**
> *Sofía's mother doesn't know (hasn't met) Wayne.*

> **No conozco la música de Andrea Bocelli.**
> *I don't know (I am not familiar with) Andrea Bocelli's music.*

> **No conozco la obra de García Márquez.**
> *I am not familiar with García Márquez' work.*

Notice the use of the personal **a** when what you know is a person.

> **Yo conozco a Ana Mari, pero no conozco a Ramón.**
> *I know Ana Mari, but I don't know Ramón.*

> **¿Ustedes conocen a mi abuela?**
> *Do you know my grandmother?*

> **Claro que conozco a Juanes. Es uno de mis mejores amigos.**
> *Of course I know Juanes. He's one of my best friends.*

411

PRÁCTICA

A. ¿Saber o conocer? Completa las conversaciones con las formas correctas de **saber** o **conocer**.

1. **Ramón**   Wayne, ¿_____ jugar tenis?

   Wayne   No, no _____ jugar, pero me gustaría aprender.

   Ramón   ¿_____ a una persona que te puede enseñar?

2. **Sofía**   Manolo, ¿ya _____ a Adriana?

   Manolo   Sí, pero no _____ de dónde es.

   Sofía   Es de Puerto Rico, pero no _____ de qué ciudad.

3. **Wayne**   No _____ ningún grupo de rock mexicano.

   Ana Mari   ¿No _____ al grupo Camila?

B. ¿Qué saben y a quién conocen? Escribe oraciones ciertas para ti usando un elemento de cada columna. Después comparte tus oraciones con un(a) compañero/a.

Modelo	Mi mamá conoce la ciudad de Nueva York.

		tocar el piano.
		la última canción de Luis Fonsi.
		a la mamá de mi novio/a.
Yo		cocinar muy bien.
Mis amigos y yo	(no) saber	la ciudad de Nueva York.
Mi mamá	(no) conocer	que los incas hablaban (*used to speak*) quechu
Mis primos		cómo llegar a tu casa.
		las pinturas de Picasso.
		el teléfono del/de la profesor(a).
		las pirámides de Tikal.

1. _____
2. _____
3. _____
4. _____
5. _____
6. _____
7. _____
8. _____

C. ¿Quieres ir? Completa la conversación. Después actúala con dos compañeros.

Ramón	¿Tienes planes para el próximo fin de semana?
Manolo	No, no tengo nada planeado, ¿por qué?
Ramón	Es que Wayne y yo no (1) _____ la isla Catalina y queremos ir. Dicen que es muy bonita. ¿Tú ya la (2) _____?
Ana Mari	Yo sí la (3) _____, es bellísima. Podemos ir a bucear.
Manolo	Pues yo no (4) _____ Catalina, ni (5) _____ bucear.
Ana Mari	No importa, ¿(6) _____ nadar?
Ramón	Ay, Ana Mari, ¡qué pregunta! Claro que Manolo (7) _____ nadar; no (8) _____ a ningún cubano que no sepa (would not know how to) nadar.
Manolo	Así es. También (9) _____ esquiar en agua; eso me gusta mucho.
Ana Mari	Pues entonces podemos nadar y esquiar. Yo te puedo enseñar a bucear.
Ramón	Tú no estás invitada, sólo vamos a ir los hombres.

D. Oraciones completas. Create sentences, using the elements and **saber** or **conocer**.

1. Eugenia / mi amiga Frances

_____

2. Pamela / hablar español muy bien

_____

3. el sobrino de Rosa / leer y escribir

_____

4. José y Laura / la ciudad de Barcelona

_____

5. nosotros no / cómo llegar a la residencia estudiantil

_____

6. yo / al profesor de literatura

_____

7. Elena y María Victoria / patinar en línea

_____

E. Situación. Talk to your partner about a place, a city, or a town you know. Describe it and identify interesting places you can visit and what you can do there.

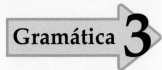

Gramática **3**

¡Siempre el trabajo!
• Por and para

Después de comer, voy a ir a la oficina por unos papeles.

¿Por qué no vas por la noche para evitar problemas de tráfico?

Santiago	¿Adónde vas?
Adriana	Voy a la oficina **por** unos papeles.
Santiago	¿Y no puedes esperar hasta mañana?
Adriana	Desgraciadamente (*unfortunately*) no. Tengo que terminar el informe (*report*) de unos clientes **para** mañana.
Santiago	¿**Por qué** no vas **por** la noche **para** evitar (*to avoid*) problemas de tráfico? ¡No sé por qué trabajas **para** una compañía que te pide tanto!

You have used **por** and **para** in different expressions such as **por la mañana, voy por ti,** and **para mañana, para mí.** This section will outline some distinctions between these prepositions.

One of the basic differences between **por** and **para** is that **por** is used to refer to a motive or a cause, whereas **para** is used for purpose and destination.

Para is used to indicate...

1. Destination.. *(toward, in the direction of)*	Salimos **para** Córdoba el sábado. *We are leaving for Córdoba on Saturday.*
2. Deadline or a specific time in the future......... *(by, for)*	Tiene que estar listo **para** mañana. *It has to be ready for tomorrow.*
3. Purpose or goal + *[infinitive]*........................ *(in order to)*	Quiero verte **para** hablar contigo. *I want to see you so we can talk.*
4. Purpose + *[noun]*..................................... *(for, used for)*	Es una llanta **para** el carro. *It's a tire for the car.*
5. The recipient of something........................ *(for)*	Compro una impresora **para** mi hijo. *I am buying a printer for my son.*
6. Comparison with others or an opinion........... *(for, considering)*	**Para** un joven, es demasiado serio. *For a young person, he is too serious.*
7. In the employ of...................................... *(for)*	Trabajo **para** el distrito escolar. *I work for the school district.*

Por is used to indicate...

8. Motion or a general location................
(around, through, along, by)

Voy a caminar **por** el parque.
I am going to walk through the park.

9. Duration of an action........................
(for, during, in)

Hago ejercicio **por** una hora todos los días.
I exercise for one hour everyday.

Ana Mari navega por Internet **por** la tarde.
Ana Mari surfs the Internet in the afternoon.

10. Reason or motive for an action............
(because of, on account of, on behalf of)

Le duele el estómago **por** comer
demasiado pozole.
*Her stomach hurts because she ate
too much pozole.*

Adriana llega tarde a casa **por** el tráfico.
Adriana arrives home late because of the traffic.

11. Object of a search...........................
(for, in search of)

Vamos a la farmacia **por** jarabe.
We are going to the pharmacy for cough syrup.

Wayne va **por** su cámara digital.
Wayne is going (in search of) his digital camera.

12. Means by which something is done.......
(by, by way of, by means of)

No me gusta viajar **por** avión.
I don't like traveling by plane.

¿Hablaste con la policía **por** teléfono?
Did you talk to the police by (on the) phone?

13. Exchange or substitution...................
(for, in exchange for)

Le doy dinero **por** la videocasetera.
I give him money for the VCR.

Muchas gracias **por** el cederrón.
Thank you very much for the CD-ROM.

14. Unit of measure..............................
(per, by)

José maneja a 120 kilómetros **por** hora.
José drives 120 kilometers per hour.

- **Por** is also used in several idiomatic expressions, such as these.

> **por aquí** *around here*   **por eso** *that's why*
> **por ejemplo** *for example*   **por fin** *finally*

- Remember that when giving an exact time, **de** is used instead of **por** before **la mañana**, **la tarde**, or **la noche**.

La clase empieza a las nueve de la mañana.

- In addition to **por, durante** is also commonly used to mean *for* when referring to time.

Esperé al mecánico durante cincuenta minutos.

PRÁCTICA

A. ¿Por qué? Lee estas oraciones. Luego usa las reglas anteriores para seleccionar el número que explica cada uso de **por** y **para.**

_____ a. No toques eso, es para tu tía Adriana.

_____ b. Emilio, ¿me vas a mandar la información por fax o por correo electrónico?

_____ c. Mi papá trabaja para la NASA.

_____ d. Voy a pasar a la biblioteca por un libro de arquitectura moderna.

_____ e. Lalo, necesitas levantarte más temprano para llegar a tiempo a tus clases.

_____ f. Saqué F en el examen por no estudiar lo suficiente.

_____ g. El trabajo de investigación es para el lunes, 12 de octubre.

_____ h. La carretera panamericana pasa por casi todos los países de Latinoamérica.

B. ¿Por o para? Completa las oraciones con **por** o **para.**

1. Quiero la tarea _____ mañana, por favor.

2. Sofía, ayer pasé _____ tu casa, pero no te encontré.

3. Ayer fui al supermercado _____ pan, leche y chocolates.

4. Estoy enfermo del estómago _____ comerme todos los chocolates.

5. La blusa verde es _____ Ana Mari.

6. Wayne, es necesario practicar mucho _____ hablar bien el español, ¿verdad?

7. Mañana vienes _____ mí, ¿no? Te espero.

8. Voy a comprar estos tenis _____ jugar fútbol los domingos con Ramón.

9. Vamos a ir _____ avión. No volvemos a viajar _____ carretera.

10. Necesito tomar tres clases más _____ recibirme (_to graduate_).

C. ¡Las preguntas de los niños! Imagínate que estás cuidando a los tres hijos de tu vecina. Contesta las preguntas que te hacen. Después comparte tus respuestas con un(a) compañero/a.

1. ¿Por qué tenemos que comer verduras todos los días?

_____

2. ¿Por qué tengo que acostarme temprano?

_____

3. ¿Para quién compraste esa camisa?

_____

4. ¿Para qué son los faxes? ¿Por qué tú no tienes uno en tu casa?

_____

5. ¿Por qué vas a viajar en avión?

_____

6. ¿Para qué quieres hablar con mi abuela?

_____

Gramática 4

Lo que me gusta es...
• Relative pronouns

In both English and Spanish, relative pronouns are used to combine two sentences or clauses that share a common element, such as a noun or pronoun. Study these diagrams.

| **Adriana toma muchas classes.**
Adriana takes a lot of classes. | | **Las clases son muy difíciles.**
The classes are very difficult. |

Las clases que toma Adriana son muy difíciles.
The classes that Adriana takes are very difficult.

| **Ana Mari es muy inteligente.**
Ana Mari is very intelligent. | | **Ana Mari es la hermana de Ramón.**
Ana Mari is Ramón's sister. |

Ana Mari, quien es la hermana de Ramón, es muy inteligente.
Ana Mari, who is Ramón's sister, is very intelligent.

A Sofía le gusta la ropa que venden en esta tienda.

Manolo, quien está al lado de Sofía, estudia cálculo.

1. Spanish has three frequently-used relative pronouns. **¡Atención!** Interrogative words **(qué, quién, etc.)** always carry an accent. Relative pronouns, however, do not.

Pronombres relativos	
que	*that; which; who*
quien(es)	*who; whom; that*
lo que	*that which; what*

2. **Que** is the most frequently used relative pronoun. It can refer to things or to people. Notice that, though its English counterpart, *that*, may be omitted in speech or writing, **que** is never omitted.

¿Dónde está la cafetera **que** necesito comprar?
Where is the coffee maker (that) I need to buy?

El hombre **que** limpia es Pedro.
The man who is cleaning is Pedro.

3. The relative pronoun **quien** refers only to people, and is often used after a preposition or the personal **a**. **Quien** has two forms: **quien** (singular) and **quienes** (plural).

¿Son las chicas **de quienes** me hablaste la semana pasada?
Are they the girls (that) you told me about last week?

Eva, **a quien** conozco muy bien, es mi nueva vecina.
Eva, whom I know very well, is my new neighbor.

4. **Quien(es)** is occasionally used in written Spanish instead of **que** in clauses set off by commas.

Manolo, **quien** es cubano, es estudiante.
Manolo, who is Cuban, is a student.

Emilio, **que** es español, ya llegó.
Emilio, who is Spanish, already arrived.

5. **Lo que** doesn't refer to a specific noun. It refers to a specified or unspecified object, idea, situation, or past event and means *what, that which,* or *the thing that.*

¡Fíjate!

In English, it is generally recommended that *who(m)* be used to refer to people, and that *that* and *which* be used to refer to things. In Spanish, however, it is perfectly acceptable to use **que** when referring to people.

Lo que necesita es un nuevo compañero de cuarto.

A Wayne no le gusta lo que ve.

PRÁCTICA

A. Inténtalo. Completa estas oraciones con pronombres relativos.

1. Voy a usar los platos _____ me regaló mi abuela.

2. Ana comparte un apartamento con la chica a _____ conocimos en la fiesta de Jorge.

3. Esta oficina tiene todo _____ necesitamos.

4. Puedes estudiar en el cuarto _____ está a la derecha de la cocina.

5. Los señores _____ viven en esa casa acaban de llegar de Centroamérica.

6. Los niños, a _____ ves en nuestro jardín, son mis sobrinos.

7. La piscina _____ ves desde la ventana es de mis vecinos.

8. Úrsula es _____ ayuda a mamá a limpiar el refrigerador.

9. _____ te dice Pablo no es cierto.

10. Tengo que buscar el suéter azul _____ está en el altillo (*attic*).

11. No entiendo _____ me dices.

12. La señora Ortiz, a _____ saludas todas las tardes, vive en San Juan.

13. ¿Sabes _____ necesita esta clase? ¡Otro profesor!

14. No me gusta vivir con personas a _____ no conozco.

B. Completar. Completa la historia sobre la casa que Jaime y Tina quieren comprar, usando los pronombres relativos **que, quien, quienes** o **lo que**.

1. Jaime y Tina son los chicos a _____ conocí (*I met*) la semana pasada.

2. Quieren comprar una casa _____ está en el centro de la ciudad.

3. Es una casa _____ está cerca de la universidad.

4. Jaime, _____ quiere ser médico, estudia en esta universidad.

5. _____ le encanta a Tina es el jardín de la casa.

C. Entrevista. En parejas, túrnense para hacerse estas preguntas.

1. ¿Qué es lo que más te gusta de vivir aquí?

_____

2. ¿Cómo son las personas que viven en tu barrio (*neighborhood*)?

_____

3. ¿Cuál es la clase que menos te gusta? ¿Y la que más te gusta?

_____

4. ¿Quién es la persona que hace los quehaceres domésticos (*chores*) en tu casa?

_____

5. ¿Quiénes son las personas con quienes más sales los fines de semana?

_____

6. ¿Quién es la persona a quien más llamas por teléfono?

_____

7. ¿Cuál es el deporte que más te gusta?

_____

8. ¿Cuál es el barrio de tu ciudad que más te gusta y por qué?

_____

9. ¿Quién es la persona a quien más llamas cuando tienes problemas?

_____

10. ¿Quién es la persona a quien más admiras? ¿Por qué?

_____

11. ¿Qué es lo que más te gusta de tu casa?

_____

12. ¿Qué es lo que más te molesta de tus amigos/as?

_____

D. Adivinanza. En grupos, túrnense para describir los objetos en la clase o los lugares de la universidad usando pronombres relativos. Los demás compañeros tienen que hacer preguntas hasta que adivinen la cosa o el lugar descrito/a.

Modelo	Estudiante 1: **Es lo que tenemos en la mochila.**
	Estudiante 2: **¿Es la computadora?**
	Estudiante 1: **No. Es lo que usamos para hablar con los amigos.**
	Estudiante 3: **Lo sé. Es el teléfono.**

Glossary of Grammatical Terms

ADJECTIVE A word that modifies or describes a noun or pronoun.

muchos libros
many books

un hombre **rico**
*a **rich** man*

las mujeres **altas**
*the **tall** women*

Demonstrative adjective An adjective that points out a specific noun.

esta fiesta
this party

ese chico
that boy

aquellas flores
those flowers

Possessive adjective An adjective that indicates ownership or possession.

mi mejor vestido
my best dress

Éste es **mi** hermano.
*This is **my** brother*

Stressed possessive adjective A possessive adjective that emphasizes the owner or possessor.

Es un libro **mío**.
*It's **my** book./It's a book **of mine**.*

Es amiga **tuya**; yo no la conozco.
*She's a friend **of yours**; I don't know her.*

ADVERB A word that modifies or describes a verb, adjective, or another adverb.

Pancho escribe **rápidamente**.
*Pancho writes **quickly**.*

Este cuadro es **muy** bonito.
*This picture is **very** pretty.*

ARTICLE A word that points out either a specific (definite) noun or a non-specific (indefinite) noun.

Definite article An article that points out a specific noun.

el libro
the book

la maleta
the suitcase

los diccionarios
the dictionaries

las palabras
the words

Indefinite article An article that points out a noun in a general, non-specific way.

un lápiz
a pencil

una computadora
a computer

unos pájaros
some birds

unas escuelas
some schools

CLAUSE A group of words that contains both a conjugated verb and a subject, either expressed or implied.

Main (or Independent) clause A clause that can stand alone as a complete sentence.

Pienso ir a cenar pronto.
I plan to go to dinner soon.

Subordinate (or Dependent) clause A clause that does not express a complete thought and therefore cannot stand alone as a sentence.

Trabajo en la cafetería **porque necesito dinero para la escuela**.
*I work in the cafeteria **because I need money for school**.*

COMPARATIVE A word or construction used with an adjective or adverb to express a comparison between two people, places, or things.

Este programa es **más interesante que** el otro.
*This program is **more interesting than** the other one.*

Tomás no es **tan alto como** Alberto.
*Tomás is not **as tall as** Alberto.*

CONJUGATION A set of the forms of a verb for a specific tense or mood or the process by which these verb forms are presented.

Preterit conjugation of **cantar**

cant**é**	cant**amos**
cant**aste**	cant**asteis**
cant**ó**	cant**aron**

CONJUNCTION A word or phrase used to connect words, clauses, or phrases.

Susana es de Cuba **y** Pedro es de España.
*Susana is from Cuba **and** Pedro is from Spain.*

No quiero estudiar, **pero** tengo que hacerlo.
*I don't want to study, **but** I have to do it.*

CONTRACTION The joining of two words into one. The only contractions in Spanish are **al** and **del**.

Mi hermano fue **al** concierto ayer.
*My brother went **to the** concert yesterday.*

Saqué dinero **del** banco.
*I took money **from the** bank.*

DIRECT OBJECT A noun or pronoun that directly receives the action of the verb.

Tomás lee **el libro**.   **La** pagó ayer.
*Tomás reads **the book**.*   *She paid **it** yesterday.*

GENDER The grammatical categorizing of certain kinds of words, such as nouns and pronouns, as masculine, feminine, or neuter.

Masculine
articles **el**, un**o**
pronouns **él**, **lo**, **mío**, ést**e**, és**e**
adjective simpátic**o**

Feminine
articles **la**, un**a**
pronouns **ella**, **la**, **mía**, ést**a**, és**a**, aquéll**a**
adjective simpátic**a**

GERUND See Present Participle on next page.

IMPERSONAL EXPRESSION A third-person pl. and sing. expression with no expressed or specific subject.

Es muy importante.   **Llueve** mucho.
It's very important.   *It's raining hard.*

Aquí **se habla** español.   **Sirven** lasaña.
Spanish is spoken here.   *They serve lasagna.*

INDIRECT OBJECT A noun or pronoun that receives the action of the verb indirectly; the object, often a living being, to or for whom an action is performed.

Eduardo **le** dio un libro **a Linda**.
*Eduardo gave a book **to Linda**.*

La profesora **me** dio una C en el examen.
*The professor gave **me** a C on the test.*

INFINITIVE The basic form of a verb. Infinitives in Spanish end in **-ar**, **-er**, or **-ir**.

hablar   **correr**   **abrir**
to speak   *to run*   *to open*

INTERROGATIVE An adjective or pronoun used to ask a question.

¿Quién habla?   **¿Cuántos** compraste?
Who is speaking?   *How many did you buy?*

¿Qué piensas hacer hoy?
What do you plan to do today?

INVERSION Changing the word order of a sentence, often to form a question.

Statement: Tu mamá vive en Boston.

Inversion: ¿Vive en Boston tu mamá?

MOOD A grammatical distinction of verbs that indicates whether the verb is intended to make a statement or command, or to express a doubt, emotion, or condition contrary to fact.

Imperative mood Verb forms used to make commands.

Diga la verdad.   **Caminen** Uds. conmigo.
Tell the truth.   *Walk with me.*

¡Comamos ahora!
Let's eat now!

Indicative mood Verb forms used to state facts, actions, and states considered to be real.

Sé que **tienes** el dinero.
I know that you have the money.

Subjunctive mood Verb forms used principally in subordinate (or dependent) clauses to express wishes, desires, emotions, doubts, and certain conditions, such as contrary-to-fact situations.

Prefieren que **hables** en español.
*They prefer that **you speak** in Spanish.*

Dudo que Luis **tenga** el dinero necesario.
*I doubt that Luis **has** the necessary money.*

NOUN A word that identifies people, animals, places, things, and ideas.

hombre	**gato**
man	*cat*
México	**casa**
Mexico	*house*
libertad	**libro**
freedom	*book*

NUMBER A grammatical term that refers to singular or plural. Nouns in Spanish and English have number. Other parts of a sentence, such as adjectives, articles, and verbs, can also have number.

Singular	Plural
una cosa	**unas** cosas
a thing	*some things*
el profesor	**los** profesores
the professor	*the professors*

NUMBERS Words that represent amounts.

Cardinal numbers Words that show specific amounts.

cinco minutos
five minutes

el año **dos mil quince**
the year 2015

Ordinal numbers Words that indicate the order of a noun in a series.

el **cuarto** jugador   la **décima** hora
the fourth player   *the tenth hour*

PAST PARTICIPLE A past form of the verb used in compound tenses. The past participle may also be used as an adjective, but it must then agree in number and gender with the word it modifies.

Han **buscado** por todas partes.
They have searched everywhere.

Yo no había **estudiado** para el examen.
I hadn't studied for the exam.

Hay una **ventana rota** en la sala.
There is a broken window in the living room.

PERSON The form of the verb or pronoun that indicates the speaker, the one spoken to, or the one spoken about. In Spanish, as in English, there are three persons: first, second, and third.

Person	Singular	Plural
1st	**yo** *I*	**nosotros/as** *we*
2nd	**tú, Ud.** *you*	**vosotros/as, Uds.** *you*
3rd	**él, ella** *he/she*	**ellos, ellas** *they*

PREPOSITION A word that describes the relationship, most often in time or space, between two words.

Anita es **de** California.
Anita is from California.

La chaqueta está **en** el carro.
The jacket is in the car.

¿Quieres hablar **con** ella?
Do you want to speak to her?

PRESENT PARTICIPLE In English, a verb form that ends in *-ing*. In Spanish, the present participle ends in **–ndo**, and is often used with **estar** to form a progressive tense.

Mi hermana está **hablando** por teléfono ahora mismo.
My sister is talking on the phone right now.

PRONOUN A word that takes the place of a noun or nouns.

Demonstrative pronoun A pronoun that takes the place of a specific noun.

Quiero **ésta**.
I want this one.

¿Vas a comprar **ése**?
Are you going to buy that one?

Juan prefirió **aquéllos**.
Juan preferred those (over there).

Object pronoun A pronoun that functions as a direct or indirect object of the verb. Object pronouns may be placed before conjugated verbs or attached to an infinitive or present participle.

Te digo la verdad.
I'm telling you the truth.

Me lo trajo Juan.
Juan brought it to me.

Lo voy a llevar a la escuela.
Voy a **llevarlo** a la escuela.
I'm going to bring him to school.

Me estaba llamando por teléfono.
Estaba **llamándome** por teléfono.
She was calling me on the phone.

Reflexive pronoun A pronoun that indicates that the action of a verb is performed by the subject on itself. These pronouns are often expressed in English with *-self: myself, yourself*, etc.

Yo **me bañé** antes de salir.
I bathed (myself) before going out.

Elena **se acostó** a las once y media.
Elena went to bed at eleven-thirty.

Relative pronoun A pronoun that connects a subordinate clause to a main clause.

El chico **que** nos escribió viene a visitarnos mañana.
The boy who wrote to us is coming to visit us tomorrow.

Ya sé **lo que** tenemos que hacer.
I already know what we have to do.

Subject pronoun A pronoun that replaces the name or title of a person or thing and acts as the subject of a verb.

Tú debes estudiar más.
You should study more.

Él llegó primero.
He arrived first.

SUBJECT A noun or pronoun that performs the action of a verb and is often implied by the verb.

María va al supermercado.
María goes to the supermarket.

(Ellos) Trabajan mucho.
They work hard.

Esos **libros** son muy caros.
Those books are very expensive.

SUPERLATIVE A word or construction used with an adjective or adverb to express the highest or lowest degree of a specific quality among three or more people, places, or things.

Entre todas mis clases, ésta es la **más interesante**.
Among all my classes, this is the most interesting.

Raúl es el **menos simpático** de los chicos.
Raúl is the least pleasant of the boys.

TENSE A set of verb forms that indicates the time of an action or state: past, present, or future.

Compound tense A two-word tense made up of an auxiliary verb and a present or past participle. In Spanish, there are two auxiliary verbs: **estar** and **haber**.

En este momento, **estoy estudiando**.
At this time, I am studying.

El paquete no **ha llegado** todavía.
The package has not arrived yet.

Simple tense A tense expressed by a single verb form.

María **estaba** mal anoche.
María was ill last night.

Juana **hablará** con su mamá mañana.
Juana will speak with her mom tomorrow.

VERB A word that expresses actions or states-of-being.

Auxiliary verb A verb used with a present or past participle to form a compound tense. **Haber** is the most commonly used auxiliary verb in Spanish.

Los chicos **han** visto los elefantes.
The children have seen the elephants.

Espero que **hayas** comido.
I hope you have eaten.

Reflexive verb A verb that describes an action performed by the subject on itself and is always used with a reflexive pronoun.

Me compré un carro nuevo.
I bought myself a new car.

Pedro y Adela **se levantan** muy temprano.
Pedro and Adela get (themselves) up very early.

Spelling change verb A verb that undergoes a predictable change in spelling in order to reflect its actual pronunciation in the various conjugations.

practicar	c ➤ qu	practico	practi**qué**
dirigir	g ➤ j	diri**j**o	dirig**í**
almorzar	z ➤ c	almorzó	almor**cé**

Stem-changing verb A verb whose stem vowel undergoes one or more predictable changes in the various conjugations.

entender (i ➤ ie)   enti**e**ndo
pedir (e ➤ i)   p**i**den
dormir (o ➤ ue, u) d**ue**rmo, d**u**rmieron

Verb Conjugation Tables

The verb lists

The list of verbs below and the model-verb tables that start on page 426 show you how to conjugate every verb taught in **INVITACIONES**. Each verb in the list is followed by a model verb conjugated according to the same pattern. The number in parentheses indicates where in the tables you can find the conjugated forms of the model verb. If you want to find out how to conjugate **divertirse**, for example, look up number 29, **sentir**, the model for verbs that follow the **i ➤ ie** stem-change pattern.

How to use the verb tables

In the tables you will find the infinitive, past and present participles, and all the simple forms of each model verb. The formation of the compound tenses of any verb can be inferred from the table of compound tenses, pages 426–427, either by combining the past participle of the verb with a conjugated form of **haber** or combining the present participle with a conjugated form of **estar**.

---

abrir like vivir (3) *except* past participle is abierto
acabar de like hablar (1)
aceptar like hablar (1)
aconsejar like hablar (1)
acostarse (o ➤ ue) like contar (21)
afeitarse like hablar (1)
ahorrar like hablar (1)
almorzar (o ➤ ue) like contar (21) *except* (z ➤ c)
alquilar like hablar (1)
andar like hablar (1) *except* preterit stem is anduv-
aprender like comer (2)
armar like hablar (1)
ayudar(se) like hablar (1)

bailar like hablar (1)
bañarse like hablar (1)
barrer like comer (2)
beber like comer (2)
besar(se) like hablar (1)
bucear like hablar (1)
buscar (c ➤ qu) like tocar (35)

cambiar like hablar (1)
cantar like hablar (1)
casarse like hablar (1)
castigar like hablar (1)
cenar like hablar (1)

chocar (c ➤ qu) like tocar (35)
colorear like hablar (1)
comer (2)
compartir like vivir (3)
comprar like hablar (1)
conocer (c ➤ zc) (30)
contar (o ➤ ue) (21)
correr like comer (2)
cortar like hablar (1)
costar (o ➤ ue) like contar (21)
creer (y) (31)
cruzar (z ➤ c) (32)
cuidar(se) like hablar (1)

dar(se) (4)
deber like comer (2)
decidir like vivir (3)
decir (e ➤ i) (5)
dejar like hablar (1)
desayunar like hablar (1)
descansar like hablar (1)
descomponerse like poner(se) (12)
dibujar like hablar (1)
discutir like vivir (3)
disfrazar(se) like hablar (1)
divertirse (e ➤ ie) like sentir (29)
divorciarse like hablar (1)
dormir(se) (o ➤ ue) (22)
ducharse like hablar (1)
dudar like hablar (1)

embarazar(se) like hablar (1)
empezar (e ➤ ie) (z ➤ c) (23)
empujar like hablar (1)
enamorarse like hablar (1)
encantar like hablar (1)
encontrar(se) (o ➤ ue) like contar (21)
enfermarse like hablar (1)
enseñar like hablar (1)
entender (e ➤ ie) (24)
entrar like hablar (1)
entregar like hablar (1) *except* (g ➤ gu)
entrenarse like hablar (1)
escribir like vivir (3) *except* past participle is escrito
escuchar like hablar (1)
esperar like hablar (1)
esquiar (esquío) (33)
estacionar(se) like hablar (1)
estar (6)
estudiar like hablar (1)
explicar (c ➤ qu) like tocar (35)

fascinar like hablar (1)
frenar like hablar (1)
fumar like hablar (1)

ganar like hablar (1)
gastar like hablar (1)
gustar like hablar (1)

haber (hay) (7)
hablar (1)
hacer (8)

iluminar like hablar (1)
importar like hablar (1)
interesar like hablar (1)
invitar like hablar (1)
ir(se) (9)

jugar (u→ue) (g→gu) (25)
juntar(se) like hablar (1)

lastimarse like hablar (1)
lavar(se) like hablar (1)
leer (y) like creer (31)
levantar(se) like hablar (1)
limpiar like hablar (1)
llamar(se) like hablar (1)
llegar (g→gu) (34)
llenar like hablar (1)
llevar(se) like hablar (1)
mandar like hablar (1)
manejar like hablar (1)
mirar like hablar (1)
molestar like hablar (1)
montar like hablar (1)
morir (o→ue) like dormir (22)
  except past participle is muerto
mudarse like hablar (1)

necesitar like hablar (1)
nevar (e→ie) like pensar (27)

obedecer (c→zc) like conocer (30)
ofrecer (c→zc) like conocer (30)
oír (10)

pagar (g→gu) like llegar (34)
parar(se) like hablar (1)
pasar(se) like hablar (1)
pasear like hablar (1)
patinar like hablar (1)
pedir (e→i) (26)
pegar like hablar (1) *except* (g→gu)
pelearse like hablar (1)
pensar (e→ie) (27)
perder (e→ie) like entender (24)
pintar(se) like hablar (1)
planchar like hablar (1)
poder (o→ue) (11)
poner(se) (12)

ponchar(se) like hablar (1)
portar(se) like hablar (1)
practicar (c→qu) like tocar (35)
preferir (e→ie) like sentir (29)
prestar like hablar (1)
prometer like comer (2)

quedar(se) like hablar (1)
querer (e→ie) (13)
quitar(se) like hablar (1)

rasurar(se) like hablar (1)
recibir(se) like vivir (3)
recomendar (e→ie) like pensar (27)
recordar (o→ue) like contar (21)
regalar like hablar (1)
regañar like hablar (1)
romper(se) like comer (2) *except* past
  participle is roto

saber (14)
sacar (c→qu) like tocar (35)
salir(se) (15)
saltar like hablar (1)
seguir (e→i) (28)
sentir(se) (e→ie) (29)
separarse like hablar (1)
ser (16)
servir (e→i) like pedir (26)
solicitar like hablar (1)
subir(se) like vivir (3)

tener (e→ie) (17)
terminar like hablar (1)
tocar (c→qu) (35)
tomar like hablar (1)
trabajar like hablar (1)
traer (18)

usar like hablar (1)

vender like comer (2)
venir (e→ie) (19)
ver (20)
vestir(se) (e→i) (36)
viajar like hablar (1)
visitar like hablar (1)
vivir (3)

425

Regular verbs: simple tenses

Infinitive	INDICATIVE					SUBJUNCTIVE		IMPERATIVE
	Present	Imperfect	Preterit	Future	Conditional	Present	Past	
1 hablar	hablo	hablaba	hablé	hablaré	hablaría	hable	hablara	
	hablas	hablabas	hablaste	hablarás	hablarías	hables	hablaras	habla tú (no hables)
	habla	hablaba	habló	hablará	hablaría	hable	hablara	hable Ud.
Participles:	hablamos	hablábamos	hablamos	hablaremos	hablaríamos	hablemos	habláramos	hablemos
hablando	habláis	hablabais	hablasteis	hablaréis	hablaríais	habléis	hablarais	hablad (no habléis)
hablado	hablan	hablaban	hablaron	hablarán	hablarían	hablen	hablaran	hablen Uds.
2 comer	como	comía	comí	comeré	comería	coma	comiera	
	comes	comías	comiste	comerás	comerías	comas	comieras	come tú (no comas)
	come	comía	comió	comerá	comería	coma	comiera	coma Ud.
Participles:	comemos	comíamos	comimos	comeremos	comeríamos	comamos	comiéramos	comamos
comiendo	coméis	comíais	comisteis	comeréis	comeríais	comáis	comierais	comed (no comáis)
comido	comen	comían	comieron	comerán	comerían	coman	comieran	coman Uds.
3 vivir	vivo	vivía	viví	viviré	viviría	viva	viviera	
	vives	vivías	viviste	vivirás	vivirías	vivas	vivieras	vive tú (no vivas)
	vive	vivía	vivió	vivirá	viviría	viva	viviera	viva Ud.
Participles:	vivimos	vivíamos	vivimos	viviremos	viviríamos	vivamos	viviéramos	vivamos
viviendo	vivís	vivíais	vivisteis	viviréis	viviríais	viváis	vivierais	vivid (no viváis)
vivido	viven	vivían	vivieron	vivirán	vivirían	vivan	vivieran	vivan Uds.

All verbs: compound tenses

PERFECT TENSES

INDICATIVE				SUBJUNCTIVE	
Present Perfect	Past Perfect	Future Perfect	Conditional Perfect	Present Perfect	Past Perfect
he	había	habré	habría	haya	hubiera
has	habías	habrás	habrías	hayas	hubieras
ha hablado	había hablado	habrá hablado	habría hablado	haya hablado	hubiera hablado
hemos comido	habíamos comido	habremos comido	habríamos comido	hayamos comido	hubiéramos comido
habéis vivido	habíais vivido	habréis vivido	habríais vivido	hayáis vivido	hubierais vivido
han	habían	habrán	habrían	hayan	hubieran

PROGRESSIVE TENSES

	INDICATIVE				SUBJUNCTIVE	
	Present Progressive	Past Progressive	Future Progressive	Conditional Progressive	Present Progressive	Past Progressive
	estoy	estaba	estaré	estaría	esté	estuviera
	estás	estabas	estarás	estarías	estés	estuvieras
	está	estaba	estará	estaría	esté	estuviera
	estamos	estábamos	estaremos	estaríamos	estemos	estuviéramos
	estáis	estabais	estaréis	estaríais	estéis	estuvierais
	estan	estaban	estarán	estarían	estén	estuvieran
	hablando comiendo viviendo	hablando comiendo viviendo	hablando comiendo viviendo	hablando comiendo viviendo	hablando comiendo viviendo	hablando comiendo viviendo

Irregular verbs

		INDICATIVE					SUBJUNCTIVE		IMPERATIVE
Infinitive	Present	Imperfect	Preterit	Future	Conditional	Present	Past		
4 dar	**doy**	daba	**di**	daré	daría	**dé**	**diera**		
	das	dabas	**diste**	darás	darías	**des**	**dieras**	da tú (no **des**)
Participles:	da	daba	**dio**	dará	daría	**dé**	**diera**	**dé** Ud.
dando	damos	dábamos	**dimos**	daremos	daríamos	**demos**	**diéramos**	**demos**
dado	dais	dabais	**disteis**	daréis	daríais	**deis**	**dierais**	dad (no **deis**)
	dan	daban	**dieron**	darán	darían	**den**	**dieran**	**den** Uds.
5 decir (e → i)	**digo**	decía	**dije**	**diré**	**diría**	**diga**	**dijera**	
	dices	decías	**dijiste**	**dirás**	**dirías**	**digas**	**dijeras**	**di** tú (no **digas**)
Participles:	**dice**	decía	**dijo**	**dirá**	**diría**	**diga**	**dijera**	**diga** Ud.
diciendo	decimos	decíamos	**dijimos**	**diremos**	**diríamos**	**digamos**	**dijéramos**	**digamos**
dicho	decís	decíais	**dijisteis**	**diréis**	**diríais**	**digáis**	**dijerais**	decid (no **digáis**)
	dicen	decían	**dijeron**	**dirán**	**dirían**	**digan**	**dijeran**	**digan** Uds.
6 estar	**estoy**	estaba	**estuve**	estaré	estaría	esté	**estuviera**	
	estás	estabas	**estuviste**	estarás	estarías	estés	**estuvieras**	está tú (no estés)
Participles:	está	estaba	**estuvo**	estará	estaría	esté	**estuviera**	esté Ud.
estando	estamos	estábamos	**estuvimos**	estaremos	estaríamos	estemos	**estuviéramos**	estemos
estado	estáis	estabais	**estuvisteis**	estaréis	estaríais	estéis	**estuvierais**	estad (no estéis)
	están	estaban	**estuvieron**	estarán	estarían	estén	**estuvieran**	estén Uds.

	Infinitive	INDICATIVE					SUBJUNCTIVE		IMPERATIVE
		Present	Imperfect	Preterit	Future	Conditional	Present	Past	
7	haber	**he**	había	**hube**	**habré**	**habría**	**haya**	**hubiera**	
		has	habías	**hubiste**	**habrás**	**habrías**	**hayas**	**hubieras**	
	Participles:	**ha**	había	**hubo**	**habrá**	**habría**	**haya**	**hubiera**	
	habiendo	**hemos**	habíamos	**hubimos**	**habremos**	**habríamos**	**hayamos**	**hubiéramos**	
	habido	**habéis**	habíais	**hubisteis**	**habréis**	**habríais**	**hayáis**	**hubierais**	
		han	habían	**hubieron**	**habrán**	**habrían**	**hayan**	**hubieran**	
8	hacer	**hago**	hacía	**hice**	**haré**	**haría**	**haga**	**hiciera**	
		haces	hacías	**hiciste**	**harás**	**harías**	**hagas**	**hicieras**	**haz** tú (no **hagas**)
	Participles:	hace	hacía	**hizo**	**hará**	**haría**	**haga**	**hiciera**	**haga** Ud.
	haciendo	hacemos	hacíamos	**hicimos**	**haremos**	**haríamos**	**hagamos**	**hiciéramos**	**hagamos**
	hecho	hacéis	hacíais	**hicisteis**	**haréis**	**haríais**	**hagáis**	**hicierais**	haced (no **hagáis**)
		hacen	hacían	**hicieron**	**harán**	**harían**	**hagan**	**hicieran**	**hagan** Uds.
9	ir	**voy**	**iba**	**fui**	iré	iría	**vaya**	**fuera**	
		vas	**ibas**	**fuiste**	irás	irías	**vayas**	**fueras**	**ve** tú (no **vayas**)
	Participles:	**va**	**iba**	**fue**	irá	iría	**vaya**	**fuera**	**vaya** Ud.
	yendo	**vamos**	**íbamos**	**fuimos**	iremos	iríamos	**vayamos**	**fuéramos**	**vamos**
	ido	**vais**	**ibais**	**fuisteis**	iréis	iríais	**vayáis**	**fuerais**	id (no **vayáis**)
		van	**iban**	**fueron**	irán	irían	**vayan**	**fueran**	**vayan** Uds.
10	oír (y)	**oigo**	oía	**oí**	oiré	oiría	**oiga**	**oyera**	
		oyes	oías	**oíste**	oirás	oirías	**oigas**	**oyeras**	**oye** tú (no **oigas**)
	Participles:	**oye**	oía	**oyó**	oirá	oiría	**oiga**	**oyera**	**oiga** Ud.
	oyendo	**oímos**	oíamos	**oímos**	oiremos	oiríamos	**oigamos**	**oyéramos**	**oigamos**
	oído	**oís**	oíais	**oísteis**	oiréis	oiríais	**oigáis**	**oyerais**	oíd (no **oigáis**)
		oyen	oían	**oyeron**	oirán	oirían	**oigan**	**oyeran**	**oigan** Uds.
11	poder (o → ue)	**puedo**	podía	**pude**	**podré**	**podría**	**pueda**	**pudiera**	
		puedes	podías	**pudiste**	**podrás**	**podrías**	**puedas**	**pudieras**	**puede** tú (no **puedas**)
	Participles:	**puede**	podía	**pudo**	**podrá**	**podría**	**pueda**	**pudiera**	**pueda** Ud.
	pudiendo	podemos	podíamos	**pudimos**	**podremos**	**podríamos**	podamos	**pudiéramos**	podamos
	podido	podéis	podíais	**pudisteis**	**podréis**	**podríais**	podáis	**pudierais**	poded (no podáis)
		pueden	podían	**pudieron**	**podrán**	**podrían**	**puedan**	**pudieran**	**puedan** Uds.
12	poner	**pongo**	ponía	**puse**	**pondré**	**pondría**	**ponga**	**pusiera**	
		pones	ponías	**pusiste**	**pondrás**	**pondrías**	**pongas**	**pusieras**	**pon** tú (no **pongas**)
	Participles:	pone	ponía	**puso**	**pondrá**	**pondría**	**ponga**	**pusiera**	**ponga** Ud.
	poniendo	ponemos	poníamos	**pusimos**	**pondremos**	**pondríamos**	**pongamos**	**pusiéramos**	**pongamos**
	puesto	ponéis	poníais	**pusisteis**	**pondréis**	**pondríais**	**pongáis**	**pusierais**	poned (no **pongáis**)
		ponen	ponían	**pusieron**	**pondrán**	**pondrían**	**pongan**	**pusieran**	**pongan** Uds.

428

13 — querer (e → ie)

Participles: queriendo, querido

	Present	Imperfect	Preterit	Future	Conditional	Subj. Present	Subj. Past	Imperative
yo	quiero	quería	quise	querré	querría	quiera	quisiera	
tú	quieres	querías	quisiste	querrás	querrías	quieras	quisieras	quiere tú (no quieras)
Ud./él/ella	quiere	quería	quiso	querrá	querría	quiera	quisiera	quiera Ud.
nosotros	queremos	queríamos	quisimos	querremos	querríamos	queramos	quisiéramos	queramos
vosotros	queréis	queríais	quisisteis	querréis	querríais	queráis	quisierais	quered (no queráis)
Uds./ellos	quieren	querían	quisieron	querrán	querrían	quieran	quisieran	quieran Uds.

14 — saber

Participles: sabiendo, sabido

	Present	Imperfect	Preterit	Future	Conditional	Subj. Present	Subj. Past	Imperative
yo	sé	sabía	supe	sabré	sabría	sepa	supiera	
tú	sabes	sabías	supiste	sabrás	sabrías	sepas	supieras	sabe tú (no sepas)
Ud./él/ella	sabe	sabía	supo	sabrá	sabría	sepa	supiera	sepa Ud.
nosotros	sabemos	sabíamos	supimos	sabremos	sabríamos	sepamos	supiéramos	sepamos
vosotros	sabéis	sabíais	supisteis	sabréis	sabríais	sepáis	supierais	sabed (no sepáis)
Uds./ellos	saben	sabían	supieron	sabrán	sabrían	sepan	supieran	sepan Uds.

15 — salir

Participles: saliendo, salido

	Present	Imperfect	Preterit	Future	Conditional	Subj. Present	Subj. Past	Imperative
yo	salgo	salía	salí	saldré	saldría	salga	saliera	
tú	sales	salías	saliste	saldrás	saldrías	salgas	salieras	sal tú (no salgas)
Ud./él/ella	sale	salía	salió	saldrá	saldría	salga	saliera	salga Ud.
nosotros	salimos	salíamos	salimos	saldremos	saldríamos	salgamos	saliéramos	salgamos
vosotros	salís	salíais	salisteis	saldréis	saldríais	salgáis	salierais	salid (no salgáis)
Uds./ellos	salen	salían	salieron	saldrán	saldrían	salgan	salieran	salgan Uds.

16 — ser

Participles: siendo, sido

	Present	Imperfect	Preterit	Future	Conditional	Subj. Present	Subj. Past	Imperative
yo	soy	era	fui	seré	sería	sea	fuera	
tú	eres	eras	fuiste	serás	serías	seas	fueras	sé tú (no seas)
Ud./él/ella	es	era	fue	será	sería	sea	fuera	sea Ud.
nosotros	somos	éramos	fuimos	seremos	seríamos	seamos	fuéramos	seamos
vosotros	sois	erais	fuisteis	seréis	seríais	seáis	fuerais	sed (no seáis)
Uds./ellos	son	eran	fueron	serán	serían	sean	fueran	sean Uds.

17 — tener (e → ie)

Participles: teniendo, tenido

	Present	Imperfect	Preterit	Future	Conditional	Subj. Present	Subj. Past	Imperative
yo	tengo	tenía	tuve	tendré	tendría	tenga	tuviera	
tú	tienes	tenías	tuviste	tendrás	tendrías	tengas	tuvieras	ten tú (no tengas)
Ud./él/ella	tiene	tenía	tuvo	tendrá	tendría	tenga	tuviera	tenga Ud.
nosotros	tenemos	teníamos	tuvimos	tendremos	tendríamos	tengamos	tuviéramos	tengamos
vosotros	tenéis	teníais	tuvisteis	tendréis	tendríais	tengáis	tuvierais	tened (no tengáis)
Uds./ellos	tienen	tenían	tuvieron	tendrán	tendrían	tengan	tuvieran	tengan Uds.

18 — traer

Participles: trayendo, traído

	Present	Imperfect	Preterit	Future	Conditional	Subj. Present	Subj. Past	Imperative
yo	traigo	traía	traje	traeré	traería	traiga	trajera	
tú	traes	traías	trajiste	traerás	traerías	traigas	trajeras	trae tú (no traigas)
Ud./él/ella	trae	traía	trajo	traerá	traería	traiga	trajera	traiga Ud.
nosotros	traemos	traíamos	trajimos	traeremos	traeríamos	traigamos	trajéramos	traigamos
vosotros	traéis	traíais	trajisteis	traeréis	traeríais	traigáis	trajerais	traed (no traigáis)
Uds./ellos	traen	traían	trajeron	traerán	traerían	traigan	trajeran	traigan Uds.

19 venir (e→ie)
Participles: viniendo, venido

Infinitive	INDICATIVE					SUBJUNCTIVE		IMPERATIVE
	Present	Imperfect	Preterit	Future	Conditional	Present	Past	
venir (e→ie)	vengo	venía	vine	vendré	vendría	venga	viniera	
	vienes	venías	viniste	vendrás	vendrías	vengas	vinieras	ven tú (no vengas)
	viene	venía	vino	vendrá	vendría	venga	viniera	venga Ud.
Participles:	venimos	veníamos	vinimos	vendremos	vendríamos	vengamos	viniéramos	vengamos
viniendo	venís	veníais	vinisteis	vendréis	vendríais	vengáis	vinierais	venid (no vengáis)
venido	vienen	venían	vinieron	vendrán	vendrían	vengan	vinieran	vengan Uds.

20 ver
Participles: viendo, visto

Infinitive	INDICATIVE					SUBJUNCTIVE		IMPERATIVE
	Present	Imperfect	Preterit	Future	Conditional	Present	Past	
ver	veo	veía	vi	veré	vería	vea	viera	
	ves	veías	viste	verás	verías	veas	vieras	ve tú (no veas)
	ve	veía	vio	verá	vería	vea	viera	vea Ud.
Participles:	vemos	veíamos	vimos	veremos	veríamos	veamos	viéramos	veamos
viendo	veis	veíais	visteis	veréis	veríais	veáis	vierais	ved (no veáis)
visto	ven	veían	vieron	verán	verían	vean	vieran	vean Uds.

Stem–changing verbs

21 contar (o→ue)
Participles: contando, contado

Infinitive	INDICATIVE					SUBJUNCTIVE		IMPERATIVE
	Present	Imperfect	Preterit	Future	Conditional	Present	Past	
contar (o→ue)	cuento	contaba	conté	contaré	contaría	cuente	contara	
	cuentas	contabas	contaste	contarás	contarías	cuentes	contaras	cuenta tú (no cuentes)
	cuenta	contaba	contó	contará	contaría	cuente	contara	cuente Ud.
Participles:	contamos	contábamos	contamos	contaremos	contaríamos	contemos	contáramos	contemos
contando	contáis	contabais	contasteis	contaréis	contaríais	contéis	contarais	contad (no contéis)
contado	cuentan	contaban	contaron	contarán	contarían	cuenten	contaran	cuenten Uds.

22 dormir (o→ue)
Participles: durmiendo, dormido

Infinitive	INDICATIVE					SUBJUNCTIVE		IMPERATIVE
	Present	Imperfect	Preterit	Future	Conditional	Present	Past	
dormir (o→ue)	duermo	dormía	dormí	dormiré	dormiría	duerma	durmiera	
	duermes	dormías	dormiste	dormirás	dormirías	duermas	durmieras	duerme tú (no duermas)
	duerme	dormía	durmió	dormirá	dormiría	duerma	durmiera	duerma Ud.
Participles:	dormimos	dormíamos	dormimos	dormiremos	dormiríamos	durmamos	durmiéramos	durmamos
durmiendo	dormís	dormíais	dormisteis	dormiréis	dormiríais	durmáis	durmierais	dormid (no durmáis)
dormido	duermen	dormían	durmieron	dormirán	dormirían	duerman	durmieran	duerman Uds.

23 empezar (e→ie) (z:c)
Participles: empezando, empezado

Infinitive	INDICATIVE					SUBJUNCTIVE		IMPERATIVE
	Present	Imperfect	Preterit	Future	Conditional	Present	Past	
empezar (e→ie) (z:c)	empiezo	empezaba	empecé	empezaré	empezaría	empiece	empezara	
	empiezas	empezabas	empezaste	empezarás	empezarías	empieces	empezaras	empieza tú (no empieces)
	empieza	empezaba	empezó	empezará	empezaría	empiece	empezara	empiece Ud.
Participles:	empezamos	empezábamos	empezamos	empezaremos	empezaríamos	empecemos	empezáramos	empecemos
empezando	empezáis	empezabais	empezasteis	empezaréis	empezaríais	empecéis	empezarais	empezad (no empecéis)
empezado	empiezan	empezaban	empezaron	empezarán	empezarían	empiecen	empezaran	empiecen Uds.

24 entender (e→ie) — Participles: entendiendo, entendido

	INDICATIVE					SUBJUNCTIVE		IMPERATIVE
	Present	Imperfect	Preterit	Future	Conditional	Present	Past	
	entiendo	entendía	entendí	entenderé	entendería	entienda	entendiera	
	entiendes	entendías	entendiste	entenderás	entenderías	entiendas	entendieras	entiende tú (no entiendas)
	entiende	entendía	entendió	entenderá	entendería	entienda	entendiera	entienda Ud.
	entendemos	entendíamos	entendimos	entenderemos	entenderíamos	entendamos	entendiéramos	entendamos
	entendéis	entendíais	entendisteis	entenderéis	entenderíais	entendáis	entendierais	entended (no entendáis)
	entienden	entendían	entendieron	entenderán	entenderían	entiendan	entendieran	entiendan Uds.

25 jugar (u→ue) (g:gu) — Participles: jugando, jugado

	INDICATIVE					SUBJUNCTIVE		IMPERATIVE
	Present	Imperfect	Preterit	Future	Conditional	Present	Past	
	juego	jugaba	jugué	jugaré	jugaría	juegue	jugara	
	juegas	jugabas	jugaste	jugarás	jugarías	juegues	jugaras	juega tú (no juegues)
	juega	jugaba	jugó	jugará	jugaría	juegue	jugara	juegue Ud.
	jugamos	jugábamos	jugamos	jugaremos	jugaríamos	juguemos	jugáramos	juguemos
	jugáis	jugabais	jugasteis	jugaréis	jugaríais	juguéis	jugarais	jugad (no juguéis)
	juegan	jugaban	jugaron	jugarán	jugarían	jueguen	jugaran	jueguen Uds.

26 pedir (e→i) — Participles: pidiendo, pedido

	INDICATIVE					SUBJUNCTIVE		IMPERATIVE
	Present	Imperfect	Preterit	Future	Conditional	Present	Past	
	pido	pedía	pedí	pediré	pediría	pida	pidiera	
	pides	pedías	pediste	pedirás	pedirías	pidas	pidieras	pide tú (no pidas)
	pide	pedía	pidió	pedirá	pediría	pida	pidiera	pida Ud.
	pedimos	pedíamos	pedimos	pediremos	pediríamos	pidamos	pidiéramos	pidamos
	pedís	pedíais	pedisteis	pediréis	pediríais	pidáis	pidierais	pedid (no pidáis)
	piden	pedían	pidieron	pedirán	pedirían	pidan	pidieran	pidan Uds.

27 pensar (e→ie) — Participles: pensando, pensado

	INDICATIVE					SUBJUNCTIVE		IMPERATIVE
	Present	Imperfect	Preterit	Future	Conditional	Present	Past	
	pienso	pensaba	pensé	pensaré	pensaría	piense	pensara	
	piensas	pensabas	pensaste	pensarás	pensarías	pienses	pensaras	piensa tú (no pienses)
	piensa	pensaba	pensó	pensará	pensaría	piense	pensara	piense Ud.
	pensamos	pensábamos	pensamos	pensaremos	pensaríamos	pensemos	pensáramos	pensemos
	pensáis	pensabais	pensasteis	pensaréis	pensaríais	penséis	pensarais	pensad (no penséis)
	piensan	pensaban	pensaron	pensarán	pensarían	piensen	pensaran	piensen Uds.

28 seguir (e→i) (g:gu) — Participles: siguiendo, seguido

	INDICATIVE					SUBJUNCTIVE		IMPERATIVE
	Present	Imperfect	Preterit	Future	Conditional	Present	Past	
	sigo	seguía	seguí	seguiré	seguiría	siga	siguiera	
	sigues	seguías	seguiste	seguirás	seguirías	sigas	siguieras	sigue tú (no sigas)
	sigue	seguía	siguió	seguirá	seguiría	siga	siguiera	siga Ud.
	seguimos	seguíamos	seguimos	seguiremos	seguiríamos	sigamos	siguiéramos	sigamos
	seguís	seguíais	seguisteis	seguiréis	seguiríais	sigáis	siguierais	seguid (no sigáis)
	siguen	seguían	siguieron	seguirán	seguirían	sigan	siguieran	sigan Uds.

29 sentir (e→ie) — Participles: sintiendo, sentido

	INDICATIVE					SUBJUNCTIVE		IMPERATIVE
	Present	Imperfect	Preterit	Future	Conditional	Present	Past	
	siento	sentía	sentí	sentiré	sentiría	sienta	sintiera	
	sientes	sentías	sentiste	sentirás	sentirías	sientas	sintieras	siente tú (no sientas)
	siente	sentía	sintió	sentirá	sentiría	sienta	sintiera	sienta Ud.
	sentimos	sentíamos	sentimos	sentiremos	sentiríamos	sintamos	sintiéramos	sintamos
	sentís	sentíais	sentisteis	sentiréis	sentiríais	sintáis	sintierais	sentid (no sintáis)
	sienten	sentían	sintieron	sentirán	sentirían	sientan	sintieran	sientan Uds.

Reflexive verbs and verbs with spelling changes

30 conocer (c → zc)
Participles: conociendo, conocido

Infinitive	INDICATIVE					SUBJUNCTIVE		IMPERATIVE
	Present	Imperfect	Preterit	Future	Conditional	Present	Past	
conocer	**conozco**	conocía	conocí	conoceré	conocería	**conozca**	conociera	
	conoces	conocías	conociste	conocerás	conocerías	**conozcas**	conocieras	conoce tú (no **conozcas**)
	conoce	conocía	conoció	conocerá	conocería	**conozca**	conociera	**conozca** Ud.
	conocemos	conocíamos	conocimos	conoceremos	conoceríamos	**conozcamos**	conociéramos	**conozcamos**
	conocéis	conocíais	conocisteis	conoceréis	conoceríais	**conozcáis**	conocierais	conoced (no **conozcáis**)
	conocen	conocían	conocieron	conocerán	conocerían	**conozcan**	conocieran	**conozcan** Uds.

31 creer (y)
Participles: **creyendo**, **creído**

Infinitive	INDICATIVE					SUBJUNCTIVE		IMPERATIVE
	Present	Imperfect	Preterit	Future	Conditional	Present	Past	
creer	creo	creía	**creí**	creeré	creería	**crea**	**creyera**	
	crees	creías	**creíste**	creerás	creerías	**creas**	**creyeras**	cree tú (no creas)
	cree	creía	**creyó**	creerá	creería	**crea**	**creyera**	crea Ud.
	creemos	creíamos	**creímos**	creeremos	creeríamos	**creamos**	**creyéramos**	creamos
	creéis	creíais	**creísteis**	creeréis	creeríais	**creáis**	**creyerais**	creed (no creáis)
	creen	creían	**creyeron**	creerán	creerían	**crean**	**creyeran**	crean Uds.

32 cruzar (z:c)
Participles: cruzando, cruzado

Infinitive	INDICATIVE					SUBJUNCTIVE		IMPERATIVE
	Present	Imperfect	Preterit	Future	Conditional	Present	Past	
cruzar	cruzo	cruzaba	**crucé**	cruzaré	cruzaría	**cruce**	cruzara	
	cruzas	cruzabas	cruzaste	cruzarás	cruzarías	**cruces**	cruzaras	cruza tú (no **cruces**)
	cruza	cruzaba	cruzó	cruzará	cruzaría	**cruce**	cruzara	**cruce** Ud.
	cruzamos	cruzábamos	cruzamos	cruzaremos	cruzaríamos	**crucemos**	cruzáramos	**crucemos**
	cruzáis	cruzabais	cruzasteis	cruzaréis	cruzaríais	**crucéis**	cruzarais	cruzad (no **crucéis**)
	cruzan	cruzaban	cruzaron	cruzarán	cruzarían	**crucen**	cruzaran	**crucen** Uds.

33 esquiar (esquío)
Participles: esquiando, esquiado

Infinitive	INDICATIVE					SUBJUNCTIVE		IMPERATIVE
	Present	Imperfect	Preterit	Future	Conditional	Present	Past	
esquiar	**esquío**	esquiaba	esquié	esquiaré	esquiaría	**esquíe**	esquiara	
	esquías	esquiabas	esquiaste	esquiarás	esquiarías	**esquíes**	esquiaras	**esquía** tú (no **esquíes**)
	esquía	esquiaba	esquió	esquiará	esquiaría	**esquíe**	esquiara	**esquíe** Ud.
	esquiamos	esquiábamos	esquiamos	esquiaremos	esquiaríamos	**esquiemos**	esquiáramos	esquiemos
	esquiáis	esquiabais	esquiasteis	esquiaréis	esquiaríais	**esquiéis**	esquiarais	esquiad (no **esquiéis**)
	esquían	esquiaban	esquiaron	esquiarán	esquiarían	**esquíen**	esquiaran	**esquíen** Uds.

34 llegar (g:gu)
Participles: llegando, llegado

Infinitive	INDICATIVE					SUBJUNCTIVE		IMPERATIVE
	Present	Imperfect	Preterit	Future	Conditional	Present	Past	
llegar	llego	llegaba	**llegué**	llegaré	llegaría	**llegue**	llegara	
	llegas	llegabas	llegaste	llegarás	llegarías	**llegues**	llegaras	llega tú (no **llegues**)
	llega	llegaba	llegó	llegará	llegaría	**llegue**	llegara	**llegue** Ud.
	llegamos	llegábamos	llegamos	llegaremos	llegaríamos	**lleguemos**	llegáramos	**lleguemos**
	llegáis	llegabais	llegasteis	llegaréis	llegaríais	**lleguéis**	llegarais	llegad (no **lleguéis**)
	llegan	llegaban	llegaron	llegarán	llegarían	**lleguen**	llegaran	**lleguen** Uds.

	Infinitive	INDICATIVE					SUBJUNCTIVE		IMPERATIVE
		Present	Imperfect	Preterit	Future	Conditional	Present	Past	
35	tocar (c:qu)	toco	tocaba	**toqué**	tocaré	tocaría	**toque**	tocara	
		tocas	tocabas	tocaste	tocarás	tocarías	**toques**	tocaras	toca tú (no **toques**)
		toca	tocaba	**tocó**	tocará	tocaría	**toque**	tocara	**toque** Ud.
	Participles:	tocamos	tocábamos	tocamos	tocaremos	tocaríamos	**toquemos**	tocáramos	**toquemos**
	tocando	tocáis	tocabais	tocasteis	tocaréis	tocaríais	**toquéis**	tocarais	tocad (no **toquéis**)
	tocado	tocan	tocaban	tocaron	tocarán	tocarían	**toquen**	tocaran	**toquen** Uds.
36	vestir(se) (e→i)	**me visto**	me vestía	me vestí	me vestiré	me vestiría	**me vista**	**me vistiera**	
		te vistes	te vestías	te vestiste	te vestirás	te vestirías	**te vistas**	**te vistieras**	**vístete** tú (no te **vistas**)
		se viste	se vestía	**se vistió**	se vestirá	se vestiría	**se vista**	**se vistiera**	**vístase** Ud.
	Participles:	nos vestimos	nos vestíamos	nos vestimos	nos vestiremos	nos vestiríamos	**nos vistamos**	**nos vistiéramos**	**vistámonos**
	vistiendo	os vestís	os vestíais	os vestisteis	os vestiréis	os vestiríais	**os vistáis**	**os vistierais**	vestíos (no os **vistáis**)
	vestido	**se visten**	se vestían	**se vistieron**	se vestirán	se vestirían	**se vistan**	**se vistieran**	**vístanse** Uds.

433

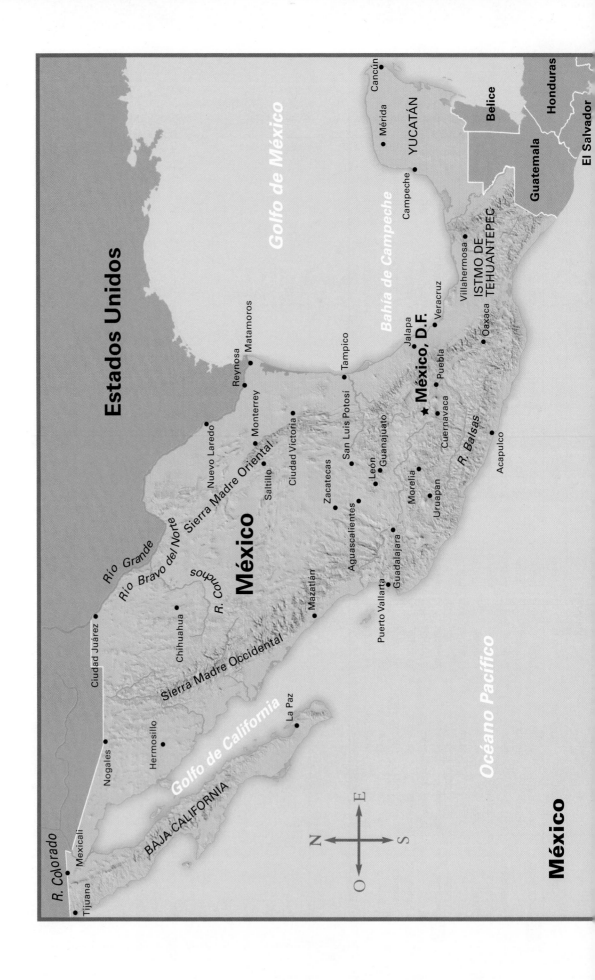

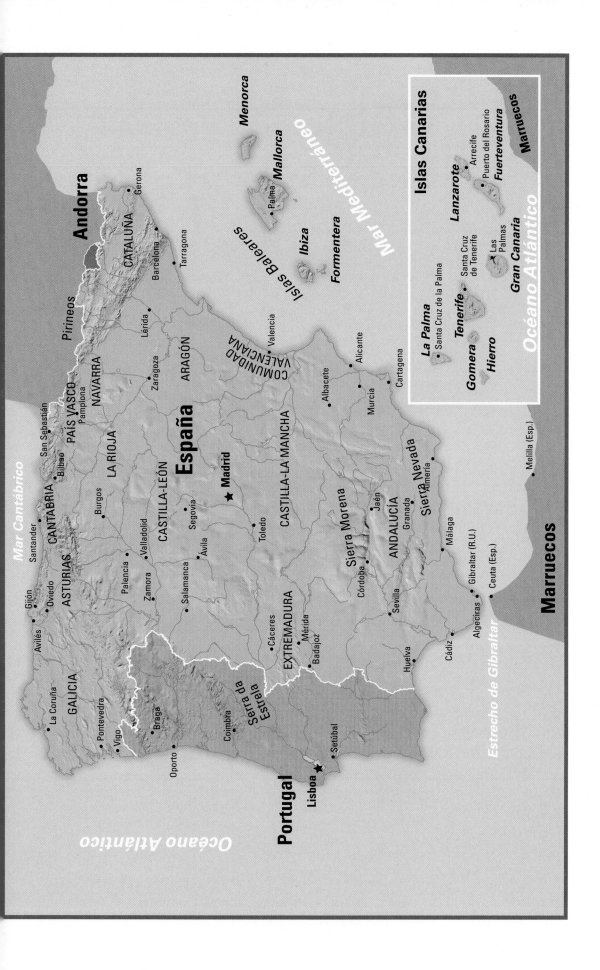

América del Sur

436

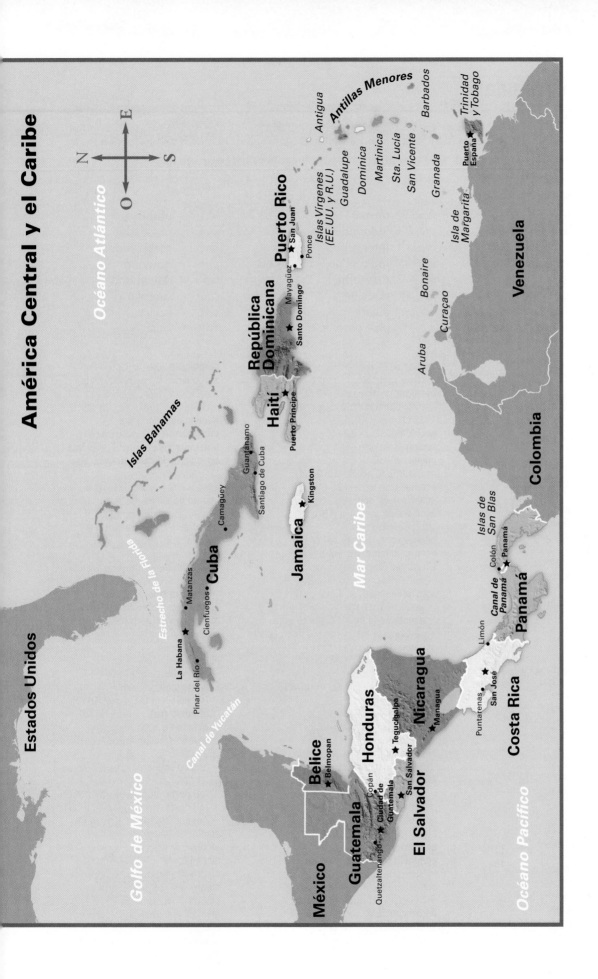

América Central y el Caribe

Estados Unidos

Golfo de México

Océano Atlántico

Estrecho de la Florida

Islas Bahamas

México

Canal de Yucatán

Pinar del Río

La Habana

Matanzas

Cienfuegos

Camagüey

Cuba

Santiago de Cuba

Guantánamo

Jamaica

Kingston

Mar Caribe

Belice

Belmopan

Guatemala

Quetzaltenango

Ciudad de Guatemala

Copán

El Salvador

San Salvador

Honduras

Tegucigalpa

Nicaragua

Managua

Costa Rica

San José

Puntarenas

Limón

Panamá

Canal de Panamá

Colón

Panamá

Islas de San Blas

Océano Pacífico

Colombia

Venezuela

Haití

Puerto Príncipe

República Dominicana

Santo Domingo

Puerto Rico

San Juan

Ponce

Mayagüez

Islas Vírgenes (EE.UU. y R.U.)

Antillas Menores

Antigua

Guadalupe

Dominica

Martinica

Sta. Lucía

San Vicente

Granada

Barbados

Trinidad y Tobago

Puerto España

Isla de Margarita

Aruba

Bonaire

Curaçao

N

E

S

O

Guide to Vocabulary

Note on alphabetization

For purposes of alphabetization, **ch** and **ll** are not treated as separate letters, but **ñ** still follows **n**. Therefore, in this glossary you will find that **año**, for example, appears after **anuncio**.

Abbreviations used in this glossary

adj.	adjective	*form.*	formal	*pl.*	plural
adv.	adverb	*indef.*	indefinite	*poss.*	possessive
art.	article	*interj.*	interjection	*prep.*	preposition
conj.	conjunction	*i.o.*	indirect object	*pron.*	pronoun
def.	definite	*m.*	masculine	*ref.*	reflexive
d.o.	direct object	*n.*	noun	*sing.*	singular
f.	feminine	*obj.*	object	*sub.*	subject
fam.	familiar	*p.p.*	past participle	*v.*	verb

Spanish-English

A

a *prep.* at; to
  ¿A qué hora...? At what time...? **2 (1)**
  a bordo aboard
  a dieta on a diet
  a la derecha de to the right of
  a la izquierda de to the left of
  a la plancha grilled
  a la(s) + *time* at + *time*
  a menos que unless **30 (2)**
  a menudo often **22 (2)**
  a mi nombre in my name
  a nombre de in the name of
  a plazos in installments
  A sus órdenes. At your service.
  a tiempo on time
  a veces sometimes **8 (1)**, **15 (1)**
  a ver let's see
al *conj., m., sing.* to the **8 (1)**
a la *f.,sing.* to the **8 (1)**
a las *f.,pl.* to the **8 (1)**
a los *m.,pl.* to the **8 (1)**
¡Abajo! *adv.* Down!
abeja *f.* bee
abierto/a *adj.* open; *p.p.* opened **28 (2)**
abogado/a *m., f.* lawyer **12 (1)**
abrazar(se) *v.* to hug; to embrace (each other)
abrazo *m.* hug
abrigo *m.* coat **13 (1)**
abril *m.* April **13 (1)**
abrir *v.* to open **8 (1)**
  abrir *v.* **los regalos** to open presents **20 (2)**
abuelo/a *m., f.* grandfather; grandmother **4 (1)**
abuelos *pl.* grandparents **4 (1)**
aburrido/a *adj.* bored; boring **6 (1)**, **15 (1)**
aburrir *v.* to bore
aburrirse *v.* to get bored

acabar de *(+ inf.)* *v.* to have just *(done something)* **21 (2)**
acampar *v.* to camp **18 (2)**
  ir de campamento to go camping **18 (2)**
accidente *m.* accident
acción *f.* action
aceite *m.* oil
acelerar *v.* to accelerate **26 (2)**
aceptar *v.* to accept **28 (2)**
ácido/a *adj.* acid
acompañar *v.* to go with; to accompany
aconsejar *v.* to advise **27 (2)**
acontecimiento *m.* event
acordarse (de) (o:ue) *v.* to remember
acostarse (o:ue) *v.* to lie down; to go to bed **17 (2)**
  acostarse (o:ue) *v.* **tarde** to go to bed late **14 (1)**
activo/a *adj.* active **3 (1)**
actor *m.* actor
actriz *f.* actress
actualidades *f., pl.* news; current events
acuático/a *adj.* aquatic
adelgazar *v.* to lose weight; to slim down
además (de) *adv.* furthermore; besides; in addition (to)
(a)dentro *adv.* inside **15 (1)**
  estar adentro/dentro de to be inside **15 (1)**
adicional *adj.* additional
adiós *m.* goodbye **1 (1)**
adjetivo *m.* adjective
administración de empresas *f.* business administration
administrador/a de empresas *m.f.* business administrator **12 (1)**
adolescencia *f.* adolescence
adolorido/a *adj.* sore **21 (2)**
¿adónde? *adv.* where (to)? *(destination)*
aduana *f.* customs

aeróbico/a *adj.* aerobic
aeropuerto *m.* airport **8 (1)**
afectado/a *adj.* affected
afeitarse *v.* to shave **23 (2)**
aficionado/a *adj.* fan
afirmativo/a *adj.* affirmative
afueras *f., pl.* suburbs; outskirts
agencia de bienes raíces *f.* real estate agency
agencia de viajes *f.* travel agency
agente de viajes *m., f.* travel agent
agosto *m.* August **13 (1)**
agradable *adj.* pleasant **6 (1)**
agrio/a *adj.* sour
agua *f.* water **9 (1)**
  agua mineral mineral water
ahora *adv.* now
  ahora mismo right now
ahorrar *v.* to save money **28 (2)**
ahorros *m., pl.* savings
aire *m.* air
ajo *m.* garlic
al *(contraction of a + el)*
  al aire libre open-air
  al contado in cash
  (al) este (to the) east **26 (2)**
  al fondo (de) at the end (of)
  al lado de next to; beside
  al lado derecho on the right side **23 (2)**
  al lado izquierdo on the left side **23 (2)**
  (al) norte (to the) north **26 (2)**
  (al) oeste (to the) west **26 (2)**
  (al) sur (to the) south **26 (2)**
alcoba *f.* bedroom
alcohol *m.* alcohol
alcohólico/a *adj.* alcoholic
alegrarse (de) *v.* to be happy
alegre *adj.* happy; joyful
alegría *f.* happiness
alemán, alemana *adj.* German
alérgico/a *adj.* allergic
alfombra *f.* carpet; rug **18 (2)**
algo *pron.* something; anything **18 (2)**

algodón *m.* cotton
alguien *pron.* someone; anyone 18 (2)
algún, alguno/a(s) *adj.* any; some 18 (2)
  alguna vez ever 28 (2)
aliviar *v.* to relieve
  aliviar el estrés/la tensión to relieve stress/tension
allí *adv.* there
  allí mismo right there
almacén *m.* department store
almohada *f.* pillow
almorzar (o:ue) *v.* to have lunch 9 (1)
almuerzo *m.* lunch 9 (1)
¿Aló? *interj.* Hello? (*on the telephone*)
alojamiento *m.* lodging
alquilar *v.* to rent
alquiler *m.* rent
alternador *m.* alternator
altillo *m.* attic
alto/a *adj.* tall 6 (1)
alto *m.* red light 26 (2)
aluminio *m.* aluminum
amable *adj.* nice; friendly 6 (1)
ama *m., f.* **de casa** homemaker; housekeeper; housewife 11 (1)
amarillo/a *adj.* yellow 13 (1)
ambicioso/a *adj.* ambitious 3 (1)
amigo/a *m., f.* friend 4 (1)
amistad *f.* friendship
amor *m.* love
analista de sistemas *m., f.* systems analyst 12 (1)
anaranjado/a *adj.* orange
andar *v.* **en bicicleta** to ride a bike 18 (2), 20 (2)
anillo (de compromiso) *m.* (engagement) ring 27 (2)
animal *m.* animal
aniversario (de bodas) *m.* (wedding) anniversary
anoche *adv.* last night 15 (1), 17 (2)
anteayer *adv.* the day before yesterday
antes *adv.* before 22 (2)
  antes de *prep.* before
  antes (de) que *conj.* before 30 (2)
antropología *f.* anthropology 1 (1)
antibiótico *m.* antibiotic 21 (2)
antipático/a *adj.* unpleasant 6 (1)
anunciar *v.* to announce; to advertise
anuncio *m.* advertisement
año *m.* year
  el año pasado last year 15 (1), 17 (2)
  el año que viene next year 7 (1)
apagar *v.* to turn off
  apagar *v.* **el coche** to turn off the car 26 (2)
aparato *m.* appliance
apartamento *m.* apartment 18 (2)

apellido *m.* last name
apenas *adv.* hardly; scarcely; just
aplaudir *v.* to applaud
apreciar *v.* to appreciate
aprender *v.* to learn
  aprender (+ *verb*) learn (how) 19 (2)
  aprender cosas nuevas to learn new things 19 (2)
apurarse *v.* to hurry; to rush
aquel, aquella *adj.* that; those (over there)
aquél, aquélla *pron.* that; those (over there)
aquello *neuter, pron.* that; that thing; that fact
aquellos/as *pl. adj.* that; those (over there)
aquéllos/as *pl. pron.* those (ones) (over there)
aquí *adv.* here
  Aquí está... Here it is…
  Aquí estamos en... Here we are at/in…
  aquí mismo right here
árbol *m.* tree 22 (2)
  subir(se) a los árboles to climb trees 22 (2)
archivo *m.* file
armar rompecabezas *v.* to do puzzles 22 (2)
armario *m.* closet
arqueólogo/a *m., f.* archaeologist
arquitecto/a *m., f.* architect
arrancar *v.* to start (a car)
arreglar *v.* to fix; to arrange; to neaten; to straighten up 18 (2)
arreglado/a *adj.* tidy 18 (2)
  estar arreglado/a to be tidy 18 (2)
arriba *adv.* up
arrogante *adj.* arrogant 3 (1)
arroz *m.* rice 9 (1)
arte *m.* art
artes *f., pl.* arts
artesanía *f.* craftsmanship; crafts
artículo *m.* article
artista *m., f.* artist
artístico/a *adj.* artistic
arveja *m.* pea
asado/a *adj.* roasted
asador *m.* grill 18 (2)
ascenso *m.* promotion
ascensor *m.* elevator
así *adj.* like this; so (*in such a way*)
  así así so-so
asistir (a) *v.* to attend
aspiradora *f.* vacuum cleaner
  pasar la aspiradora to vacuum 18 (2)
aspirante *m., f.* candidate; applicant
aspirina *f.* aspirin 21 (2)
astronomía *f.* astronomy 1 (1)

atender(e:ie) *v.* **a los clientes** attend to the customers/clients 11 (1)
atractivo/a *adj.* attractive 3 (1)
atrás *adv.* behind 25 (2)
  por atrás from behind 25 (2)
atún *m.* tuna
  sandwich de atún *m.* tuna sándwich 9 (1)
auditorio *m.* auditorium 2 (1)
aumentar *v.* **de peso** to gain weight
aumento *m.* increase
  aumento de sueldo pay raise
aunque *conj.* although
autobús *m.* bus
automático/a *adj.* automatic
auto(móvil) *m.* auto(mobile)
autopista *f.* highway; freeway; expressway 26 (2)
ave *f.* bird
avenida *f.* avenue 26 (2)
aventura *f.* adventure
avergonzado/a *adj.* embarrassed
avión *m.* airplane
  ir en avión to go by plane 20 (2)
¡Ay! *interj.* Oh!
  ¡Ay, qué dolor! Oh, what pain!
ayer *adv.* yesterday 15 (1), 17 (2)
ayudar *v.* to help 11 (1)
ayudarse *v.* to help each other
azúcar *m.* sugar
azul *adj.* blue 13 (1)

B

bailar *v.* to dance 5 (1)
bailarín/bailarina *m., f.* dancer
baile *m.* dance
bajar *v.* to go down
bajar(se) de *v.* to get off of/out of (a vehicle)
bajo/a *adj.* short (*in height*) 6 (1)
  bajo control under control
balcón *m.* balcony
ballena *f.* whale
ballet *m.* ballet
baloncesto *m.* basketball
banana *f.* banana 9 (1)
banco *m.* bank
banda *f.* band
bandera *f.* flag 2 (1)
bañarse *v.* to bathe; to take a bath 14 (1)
  bañarse *v.* **por la noche** take a bath/shower at night 14 (1)
baño *m.* bathroom 2 (1), 18 (2)
barato/a *adj.* cheap
barco *m.* boat
barrer *v.* to sweep
  barrer el suelo to sweep the floor 18 (2)
  barrer el garaje to sweep the garage 18 (2)
barrio *m.* neighborhood
bastante *adv.* enough; quite; pretty

basura *f.* trash 18 (2)
  sacar *v.* **la basura** take out the trash 18 (2)
baúl *m.* trunk
beber *v.* to drink 8 (1)
bebida *f.* drink
  bebida alcohólica alcoholic beverage
béisbol *m.* baseball
bellas artes *f., pl.* fine arts
belleza *f.* beauty
beneficio *m.* benefit
berrinche *m.* tantrum 22 (2)
  hacer *v.* **berrinches** to throw tantrums 22 (2)
besar(se) *v.* to kiss (each other)
beso *m.* kiss
  dar *v.* **un beso** to give a kiss 20 (2)
biblioteca *f.* library 2 (1)
bicicleta *f.* bicycle
  andar *v.* **en bicicleta** to ride a bike 18 (2)
bien *adj.* fine 1 (1); well *adj.* 21 (2)
bienestar *m.* well-being
¡Bienvenido(s)/a(s)! *adj.* Welcome!
bikini *m.* bikini 13 (1)
billete *m.* paper money
billón trillion
biología *f.* biology 1 (1)
bistec *m.* steak
bistec de res *m.* roast beef 9 (1)
bizcocho *m.* biscuit
blanco/a *adj.* white 13 (1)
bluejeans *m., pl.* jeans 13 (1)
blusa *f.* blouse 13 (1)
boca *f.* mouth 21 (2)
boda *f.* wedding
boleto *m.* ticket
boliche *m.* bowling alley 8 (1)
bolsa *f.* bag; purse 13 (1)
bombero/a *m., f.* firefighter 12 (1)
bonito(a) *adj.* pretty 6 (1)
borracho(a) *adj.* drunk 15 (1)
borrador *m.* eraser
bosque *m.* forest
  bosque tropical tropical forest; rainforest
bota *f.* boot
botella *f.* bottle
  botella de vino bottle of wine
botones *m., f., sing.* bellhop
brazo *m.* arm 21 (2)
brindar *v.* to toast (drink)
brócoli *m.* broccoli 9 (1)
bucear *v.* to scuba dive/snorkel 18 (2)
bueno... *adv.* well...
buen, bueno/a *adj.* good 6 (1)
  ¡Buen viaje! Have a good trip!
  buena forma good shape *(physical)*
  ¡Buena idea! Good idea!
  Buenas noches. Good evening; Good night. 1 (1)

Buenas tardes. Good afternoon. 1 (1)
buenísimo extremely good
¿Bueno? Hello? *(on telephone)*
Buenos días. Good morning. 1 (1)
bufanda *f.* scarf 13 (1)
bulevar *m.* boulevard
buscar *v.* to look for 5 (1)
buzón *m.* mailbox

C

caballo *m.* horse
cabaña *f.* cabin
cabe: no cabe duda de there's no doubt
cabeza *f.* head 21 (2)
cada *adj.* each 22 (2)
  cada año *adj.* each year 22 (2)
caerse *v.* to fall (down)
café *m.* café 8 (1); *adj.* brown 13 (1); **coffee** *m.* 9 (1)
cafetera *f.* coffee maker
cafetería *f.* cafeteria 2 (1)
caído/a *p.p.* fallen
caja *f.* cash register
cajero/a *m., f.* cashier
  cajero automático automatic teller machine (ATM)
calcetín *m.* sock 13 (1)
calculadora *f.* calculator 2 (1)
caldo *m.* soup
  caldo de patas beef soup
calentamiento global *m.* global warming
calentarse (e:ie) *v.* to warm up
calidad *f.* quality
calle *f.* street 26 (2)
calor *m.* heat
caloría *f.* calorie
calzar *v.* to take size . . . shoes
cama *f.* bed 18 (2)
cámara *f.* camera
  cámara de video videocamera
  cámara digital digital camera
camarero/a *m., f.* waiter/waitress 9 (1), 11 (1)
camarón *m.* shrimp 9 (1)
cambiar (de) *v.* to change 28 (2)
cambio *m.* **de moneda** currency exchange
caminar *v.* to walk
camino *m.* route
camión *m.* truck; bus
camisa *f.* shirt 13 (1)
camiseta *f.* t-shirt 13 (1)
campo *m.* countryside
canadiense *adj.* Canadian
canal *m.* channel (TV)
cancha de tenis *f.* tennis court 2 (1)
cancha de vóleibol *f.* volleyball court 2 (1)
canción *f.* song
candidato/a *m., f.* candidate

cansado/a *adj.* tired 15 (1)
cantante *m., f.* singer
cantar *v.* to sing
  cantar *v.* **villancicos** sing carols 20 (2)
  cantar *v.* **las mañanitas** sing a birthday song 20 (2)
capital *f.* capital city
capó *m.* (car) hood
cara *f.* face 21 (2)
caramelo *m.* caramel
cariñoso/a *adj.* affectionate 6 (1)
carne *f.* meat
  carne de res *m.* beef 9 (1)
  carne de cerdo *m.* pork 9 (1)
carnicería *f.* butcher shop
caro/a *adj.* expensive
carpintero/a *m., f.* carpenter
carrera *f.* career
carretera *f.* highway 26 (2)
carro *m.* car
carta *f.* letter; (playing) card
cartel *m.* poster
cartera *f.* wallet
cartero *m.* mail carrier
casa *f.* house; home
  la casa de mi novio/a my boyfriend's/girlfriend's house 8 (1)
  la casa de mis amigos/padres my friends'/parents' house 8 (1)
casado/a *adj.* married 6 (1)
casarse (con) *v.* to get married (to) 27 (2)
casi *adv.* almost 8 (1)
castigar *v.* to punish 22 (2)
catarro *m.* cold 21 (2)
  tener (el) catarro to have a cold 21 (2)
catorce fourteen 1 (1)
caza *f.* hunting
cebolla *f.* onion
celebrar *v.* to celebrate 28 (2)
celular *adj.* cellular
cena *f.* dinner 9 (1)
cenar *v.* to have dinner 9 (1)
centro *m.* downtown
  centro comercial *m.* mall 8 (1)
cepillarse los dientes/el pelo *v.* to brush one's teeth/one's hair
cerámica *f.* pottery
cerca de *prep.* near
cerdo *m.* pork 9 (1)
cereales *m., pl.* cereal; grains 9 (1)
cero zero 1 (1)
cerrado/a *adj.* closed
cerrar (e:ie) *v.* to close
cerveza *f.* beer 9 (1)
césped *m.* grass
ceviche *m.* lemon-marinated fish dish
  ceviche de camarón lemon-marinated shrimp
chaleco *m.* vest
champán *m.* champagne
champiñón *m.* mushroom

champú *m.* shampoo
chaqueta *f.* jacket 13 (1)
chau *fam., interj.* bye
cheque *m.* (bank) check
　cheque de viajero traveler's check
chévere *adj., fam.* terrific
chico/a *m., f.* boy/girl 4 (1)
chino/a *adj.* Chinese
chocar *v.* (con) to run into; to crash; to shock 29 (2); to hit (a car) 26(2); to hate; to dislike 19 (2)
chocolate *m.* chocolate
chofer *m., f.* driver, chauffeur 11 (1)
choque *m.* collision
chuleta *f.* chop *(food)*
　chuleta de cerdo pork chop
ciclismo *m.* cycling
cielo *m.* sky
cien(to) one hundred 4 (1),
　por ciento percent
ciencia *f.* science
　ciencia ficción science fiction
científico/a *m., f.* scientist
cierto *m.* certain; true
　es cierto it's true/certain
　no es cierto it's not true/certain
cifra *f.* figure
cinco five 1(1)
cincuenta fifty 4 (1)
cine *m.* movie theater 8(1)
cinta *f.* (audio) tape
cinturón *m.* belt
　cinturón *m.* **de seguridad** seat belt 26 (2)
　ponerse *v.* **el cinturón de seguridad** to wear the seat belt 26 (2)
circulación *f.* traffic
cita *f.* date; appointment
ciudad *f.* city
ciudadano/a *adj.* citizen
claro que sí *fam.* of course
clase *f.* class
　clase de ejercicios aeróbicos aerobics class
clásico/a *adj.* classical
cliente/a *m., f.* client
clínica *f.* clinic
clóset *m.* closet 18 (2)
cobrar *v.* to cash a check; to charge for a product or service
coche *m.* car
　ir *v.* **en coche** to go by car 20 (2)
cocina *f.* kitchen 18 (2); stove
cocinar *v.* to cook
cocinero/a *m., f.* cook, chef
cola *f.* line
colegio *m.* school 22 (2)
　colegio católico *m.* catholic school 22 (2)
colesterol *m.* cholesterol
color *m.* color 13 (1)
colorear *v.* to color 22 (2)
columpio *m.* swing (leisure) 22 (2)
comedia *f.* comedy; play
comedor *m.* dining room 18 (2)

comenzar (e:ie) *v.* to begin
comer *v.* to eat 8 (1), 9 (1)
comercial *adj.* commercial; business-related
comida *f.* food; meal 5 (1)
como *prep.* like, as
¿cómo? what?; how? 6 (1)
¿Cómo es...? What's... like? 3 (1)
　¿Cómo está usted? How are you? *(form.)*
　¿Cómo estás? How are you? *(fam.)* 1 (1)
　¿Cómo les fue...? *pl.* How did... go for you?
　¿Cómo se llama usted? What's your name? *(form.)*
　¿Cómo te llamas (tú)? What's your name? *(fam.)* 1 (1)
　¿Cómo son...? What are... like? (1)
cómoda *f.* chest of drawers
cómodo/a *adj.* comfortable 20 (2)
compañero/a de clase *m., f .pl.* classmate 2 (1)
compañero/a de cuarto *m., f.* roommate
compañía *f.* company; firm
compartir *v.* to share 22 (2)
　compartir *v.* **los juguetes** share toys 22 (2)
competente *adj.* competent; able 3 (1)
completamente *adv.* completely
compositor(a) *m., f.* composer
comprar *v.* to buy 5 (1)
compras *f., pl.* purchases
　ir de compras go shopping
comprender *v.* to understand
comprobar *v.* to check
comprometerse (con) *v.* to get engaged (to)
computación *f.* computer science
computadora *f.* computer
computadora portátil *f.* laptop; portable computer
comunicación *f.* communication
comunicarse (con) *v.* to communicate (with)
comunidad *f.* community
con *prep.* with
　Con él/ella habla This is he/she *(on telephone)*
　con frecuencia *adv.* frequently 8 (1)
　Con permiso Pardon me, Excuse me.
　con tal (de) que provided that
concierto *m.* concert
concordar *v.* to agree
concurso *m.* contest; game show
conducir *v.* to drive
conductor(a) *m., f.* driver 26 (2), chauffeur 11 (1)
confirmar *v.* to confirm
　confirmar una reservación to confirm a reservation

congelador *m.* freezer
congestionado/a *adj.* congested; stuffed-up
conmigo *pron.* with me 10 (1)
conocer *v.* to know; to be acquainted with; to meet someone 12 (1)
conocido/a *adj.* known
conseguir (e:i) *v.* to get; to obtain
consejero/a *m., f.* counselor; advisor 2 (1)
consejo *m.* advice
consentido/a *adj.* spoiled 22 (2)
　ser consentido/a to be spoiled 22 (2)
conservación *f.* conservation
conservar *v.* to conserve
construir *v.* to build
consultorio *m.* doctor's office
consumir *v.* to consume
contabilidad *f.* accounting
contador(a) *m., f.* accountant 12 (1)
contaminación *f.* pollution; contamination
　contaminación del aire/del agua air/water pollution
contaminado/a *adj.* polluted
contaminar *v.* to pollute
contar (con) *v.* to count (on)
　contar (o:ue) *v.* **los problemas** to tell your problems 11 (1), 24 (2)
contento/a *adj.* happy; content 15 (1)
contestadora *f.* answering machine
contestar *v.* to answer
　contestar *v.* **los teléfonos/los correos** to answer the phone/e-mails 11 (1)
contigo *pron.* with you 10 (1)
contratar *v.* to hire
control *m.* control
　control remoto remote control
controlar *v.* to control
conversación *f.* conversation
conversar *v.* to talk; to chat
copa *f.* wineglass; goblet
corazón *m.* heart
corbata *f.* tie 13 (1)
cortar *v.* **el pasto** to mow the lawn 18 (2)
corredor(a) *m., f.* **de bolsa** stockbroker
correo *m.* post office; mail
　correo electrónico e-mail
correr *v.* to run 8 (1)
cortesía *f.* courtesy
cortinas *f., pl.* curtains
corto/a *adj.* short *(in length)*
cosa *f.* thing 5 (1)
costar (o:ue) *f.* to cost
cráter *m.* crater
creativo/a *adj.* creative 3 (1)
creer *v.* to believe; to think 17 (2)
　creer (en) *v.* to believe *(in)*
creído/a *p.p.* believed
crema de afeitar *f.* shaving cream

crimen *m.* crime; murder
cruzar *v.* to cross
  cruzar *v.* **la calle** to cross the street **26 (2)**
cuaderno *m.* notebook **2 (1)**
cuadra *f.* city block **26 (2)**
cuadro *m.* picture
cuadros *m., pl.* plaid
¿cuál(es)? which?; which one(s)?; what? **6 (1)**
  ¿Cuál es la fecha de hoy? What is today's date?
cuando *conj.* when **30 (2)**
  cuando era niño/a when I was a child **22 (2)**
  cuando tenía… años when I was … years old **22 (2)**
¿cuándo? *adv.* when? **6 (1)**
¿cuánto(s)/a(s)? *adv.* how much?, how many? **6 (1)**
  ¿Cuántas classes tomas? How many classes are you taking? **1 (1)**
  ¿Cuántas horas trabajas? How many hours do you work? **1 (1)**
  ¿Cuánto cuesta…? How much does… cost?
  ¿Cuántos años tienes/tiene? 4 (1) How old are you?
  ¿Cuánto tiempo hace que…? How long has it been since…? **21 (2)**
cuarenta forty **4 (1)**
cuarto *m.* room **18 (2)**
cuarto/a *adj.* quarter; fourth
  menos cuarto quarter to (time)
  y cuarto quarter after (time)
cuarto de baño *m.* bathroom
cuatro four **1 (1)**
cuatrocientos/as four hundred
cubiertos *m., pl.* silverware
cubierto/a *p.p.* covered
cubrir *v.* to cover
cuchara *f.* spoon
cuchillo *m.* knife
cuello *m.* neck **21 (2)**
cuenta *f.* bill **9 (1)**; account
  cuenta corriente *f.* checking account
  cuenta de ahorros *f.* savings account
cuento *m.* story
cuerda *f.* rope **22 (2)**
  saltar *v.* **la cuerda** to jump rope **22 (2)**
cuerpo *m.* body **21 (2)**
cuidado *m.* care
cuidar *v.* to take care of
  cuidar *v.* **a los niños/ancianos** to take care of (to watch) kids/the elderly **11 (1)**
cuidarse *v.* take care of oneself **21 (2)**
¡Cuídense! Take care!
culpa *f.* fault **25 (2)**
cultura *f.* culture
cumpleaños *m., sing.* birthday

cumplir años *v.* to have a birthday
cuñado/a *m., f.* brother-in-law; sister-in-law **4 (1)**
currículum *m.* résumé; curriculum vitae **28 (2)**
curso *m.* course

D

damas chinas *f., pl. (game)* checkers **22 (2)**
  jugar a las damas chinas to play checkers **22 (2)**
danza *f.* dance
dañar *v.* to damage; to breakdown
dar *v.* to give **20 (2), 24 (2)**
  dar *v.* **consejos** to give advice **11 (1)**
  dar *v.* **un beso** to give a kiss **20 (2)**
  dar *v.* **un paseo** go for a walk **18 (2)**
  dar *v.* **vuelta a la derecha/izquierda en la avenida/calle…** to turn right/left at … Avenue/Street **26 (2)**
  darle *v.* **de comer al gato** to feed the cat **18 (2)**
  darse *v.* **con** to bump into; to run into
  darse *v.* **cuenta** to realize **25 (2)**
  darse *v.* **prisa** to hurry; to rush
de *prep.* of; from
  ¿de dónde? from where?
  ¿De dónde eres? *fam.* Where are you from? **4 (1)**
  ¿De dónde es usted? *form.* Where are you from?
  ¿De parte de quién? Who is calling? *(on telephone)*
  ¿de quién…? whose…? *(sing.)*
  ¿de quiénes…? whose…? *(pl.)*
  de algodón (made of) cotton
  de aluminio (made of) aluminum
  de compras shopping
  de cuadros plaid
  de excursión hiking **18 (2)**
  de hecho in fact
  de ida y vuelta round-trip
  de la mañana in the morning; A.M.
  de la noche in the evening; at night; P.M.
  de la tarde in the afternoon; in the early evening; P.M. **1 (1)**
  de lana (made of) wool
  de lunares polka-dotted
  de mi vida of my life
  de moda in fashion
  De nada. You're welcome. **1 (1)**
  de ninguna manera no way
  de niño/a as a child **22 (2)**
  de parte de on behalf of
  de plástico (made of) plastic
  de rayas striped

  de repente *adv.* suddenly; all of a sudden **25 (2)**
  de seda (made of) silk
  de vaqueros western (genre)
  de vez en cuando from time to time **22 (2)**
  de vidrio (made of) glass
debajo de *prep.* below; under
deber *(+ inf.)* *v.* to have to (do something), should (do something)
  Debe ser… It must be…
deber *m.* responsibility; obligation
debido a due to; the fact that
débil *adj.* weak
decidido/a *adj.* decided
decidir *v.* to decide
décimo/a *adj.* tenth
decir *v.* to say; to tell **20 (2), 24 (2)**
  decir *v.* **mentiras** to lie **24 (2)**
declarar *v.* to declare; to say
dedo *m.* finger
deforestación *f.* deforestation
dejar *v.* to let; to quit; to leave behind
  dejar de *(+ inf.)* to stop *(doing something)*
  dejar una propina to leave a tip
  dejar usar su coche let someone use on'es car **11 (1)**
del *(contraction of de + el)* of the; from the
  del/al lado derecho from/on the right side **23 (2)**
  del/al lado izquierdo from/on the left side **23 (2)**
delante de *prep.* in front of
delgado/a *adj.* thin; slender **6 (1)**
delicioso/a *adj.* delicious
demás *pron.* the rest
demasiado *adv.* too much
dentista *m., f.* dentist
  higienista dental *m., f.* dental hygienist **12 (1)**
dentro de *adv.* within
dependiente/a *m., f.* clerk
deporte *m.* sport
deportista *m.* sports person
deportivo/a *adj.* sports-related
depositar *v.* to deposit
deprimido/a *adj.* depressed **15 (1)**
derecha *f.* right
  a la derecha de to the right of
derecho *adj.* straight **26 (2)**
  del/al lado derecho from/on the right side **23 (2)**
derechos *m., pl.* rights
desarreglado/a *adj.* messy **18 (2)**
  estar desarreglado/a to be messy **18 (2)**
desarrollar *v.* to develop
desastre natural *m.* natural disaster
desayunar *v.* to have breakfast **9 (1)**
desayuno *m.* breakfast **9 (1)**
descafeinado/a *adj.* decaffeinated
descansar *v.* to rest **5 (1)**
descanso *m.* rest **21 (2)**

descompuesto/a *adj.* not working; out of order
describir *v.* to describe
descrito/a *p.p.* described
descubierto/a *p.p.* discovered
descubrir *v.* to discover
desde *prep.* from
desear *v.* to want; to wish; to desire
desempleo *m.* unemployment
desfile *m.* parade **20 (2)**
deshonesto/a *adj.* dishonest **3 (1)**
desierto *m.* desert
desilusionado/a *adj.* disappointed **15 (1)**
desigualdad *f.* inequality
desobedecer (c:zc) *v.* to disobey **22 (2)**
desordenado/a *adj.* disorderly; messy **6 (1)**
despacio *adj.* slowly
despedida *f.* farewell; goodbye
despedir (e:i) *v.* to fire
despedirse (de) (e:i) *v.* to say goodbye (to)
despejado/a *adj.* clear (weather)
despertador *m.* alarm clock
despertarse (e:ie) *v.* to wake up
después *adv.* afterwards; then
    después de after
    después (de) que *conj.* after
destruir *v.* to destroy
desventaja *f.* disadvantage **11 (1)**
detrás de *prep.* behind
devolver *v.* to return **27 (2)**
día *m.* day
    día de fiesta holiday
diario *m.* diary; newspaper
    diario/a *adj.* daily
dibujar *v.* to draw **22 (2)**
dibujo *m.* drawing
    dibujos animados *m., pl.* cartoons **22 (2)**
    ver *v.* **los dibujos animados** to watch cartoons **22 (2)**
diccionario *m.* dictionary **2 (1)**
dicho/a *p.p.* said **28 (2)**
diciembre *m.* December **13 (1)**
dictadura *f.* dictatorship
diecinueve nineteen **1 (1)**
dieciocho eighteen **1 (1)**
dieciséis sixteen **1 (1)**
diecisiete seventeen **1 (1)**
diente *m.* tooth
dieta *f.* diet
    dieta equilibrada balanced diet
diez ten **1 (1)**
difícil *adj.* difficult; hard **6 (1)**
¿Diga? Hello? *(on telephone)*
diligencia *f.* errand
dinero *m.* money
dirección *f.* address
director(a) *m., f.* director; (musical) conductor
disco *m.* disk
discoteca *f.* nightclub (disco) **8 (1)**

disco compacto compact disc (CD)
discreto/a *adj.* discreet **3 (1)**
discriminación *f.* discrimination
discurso *m.* speech
discutir *v.* **(de/con)** to discuss, argue (about/with) **8 (1)**
diseñador(a) *m., f.* designer
    diseñador(a) gráfico/a *m., f.* graphic designer **12 (1)**
diseño *m.* design
disfraz *m.* costume **20 (2)**
    disfrazarse *v.* **de…** to wear a … costume **20 (2)**
disfrutar (de) *v.* to enjoy; to reap the benefits (of)
diversión *f.* entertainment; fun activity
divertido/a *adj.* fun **6 (1)**
divertirse (e:ie) *v.* to have fun **14 (1)**
divorciado/a *adj.* divorced
divorciarse (de) *v.* to get divorced (from) **28 (2)**
divorcio *m.* divorce
doblar *v.* to turn
    doblar *v.* **a la derecha/izquierda en la avenida/calle…** to turn right/left at…Avenue/Street. **26 (2)**
doble *adj.* double
doce twelve **1 (1)**
doctor(a) *m., f.* doctor **1 (1), 8 (1)**
doctorado *n.* PhD **28 (2)**
documental *m.* documentary
documentos de viaje *m., pl.* travel documents
doler (o:ue) *v.* to hurt; to ache **21 (2)**
    Me duele la espalda. My back hurts. **21 (2)**
    Me duelen las piernas. My legs hurt. **21 (2)**
dolor *m.* ache; pain **21 (2)**
    tener (el) dolor de… to have a(n) ache **21 (2)**
dolor de cabeza *m.* headache
doméstico/a *adj.* domestic
domingo *m.* Sunday **5 (1)**
    los domingos *m., pl.* on Sundays **5 (1)**
don/doña *title of respect used with a person's first name*
dona *f.* donut **9 (1)**
donde *prep.* where
    ¿De dónde eres? *fam.* Where are you from? **4 (1)**
    ¿dónde? where? **6 (1)**
    ¿Dónde está…? Where is…?
dormir (o:ue) *v.* to sleep **10 (1)**
dormirse (o:ue) *v.* to go to sleep; to fall asleep
dos two **1 (1)**
    dos veces twice; two times
    dos veces al mes twice a month **8 (1)**
doscientos/as two hundred

drama *m.* drama; play **1 (1)**
dramático/a *adj.* dramatic
dramaturgo/a *m., f.* playwright
droga *f.* drug
drogadicto/a *m., f.* drug addict
ducha *f.* shower **18 (2)**
ducharse *v.* to shower; to take a shower
duda *f.* doubt
dudar *v.* to doubt
dueño/a *m., f.* owner; landlord
dulce *adj.* sweet
dulces *m., pl.* sweets; candy **9 (1)**
durante *prep.* during
    durante (cinco) años for (five years) **15 (1)**
durar *v.* to last

E

e *conj. (used instead of **y** before words beginning with **i** and **hi**)* and
echar *v.* to throw
    echar una carta al buzón to put a letter in the mailbox; to mail a letter
ecología *f.* ecology
ecologista *adj.* ecological; ecologist
economía *f.* economics **1 (1)**
ecoturismo *m.* ecotourism
Ecuador *m.* Ecuador
ecuatoriano/a *adj.* Ecuadorian
edad *f.* age
edificio *m.* building **2 (1)**
    edificio de apartamentos apartment building
educación física *f.* physical education **1 (1)**
educador(a) *m., f.* pre-school teacher **12 (1)**
efectivo *m.* cash
ejercicio *m.* exercise
    ejercicios aeróbicos aerobic exercises
    ejercicios de estiramiento stretching exercises
ejército *m.* army
el *m., sing., def. art.* the **2 (1)**
él *sub. pron.* he; *adj. pron.* him
elección *f.* election
electricista *m., f.* electrician
electrodoméstico *m.* electric appliance
elegante *adj. m., f.* elegant
elegir *v.* to elect
ella *sub. pron.* she; *obj. pron.* her
ellos/as *sub. pron.* they; them
embarazada *adj.* pregnant
embarazarse *v.* to get pregnant **28 (2)**
emergencia *f.* emergency
emitir *v.* to broadcast
emocionado/a *adj.* excited **15 (1)**
emocionante *adj.* exciting

empezar (e:ie) *v.* to begin **10 (1)**

empleado/a *m., f.* employee; clerk **11 (1)**

empleo *m.* job; employment

empresa *f.* company; firm **28 (2)**

empujar *v.* to push **25 (2)**

en *prep.* in; on; at

en aquel entonces at that time **22 (2)**

en casa at home

en caso (de) que in case (that)

en cuanto as soon as **30 (2)**

en efectivo in cash

en esos tiempos back then **22 (2)**

en exceso in excess; too much

en línea in-line

¡En marcha! Let's get going!

en mi nombre in my name

en punto on the dot; exactly; sharp (time)

en qué in which; in what; how

¿En qué puedo servirles? How can I help you?

enamorado/a *adj.* **(de)** in love (with)

enamorarse (de) *v.* to fall in love (with) **28 (2)**

encantado/a *adj.* delighted; pleased to meet you **1 (1)**

encantar *v.* to like very much; to love *(inanimate objects)* **19 (2)**

encima de *prep.* on top of

encontrar (o:ue) *v.* to find **10 (1)**, **17 (2)**

encontrar(se) *v.* to meet (each other); to find (each other)

encuesta *f.* poll; survey

energía *f.* energy

energía nuclear nuclear energy

energía solar solar energy

enero *m.* January **13 (1)**

enfermarse *v.* to get sick **21 (2)**

enfermedad *f.* illness; sickness

enfermería *f.* health center; infirmary **2 (1)**

enfermero/a *m., f.* nurse **12 (1)**

enfermo/a *adj.* sick **15 (1)**

enfrente de *adv.* opposite; facing; in front of **26 (2)**

engordar *v.* to gain weight

enojado/a *adj.* mad; angry **15 (1)**

enojarse (con) *v.* to get angry (with)

ensalada *f.* salad

la ensalada de lechuga y tomate lettuce and tomato salad **9 (1)**

enseguida *adv.* right away

enseñar *v.* **a** to teach; to show **24 (2)**

ensuciar *v.* to get (something) dirty; to dirty

entender (e:ie) *v.* to understand **10 (1)**, **17 (2)**

entonces *adv.* then

en aquel entonces at that time **22 (2)**

entrada *f.* entrance **26 (2)**; ticket

la primera/segunda entrada the first/second entrance **26 (2)**

entrar *v.* to enter **28 (2)**

entre *prep.* between; among

entregar *v.* to turn something in **24 (2)**

entremeses *m., pl.* hors d'oeuvres; appetizers

entrenarse *v.* to practice; to train

entrevista *f.* interview **28 (2)**

entrevistador(a) *m., f.* interviewer

entrevistar *v.* to interview

envase *m.* container

enviar *v.* to send ; to mail

equilibrado/a *adj.* balanced

equipado/a *adj.* equipped

equipaje *m.* luggage

equipo *m.* team

equivocado/a *adj.* wrong; mistaken

eres you are *fam.* **3 (1)**

es you are *form.*; he/she/it is **3 (1)**

Es a la(s)… de la mañana/tarde/noche. It's at…in the morning/afternoon/evening. **2 (1)**

Es bueno que… It's good that…

Es de… He/She is from…

Es extraño… It's strange…

Es importante que… It's important that…

Es imposible… It's impossible…

Es improbable… It's improbable…

Es la una. It's one o'clock.

Es malo que… It's bad that…

Es mejor que… It's better that…

Es necesario que… It's necessary that…

Es obvio… It's obvious…

Es ridículo… It's ridiculous…

Es seguro… It's sure…

Es terrible… It's terrible…

Es triste… It's sad…

Es una lástima… It's a shame…

Es urgente que… It's urgent that…

Es verdad… It's true…

esa(s) *f., adj.* that; those **6 (1)**

ésa(s) *f., pron.* those (ones)

escalar *v.* to climb

escalar montañas *f., pl.* to climb mountains

escalera *f.* stairs; stairway

escoger *v.* choose

escondite *m.* hideout; hiding place **22 (2)**

jugar a las escondidillas/al escondite to play hide-and-seek **22 (2)**

escribir *v.* to write **24 (2)**

escribir una carta to write a letter **8 (1)**

escribir un mensaje electrónico to write an e-mail message

escribir un trabajo to write a paper **8 (1)**

escribir una (tarjeta) postal to write a postcard

escrito/a *p.p.* written **28 (2)**

escritor(a) *m., f.* writer

escritorio *m.* desk (teacher's) **2 (1)**

escuchar *v.* to listen

escuchar la radio to listen to the radio

escuchar música to listen to music **5 (1)**

escuela *f.* school **8 (1)**, **22 (2)**

colegio católico *m.* catholic school **22 (2)**

escuela particular *f.* private school **22 (2)**

escuela pública *f.* public school **22 (2)**

escuela secundaria *f.* high school; middle school (in Mexico) **22 (2)**

preparatoria (prepa) *f.* high school **22 (2)**

primaria *f.* elementary school **22 (2)**

esculpir *v.* to sculpt

escultor(a) *m., f.* sculptor

escultura *f.* sculpture

ese *m., sing., adj.* that **6 (1)**

ése *m., sing., pron.* that (one)

eso *neuter, pron.* that; that thing

esos *m., pl., adj.* those **6 (1)**

ésos *m., pl., pron.* those (ones)

espagueti *m.* spaghetti **9 (1)**

espalda *f.* back **21 (2)**

España *f.* Spain

español *m.* Spanish (language) **1 (1)**

español(a) *adj.* Spanish

espárragos *m., pl.* asparagus

especialización *f.* field of study; specialization

espectacular *adj.* spectacular

espectáculo *m.* show

espejo *m.* mirror **18 (2)**

esperar *v.* to wait (for); to hope; to wish **27 (2)**

esposo/a *m., f.* husband/wife; spouse **4 (1)**

esquí (acuático) *m.* (water) skiing

esquiar *v.* to ski **18 (2)**

esquina *m.* corner **26 (2)**

está he/she/it is, you are *form.*

Está despejado. It's clear. *(weather)*

Está (muy) nublado. It's (very) cloudy. *(weather)* **13 (1)**

Está bien. That's fine.

esta(s) *f., adj.* this; these **6 (1)**

esta noche tonight **7 (1)**

ésta(s) *f., pron.* this (one); these (ones)

Ésta es… *f.* This is… (introducing someone)

establecer *v.* to establish

estación *f.* station; season

estación de autobuses bus station

estación del metro subway station

estación del tren train station

estacionamiento *m.* parking lot 2 (1)
estacionar *v.* to park
 estacionarse *v.* **enfrente de** to park in front of 26 (2)
estadio *m.* stadium 2 (1)
estado civil *m.* marital status
Estados Unidos *m.* (EE.UU.) United States
estadounidense *adj.* from the United States
estampado/a *adj.* print
estampilla *f.* stamp
estante *m.* bookcase; bookshelf
estar *v.* to be 20 (2)
 estar a (veinte kilómetros) de aquí to be (kilometers) from here
 estar a dieta to be on a diet
 estar aburrido/a to be bored 15 (1)
 estar adentro/dentro de to be inside 15 (1)
 estar adolorido/a to be sore 21 (2)
 estar afectado/a (por) to be affected (by)
 estar afuera/fuera de to be outside 15 (1)
 estar arreglado/a to be tidy 18 (2)
 estar bajo control to be under control
 estar cansado/a to be tired 15 (1)
 estar contaminado/a to be polluted
 estar de acuerdo to agree
 estar de moda to be in fashion
 estar de vacaciones to be on vacation 15 (1)
 estar desarreglado/a to be messy 18 (2)
 estar en to be at/in/on 8 (1)
 estar en buena forma to be in good shape
 estar en cama to be in bed 15 (1)
 estar en clase to be in class 15 (1)
 estar enfermo/a to be sick 15 (1)
 estar limpio/a to be clean 18 (2)
 estar listo/a to be ready
 estar mareado/a to be dizzy 21 (2)
 estar perdido/a to be lost
 estar roto/a to be broken
 estar seguro/a (de) to be sure (of)
 estar sucio/a to be dirty 18 (2)
 estar torcido/a to be twisted; to be sprained
estatua *f.* statue
este *m.* east 26 (2); umm
este *m., sing., adj.* this 6 (1)
 este lunes/jueves (etc.) this Monday/Tuesday (etc.) 7 (1)

éste *m., sing., pron.* this (one)
 Éste es... *m.* This is... *(introducing someone)*
estéreo *m.* stereo
estilo *m.* style
estiramiento *m.* stretching
esto *neuter, pron.* this; this thing
estómago *m.* stomach 21 (2)
estornudar *v.* to sneeze
estos *m., pl., adj.* these 6 (1)
éstos *m., pl., pron.* these (ones)
estrella *f.* star
 estrella de cine *m., f.* movie star
estrés *m.* stress
estresado/a *adj.* stressed 15 (1)
estudiante *m., f.* student 2 (1)
estudiantil *adj. m., f.* student
estudiar *v.* to study
 estudiar mucho/poco to study a lot/a little 5 (1)
estudioso/a *adj.* studious 3 (1)
estufa *f.* stove 18 (2)
estupendo/a *adj.* stupendous
etapa *f.* stage; step
evitar *v.* to avoid
 evitar *v.* **las multas** to avoid fines; tickets 26 (2)
examen *m.* test; exam
 examen médico physical exam
excelente *adj.* excellent 3 (1)
exceso *m.* excess; too much
excursión *f.* hike; tour; excursion 18 (2)
excursionista *m., f.* hiker
exhibición de arte *f.* art exhibition 8 (1)
éxito *m.* success
experiencia *f.* experience
explicar *v.* to explain 24 (2)
explorar *v.* to explore
 explorar un pueblo to explore a town
 explorar una ciudad to explore a city
expresión *f.* expression
extinción *f.* extinction
extranjero/a *adj.* foreign
extraño/a *adj.* strange
extrovertido/a *adj.* extrovert; outgoing 3 (1)

F

fábrica *f.* factory
fabuloso/a *adj* fabulous
fácil *adj.* easy 6 (1)
 facilísimo extremely easy
falda *f.* skirt
faltar *v.* to lack; to need
familia *f.* family
familiares *m., pl* relatives 4 (1)
famoso/a *adj.* famous
farmacia *f.* pharmacy

fascinar *v.* to fascinate; to like very much; to love (to be fascinated by) 19 (2)
fatal *adj.* (*accident/injury/illness*) horrible 21 (2); mortal
favorito/a *adj.* favorite
fax *m.* fax (machine)
febrero *m.* February 13 (1)
fecha *f.* date
feliz *adj.* happy 20 (2)
 ¡Felicidades! Congratulations! *(for an event such as a birthday or anniversary)*
 ¡Felicitaciones! Congratulations! *(for an event such as an engagement or a good grade on a test)*
 ¡Feliz cumpleaños! Happy birthday!
 ponerse *v.* **feliz** to get/become happy 20 (2)
fenomenal *adj.* great; phenomenal
feo/a *adj.* ugly 6 (1)
festival *m.* festival
fiebre *f.* fever 21 (2)
 tener (la) fiebre to have a fever 21 (2)
fiesta *f.* party 18 (2)
 hacer una fiesta to throw a party 18 (2)
fijo/a *adj.* set, fixed
filosofía *f.* philosophy 1 (1)
fin *m.* end
 fin de semana weekend
finalmente *adv.* finally
firmar *v.* to sign (*a document*)
física *f.* physics
 fisioterapeuta *m., f.* physical therapist 12 (1)
flan *m.* baked custard; flan 9 (1)
flexible *adj.* flexible 3 (1)
flor *f.* flower
folklórico/a *adj.* folk; folkloric
folleto *m.* brochure
fondo *m.* end
forma *f.* shape
formal *adj.* formal 20 (2)
formulario *m.* form
foto(grafía) *f.* photograph
francés, francesa *adj.* French
frecuentemente *adv.* frequently
fregadero *m.* sink (*in a kitchen*) 18 (2)
frenar *v.* to brake 26 (2)
frenos *m., pl.* brakes
fresco/a *adj.* cool
frijoles *m., pl.* beans 9 (1)
frío *m.* cold
fritada *f.* fried dish (pork, fish, etc.)
frito/a *adj.* fried
fruta *f.* fruit 9 (1)
frutería *f.* fruit shop
frutilla *f.* strawberry
fuente de fritada *f.* platter of fried food

fuegos artificiales *pl., m.* fireworks 20 (2)

fuera *adv.* outside

fuerte *adj.* strong

fumar *v.* to smoke 19 (2)
  no fumar not to smoke 19 (2)

funcionar *v.* to work; to function

fútbol *m.* soccer
  partido de fútbol *m.* soccer game 8 (1)

fútbol americano football

futuro/a *adj.* future
  en el futuro in the future

G

gafas (de sol) *f., pl.* (sun)glasses

gafas (oscuras) *f., pl.* (sun)glasses

galleta *f.* cookie 9 (1)

ganar *v.* to win; to earn (money)
  ganar *v.* **bien** to make a good living, to make good money 12 (1)

ganga *f.* bargain

garaje *m.* garage 18 (2); (mechanic's) repair shop; garage

garganta *f.* throat 21 (2)

gasolina *f.* gasoline 26 (2)
  quedarse *v.* **sin gasolina** to run out of gas 26 (2)

gasolinera *f.* gas station

gastar *v.* to spend (money) 19 (2)

gato/a *m., f.* cat 4 (1), 18 (2)
  darle de comer al gato to feed the cat 18 (2)

generoso/a *adj.* generous 3 (1)

gente *f.* people

geografía *f.* geography 1 (1)

gerente *m., f.* manager 12 (1)

gimnasio *m.* gym, gymnasium 2 (1)

gobierno *m.* government 28 (2)

golf *m.* golf

golpe *m.* bump, blow, dent 25 (2)

gordo/a *adj.* fat 6 (1)

grabadora *f.* tape recorder

gracias *f., pl.* thank you; thanks 1 (1)
  Gracias por todo. Thanks for everything.
  Gracias una vez más. Thanks once again.

gracioso/a *adj.* funny 6 (1)

graduación *f.* graduation 28 (2)

graduarse (de) *v.* to graduate (from)

gran, grande *adj.* big; large 6 (1); great

grasa *f.* fat

gratis *adj.* free of charge

grave *adj.* grave; serious

gravísimo/a *adj.* extremely serious

grillo *m.* cricket

gripe *f.* flu 21 (2)
  tener (la) gripe to have the flu 21 (2)

gris *adj.* gray 13 (1)

gritar *v.* to scream

grosero/a *adj.* rude 6 (1)

guantes *m., pl.* gloves 13 (1)

guapo/a *adj.* handsome; good-looking 6 (1)

guardar *v.* to save (on a computer)

guerra *f.* war

guía *m., f.* guide

gustar *v.* to be pleasing to; to like 19 (2)
  Me gustaría(n)… I would like…

gusto *m.* pleasure
  El gusto es mío. The pleasure is mine.
  Gusto de (+ *inf.*) It's a pleasure to…
  Mucho gusto. Pleased to meet you.

H

haber (aux.) *v.* to have (*done something*)
  ha sido un placer it's been a pleasure

habitación *f.* room
  habitación doble double room
  habitación individual single room

habitantes *m., pl.* inhabitants

hablar *v.* to talk; to speak 5 (1)
  hablar con los amigos to talk with friends 5 (1)
  hablar por teléfono to talk on the phone 5 (1)

hacer *v.* to do; to make 8 (1), 20 (2)
  Hace buen tiempo It's nice weather; The weather is good. 13 (1)
  Hace (mucho) calor. It's (very) hot. (*weather*) 13 (1)
  Hace (tres) días que (yo)… (I) have been… for (three) days 21 (2)
  Hace (dos) semanas/meses/años (two) weeks/months/years ago 15 (1), 17 (2)
  Hace fresco. It's cool. (*weather*) 13 (1)
  Hace (mucho) frío It's (very) cold. (*weather*) 13 (1)
  Hace mal tiempo It's bad weather; The weather is bad. 13 (1)
  Hace (mucho) sol. It's (very) sunny. (*weather*) 13 (1)
  Hace (mucho) viento. It's (very) windy. (*weather*) 13 (1)
  hacer *v.* **berrinches** to throw tantrums 22 (2)
  hacer cola to stand in line
  hacer diligencias to do errands; to run errands
  hacer ejercicio to exercise 8 (1)
  hacer ejercicios aeróbicos to do aerobics
  hacer ejercicios de estiramiento to do stretching exercises

hacer el papel to play a role

hacer gimnasia to work out

hacer juego (con) to match

hacer la cama to make the bed 18 (2)

hacer la tarea to do homework 8 (1)

hacer las maletas to pack (one's suitcases) 20 (2)

hacer los quehaceres domésticos to do household chores

hacer *v.* **travesuras** to get into trouble 22 (2)

hacer turismo to go sightseeing

hacer una excursión to go on a hike 18 (2); to go on a tour

hacer una fiesta to throw a party 18 (2)

hacer un picnic to have a picnic 18 (2)

hacer un viaje to take a trip 18 (2)

hacha *f.* ax

hacia *prep.* toward

hambre *f.* hunger

hamburguesa *f.* hamburger 8 (1), 9 (1)

hasta *prep.* until; toward
  hasta ahora until now, so far 28 (2)
  hasta el momento until this moment 28 (2)
  Hasta la vista See you later.
  Hasta luego See you later. 1 (1)
  Hasta mañana See you tomorrow 1 (1)
  hasta que until 30 (2)
  Hasta pronto. See you soon.

hay there is; there are 2 (1)
  Hay (mucha) contaminación. It's (very) smoggy.
  Hay (mucha) niebla. It's (very) foggy.
  Hay que It is necessary that
  No hay duda de There's no doubt
  No hay de qué. You're welcome.

hecho/a *p.p.* done 28 (2)

heladería *f.* ice cream shop

helado/a *adj.* iced

helado *m.* ice cream 9 (1)

hermanastro/a *m., f.* stepbrother/stepsister

hermano/a *m., f.* brother/sister 4 (1)
  hermano/a mayor/menor *m., f.* older/younger brother/sister
  hermanos *m., pl.* siblings (brothers and sisters) 4 (1)

hermoso/a *adj.* beautiful

hierba *f.* grass

higienista dental *m., f.* dental hygienist 12 (1)

hijastro/a *m., f.* stepson/stepdaughter

hijo/a *m., f.* son/daughter 4 (1)
  hijo/a único/a only child 4 (1)

hijos *m., pl.* children 4 (1)
historia *f.* history 1 (1); story
hockey *m.* hockey
hogar *m.* home
hola *interj.* hello; hi 1 (1)
hombre *m.* man
  hombre de negocios businessman
honesto/a *adj.* honest; honorable
  3 (1)
hora *f.* hour
horario *m.* schedule
  el horario flexible/fijo flexible/fixed
  schedule 11 (1)
horno *m.* oven 18 (2)
  horno de microondas microwave
  oven
hospital *m.* hospital
hotel *m.* hotel
hoy *adv.* today 7 (1)
  hoy día nowadays
  Hoy es... Today is…
huelga *f.* strike (labor)
hueso *m.* bone
huésped *m., f.* guest
huevo *m.* egg 9 (1)
humanidades *f., pl.* humanities
huracán *m.* hurricane

I

ida *f.* one way *(travel)*
idea *f.* idea
idealista *adj.* idealistic 3 (1)
iglesia *f.* church 8 (1)
igual *adj.* the same 21 (2)
  sentirse(e:ie) igual feel the same
  21 (2)
igualdad *f.* equality
igualmente *adv.* Nice to meet you,
  too. 1 (1)
impaciente *m., f.* impatient 3 (1)
impermeable *m.* raincoat 13 (1)
importante *adj.* important
importar *v.* to be important (to); to
  matter
imposible *adj.* impossible
impresora *f.* printer
imprimir *v.* to print
improbable *adj.* improbable
impuesto *m.* tax
incendio *m.* fire
increíble *adj.* incredible 3 (1)
indicar cómo llegar *v.* to give
  directions
individual *adj.* private (room)
infección *f.* infection 21 (2)
  tener una Infección to have an
  infection 21 (2)
informar *v.* to inform
informal *adj.* informal 20 (2)
informe *m.* report; paper *(written
  work)*
ingeniero/a *m., f.* engineer
  ingeniero/a ambientalista *m., f.*
  environmental engineer 12 (1)

ingeniero/a en computación *m., f.*
  computer engineer 12 (1)
inglés *m.* English *(language)* 1 (1)
inglés, inglesa *adj.* English
inmaduro/a *adj.* inmature 3 (1)
insistir (en) *v.* to insist (on)
inspector(a) de aduanas *m., f.*
  customs inspector
inteligente *adj.* intelligent
intercambiar *v.* exchange
interesante *adj.* interesting 3 (1)
interesar *v.* to be interesting to; to
  interest; to be interested in 19 (2)
internacional *adj.* international
Internet *m.* Internet
intersección *f.* intersection 26 (2)
inundación *f.* flood
invertir (e:ie) *v.* to invest
investigador(a) forense *m., f.*
  forensic investigator 12 (1)
invierno *m.* winter 13 (1)
invitado/a *m., f.* guest (at a function)
invitar *v.* to invite; to treat 10 (1)
  invitar a alguien to invite someone
  20 (2)
  invitar a salir to ask someone out
  11 (1)
inyección *f.* injection
ir *v.* to go 20 (2)
  ir a (+ inf.) to be going to do
  something 7 (1)
  ir a (+ place) to go to 8 (1)
  ir *v.* **a exceso de velocidad** to
  speed 26 (2)
  ir a la playa to go to the beach
  ir de campamento to go camping
  18 (2)
  ir de compras to go shopping
  ir de excursión (a las montañas) to
  go for a hike (in the mountains)
  18 (2)
  ir de pesca to go fishing
  ir de vacaciones to go on vacation
  ir en autobús to go by bus
  ir en auto(móvil) to go by car; to
  go by auto(mobile) 20 (2)
  ir en avión to go by plane 20 (2)
  ir en barco to go by ship
  ir *v.* **en coche** to go by car 20 (2)
  ir en metro to go by subway
  ir en motocicleta to go by
  motorcycle
  ir en taxi to go by taxi
  ir en tren to go by train
irresponsable *adj.* irresponsible 3 (1)
irse *v.* to go away; to leave 14 (1)
  irse *v.* **de vacaciones** to go on
  vacation 14 (1)
italiano/a *adj.* Italian
izquierdo/a *adj.* left
  a la izquierda de to the left of
  del/al lado izquierdo from/on
  the left side 23 (2)

J

jabón *m.* soap
jamás *adv.* never; not ever
jamón *m.* ham 9 (1)
japonés, japonesa *adj.* Japanese
jarabe para la tos *m.* cough syrup
  21 (2)
jardín *m.* garden; yard 18 (2)
jeans *m., pl.* jeans 13 (1)
jefe, jefa *m., f.* boss 11 (1)
joven *adj.* young 6 (1)
joven *m., f.* youth; young person
joyería *f.* jewelry store 27 (2)
jubilarse *v.* to retire (from work)
juego *m.* game
jueves *m., sing.* Thursday 5 (1)
  los jueves *m., pl.* on Thursdays
  5 (1)
jugador(a) *m., f.* player
jugar (u:ue) *v.* to play 10 (1), 22 (2)
  jugar a las cartas to play cards
  jugar a las damas chinas to play
  checkers 22 (2)
  jugar a las escondidillas/al escondite
  to play hide-and-seek 22 (2)
  jugar a las muñecas to play with
  dolls 22 (2)
  jugar Nintendo to play Nintendo
  22 (2)
  jugar a la pelota to play ball
  22 (2)
jugo *m.* juice
  jugo de fruta fruit juice
  jugo de naranja *m.* orange juice
  9 (1)
juguete *m.* toy 22 (2)
julio *m.* July 13 (1)
jungla *f.* jungle
junio *m.* June 13 (1)
juntarse *v.* to get together 14 (1)
juntos/as *adj.* together
juventud *f.* youth

K

kilómetro *m.* kilometer

L

la *f., sing., def. art.* the
la *f., sing., d.o. pron.* her, it, 2 (1)
  form. you
laboratorio *m.* laboratory
lado *m.* side 23 (2)
  del/al lado derecho from/on the
  right side 23 (2)
  del/al lado izquierdo from/on the
  left side 23 (2)
lago *m.* lake
lámpara *f.* lamp 18 (2)
lana *f.* wool
langosta *f.* lobster 9 (1)
lápiz *m.* pencil 2 (1)

largo/a *m.* long *(in length)*
las *f., pl., def. art.* the **2 (1)**
las *f., pl., d.o. pron.* them; *form.* you
lástima *f.* shame
lastimarse *v.* to injure/hurt oneself **21 (2)**
  lastimarse el pie to injure one's foot
lata *f.* *(tin)* can
lavabo *m.* sink *(in a bathroom)* **18 (2)**
lavadora *f.* washing machine
lavandería *f.* laundromat
lavaplatos *m., sing.* dishwasher
lavar *v.* to wash
  lavar el coche to wash the car **5 (1)**
  lavar la ropa to do the laundry **5 (1)**
  lavar los platos to do (wash) the dishes **18 (2)**
lavarse *v.* to wash oneself
  lavarse la cara to wash one's face **14 (1)**
  lavarse las manos to wash one's hands **14 (1)**
  lavarse los dientes to brush one's teeth **14 (1)**
le *sing., i.o. pron.* to/for him, her, you *form.* **19 (2)**
  Le presento a… *form.* I would like to introduce… to you. **1 (1)**
  ¿Le gusta(n)…? *form.* Do you like… ? **3 (1)**
lección *f.* lesson
leche *f.* milk **9 (1)**
lechuga *f.* lettuce
leer *v.* to read **8 (1), 17 (2)**
  leer el correo electrónico to read e-mail
  leer un periódico to read a newspaper **8 (1)**
  leer una revista to read a magazine
leído/a *p.p.* read
lejos de *prep.* far from
lengua *f.* language
  lenguas extranjeras *f., pl.* foreign languages
lentes de contacto *m., pl.* contact lenses
  lentes de sol *m., pl.* sunglasses **13 (1)**
lento/a *adj.* slow
les *pl., i.o. pron.* to/for them, you *form.* **19 (2)**
letrero *m.* sign
levantar *v.* to lift
  levantar pesas to lift weights **18 (2)**
levantarse *v.* to get up
  levantarse *v.* **temprano** get up early **14 (1)**
ley *f.* law
libertad *f.* liberty; freedom
libre *adj.* free

librería *f.* bookstore **2 (1)**
libro *m.* book **2 (1)**
licencia de conducir/manejar *f.* driver's license **26 (2)**
limón *m.* lemon
limonada *f.* lemonade **9 (1)**
limpiar *v.* to clean
  limpiar el cuarto to clean the (one's) room **5 (1)**
  limpiar la casa to clean the house **5 (1)**
limpio/a *adj.* clean **18 (2)**
  estar limpio/a to be clean **18 (2)**
línea *f.* line
líquido *m.* liquid **21 (2)**
listo/a *adj.* smart **6 (1)**; ready
literatura *f.* literature **1 (1)**
llamar *v.* to call **11 (1)**
  llamar a la policía call the police **23 (2)**
  llamar por teléfono to call on the phone
  llamarse to be called; to be named
llanta *f.* tire **26 (2)**
  revisar *v.* **las llantas** to check the tires **26 (2)**
llave *f.* key
llegada *f.* arrival
llegar *v.* to arrive
  llegar a tiempo/tarde/temprano a casa to get home on time/late/early **5 (1)**
llenar *v.* to fill
  llenar el tanque to fill up the tank
  llenar un formulario to fill out a form
  llenar una solicitud to fill out an application **28 (2)**
lleno/a *adj.* full
llevar *v.* to carry; to take; to wear **13 (1)**; to bring
  llevar a (+ *person/object.***)** to bring (someone/an animal/something inanimate) **7 (1)**
  llevar *v.* **algo** take something **24 (2)**
  llevar una vida sana to lead a healthy lifestyle
  llevarse bien/mal (con) to get along well/badly (with) **22 (2)**
llorón/llorona *m., f.* crybaby **22 (2)**
  ser llorón/llorona to be a crybaby **22 (2)**
llover (o:ue) *v.* to rain **13 (1)**
  Llueve. It's raining; It rains **13 (1)**
lluvia *f.* rain
lo *m., sing. d.o. pronoun* him, it, you *form.*
  lo mejor the best (thing)
  Lo pasamos de película. We had a great time.
  lo peor the worst (thing)
  lo que what; that; which
  Lo siento. I'm sorry.
  Lo siento muchísimo. I'm so sorry.
loco/a *adj.* crazy

locutor(a) *m., f.* TV or radio announcer
lomo a la plancha *m.* grilled flank steak
los *m., pl., def. art.* the
los *m., pl., do. pron.* them; you *form.*
luchar (contra), (por) *v.* to fight; to struggle (against), (for)
luego *adv.* afterwards; then; later
lugar *m.* place
luna *f.* moon
lunar *m.* polka dot; mole
lunes *m., sing.* Monday **5 (1)**
  los lunes *m., pl.* on Mondays **5 (1)**
luz *f.* light; electricity

M

madrastra *f.* stepmother
madre *f.* mother
madurez *f.* maturity; middle age
maduro/a *adj.* mature **3 (1)**
maestría *f.* Master's degree **28 (2)**
maestro/a *m., f.* teacher *(elementary school)* **12 (1)**
magnífico/a *adj.* magnificent
maíz *m.* corn
mal, malo/a *adj.* bad **6 (1)**; sick; ill **21 (2)**
  malísimo very bad
maleta *f.* suitcase **13 (1), 20 (2)**
mamá *f.* mom
mandar *v.* to order; to send; to mail **24 (2)**
  mandar *v.* **mensajes** to send text messages **11 (1)**
  mandar un regalo to send a present **11 (1)**
manejar *v.* to drive **10 (1)**
  manejar *v.* **a excceso de velocidad** to speed **26 (2)**
manera *f.* way
mano *f.* hand **21 (2)**
  ¡Manos arriba! Hands up!
manta *f.* blanket
mantener *v.* to maintain
  mantenerse en forma to stay in shape
mantequilla *f.* butter
manzana *f.* apple **9 (1)**
mañana *f.* morning, A.M.; tomorrow **7 (1)**
  esta mañana this morning **15 (1)**
  por la mañana in the morning **5 (1)**
mañanitas *f., pl.* birthday song **20 (2)**
mapa *m.* map **2 (1)**
maquillaje *m.* makeup
  pintarse *v.* to put on makeup **14 (1)**
maquillarse *v.* to put on makeup
mar *m.* ocean; sea

maravilloso/a *adj.* marvelous
mareado/a *adj.* dizzy; nauseated 21 (2)
   estar mareado/a to be dizzy 21 (2)
margarina *f.* margarine
mariscos *m., pl.* seafood 9 (1)
marrón *adj. m., f.* brown 13 (1)
martes *m., sing.* Tuesday 5 (1)
   los martes *m., pl.* on Tuesdays 5 (1)
marzo *m.* March 13 (1)
más *adj.* more
   el/la/los/las más the most
   más de (+ number) more than (+ number)
   más o menos *adv.* so-so 1 (1)
   más tarde later (on)
   más... que more... than 17 (2)
masaje *m.* massage
matemáticas *f., pl.* mathematics 1 (1)
materia *f.* course
materialista *adj.* materialistic 3 (1)
matrimonio *m.* marriage; married couple
máximo/a *m., f.* maximum
mayo *m.* May 13 (1)
mayonesa *f.* mayonnaise
mayor *adj.* older; bigger 6 (1)
   el/la mayor *adj.* the oldest; the biggest
me *pron.* me; *i.o. pron.* to/for me 19 (2)
   Me duele mucho It hurts me a lot
   Me gusta(n)... I like... 3 (1)
   No me gusta(n)... I don't like... 3 (1)
   Me gustaría(n)... I would like...
   Me llamo... My name is...
   Me muero por... I'm dying to (for)...
mecánico/a *m., f.* mechanic
mediano/a *adj.* medium
medianoche *f.* midnight
medias *f., pl.* pantyhose, stockings
medicamento *m.* medication
medicina *f.* medicine
médico/a *m., f.* doctor; physician 12 (1); *adj.* medical
medio/a *m. adj.* half
   medio ambiente environment
   medio/a hermano/a half-brother/half-sister
   medios de comunicación *m., pl.* means of communication; media
   y media thirty minutes past the hour (time)
mediodía *m.* noon
mejor *adj.* better 21 (2)
   el/la mejor *m., f.* the best
   mejor que *adj.* better than 17 (2)
   sentirse (e:ie) mejor feel better 21 (2)
mejorar *v.* to improve

melocotón *m.* peach
menor *adj.* younger 6 (1); smaller
   el/la menor *m., f.* the youngest; the smallest
menos *adv.* less
   el/la/los/las menos the least
   menos cuarto/menos quince quarter to *(time)*
   menos de (+ number) less than (+ number)
   menos... que less... than 17 (2)
mensaje de texto text message
mensaje electrónico *m.* e-mail message
mentira *f.* lie 24 (2)
   decir *v.* **mentiras** to lie 24 (2)
menú *m.* menu
mercado *m.* market
   mercado al aire libre open-air market
merendar (e:ie) *v.* to snack in the afternoon; to have a(n) (afternoon) snack
merienda *f.* (afternoon) snack
mes *m.* month 13 (1)
   el mes pasado last month 15 (1), 17 (2)
mesa *f.* table 18 (2)
   mesa *f.* **de noche** night table 18 (2)
   mesita *f.* side table 18 (2)
   poner *v.* **la mesa** to set the table 18 (2)
mesero/a *m., f.* waiter/waitress 9 (1), 11 (1)
mesita *f.* end table; side table 18 (2)
   mesita de noche night stand
metro *m.* subway
mexicano/a *adj.* Mexican
México *m.* Mexico
mí *pron. obj. of prep.* me 19 (2)
mi(s) *poss. adj.* my 4 (1)
microonda *f.* microwave oven 18 (2)
   horno de microondas microwave oven
miedo *m.* fear
mientras *adv.* while
miércoles *m., sing.* Wednesday 5 (1)
   los miércoles *m., pl.* on Wednesdays 5 (1)
mil one thousand
   mil millones billion
   Mil perdones. I'm so sorry. *(lit. A thousand pardons.)*
milla *f.* mile
millón million
millones (de) millions (of)
mineral *m.* mineral
minifalda *f.* mini-skirt 13 (1)
minuto *m.* minute
mío(s)/a(s) *poss.* my; (of) mine
mirar *v.* to look (at); to watch

mirar (la) televisión to watch television 5 (1)
misa *f.* Mass; religious service 8 (1)
mismo/a *adj.* same
mochila *f.* backpack 2 (1)
moda *f.* fashion
módem *m.* modem
moderno/a *adj.* modern 20 (2)
molestar *v.* to bother; to annoy; to be bothered by 19 (2)
molesto/a *adj.* upset 15 (1)
monitor *m.* monitor
mono *m.* monkey
montaña *f.* mountain
montar *v.* **a caballo** to ride a horse 18 (2)
monumento *m.* monument
mora *f.* blackberry
morado/a *adj.* purple 13 (1)
moreno/a *adj.* dark (skin/hair) 6 (1)
morir (o:ue) *v.* to die
mostrar (o:ue) *v.* to show
moto(cicleta) *f.* motorcycle
motor *m.* motor
muchacho/a *m., f.* boy; girl
mucho/a *adj., adv.* many; a lot of; much
   muchas veces a lot; many times
   Muchísimas gracias. Thank you very, very much.
   muchísimo *adj., adv.* very much
   Mucho gusto Pleased to meet you. 1 (1)
   (Muchas) gracias Thank you (very much); Thanks (a lot).
mudarse *v.* to move (from one house to another) 28 (2)
muebles *m., pl.* furniture 18 (2)
muela *f.* tooth
muerte *f.* death
muerto/a *p.p.* died 28 (2)
mujer *f.* woman
   mujer de negocios business woman
   mujer policía female police officer
multa *f.* fine; ticket 26 (2)
   evitar *v.* **las multas** to avoid fines; tickets 26 (2)
mundial *adj.* worldwide
mundo *m.* world
municipal *adj.* municipal
muñeca *f.* doll 22 (2)
   jugar a las muñecas to play with dolls 22 (2)
músculo *m.* muscle
museo *m.* museum 8 (1)
música *f.* music 1 (1)
musical *adj.* musical
músico/a *m., f.* musician
muy *adv.* very
   Muy amable. That's very kind of you.
   Muy bien. Very well. 1 (1)

N

nacer *v.* to be born
nacimiento *m.* birth
nacional *adj.* national
nacionalidad *f.* nationality
nada *pron., adv.* nothing; not anything **18 (2)**
  nada mal not bad at all
nadar *v.* to swim **18 (2)**
nadie *pron.* no one, not anyone **18 (2)**
naranja *m.* orange **13 (1)**
nariz *f.* nose **21 (2)**
natación *f.* swimming
natural *adj.* natural
naturaleza *f.* nature
navegador GPS GPS
navegar en Internet *v.* to surf the Internet
Navidad *f.* Christmas
necesario/a *adj.* necessary
necesitar *v.* to need
  necesitar libros to need books **5 (1)**
negar (e:ie) *v.* to deny
negativo/a *m.* negative
negocios *m., pl.* business; commerce
negro/a *adj.* black **13 (1)**
nervioso/a *adj.* nervous **3 (1)**, **15 (1)**
nevar (e:ie) *v.* to snow **13 (1)**
  Nieva. It's snowing; It snows. **13 (1)**
ni…ni *conj.* neither… nor
niebla *f.* fog
nieto/a *m., f.* grandson/granddaughter **4 (1)**
nieve *f.* snow
ningún, ninguno/a(s) *adj.* no; none; not any **18 (2)**
  Ningún problema. No problem.
  ninguna parte, (a) *adv.* nowhere **8 (1)**
niñero/a *m., f.* baby-sitter **11 (1)**
niñez *f.* childhood
niño/a *m., f.* child; boy/girl **4 (1)**
  de niño/a as a child **22 (2)**
no *adv.* no; not
  No cabe duda de There is no doubt
  No es así. That's not the way it is.
  No es para tanto. It's not a big deal.
  No es seguro… It's not sure…
  No es verdad… It's not true…
  No está. It's not here.
  No está nada mal. It's not bad at all.
  no estar de acuerdo to disagree
  no estar seguro/a (de) not to be sure (of)
  No estoy seguro. I'm not sure.
  no hay there is not; there are not
  No hay de qué. You're welcome.
  No hay duda de There is no doubt

  ¡No me diga(s)! You don't say!
  No me gustan nada. I don't like them at all.
  no muy bien not very well
  ¿no? right?
  no quiero I don't want to
  no sé I don't know
  No te/se preocupe(s). Don't worry.
  no tener razón to be wrong
noche *f.* night
nombre *m.* name
norte *m.* north **26 (2)**
norteamericano/a *adj.* (North) American
nos *pron.* us; *pl., i.o. pron.* to/for us
  Nos vemos mañana. See you tomorrow. **1 (1)**
nosotros/as *sub. pron.* we; *ob. pron.* us
noticias *f., pl.* news
noticiero *m.* newscast
novecientos/as nine hundred
noveno/a *adj.* ninth
noventa ninety **4 (1)**
noviembre *m.* November **13 (1)**
novio/a *m., f.* boyfriend/girlfriend **4 (1)**
nube *f.* cloud
nublado/a *adj.* cloudy
  Está (muy) nublado. It's (very) cloudy. **13 (1)**
nuclear *adj.* nuclear
nuera *f.* daughter-in-law
nuestro(s)/a(s) *poss. adj.* our; of ours **4 (1)**
nueve nine **1 (1)**
nuevo/a *adj.* new **6 (1)**
número *m.* number; (shoe) size
nunca *adj.* never; not ever **8 (1)**, **18 (2)**
nutrición *f.* nutrition

O

o *conj.* or
o… o *conj.* either . . . or
obedecer (c:zc) *v.* to obey **22 (2)**
  obedecer (c:zc) *v.* **las señales de tránsito** to obey the traffic signs **26 (2)**
obra *f.* work *(of art, literature, music, etc.)*
  obra maestra masterpiece
obtener *v.* to obtain; to get
obvio/a *adj.* obvious
océano *m.* ocean; sea
ochenta eighty **4 (1)**
ocho eight **1 (1)**
ochocientos/as eight hundred
octavo/a *adj.* eighth
octubre *m.* October **13 (1)**
ocupación *f.* occupation
ocupado/a *adj.* busy **15 (1)**
ocurrir *v.* to occur; to happen
odiar *v.* to hate

oeste *m.* west **26 (2)**
oferta *f.* offer
oficial de prisión *m., f.* prison guard; parole officer **12 (1)**
oficina *f.* office **2 (1)**
oficio *m.* trade
ofrecer (c:zc) *v.* to offer **24 (2)**
oído *m.* sense of hearing; inner ear **21 (2)**
oído *p.p.* heard
oír *v.* to hear **17 (2)**
  oiga *form., sing.* listen *(in conversation)*
  oigan *form., pl.* listen *(in conversation)*
  Oye *fam., sing.* listen *(in conversation)*
ojalá (que) *interj.* I hope (that); I wish (that) **27 (2)**
ojo *m.* eye **21 (2)**
olvidar *v.* to forget
once eleven **1 (1)**
ópera *f.* opera
operación *f.* operation
optimista *adj.* optimistic **3 (1)**
ordenado/a *adj.* orderly; well organized **6 (1)**
ordinal *adj.* ordinal (number)
oreja *f.* (outer) ear
orquesta *f.* orchestra
ortográfico/a *adj.* spellling
os *fam., pl. pron.* you
otoño *m.* fall, autumn **13 (1)**
otro/a *adj.* other; another
  otra vez again

P

paciente *m., f.* patient **3 (1)**
padrastro *m.* stepfather
padre *m.* father **4 (1)**
  padres *m., pl.* parents **4 (1)**
pagar *v.* to pay **11 (1)**, **24 (2)**
  pagar a plazos to pay in installments
  pagar al contado to pay in cash
  pagar con to pay with
  pagar en efectivo to pay in cash
  pagar la cuenta to pay the bill
  pagar la cuenta del celular to pay the cell phone bill **7 (1)**
página *f.* page
  página principal home page
país *m.* country
paisaje *m.* landscape; countryside
pájaro *m.* bird **4 (1)**
palabra *f.* word
pan *m.* bread
  pan tostado toasted bread; toast **9 (1)**
panadería *f.* bakery
pantalla *f.* screen
pantalones *m., pl.* pants **13 (1)**
  pantalones cortos shorts **13 (1)**

papa *f.* potato
papa al horno *f.* baked potato 9 (1)
papas fritas *f., pl.* French fries 9 (1)
papá *m.* dad
papás *m., pl.* parents
papel *m.* paper 2 (1); role
papelera *f.* wastebasket 2 (1)
paquete *m.* package
par *m.* pair
par de zapatos pair of shoes
para *prep.* for; in order to; toward; in the direction of; by; used for; considering
para que so that 30 (2)
parabrisas *m., sing.* windshield
paraguas *m.* umbrella 13 (1)
parar *v.* to stop 26 (2)
parecer *v.* to seem; to appear
pared *f.* wall
pareja *f.* couple; partner
parientes *m., pl.* relatives
parque *m.* park 8 (1)
párrafo *m.* paragraph
parte: de parte de on behalf of
partido *m.* game; match *(sports)*
partido de fútbol *m.* soccer game 8 (1)
pasado/a *adj.* last; past
pasado *p.p.* passed
pasaje *m.* ticket
pasaje de ida y vuelta *m.* round-trip ticket
pasajero/a *m., f.* passenger
pasaporte *m.* passport
pasar *v.* to go through; to pass 20 (2)
pasar (dos) semáforos to pass (two) traffic lights 26 (2)
pasar *v.* **el día** to spend the day 20 (2)
pasar la aspiradora to vacuum 18 (2)
pasar por el banco to go by the bank
pasar por la aduana to go through customs
pasar el tiempo to spend time
pasarlo bien/mal to have a good/bad time
pasarse *v.* **el alto/el semáforo en rojo** run a red light 26 (2)
pasatiempo *m.* pastime, hobby
pasear *v.* to take a walk; to stroll
pasear en bicicleta to ride a bicycle
pasear por la ciudad/el pueblo to walk around the city/town
pasillo *m.* hallway
pastel *m.* cake 9 (1)
pastel de chocolate chocolate cake
pastel de cumpleaños birthday cake
pastelería *f.* pastry shop
pastilla *f.* pill; tablet 21 (2)

pasto *m.* lawn, grass 18 (2)
cortar *v.* **el pasto** to mow the lawn 18 (2)
patata *f.* potato
patatas fritas *f., pl.* French fries
patinar (en línea) *v.* to rollerblade 18 (2)
patinar (sobre hielo) *v.* to (ice) skate 18 (2)
patio *m.* patio 18 (2); yard
pavo *m.* turkey 9 (1)
paz *f.* peace
pedir (e:i) *v.* to ask for; to request; 24 (2) to order *(food)* 9 (1)
pedir (e:i) cosas prestadas to borrow things 11 (1)
pedir prestado to borrow
pedir un préstamo to apply for a loan
peinarse *v.* to comb one's hair
pegarle *v.* **(por atrás)** hit someone (from behind) 25 (2)
pelearse *v.* to fight 22 (2)
película *f.* movie
peligro *m.* danger
peligroso/a *adj.* dangerous
pelirrojo/a *adj.* red-haired 6 (1)
pelo *m.* hair 21 (2)
pelota *f.* ball 22 (2)
jugar a la pelota to play ball 22 (2)
peluquería *f.* hairdressing salon
peluquero/a *m., f.* hairdresser
penicilina *f.* penicillin
pensar (e:ie) *v.* to think 10 (1), 17 (2)
pensar (+ *inf.*) to intend; to plan *(to do something)*
pensar en to think about 10 (1)
pensión *f.* boarding house
peor *adj.* worse 21 (2)
el/la peor the worst
peor que *adj.* worse than 17 (2)
sentirse (e:ie) peor feel worse 21 (2)
pequeño/a *adj.* small 6 (1)
pera *f.* pear 9 (1)
perder (e:ie) *v.* to lose 17 (2); to miss
perdido/a *adj.* lost
Perdón. Pardon me; Excuse me.
perezoso/a *adj.* lazy 6 (1)
perfecto/a *adj.* perfect
periódico *m.* newspaper
periodismo *m.* journalism
periodista *m., f.* journalist 12 (1)
permiso *m.* permission
pero *conf.* but
perro/a *m., f.* dog 4 (1)
persona *f.* person
personaje *m.* character
personaje principal main character
pesas *f., pl.* weights
pesca *f.* fishing
pescadería *f.* fish market
pescado *m.* fish *(cooked)* 9 (1)

pescador(a) *m., f.* fisherman/fisherwoman
pescar *v.* to fish
pesimista *adj.* pessimistic 3 (1)
peso *m.* weight
pez *m.* fish *(live)* 4 (1)
picante *adj.* hot, spicy
picnic *m.* picnic 18 (2)
hacer un picnic to have a picnic 18 (2)
pie *m.* foot 21 (2)
piedra *f.* rock; stone
pierna *f.* leg 21 (2)
pijama *m., f.* pajamas 13 (1)
pimienta *f.* pepper 9 (1)
piña *f.* pineapple
pintar *v.* to paint
pintar *v.* to paint
pintarse *v.* to put on makeup 14 (1)
pintura *f.* painting; picture
piscina *f.* swimming pool 2 (1)
piso *m.* floor *(of a building)*
pizzara *f.* chalkboard
pizzarón *f.* chalkboard 2 (1)
placer *m.* pleasure
Ha sido un placer. It's been a pleasure.
planchar *v.* to iron 18 (2)
planchar *v.* **la ropa** to iron clothes 18 (2)
planes *m., pl.* plans
planta *f.* plant
planta baja ground floor
plástico *m.* plastic
platillo *m.* dish 9 (1)
plato *m.* dish *(in a meal)* 9 (1); *m.* plate
plato principal main dish
lavar los platos to do (wash) the dishes 18 (2)
playa *f.* beach 8 (1)
plazos *m., pl.* periods; time
pluma *f.* pen 2 (1)
población *f.* population
pobre *m., f., adj.* poor 6 (1)
pobreza *f.* poverty
poco/a *adj.* little; few
poder (o:ue) *v.* to be able to; can 10 (1), 20 (2)
poema *m.* poem
poesía *f.* poetry
poeta *m., f.* poet
policía *f.* police (force); *m.* (male) police officer 12 (1), 23 (2)
llamar a la policía call the police 23 (2)
política *f.* politics
político/a *m., f.* politician
pollo *m.* chicken 9 (1)
pollo asado roast chicken
ponchar *v.* to deflate; to get a flat (tire)
poner *v.* to put; to place; to turn on *(electrical appliances)* 20 (2)
poner *v.* **atención** to pay attention 11 (1)

poner *v.* **el árbol** to decorate the tree 20 (2)

poner *v.* **la mesa** to set the table 18 (2)

poner la música muy alta play loud music 23 (2)

poner *v.* **las cosas en su lugar** to place (put) things in their place 11 (1)

poner *v.* **una inyección** to give an injection 24 (2)

ponerse *(+ adj.)* to become *(+ adj.)*; to put on

ponerse *v.* **el cinturón de seguridad** to wear the seat belt 26 (2)

ponerse *v.* **la ropa** to put on/wear clothing 14 (1), 20 (2)

ponerse *v.* **triste/feliz** to get/become sad/happy 20 (2)

por *prep.* in exchange for; for; by; in; through; by means of; along; during; around; in search of; by way of; per

por aquí around here

por avión by plane

por ciento percent

por ejemplo for example

por eso that's why; therefore

Por favor. Please.

por fin finally

por la mañana in the morning 5 (1)

por la noche at night 5 (1)

por la tarde in the afternoon; in the evening 1 (1), 5 (1)

por lo menos at least

¿por qué? why? 6 (1)

por supuesto of course

por teléfono by phone; on the phone

por último finally

porque *conj.* because

portarse *v.* **bien/mal** to behave/ misbehave 22 (2)

portátil *adj.* portable

porvenir *m.* future

posesivo/a *adj.* possessive

posible *adj.* possible

es posible it's possible

no es posible it's not possible

postal *f.* postcard

postre *m.* dessert

practicar *v.* to practice

practicar deportes *m., pl.* to play sports

precio (fijo) *m.* (fixed, set) price

preferir (e:ie) *v.* to prefer 10 (1)

pregunta *f.* question

preguntar *v.* to ask *(a question)*

premio *m.* prize; award

prender *v.* to turn on

prender *v.* **el coche** to turn on the car 26 (2)

prensa *f.* press

preocupado/a (por) *adj.* worried (about) 15 (1)

preocuparse (por) *v.* to worry (about)

preparar *v.* to prepare

preparatoria (prepa) *f.* high school 22 (2)

preposición *f.* preposition

presentación *f.* introduction

presentar *v.* to introduce; to put on *(a performance)*

presiones *f., pl.* pressure

prestaciones *f., pl.* fringe benefits 11 (1)

prestado/a *adj.* borrowed

préstamo *m.* loan

prestar *v.* to lend

prestar *v.* **dinero** to lend money 11 (1), 24 (2)

primaria *f.* elementary school 22 (2)

primavera *f.* spring 13 (1)

primer, primero/a *adj.* first

primo/a *m., f.* cousin 4 (1)

principal *adj.* main

prisa *f.* haste

probable *adj. m., f.* probable

es probable it's probable

no es probable it's not probable

probar (o:ue) *v.* to taste; to try

probarse (o:ue) *v.* to try on

problema *m.* problem

profesión *f.* profession

profesor(a) *m., f.* teacher; professor 1 (1)

profesor(a) de idiomas *m., f.* language professor 12 (1)

programa *m.* program

programa de capacitación training program 28 (2)

programa de computación software

programa de entrevistas talk show

programador(a) *m., f.* computer programmer 12 (1)

prohibir *v.* to prohibit; to forbid

prometer *v.* to promise 24 (2)

pronombre *m.* pronoun

pronto *adj.* soon

propina *f.* tip

propio/a *adj.* own

proteger *v.* to protect

proteína *f.* protein

próximo/a *adj.* next 7 (1)

el próximo lunes/martes/miércoles (etc.) next Monday/Tuesday/ Wednesday (etc.) 7 (1)

la próxima semana next week 7 (1)

prueba *f.* test; quiz 2 (1)

publicar *v.* to publish

público *m.* audience

pueblo *m.* town

puerta *f.* door 2 (1)

Puerto Rico *m.* Puerto Rico

puertorriqueño/a *adj.* Puerto Rican

pues *conj.* well; then

puesto *m.* position; job 11 (1), 28 (2)

puesto/a *p.p.* put 28 (2)

pupitre *m.* desk (student's) 2 (1)

puro/a *adj.* pure

Q

que *pron.* that; who; which

¡Qué…! How…!

¡Qué dolor! What pain!

¡Qué gusto *(+ inf.)!* What a pleasure to… !

¡Qué ropa más bonita! What pretty clothes!

¡Qué sorpresa! What a surprise!

¿qué? what?; which? 6 (1)

¿Qué día es hoy? What day is it?

¿Qué es? What is it?

¿Qué hay de nuevo? What's new?

¿Qué hicieron ellos/ellas? What did they do?

¿Qué hicieron ustedes? *form., pl.* What did you do?

¿Qué hiciste? *fam., sing.* What did you do?

¿Qué hizo él/ella? What did he/she do?

¿Qué hizo usted? *form., sing.* What did you do?

¿Qué hora es? What time is it?

¿Qué les parece? What do you guys think?

¿Qué pasa? What's happening?; What's going on?

¿Qué pasó? What happened? ; What's wrong?

¿Qué precio tiene? What is the price?

¿Qué tal? How are you?; How is it going?; How is/are…?

¿Qué talla lleva/usa usted? What size do you wear?

¡Qué le vaya bien! *form.* Have a nice day! 1 (1)

¡Qué te vaya bien! *fam.* Have a nice day! 1 (1)

¿Qué tiempo hace? How's the weather?; What's the weather like?

quedar *v.* to be left over; to fit *(clothing)*; to be left behind; to be located

quedarse *v.* to stay; to remain

quedarse *v.* **en casa** to stay home 14 (1)

quedarse *v.* **sin gasolina** to run out of gas 26 (2)

quehaceres domésticos *m., pl.* household chores

quemado/a *adj.* burned (out)

querer (e:ie) *v.* to want; to love 10 (1), 20 (2)

queso *m.* cheese 9 (1)

quien(es) *pron.* who; whom; that
  ¿Quién es...? Who is…?
  ¿Quién habla? Who is speaking? (*telephone*)
  ¿quién(es)? who?; whom? **6 (1)**
química *f.* chemistry **1 (1)**
quince fifteen **1 (1)**
  menos quince quarter to (time)
  y quince quarter after (time)
quinceañera *f.* young woman celebrating her fifteenth birthday
quinientos/as five hundred
quinto/a *adj.* fifth
quisiera *v.* I would like
quitar la mesa *v.* to clear the table
quitarse *v.* to take off
  quitarse *v.* **los zapatos** take off one's shoes **14 (1)**
quizás *adv.* maybe

R

racismo *m.* racism
radio *f.* radio (*medium*)
radio *m.* radio (set)
radiografía *f.* X-ray **24 (2)**
  sacar *v.* **una radiografía** to take an X-ray **24 (2)**
rápido/a *adj.* fast
rara vez *adv.* rarely **22 (2)**
rasurarse *v.* to shave **23 (2)**
ratón *m.* mouse
ratos libres *m., pl.* spare time
raya *f.* stripe
razón *f.* reason
rebaja *f.* sale
rebelde *adj.* rebellious **22 (2)**
  ser rebelde to be rebellious **22 (2)**
recado *m.* (telephone) message
receta *f.* prescription
recetar *v.* to prescribe
recibir *v.* to receive
  recibir *v.* **correo electrónico** to receive (get) e-mail **8 (1)**
  recibir *v.* **regalos** to receive (get) gifts **8 (1)**
recibirse *v.* to graduate **28 (2)**
reciclaje *m.* recycling
reciclar *v.* to recycle
recién casado/a *m., f.* newlywed
recoger *v.* to pick up **18 (2)**
  recoger *v.* **la mesa** to clear the table **18 (2)**
  recoger *v.* **las cosas/la ropa** to pick up one's things/clothes **18 (2)**
recomendar (e:ie) *v.* to recommend **27 (2)**
recordar (o:ue) *v.* to remember **10 (1)**
recorrer *v.* to tour an area
recurso *m.* resource
  recurso natural natural resource
red *f.* network; Web

reducir *v.* to reduce
refresco *m.* soft drink; soda **9 (1)**
refrigerador *m.* refrigerator **18 (2)**
regalar *v.* to give (*as a gift*) **20 (2)**
regalo *m.* gift; present **20 (2)**
  abrir *v.* **los regalos** to open presents **20 (2)**
regañar *v.* to scold; to reprimand **22 (2)**
regatear *v.* to bargain
región *f.* region; area
regresar *v.* to return
regular *adj. m., f.* so-so; OK
reído *p.p.* laughed
reírse (e:i) *v.* to laugh
relaciones *f., pl.* relationships
relajarse *v.* to relax
reloj *m.* clock; watch **2 (1)**
renovable *adj.* renewable
renunciar (a) *v.* to resign (from)
repetir (e:i) *v.* to repeat
reportaje *m.* report
reportero/a *m., f.* reporter; journalist
representante *m., f.* representative
reproductor de CD *m.* CD player
reproductor de DVD *m.* DVD player **2 (1)**
reproductor de MP3 *m.* MP3 player
reservado/a *adj.* reserved **3 (1), 6 (1)**
resfriado *m.* cold (*illness*)
residencia estudiantil *f.* dormitory **2 (1)**
resolver (o:ue) *v.* to resolve; to solve
respirar *v.* to breathe
responsable *adj.* responsible **3 (1)**
respuesta *f.* answer
restaurante *m.* restaurant **8 (1)**
resuelto/a *p.p.* resolved **28 (2)**
reunión *f.* meeting
revisar *v.* to check
  revisar *v.* **el aceite** to check the oil
  revisar *v.* **las llantas** to check the tires **26 (2)**
revista *f.* magazine
rico/a *adj.* rich; tasty; delicious **6 (1)**
ridículo *adj.* ridiculous
río *m.* river
riquísimo/a *adj.* extremely delicious
rodilla *f.* knee
rogar (o:ue) *v.* to beg; to plead
rojo/a *adj.* red **13 (1)**
romántico/a *adj.* romantic **3 (1)**
rompecabezas *m., pl.* puzzles **22 (2)**
romper (con) *v.* to break up (with)
  romper *v.* **la piñata** to break a piñata **22 (2)**
romper(se) *v.* to break **21 (2)**
  romperse la pierna/un abrazo to break one's leg/an arm **21 (2)**
ropa *f.* clothing; clothes **20 (2)**
  ropa interior underwear
rosado/a *adj.* pink
roto/a *adj.* broken; *p.p.* broken **28 (2)**

rubio/a *adj.* blond(e) **6 (1)**
ruso/a *adj.* Russian
rutina *f.* routine
  rutina diaria daily routine

S

sábado *m.* Saturday **5 (1)**
  los sábados *m., pl.* on Saturdays **5 (1)**
saber *v.* to know; to know how
  saber (+ *verb*) *v.* to know how (+ *verb*) **11 (1)**
sabrosísimo/a *adj.* extremely delicious
sabroso/a *adj.* tasty; delicious
sacar *v.* to take (out)
  sacar al perro a pasear take out (walk) the dog **18 (2)**
  sacar buenas notas to get good grades **5 (1)**
  sacar fotos to take pictures
  sacar la basura to take out the trash **18 (2)**
  sacar *v.* **una radiografía** to take an X-ray **24 (2)**
  sacar(se) una muela to have a tooth pulled
sacudir *v.* to dust
  sacudir los muebles to dust the furniture
sal *f.* salt **9 (1)**
sala *f.* living room **18 (2)**; room
  sala de emergencia(s) emergency room
salado/a *adj.* salty
salario *m.* salary
salchicha *f.* sausage
salida *f.* departure; exit
salir *v.* to leave; to go out
  salir a cenar (con los amigos) to go out to dinner (with friends) **8 (1)**
  salir bien/mal en las clases/los exámenes to do well/badly in class/exams **11 (1)**
  salir con to leave with; to go out with; to date (*someone*)
  salir de to leave from
  salir para to leave for (*a place*)
  salir temprano/tarde to leave/get off early/late **11 (1)**
  salirse *v.* **en...**to get off at...**26 (2)**
salmón *m.* salmon
salón de belleza *m.* beauty salon
salón de clase *m.* classroom **2 (1)**
saltar *v.* **la cuerda** to jump rope **22 (2)**
salud *f.* health **21 (2)**
  tener buena salud to have/enjoy good health **21 (2)**
saludable *adj.* healthy
saludar(se) *v.* to greet (each other)
saludo *m.* greeting
  saludos a... greetings to…

sandalia *f.* sandal 13 (1)
sándwich *m.* sandwich
sano/a *adj.* healthy
se *ref. pron.* himself, herself, itself, *form.* yourself, themselves, yourselves
se *impersonal* one
  Se nos dañó... The... broke down.
  Se hizo... He/she/it became...
  Se nos pinchó una llanta. We got a flat tire.
secadora *f.* clothes dryer
sección de (no) fumadores *f.* (non) smoking section
secretario/a *m., f.* secretary
secuencia *f.* sequence
sed *f.* thirst
seda *f.* silk
sedentario/a *adj.* sedentary; related to sitting
seguir (e:i) *v.* to follow; to continue; to keep (doing something)
  seguir *v.* **derecho (tres) cuadras** to go straight ahead for (three) blocks 26 (2)
  seguir *v.* **una dieta equilibrada** to eat a balanced diet
  seguir estudiando *v.* to continue studying 28 (2)
según *prep.* according to
segundo/a *adj.* second
seguro/a *adj.* sure; safe; confident
  seguro *m.* insurance 26 (2)
  tener *v.* **seguro** *m.* to have insurance 26 (2)
seis six 1 (1)
seiscientos/as six hundred
sello *m.* stamp
selva *f.* jungle
semáforo *m.* traffic light 26 (2)
  semáforo *m.* **en rojo** red light 26 (2)
semana *f.* week
  entre semana on weekdays 5(1)
  fin *m.* **de semana** weekend
  la semana pasada last week 15 (1), 17 (2)
  los fines de semana on weekends 5 (1)
semestre *m.* semester
señales de tránsito *pl., f.* traffic signs 26 (2)
  obedecer (c:zc) *v.* **las señales de tránsito** to obey the traffic signs 26 (2)
sendero *m.* trail; trailhead
sentarse (e:ie) *v.* to sit down
sentimental *adj.* sentimental 3 (1)
sentir(se) (e:ie) *v.* to feel; to be sorry; to regret 29 (2) , 15 (1)
  sentirse(e:ie) bien/mal/fatal feel well/ill/horrible 21 (2)
  sentirse(e:ie) igual feel the same 21 (2)

sentirse(e:ie) mejor/peor feel better/worse 21 (2)
señor (Sr.) *m.* Mr.; sir 1 (1)
señora (Sra.) *f.* Mrs.; ma'am 1 (1)
señorita (Srta.) *f.* Miss; young woman 1 (1)
separado/a *adj.* separated
separarse (de) *v.* to separate (from) 28 (2)
septiembre *m.* September 13 (1)
séptimo/a *adj.* seventh
ser *v.* to be 4 (1), 20 (2)
  ser aficionado/a (a) to be a fan (of)
  ser alérgico/a (a) to be allergic (to)
  ser consentido/a to be spoiled 22 (2)
  ser gratis to be free of charge
  ser llorón/llorona to be a crybaby 22 (2)
  ser rebelde to be rebellious 22 (2)
  ser travieso/a to be mischievous 22 (2)
serio/a *adj.* serious 3 (1), 6 (1)
servilleta *f.* napkin
servir (e:i) *v.* to help; to serve 9 (1)
sesenta sixty 4 (1)
setecientos/as seven hundred
setenta seventy 4 (1)
sexismo *m.* sexism
sexto/a *adj.* sixth
sí *adv.* yes
si *conj.* if
sicología *f.* psychology 1 (1)
sicólogo/a *m., f.* psychologist 12 (1)
SIDA *m.* AIDS
sido *p.p.* been
siempre *adv.* always 8 (1), 18 (2)
siete seven 1 (1)
silla *f.* chair 2 (1), 18 (2)
sillón *m.* arm chair 18 (2)
similar *adj. m., f.* similar
simpático/a *adj.* nice; likeable
sin *prep.* without
  sin duda without a doubt
  sin embargo *adv.* however
  sin que *conj.* without
sino *conj.* but
síntoma *m.* symptom
sitio *m.* **web** website
situado/a *p.p.* located
sobre *m.* envelope; *prep.* on; over
sobrino/a *m., f.* nephew/niece 4 (1)
sociable *adj.* sociable 3 (1)
sociología *f.* sociology
sofá *m.* couch; sofa 18 (2)
sois *fam.* you are
sol *m.* sun
solar *adj.* solar
solicitar *v.* to apply *(for a job)* 28 (2)
solicitud (de trabajo) *f.* (job) application
sólo *adv.* only

soltero/a *adj.* single; unmarried 6 (1)
solución *f.* solution
sombrero *m.* hat 13 (1)
somos we are 3 (1)
son you/they are 3 (1)
  Son las... It's... o'clock.
sonar (o:ue) *v.* to ring
sonreído *p.p.* smiled
sonreír (e:i) *v.* to smile
sopa *f.* soup 9 (1)
sorprender *v.* to surprise
sorpresa *f.* surprise
sótano *m.* basement; cellar
soy I am
  Soy yo. That's me.
  soy de... I'm from...
su(s) *poss. adj.* his; her; its; *form.* your; their;
subir *v.* to go up
subir(se) a to get on/into (a vehicle)
  subir(se) a los árboles to climb trees 22 (2)
  subir(se) a los columpios to go on the swings 22 (2)
  subir(se) a los juegos to go on rides 20 (2)
sucio/a *adj.* dirty 18 (2)
  estar sucio/a to be dirty 18 (2)
sucre *m.* former Ecuadorian currency
sudar *v.* to sweat
suegro/a *m., f.* father-in-law; mother-in-law 4 (1)
sueldo *m.* salary
  sueldo alto/bajo *m.* high/low salary 11 (1)
suelo *m.* floor
sueño *m.* sleep
suerte *f.* luck
suéter *m.* sweater 13 (1)
sufrir *v.* to suffer
  sufrir muchas presiones to be under a lot of pressure
  sufrir una enfermedad to suffer (from) an illness
sugerir (e:ie) *v.* to suggest
supermercado *m.* supermarket 8 (1)
supervisor/a *m.f.* supervisor 11 (1)
suponer *v.* to suppose
sur *m.* south 26 (2)
sustantivo *m.* noun
su(s) *poss.* his/hers; hers; its; *form.* your, yours, theirs; their 4 (1)
suyo(s)/a(s) *poss.* (of) his/her; (of) hers; (of) its; (of) *form.* your, (of) yours, (of) theirs; their

---

T

tal vez *adv.* maybe
talentoso/a *adj.* talented
talla *f.* size
  talla grande large

taller *m.* **(mecánico)** (mechanic's) repair shop

también *adv.* also; too 18 (2)

tampoco *adv.* neither; not either 18 (2)

tan *adv.* so
  tan pronto como as soon as
  tan… (*adj.*) como as… (*adj.*) as 17 (2)

tanque *m.* tank

tanto *adv.* so much
  tanto como as much as 17 (2)
  tantos/as… (*noun*) como as much/many…(*noun*) as 17 (2)

tarde *adv.* late

tarde *f.* afternoon; evening; P.M.
  por la tarde in the afternoon 5 (1)
  por la noche in the evening 5 (1)

tarea *f.* homework

tarjeta *f.* (post) card
  tarjeta de crédito credit card
  tarjeta postal postcard

taxi *m.* taxi(cab)

taza *f.* cup; mug

te *fam. pron.* you; *i.o. pron., fam* to/for you 19 (2)
  Te presento a... I would like to introduce… to you. (*fam.*) 1 (1)
  ¿Te gustaría? Would you like to?
  ¿Te gusta(n)... ? Do you like…? (*fam.*) 3 (1)

té *m.* tea 9 (1)
  té helado iced tea

teatro *m.* theater

teclado *m.* keyboard

técnico/a *m., f.* technician
  técnico/a en computación *m., f.* computer technician 12 (1)

tejido *m.* weaving

teleadicto/a *m., f.* couch potato

teléfono (celular) *m.* (cellular) telephone

telenovela *f.* soap opera

teletrabajo *m.* telecommuting

televisión *f.* television 2 (1)
  televisión por cable cable television

televisor *m.* television set

temer *v.* to be afraid/concerned; to fear

temperatura *f.* temperature

temprano *adv.* early

tenedor *m.* fork

tener *v.* to have 4 (1), 20 (2)
  cuando tenía… años when I was … years old 22 (2)
  tener… años to be… years old
  Tengo… años. I'm… years old. 4 (1)
  tener buena salud to have/enjoy good health 21 (2)
  tener (el) catarro to have a cold 21 (2)

tener (mucho) calor to be (very) hot

tener (mucho) cuidado to be (very) careful

tener (el) dolor de… to have a(n)… ache 21 (2)

tener éxito to be successful

tener (la) fiebre to have a fever 21 (2)

tener (mucho) frío to be (very) cold

tener ganas de (+ *inf.*) to feel like (*doing something*) 7 (1)

tener (la) gripe to have the flu 21 (2)

tener (mucha) hambre *f.* to be (very) hungry 9 (1)

tener la música muy alta play loud music 23 (2)

tener (mucho) miedo to be (very) afraid/scared of

tener miedo (de) que to be afraid that

tener planes to have plans

tener (mucha) prisa to be in a (big) hurry

tener que (+ *inf.*) *v.* to have to (*do something*) 7 (1)

tener razón to be right

tener (mucha) sed to be (very) thirsty 9 (1)

tener *v.* **seguro** *m.* to have insurance 26 (2)

tener (mucho) sueño to be (very) sleepy

tener (mucha) suerte to be (very) lucky

tener tiempo to have time

tener (la) tos to have a cough 21 (2)
  tener una cita to have a date; an appointment
  tener una infección to have an infection 21 (2)

tenis *m.* tennis

tensión *f.* tension

tercer, tercero/a *adj.* third

terminar *v.* to end; to finish 28 (2)
  terminar de (+ *inf.*) to finish (*doing something*)

terremoto *m.* earthquake

terrible *adj.* terrible 3 (1)

terror *m.* horror

ti *prep., obj. of prep., fam.* you 10 (1), 19 (2)

tiempo *m.* time; weather
  tiempo completo *m.* full-time 11 (1)
  tiempo libre *m.* free time 11 (1)
  tiempo parcial *m.* part-time 11 (1)

tienda *f.* shop; store 8 (1)
  tienda de campaña *f.* tent

tierra *f.* land; soil

tímido/a *adj.* shy 3 (1)

tina *f.* bathtub 18 (2)

tinto/a *adj.* red (wine) 9 (1)

tío/a *m., f.* uncle/aunt 4 (1)

tíos *m.* aunts and uncles 4 (1)

título *m.* title

tiza *f.* chalk

toalla *f.* towel 18 (2)

tobillo *m.* ankle

tocar *v.* to play (*a musical instrument*); to touch
  tocar la guitarra to play the guitar 5 (1)

todavía *adv.* yet; still 28 (2)
  todavía no *adv.* not yet 28 (2)

todo *m.* everything
  en todo el mundo throughout the world
  Todo está bajo control. Everything is under control.
  (todo) derecho straight ahead
  ¡Todos a bordo! All aboard!

todo(s)/a(s) *adj.* all; whole

todos *m., pl.* all of us; *m., pl.* everybody; everyone
  todos los días every day 5 (1), 8 (1)

tomar *v.* to take; to drink
  tomar *v.* **café** to drink coffee 5 (1)
  tomar *v.* **clases** to take classes 5 (1)
  tomar *v.* **el autobús** to take the bus 5 (1)
  tomar *v.* **el sol** to sunbathe
  tomar *v.* **en cuenta** to take into account
  tomar *v.* **fotos** to take pictures
  tomar *v.* **la autopista al norte/al sur/al este/al oeste** to take the freeway north/south/east/west 26 (2)
  tomar(le) *v.* **la temperatura (a alguien)** to take (someone's) temperature

tomate *m.* tomato

tonto/a *adj.* silly; foolish; dumb 6 (1)

torcerse (el tobillo) *v.* to sprain (one's ankle)

torcido/a *adj.* twisted; sprained

tormenta *f.* storm

tornado *m.* tornado

tortilla *f.* tortilla
  tortillas de maíz tortilla made of corn flour

tortuga marina *f.* marine turtle

tos *f., sing.* cough 21 (2)
  jarabe para la tos *m.* cough syrup 21 (2)
  tener (la) tos to have a cough 21 (2)

toser *v.* to cough

tostado/a *adj.* toasted

tostadora *f.* toaster

trabajador(a) *adj.* hard-working 6 (1)

trabajar *v.* to work

trabajar *v.* **en casa** to work at home **5 (1)**

trabajo *m.* job; work **8 (1);** written work

traducir *v.* to translate

traer *v.* to bring **20 (2)** , **24 (2)**

tráfico *m.* traffic

tragedia *f.* tragedy

traído/a *p.p.* brought

traje *m.* suit **13 (1)**

traje de baño bathing suit **13 (1)**

tranquilo/a *adj.* calm; quiet **3 (1),** **15 (1)**

¡Tranquilo! Stay calm!

transmitir to broadcast

tratar de (+ inf.) *v.* to try *(to do something)*

Trato hecho. It's a deal.

travesura *f.* prank **22 (2)**

hacer *v.* **travesuras** to get into trouble **22 (2)**

travieso/a *adj.* mischievous **22 (2)**

ser travieso/a to be mischievous **22 (2)**

trece thirteen **1 (1)**

treinta thirty **1 (1)**

y treinta thirty minutes past the hour (time)

treinta y cinco thirty five **1 (1)**

treinta y cuatro thirty four **1 (1)**

treinta y dos thirty two **1 (1)**

treinta y nueve thirty nine **1 (1)**

treinta y ocho thirty eight **1 (1)**

treinta y seis thirty six **1 (1)**

treinta y siete thirty seven **1 (1)**

treinta y tres thirty three **1 (1)**

treinta y uno thirty one **1 (1)**

tren *m.* train

tres three **1 (1)**

trescientos/as three hundred

trimestre *m.* trimester; quarter

triste *adj.* sad **15 (1), 20 (2)**

ponerse *v.* **triste** to get/become sad **20 (2)**

tú *fam., sing. sub. pron.* you

Tú eres… You are…

tu(s) *fam., poss. adj.* your **4 (1)**

turismo *m.* tourism

turista *m., f.* tourist

turístico/a *adj.* touristic

turno de la manana/tarde/noche *m.* morning/afternoon/evening shift **11 (1)**

tuyo(s)/a(s) *fam., poss. pron.* your; (of) yours

U

Ud. *form., sing. sub. pron.* you

Uds. *form., pl. sub. pron.* you

últimamente *adv.* lately **28 (2)**

último/a *adj.* last

un, uno/a *indef. art.* a **2 (1);** one **1 (1)**

una vez once; one time

una vez más once again

una vez a la semana once a week **8 (1)**

único/a *adj.* only

universidad *f.* university; college

unos/as *pron. indef. art.* some **2 (1)**

urgente *adj.* urgent

usar *v.* to wear **13 (1);** to use

usar *v.* **la computadora** to use the computer **5 (1)**

usted *form., sing. sub. pron.* you

ustedes *form., pl. sub. pron.* you

útil *adj.* useful

uva *f.* grape **9 (1)**

V

vaca *f.* cow

vacaciones *f., pl.* vacation **11 (1)**

irse *v.* **de vacaciones** to go on vacation **14 (1)**

valle *m.* valley

vamos let's go

vaquero *m.* cowboy

de vaqueros *m., pl.* western

varios/as *adj., pl.* several

vaso *m.* glass

veces *f., pl.* times

vecino/a *m., f.* neighbor **23 (2)**

veinte twenty **1 (1)**

veinticinco twenty-five **1 (1)**

veinticuatro twenty-four **1 (1)**

veintidós twenty-two **1 (1)**

veintinueve twenty-nine **1 (1)**

veintiocho twenty-eight **1 (1)**

veintiséis twenty-six **1 (1)**

veintisiete twenty-seven **1 (1)**

veintitrés twenty-three **1 (1)**

veintiún, veintiuno/a twenty-one **1 (1)**

vejez *f.* old age

velocidad *f.* speed **26 (2)**

manejar/ir *v.* **a exceso de velocidad** to speed **26 (2)**

velocidad máxima speed limit

vendedor(a) *m., f.* salesperson

vender *v.* to sell

vender *v.* **comida** to sell food **8 (1)**

venir *v.* to come **10 (1), 20 (2)**

ventaja *f.* advantage **11 (1)**

ventana *f.* window **2 (1)**

ver *v.* to see **20 (2)**

ver *v.* **el desfile/los fuegos artificiales** see the parade/fireworks **20 (2)**

ver *v.* **los dibujos animados** to watch cartoons **22 (2)**

ver *v.* **una película en casa** to watch a movie at home **8 (1)**

ver *v.* **películas** *f., pl.* to see movies

a ver let's see

verano *m.* summer **13 (1)**

verbo *m.* verb

verdad *f.* truth

¿verdad? right?

verde *adj.,* green **13 (1);** not ripe

verduras *pl., f.* vegetables

vestido *m.* dress **13 (1)**

vestirse (e:i) *v.* to get dressed

veterinario/a *m., f.* veterinarian **12 (1)**

vez *f.* time

viajar *v.* to travel

viaje *m.* trip **18 (2)**

hacer un viaje to take a trip **18 (2)**

viajero/a *m., f.* traveler

vida *f.* life

video *m.* video

videocasete *m.* video cassette

videocasetera *f.* VCR **2 (1)**

videoconferencia *f.* video conference

vidrio *m.* glass

viejo/a *adj.* old **6 (1)**

viento *m.* wind

viernes *m., sing.* Friday **5 (1)**

los viernes *m., pl.* on Fridays **5 (1)**

villancico *m.* carol **20 (2)**

cantar villancicos sing carols **20 (2)**

vinagre *m.* vinegar

vino *m.* wine

vino blanco *m.* white wine

vino tinto *m.* red wine **9 (1)**

violencia *f.* violence

visitar *v.* to visit

visitar un monumento to visit a monument

visitar *v.* **a los abuelos** visit one's grandparents **5 (1)**

visto/a *p.p.* seen **28 (2)**

vitamina *f.* vitamin

viudo/a *adj.* widowed

vivienda *f.* housing

vivir *v.* to live

vivir *v.* **en/con** to live in/with **8 (1)**

vivo/a *adj.* lively; alive; bright

volante *m.* steering wheel

volcán *m.* volcano

vóleibol *m.* volleyball

volver (o:ue) *v.* to return

volver a ver(te, lo, la) *v.* to see (you) again

vos *pron.* you

vosotros/as *fam., pl. sub. pron.* you

votar *v.* to vote

vuelta *f.* return trip

vuelto/a *p.p.* returned **28 (2)**

vuestro(s)/a(s) *poss. adj.* your; (of) yours

W

walkman *m.* Walkman

Y

y *conj.* and
  y cuarto quarter after (time)
  y media half-past (time)
  y quince quarter after (time)
  y treinta thirty (minutes past the hour)
  ¿Y tú? *fam.* And you? **1 (1)**
  ¿Y usted? *form.* And you?
ya *adv.* already **28 (2)**
yerno *m.* son-in-law
yo *sub. pron.* I
  Yo soy… I'm… **3 (1)**
yogur *m.* yogurt **9 (1)**

Z

zanahoria *f.* carrot **9 (1)**
zapatería *f.* shoe store
zapato *m.* shoe
  par de zapatos pair of shoes
  zapatos (de tacón) *m., pl.* (high-heeled) shoes **13 (1)**
  zapatos de tenis sneakers **13 (1)**

English–Spanish

A

a/an un *m.*, una *f. sing., indef. art.*
2 (1)
A.M. mañana *f.*
able: be able to poder (o:ue) *v.*
able competente *adj.* 3 (1)
aboard a bordo
accelerate acelerar *v.* 26 (2)
accept aceptar *v.* 28 (2)
accident accidente *m.*
accompany acompañar *v.*
account cuenta *f.*
accountant contador(a) *m., f.* 12 (1)
accounting contabilidad *f.*
ache dolor *m.* 21 (2)
 have a(n)… ache tener (el) dolor
 de… 21 (2)
acquainted: be acquainted with
 conocer *v.* 12 (1)
action acción *f.*
active activo/a *adj.* 3 (1)
actor actor *m.*
actress actriz *f.*
addict (drug) drogadicto/a *adj.*
additional adicional *adj.*
address dirección *f.*
adjective adjetivo *m.*
adolescence adolescencia *f.*
adolescent chico/a 4 (1)
advantage ventaja *f.* 11 (1)
adventure aventura *f.*
advertise anunciar *v.*
advertisement anuncio *m.*
advice consejo *m.*
 give advice dar *v.* consejos 11 (1)
advise aconsejar *v.* 27 (2)
advisor consejero/a *m., f.*
aerobic aeróbico/a *adj.*
 aerobic exercises ejercicios
 aeróbicos
 aerobics class clase de ejercicios
 aeróbicos
affected afectado/a *adj.*
 be affected (by) estar *v.*
 afectado/a (por)
affectionate cariñoso/a *adj.* 6 (1)
affirmative afirmativo/a *adj.*
afraid: be (very) afraid tener
 (mucho) miedo
 be afraid temer *v.*
after después de *prep.;* después
 (de) que *conj.*
afternoon tarde *f.*
 in the afternoon por la tarde 5 (1)
afterward después *adv.;* luego *adv.*
again otra vez *adv.*
age edad *f.*

**ago (two weeks/three months/four
 years ago).** Hace (dos) semanas/
 (tres)meses/(cuatro) años.
 15 (1), 17(2)
agree concordar *v.;* estar *v.* de acuerdo
agreement acuerdo *m.*
AIDS SIDA *m.*
air aire *m.*
 air pollution contaminación del aire
airplane avión *m.* 20 (2)
 go by plane ir *v.* en avión 20 (2)
airport aeropuerto *m.* 8 (1)
alarm clock despertador *m.*
alcohol alcohol *m.*
alcoholic alcohólico/a *adj.*
 alcoholic beverage bebida
 alcohólica
all todo(s)/toda(s) *adj.*
 All aboard! ¡Todos a bordo!
 all of a sudden de repente *adv.*
 25 (2)
 all of us todos
 all over the world en todo el mundo
allergic alérgico/a *adj.*
 be allergic (to) ser alérgico/a (a)
alleviate aliviar *v.*
almost casi *adv.* 8 (1)
alone solo/a *adj.*
along por *prep.*
already ya *adv.* 28 (2)
also también *adv.* 18 (2)
alternator alternador *m.*
although aunque *conj.*
aluminum aluminio *m.*
 (made of) aluminum de aluminio
always siempre *adv.* 8 (1), 18 (2)
ambitious ambicioso/a *adj.* 3 (1)
American (North) norteamericano/a
 adj.
among entre *prep.*
amusement diversión *f.*
and y; e (*before words beginning with
 i or hi*)
 And you? ¿Y tú? *fam.* 1 (1); ¿Y
 usted? *form.* 1 (1)
angry enojado/a *adj.* 15 (1)
 get angry (with) enojarse *v.* (con)
animal animal *m.*
ankle tobillo *m.*
anniversary aniversario *m.*
 wedding anniversary aniversario
 de bodas
announce anunciar *v.*
announcer (TV/radio) locutor(a) *m., f.*
annoy molestar *v.* 19 (2)
another otro/a *adj.*
answer contestar *v.;* respuesta *f.*
 answer the phone/e-mails
 contestar *v.* los teléfonos/los
 correos 11 (1)
answering machine contestadora *f.*
anthropology antropología *f.* 1 (1)
antibiotic antibiótico *m.* 21 (2)
any algún, alguno/a(s) *adj.* 18 (2)
anyone alguien *pron.*

anything algo *pron.* 18 (2)
apartment apartamento *m.* 18 (2)
apartment building edificio de
 apartamentos
appear parecer *v.*
appetizers entremeses *m., pl.*
applaud aplaudir *v.*
apple manzana *f.* 9 (1)
appliance (electric)
 electrodoméstico *m.*
applicant aspirante *m., f.*
application solicitud *f.* 28 (2)
 job application solicitud de trabajo
apply (for a job) solicitar *v.* 28 (2)
 apply for a loan pedir *v.* un
 préstamo
appointment cita *f.*
 have an appointment tener *v.*
 una cita
appreciate apreciar *v.*
April abril *m.* 13 (1)
aquatic acuático/a *adj.*
archaeologist arqueólogo/a *m., f.*
architect arquitecto/a *m., f.*
area región *f.*
argue (about/with) discutir *v.*
 (de/con) 8 (1)
arm brazo *m.* 21 (2)
arm chair sillón *m.* 18 (2)
army ejército *m.*
around por *prep.*
around here por aquí
arrange arreglar *v.*
arrival llegada *f.*
arrive llegar *v.*
 **arrive (get) home on
 time/late/early** llegar a tiempo/
 tarde/temprano a casa 5 (1)
arrogant arrogante *adj.* 3 (1)
art arte *m.*
 fine arts bellas artes *f., pl.*
article *m.* artículo
artist artista *m., f.*
artistic artístico/a *adj.*
art exhibition exhibición de arte *f.*
 8 (1)
arts artes *f., pl.*
as como *conj.*
 as… (*adj.*) as tan… (*adj.*) como
 17 (2)
 as a child de niño/a 22 (2)
 as much/many… (*noun*) **as**
 tantos/as…(*noun*) como 17 (2)
 as much as tanto como 17 (2)
 as soon as en cuanto *conj.* 30 (2);
 tan pronto como *conj.*
ask (a question) preguntar *v.*
 ask for pedir (e:i) *v.* 9 (1), 24 (2)
 ask someone out invitar a salir
 11 (1)
asparagus espárragos *m., pl.*
aspirin aspirina *f.* 21 (2)
astronomy astronomía *f.* 1 (1)
at a *prep.;* en *prep.*
 at + time a la(s) + *time*

at home en casa
at least por lo menos
at night por la noche 5 (1)
at that time en aquel entonces 22 (2)
at the end (of) al fondo (de)
At what time…? ¿A qué hora…? 2 (1)
At your service A sus órdenes.
attend asistir (a) *v.*
attend to the customers/clients atender(e:ie) *v.* a los clientes 11 (1)
attic altillo *m.*
attract atraer *v.*
attractive atractivo/a *adj.* 3 (1)
audience público *m.*
auditorium auditorio *m.* 2 (1)
August agosto *m.* 13 (1)
aunt tía *f.* 4 (1)
aunts and uncles tíos *m., pl.* 4 (1)
automatic automático/a *adj.*
automatic teller machine (ATM) cajero automático
automobile automóvil *m.*
autumn otoño *m.*
avenue avenida *f.* 26 (2)
avoid evitar *v.* 26 (2)
avoid fines; tickets evitar *v.* las multas 26 (2)
award premio *m.*

B

back espalda *f.* 21 (2)
back then en esos tiempos 22 (2)
baby-sitter niñero/a *m. f.* 11 (1)
backpack mochila *f.* 2 (1)
bad mal, malo/a *adj.* 6 (1)
It's bad that… Es malo que…
It's not bad at all. No está nada mal.
bag bolsa *f.* 13 (1)
baked potato papa al horno *f.* 9 (1)
bakery panadería *f.*
balanced equilibrado/a *adj.*
balanced diet dieta equilibrada
balcony balcón *m.*
ball pelota *f.* 22 (2)
play ball jugar a la pelota 22 (2)
ballet ballet *m.*
banana banana *f.* 9 (1)
band banda *f.*
bank banco *m.*
bargain ganga *f.;* regatear *v.*
baseball (game) béisbol *m.*
basement sótano *m.*
basketball (game) baloncesto *m.*
bath baño *m.*
bathtub tina *f.* 18 (2)
take a bath bañarse *v.*
take a bath/shower at night bañarse *v.* por la noche 14 (1)
bathe bañarse *v.*

take a bath/shower at night bañarse *v.* por la noche 14 (1)
bathing suit traje *m.* de baño 13 (1)
bathroom baño *m.* 18 (2); cuarto de baño *m.*
bathtub tina *f.* 18 (2)
be ser *v.* 4 (1), 20 (2); estar *v.* 15 (1), 20 (2)
be at/in/on estar *v.* en 8 (1)
be clean estar limpio/a 18 (2)
be a crybaby ser llorón/llorona 22 (2)
be dirty estar sucio/a 18 (2)
be dizzy estar mareado/a 21 (2)
be in bed estar en cama 15 (1)
be in class estar en clase 15 (1)
be mischievous ser travieso/a 22 (2)
be rebellious ser rebelde 22 (2)
be spoiled ser consentido/a 22 (2)
be inside estar adentro/dentro de 15 (1)
be messy estar desarreglado/a 18 (2)
be on vacation estar de vacaciones 15 (1)
be outside estar afuera/fuera de 15 (1)
be rebellious ser rebelde 22 (2)
be sore estar adolorido/a 21 (2)
be tidy estar arreglado/a 18 (2)
be… years old tener… años
beach playa *f.* 8 (1)
go to the beach ir a la playa
beans frijoles *m., pl.* 9 (1)
beautiful hermoso/a *adj.*
beauty belleza *f.*
beauty salon peluquería *f.;* salón *m.* de belleza
because porque *conj.*
because of por *prep.*
become (+ *adj.*) ponerse (+ *adj.*); convertirse *v.*
get/become sad/happy ponerse *v.* triste/feliz 20 (2)
bed cama *f.* 18 (2)
go to bed acostarse (o:ue) *v.* 17 (2)
go to bed late acostarse (o:ue) *v.* tarde 14 (1)
be in bed estar en cama 15 (1)
bedroom alcoba *f.;* cuarto *m.;* recámara *f.*
beef carne *f.* de res 9 (1)
beef soup caldo *m.* de patas
been sido *p.p.*
beer cerveza *f.* 9 (1)
before antes *adv.* 22 (2); antes de *prep.;* antes (de) que *conj.* 30 (2)
beg rogar (o:ue) *v.*
begin comenzar (e:ie) *v.;* empezar (e:ie) *v.*
behalf: on behalf of de parte de
behave portarse *v.* bien 22 (2)

behind detrás de *prep.* atrás *adv.* 25 (2)
from behind por atrás 25 (2)
believe creer *v.* 17 (2)
believe (in) creer *v.* (en)
believed creído *p.p.*
bellhop botones *m., f., sing.*
beloved enamorado/a *adj.*
below debajo de *prep.*
belt cinturón *m.*
benefit beneficio *m.*
beside al lado de *prep.*
besides además (de) *adv.*
best mejor *adj.*
better than mejor que *adj.* 17 (2)
the best el/la mejor *m., f.;* lo mejor *neuter*
better mejor *adj.* 21 (2)
feel better sentirse(e:ie) mejor 21 (2)
It's better that… Es mejor que…
between entre *prep.*
bicycle bicicleta *f.* 18 (2)
ride a bike andar *v.* en bicicleta 18 (2) , 20 (2)
big gran, grande *adj.*
bigger mayor *adj.*
biggest, (the) el/la mayor *m., f.*
bikini bikini *m.* 13 (1)
bill cuenta *f.* 9 (1)
billion mil millones
biology biología *f.* 1 (1)
bird pájaro *m.* 4 (1); ave *f.*
birth nacimiento *m.*
birthday cumpleaños *m., sing.*
birthday cake pastel de cumpleaños
birthday song mañanitas *f., pl.* 20 (2)
have a birthday cumplir *v.* años
biscuit bizcocho *m.*
black negro/a *adj.* 13 (1)
blackberry mora *f.*
blanket manta *f.*
block (city) cuadra *f.* 26 (2)
blond(e) rubio/a *adj.* 6 (1)
blouse blusa *f.* 13 (1)
blow golpe *m.* 25 (2)
blue azul *adj.* 13 (1)
boarding house pensión *f.*
boat barco *m.*
body cuerpo *m.* 21 (2)
bone hueso *m.*
book libro *m.* 2 (1)
bookcase estante *m.*
bookshelves estante *m.*
bookstore librería *f.* 2 (1)
boot bota *f.*
bore aburrir *v.*
bored aburrido/a *adj.* 15 (1)
be bored estar *v.* aburrido/a 15 (1)
get bored aburrirse *v.*
boring aburrido/a *adj.* 6 (1)
born: be born nacer *v.*
borrow pedir prestado

borrow things pedir (e:i) cosas prestadas **11 (1)**
borrowed prestado/a *adj.*
boss jefe *m.*, jefa *f.* **11 (1)**
bottle botella *f.*
  bottle of wine botella de vino
bother molestar *v.* **19 (2)**
bottom fondo *m.*
boulevard bulevar *m.*
bowling alley boliche *m.* **8 (1)**
boy chico *m.* **4 (1)**; muchacho; niño *m.* **4 (1)**
boyfriend novio *m.* **4 (1)**
brake frenar *v.* **26 (2)**
brakes frenos *m., pl.*
bread pan *m.*
break romper(se) *v.* **21 (2)**
  break a piñata romper *v.* la piñata **22 (2)**
  break (one's leg)/an arm romperse (la pierna)/(un brazo) **21 (2)**
breakdown dañar *v.*
  The bus broke down. Se nos dañó el autobús.
  break up (with) romper *v.* (con)
breakfast desayuno *m.* **9 (1)**
  have breakfast desayunar *v.* **9 (1)**
breathe respirar *v.*
bring traer *v.* **20 (2)**, **24 (2)**; **(someone/ an animal/something inanimate)** llevar *v.* a (+person/object)
broadcast transmitir *v.*; emitir *v.*
broccoli brócoli *m.* **9 (1)**
brochure folleto *m.*
broken roto/a *adj.*; roto/a *p.p.* **28 (2)**
  be broken estar roto/a
brother hermano *m.* **4 (1)**
  brother-in-law cuñado *m., f.* **4 (1)**
  brothers and sisters hermanos *m., pl.* **4 (1)**
brought traído/a *p.p.*
brown café *adj.* **13 (1)**; marrón *adj.* **13 (1)**
brunet(te) moreno/a *adj.* **6 (1)**
brush cepillar *v.*
  brush one's hair cepillarse el pelo
  brush one's teeth cepillarse *v.* los dientes; lavarse *v.* los dientes **14 (1)**
build construir *v.*
building edificio *m.*
bullfight corrida *f.* de toros
bump golpe *m.* **25 (2)**
bump into (meet accidentally) darse con
burned (out) quemado/a *adj.*
bus autobús *m.*
  bus station estación *f.* de autobuses
business negocios *m., pl.*
  business administration administración *f.* de empresas

business administrator administrador/a de empresas *m., f.* **12 (1)**
  business-related comercial *adj.*
businessman hombre *m.* de negocios
businesswoman mujer *f.* de negocios
busy ocupado/a *adj.* **15 (1)**
but pero *conj.*; sino *conj. (in negative sentences)*
butcher shop carnicería *f.*
butter mantequilla *f.*
buy comprar *v.* **5 (1)**
by por *conj.*; para *prep.*
  by car en coche **20 (2)**
  by means of por *prep.*
  by phone por teléfono
  by plane en avión **20 (2)**
  by way of por *prep.*
Bye. Chau. *interj. fam.*

C

cabin cabaña *f.*
cable television televisión *f.* por cable *m.*
café café *m.* **8 (1)**
cafeteria cafetería *f.* **2 (1)**
cake pastel *m.* **9 (1)**
calculator calculadora *f.* **2 (1)**
call llamar *v.* **11 (1)**
  call on the phone llamar por teléfono
  call the police llamar a la policía **23 (2)**
  be called llamarse *v.*
calm tranquilo/a *adj.* **3 (1)**
  Stay calm! ¡Tranquilo/a!
calorie caloría *f.*
camera cámara *f.*
  digital camera cámara digital
camp acampar *v.* **18 (2)**
  to go camping ir de campamento **18 (2)**
can lata *f.*
can poder (o:ue) *v.* **10 (1)**, **20 (2)**
Canadian canadiense *adj.*
candidate aspirante *m. f.*; candidato/a *m., f.*
candy dulces *m., pl.* **9 (1)**
capital city capital *f.*
car coche *m.*; carro *m.*; auto(móvil) *m.*
  go by car ir *v.* en coche **20 (2)**
caramel caramelo *m.*
card tarjeta *f.*; (playing) carta *f.*
care cuidado *m.*
  take care of cuidar *v.*
career carrera *f.*
careful: be (very) careful tener *v.* (mucho) cuidado
caretaker ama *m., f.* de casa **11 (1)**
carpenter carpintero/a *m., f.*
carpet alfombra *f.* **18 (2)**

carrot zanahoria *f.* **9 (1)**
carry llevar *v.*
cartoons dibujos *m., pl.* animados **22 (2)**
  watch cartoons ver *v.* los dibujos animados **22 (2)**
case: in case (that) en caso (de) que
cash (a check) cobrar *v.*; efectivo *m.*
  cash register caja *f.*
  pay in cash pagar *v.* al contado pagar en efectivo
cashier cajero/a *m., f.*
cat gato/a *m., f.* **4 (1)**, **18 (2)**
  feed the cat darle de comer al gato **18 (2)**
Catholic school colegio católico *m.* **22 (2)**
CD player reproductor *m.* de CD
celebrate celebrar *v.* **28 (2)**
cellar sótano *m.*
cellular celular *adj.*
  cellular telephone teléfono *m.* celular
cereal cereales *m., pl.* **9 (1)**
certain cierto *m.*; seguro *m.*
  it's (not) certain (no) es seguro/cierto
chair silla *f.* **2 (1)**, **18 (2)**
chalk tiza *f.*
chalkboard pizzara *f.*
chalkboard pizzarón *f.* **2 (1)**
champagne champán *m.*
change cambiar *v.* (de) **28 (2)**
channel (TV) canal *m.*
character (fictional) personaje *m.*
  main character personaje principal
charge (for a product or service) cobrar *v.*
chauffeur conductor(a) *m., f.*
chat conversar *v.*
cheap barato/a *adj.*
check comprobar *v.*; revisar *v.*; (bank) cheque *m.*
  check the oil revisar *v.* el aceite
  check the tires revisar *v.* las llantas **26 (2)**
checkers (game) damas chinas *f., pl.* **22 (2)**
  play checkers jugar a las damas chinas **22 (2)**
checking account cuenta *f.* corriente
cheese queso *m.* **9 (1)**
chef cocinero/a *m., f.*
chemistry química *f.* **1 (1)**
chest of drawers cómoda *f.*
chicken pollo *m.* **9 (1)**
child niño/a *m., f.* **4 (1)**
  as a child de niño/a **22 (2)**
childhood niñez *f.*
children hijos *m., pl* **4 (1)**
Chinese chino/a *adj.*
chocolate chocolate *m.*
  chocolate cake pastel *m.* de chocolate

cholesterol colesterol *m.*
choose escoger *v.*
chop (food) chuleta *f.*
Christmas Navidad *f.*
church iglesia *f.* **8 (1)**
citizen ciudadano/a *m., f.*
city ciudad *f.*
class clase *f.*
  take classes tomar *v.* clases **5 (1)**
  be in class estar en clase **15 (1)**
classroom salón de clase *m.* **2 (1)**
classical clásico/a *adj.*
classmate compañero/a *m., f.* de
  clase **2 (1)**
clean limpio/a *adj.* **18 (2)**; limpiar *v.*
  be clean estar limpio/a **18 (2)**
  clean the house *v.* limpiar la casa
  clean the (one's) room limpiar el
  cuarto **5 (1)**
clear (weather) despejado/a *adj.*
  clear the table quitar *v.* la mesa;
  recoger *v.* la mesa **18 (2)**
  It's clear. (weather) Está
  despejado.
clerk dependiente/a *m., f.*
  empleado/a *m., f.* **11 (1)**
client cliente/a *m., f.*
climb escalar *v.*
  climb mountains escalar montañas
  climb trees subir(se) a los
  árboles **22 (2)**
clinic clínica *f.*
clock reloj *m.* **2 (1)**
close cerrar (e:ie) *v.*
closed cerrado/a *adj.*
closet armario *m.;* clóset *m.* **18 (2)**
clothes ropa *f.* **20 (2)**
  clothes dryer secadora *f.*
clothing ropa *f.*
cloud nube *f.*
cloudy nublado/a *adj.*
  It's (very) cloudy Está (muy)
  nublado
coat abrigo *m.* **13 (1)**
coffee café *m.* **9 (1)**
  coffee maker cafetera *f.*
cold frío *m.;* **(disease)** resfriado *m.;*
  (sickness) catarro *m.* **21 (2)**
  be (very) cold (feel) tener
  (mucho) frío
  It's (very) cold. (weather) Hace
  (mucho) frío. **13 (1)**
  have a cold tener (el) catarro
  21 (2)
college universidad *f.*
collision choque *m.*
color color *m.* **13 (1)**; colorear *v.*
  22 (2)
comb one's hair peinarse *v.*
come venir *v.* **10 (1), 20 (2)**
comedy comedia *f.*
comfortable cómodo/a *adj.* **20 (2)**
commerce negocios *m., pl.*
commercial comercial *adj.*

communicate (with) comunicarse *v.*
  (con)
communication comunicación *f.*
  means of communication medios
  m., pl. de comunicación
community comunidad *f.*
compact disc (CD) disco *m.* compacto
  compact disc player reproductor
  m. de CD
company compañía *f.;* empresa *f.*
  28 (2)
comparison comparación *f.*
competent competente *adj.* **3(1)**
completely completamente *adv.*
composer compositor(a) *m., f.*
computer computadora *f.*
  computer disc disco *m.*
  computer monitor monitor *m.*
  computer programmer
  programador(a) *m., f.* **12 (1)**
  computer science computación *f.*
  computer technician técnico/a
  en computación *m., f.* **12 (1)**
concerned: to be concerned temer *v.*
concert concierto *m.*
conductor (musical) director(a) *m., f.*
confirm confirmar *v.*
  confirm a reservation confirmar
  una reservación
congested congestionado/a *adj.*
Congratulations! (for an event such
  as a birthday or anniversary)
  ¡Felicidades!; **(for an event such**
  as an engagement or a good grade
  on a test) *f., pl.* ¡Felicitaciones!
conservation conservación *f.*
conserve conservar *v.*
considering para *prep.*
consume consumir *v.*
contact lenses lentes *m. pl.* de
  contacto
container envase *m.*
contamination contaminación *f.*
content contento/a *adj.*
contest concurso *m.*
continue (studying) seguir (e:i)
  (estudiando) *v.* **28 (2)**
control control *m.;* controlar *v.*
  be under control estar bajo
  control
conversation conversación *f.*
converse conversar *v.*
cook cocinar *v.;* cocinero/a *m., f.*
cookie galleta *f.* **9 (1)**
cool fresco/a *adj.*
  It's cool. (weather) Hace fresco.
  13 (1)
corn maíz *m.*
corner esquina *m.* **26 (2)**
cost costar (o:ue) *v.*
costume disfraz *m.* **20 (2)**
  wear a ... costume disfrazarse *v.*
  de... **20 (2)**
cotton algodón *m.*
  (made of) cotton de algodón

couch sofá *m.* **18 (2)**
couch potato teleadicto/a *m., f.*
cough tos *f.* **21 (2);** toser *v.*
  cough syrup jarabe para la tos *m.*
  21 (2)
  have a cough tener (la) tos **21 (2)**
counselor consejero/a *m., f.* **2 (1)**
count (on) contar *v.* (con)
country (nation) país *m.*
countryside campo *m.;* paisaje *m.*
couple pareja *f.*
  couple (married) matrimonio *m.*
course curso *m.;* materia *f.*
courtesy cortesía *f.*
cousin primo/a *m., f.* **4 (1)**
depressed deprimido/a *adj.* **15 (1)**
cover cubrir *v.*
covered cubierto *p.p.*
cow vaca *f.*
cowboy vaquero *m.*
crafts artesanía *f.*
craftsmanship artesanía *f.*
crash chocar *v.* (con)
crater cráter *m.*
crazy loco/a *adj.*
create crear *v.*
creative creativo/a *adj.* **3 (1)**
credit crédito *m.*
  credit card tarjeta *f.* de crédito
crime crimen *m.*
cross cruzar *v.*
  cross the street cruzar *v.* la calle
  26 (2)
crybaby llorón/llorona *m.f.* **22 (2)**
  be a crybaby ser llorón/llorona
  22 (2)
culture cultura *f.*
cup taza *f.*
currency exchange cambio *m.* de
  moneda
current events actualidades *f., pl.*
curriculum vitae currículum *m.*
curtains cortinas *f., pl.*
custard (baked) flan *m.* **9 (1)**
custom costumbre *f.*
customer cliente/a *m., f.*
customs aduana *f.*
  customs inspector inspector(a)
  m., f. de aduanas
cycling ciclismo *m.*

D

dad papá *m.*
daily diario/a *adj.*
  daily routine rutina *f.* diaria
damage dañar *v.*
dance bailar *v.* **5(1)**; danza *f.* baile *m.*
dancer bailarín/bailarina *m., f.*
danger peligro *m.*
dangerous peligroso/a *adj.*
dark-haired moreno/a *adj.* **6 (1)**
dark-skinned moreno/a *adj.* **6 (1)**

date (appointment) cita *f.*; **(calendar)** fecha *f.*; **(someone)** salir *v.* con (alguien)
  date: have a date tener *v.* una cita
daughter hija *f.* **4 (1)**
  daughter-in-law nuera *f.*
day día *m.*
  day before yesterday anteayer *adv.*
dead muerto/a *p.p.* **28 (2)**
deal trato *m.*
  It's a deal. Trato hecho.
  It's not a big deal. No es para tanto.
death muerte *f.*
decaffeinated descafeinado/a *adj.*
December diciembre *m.* **13 (1)**
decide decidir *v.*
decided decidido/a *adj.*
declare declarar *v.*
decorate the tree poner *v.* el árbol **20 (2)**
deforestation deforestación *f.*
delicious delicioso/a *adj.*; rico/a *adj.* **6 (1)**; sabroso/a *adj.*
delighted encantado/a *adj.*
dent golpe *m.* **25 (2)**
dental hygienist higienista dental *m., f.* **12 (1)**
dentist dentista *m., f.*
deny negar (e: ie) *v.*
department store almacén *m.*
departure salida *f.*
deposit depositar *v.*
describe describir *v.*
described descrito/a *p.p.*
desert desierto *m.*
design diseño *m.*
designer diseñador(a) *m., f.*
  graphic designer diseñador(a) gráfico/a *m., f.* **12 (1)**
desire desear *v.*
desk escritorio **(teacher's)** *m.* **2 (1)**; pupitre **(student's)** *m.* **2 (1)**
dessert postre *m.*
destroy destruir *v.*
develop desarrollar *v.*
diary diario *m.*
dictatorship dictadura *f.*
dictionary diccionario *m.* **2 (1)**
did hecho/a *p.p.* **28 (2)**
die morir (o:ue) *v.*
died muerto/a *p.p.*
diet dieta *f.*
  balanced diet dieta equilibrada
  be on a diet estar *v.* a dieta
  eat a balanced diet seguir una dieta equilibrada
difficult difícil *adj.* **6 (1)**
dining room comedor *m.* **18 (2)**
dinner cena *f.* **9 (1)**
  have dinner cenar *v.* **9 (1)**
direction: in the direction of para *prep.*
directions: give directions indicar cómo llegar *v.*
director director(a) *m., f.*

dirty ensuciar *v.*; sucio/a *adj.* **18 (2)**
  be dirty estar sucio/a **18 (2)**
  get (something) dirty ensuciar *v.*
disappointed desilusionado/a *adj.* **15 (1)**
disadvantage desventaja *f.* **11 (1)**
disagree no estar de acuerdo
disaster desastre *m.*
disco discoteca *f.* **8 (1)**
discover descubrir *v.*
discovered descubierto *p.p.*
discreet discreto/a *adj.* **3 (1)**
discrimination discriminación *f.*
discuss (about/with) discutir *v.* (de/con) **8 (1)**
dish plato *m.* **9 (1)**; platillo *m.* **9 (1)**
  main dish plato principal
  do (wash) the dishes lavar los platos **18 (2)**
dishonest deshonesto/a *adj.* **3 (1)**
dishwasher lavaplatos *m., sing.*
disk disco *m.*
dislike chocar *v.* **19 (2)**
disobey desobedecer (c:zc) *v.* **22 (2)**
disorderly desordenado/a *adj.* **6 (1)**
dive bucear *v.* **18 (2)**
divorce divorcio *m.*
divorced divorciado/a *adj.*
  get divorced (from) divorciarse *v.* (de) **28 (2)**
dizzy mareado/a *adj.* **21 (2)**
  be dizzy estar mareado/a **21 (2)**
do hacer *v.* **8 (1), 20 (2)**
  do aerobics hacer ejercicios aeróbicos
  do errands hacer diligencias
  do household chores hacer quehaceres domésticos
  do homework hacer la tarea **8 (1)**
  do stretching exercises hacer ejercicios de estiramiento
  do puzzles armar rompecabezas *v.* **22 (2)**
  do (wash) the dishes lavar los platos **18 (2)**
  do well/badly in class/exams salir bien/mal en las clases/los exámenes **11 (1)**
doctor médico/a *m., f.*; doctor(a) *m., f.*; **1 (1), 8 (1)**
documentary (film) documental *m.*
dog perro/a *m., f.* **4 (1), 18 (2)**
  take out (walk) the dog sacar al perro a pasear **18 (2)**
doll muñeca *f.* **22 (2)**
  play with dolls jugar a las muñecas **22 (2)**
domestic doméstico/a *adj.*
  domestic appliance electrodoméstico *m.*
done hecho/a *p.p.*
door puerta *f.* **2 (1)**
donut dona *f.* **9 (1)**

dormitory residencia *f.* estudiantil **2 (1)**
double doble *adj.*
  double room habitación *f.* doble
doubt duda *f.*; dudar *v.*
  There is no doubt… No cabe duda de…; No hay duda de…
Down with… ! ¡Abajo el/la…!
downtown centro *m.*
drama drama *m.* **1 (1)**
dramatic dramático/a *adj.*
draw dibujar *v.* **22 (2)**
drawing dibujo *m.*
dress vestido *m.* **13 (1)**
  get dressed vestirse (e:i) *v.*
drink beber *v.* **8 (1)**; bebida *f.*; tomar *v.*
  Do you want something to drink? ¿Quieres algo de tomar?
  drink coffee tomar *v.* café **5 (1)**
drive conducir *v.*; manejar *v.* **10 (1)**
driver conductor(a) *m., f.* **26 (2)**; chofer *m., f.*
  driver's license licencia *f.* de conducir/manejar **26 (2)**
drug *f.* droga
  drug addict drogadicto/a *adj.*
drunk borracho(a) *adj.* **15 (1)**
due to por *prep.*
  due to the fact that debido a
dumb tonto/a *adj.* **6 (1)**
during durante *prep.*; por *prep.*
dust sacudir *v.*
  dust the furniture sacudir los muebles
DVD player reproductor de DVD *m.* **2 (1)**
dying: I'm dying to (for)… me muero por…

E

each cada *adj.* **22 (2)**
  each year cada año *adj.* **22(2)**
eagle águila *f.*
ear (outer) oreja *f.*
early temprano *adv.*
earn ganar *v.*
earthquake terremoto *m.*
ease aliviar *v.*
east este *m.* **26 (2)**
  to the east al este **26 (2)**
easy fácil *adj.* **6 (1)**
  extremely easy facilísimo
eat comer *v.* **8 (1), 9 (1)**
ecological ecologista *adj.*
ecologist ecologista *adj.*
ecology ecología *f.*
economics economía *f.* **1 (1)**
ecotourism ecoturismo *m.*
Ecuador Ecuador *m.*
Ecuadorian ecuatoriano/a *adj.*
effective eficaz *adj. m., f.*
egg huevo *m.* **9 (1)**

eight ocho **1 (1)**
eight hundred ochocientos/as
eighteen dieciocho **1 (1)**
eighth octavo/a
eighty ochenta **4 (1)**
either… or o… o *conj.*
elect elegir *v.*
election elecciones *f., pl.*
electrician electricista *m., f.*
electricity luz *f.*
elegant elegante *adj.*
elementary school primaria *f.* **22 (2)**
elevator ascensor *m.*
eleven once **1 (1)**
e-mail correo *m.* electrónico
  e-mail message mensaje *m.*
  electrónico
  read e-mail leer *v.* el correo
  electrónico
embarrassed avergonzado/a *adj.*
embrace (each other) abrazar(se) *v.*
emergency emergencia *f.*
  emergency room sala *f.* de
  emergencia(s)
employee empleado/a *m., f.* **11 (1)**
employment empleo *m.*
end fin *m.;* terminar *v.*
  end table mesita *f.* **18 (2)**
energy energía *f.*
engaged: get engaged (to)
  comprometerse *v.* (con)
engineer ingeniero/a *m., f.*
  computer engineer ingeniero/a
  en computación *m., f.* **12 (1)**
  environmental engineer
  ingeniero/a ambientalista *m., f.*
  12 (1)
English (language) inglés *m.* **1 (1);**
  inglés, inglesa *adj.*
enjoy disfrutar *v.* (de)
have/enjoy good health tener buena
  salud **21 (2)**
enough bastante *adj.*
enter entrar *v.* **28 (2)**
entertainment diversión *f.*
entrance entrada *f.* **26 (2)**
  first/second entrance la
  primera/segunda entrada **26 (2)**
envelope sobre *m.*
environment medio ambiente *m.*
equality igualdad *f.*
equipped equipado/a *adj.*
eraser borrador *m.*
errand diligencia *f.*
establish establecer *v.*
evening tarde *f.*
event acontecimiento *m.*
ever alguna vez *adv.* **28 (2)**
every day todos los días **5 (1), 8 (1)**
everybody todos *m., pl.*
everything todo *m.*
  Everything is under control Todo
  está bajo control
exactly en punto *adv.*
exam examen *m.*

excellent excelente *adj.* **3 (1)**
excess exceso *m.*
  in excess en exceso
exchange intercambiar *v.*
  in exchange for por
excited emocionado/a *adj.* **15 (1)**
exciting emocionante *adj. m., f.*
excursion excursión *f.* **18 (2)**
excuse disculpar *v.*
Excuse me. (May I?) Con permiso;
  (I beg your pardon.) Perdón.
exercise ejercicio *m.* hacer *v.*
  ejercicio **8 (1)**
exit salida *f.*
expensive caro/a *adj.*
experience experiencia *f.*
explain explicar *v.* **24 (2)**
explore explorar *v.*
  explore a city/town explorar una
  ciudad/pueblo
expression expresión *f.*
expressway autopista *f.* **26 (2)**
extinction extinción *f.*
extrovert extrovertido/a *adj.* **3 (1)**
eye ojo *m.* **21 (2)**

F

fabulous fabuloso/a *adj*
face cara *f.* **21 (2)**
facing enfrente de *prep.*
fact: in fact de hecho
factory fábrica *f.*
fall (down) caerse *v.*
  fall asleep dormirse (o:ue) *v.*
  fall in love (with) enamorarse *v.*
  (de) **28 (2)**
  fall (season) otoño *m.* **13 (1)**
fallen caído/a *p.p.*
family familia *f.*
famous famoso/a *adj.*
fan aficionado/a *adj.*
  be a fan (of) ser aficionado/a (a)
far from lejos de *prep.*
farewell despedida *f.*
fascinate fascinar *v.* **19 (2)**
fashion moda *f.*
  be in fashion estar *v.* de moda
fast rápido/a *adj.*
fat gordo/a *adj.* **6 (1); grasa *f.***
father padre *m.* **4 (1)**
father-in-law suegro *m.* **4 (1)**
fault culpa *f.* **25 (2)**
favorite favorito/a *adj.*
fax (machine) fax *m.*
fear miedo *m.;* temer *v.*
February febrero *m.* **13 (1)**
feed the cat darle de comer al gato
  18 (2)
feel *v.* sentir(se) (e:ie) **15 (1), 21 (2)**
  feel better/worse sentirse (e:ie)
  mejor/peor **21 (2)**
  feel like (doing something) tener
  ganas de (+ *inf.*) **7 (1)**

feel the same sentirse(e:ie) igual
  21 (2)
  feel well/ill/horrible sentirse(e:ie)
  bien/mal/fatal **21 (2)**
festival festival *m.*
fever fiebre *f.* **21 (2)**
  have a fever tener *v.* (la) fiebre
  21 (2)
few pocos/as *adj. pl.*
field: field of study especialización *f.*
fight pelearse *v.* **22 (2)**
fifteen quince **1 (1)**
  young woman celebrating her
  fifteenth birthday quinceañera *f.*
fifth quinto/a *adj.*
fifty cincuenta **4 (1)**
fight luchar *v.* (por)
figure (number) cifra *f.*
file archivo *m.*
fill llenar *v.*
  fill out a form llenar un formulario
  fill up the tank llenar el tanque
finally finalmente *adv;* por último;
  por fin
find encontrar (o:ue) *v.* **17 (2)**
  find (each other) encontrar(se) *v.*
fine arts bellas artes *f., pl.*
fine multa *f.* **26 (2);** bien *adv.*
  avoid fines evitar *v.* las multas
  26 (2)
  That's fine. Está bien.
finger dedo *m.*
finish terminar *v.* **28 (2)**
  finish (doing something) terminar
  v. de (+ *inf.*)
fire incendio *m.;* despedir (e:i) *v.*
fireworks fuegos artificiales *pl., m.*
  20 (2)
firefighter bombero/a *m., f.* **12 (1)**
firm compañía *f.;* empresa *f.*
first primer, primero/a *adj.*
fish (food) pescado *m.* **9 (1);** pescar
  v.; **(live)** pez *m.* **4 (1)**
  fish market pescadería *f.*
fisherman pescador *m.*
fisherwoman pescadora *f.*
fishing pesca *f.*
fit (clothing) quedar *v.*
five cinco
five hundred quinientos/as
fix (put in working order) arreglar *v.*
fixed fijo/a *adj.*
flag bandera *f.* **2 (1)**
flan flan *m.* **9 (1)**
flank steak lomo *m.*
flat tire: We got a flat tire. Se nos
  pinchó una llanta.
flexible flexible *adj.* **3 (1)**
flood inundación *f.*
floor (story in a building) piso *m.;*
  suelo *m.*
  ground floor planta *f.* baja
  top floor planta *f.* alta
flower flor *f.*
flu gripe *f.* **21 (2)**

have the flu tener (la) gripe 21 (2)

fog niebla *f.*

foggy: It's (very) foggy. Hay (mucha) niebla.

folk folklórico/a *adj.*

follow seguir (e:i) *v.*

food comida *f.* 5 (1)

foolish tonto/a *adj.* 6 (1)

foot pie *m.*

football fútbol *m.* americano

for para *prep.*; por *prep.*
  for example por ejemplo
  for me para mí
  for (five years) durante (cinco) años 15 (1)

forbid prohibir *v.*

foreign extranjero/a *adj.*
  foreign languages lenguas *f,. pl.* extranjeras

forensic investigator investigador(a) forense *m., f.* 12 (1)

forest bosque *m.*

forget olvidar *v.*

fork tenedor *m.*

form formulario *m.*

formal *adj.* formal 20 (2)

forty cuarenta 4 (1)

forward en marcha *adv.*

four cuatro 1 (1)

four hundred cuatrocientos/as

fourteen catorce 1 (1)

fourth cuarto/a *adj.*

free libre *adj.*
  be free of charge ser gratis
  free time tiempo *m.* libre; ratos *m., pl.* libres

freedom libertad *f.*

freeway autopista *f.* 26 (2)

freezer congelador *m.*

French francés, francesa *adj.*
  French fries papas *f., pl* fritas; patatas *f., pl* fritas 9 (1)

frequently frecuentemente *adv.*; con frecuencia 8 (1)

Friday viernes *m., sing.* 5 (1)
  (on) Fridays los viernes *m., pl.* 5 (1)

fried frito/a *adj.*
  fried potatoes papas *f., pl.* fritas; patatas *f., pl.* fritas

friend amigo/a *m., f.* 4 (1)

friendly amable *adj.* 6 (1)

friendship amistad *f.*

fringe benefits prestaciones *f., pl.* 11 (1)

from de *prep.*; desde *prep.*
  from behind por atrás 25 (2)
  from where? ¿de dónde?
  from the left side del lado izquierdo 23 (2)
  from the right side del lado derecho 23 (2)

from the United States estadounidense *adj.*

from time to time de vez en cuando 22 (2)

He/She/It is from… Es de…

I'm from… Soy de…

fruit fruta *f.* 9 (1)
  fruit juice jugo *m.* de fruta
  fruit shop frutería *f.*

full lleno/a *adj.*

fun divertido/a *adj.* 6 (1)
  fun activity diversión *f.*
  have fun divertirse (e:ie) *v.* 14 (1)

function funcionar *v.*

funny gracioso/a *adj.* 6 (1)

furniture muebles *m., pl.* 18 (2)

furthermore además (de) *adv.*

future futuro *m.*; porvenir *m.*
  in the future en el futuro

G

gain weight aumentar *v.* de peso; engordar *v.*

game (match) partido *m.*; juego *m.*
  soccer game partido de fútbol *m.* 8(1)
  game show concurso *m.*

garage garaje *m.* 18 (2)

garden jardín *m.* 18 (2)

garlic ajo *m.*

gas station gasolinera *f.*

gasoline gasolina *f.* 26 (2)
  run out of gas quedarse *v.* sin gasolina 26 (2)

generous generoso/a *adj.* 3 (1)

geography geografía *f.* 1 (1)

German alemán, alemana *adj.*

get conseguir (e:i) *v.*; obtener *v.*
  get along well/badly (with) llevarse bien/mal (con) 22 (2)
  get/become sad/happy ponerse *v.* triste/feliz 20 (2)
  get bored aburrirse *v.*
  get e-mail recibir *v.* correo electrónico 8 (1)
  get gifts recibir *v.* regalos 8 (1)
  get good grades sacar buenas notas 5 (1)
  get home on time/late/early llegar a tiempo/tarde/temprano a casa 5 (1)
  get into trouble hacer *v.* travesuras 22 (2)
  get off at… salirse *v.* en… 26 (2)
  get off of/out of (a vehicle) bajar(se) *v.* de
get off, leave early/late salir temprano/tarde 11 (1)
  get on/into (a vehicle) subir(se) *v.* a
  get together juntarse *v.* 14 (1)
  get up levantarse *v.* 14 (1)
  get up early levantarse *v.* 14 (1)

gift regalo *m.*

girl chica *f.* 4 (1); muchacha; niña *f.* 4 (1)

girlfriend novia *f.* 4 (1)

give dar *v.* 20 (2), 24 (2); **(as a gift)** regalar 20 (2)
  give directions indicar cómo llegar *v.*
  give a kiss dar *v.* un beso 20 (2)

glass (drinking) vaso *m.*; vidrio *m.*

(made of) glass de vidrio

glasses gafas *f., pl.*
  sunglasses gafas de sol

global warming calentamiento global *m.*

gloves guantes *m., pl.* 13 (1)

go ir *v.* 20 (2)
  go away irse
  go camping ir de campamento 18 (2)
  go by boat ir en barco
  go by bus ir en autobús
  go by car ir en auto(móvil)/coche 20 (2)
  go by motorcycle ir en motocicleta
  go by plane ir en avión 20 (2)
  go by subway ir en metro
  go by taxi ir en taxi
  go by the bank pasar por el banco
  go by train ir en tren
  go by pasar *v.* por
  go down bajar *v.*
  go fishing ir de pesca
  go for a hike (in the mountains) ir de excursión (a las montañas) 18 (2)
  go for a walk dar *v.* un paseo 18 (2)
  go on rides subir(se) a los juegos 20 (2)
  go on the swings subir(se) a los columpios 22 (2)
  go on vacation irse *v.* de vacaciones 14 (1)
  go out salir *v.*
  go out to dinner (with friends) salir a cenar (con los amigos) 8 (1)
  go out with salir con
  go straight ahead for (three) blocks seguir derecho (tres) cuadras 26 (2)
  go through customs pasar por la aduana
  go to ir a (+ place) 8 (1)
  go to bed late acostarse (o:ue) *v.* tarde 14 (1)
  go up subir *v.*
  go with acompañar *v.*
  Let's get going. En marcha.
  Let's go. Vamos.

goblet copa *f.*

going to: be going to (do something) ir a (+ *inf.*) 7 (1)

golf golf *m.*

good buen, bueno/a *adj.* **6 (1)**
  Good afternoon. Buenas tardes. **1 (1)**
  Good evening. Buenas noches. **1 (1)**
  Good idea! ¡Buena idea!
  Good morning. Buenos días. **1 (1)**
  Good night. Buenas noches.
  I'm good, thanks. Bien, gracias.
  It's good that… Es bueno que…
goodbye adiós *m.* **1 (1)**
  say goodbye (to) despedirse *v.* (de) (e:i)
good-looking guapo/a *adj.* **6 (1)**
government gobierno *m.* **28 (2)**
GPS navegador GPS *m.*
graduate (from) graduarse *v.* (de); recibirse *v.* **28 (2)**
graduation graduación *f.* **28 (2)**
grains cereales *m., pl.*
granddaughter nieta *f.* **4 (1)**
grandfather abuelo *m.* **4 (1)**
grandmother abuela *f.* **4 (1)**
grandparents abuelos *m., pl.* **4 (1)**
grandson nieto *m.* **4 (1)**
grape uva *f.* **9 (1)**
graphic designer diseñador/a gráfico/a *m., f.* **12 (1)**
grass hierba *f.;* césped *m.;* pasto *m.* **18 (2)**
grave grave *adj.*
gray gris *adj. m., f.* **13 (1)**
great gran, grande *adj.;* fenomenal *adj.*
green verde *adj. m., f.* **13 (1)**
greet (each other) saludar(se) *v.*
greeting saludo *m.*
  Greetings to… Saludos a…
grill asador *m.* **18 (2)**
grilled (food) a la plancha
  grilled flank steak lomo a la plancha
ground floor planta *f.* baja
guest (at a house/hotel) huésped *m., f.;* **(invited to a function)** invitado/a *m., f.*
guide guía *m., f.*
gym gimnasio *m.* **2 (1)**
gymnasium gimnasio *m.*

H

hair pelo *m.* **21 (2)**
hairdresser peluquero/a *m., f.*
hairdressing salon peluquería *f.*
half medio/a *adj.*
  half-brother medio hermano
  half-sister media hermana
  half-past (time) y media
hallway pasillo *m.*
ham jamón *m.* **9 (1)**
hamburger hamburguesa *f.* **8 (1), 9 (1)**
hand mano *f.* **21 (2)**

Hands up! ¡Manos arriba!
handsome guapo/a *adj.*
happen ocurrir *v.*
happiness alegría *f.*
Happy birthday! ¡Feliz cumpleaños!
happy alegre *adj.;* contento/a *adj.* **15 (1);** feliz *adj.* **20 (2)**
  be happy alegrarse *v.* (de)
  get/become happy ponerse *v.* feliz **20 (2)**
hard difícil *adj.*
hard-working trabajador(a) *adj.* **6 (1)**
hardly apenas *adv.*
haste prisa *f.*
hat sombrero *m.* **13 (1)**
hate odiar *v.;* chocar *v.* **19 (2)**
have tener *v.* **4 (1), 20 (2)**
  have a(n)… ache tener (el) dolor de… **21 (2)**
  have a cold tener (el) catarro **21 (2)**
  have a cough tener (la) tos **21 (2)**
  have a fever tener (la) fiebre **21 (2)**
  Have a good trip! ¡Buen viaje!
  Have a nice day! ¡Que te vaya bien! *fam.* **1 (1)**
  Have a nice day! ¡Que le vaya bien! *form.* **1 (1)**
  have a picnic hacer un picnic **18 (2)**
  have a tooth pulled sacar(se) una muela
  have an infection tener una infección **21 (2)**
  have/enjoy good health tener buena salud **21 (2)**
  have insurance tener *v.* seguro *m.* **26 (2)**
  have the flu tener (la) gripe **21 (2)**
  have to (do something) tener que (+ *inf.*) **7 (1);** deber (+ *inf.*)
(I) have been… for (three) days Hace (tres) días que (yo)… **21 (2)**
he él *sub. pron.*
he is él es **3 (1)**
he/she/it is, you *form., sing.* **are** está
head cabeza *f.* **21 (2)**
headache dolor de cabeza *m.*
health salud *f.* **21 (2)**
  health center enfermería, *f.* **2 (1)**
  have/enjoy good health tener buena salud **21 (2)**
healthful saludable *adj.*
healthy sano/a, saludable *adj.*
  lead a healthy life llevar *v.* una vida sana
hear oír *v.* **17 (2)**
heard oído/a *p.p.*
hearing: sense of hearing oído *m.*
heart corazón *m.*
heat calor *m.*

Hello. Hola. *interj.;* **(on the telephone)** Aló.; ¿Bueno?; Diga.
help ayudar *v.* **11 (1);** servir (e:i) *v.*
  help each other ayudarse *v.*
her su(s) *poss. adj.* **4 (1);** la *pron.;* le *pron.; i.o. pron.* **19 (2)**
hers suyo(s)/a(s) *poss. pron.*
here aquí *adv.*
  Here it is… Aquí está…
  Here we are at/in… Aquí estamos en…
  It's not here. No está.
Hi. Hola. *interj.* **1 (1)**
hideout, hiding place escondite *m.* **22 (2)**
  play hide-and-seek jugar a las escondidillas/al escondite **22 (2)**
highway autopista *f.* **26 (2);** carretera *f.* **26 (2)**
high-heeled shoes zapatos de tacón *m., pl.* **13 (1)**
high school preparatoria (prepa) *f.* **22 (2);** escuela secundaria *f.* **22 (2)**
hike excursión *f.* **18 (2)**
  go on a hike hacer una excursión; ir de excursión **18 (2)**
hiker excursionista *m., f.*
hiking de excursión **18 (2)**
him lo *pron.;* le *pron., i.o. pron.* **19 (2)**
hire contratar *v.*
his su(s) *poss. adj.* **4 (1);** suyo(s)/a(s) *poss. pron.*
history historia *f.* **1 (1)**
hit (a car) chocar *v.* con **26 (2)**
hit someone (from behind) pegarle *v.* (por atrás) **25 (2)**
hobby pasatiempo *m.*
hockey hockey *m.*
holiday día *m.* de fiesta
home hogar *m.*
  home page página *f.* principal
  stay home quedarse *v.* en casa **14 (1)**
homemaker ama (*m., f.*) de casa **11 (1)**
homework tarea *f.*
honest honesto/a *adj.* **3 (1)**
honorable honesto/a *adj.* **3 (1)**
hood (car) capó *m.*
hope esperar *v.* **27 (2)**
  I hope (that) ojalá (que) *interj.* **27 (2)**
horrible *adj.* horrible; *(accident/injury/ illness)* fatal **21 (2);** mortal
horror terror *m.*
hors d'oeuvres entremeses *m., pl.*
horse caballo *m.*
hospital hospital *m.*
hot picante *adj.*
hot: be (very) hot (feel) tener (mucho) calor; **(weather)** hacer (mucho) calor **13 (1)**
hotel hotel *m.*

hour hora *f.*
house casa *f.*
  my boyfriend's/girlfriend's house
  la casa de mi novio/a **8 (1)**
  my friends'/parents' house la
  casa de mis amigos/padres **8 (1)**
household chores quehaceres *m., pl.*
  domésticos
housekeeper ama *m., f.* de casa
housing vivienda *f.*
How…! ¡Qué…!
  how ¿cómo? *adv.* **6 (1)**
  How are you? ¿Qué tal?
  How are you? ¿Cómo estás? *fam.*
  1 (1)
  How are you? ¿Cómo está usted?
  form. **1 (1)**
  How can I help you? ¿En qué
  puedo servirles?
  How did… go for you? ¿Cómo les
  fue…?
  How is it going? ¿Qué tal?
  How is/are . . . ? ¿Qué tal…?
  How long has it been since…?
  ¿Cuánto tiempo hace que…?
  21 (2)
  How much/many? ¿Cuánto(s)/a(s)?
  6 (1)
  How many classes are you taking?
  ¿Cuántas clases tomas? *fam.*
  1 (1)
  How many hours do you work?
  ¿Cuántas horas trabajas? *fam.*
  1 (1)   **How much does… cost?**
  ¿Cuánto cuesta…?
  How old are you? ¿Cuántos años
  tienes? *fam.* **4 (1)**
  How's the weather? ¿Qué tiempo
  hace?
however sin embargo *adv.*
hug (each other) abrazar(se) *v.*
humanities humanidades *f., pl.*
hunger hambre *f.*
hundred cien, ciento **4 (1)**
hungry: be (very) hungry tener *v.*
  (mucha) hambre **9 (1)**
hunting caza *f.*
hurricane huracán *m.*
hurry apurarse; darse prisa *v.*
  be in a (big) hurry tener *v.*
  (mucha) prisa
hurt doler (o:ue) *v.* **21 (2)**; **(hurt**
  oneself) lastimarse *v.* **21 (2)**
  It hurts me a lot. Me duele
  mucho.
  My back hurts. Me duele la
  espalda. **21 (2)**
  My legs hurt. Me duelen las
  piernas. **21 (2)**
husband esposo *m.* **4 (1)**

I yo *sub. pron.*

I am… Yo soy… **3 (1)**
I don't like them at all. No me
  gustan nada.
I hope (that) Ojalá (que) *interj.*
I wish (that) Ojalá (que) *interj.*
I would like… me gustaría(n)…
I would like you to meet… Le
  presento a… *form.* **1 (1)**; Te
  presento a… *fam.* **1 (1)**
ice cream helado *m.* **9 (1)**
  ice cream shop heladería *f.*
ice skate patinar *v.* (sobre hielo)
  18 (2)
iced helado/a *adj.*
  iced tea té helado
idea idea *f.*
idealistic idealista *adj.* **3 (1)**
if si *conj.*
illness enfermedad *f.*
impatient impaciente *m., f.* **3 (1)**
important importante *adj.*
  be important to importar *v*
  It's important that… Es
  importante que…
impossible imposible *adj.*
  It's impossible… Es imposible…
improbable improbable *adj.*
  It's improbable… Es improbable…
improve mejorar *v.*
in en *prep.*; por *prep.*
  in the afternoon de la tarde; por
  la tarde **5 (1)**
  in the evening de la noche;
  (early) por la tarde **5 (1)**
  in the morning de la mañana;
  por la mañana **5 (1)**
  in love (with) enamorado/a (de)
  in which en qué
  in front of delante de *prep.*;
  enfrente **26 (2)**
increase aumento *m.*
incredible increíble *adj.* **3 (1)**
inequality desigualdad *f.*
infection infección *f.* **21 (2)**
  have an infection tener una
  infección **21 (2)**
infirmary enfermería, *f.* **2 (1)**
inform informar *v.*
informal *adj.* informal **20 (2)**
inhabitants habitantes *m., pl*
injection inyección *f.*
  give an injection poner *v.* una
  inyección **24 (2)**
injure (oneself) lastimarse *v.* **21 (2)**
  injure (one's foot) lastimarse (el pie)
inmature inmaduro/a *adj.* **3 (1)**
inner ear oído *m.* **21 (2)**
inside (a)dentro *adv.* **15 (1)**
  be inside estar adentro/dentro
  de **15 (1)**
insist (on) insistir *v.* (en)
installments: pay in installments
  pagar *v.* a plazos
insurance seguro *m.* **26 (2)**

have insurance tener *v.* seguro *m.*
  26 (2)
intelligent inteligente *adj.*
intend pensar *v.* (+ *inf.*)
interest interesar *v.* **19 (2)**
interesting interesante *adj.* **3 (1)**
  be interesting to interesar *v.*
  19 (2)
  be interested in interesar *v.* **19 (2)**
international internacional *adj. m., f.*
Internet red *f.*; Internet *m.*
intersection intersección *f.* **26 (2)**
interview entrevista *f.* **28 (2)**;
  interview entrevistar *v.*
interviewer entrevistador(a) *m., f.*
introduction presentación *f.*
invest invertir (e:ie) *v.*
invite invitar *v.* **10 (1), 20 (2)**
  invite someone invitar a alguien
  20 (2)
iron planchar *v.* **18 (2)**
iron clothes planchar *v.* la ropa
  18 (2)
irresponsible irresponsable *adj.*
  3 (1)
it lo/la *pron.*
It's at … in the morning/afternoon/
  evening. Es a la(s)… de la
  mañana/tarde/noche. **2 (1)**
Italian italiano/a *adj.*
its su(s) *poss. adj.*, suyo(s)/a(s)
  poss. pron.

jacket chaqueta *f.* **13 (1)**
January enero *m.* **13 (1)**
Japanese japonés, japonesa *adj.*
jeans bluejeans *m., pl.* **13 (1)**
jewelry store joyería *f.*
job empleo *m.*; puesto *m.*; trabajo
  m. **8 (1)**
  job application solicitud *f.* de
  trabajo
jog correr *v.* **8 (1)**
journalism periodismo *m.*
journalist periodista *m., f.* **12 (1)**;
  reportero/a *m., f.*
joy alegría *f.*
  give joy dar *v.* alegría
joyful alegre *adj.*
juice jugo *m.*
  orange juice jugo de naranja *m.*
  9 (1)
July julio *m.* **13 (1)**
jump rope saltar *v.* la cuerda **22 (2)**
June junio *m.* **13 (1)**
jungle selva *f.*, jungla *f.*
just apenas *adv.*
  have just done something acabar
  de (+ *inf.*) **21 (2)**

K

keep (doing something) seguir (e:ie) *v.*
key llave *f.*
keyboard teclado *m.*
kilometer kilómetro *m.*
kind: That's very kind of you. Muy amable. *adj.*
kiss beso *m.* **20 (2)**
  kiss (each other) besar(se) *v.*
  give a kiss dar *v.* un beso **20 (2)**
kitchen cocina *f.* **18 (2)**
knee rodilla *f.*
knife cuchillo *m.*
know saber *v.*; conocer *v.* **12 (1)**
know how (+ *verb*) saber (+ *verb*) *v.* **11 (1)**

L

laboratory laboratorio *m.*
lack faltar *v.*
lake lago *m.*
lamp lámpara *f.* **18 (2)**
land tierra *f.*
landlord dueño/a *m., f.*
landscape paisaje *m.*
language lengua *f.*
  language professor profesor(a) de idiomas *m., f.* **12 (1)**
laptop (computer) computadora *f.* portátil
large gran, grande *adj.* **6 (1)**
large (clothing size) talla *f.* grande *adj.*
last durar *v.*; pasado/a *adj.*; último/a *adj.*
  last month el mes pasado **15 (1)**
  last name apellido *m.*
  last night anoche *adv.* **15 (1), 17 (2)**
  last week la semana pasada **15 (1), 17 (2)**
  last year el año pasado **15 (1), 17 (2)**
late tarde *adv.*
lately últimamente *adv.* **28 (2)**
later (on) más tarde *adv.*
  See you later. Hasta la vista.; Hasta luego.
laugh reírse (e:i) *v.*
laughed reído *p.p.*
laundromat lavandería *f.*
law ley *f.*
lawn pasto *m.* **18 (2)**
  mow the lawn cortar *v.* el pasto **18 (2)**
lawyer abogado/a *m., f.* **12 (1)**
lazy perezoso/a *adj.* **6 (1)**
learn aprender *v.*
  learn (how) aprender (+ *verb*) **19 (2)**
  learn new things aprender cosas nuevas **19 (2)**
least, (the) el/la/los/las menos

leave salir *v.*; irse *v.* **14 (1)**
  leave, get off early/late salir temprano/tarde **11 (1)**
  leave a tip dejar una propina
  leave for (a place) salir para
  leave from salir de
  leave behind dejar *v.*
left izquierdo/a *adj.*
  from/on the left side del/al lado izquierdo **23 (2)**
  be left behind quedar *v.*
  be left over quedar *v.*
  to the left of a la izquierda de
leg pierna *f.* **21 (2)**
lemon limón *m.*
lemonade limonada *f.* **9 (1)**
lend prestar *v.*
  lend money prestar *v.* dinero **11 (1), 24 (2)**
less menos *adv.*
  less… than menos… que **17 (2)**
  less than (+ number) menos de (+ *number*)
lesson lección *f.*
let dejar *v.*
  let someone use one's car dejar usar su coche **11 (1)**
  let's see a ver
letter carta *f.*
lettuce lechuga *f.*
liberty libertad *f.*
library biblioteca *f.* **2 (1)**
license (driver's) licencia *f.* de conducir/manejar **26 (2)**
lie mentira *f.*; decir *v.* mentiras **24 (2)**
lie down acostarse (o:ue) *v.* **17 (2)**
life vida *f.*
  of my life de mi vida
lifestyle: lead a healthy lifestyle llevar una vida sana
lift levantar *v.*
  lift weights levantar pesas **18 (2)**
light luz *f.*
like como *prep.*; gustar *v.* **19 (2)**
  like this así *adv.*
  like very much encantar *v.* **19 (2)** fascinar *v.* **19 (2)**
  I like… me gusta(n)… **3 (1)**
  I like… very much Me encanta…*v.*
  Do you like… ? ¿Te gusta(n)…? **3 (1)**
  Do you like… ? ¿Le gusta(n)…? *(form.)* **3 (1)**
likeable simpático/a *adj.*
likewise igualmente *adv.*
line línea *f.*; cola **(queue)** *f.*
liquid líquido *m.* **21 (2)**
listen to escuchar *v.*
  Listen! (command) ¡Oye! *fam., sing.*; ¡Oigan! *form., pl.*
  listen to music escuchar música **5 (1)**

  listen to the radio escuchar la radio
literature literatura *f.* **1 (1)**
little (quantity) poco/a *adj.*; poco *adv.*
live vivir *v.*
  live in/with vivir *v.* en/con **8 (1)**
living room sala *f.* **18 (2)**
loan préstamo *m.*; prestar *v.*
  loan money prestar *v.* dinero **24 (2)**
lobster langosta *f.* **9 (1)**
located situado/a *adj.*
  be located quedar *v.*
lodging alojamiento *m.*
long largo/a *adj.*
  How long has it been since…? ¿Cuánto tiempo hace que…? **21 (2)**
look (at) mirar *v.*
look for buscar *v.* **5 (1)**
lose perder (e:ie) *v.* **17 (2)**
  lose weight adelgazar *v.*
lost perdido/a *adj.*
  be lost estar perdido/a
lot, a muchas veces
lot of, a mucho/a *adj.*
love (another person) querer (e:ie) *v.* **20 (2)**; (things) encantar *v.* **19 (2)**; amor *m.*; **in love (with)** enamorado/a (de) *adj.*; fascinar *v.* **19 (2)**
luck suerte *f.*
lucky: be (very) lucky tener (mucha) suerte
luggage equipaje *m.*
lunch almuerzo *m.* **9 (1)**
  have lunch almorzar (o:ue) *v.* **10 (1), 9 (1)**

M

ma'am señora (Sra.) *f.*
mad enojado/a *adj.*
made hecho *p.p.* **28 (2)**
magazine revista *f.*
  read a magazine leer una revista
magnificent magnífico/a *adj.*
mail correo *m.*; enviar *v.*, mandar *v.* **24 (2)**
  mail a letter echar una carta al buzón
  mail carrier cartero/a *m.*
mailbox buzón *m.*
main principal *adj. m., f.*
maintain mantener *v.*
make hacer *v.* **8 (1), 20 (2)**
  make a good living, to make good money ganar *v.* bien **12 (1)**
  make the bed hacer la cama **18 (2)**
makeup maquillaje *m.*
  put on makeup pintarse *v.* **14 (1)**
mall centro comercial *m.* **8 (1)**
man hombre *m.*

manager gerente *m.*, *f.* **12 (1)**
many mucho/a *adj.*
　many times muchas veces
map mapa *m.* **2 (1)**
March marzo *m.* **13 (1)**
margarine margarina *f.*
marinated fish ceviche *m.*
　lemon-marinated shrimp ceviche
　de camarón
marine turtle tortuga marina *f.*
marital status estado *m.* civil
market mercado *m.*
　open-air market mercado al aire
　libre
marriage matrimonio *m.*
married casado/a *adj.* **6 (1)**
　get married (to) casarse *v.* (con)
　27 (2)
marvelous maravilloso/a *adj.*
marvelously maravillosamente *adv.*
Mass (religious service) misa *f.* **8 (1)**
massage masaje *m.*
Master's degree maestría *m.* **28 (2)**
masterpiece obra *f.* maestra
match (sports) partido *m.*
　match hacer *v.* juego (con)
materialistic materialista *adj.* **3 (1)**
mathematics matemáticas *f.*, *pl.*
　1 (1)
matter importar *v.*
mature maduro/a *adj.* **3 (1)**
maturity madurez *f.*
maximum máximo/a *m.*
May mayo *m.* **13 (1)**
maybe tal vez *adv.*; quizás *adv.*
mayonnaise mayonesa *f.*
me me *pron; i.o. pron.* **19 (2)**; mí
　pron. **10 (1)**, **19 (2)**
meal comida *f.*
means of communication medios *m.*,
　pl. de comunicación
meat carne *f.*
mechanic mecánico/a *m.*, *f.*
　(mechanic's) repair shop taller *m.*
　mecánico; garaje *m.*
media medios *m.*, *pl.* de comunicación
medical médico/a *adj.*
medication medicamento *m.*
medicine medicina *f.*
medium mediano/a *adj.*
meet (each other) encontrar(se) *v.*;
　(someone) conocer *v.* **12 (1)**
meeting reunión *f.*
menu menú *m.*
message (telephone) recado *m.*
messy desordenado/a *adj.* **6 (1)**;
　desarreglado/a *adj* **18 (2)**
　be messy estar desarreglado/a
　18 (2)
Mexican mexicano/a *adj.*
Mexico México *m.*
microwave microonda *f.* **18 (2)**
　microwave oven horno *m.* de
　microondas
middle age madurez *f.*

middle school (in Mexico) escuela
　secundaria *f.* **22 (2)**
midnight medianoche *f.*
mile milla *f.*
milk leche *f.* **9 (1)**
million millón
　million of millón de
mine mío/a(s) *poss. pron.*
mineral mineral *m.*
　mineral water agua *f.* mineral
mini-skirt minifalda *f.* **13 (1)**
minute minuto *m.*
mirror espejo *m.* **18 (2)**
misbehave portarse *v.* mal **22 (2)**
mischievous travieso/a *adj.* **22 (2)**
　be mischievous ser travieso/a
　22 (2)
mistaken equivocado/a *adj.*
Miss señorita (Srta.) *f.* **1 (1)**
miss perder (e:ie) *v.*
modem módem *m.*
modern moderno/a *adj.* **20 (2)**
mom mamá *f.*
Monday lunes *m.*, *sing.* **5 (1)**
　(on) Mondays los lunes *m.*, *pl.*
　5 (1)
money dinero *m.*
monitor monitor *m.*
monkey mono *m.*
month mes *m.* **13 (1)**
　last month el mes pasado **15 (1)**,
　17 (2)
monument monumento *m.*
moon luna *f.*
more más *adj.*
　more... than más... que **17 (2)**
　more than (+ number) más de
　(+ *number*)
　most, (the) el/la/los/las más
morning mañana *f.*
　in the morning por la manana
　5 (1)
mother madre *f.* **4 (1)**
mother-in-law suegra *f.* **4 (1)**
motor motor *m.*
motorcycle moto(cicleta) *f.*
mountain montaña *f.*
mouse ratón *m.*
mouth boca *f.* **21 (2)**
move (to another house/city/country)
　mudarse *v.* **28 (2)**
movie película *f.*
　movie star estrella *f.* de cine
　movie theater cine *m.* **8 (1)**
mow the lawn cortar *v.* el pasto
　18 (2)
MP3 player reproductor de MP3 *m.*
Mr. señor (Sr.) *m.* **1 (1)**
Mrs. señora (Sra.) *f.* **1 (1)**
much mucho/a *adj.*
mug taza *f.*
municipal municipal *adj.*
murder crimen *m.*
muscle músculo *m.*
museum museo *m.* **8 (1)**

mushroom champiñón *m.*
music música *f.* **1 (1)**, **23 (2)**
　play loud music tener/poner la
　música muy alta **23 (2)**
musical musical *adj.*
musician músico/a *m.*, *f.*
must: It must be . . . Debe ser…
my mi(s) *poss. adj.* **4 (1)**; mío(s)/a(s)
　poss. pron.

N

name nombre *m.*
　in my name a mi nombre
　in the name of a nombre de
　last name apellido *m.*
　My name is... Me llamo…
　be named llamarse *v.*
napkin servilleta *f.*
national nacional *adj.*, *m.*, *f.*
nationality nacionalidad *f.*
natural natural *adj.*, *m.*, *f.*
　natural disaster desastre *m.* natural
　natural resource recurso *m.* natural
nature naturaleza *f.*
nauseated mareado/a *adj.*
near cerca de *prep.*
neaten arreglar *v.*
necessary necesario/a *adj.*
　It's necessary that... Es necesario
　que…; Hay que…
neck cuello *m.* **21 (2)**
need faltar *v.*; necesitar *v.*
　need books necesitar libros **5 (1)**
negative negativo/a *adj.*
neighbor vecino/a *m.*, *f.* **23 (2)**
neighborhood barrio *m.*
neither... nor ni… ni *conj.*; **neither**
　tampoco *adv.* **18 (2)**
nephew sobrino *m.* **4 (1)**
nervous nervioso/a *adj.* **3 (1)** ,
　15 (1)
network red *f.*
never nunca *adv.* **8 (1)**, **18 (2)**;
　jamás *adv.*
new nuevo/a *adj.* **6 (1)**
newlywed recién casado/a *m.*, *f.*
news noticias *f.*, *pl.*; actualidades *f.*, *pl.*
newscast noticiero *m.*
newspaper periódico *m.*; diario *m.*
　read a newspaper leer un
　periódico **8 (1)**
next próximo/a *adj.* **7 (1)**
next Monday/Tuesday/Wednesday
　(etc.) el próximo lunes/martes/
　miércoles (etc.) **7 (1)**
　next week la próxima semana
　7 (1)
　next year el año que viene **7 (1)**
next to al lado de
nice simpático/a *adj.*; amable *adj.*;
　bueno/a *adj* **6 (1)**
　Nice to meet you. Mucho gusto.
　1 (1)

Nice to meet you, too. Igualmente. 1 **(1)**
niece sobrina *f.* 4 **(1)**
night noche *f.*
  night stand mesita *f.* de noche; mesa *f.* de noche 18 **(2)**
nightclub discoteca *f.* 8 **(1)**
nine nueve 1 **(1)**
nine hundred novecientos/as
nineteen diecinueve 1 **(1)**
ninety noventa 4 **(1)**
ninth noveno/a
no no; ningún, ninguno/a(s) *adj.* 18 **(2)**
  No, I don't like it. No, no me gusta. 3 **(1)**
  no one nadie *pron.* 18 **(2)**
  No problem. No hay problema.
  no way de ninguna manera
none ningún, ninguno/a(s) *adj.* 18 **(2)**
noon mediodía *m.*
nor ni *conj.*
north norte *m.* 26 **(2)**
  to the north al norte 26 **(2)**
nose nariz *f.* 21 **(2)**
not no
  not any ningún, ninguno/a(s) *adj.* 18 **(2)**
  not anyone nadie *pron.* 18 **(2)**
  not anything nada *pron.* 18 **(2)**
  not bad at all nada mal
  not either tampoco *adv.* 18 **(2)**
  not ever nunca *adv.* 18 **(2)**; jamás *adv.*
  Not very well. No muy bien.
  not working descompuesto/a *adj.*
notebook cuaderno *m.* 2 **(1)**
nothing nada *pron.* 18 **(2)**
noun sustantivo *m.*
November noviembre *m.* 13 **(1)**
now ahora *adv.*
nowadays hoy día *adv.*
nowhere ninguna parte, (a) *adv.* 8 **(1)**
nuclear energy energía nuclear *f.*
number número *m.*
nurse enfermero/a *m., f.* 12 **(1)**
nutrition nutrición *f.*

O

o'clock: It's… o'clock Son las…
  It's one o'clock. Es la una.
obey obedecer (c:zc) *v.* 22 **(2)**
  obey the traffic signs obedecer (c:zc) *v.* las señales de tránsito 26 **(2)**
obligation deber *m.*
obtain conseguir (e:i) *v.*; obtener *v.*
obvious obvio *adj.*
  it's obvious es obvio
occupation ocupación *f.*
occur ocurrir *v.*
ocean mar *m.*; océano *m.*

October octubre *m.* 13 **(1)**
of de *prep.*
  of course claro que sí; por supuesto
offer oferta *f.*; ofrecer (c:zc) *v.* 24 **(2)**
office oficina *f.* 2 **(1)**
  doctor's office consultorio *m.*
often a menudo *adv.* 22 **(2)**; con frecuencia *adv.* 8 **(1)**
Oh! ¡Ay!
oil aceite *m.*
okay regular *adj.*
  It's okay. Está bien.
old viejo/a *adj.* 6 **(1)**
  old age vejez *f.*
older mayor *adj., m., f.* 6 **(1)**
  older brother, sister hermano/a mayor *m., f.*
oldest el/la mayor
on en *prep.*; sobre *prep.*
  on behalf of de parte de *prep.*
  on the dot en punto *adv.*
  on the left side al lado izquierdo 23 **(2)**
  on the right side al lado derecho 23 **(2)**
  on time a tiempo *adv.*
  on top of encima de *prep.*
once una vez
  once a week una vez a la semana 8 **(1)**
  once again una vez más
one un, uno/a 1 **(1)**
  one hundred cien(to)
  one million un millón
  one thousand mil
  one time una vez
  one way (travel) ida *f.*
onion cebolla *f.*
only sólo *adv.*; único/a *adj.*
  only child hijo/a único/a *m., f.* 4 **(1)**
open abrir *v.* 8(1); abierto/a *adj.*
  open presents abrir *v.* los regalos 20 **(2)**
open-air al aire libre
opened abierto/a *p.p.* 28 **(2)**
opera ópera *f.*
operation operación *f.*
opposite en frente de *prep.*
optimistic optimista *adj.* 3 **(1)**
or o *conj.*
orange anaranjado/a *adj.*; naranja *f.* 13 **(1)**
  orange juice jugo de naranja *m.* 9 **(1)**
orchestra orquesta *f.*
order mandar; **(food)** pedir (e:i) *v.* 9 **(1)**
  in order to para *prep.*
orderly ordenado/a *adj.* 6 **(1)**
ordinal (numbers) ordinal *adj.*
other otro/a *adj.*
our nuestro(s)/a(s) *poss. adj.* 4 **(1)**; *poss. pron.*
outgoing extrovertido/a *adj.* 3 **(1)**

out of order descompuesto/a *adj.*
outside fuera *adv.*
  be outside estar afuera/fuera de 15 **(1)**
outskirts afueras *f., pl.*
oven horno *m.* 18 **(2)**
over sobre *prep.*
own propio/a *adj.*
owner dueño/a *m., f.*

P

P.M. tarde *f.*
pack (one's suitcases) hacer *v.* las maletas 20 **(2)**
package paquete *m.*
page página *f.*
pain dolor *m.*
  have a pain in the (knee) tener *v.* dolor de (rodilla)
  have a(n)… ache/pain tener (el) dolor de… 21 **(2)**
paint pintar *v.*
painter pintor(a) *m., f.*
painting pintura *f.*
pair par *m.*
  pair of shoes par de zapatos
pajamas pijama *m., f.* 13 **(1)**
pants pantalones *m., pl.* 13 **(1)**
pantyhose medias *f., pl.*
paper papel *m.* 2 **(1)**; **(report)** informe *m.*
  paper money billete *m.*
paragraph párrafo *m.*
Pardon me. (May I?) Con permiso.; **(Excuse me.).** Perdón.
parents padres *m., pl.* 4 **(1)**; papás *m., pl.*
park parque *m.* 8 **(1)**; estacionar *v.*
  park in front of estacionarse *v.* enfrente de 26 **(2)**
parking lot estacionamiento *m.* 2 **(1)**
parole officer/prison guard oficial de prisión *m., f.* 12 **(1)**
partner (one of a couple) pareja *f.*
party fiesta *f.* 18 **(2)**
  throw a party hacer una fiesta 18 **(2)**
pass pasar *v.*
  pass (two) traffic lights pasar (dos) semáforos 26 **(2)**
passed pasado/a *p.p.*
passenger pasajero/a *m., f.*
passport pasaporte *m.*
past pasado/a *adj.*
pastime pasatiempo *m.*
pastry shop pastelería *f.*
patient paciente *m., f.* 3 **(1)**
patio patio *m.* 18 **(2)**
pay pagar *v.* 11 **(1)**, 24 **(2)**
  pay attention poner *v.* atención 11 **(1)**
  pay the cell phone bill pagar la cuenta del celular 7 **(1)**

pay with pagar con
pay in cash pagar *v.* al contado; pagar en efectivo
pay in installments pagar *v.* a plazos
pay the bill pagar *v.* la cuenta
pea arveja *m.*
peace paz *f.*
peach melocotón *m.*
pear pera *f.* **9 (1)**
pen pluma *f.* **2 (1)**
pencil lápiz *m.* **2 (1)**
penicillin penicilina *f.*
people gente *f.*
pepper pimienta *f.* **9 (1)**
per por *prep.*
percent por ciento
perfect perfecto/a *adj.*
perhaps quizás *adv.;* tal vez *adv.*
periods plazos *m., pl.*
permission permiso *m.*
person persona *f.*
pessimistic pesimista *adj.* **3 (1)**
pharmacy farmacia *f.*
PhD doctorado *m.* **28 (2)**
phenomenal fenomenal *adj.*
philosophy filosofía *f.* **1 (1)**
photograph foto(grafía) *f.*
physical (exam) examen *m.* médico
  physical education educación física *f.* **1 (1)**
  physical therapist fisioterapeuta *m., f.* **12 (1)**
physician médico/a *m., f.* **12 (1);** doctor(a) *m., f.*
physics física *f., sing.* **1 (1)**
pick up recoger *v.* **18 (2)**
  pick up one's things/clothes recoger *v.* las cosas/la ropa **18 (2)**
picnic picnic *m.* **18 (2)**
  have a picnic hacer un picnic **18 (2)**
picture foto *f.;* pintura *f.*
pie pastel *m.*
pill (tablet) pastilla *f.* **21(2)**
pillow almohada *f.*
pineapple piña *f.*
pink rosado/a *adj.*
place lugar *m.;* poner *v.*
  place (put) things in their place poner *v.* las cosas en su lugar **11 (1)**
plaid de cuadros *adj.*
plan (to do something) pensar *v.* (+ *inf.*)
plane avión *m.* **20 (2)**
  go by plane ir *v.* en avión **20 (2)**
plans planes *m., pl.*
  have plans tener *v.* planes
plant planta *f.*
plastic plástico *m.*
  (made of) plastic de plástico
plate plato *m.*
platter of fried food fuente *f.* de fritada

play drama *m.;* comedia *f.;* jugar (u:ue) *v.* **10 (1); (a musical instrument)** tocar *v.* **(play the guitar)** tocar la guitarra **5 (1); (a role)** hacer *v.* el papel; **(cards)** jugar *v.* a (las cartas); **(sports)** practicar *v.* deportes
  play ball jugar a la pelota **22 (2)**
  play checkers jugar a las damas chinas **22 (2)**
  play hide-and-seek jugar a las escondidillas/al escondite **22 (2)**
  play Nintendo jugar Nintendo **22 (2)**
  play loud music tener/poner la música muy alta **23 (2)**
  play with dolls jugar a las muñecas **22 (2)**
player jugador(a) *m., f.*
playwright dramaturgo/a *m., f.*
plead rogar (o:ue) *v.*
pleasant agradable *adj.* **6 (1)**
Please. Por favor.
Pleased to meet you. Mucho gusto. **1 (1);** Encantado/a. *adj.* **1 (1)**
pleasing: be pleasing to gustar *v.* **19 (2)**
pleasure gusto *m.;* placer *m.*
  It's a pleasure to... Gusto de (+ *inf.*)
  It's been a pleasure. Ha sido un placer.
  The pleasure is mine. El gusto es mío.
poem poema *m.*
poet poeta *m., f.*
poetry poesía *f.*
police (force) policía *f.* **23 (2)**
  call the police llamar a la policía **23 (2)**
  police officer policía *m.,* mujer *f.* policía **12 (1)**
political político/a *adj.*
politician político/a *m., f.*
politics política *f.*
polka-dotted de lunares *adj.*
poll encuesta *f.*
pollute contaminar *v.*
polluted contaminado/a *adj.*
  be polluted estar contaminado/a
pollution contaminación *f.*
pool piscina *f.* **2 (1)**
poor pobre *adj.* **6 (1)**
population población *f.*
pork cerdo *m.* carne de cerdo *m.* **9 (1)**
  pork chop chuleta *f.* de cerdo
portable portátil *adj.*
  portable computer computadora *f.* portátil
position puesto *m.* **11 (1) , 28 (2)**
possessive posesivo/a *adj.*
possible posible *adj.*
  it's (not) possible (no) es posible
post office correo *m.*
postcard postal *f.;* tarjeta *f.* postal

poster cartel *m.*
potato papa *f.;* patata *f.*
  baked potato papa al horno *f.* **9 (1)**
pottery cerámica *f.*
practice entrenarse *v.;* practicar *v.*
prank travesura *f.* **22 (2)**
prefer preferir (e:ie) *v.* **10 (1)**
pregnant embarazada *adj. f.*
  to get pregnant embarazarse *v.* **28 (2)**
prepare preparar *v.*
preposition preposición *f.*
prescribe (medicine) recetar *v.*
prescription receta *f.*
present regalo *m.* **20 (2);** presentar *v.*
  open presents abrir *v.* los regalos **20 (2)**
press prensa *f.*
pressure: be under a lot of pressure sufrir *v.* muchas presiones
pretty bonito/a *adj.* **6 (1);** bastante *adv.*
price precio *m.*
  fixed price precio *m.* fijo
print estampado/a *adj.;* imprimir *v.*
printer impresora *f.*
prison guard/parole officer oficial de prisión *m., f.* **12 (1)**
private (room) individual *adj.*
private school escuela particular *f.* **22 (2)**
prize premio *m.*
probable probable *adj.*
  it's (not) probable (no) es probable
problem problema *m.* **10 (1)**
profession profesión *f.*
professor profesor(a) *m., f.* **1 (1)**
  language professor profesor(a) de idiomas *m., f.* **12 (1)**
program programa *m.*
  training program programa de capacitación **28 (2)**
programmer (computer) programador(a) *m., f.* **12 (1)**
prohibit prohibir *v.*
promise prometer *v.* **24 (2)**
promotion (career) ascenso *m.*
pronoun pronombre *m.*
protect proteger *v.*
protein proteína *f.*
provided that con tal (de) que *conj.*
psychologist sicólogo/a *m., f.* **12 (1)**
psychology sicología *f.* **1 (1)**
public school escuela pública *f.* **22 (2)**
publish publicar *v.*
Puerto Rican puertorriqueño/a *adj.*
Puerto Rico Puerto Rico *m.*
pull a tooth sacar *v.* una muela
purchases compras *f., pl.*
pure puro/a *adj.*
purple morado/a *adj.* **13 (1)**
purse bolsa *f.*

punish castigar *v.* **22 (2)**
push empujar *v.* **25 (2)**
put poner *v.* **20 (2)**; puesto/a *p.p.*
28 (2)
  put a letter in the mailbox echar *v.*
  una carta al buzón
  put on (a performance) presentar *v.*
  put on (clothing) ponerse *v.* la
  ropa **14 (1)**
  put on makeup maquillarse *v.;*
  pintarse *v.* **14 (1)**
  to place (put) things in their place
  poner *v.* las cosas en su lugar
  11 (1)
puzzles rompecabezas *m., pl.* **22 (2)**
  do puzzles armar rompecabezas *v.*
  22 (2)

Q

quality calidad *f.*
quarter trimestre *m.*
  quarter after (time) y cuarto; y
  quince
  quarter to (time) menos cuarto;
  menos quince
question pregunta *f.*
quickly rápido *adv.*
quiet tranquilo/a *adj.* **3 (1) , 15 (1)**
quit dejar *v.*
quite bastante *adv.*
quiz prueba *f.* **2 (1)**

R

racism racismo *m.*
radio (medium) radio *f.*
  radio (set) radio *m.*
rain llover (o:ue) *v.* **13 (1)**
  It's raining, it rains. Llueve.
  13 (1)
raincoat impermeable *m.* **13 (1)**
rainforest bosque *m.* tropical
raise (salary) aumento *v.* de sueldo
read leer *v.* **8 (1), 17 (2)**; leído/a
  p.p.
ready listo/a *adj.* **6 (1)**
real estate agency agencia *f.* de
  bienes raíces
realize darse *v.* cuenta **25 (2)**
reap the benefits (of) disfrutar *v.*
  (de)
reason razón *f.*
rebellious rebelde *adj.* **22 (2)**
  be rebellious ser rebelde **22 (2)**
receive recibir *v.*
  receive (get) e-mail recibir correo
  electrónico **8 (1)**
  receive (get) gifts recibir regalos
  8 (1)
recommend recomendar (e:ie) *v.*
  27 (2)
recycle reciclar *v.*
recycling reciclaje *m.*

red rojo/a *adj.* **13 (1)**
red-haired pelirrojo/a *adj.* **6 (1)**
red light alto *m.;* semáforo *m.* en
  rojo **26 (2)**
  run a red light pasarse *v.* el
  alto/el semáforo en rojo **26 (2)**
reduce reducir *v.*
  reduce stress/tension aliviar *v.* el
  estrés/la tensión
refrigerator refrigerador *m.* **18 (2)**
region región *f.*
regret sentir (e:ie) *v.*
related to sitting sedentario/a *adj.*
relationships relaciones *f., pl.*
relatives parientes *m., pl.* **4 (1)**
relax relajarse *v.*
relieve stress/tension aliviar el
  estrés/la tensión
remain quedarse *v.*
remember recordar (o:ue) *v.* **10 (1)**;
  acordarse (o:ue) *v.* (de)
remote control control *m.* remoto
renewable renovable *adj.*
rent alquilar *v.;* alquiler *m.*
repeat repetir (e:i) *v.*
report informe *m.;* reportaje *m.*
reporter reportero/a *m., f.*
representative representante *m., f.*
reprimand regañar *v.* **22 (2)**
request pedir (e:i) *v.* **9 (1), 24 (2)**
reservation reservación *f.*
reserved reservado/a *adj.* **3 (1),
  6 (1)**
resign (from) renunciar (a) *v.*
resolve resolver (o:ue) *v.*
resolved resuelto/a *p.p.*
resource recurso *m.*
responsibility deber *v.*
responsible responsable *adj.* **3 (1)**
rest descansar *v.* **5 (1)**; descanso
  m. **21 (2)**
  the rest lo/los/las demás *pron.*
restaurant restaurante *m.* **8 (1)**
résumé currículum *m.* **28 (2)**
retire (from work) jubilarse *v.*
return regresar *v.;* volver (o:ue) *v.;*
  devolver (o:ue) *v.* **27 (2)**
  return trip vuelta *f.*
returned vuelto/a *p.p.* **28 (2)**
rice arroz *m.* **9 (1)**
rich rico/a *adj.* **6 (1)**
ride pasear *v.*
  ride a bicycle pasear en bicicleta;
  andar *v.* en bicicleta **18 (2)**
  ride a horse montar a caballo
  18 (2)
ridiculous ridículo/a *adj.*
  it's ridiculous es ridículo
right derecha *f.*
  from/on the right side del/al
  lado derecho **23 (2)**
  right away enseguida *adv.*
  right here aquí mismo
  right now ahora mismo
  right there allí mismo

  be right tener *v.* razón
  to the right of a la derecha de
  right? *(question tag)* ¿no?;
  ¿verdad?
rights derechos *m., pl.*
ring (a doorbell) sonar (o:ue) *v.*
ring (engagement) anillo (de
  compromiso) *m.* **27 (2)**
river río *m.*
road camino *m.*
roast beef bistec de res *m.* **9 (1)**
roast chicken pollo *m.* asado
roasted asado/a *adj.*
rock piedra *f.*
role papel *m.*
rollerblade patinar v. en línea **18 (2)**
romantic romántico/a *adj.* **3 (1)**
room habitación *f.;* cuarto *m.*
  18 (2); (large, living) sala *f.*
roommate compañero/a *m., f.* de
  cuarto
rope cuerda *f.* **22 (2)**
  jump rope saltar *v.* la cuerda
  22 (2)
round-trip de ida y vuelta
  round-trip ticket pasaje *m.* de ida
  y vuelta
route camino *m.*
routine rutina *f.*
rude grosero/a *adj.* **6 (1)**
rug alfombra *f.* **18 (2)**
run correr *v.* **8 (1)**
  run a red light pasarse *v.* el
  alto/el semáforo en rojo **26 (2)**
  run errands hacer diligencias
  run into (have an accident)
  chocar *v.* (con); **(meet
  accidentally)** darse con *v.*
  run out of gas quedarse *v.* sin
  gasolina **26 (2)**
rush apurarse; darse prisa *v.*
Russian ruso/a *adj.*

S

sad triste *adj.* **15 (1)**
  it's sad es triste
  get/become sad ponerse *v.* triste
  20 (2)
safe seguro/a *adj.*
said dicho/a *p.p.* **28 (2)**
sake: for the sake of por *prep.*
salad ensalada *f.*
  lettuce and tomato salad la
  ensalada de lechuga y tomate
  9 (1)
salary salario *m.;* sueldo *m.*
  high/low salary sueldo alto/bajo
  m. **11 (1)**
sale rebaja *f.*
salesperson vendedor(a) *m., f.*
salmon salmón *m.*
salt sal *f.* **9 (1)**
salty salado/a *adj.*

same mismo/a *adj.*; igual **21 (2)**
  feel the same sentirse (e:ie) igual **21 (2)**
sandal sandalia *f.* **13 (1)**
sandwich sándwich *m.*
Saturday sábado *m.* **5 (1)**
  (on) Saturdays los sábados *m., pl.* **5 (1)**
sausage salchicha *f.*
save (on a computer) guardar *v.*
  save (money) ahorrar *v.* **28 (2)**
savings ahorros *m., pl.*
  savings account cuenta *f.* de ahorros
say decir *v.* **20 (2), 24 (2);** declarar *v.*
scarcely apenas *adv.*
scared: be (very) scared tener *v.* (mucho) miedo
scarf bufanda *f.* **13 (1)**
schedule horario *m.*
  flexible/fixed schedule el horario flexible/fijo **11 (1)**
school escuela *f.* **8 (1);** colegio *m.* **22 (2)**
  Catholic school colegio católico *m.* **22 (2)**
  elementary school primaria *f.* **22 (2)**
  high school preparatoria (prepa) *f.* **22 (2);** escuela secundaria *f.* **22 (2)**
  middle school (in Mexico) escuela secundaria *f.* **22 (2)**
  private school escuela particular *f.* **22 (2)**
  public school escuela pública *f.* **22 (2)**
science ciencia *f.*
  science fiction ciencia ficción *f.*
scientist científico/a *m., f.*
scold regañar *v.* **22 (2)**
scream gritar *v.*
screen pantalla *f.*
scuba dive bucear *v.* **18 (2)**
sculpt esculpir *v.*
sculptor escultor(a) *m., f.*
sculpture escultura *f.*
sea mar *m.*; océano *m.*
seafood mariscos *m., pl.* **9 (1)**
search: in search of por *prep.*
season estación *f.*
seat silla *f.* **2 (1), 18 (2)**
seat belt cinturón *m.* de seguridad **26 (2)**
  wear the seat belt ponerse *v.* el cinturón de seguridad to **26 (2)**
second segundo/a *adj.*
secretary secretario/a *m., f.*
sedentary sedentario/a *adj.*
see ver *v.* **20 (2)**
  see a movie at home ver *v.* una película en casa **8 (1)**
  see the parade/fireworks ver *v.* el desfile/los fuegos artificiales **20 (2)**

see (you) again volver *v.* a ver (te, lo, la)
see movies ver películas
See you. Nos vemos.
See you later. Hasta la vista.; Hasta luego. **1 (1)**
See you soon. Hasta pronto.
See you tomorrow. Hasta mañana. **1 (1);** Nos vemos mañana. **1 (1)**
seem parecer *v.*
seen visto/a *p.p.* **28 (2)**
sell vender *v.*
  sell food vender *v.* comida **8 (1)**
semester semestre *m.*
send enviar *v.*; mandar *v.*
  send a present mandar un regalo **11 (1)**
  send text messages mandar *v.* mensajes **11 (1)**
sentimental sentimental *adj.* **3 (1)**
separate (from) separarse *v.* (de) **28 (2)**
separated separado/a *adj.*
September septiembre *m.* **13 (1)**
sequence secuencia *f.*
serious grave *adj.*; serio/a *adj.* **3 (1), 6 (1)**
  extremely serious gravísimo/a *adj.*
serve servir (e:i) *v.* **9 (1)**
set (fixed) fijo *adj.*
  set the table poner *v.* la mesa **18 (2)**
seven siete **1 (1)**
seven hundred setecientos/as
seventeen diecisiete **1 (1)**
seventh séptimo/a *adj.*
seventy setenta **4 (1)**
several varios/as *adj., pl.*
sexism sexismo *m.*
shame lástima *f.*
  It's a shame. Es una lástima.
shampoo champú *m.*
shape forma *f.*
  be in good shape estar en buena forma
share compartir *v.* **22 (2)**
  share toys compartir *v.* los juguetes **22 (2)**
sharp (time) en punto
shave afeitarse *v.*; rasurarse **23 (2)**
shaving cream crema *f.* de afeitar
she ella *sub. pron.*
  she is ella es **3 (1)**
shellfish mariscos *m., pl.*
shift (morning/afternoon/evening) turno de la manana/tarde/noche *m.* **11 (1)**
ship barco *m.*
shirt camisa *f.* **13 (1)**
shock chocar *v.* **29 (2)**
shoe zapato *m.*
  (high-heeled) shoes zapatos (de tacón) *m., pl.* **13 (1)**
  pair of shoes par de zapatos

  shoe size número *m.* de zapato
  shoe store zapatería *f.*
  tennis shoes zapatos *m., pl.* de tenis **13 (1)**
shop tienda *f.* **8 (1)**
shopping, to go ir *v.* de compras
  shopping mall centro *m.* comercial
short (in height) bajo/a *adj.* **6 (1);** **(in length)** corto/a *adj.*
short story cuento *m.*
shorts pantalones cortos *m., pl.* **13 (1)**
should (do something) deber *v.* *(+ inf.)*
show mostrar (o:ue) *v.*; espectáculo *m.*; enseñar *v.* a **24 (2)**
shower ducha *f.* **18 (2);** ducharse *v.*; bañarse *v.*
  take a bath/shower at night bañarse *v.* por la noche **14 (1)**
shrimp camarón *m.* **9 (1)**
shy tímido/a *adj.* **3 (1)**
siblings hermanos *m., pl.*
sick mal, malo/a; enfermo/a *adj.* **15 (1), 21 (2)**
  be sick estar enfermo/a
  get sick enfermarse *v.* **21 (2)**
sickness enfermedad *f.*
side lado *m.* **23 (2)**
  from/on the left side del/al lado izquierdo **23 (2)**
  from/on the right side del/al lado derecho **23 (2)**
side table mesita *f.* **18 (2)**
sightseeing: go sightseeing hacer *v.* turismo
sign firmar *v.*; letrero *m.*
silk seda *f.*; **(made of)** de seda
silly tonto/a *adj.* **6 (1)**
silverware cubierto *m.*
similar similar *adj. m., f.*
since desde *prep.*
sing cantar *v.* **20 (2)**
  sing carols cantar villancicos **20 (2)**
  sing a birthday song cantar las mañanitas **20 (2)**
singer cantante *m., f.*
single soltero/a *adj.* **6 (1)**
single room habitación *f.* individual
sink (in a bathroom) lavabo *m.* **18 (2); (in a kitchen)** fregadero *m.* **18 (2)**
sir señor (Sr.) *m.*
sister hermana *f.* **4 (1)**
sister-in-law cuñada *f.* **4 (1)**
sit down sentarse (e:ie) *v.*
six seis
six hundred seiscientos/as
sixteen dieciséis **1 (1)**
sixth sexto/a *adj.*
sixty sesenta **4 (1)**
size talla *f.*
  shoe size número *m.* de zapato

skate (in-line) patinar *v.* (en línea) **18 (2)**

skate (rollerblade) patinar *v.* (en línea) **18 (2)**

skate (on ice) patinar *v.* (sobre hielo) **18 (2)**

ski esquiar *v.* **18 (2)**

skiing esquí *m.*
   water-skiing esquí acuático

skirt falda *f.*

sky cielo *m.*

sleep dormir (o:ue) *v.* **10 (1)**; sueño *m.*
   go to sleep dormirse (o:ue) *v.*

sleepy: be (very) sleepy tener *v.* (mucho) sueño

slender delgado/a *adj.*

slim down adelgazar *v.*

slow lento/a *adj.*

slowly despacio *adv.*

small pequeño/a *adj.* **6 (1)**

smaller menor *adj.*

smallest, (the) el/la menor *m., f.*

smart listo/a *adj.*

smile sonreír (e:i) *v.*

smiled sonreído *p.p.*

smoggy: It's (very) smoggy. Hay (mucha) contaminación.

smoke fumar *v.* **19 (2)**
   not to smoke no fumar *v.* **19 (2)**

smoking section sección *f.* de fumadores
   (non) smoking section sección de (no) fumadores

snack (in the afternoon) merendar *v.;* **(afternoon snack)** merienda *f.*
   have a snack merendar *v.*

sneakers zapatos de tenis **13 (1)**

sneeze estornudar *v.*

snorkel bucear *v.* **18 (2)**

snow nevar (e:ie) *v.* **13 (1)**; nieve *f.*

snowing: It's snowing; It snows Nieva. **13 (1)**

so (in such a way) así *adv.*; tan *adv.*
   so much tanto *adv.*
   so-so regular; así así
   so that para que *conj.* **30 (2)**

soap jabón *m.*
   soap opera telenovela *f.*

soccer fútbol *m.*
   soccer game partido de fútbol *m.* **8 (1)**

sociable sociable *adj.* **3 (1)**

sociology sociología *f.*

sock calcetín *m.* **13 (1)**

soda refresco *m.* **9 (1)**

sofa sofá *m.* **18 (2)**

soft drink refresco *m.* **9 (1)**

software programa *m.* de computación

soil tierra *f.*

solar energy energía solar

solution solución *f.*

solve resolver (o:ue) *v*

solved resuelto/a *p.p.* **28 (2)**

some algún, alguno/a(s) **18 (2)** *adj.*; unos/as *pron.*; unos/as *m., f.*, pl. *indef. art.*

somebody alguien *pron.* **18(2)**

someone alguien *pron.* **18 (2)**

something algo *pron.* **18 (2)**

sometimes a veces *adv.* **8 (1)**, **15 (1)**

son hijo *m.* **4 (1)**

song canción *f.*
   birthday song mañanitas *f., pl.* **20 (2)**

son-in-law yerno *m.*

soon pronto *adj.*
   See you soon. Hasta pronto.

sore adolorido/a *adj.* **21 (2)**
   be sore estar adolorido/a **21 (2)**

sorry: be sorry sentir (e:ie) *v.* **29 (2)**
   I'm sorry. Lo siento.
   I'm so sorry. Mil perdones.; Lo siento muchísimo.

So-so. Más o menos. **1 (1)**

soup caldo *m.;* sopa *f.* **9 (1)**

sour agrio/a *adj.*

south sur *m.* **26 (2)**
   to the south al sur **26 (2)**

spaghetti espagueti *m.* **9 (1)**

Spain España *f.*

Spanish (language) español *m.* **1 (1)**; español(a) *adj.; m., f.*

spare time ratos *m., pl.* libres

speak hablar *v.*

specialization especialización *f.*

spectacular espectacular *adj.*

speech discurso *m.*

speed velocidad *f.* **26 (2)**; ir *v.* manejar *v.* a exceso de velocidad **26 (2)**
   speed limit velocidad máxima

spelling ortográfico/a *adj.*

spend (money) gastar *v.* **19 (2)**
   spend time pasar *v.* el tiempo
   spend the day pasar *v.* el día **20 (2)**

spicy picante *adj.*

spoiled consentido/a *adj.* **22 (2)**
   be spoiled ser consentido/a **22 (2)**

spoon (table or large) cuchara *f.*

sport deporte *m.*
   sports-loving deportivo/a *adj.*
   sports-related deportivo/a *adj.*

spouse esposo/a *m., f.*

sprain (one's ankle) torcerse *v.* (el tobillo)

sprained torcido/a *adj.*
   be sprained estar *v.* torcido/a

spring primavera *f.* **13 (1)**

stadium estadio *m.* **2 (1)**

stage etapa *f.*

stairs escalera *f.*

stairway escalera *f.*

stamp estampilla *f.;* sello *m.*

stand in line hacer *v.* cola

star estrella *f.*

start empezar (e:ie) *v* **10 (1)**

start (a vehicle) arrancar *v.*

state estado *m.*

station estación *f.*

statue estatua *f.*

status: marital status estado *m.* civil

stay quedarse *v.*
   Stay calm! ¡Tranquilo/a! *adj.*
   stay home quedarse *v.* en casa **14 (1)**
   stay in shape mantenerse *v.* en forma

steak bistec *m.*

steering wheel volante *m.*

step etapa *f.*

stepbrother hermanastro *m.*

stepdaughter hijastra *f.*

stepfather padrastro *m.*

stepmother madrastra *f.*

stepsister hermanastra *f.*

stepson hijastro *m.*

stereo estéreo *m.*

still todavía *adv.* **28 (2)**

stock broker corredor(a) *m., f.* de bolsa

stockings medias *f., pl.*

stomach estómago *m.* **21 (2)**

stone piedra *f.*

stop parar *v.* **26 (2)**
   stop (doing something) dejar *v.* de (+ *inf.*)

store tienda *f.*

storm tormenta *f.*

story cuento *m.;* historia *f.*

stove estufa *f.* **18 (2)**

straight derecho *adj.* **26 (2)**
   straight ahead (todo) derecho
   go straight ahead for (three) blocks seguir derecho (tres) cuadras **26 (2)**

straighten up arreglar *v.*

strange extraño/a *adj.*
   It's strange… Es extraño…

strawberry frutilla *f.;* fresa *f.*

street calle *f.* **26 (2)**

stress estrés *m.*

stressed estresado/a *adj.* **15 (1)**

stretching estiramiento *m.*
   stretching exercises ejercicios *m., pl.* de estiramiento

strike (labor) huelga *f.*

stripe raya *f.*
   striped de rayas *adj.*

stroll pasear *v.*

strong fuerte *adj.*

struggle (for) luchar *v.* (por)

student estudiante *m., f.* **2 (1)**; estudiantil *adj.*

studious estudioso/a *adj.* **3 (1)**

study estudiar *v.* **5 (1)**
   to study a lot/a little estudiar mucho/poco **5 (1)**

stuffed up (sinuses) congestionado/a *adj.*

stupendous estupendo/a *adj.*

style estilo *m.*

suburbs afueras *f., pl.*
subway metro *m.*
  subway station estación *f.* del metro
success éxito *m.*
successful: be successful tener *v.* éxito
such as tales como
suddenly de repente *adv.* **25 (2)**
suffer sufrir *v.*
  suffer from an illness sufrir una enfermedad
sufficient bastante *adj.*
sugar azúcar *m.*
suggest sugerir (e:ie) *v.*
suit traje *m.* **13 (1)**
suitcase maleta *f.* **13 (1), 20 (2)**
summer verano *m.* **13 (1)**
sun sol *m.*
sunbathe tomar *v.* el sol
Sunday domingo *m.* **5 (1)**
  (on) Sundays los domingos *m., pl.* **5 (1)**
sunglasses gafas *f., pl.* de sol; gafas oscuras; lentes *m., pl.* de sol
sunny: It's (very) sunny. Hace (mucho) sol.
supermarket supermercado *m.* **8 (1)**
supervisor supervisor/a *m., f.* **11 (1)**
suppose suponer *v.*
sure seguro/a *adj.*
  be sure (of) estar *v.* seguro/a (de)
surf the Internet navegar *v.* en Internet
surprise sorprender *v.*; sorpresa *f.*
survey encuesta *f.*
sweat sudar *v.*
sweater suéter *m.* **13 (1)**
sweep the floor barrer *v.* el suelo **18 (2)**
  sweep the garage barrer *v.* el garaje **18 (2)**
sweet dulce *adj.*
sweets dulces *m., pl.*
swim nadar *v.* **18 (2)**
swimming natación *f.*
  swimming pool piscina *f.*
swing (leisure) columpio *m.* **22 (2)**
  go on the swings subir(se) a los columpios **22 (2)**
symptom síntoma *m.*
systems analyst analista de sistemas *m., f.* **12 (1)**

T

table mesa *f.* **18 (2)**
  night table mesa *f.* de noche **18 (2)**
  side table mesita *f.* **18 (2)**
  set the table poner *v.* la mesa **18 (2)**
tablespoon cuchara *f.*
tablet (pill) pastilla *f.*

take tomar *v.*; llevar *v.*
  take a bath bañarse *v.* **14 (1)**
  take a bath/shower at night bañarse *v.* por la noche **14 (1)**
  take a shower ducharse *v.* **14 (1)**
  take a trip hacer un viaje **18 (2)**
  take an x-ray sacar *v.* una radiografía **24 (2)**
  Take care! ¡Cuídense!
  take care of cuidar *v.*
  take care of oneself cuidarse *v.* **21 (2)**
  take care of (watch) kids/the elderly cuidar *v.* a los niños/ancianos **11 (1)**
  take classes tomar *v.* clases
  take into account tomar *v.* en cuenta
take off quitarse *v.*
  take off one's shoes quitarse *v.* los zapatos **14 (1)**
  take out the trash sacar *v.* la basura **18 (2)**
  take out (walk) the dog sacar al perro a pasear **18 (2)**
  take pictures sacar *v.* fotos; tomar *v.* fotos
  take (someone's) temperature tomar(le) *v.* la temperatura (a alguien)
  take something llevar *v.* algo **24 (2)**
  take the bus tomar *v.* el autobús **5 (1)**
  take the freeway north/south/east/west tomar *v.* la autopista al norte/al sur/al este/al oeste **26 (2)**
  take (wear) a shoe size calzar *v.*
talented talentoso/a *adj.*
talk hablar *v.* **5 (1)**; conversar *v.*
  talk show programa *m.* de entrevistas
  to talk with friends hablar con los amigos **5 (1)**
  to talk on the phone hablar por teléfono **5 (1)**
tall alto/a *adj.* **6 (1)**
tank tanque *m.*
tantrum berrinche *m.* **22 (2)**
  throw tantrums hacer *v.* berrinches **22 (2)**
tape (audio) cinta *f.*
  tape recorder grabadora *f.*
taste probar (o:ue) *v.*
tasty rico/a *adj.* **6 (1)**; sabroso/a *adj.*
tax impuesto *m.*
taxi(cab) taxi *m.*
tea té *m.* **9 (1)**
teach enseñar *v.* a **24 (2)**
teacher profesor(a) *m., f.* **1 (1)**; **(elementary school)** maestro/a *m., f.;* **12 (1) (pre-school teacher)** educador(a) *m., f.* **12 (1)**

team equipo *m.*
technician técnico/a *m., f.*
  computer technician técnico/a en computación *m., f.* **12 (1)**
teenager chico/a **4 (1)**
telecommuting teletrabajo *m.*
teleconference videoconferencia *f.*
telephone teléfono *m.*
  cellular telephone teléfono celular
tele(vision) televisión *f.* **2 (1)**
  television set televisor *m.*
tell decir *v.* **20 (2), 24 (2)**; contar (o:ue) *v.*
  tell your problems contar (o:ue) *v.* los problemas **11 (1), 24 (2)**
temperature temperatura *f.*
ten diez **1 (1)**
tennis tenis *m.*
tennis court cancha de tenis *f.* **2 (1)**
  tennis shoes zapatos *m., pl.* de tenis **13 (1)**
tension tensión *f.*
tent tienda *f.* de campaña
tenth décimo/a *adj.*
terrible terrible *adj., m., f.* **3 (1)**
  it's terrible es terrible
terrific chévere *adj.*
test prueba *f.*, examen *m.*
text message mensaje de texto *m.*
Thank you. Gracias. *f., pl.* **1 (1)**
  Thank you (very much). (Muchas) gracias.
  Thank you very, very much. Muchísimas gracias.
  Thanks (a lot). (Muchas) gracias.
  Thanks for everything. Gracias por todo.
  Thanks once again. Gracias una vez más.
that que; quien(es); lo que rel *pron.*
  that (one) ése, ésa, eso *pron.;* ese, esa, *adj.* **6 (1)**
  that (over there) aquél, aquélla, aquello *pron.;* aquel, aquella *adj.*
  that which lo que *conj.*
  That's me. Soy yo.
  that's why por eso
the el *m.*, la *f., sing., def., art.;* los *m.*, las *f., pl., def. art.* **2 (1)**
theater teatro *m.*
their su(s) *poss., adj.* **4 (1);** suyo(s)/ a(s) *poss., pron.*
them los/las *pron.;* les *pron.; i.o., pron.* **19 (2)**
then después **(afterward)** *adv.;* entonces **(as a result)** *adv.;* luego **(next)** *adv.;* pues *adv.*
  back then en esos tiempos **22 (2)**
there allí *adv.*
  There is/are... Hay... **2 (1);**
  There is/are not... No hay...
therefore por eso *adv.*
these éstos, éstas *pron.;* estas *adj.* **6 (1)**
they ellos/as *sub. pron.*
  they are ellos/as son **3 (1)**

thin delgado/a *adj.* **6 (1)**

thing cosa *f.* **5 (1)**

think pensar (e:ie) *v.* **10 (1), 17 (2)**; **(believe)** creer *v.* **17 (2)**; **think about** pensar en **10 (1)**

third tercer, tercero/a *adj.*

thirst sed *f.*

thirsty: be (very) thirsty tener *v.* (mucha) sed **9 (1)**

thirteen trece **1 (1)**

thirty treinta **1 (1)**; **thirty (minutes past the hour)** y treinta; y media

thirty-one treinta y uno **1 (1)**

thirty-two treinta y dos **1 (1)**

thirty-three treinta y tres **1 (1)**

thirty-four treinta y cuatro **1 (1)**

thirty-five treinta y cinco **1 (1)**

thirty-six treinta y seis **1 (1)**

thirty-seven treinta y siete **1 (1)**

thirty-eight treinta y ocho **1 (1)**

thirty-nine treinta y nueve **1 (1)**

this este, esta *adj.* **6 (1)**; éste, ésta, esto *pron.*

  This is… (introduction) Éste/a es…

  This is he/she. (on telephone) Con él/ella habla.

  this Monday/Tuesday (etc.) este lunes/jueves (etc). **7 (1)**

  this morning esta mañana **15 (1)**

those ésos, ésas *pron.*; esos, esas *adj.* **6 (1)**

those (over there) aquéllos, aquéllas *pron.*; aquellos, aquellas *adj.*

thousand mil *m.*

three tres **1 (1)**

three hundred trescientos/as

throat garganta *f.* **21 (2)**

through por *prep.*

throughout: throughout the world en todo el mundo

throw echar *v.*

  throw a party hacer una fiesta **18 (2)**

  throw tantrums hacer *v.* berrinches **22 (2)**

Thursday jueves *m., sing.* **5 (1)**

  (on) Thursdays los jueves *m., pl.* **5 (2)**

thus (in such a way) así *adj.*

ticket boleto *m.*; entrada *f.*; pasaje *m.*; **(traffic)** multa *f.* **26 (2)**

  avoid tickets evitar *v.* las multas **26 (2)**

tidy arreglado/a *adj.* **18 (2)**

  be tidy estar arreglado/a **18 (2)**

tie corbata *f.* **13 (1)**

time vez *f.*; tiempo *m.*

  buy on time comprar *v.* a plazos *m., pl.*

  have a good/bad time pasar lo *v.* bien/mal

  full-time/part-time/free time el tiempo completo/parcial/libre **11 (1)**

We had a great time. Lo pasamos de película.

times veces *f., pl.*

  many times muchas veces

tip propina *f.*

tire llanta *f.* **26 (2)**

  check the tires revisar *v.* las llantas **26 (2)**

tired cansado/a *adj.* **15 (1)**

  be tired estar *v.* cansado/a

title título *m.*

to a *prep.*

  to (the) al *m.,sing.*; a la *f.,sing.*; a los *m.,pl.*; a las *f.,pl.* **8 (1)**

toast (drink) brindar *v.*; pan *m.* tostado **9 (1)**

toasted tostado/a *adj.*

toaster tostadora *f.*

today hoy *adv.* **7 (1)**

  Today is… Hoy es…

together juntos/as *adj.*

  get together juntarse *v.* **14 (1)**

told dicho/a *pp.* **28 (2)**

tomato tomate *m.*

tomorrow mañana *adv.* **7 (1)**

  See you tomorrow. Hasta mañana.

tonight esta noche *adv.* **7 (1)**

too también *adv.*

  too much demasiado *adv.*; en exceso

tooth diente *m.*; muela *f.*

tornado tornado *m.*

tortilla tortilla *f.*

touch tocar *v.*

tour an area recorrer *v.*; excursión *f.*

  go on a tour hacer *v.* una excursión

tourism turismo *m.*

tourist turista *m., f.*; turístico/a *adj.*

toward para *prep.*; hacia *prep.*

towel toalla *f.* **18 (2)**

town pueblo *m.*

toy juguete *m.* **22 (2)**

trade oficio *m.*

traffic circulación *f.*; tráfico *m.*

  obey the traffic signs obedecer (c:zc) *v.* las señales de tránsito **26 (2)**

  traffic light semáforo *m.* **26 (2)**

  traffic signs señales de tránsito *pl., f.* **26 (2)**

tragedy tragedia *f.*

trail sendero *m.*

  trailhead sendero *m.*

train entrenarse *v.*; tren *m.*

  train station estación *f.* del tren *m.*

translate traducir *v.*

trash basura *f.* **18 (2)**

  take out the trash sacar *v.* la basura **18 (2)**

travel viajar *v.*

  travel agency agencia *f.* de viajes

  travel agent agente *m., f.* de viajes

  travel documents documentos *m., pl.* de viaje

traveler viajero/a *m., f.*

  traveler's check cheque *m.* de viajero

treat (entertain) invitar *v.*

tree árbol *m.* **22 (2)**

  climb trees subir(se) a los árboles **22 (2)**

trillion billón

trimester trimestre *m.*

trip viaje *m.* **18 (2)**

  take a trip hacer *v.* un viaje **18 (2)**

tropical forest bosque *m.* tropical

trouble problemas *m., pl.*

  get into trouble hacer *v.* travesuras **22 (2)**

truck camión *m.*

true cierto/a; verdad *adj.*

  it's (not) true (no) es cierto/ verdad

trunk baúl *m.*

truth verdad *f.*

try intentar *v.*; probar (o:ue) *v.*

  try (to do something) tratar *v.* de (+ *inf.*)

  try on probarse (o:ue) *v.*

t-shirt camiseta *f.* **13 (1)**

Tuesday martes *m., sing.*

  (on) Tuesdays los martes *m., pl.*

tuna atún *m.*

  tuna sándwich sandwich de atún *m.* **9 (1)**

turkey pavo *m.* **9 (1)**

turn doblar *v.*

  turn off (electricity/appliance) apagar *v.*

  turn off the car apagar *v.* el coche **26 (2)**

  turn on (electricity/appliance) poner *v.*; prender *v.*

  turn on the car prender *v.* el coche **26 (2)**

  turn right/left at… Avenue/Street doblar *v.* a la derecha/izquierda en la avenida/calle… **26 (2)**; dar *v.* vuelta a la derecha/izquierda en la calle/avenida… **26 (2)**

  turn something in entregar *v.* **24 (2)**

turtle tortuga *f.*

  marine turtle tortuga marina

twelve doce **1 (1)**

twenty veinte **1 (1)**

twenty-eight veintiocho **1 (1)**

twenty-five veinticinco **1 (1)**

twenty-four veinticuatro **1 (1)**

twenty-nine veintinueve **1 (1)**

twenty-one veintiún, veintiuno/a **1 (1)**

twenty-seven veintisiete **1 (1)**

twenty-six veintiséis **1 (1)**

twenty-three veintitrés **1 (1)**

twenty-two veintidós **1 (1)**

twice dos veces

twice a month dos veces al
mes **8 (1)**
twisted torcido/a *adj.*
  be twisted estar *v.* torcido/a
two dos **1 (1)**
two hundred doscientos/as
  two times dos veces

U

ugly feo/a *adj.* **6 (1)**
umbrella paraguas *m.* **13 (1)**
uncle tío *m.* **4 (1)**
under debajo de *prep.;* bajo *prep.*
understand comprender *v.;*
  entender (e:ie) *v.* **10 (1), 17 (2)**
underwear ropa *f.* interior
unemployment desempleo *m.*
United States Estados Unidos *m., pl.*
university universidad *f.*
unless a menos que *adv.* **30 (2)**
unmarried soltero/a *adj.*
unpleasant antipático/a *adj.* **6 (1)**
until hasta *prep.*
  until now; so far hasta ahora
  28 (2)
  until this moment hasta el
  momento **28 (2);** hasta que *conj.*
  30 (2)
up arriba *adv.*
upset molesto/a *adj.* **15 (1)**
urgent urgente *adj.*
  It's urgent that... Es urgente
  que...
us nos *pron.; i.o. pron.* **19 (2)**
use usar *v.*
  use the computer usar *v.* la
  computadora **5 (1)**
used for para *prep.*
useful útil *adj.*

V

vacation vacaciones *f., pl.* **11 (1)**
  be on vacation estar *v.* de
  vacaciones **15 (1)**
  go on vacation ir *v.* de vacaciones
  go on vacation irse *v.* de
  vacaciones **14 (1)**
vacuum pasar *v.* la aspiradora
  18 (2)
  vacuum cleaner aspiradora *f.*
valley valle *m.*
various varios/as *adj., pl.*
VCR videocasetera *f.* **2 (1)**
vegetables verduras *f., pl.*
verb verbo *m.*
very muy *adv.*
  very bad malísimo
  very much muchísimo *adv.*
  Very good, thank you. Muy bien,
  gracias.
  Very well. Muy bien. **1 (1)**
vest chaleco *m.*

veterinarian veterinario/a *m., f.*
  12 (1)
video video *m.*
  videocassette videocasete *m.*
  video conference
  videoconferencia *f.*
  videocamera cámara *f.* de video
vinegar vinagre *m.*
violence violencia *f.*
visit visitar *v.*
  visit a monument visitar un
  monumento
  visit one's grandparents visitar *v.*
  a los abuelos **5 (1)**
vitamin vitamina *f.*
volcano volcán *m.*
volleyball vóleibol *m.*
  volleyball court cancha de
  vóleibol *f.* **2 (1)**
vote votar *v.*

W

wait (for) esperar *v.*
waiter/waitress camarero/a *m., f.;*
  mesero/a *m., f.* **9 (1), 11 (1)**
wake up despertarse (e:ie) *v.*
walk caminar *v.*
  go for a walk dar *v.* un paseo
  18 (2)
  take a walk pasear *v.*
  take out (walk) the dog sacar al
  perro a pasear **18 (2)**
  walk around the city/town pasear
  por la ciudad/el pueblo
Walkman walkman *m.*
wall pared *f.*
wallet cartera *f.*
want desear *v.;* querer (e:ie) *v.*
  10 (1), 20 (2)
  I don't want to no quiero
war guerra *f.*
warm (oneself) up calentarse *v.*
wash lavar *v.*
  wash one's face/hands lavarse *v.*
  la cara/los manos **14 (1)**
  do (wash) the laundry lavar la
  ropa **5 (1)**
  do (wash) the dishes lavar los
  platos **18 (2)**
  wash the car lavar el coche **5 (1)**
  wash oneself lavarse
washing machine lavadora *f.*
wastebasket papelera *f.* **2 (1)**
watch mirar *v.;* reloj *m.*
  watch cartoons ver *v.* los dibujos
  animados **22 (2)**
  watch television mirar (la)
  televisión **5 (1)**
  watch a movie at home ver *v.* una
  película en casa **8 (1)**
water agua *f.* **9 (1)**
  water pollution contaminación
  del agua

water-skiing esquí *m.* acuático
way manera *f.*
we nosotros/as *sub. pron.*
  we are nosotros/as somos **3 (1)**
weak débil *adj.*
wear llevar *v.* **13 (1);** usar *v.* **13 (1);**
  (shoes) calzar *v.*
  wear a ... costume disfrazarse *v.*
  de... **20 (2)**
  wear clothing ponerse *v.* la ropa
  14 (1), 20 (2)
  wear the seat belt ponerse *v.* el
  cinturón de seguridad **26 (2)**
weather tiempo *m.*
  It's bad weather. Hace mal
  tiempo. **13 (1)**
  It's nice weather. Hace buen
  tiempo. **13 (1)**
weaving tejido *m.*
Web red *f.*
website sitio *m.* web
wedding boda *f.*
Wednesday miércoles *m., sing.* **5 (1)**
  (on) Wednesdays los miércoles
  m., pl. **5 (1)**
week semana *f.*
  (on) weekdays entre semana **5 (1)**
weekend fin *m.* de semana **5 (1)**
  (on) weekends los fines de
  semana **5 (1)**
weight peso *m.*
  lift weights levantar *v.* pesas *f.,*
  pl. **18 (2)**
Welcome! ¡Bienvenido(s)/a(s)! *adj.*
well pues *adv.;* bueno *adv.;* bien *adj.*
  21 (2)
well-being bienestar *m.*
well organized ordenado/a *adj.* **6 (1)**
west oeste *m.* **26 (2)**
  to the west al oeste **26 (2)**
western (genre) de vaqueros *adj.*
whale ballena *f.*
what lo que
  what? ¿qué? *adj., pron.* **6 (1);**
  ¿cuál(es)? **6 (1)**
  At what time...? ¿A qué hora...?
  2 (1)
  What a...! ¡Qué...!
  What a pleasure to...! ¡Qué gusto
  (+ *inf.*)...!
  What a surprise! ¡Qué sorpresa!
  What are... like? ¿Cómo son...?
  3 (1)
  What day is it? ¿Qué día es hoy?
  What did he/she do? ¿Qué hizo
  él/ella?
  What did they do? ¿Qué hicieron
  ellos/ellas?
  What did you do? ¿Qué hiciste?
  fam., sing.; ¿Qué hizo usted?
  form., sing.; ¿Qué hicieron
  ustedes? *form., pl.*
  What did you say? ¿Cómo?
  What do you guys think? ¿Qué les
  parece?

What happened? ¿Qué pasó?
What is it? ¿Qué es?
What is the date (today)? ¿Cuál es la fecha (de hoy)?
What is the price? ¿Qué precio tiene?
What is today's date? ¿Cuál es la fecha de hoy?
What pain! ¡Qué dolor!
What pretty clothes! ¡Qué ropa más bonita!
What size do you wear? ¿Qué talla lleva (usa)?
What time is it? ¿Qué hora es?
What's going on? ¿Qué pasa?
What's happening? ¿Qué pasa?
What's… like! ¿Cómo es…? **3 (1)**
What's new? ¿Qué hay de nuevo?
What's the weather like? ¿Qué tiempo hace?
What's wrong? ¿Qué pasó?
What's your name? ¿Cómo se llama usted? *form.* **1 (1)**
What's your name? ¿Cómo te llamas (tú)? *fam.* **1 (1)**
when cuando *conj.* **30 (2)**
When? ¿Cuándo? **6 (1)**
when I was a child cuando era niño/a **22 (2)**
when I was … years old cuando tenía… años **22 (2)**
where donde *adj., conj.*
where? (destination) ¿adónde?; **(location)** ¿dónde? **6 (1)**
Where are you from? ¿De dónde eres? *fam.* **4 (1)**; ¿De dónde es usted? *form.*
Where is…? ¿Dónde está…?
(to) where? ¿adónde?
which que; lo que *rel. pron.*
which? ¿cuál(es)? *adj., pron.;* ¿qué? **6 (1)**
which one(s)? ¿cuál(es)? **6 (1)**
while mientras *adv.*
white blanco/a *adj.* **13 (1)**
white wine vino *m.* blanco
who que; quien(es) *rel. pron.*
who? ¿quién(es)? *adv.* **6 (1)**
Who is…? ¿Quién es…?
Who is calling? (on telephone) ¿De parte de quién?
Who is speaking? (on telephone) ¿Quién habla?
whole todo/a *adj.*
whom quien(es) *rel. pron.*
whose…? ¿de quién(es)…?
why? ¿por qué? *adv.* **6 (1)**
widowed viudo/a *adj.*
wife esposa *f.* **4 (1)**
win ganar *v.*
wind viento *m.*
window ventana *f.* **2 (1)**
windshield parabrisas *m., sing.*
windy: It's (very) windy. Hace (mucho) viento. **13 (1)**

wine vino *m.*
red wine vino tinto *m.* **9 (1)**
white wine vino blanco *m.*
wineglass copa *f.*
winter invierno *m.* **13 (1)**
wish desear *v.;* esperar *v.*
I wish (that) Ojalá que
with con *prep.*
with me conmigo
with you contigo *fam.*
within dentro de *prep.*
without sin *prep.;* sin que *conj.*
without a doubt sin duda
woman mujer *f.*
wool lana *f.*
(made of) wool de lana
word palabra *f.*
work trabajar *v.;* funcionar *v.;* trabajo *m.* **8 (1)**
work (of art, literature, music, etc.) obra *f.*
work at home trabajar *v.* en casa **5 (1)**
work out hacer *v.* gimnasia
world mundo *m.*
worldwide mundial *adj. m., f.*
worried (about) preocupado/a (por) *adj.* **15 (1)**
worry (about) preocuparse *v.* (por)
Don't worry. No se preocupe. *form.;* No te preocupes. *fam.*
worse peor *adj. m., f.*
feel worse sentirse (e:ie) peor **21 (2)**
worse than peor que *adj.* **17 (2)**
worst el/la peor; lo peor
Would you like to? ¿Te gustaría?
write escribir *v.* **24 (2)**
write a letter/post card/e-mail message escribir una carta/(tarjeta) postal/mensaje *m.* electrónico **8 (1)**
write a paper escribir un trabajo **8 (1)**
writer escritor(a) *m., f.*
written escrito/a *p.p.* **28 (2)**
wrong equivocado/a *adj.*
be wrong no tener *v.* razón

X

X-ray radiografía *f.* **24 (2)**
take an X-ray sacar *v.* una radiografía **24 (2)**

Y

yard jardín *m.* **18 (2);** patio *m.*
year año *m.*
be… years old tener… *v.* años
yellow amarillo/a *adj.* **13 (1)**
yes sí *interj.*
yesterday ayer *adv.* **15 (1), 17 (2)**
(not) yet todavía (no); ya *adv.* **28 (2)**

yogurt yogur *m.* **9 (1)**
you tú *sub. pron., fam., sing.;* usted *sub. pron., form., sing.;* vosotros/as *sub. pron., fam., pl.;* ustedes *sub. pron., form., pl.;* te *d.o. pron., fam., sing.; i.o. pron., fam., sing.* **19 (2);** lo *d.o. pron., m., form., sing.;* la *d.o. pron., f., form., sing.;* os *d.o. pron., fam., pl.;* los *d.o. pron., m., form., pl.;* las *d.o. pron., f., form., pl.;* le(s) *i.o. pron., form.* **19 (2)**
you are tú eres *fam., sing.* **3 (1);** usted es *form., sing.* **3 (1);** vosotros/as sois *fam., pl.* **3 (1);** ustedes son *form., pl.* **3 (1)**
You don't say! ¡No me digas! *fam.;* ¡No me diga! *form.*
You're welcome. De nada. **1 (1);** No hay de qué.
young joven *adj.* **6 (1)**
young person joven *m., f.*
young woman señorita *f.*
younger menor *adj., m., f.* **6 (1)**
younger brother, sister hermano/a menor *m., f.*
youngest el/la menor *m., f.*
your su(s) *poss., adj., form.* **4 (1)**
your tu(s) *poss., adj., fam., sing.* **4 (1)**
your vuestro(s)/a(s) *poss., adj. form., pl.*
your(s) *form.* suyo(s)/a(s) *poss. pron., form.*
your(s) tuyo(s)/a(s) *poss., fam., sing.*
youth juventud *f.;* **(young person)** joven *m., f.*

Z

zero cero *m.* **1 (1)**

Each entry is followed by a citation, **(1)** or **(2)**. All entries followed by a **(1)** are found on the corresponding page in **INVITACIONES: Primera parte**; entries followed by a **(2)** are found on the page noted in **INVITACIONES: Segunda parte**.

Photo Credits: Primera parte

Cover: Alfaguara Editorial

Front Matter: xxvii Ali Burafi; **2** (tl) Courtesy Mabis Robledo; (tr) © Graham Neden; Ecoscene/Corbis; (bl) © James Marshall/Corbis; (br) © Darrell Jones/Corbis; **3** (tl) © Pablo Corral V/Corbis; (tr) © Francesco Venturi/Corbis; (bl) permission to reproduce J. Carballo; (br) © Randy Krauss.

Episodio 1: 15 © Morton Beebe/Corbis.

Episodio 2: 46 (l) © Tony Arruza/Corbis.

Episodio 3: 55 (tr, mr) Martín Bernetti; (ml) © NuStock/iStockphoto; (br) © Auris/iStockphoto; **61** (l) © Tiziana and Gianni Baldizzone/Corbis; (r) © Tim Whitby/Alamy.

Episodio 4: 75 (t) Martín Bernetti; **84** © EFE, Ballesteros/AP Images.

Episodio 5: 111 © Buddy Mays/Corbis; **121** © Blend Images/Image Source; **122** (tl) © Michele Molinari/Alamy; (tr) © Universidad de Navarra; (b) © Universidad Autónoma de Chihuahua; **123** © Universidad Nacional Autónoma de México (www.unam.mx).

Episodio 6: 137 © Schwarz Shaul/Corbis SYGMA; **145** © Jimmy Dorantes/Latin Focus; **146** © Jimmy Dorantes/Latin Focus.

Episodio 7: 154 (b) Rossy Llano.

Episodio 9: 206 (t, b) USDA, MyPyramid.gov; **210** (l, r) Ali Burafi.

Episodio 10: 235 © Hans Georg Roth/Corbis; **252** © Alfaguara; **253** (l) © Bon Appetit/Alamy; (tr) © Richard Levine/Alamy; (br) © Cheryl Zibisky/FoodPix/Getty Images; **254** (t) © Richard T. Nowitz/Corbis; (bl) © FoodPix/Jupiter Images; (br) © ACE STOCK LIMITED/Alamy; **255** (tl) Ali Burafi; (tr) José Blanco; (bl) © FoodPix/Jupiter Images; (br) © Alexandra Grablewski/FoodPix/Getty Images.

Episodio 11: 271 (t) © Wolfgang Kaehler/Corbis.

Episodio 12: 292 (l) Martín Bernetti; **297** (l) © David Frazier/PhotoEdit; (r) © jonathanparry/iStockphoto; **303** (tl, tr) Martín Bernetti; (bml) Katie Wade; **304** (mtm) © LdF/iStockphoto; (bl, br) Martín Bernetti.

Episodio 13: 315 (br) © Polka Dot Images/Jupiter Images; **316** (l) © Amos Nachoum/Corbis; **324** (t) © WWD/Condé Nast/Corbis; (m) © FREDY AMARILES/Reuters/Landov; (b) © ALBERT GEA/Reuters/Landov; **325** (t) © CARLOS BARRIA/Reuters/Landov; (b) © LUCAS JACKSON/Reuters/Landov.

Episodio 14: 357 (m) © Nik Wheeler/Corbis; **363** (l, r) Martín Bernetti; **365** (l) © Michael Freeman/Corbis.

Episodio 15: 377 (t) © Doug Wilson/Corbis; **389** (l) © Rob Lewine/Corbis; **394** © Reuters/Corbis; **395** (l) © Stock Connection Blue/Alamy; (tr) © Sue Cunningham Photographic/Alamy; (br) © Marina Spironetti/Alamy; **396** (t) © INTERFOTO/Alamy; (m) © Picture Contact BV/Alamy; (b) © Andres Leighton/AP Images; **397** (tl) © Michael Caulfield/WireImage (Awards)/Newscom; (tr) © HECTOR GUERREO/Reuters/Landov; (b) © smilingworld/iStockphoto; **398** (t) © MarkFGD/iStockphoto; (bl, br) Ali Burafi.

Photo Credits: Segunda parte

Cover: Alfaguara Editorial.

Front Matter: xxvii Ali Burafi.

Episodio 16: 20 (t) © Jacques Pavlovsky/Sygma/Corbis; (b) Christian Inaraja, Cavall Fort Num. 1.111.

Episodio 17: 47 (l) © Charles & Josette Lenars; (m) © Randy Krauss; (r) © Jeremy Horner; **48** (t) © Barnabas Bosshart/Corbis.

About the Authors

Deana Alonso was born and raised in Mexico City. After graduating from High School and studying for a year at the *Universidad Nacional Autónoma de México* (UNAM) her family moved to the United States. She earned a Bachelor of Arts Degree in Mathematics and a Master's Degree in Spanish from San Diego State University. She also holds a Master's Degree in Teaching English to Speakers of Other Languages from California State University, Los Angeles. She served for four years as consultant and teacher leader at the Los Angeles Area Site of the California Foreign Language Project before joining the team at the San Diego Area Site. She is also the new president of the Foreign Language Council of San Diego (FLCSD). In addition, Deana co-authored several texts for McGraw-Hill, Prentice Hall and National Textbook Company. She taught Spanish for five years at Citrus College and she is presently a Professor of Spanish at Southwestern College. She has traveled extensively throughout Europe and Latin America.

Esther Alonso was born and raised in Mexico City. After graduating from High School and studying for two years at the *Universidad Internacional de Turismo,* her family moved to the United States. She earned a Bachelor's Degree in Linguistics and a Master's Degree in Spanish and English Sociolinguistics from San Diego State University. Esther was a consultant and teacher leader for the Los Angeles Area Site of the California Foreign Language Project for a year. She has published her research on language assessment in professional journals. She taught Spanish for five years at California State University, San Marcos where she currently is the Language Proficiency Assessor for Spanish and Portuguese. She is presently a Professor of Spanish and Portuguese at Southwestern College. She has traveled extensively through Europe and Latin America.

Brandon Zaslow was born and educated in the United States. He holds graduate degrees in Spanish and Education from the University of California, Los Angeles where he was a University Distinguished Scholar and from California State University Los Angeles. From 1990 to 1995, he held a teaching position in UCLA's Graduate School of Education where he taught Methods of Foreign Language Instruction and Primary and English Language Development. Since 1995, he serves as Director of the Los Angeles Area Site of the California Foreign Language Project, which is funded by the legislature through the Office of the President of the University of California to improve K–16 foreign, second and heritage language programs. In addition to serving on a team that authored Entre mundos (Prentice Hall), a program for heritage speakers of Spanish and Invitaciones (Vistas), a program for second language learners, Brandon worked to develop California's Classroom Oral Competency Interview (COCI), Classroom Writing Competency Assessment (CWCA), and Classroom Receptive Competency Matrix (CRCM). In addition, he was contributor and consultant to the 2003 Foreign Language Framework for California Public Schools and served on the writing committee of the 2009 Foreign Language Standards for California Public Schools. Brandon has been repeatedly honored by his colleagues receiving California's Outstanding Teacher Award in 1996, the National Textbook Company Award for Leadership in Education in 2000, and being named California Language Teacher of the year in 2000.